Oxford
Mini
School
German
Dictionary

Editorial Manager: Valerie Grundy
Editors: Neil and Roswitha Morris

OXFORD
UNIVERSITY PRESS

OXFORD
UNIVERSITY PRESS

Great Clarendon Street, Oxford OX2 6DP

Oxford University Press is a department of the University of Oxford.
It furthers the University's objective of excellence in research, scholarship,
and education by publishing worldwide in

Oxford New York

Auckland Bangkok Buenos Aires Cape Town Chennai
Dar es Salaam Delhi Hong Kong Istanbul Karachi Kolkata
Kuala Lumpur Madrid Melbourne Mexico City Mumbai Nairobi
São Paulo Shanghai Singapore Taipei Tokyo Toronto

with an associated company in Berlin

Oxford is a registered trade mark of Oxford University Press
in the UK and in certain other countries

© Oxford University Press 1998

Database right Oxford University Press (maker)

First published in 1998
This edition 2002

British Library Cataloguing in Publication Data available

ISBN 0-19-910962-1

10 9 8 7 6 5 4 3 2 1

Typeset by Selwood Systems, Midsomer Norton
Printed & Bound in Great Britain by Charles Letts & Company Ltd

INTRODUCTION

Learning a new language is an exciting experience. It can also sometimes seem confusing and difficult. Feeling secure and at ease in using a bilingual dictionary is essential to the building of confidence in understanding and using a foreign language.

This dictionary has been specially written for students who are preparing for exams. We have paid particular attention to making the dictionary as user-friendly as possible. With the help of colour headwords, easy-to-follow signposts and simple example phrases, the right translation can quickly be found. The things students need to know about words in German are clearly shown. These include main parts of irregular verbs, noun plurals, and the case taken by prepositions.

We have adopted a simplified version of traditional bilingual entry layout. This means that the dictionary is ideal for learning basic dictionary skills, which can subsequently be built upon as the student moves towards larger, more complex dictionaries. We have done our best to make this dictionary a practical, easy-to-use tool for learning and understanding German.

Throughout the writing of this dictionary we have worked in close consultation with students, teachers, and examining boards. We gratefully acknowledge the examining boards AQA (formerly NEAB and SEG), OCR, and EDEXCEL, who have read and commented on the dictionary text.

HOW A BILINGUAL DICTIONARY WORKS

A bilingual dictionary is a dictionary that has two languages in it. When you look up a word in one of the languages, the dictionary gives the translation for that word in the other language. The two languages in this dictionary are English and German. This dictionary is divided into two halves separated by red-edged pages in the middle. In the first half you look up German words to find out what they mean in English and in the second half you look up English words and find out how to say them in German.

The words you look up are in red and in the first half of the dictionary you will find **German** words in alphabetical order from a to z and in the second half **English** words from a to z. In a dictionary, these are called **headwords** because each one of them comes at the **head** of an **entry**. In the **entry** you can find **translations** but also other sorts of information which you can use to make sure you get the correct translation. The different sorts of information are typed in different ways to help you see clearly which is which. Here is a guide to the different things you will find in an entry:

headword	a word you look up in the dictionary
translation	translations are the only things that are in 'ordinary' type in an entry. They are always typed like this, and something that is typed in a different way can never be a translation
part of speech	tells you whether the word you are looking up is a verb, an adjective, or another part of speech. One headword can have more than one part of speech. **Book** can be a noun *(she was reading a book)* or a verb *(remember to book a table)*
(signpost)	helpful information to guide you to the right translation, to show you how to use the translation, or to give you essential information about either the headword or the translation
example	a phrase using the word you have looked up. If these appear in the entry you are looking at, you should read through them carefully to see if one of them is close to what you want to understand or say
der/die/das	gender: after a German noun to tell you whether it is masculine *(der)*, feminine *(die)*, or neuter *(das)*
(PL *die........*)	plural: shows the plural form of a German noun
●	indicates a phrasal verb such as *to carry on*
★	indicates an idiomatic expression such as *to look on the bright side*
◇	indicates an irregular German verb
SEP	indicates that a German verb is separable such as *ablenken* (PERF *lenkt ab*)
Δ	indicates a new spelling of a German word (see page xii)

vi

You can think of a dictionary entry as being made out of different sorts of building bricks. In the entries below you can see how they fit together to help you to find what you need. The more you use your dictionary the more confident you will feel about finding your way around it.

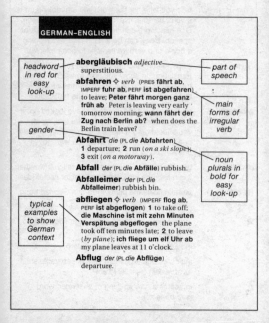

GERMAN–ENGLISH

headword in red for easy look-up →

abergläubisch *adjective*
superstitious.

abfahren ◊ *verb* (PRES **fährt ab**, IMPERF **fuhr ab**, PERF **ist abgefahren**) to leave; **Peter fährt morgen ganz früh ab** Peter is leaving very early tomorrow morning; **wann fährt der Zug nach Berlin ab?** when does the Berlin train leave?

gender →

Abfahrt *die* (PL *die* **Abfahrten**) **1** departure; **2** run (*on a ski slope*); **3** exit (*on a motorway*).

Abfall *der* (PL *die* **Abfälle**) rubbish.

Abfalleimer *der* (PL *die* **Abfalleimer**) rubbish bin.

typical examples to show German context →

abfliegen ◊ *verb* (IMPERF **flog ab**, PERF **ist abgeflogen**) **1** to take off; **die Maschine ist mit zehn Minuten Verspätung abgeflogen** the plane took off ten minutes late; **2** to leave (*by plane*); **ich fliege um elf Uhr ab** my plane leaves at 11 o'clock.

Abflug *der* (PL *die* **Abflüge**) departure.

part of speech ←

main forms of irregular verb ←

noun plurals in bold for easy look-up ←

ENGLISH–GERMAN

case governed by German preposition

essential structures for expression in German

based *adjective* **1** to be based on basieren auf (+DAT); **the film is based on a true story** der Film basiert auf einer wahren Geschichte; **2** to be based in wohnen in (+DAT); **he's based in Bristol** er wohnt in Bristol.

new spelling

basement *noun* Kellergeschoss △ das (PL die Kellergeschosse).

plural form

irregular verb

bear *noun* Bär der (PL die Bären). *verb* **1** ertragen ◇; **I can't bear the idea** ich kann den Gedanken nicht ertragen; **2** to bear something in mind an etwas +(ACC) denken; **I'll bear it in mind** ich denke daran.

case of 'etwas' shown in translation of example

perfect formed with 'sein'

blush *verb* erröten (PERF sein).

bolt *noun* (on a door) Riegel der (PL die Riegel). *verb* **1** (lock) verriegeln; **2** (gobble down) runterschlingen ◇ SEP (informal).

gender

separable verb

informal word or expression

◇ IRREGULAR VERB: See the verb tables in the centre of the dictionary

A STEP-BY-STEP GUIDE TO FINDING THE TRANSLATION YOU NEED

Finding a word in the dictionary

You will be using this dictionary to do one of the following things:

1 look up a German word or phrase to find out what it means
2 look up an English word or phrase to find out how to say it in German.

1 Finding out what a German word means

First of all, look it in the first half of the dictionary where you can find the German words and expressions with their English translations. You will see that the top of every page is marked with this red box.

No matter what you are using the dictionary to find out, you will always start by looking up a headword. Here are the German headwords **Ampel, Amsel, Amt, amtlich,** and **amüsant** with their entries.

> **Ampel** *die* (PL *die* **Ampeln**) traffic lights.
>
> **Amsel** *die* (PL *die* **Amseln**) blackbird.
>
> **Amt** *das* (PL *die* **Ämter**) **1** office; **2** exchange (*telephone*).
>
> **amtlich** *adjective* official.
>
> **amüsant** *adjective* amusing.

Suppose you want to find out what the German word **Bürste** means. You will look through the first half of your dictionary until you come to the bit which has all the German words beginning with **b**. You now need to find the page or pages containing German words beginning with **bu**, then **bur**, then **burs**, then **burst**. The dictionary helps you to do this by showing you the alphabetical range of words that you can find on the two pages that you can see when you have the dictionary open.

For instance, if you look at pages 52-53, you will see **Brühwürfel** and **campen** at the top of the pages. If you look down the first column on page 53, you will find **Bürste** between **Büroklammer** and **bürsten**. You will know that all German nouns start with a capital letter. Notice that this makes no difference to the alphabetical order, nor do accented letters like **ü**.

Büro *das* (PL *die* Büros) office.

Büroklammer *die* (PL *die* Büroklammern) paper clip.

Bürste *die* (PL *die* Bürsten) brush.

bürsten *verb* (PERF hat gebürstet) to brush.

When you look at the entry for **Bürste** you will find the translation you are looking for: **Bürste** means **brush**.

Bürste *die* (PL *die* Bürsten) brush.

You can also see what the gender of **Bürste** is. Nouns in German are either masculine, feminine, or neuter. These are shown in the dictionary as *der*, *die*, or *das*. You can see that **Bürste** says *die*. **Bürste** is a feminine noun.

It often happens that a German word has more than one translation in English. If you look at the entry for **Tor** on page 235 you will see that it is divided into sections numbered **1** and **2**.

Tor *das* (PL *die* Tore) **1** gate; **2** goal.

The first translation is **gate** and the second is **goal**. You will need to look at both translations and see which fits best in the German sentence you are trying to understand, so:

Uli hat das Tor geöffnet *means* Uli opened the gate

BUT

Uli steht im Tor *means* Uli's in goal

In English, the plural of most nouns is formed by adding **-s** (**book/books**). In German there are quite a lot of ways of forming the plural and these are not always easy to recognize. To help you with this, we show the plural form after every noun headword.

For instance, if you are trying to find out what the German word **Häuser** means, you can see immediately that it is the plural of **Haus** and so it means **houses**.

> **Haus** *das* (PL *die* **Häuser**) **1** house;
> **2 nach Hause** home; **zu Hause** at
> home.

German like English has certain words that you would use when chatting with friends but not in more formal situations. German words like this are marked (*informal*) like **flitzen** here:

> **flitzen** *verb* (*informal*) (PERF **ist**
> **geflitzt**) **1** to dash; **2** to whizz.

2 Finding an English word and how to say it in German

You can see that it is quite easy once you know how the dictionary works to look up a German word and find out what it means. Students usually find it harder to use the dictionary to find out how to say something in German. This dictionary is written specially to help you do this and to make it easy to find the right way of saying things in German.

Suppose you want to know how to say **garden** in German. Look up the word in the second part of the dictionary where the top of every page is marked with this box framed in red.

If you follow the same way of going through the alphabetical order of the headwords as you did when you were looking up a German word, you will find **garden** on page 417.

Now you can see that the German word for **garden** is **Garten**. But if you want to make a sentence using a noun like **Garten** you need to know its gender. The dictionary shows you that it is *der* **Garten** so **in the garden** will be **im Garten**.

It is not always as easy as this to know which German word you need. Sometimes there will be more than one German word for the English word you are looking up. When the dictionary entry gives you more than just one translation, it is very important to take the time to read through the whole entry. If you look up **plug** the entry looks like this:

> **plug** noun 1 (*electrical*) Stecker der
> (PL die Stecker); 2 (*in a bath or sink*)
> Stöpsel der (PL die Stöpsel); **to pull
> out the plug** den Stöpsel
> herausziehen.

You can see that **1** tells you that the German word for an electrical plug is **Stecker** and **2** tells you that the word for a plug in a bath or a sink is **Stöpsel**.

Remember that information which is either in brackets or italics or both is there to help you, but it *will never be* the translation itself. Wherever there is more than one translation, depending on what meaning of the English word you are looking for, the dictionary will always help you to choose the right one.

Often it is not enough to find the translation of one word. In the case of more common words the dictionary also gives you a selection of phrases you will often want to use. In the entry for **hair** below you can find out how to use the translation **Haare** in different expressions:

> **hair** noun 1 Haare (*plural*); **to comb
> your hair** sich ⋅(DAT) die Haare
> kämmen; **to wash your hair** sich
> ⋅(DAT) die Haare waschen; **to have
> your hair cut** sich ⋅(DAT) die Haare
> schneiden lassen; **she's had her hair
> cut** sie hat sich die Haare schneiden
> lassen; **2 a hair** ein Haar.

THE GERMAN SPELLING REFORM

The German spelling reform was adopted by German-speaking countries in July 1996. It was agreed that both old and new spellings would be acceptable until 2005, by which time the new spellings should be included in all written texts.

The main changes to the spelling of German words include:
- After a short vowel, **ss** is used instead of **ß**. For example: **daß** becomes **dass**, **Schloß** becomes **Schloss**.
- Capital letters are now used more often, especially for adjectives used as nouns. For example: **recht haben** becomes **Recht haben**, **es tut mir leid** becomes **es tut mir Leid**.
- Words which were previously one word are now often spelt as two words. For example: **stehenlassen** becomes **stehen lassen**, **wieviel** becomes **wie viel**.

In the headword list of this dictionary you will find all the new spellings. They are marked Δ and there is a note at the foot of each page explaining that this symbol signals a new spelling. However, since you may come across old spellings if you are reading pre-reform German material, we have also given as headwords all the most frequent old spellings which could cause problems in looking up. These are cross-referred to the new spellings.

The same symbol Δ is used on the English-German side of the dictionary to signal new spellings in translations of English headwords.

A a

Aal der (PL die **Aale**) eel.

ab preposition ←(+DAT) from; **ab Montag** from Monday; **Kinder ab sechs Jahren** children from the age of six.
adverb 1 off; **der Henkel ist ab** the handle has come off; **ab ins Bett!** (informal) off (you go) to bed!; 2 **ab und zu** now and again.

abbiegen ◇ verb (IMPERF **bog ab**, PERF **ist abgebogen**) 1 to turn off; **nach rechts abbiegen** to turn off to the right; 2 **biegen Sie an der Ampel (nach) links ab** turn left at the lights.

Abbildung die (PL die **Abbildungen**) illustration.

abbrechen ◇ verb (PRES **bricht ab**, IMPERF **brach ab**, PERF **hat abgebrochen**) 1 to break off (a branch, negotiations); **Ruth brach ein paar Zweige ab** Ruth broke off a few branches; 2 to pull down (a building); 3 to cut short; **leider mussten wir unsere Ferien vorzeitig abbrechen** unfortunately we had to cut short our holidays; **er hat sein Studium aus finanziellen Gründen abgebrochen** he left university for financial reasons; 4 (PERF **ist abgebrochen**) **der Ast ist abgebrochen** the branch has broken off.

Abend der (PL die **Abende**) evening; **am Abend** in the evening; **heute Abend** △ this evening, tonight; **gestern Abend** △ yesterday evening, last night; **wann esst ihr zu Abend?** when do you have dinner?

Abendessen das (PL die **Abendessen**) dinner (in the evening); **was gibt es zum Abendessen?** what are we having for dinner?

Abendbrot das evening meal.

Abendkurs der (PL die **Abendkurse**) evening course.

abends adverb in the evening.

Abenteuer das (PL die **Abenteuer**) adventure.

aber conjunction but; **es ist zwar nützlich, aber zu teuer** it's useful, but too expensive.
adverb really; **das ist aber sehr nett von dir** that's really nice of you; **du bist aber groß!** aren't you tall!; **aber ja!** but of course!; **jetzt ist aber Schluss!** that's it now!

abergläubisch adjective superstitious.

abfahren ◇ verb (PRES **fährt ab**, IMPERF **fuhr ab**, PERF **ist abgefahren**) to leave; **Peter fährt morgen ganz früh ab** Peter is leaving very early tomorrow morning; **wann fährt der Zug nach Berlin ab?** when does the Berlin train leave?

Abfahrt die (PL die **Abfahrten**) 1 departure; 2 run (on a ski slope); 3 exit (on a motorway).

Abfall der (PL die **Abfälle**) rubbish.

△ NEW SPELLING: See page xii

Abfalleimer der (PL die Abfalleimer) rubbish bin.

abfliegen ◇ verb (IMPERF **flog ab**, PERF **ist abgeflogen**) **1** to take off; **die Maschine ist mit zehn Minuten Verspätung abgeflogen** the plane took off ten minutes late; **2** to leave (by plane); **ich fliege um elf Uhr ab** my plane leaves at 11 o'clock.

Abflug der (PL die **Abflüge**) departure.

abfragen verb (PERF **hat abgefragt**) **1** to test; **sie fragt ihn Vokabeln ab** she's testing him on his vocabulary; **2** to call up (on a computer); **Adressen am Computer abfragen** to call up addresses on the computer.

Abgase (plural noun) exhaust fumes.

abgeben ◇ verb (PRES **gibt ab**, IMPERF **gab ab**, PERF **hat abgegeben**) **1** to hand in (homework, an application, lost property); **2** to pass (in football); **den Ball abgeben** to pass the ball; **3** sich mit etwas abgeben to spend time on something; **mit solchen Typen würde ich mich nicht abgeben** I wouldn't associate with blokes like that; **4** jemandem etwas abgeben to give someone something; **gib mir ein Stück von deiner Schokolade ab** give me a piece of your chocolate; **5** er wird einen guten Lehrer abgeben he'll make a good teacher.

abgelegen adjective remote.

abgemacht adjective agreed.

Abgeordnete der/die (PL die Abgeordneten) member of parliament.

Abhang der (PL die **Abhänge**) slope.

abhängen[1] ◇ verb (IMPERF **hing ab**, PERF **hat abgehangen**) **von jemandem abhängen** to depend on somebody; **von etwas abhängen** to depend on something; **es hängt vom Wetter ab, ob wir am Wochenende nach Wales fahren** whether or not we are going to Wales at the weekend depends on the weather.

abhängen[2] verb (PERF **hat abgehängt**) **1** to unhitch (a trailer); **2** to uncouple (a train carriage); **3** (informal) to shake off; **die Einbrecher hängten die Polizei schnell ab** the burglars soon shook off the police.

abheben ◇ verb (IMPERF **hob ab**, PERF **hat abgehoben**) **1** to lift up; **2** to withdraw (money); **3** to answer the phone; **ich habe schon zweimal angerufen, aber niemand hat abgehoben** I've rung twice before, but nobody answered.

abholen verb (PERF **hat abgeholt**) **1** to collect; **2** to pick up; **ich hole dich am Bahnhof ab** I'll pick you up at the station.

Abitur das (PL die **Abiture**) A levels (German students usually take Abitur at 19, sitting exams in four subjects, which they have to pass to go on to university); **sein Abitur machen** to do your A levels.

Abiturient der (PL die **Abiturienten**) A-level student.

◇ IRREGULAR VERB: See the verb table in the centre of the dictionary

Abiturientin *die* (PL *die* Abiturientinnen) A-level student.

Abkommen *das* (PL *die* Abkommen) agreement.

abkürzen *verb* (PERF hat abgekürzt) 1 to abbreviate; **wie kürzt man das Wort ab?** how do you abbreviate that word?; 2 **den Weg abkürzen** to take a short cut.

Abkürzung *die* (PL *die* Abkürzungen) 1 abbreviation; **die Abkürzung für Europäische Union ist EU** the abbreviation for European Union is EU; 2 short cut.

abladen ◇ *verb* (PRES lädt ab, IMPERF lud ab, PERF hat abgeladen) to unload.

ablaufen ◇ *verb* (PRES läuft ab, IMPERF lief ab, PERF ist abgelaufen) 1 to expire (*passport, contract*); 2 to drain off; **das Badewasser ablaufen lassen** to let the bathwater out; 3 to go off; **wie ist die Besprechung abgelaufen?** how did the meeting go?

ablegen *verb* (PERF hat abgelegt) 1 to take off; 2 **abgelegte Kleidung** cast-offs.

ablehnen *verb* (PERF hat abgelehnt) 1 to turn down (*a position, money, an invitation*); 2 to reject (*an applicant, a suggestion*).

ablenken *verb* (PERF hat abgelenkt) 1 to distract; **jemanden von seiner Arbeit ablenken** to distract somebody from their work; 2 **jemanden von seinen Sorgen ablenken** to take somebody's mind off their worries; 3 to divert (*attention, suspicion*); **vom Thema ablenken** to change the subject.

abliefern *verb* (PERF hat abgeliefert) 1 to deliver; 2 to hand in (*an essay, a form, lost property*); 3 to drop off; **die Kinder abliefern** to drop the children off.

abmachen *verb* (PERF hat abgemacht) 1 to take off; **kannst du den Deckel abmachen?** can you take off the lid?; 2 to agree; **wir müssen noch einen Termin für unser nächstes Treffen abmachen** we still have to agree on a date for our next meeting; **abgemacht!** agreed!; 3 to sort out; **das müsst ihr untereinander abmachen** you'll have to sort that out amongst yourselves.

Abmachung *die* (PL *die* Abmachungen) agreement.

abnehmen ◇ *verb* (PRES nimmt ab, IMPERF nahm ab, PERF hat abgenommen) 1 to take off (*remove*); 2 **kann ich dir etwas abnehmen?** (*carry*) can I take something (for you)?; (*help*) can I do anything for you?; 3 **jemandem etwas abnehmen** to take something off somebody; **sie nehmen einem schnell zwanzig Mark ab** they'll soon take 20 marks off you; 4 to buy; 5 to decrease (*in number*); 6 to lose weight; **er hat schon vier Kilo abgenommen** he's already lost four kilos; 7 to answer the phone; 8 **das nehme ich dir nicht ab** (*informal*) I don't buy that.

Abonnement *das* (PL *die* Abonnements) subscription.

△ NEW SPELLING: *See page xii*

abonnieren verb (PERF hat abonniert) to subscribe to.

abraten ◊ verb (PRES rät ab, IMPERF riet ab, PERF hat abgeraten) jemandem von etwas abraten to advise somebody against something.

abräumen verb (PERF hat abgeräumt) to clear away.

abreagieren verb (PERF hat abreagiert) 1 seine Wut an jemandem abreagieren to take your anger out on somebody; 2 sich abreagieren to calm down.

Abreise die departure.

abreisen verb (PERF ist abgereist) to leave.

abreißen ◊ verb (IMPERF riss ab △, PERF hat abgerissen) 1 to tear down (a poster, notice); 2 **abreißen** to come off (a button, for example).

Absage die (PL die Absagen) refusal.

absagen verb (PERF hat abgesagt) 1 to cancel; 2 eine Einladung absagen to turn down an invitation.

Absatz der (PL die Absätze) 1 heel (of a shoe); 2 paragraph.

abschaffen verb (PERF hat abgeschafft) 1 to abolish (a regulation, capital punishment); 2 to get rid of; wir haben unseren Hund abgeschafft we got rid of our dog.

abscheulich adjective horrible.

abschicken verb (PERF hat abgeschickt) to send off.

Abschied der (PL die Abschiede) 1 parting; 2 farewell; 3 Abschied nehmen to say goodbye.

Abschleppdienst der breakdown service.

abschleppen verb (PERF hat abgeschleppt) 1 to tow away; 2 sich mit den Koffern abschleppen (informal) to struggle along with the suitcases; 3 jemanden abschleppen (informal) to pick somebody up.

abschließen ◊ verb (IMPERF schloss ab △, PERF hat abgeschlossen) to lock.

Abschlussprüfung △ die (PL die Abschlussprüfungen) final exam.

abschneiden ◊ verb (IMPERF schnitt ab, PERF hat abgeschnitten) 1 to cut off; ich schneide dir eine Scheibe Brot ab I'll cut you a slice of bread; 2 gut/schlecht abschneiden to do well/badly.

abschrecken verb (PERF hat abgeschreckt) to deter.

abschreiben ◊ verb (IMPERF schrieb ab, PERF hat abgeschrieben) to copy.

abseits adverb 1 far away; etwas abseits a little way away; 2 offside (in soccer).

Absender der (PL die Absender) sender.

absetzen verb (PERF hat abgesetzt) 1 to take off (your hat, glasses); 2 to put down (a bag, suitcase); 3 to drop off; ich setze euch am Bahnhof ab I'll drop you off at the station; 4 die

◊ IRREGULAR VERB: See the verb table in the centre of the dictionary

Pille absetzen to stop taking the pill.

Absicht die (PL die **Absichten**) intention.

absichtlich adverb intentionally.

absolut adjective absolute. adverb absolutely; **das ist absolut unmöglich** that's absolutely impossible.

abspülen verb (PERF hat abgespült) 1 to rinse, to rinse off; 2 to do the washing up.

Abstand der (PL die **Abstände**) 1 distance; **in zwanzig Meter Abstand** at a distance of 20 metres; **Abstand halten** to keep your distance; 2 interval.

abstauben verb (PERF hat abgestaubt) to dust.

abstellen verb (PERF hat abgestellt) 1 to turn off (the radio, a tap); 2 to put down (a suitcase, the shopping); 3 to park (the car).

Abstimmung die (PL die **Abstimmungen**) vote.

abstreiten ◇ verb (IMPERF stritt ab, PERF hat abgestritten) to deny.

abstürzen verb (PERF ist abgestürzt) 1 to fall; 2 to crash (a plane).

Abteil das (PL die **Abteile**) compartment.

Abteilung die (PL die **Abteilungen**) department.

Abtreibung die (PL die **Abtreibungen**) abortion.

abtrocknen verb (PERF hat abgetrocknet) 1 to dry up; 2 **sich abtrocknen** to dry yourself.

abwägen verb (IMPERF wog ab, PERF hat abgewogen) to weigh up.

abwärts adverb down.

Abwasch der washing-up.

abwaschen ◇ verb (PRES wäscht ab, IMPERF wusch ab, PERF hat abgewaschen) 1 to wash up (the dishes); 2 to wash off (dirt, marks).

Abwasser das (PL die **Abwässer**) sewage.

Abwechslung die (PL die **Abwechslungen**) change; **zur Abwechslung** for a change.

abwerten verb (PERF hat abgewertet) to devalue.

abwertend adjective pejorative.

abwesend adjective absent.

Abwesenheit die absence.

abwischen verb (PERF hat abgewischt) to wipe.

abzählen verb (PERF hat abgezählt) to count.

Abzeichen das (PL die **Abzeichen**) badge.

abziehen ◇ verb (IMPERF zog ab, PERF hat abgezogen) 1 to take off (a sheet, backing); **die Betten abziehen** to strip the beds; 2 to take out (a key); 3 to deduct, to take away; 4 to withdraw (troops); 5 (PERF ist abgezogen) to escape (steam or smoke, for example); 6 (PERF ist abgezogen) sie sind

△ NEW SPELLING: See page xii

gleich nach dem Essen
abgezogen (*informal*) they pushed
off straight after the meal.

abzielen verb (PERF hat abgezielt)
etwas zielt auf etwas ab
something is aimed at something.

ach exclamation oh!

Achsel die (PL die Achseln) shoulder.

acht number eight; **um acht (Uhr)**
at eight (o'clock); **um halb acht** at
half past seven.

Acht[1] die (PL die Achten) eight; **eine
Acht schreiben** to write an eight.

Acht[2] die 1 **Acht geben** △ to pay
attention; **er sollte in der Schule
besser Acht geben** he should pay
more attention at school; 2 **auf
etwas/jemanden Acht geben** to
look after something/somebody;
3 **gib Acht!** watch out!; 4 **sich in
Acht nehmen** △ to be careful;
5 **etwas außer Acht lassen** △ to
disregard something.

Achtel das (PL die Achtel) eighth.

achten verb (PERF hat geachtet)
1 to respect (*a person, an opinion*);
2 **auf etwas achten** to pay attention
to something; 3 **auf jemanden
achten** to look after somebody;
4 **achte nicht darauf!** don't take
any notice of it!

achter, achte, achtes adjective
eighth; **jede achte Kiste** every
eighth crate; **mein achter
Geburtstag** my eighth birthday; **sie
ging als Achte durchs Ziel** she
finished eighth.

Achterbahn die (PL die
Achterbahnen) roller coaster.

achtgeben SEE **Acht**[2].

achthundert number eight
hundred.

achtmal adverb eight times.

Achtung die 1 respect; **Achtung
vor jemandem haben** to have
respect for somebody; 2 **Achtung!**
look out!; **Achtung, fertig, los!** on
your marks, get set, go!; '**Achtung
Stufe**' 'mind the step'.

achtzehn number eighteen.

achtzig number eighty.

Acker der (PL die Äcker) field.

addieren verb (PERF hat addiert) to
add.

Ader die (PL die Adern) vein.

Adjektiv das (PL die Adjektive)
adjective.

Adler der (PL die Adler) eagle.

adoptieren verb (PERF hat
adoptiert) to adopt.

Adoption die (PL die Adoptionen)
adoption.

Adoptiveltern plural noun
adoptive parents.

Adoptivkind das (PL die
Adoptivkinder) adopted child.

Adresse die (PL die Adressen)
address.

adressieren verb (PERF hat
adressiert) to address; **an wen soll
ich den Brief adressieren?** who
shall I address the letter to?

✧ IRREGULAR VERB: *See the verb table in the centre of the dictionary*

Advent der Advent.

Adventskalender der (PL die Adventskalender) Advent calendar.

Adventskranz der (PL die Adventskränze) Advent wreath.

Adverb das (PL die Adverbien) adverb.

Aerobic das aerobics.

Affe der (PL die Affen) 1 monkey; 2 ape.

Afrika das Africa; aus Afrika from Africa; nach Afrika to Africa.

Afrikaner der (PL die Afrikaner) African.

Afrikanerin die (PL die Afrikanerinnen) African.

afrikanisch adjective African.

Agentur die (PL die Agenturen) agency.

aggressiv adjective aggressive.

ähneln verb (PERF hat geähnelt) 1 to resemble; er ähnelt seinem Vater sehr he's very like his father; 2 sich ähneln to be alike.

ahnen verb (PERF hat geahnt) 1 to know; das konnte ich wirklich nicht ahnen I had no way of knowing that; wer soll denn ahnen, dass ...? who would know that ...?; 2 to suspect; so etwas habe ich doch schon geahnt I did suspect something like that.

ähnlich adjective 1 similar; 2 jemandem ähnlich sein to be like somebody; jemandem ähnlich sehen to look like somebody;

3 ähnlich wie like; 4 das sieht dir ähnlich! (informal) that's just like you!

Ähnlichkeit die (PL die Ähnlichkeiten) similarity.

Ahnung die 1 idea; hast du eine Ahnung, wie er heißt? have you got any idea what he's called?; 2 keine Ahnung! no idea!; er hat von Mode absolut keine Ahnung he doesn't know a thing about fashion; 3 premonition.

ahnungslos adjective unsuspecting.

Ahorn der (PL die Ahorne) maple.

Aids das Aids.

Akademiker der (PL die Akademiker) university graduate.

Akademikerin die (PL die Akademikerinnen) university graduate.

akademisch adjective academic.

Akkusativ der (PL die Akkusative) accusative.

Akne die acne.

Akte die (PL die Akten) file.

Aktentasche die (PL die Aktentaschen) briefcase.

Aktion die (PL die Aktionen) 1 action; in Aktion treten to go into action; 2 campaign.

aktiv adjective active.

Aktiv das active.

aktuell adjective 1 topical; ein aktuelles Thema a topical issue;

△ NEW SPELLING: See page xii

2 nicht mehr aktuell no longer relevant; **3** current; eine aktuelle Sendung a current-affairs programme.

Akzent der (PL die Akzente) **1** accent; mit starkem Akzent sprechen to speak with a strong accent; **2** accent (on a letter); **3** stress; den Akzent auf etwas legen to stress something.

albern adjective silly. adverb in a silly way.

Album das (PL die Alben) album.

Algebra die algebra.

Alkohol der alcohol.

alkoholfrei adjective non-alcoholic.

Alkoholiker der (PL die Alkoholiker) alcoholic.

Alkoholikerin die (PL die Alkoholikerinnen) alcoholic.

alkoholisch adjective alcoholic.

All das space; einen Satelliten ins All schicken to send a satellite into space.

alle SEE aller.

Allee die (PL die Alleen) avenue.

allein adjective, adverb **1** alone; sie waren allein im Zimmer they were alone in the room; jemanden allein lassen to leave somebody alone; **2** on your own; sie hat das ganz allein gezeichnet she drew it all on her own; **3** von allein by yourself, by itself (automatically); **4** allein stehend △ single; **5** eine allein

erziehende Mutter △ a single mother; der/die allein Erziehende △ single parent; **6** nicht allein not only; **7** allein der Gedanke the mere thought.

alleinerziehend, alleinstehend SEE allein.

aller, alle, alles pronoun **1** all; alle meine Freunde all my friends; alles Geld all the money; alle miteinander all together; **2** alle Jungen in der Schule all the boys in the school; alle Bewohner der Stadt sind dagegen all the people of the town are against it; alles Gute! all the best!; Getränke aller Art all kinds of drinks; **3** alle (plural) all; alle waren da they were all there; wir alle we all, all of us; wir haben alle gesehen we saw all of them; **4** ohne allen Grund without any reason; **5** alle beide both of them; **6** every; alle Tage every day; alle fünf Minuten every five minutes; **7** alles everything, everybody (people). adjective alle sein (informal) to be all gone.

allerbester, allerbeste, allerbestes adjective **1** very best; **2** am allerbesten best of all.

allerdings adverb **1** though; das Essen ist gut, allerdings ziemlich teuer the food's good, though rather expensive; **2** certainly (yes); 'tut das weh?' – 'allerdings!' 'does it hurt?' – 'it certainly does!'.

Allergie die (PL die Allergien) allergy.

allergisch adjective allergic.

$\diamondsuit$ IRREGULAR VERB: See the verb table in the centre of the dictionary

Allerheiligen *das* All Saints' Day.

allerlei *adjective* all sorts of; **allerlei Ausreden** all sorts of excuses.

allerletzter, allerletzte, allerletztes *adjective* very last.

alles SEE **aller**.

allgemein *adjective* 1 general; 2 **im Allgemeinen**△ in general.
adverb 1 generally; 2 **es ist allgemein bekannt, dass ...** it is common knowledge that ...

allmählich *adjective* gradual.
adverb gradually; **wir sollten allmählich gehen** it's time we got going.

alltäglich *adjective* everyday (*event, sight*).

Alltag *der* 1 daily routine; 2 weekday.

alltags *adverb* on weekdays.

Alpen *plural noun* **die Alpen** the Alps.

Alphabet *das* (PL **die Alphabete**) alphabet.

alphabetisch *adjective* alphabetical.

Alptraum *der* (PL **die Alpträume**) nightmare.

als *conjunction* 1 when; **als meine Freundin hier war** when my friend was here; **erst als** only when; 2 than (*as a comparison*); **er ist jünger als sie** he's younger than her; 3 **lieber ... als ...** rather ... than ...; **ich ginge lieber ins Kino als zum Essen** I'd rather go to the cinema than for a meal; 4 as; **als Frau kann ich das verstehen** as a woman, I can sympathize; **gerade als ich gehen wollte** just as I was about to leave; 5 **als ob** as if; **als ob ich das nicht wüsste!** as if I didn't know that!

also *adverb, conjunction* 1 so; **ich konnte ihn telefonisch nicht erreichen, also habe ich ihm ein Fax geschickt** I couldn't get through to him on the phone, so I sent him a fax; 2 then; **also kommst du mit?** you're coming too, then?; **also gut** all right then; 3 well; **also, wie gesagt** well, as I said before; 4 **na also!** there you are!

alt *adjective* 1 old; **wie alt bist du?** how old are you?; **alt werden** to grow old; 2 **alles beim Alten lassen** to leave everything as it was.

Altar *der* (PL **die Altäre**) altar.

Alter *das* (PL **die Alter**) 1 age; **in deinem Alter** at your age; **im Alter von zwanzig** at the age of twenty; 2 old age; **im Alter** in old age.

älter *adjective* 1 older; **mein Rad ist älter als deins** my bike is older than yours; 2 elder; **mein älterer Bruder** my elder brother; 3 elderly.

altern *verb* (PERF **ist gealtert**) to age.

Alternative *die* (PL **die Alternativen**) alternative.

Altersgrenze *die* (PL **die Altersgrenzen**) age limit.

Altersheim *das* (PL **die Altersheime**) old people's home.

△ NEW SPELLING: *See page xii*

ältester, älteste, ältestes
adjective 1 oldest; 2 eldest; **der
älteste Sohn** the eldest son.

Altglas *das* used glass.

Altglascontainer *der* (PL *die*
Altglascontainer) bottle bank.

altmodisch *adjective* old-
fashioned.

Altpapier *das* waste paper.

Altstadt *die* (PL *die* **Altstädte**) old
town.

Alufolie *die* tin foil.

Aluminium *das* aluminium.

am = an dem; 1 **am Freitag** on
Friday; 2 **am besten** the best; 3 **am
teuersten** (the) most expensive;
4 **am höchsten** the highest; 5 **am
Abend** in the evening.

Ameise *die* (PL *die* **Ameisen**) ant.

Amerika *das* America.

Amerikaner *der* (PL *die*
Amerikaner) American.

Amerikanerin *die* (PL *die*
Amerikanerinnen) American.

amerikanisch *adjective* American.

Ampel *die* (PL *die* **Ampeln**) traffic
lights.

Amsel *die* (PL *die* **Amseln**) blackbird.

Amt *das* (PL *die* **Ämter**) 1 office;
2 exchange (*telephone*).

amtlich *adjective* official.

amüsant *adjective* amusing.

amüsieren *verb* (PERF **hat
amüsiert**) 1 to amuse; 2 **sich
amüsieren** to enjoy oneself;

amüsier dich gut! enjoy yourself!;
3 **sich über etwas amüsieren** to
find something funny.

an *preposition* ←(+DAT or +ACC) (*the
dative is used when talking about
position; the accusative shows
movement or a change of place*) 1 at;
an der Spitze at the top; **sich an
den Tisch setzen** to sit down at the
table; **er arbeitet an der Schule** he
works at the school; 2 on (*attached
to, when talking about time*); **das
Bild hängt an der Wand** the picture
is on the wall; **an dem Tag** on that
day; **ich habe am fünften März
Geburtstag** my birthday is on the
fifth of March; 3 to; **einen Brief an
jemanden schicken** to send a letter
to somebody; 4 **an einer Krankheit
sterben** to die of a disease; 5 **an
jemanden denken** to think of
somebody; 6 **sich an etwas
erinnern** to remember something;
7 **an (und für) sich** actually; **an sich
ist das kein Problem** actually, it's
no problem; 8 **es liegt an dir, jetzt
etwas zu unternehmen** it's up to
you to do something now.
adverb 1 on; **das Licht ist an** the
light's on; 2 **ohne etwas an** with
nothing on; 3 **an die dreißig Mark**
about thirty marks; 4 **von heute an**
from today.

Ananas *die* (PL *die* **Ananas**)
pineapple.

anbieten ◇ *verb* (IMPERF **bot an**,
PERF **hat angeboten**) to offer; **Anna
bot mir an, mich nach Hause zu
bringen** Anna offered to take me
home.

◇ IRREGULAR VERB: *See the verb table in the centre of the dictionary.*

Anblick der (PL die Anblicke) sight.

anbrennen ◇ verb (IMPERF **brannte an**, PERF **ist angebrannt**) to burn; **das Essen ist angebrannt** the food's burnt.

Andenken das (PL die Andenken) 1 souvenir; 2 **zum Andenken an unsere Ferien** to remind us of our holiday.

anderer, andere, anderes adjective 1 other; **ich nehme das andere T-Shirt** I'll have the other T-shirt; 2 different; 3 **ein anderer/eine andere/ein anderes** another; **ein anderes Mal** another time. pronoun 1 **der/die/das andere** the other one; **nicht dieses Buch, sondern das andere** not that book, but the other one; **die anderen** the others; **die anderen kommen später** the others are coming later; 2 **andere** other ones (things, toys, etc.); 3 **ein anderer/eine andere/ein anderes** a different one (thing); someone else (person); 4 **kein anderer** no one else; 5 **unter anderem** among other things; 6 **etwas anderes** something else; 7 **alles andere** everything else.

andererseits adverb on the other hand.

andermal adverb **ein andermal** another time.

ändern verb (PERF **hat geändert**) 1 to change; 2 to alter (a garment); 3 **sich ändern** to change; **sie hat sich sehr geändert** she's changed a lot.

anders adverb 1 differently;

2 **anders aussehen** to look different; 3 **niemand anders** nobody else; **jemand anders** somebody else; 4 **anders als** different from; **du bist ganz anders als ich** you're quite different from me; 5 **irgendwo anders** somewhere else.

anderthalb number one and a half.

Anerkennung die 1 appreciation; 2 recognition (of a king, state).

Anfall der (PL die Anfälle) fit.

Anfang der (PL die Anfänge) 1 beginning, start; **am Anfang** at the beginning; **von Anfang an** from the start; 2 **zu Anfang** at first.

anfangen ◇ verb (PRES **fängt an**, IMPERF **fing an**, PERF **hat angefangen**) 1 to begin, to start; **die Schule fängt um acht an** school starts at eight; **mit etwas anfangen** to start (on) something; 2 **bei einer Firma anfangen** to start working for a firm; 3 **was soll ich damit anfangen?** what am I supposed to do with that?; 4 **damit kann ich nichts anfangen** that's no good to me (it's no use); it doesn't mean anything to me (I don't understand it).

Anfänger der (PL die Anfänger) beginner.

Anfängerin die (PL die Anfängerinnen) beginner.

anfassen verb (PERF **hat angefasst**△) 1 to touch; 2 to tackle (a problem, a task); 3 to treat (a person); 4 **mit anfassen** to lend a hand; **5 sich anfassen** to feel; **es fasst sich weich an** it feels soft; **6 jemanden anfassen** to take somebody's hand; **sie hat ihre Mutter angefasst** she took her mother's hand; **fasst euch an!** hold hands!

anfragen verb (PERF **hat angefragt**) to enquire, to ask.

anfreunden verb (PERF **hat sich angefreundet**) **1 sich anfreunden** to make friends; **sie freundet sich mit allen möglichen Leuten an** she makes friends with all sorts of people; **2 sich anfreunden** to become friends; **wir haben uns angefreundet** we've become friends.

Anführungszeichen plural noun inverted commas.

Angabe die (PL die **Angaben**) **1** piece of information; **2** serve (in tennis); **3** showing off; **das ist nur Angabe** he is/she is/they are only showing off.

angeben ◇ verb (PRES **gibt an**, IMPERF **gab an**, PERF **hat angegeben**) **1** to give (your name, a reason); **2** to show off; **3** to indicate (on a map); **4** to serve (in tennis).

Angeber der (PL die **Angeber**) show-off.

Angeberin die (PL die **Angeberinnen**) show-off.

Angebot das (PL die **Angebote**) offer.

angehen ◇ verb (IMPERF **ging an**, PERF **ist angegangen**) **1** to come on (a radio, heating, a light); **2** to

concern; **das geht auch dich etwas an** it concerns you too; **das geht dich nichts an** it's none of your business; **3** (PERF **hat angegangen**) to tackle (problems, difficulty, work).

Angehörige der/die (PL die **Angehörigen**) relative.

Angel die (PL die **Angeln**) fishing rod.

Angelegenheit die (PL die **Angelegenheiten**) **1** matter; **2** business; **das ist meine Angelegenheit** that's my business.

angeln verb (PERF **hat geangelt**) **1** to fish; **angeln gehen** to go fishing; **2** to catch (a fish).

Angelrute die (PL die **Angelruten**) fishing rod.

angenehm adjective pleasant. exclamation pleased to meet you! (when introduced to somebody).

Angestellte der/die (PL die **Angestellten**) employee.

angewiesen adjective dependent; **auf etwas angewiesen sein** to be dependent on something; **auf jemanden angewiesen sein** to be dependent on somebody.

angewöhnen verb (PERF **hat angewöhnt**) **1 jemandem etwas angewöhnen** to get somebody used to something; **2 sich etwas angewöhnen** to get into the habit of doing something; **ich habe es mir angewöhnt, früh aufzustehen** I've got into the habit of getting up early.

Angewohnheit die (PL die **Angewohnheiten**) habit.

◇ IRREGULAR VERB: See the verb table in the centre of the dictionary

angreifen ◇ verb (IMPERF griff an, PERF hat angegriffen) 1 to attack; 2 to affect (your health, voice).

Angriff der (PL die Angriffe) attack.

Angst die (PL die Ängste) 1 fear; 2 Angst haben to be afraid; vor jemandem Angst haben to be afraid of somebody; mir ist Angst I'm afraid; 3 jemandem Angst machen to frighten somebody; 4 Angst vor einer Prüfung haben to be worried about an exam; Angst um jemanden haben to be worried about somebody.

ängstlich adjective 1 nervous; 2 frightened; 3 anxious.

anhaben ◇ verb (informal) (PRES hat an, IMPERF hatte an, PERF hat angehabt) to have on; sie hat heute das neue Kleid an she's got her new dress on today.

anhalten ◇ verb (PRES hält an, IMPERF hielt an, PERF hat angehalten) 1 to stop; 2 den Atem anhalten to hold your breath; 3 to last; das schöne Wetter wird nicht lange anhalten the nice weather won't last long; 4 jemanden zur Arbeit anhalten to urge somebody to work.

Anhalter der (PL die Anhalter) hitchhiker; per Anhalter fahren to hitchhike.

Anhalterin die (PL die Anhalterinnen) hitchhiker.

Anhang der (PL die Anhänge) appendix.

Anhänger der (PL die Anhänger) 1 supporter; 2 trailer; 3 label (on a suitcase); 4 pendant; 5 loop (for hanging up).

Anhängerin die (PL die Anhängerinnen) supporter.

anhören verb (PERF hat angehört) 1 to listen to (music, a CD); sich etwas anhören to listen to something; ich kann ihn mir nicht länger anhören I can't listen to him any longer; 2 sich anhören to sound; sich gut anhören to sound good; 3 jemandem etwas anhören to hear something in somebody's voice; man hörte ihr die Verzweifung an you could hear the despair in her voice.

anklagen verb (PERF hat angeklagt) to accuse.

Ankleidekabine die (PL die Ankleidekabinen) changing cubicle.

ankommen ◇ verb (IMPERF kam an, PERF ist angekommen) 1 to arrive; gut ankommen to arrive safely; 2 (bei jemandem) gut ankommen (informal) to go down well (with somebody); 3 ankommen auf to depend on; es kommt ganz darauf an it all depends; 4 es drauf ankommen lassen (informal) to take a chance; 5 auf ein paar Minuten kommt es nicht an a few minutes don't matter.

ankündigen verb (PERF hat angekündigt) to announce.

Ankunft die (PL die Ankünfte) arrival.

Ankunftstafel die (PL die Ankunftstafeln) arrivals board.

△ NEW SPELLING: See page xii

Ankunftszeit die (PL die Ankunftszeiten) time of arrival.

Anlage die (PL die Anlagen) 1 gardens; 2 investment; das Haus ist eine gute Anlage the house is a good investment; 3 plant (industrial, for recycling, for example); 4 enclosure; als Anlage enclosed; 5 system (music, loudspeakers, etc.); 6 installation (military).

Anlass Δ der (PL die Anlässe) 1 cause; der Anlass ihres Streits the cause of their row; Anlass zu etwas geben to give cause for something; 2 occasion; ein festlicher Anlass a festive occasion; aus Anlass ihres Geburtstags on the occasion of her birthday.

Anleitung die (PL die Anleitungen) instructions.

anmachen verb (PERF hat angemacht) 1 to turn on (the light, radio, TV); 2 to light (a fire); 3 to dress (salad); 4 (informal) to chat up (a person).

Anmeldeformular das (PL die Anmeldeformulare) registration form.

anmelden verb (PERF hat angemeldet) 1 to register (a car, change of address); 2 jemanden anmelden to enrol somebody; 3 jemanden anmelden to make an appointment for somebody; sind Sie angemeldet? do you have an appointment? 4 ein Gespräch anmelden to book a call (on the phone); 5 sich anmelden to say that you're coming; 6 sich anmelden to register your new address (in Germany a change of address has to be registered at the 'Einwohnermeldeamt'); sich polizeilich anmelden to register with the police; 7 sich anmelden to make an appointment; sich beim Arzt anmelden to make an appointment with the doctor; 8 sich anmelden to enrol; sich zu einem Abendkurs anmelden to enrol for an evening course.

Anmeldung die (PL die Anmeldungen) 1 registration; 2 appointment.

annehmen Φ verb (PRES nimmt an, IMPERF nahm an, PERF hat angenommen) 1 to accept (an invitation, help, a verdict); 2 to take (a call, name); 3 to adopt (a child, habit); 4 to assume; angenommen, dass ... assuming that ...; 5 to suppose.

annehmbar adjective acceptable.

Annonce die (PL die Annoncen) (small) ad.

anordnen verb (PERF hat angeordnet) 1 to arrange; 2 to order.

anpassen verb (PERF hat sich angepasst Δ) sich anpassen to adapt.

anpassungsfähig adjective adaptable.

anprobieren verb (PERF hat anprobiert) to try on.

Φ IRREGULAR VERB: See the verb table in the centre of the dictionary

Anruf der (PL die **Anrufe**) (phone) call.

Anrufbeantworter der (PL die **Anrufbeantworter**) answering machine.

anrufen ◇ verb (IMPERF **rief an**, PERF **hat angerufen**) 1 to ring, to phone; **ich rufe schnell mal meine Mutter an** I'll just quickly ring my mother; 2 to call to (a passer-by).

ans = an das; **ans Telefon gehen** to answer the phone.

Ansage die (PL die **Ansagen**) announcement.

Ansager der (PL die **Ansager**) announcer.

Ansagerin die (PL die **Ansagerinnen**) announcer.

anschalten verb (PERF **hat angeschaltet**) to switch on.

anschauen verb (PERF **hat angeschaut**) 1 to look at; 2 **sich etwas anschauen** to look at something, to watch something (on TV); **sie schauten sich den neuen Film an** they saw the new film.

anscheinend adverb apparently.

Anschlag der (PL die **Anschläge**) 1 notice; 2 attack; **ein Anschlag auf den Präsidenten** an attack on the president.

Anschlagbrett das (PL die **Anschlagbretter**) notice board.

anschlagen ◇ verb (PRES **schlägt an**, IMPERF **schlug an**, PERF **hat angeschlagen**) 1 to put up (a notice, an announcement); 2 to chip.

anschließen ◇ verb (IMPERF **schloss an** △, PERF **hat angeschlossen**) 1 to connect; 2 **sich an etwas anschließen** to follow something; **an den Vortrag schließt sich eine Diskussion an** the talk will be followed by a discussion; 3 **sich jemandem anschließen** to join somebody; **sich einer Gruppe anschließen** to join a group.

anschließend adverb 1 afterwards; 2 **anschließend an das Essen** after the meal.

Anschluss △ der (PL die **Anschlüsse**) 1 connection; 2 **Anschluss finden** to make friends; 3 **den Anschluss verlieren** to lose contact; 4 **im Anschluss an** after.

anschnallen verb (PERF **hat sich angeschnallt**) **sich anschnallen** to fasten your seat belt.

Anschrift die (PL die **Anschriften**) address.

Anschuldigung die (PL die **Anschuldigungen**) accusation.

ansehen ◇ verb (PRES **sieht an**, IMPERF **sah an**, PERF **hat angesehen**) 1 to look at; **sie sah mich nicht an** she didn't look at me; 2 **sich etwas ansehen** to look at something (on TV) to watch something; **sich einen Film ansehen** to see a film; 3 **sich eine Stadt ansehen** to look round a town; 4 to regard; **ich sehe ihn als meinen Freund an** I regard him as a friend.

Ansehen das 1 respect; 2 reputation.

Ansicht die (PL die Ansichten) view; meiner Ansicht nach in my view.

Ansichtskarte die (PL die Ansichtskarten) picture postcard.

ansprechen ◇ verb (PRES spricht an, IMPERF sprach an, PERF hat angesprochen) 1 to speak to; 2 to appeal to; die Musik spricht mich an the music appeals to me; 3 to mention; er hat den Skandal, in den sie verwickelt war, angesprochen he mentioned the scandal she was involved in; 4 auf etwas ansprechen to respond to something (a treatment, for example).

Anspruch der (PL die Ansprüche) 1 demand; keine Ansprüche stellen to make no demands; 2 claim; Anspruch auf etwas haben to be entitled to something; 4 viel Zeit in Anspruch nehmen to take up a lot of time; 5 etwas in Anspruch nehmen to take advantage of something (an offer, for example).

anständig adjective 1 decent; 2 respectable.

anstarren verb (PERF hat angestarrt) to stare at.

anstatt preposition ←(+GEN) instead of.
conjunction anstatt zu arbeiten instead of working.

ansteckend adjective infectious.

anstelle preposition ←(+GEN) instead of.

anstellen verb (PERF hat angestellt) 1 to employ; 2 to turn on (the TV, radio); 3 to do; was stellt ihr heute Abend noch an? what are you doing tonight?; wie kann ich es nur anstellen, dass ...? what can I do to ...?; 4 sich anstellen to queue; 5 sich anstellen to make a fuss; stell dich nicht so an! don't make such a fuss!

anstreichen ◇ verb (IMPERF strich an, PERF hat angestrichen) to paint.

anstrengen verb (PERF hat angestrengt) 1 to tire; ihr Besuch hat mich sehr angestrengt their visit tired me out; 2 sich anstrengen to make an effort.

anstrengend adjective tiring.

Anstrengung die (PL die Anstrengungen) effort.

Antarktis die die Antarktis the Antarctic.

Anteil der (PL die Anteile) 1 share; mein Anteil an dem Gewinn my share of the profit; 2 Anteil nehmen to sympathize; 3 Anteil nehmen an to take an interest in.

Antenne die (PL die Antennen) aerial.

Antibiotikum das (PL die Antibiotika) antibiotic.

antik adjective antique.

Antiquitäten plural noun antiques.

Antrag der (PL die Anträge)

◇ IRREGULAR VERB: See the verb table in the centre of the dictionary

application; **einen Antrag stellen** to make an application.

Antragsformular das (PL die **Antragsformulare**) application form.

Antwort die (PL die **Antworten**) answer, reply; **jemandem eine Antwort geben** to give somebody an answer.

antworten verb (PERF hat **geantwortet**) to answer, to reply; **auf etwas antworten** to answer something; **jemandem antworten** to reply to somebody.

Anwalt der (PL die **Anwälte**) lawyer.

Anwältin die (PL die **Anwältinnen**) lawyer.

Anweisung die (PL die **Anweisungen**) instruction.

anwenden verb (PERF hat **angewendet**) 1 to use (a method, process, medicine); 2 to apply (a rule, law).

anwesend adjective present.

Anzahl die number.

anzahlen verb (PERF hat angezahlt) to pay a deposit; **hundert Mark anzahlen** to pay a hundred marks deposit; **ein Auto anzahlen** to pay a deposit on a car.

Anzahlung die (PL die **Anzahlungen**) deposit.

Anzeichen das (PL die **Anzeichen**) sign.

Anzeige die (PL die **Anzeigen**) 1 advertisement; 2 report (to the

police); **(eine) Anzeige gegen jemanden erstatten** to report somebody to the police.

anzeigen verb (PERF hat angezeigt) 1 to report; **jemanden anzeigen** to report somebody to the police; 2 to show (the time, a date).

anziehen ◇ verb (IMPERF zog an, PERF hat angezogen) 1 to attract; 2 to put on (clothes, the brakes); 3 to dress (a child or doll); **gut angezogen** well dressed; 4 **sich anziehen** to get dressed; 5 **was soll ich anziehen?** what shall I wear?

Anzug der (PL die **Anzüge**) suit.

anzünden verb (PERF hat angezündet) to light.

Apfel der (PL die **Äpfel**) apple.

Apfelsaft der (PL die **Apfelsäfte**) apple juice.

Apfelsine die (PL die **Apfelsinen**) orange.

Apotheke die (PL die **Apotheken**) chemist's, pharmacy.

Apotheker der (PL die **Apotheker**) chemist, pharmacist.

Apothekerin die (PL die **Apothekerinnen**) chemist, pharmacist.

Apparat der (PL die **Apparate**) 1 set (TV, radio); 2 camera; 3 phone; **am Apparat!** speaking!; 4 gadget.

Appartement das (PL die **Appartements**) flat.

Appetit der appetite; **guten Appetit!** enjoy your meal!

△ NEW SPELLING: See page xii

Aprikose die (PL die **Aprikosen**) apricot.

April der April; **am ersten April** on the first of April; **April, April!** April fool!; **jemanden in den April schicken** to play an April fool trick on somebody.

Äquator der equator.

Araber der (PL die **Araber**) Arab.

Araberin die (PL die **Araberinnen**) Arab.

arabisch adjective **1** Arab; **2** Arabian; **3** Arabic (number); **die arabische Sprache** Arabic.

Arbeit die (PL die **Arbeiten**) **1** work; **viel Arbeit haben** to have a lot of work; **von der Arbeit kommen** to come from work; **2** job; **3** test (at school); **4** **sich viel Arbeit machen** to go to a lot of trouble.

arbeiten verb (PERF **hat gearbeitet**) to work.

Arbeiter der (PL die **Arbeiter**) worker.

Arbeiterin die (PL die **Arbeiterinnen**) worker.

Arbeitgeber der (PL die **Arbeitgeber**) employer.

Arbeitnehmer der (PL die **Arbeitnehmer**) employee.

Arbeitsamt das (PL die **Arbeitsämter**) job centre.

arbeitslos adjective unemployed.

Arbeitslose der/die (PL die **Arbeitslosen**) unemployed person; **die Arbeitslosen** the unemployed.

Arbeitslosigkeit die unemployment.

Arbeitspraktikum das (PL die **Arbeitspraktika**) work experience.

Arbeitsplatz der (PL die **Arbeitsplätze**) **1** job; **2** desk.

Architekt der (PL die **Architekten**) architect.

Architektin die (PL die **Architektinnen**) architect.

Architektur die architecture.

Ärger der **1** annoyance; **2** trouble; **Ärger mit dem Auto haben** to have trouble with the car.

ärgerlich adjective **1** annoying; **2** annoyed; **er war darüber sehr ärgerlich** he was very annoyed about it.

ärgern verb (PERF **hat geärgert**) **1** to annoy; **2** **sich ärgern** to be annoyed, to get annoyed; **ich habe mich darüber geärgert** I was annoyed about it; **sich über jemanden ärgern** to get annoyed with somebody.

artig adjective well-behaved.

Arktis die die Arktis the Arctic; **in der Arktis** in the Arctic.

arm adjective poor.

Arm der (PL die **Arme**) arm; **jemanden auf den Arm nehmen** (informal) to pull somebody's leg.

Armband das (PL die **Armbänder**) bracelet.

Armbanduhr die (PL die **Armbanduhren**) wrist-watch.

◊ IRREGULAR VERB: See the verb table in the centre of the dictionary

Armee die (PL die Armeen) army.

Ärmel der (PL die Ärmel) sleeve.

Ärmelkanal der (English) Channel.

Armut die poverty.

arrangieren verb (PERF hat arrangiert) 1 to arrange; 2 sich arrangieren to come to an arrangement.

Art die (PL die Arten) 1 way; auf diese Art in this way; auf seine Art in his own way; 2 kind; diese Art (von) Buch this kind of book; Bücher aller Art all kinds of books; 3 species; 4 nature; es ist nicht seine Art, das zu tun it's not (in) his nature to do that.

Artikel der (PL die Artikel) article.

Arznei die medicine.

Arzneimittel das (PL die Arzneimittel) drug.

Arzt der (PL die Ärzte) doctor.

Ärztin die (PL die Ärztinnen) doctor.

ärztlich adjective medical. adverb sich ärztlich behandeln lassen to have medical treatment.

As SEE Ass.

Asche die (PL die Aschen) ash.

Aschenbecher der (PL die Aschenbecher) ashtray.

Aschermittwoch der Ash Wednesday.

Asiat der (PL die Asiaten) Asian.

Asiatin die (PL die Asiatinnen) Asian.

asiatisch adjective Asian.

Asien das Asia; nach Asien to Asia.

aß SEE essen.

Ass △ das (PL die Asse) ace.

Assistent der (PL die Assistenten) assistant.

Assistentin die (PL die Assistentinnen) assistant.

Ast der (PL die Äste) branch.

Asthma das asthma.

Astrologie die astrology.

Astronaut der (PL die Astronauten) astronaut.

Astronomie die astronomy.

Asyl das (PL die Asyle) 1 asylum; um politisches Asyl bitten to apply for political asylum; 2 hostel (for the homeless).

Asylant der (PL die Asylanten) asylum-seeker.

Atelier das (PL die Ateliers) (artist's) studio.

Atem der breath; außer Atem sein to be out of breath.

atemlos adjective breathless.

Athlet der (PL die Athleten) athlete.

Athletin die (PL die Athletinnen) athlete.

Atlantik der der Atlantik the Atlantic (Ocean); im Atlantik in the Atlantic.

Atlas der (PL die Atlanten) atlas.

atmen verb (PERF hat geatmet) to breathe.

△ NEW SPELLING: See page xii

Atmosphäre *die* (PL *die* **Atmosphären**) atmosphere.

Atom *das* (PL *die* **Atome**) atom.

atomar *adjective* atomic.

Atomwaffen *plural noun* nuclear weapons.

atomwaffenfrei *adjective* nuclear-free.

attraktiv *adjective* attractive.

ätzend *adjective* 1 corrosive; 2 caustic (*wit, remark*).

au *exclamation* 1 ouch!; 2 oh! (*when surprised or enthusiastic*); **au ja!** oh yes!

auch *adverb* 1 also, too; **Sophie war auch dabei** Sophie was also there, Sophie was there too; **ich auch** me too; **nicht nur ... sondern auch ...** not only ... but also ...; 2 **'ich gehe jetzt' – 'ich auch'** 'I'm going now' – 'so am I'; **'er schläft' – 'sie auch'** 'he's asleep' – 'so is she'; 3 **'ich bin nicht müde' – 'ich auch nicht'** 'I'm not tired'–'neither am I'; **das weiß ich auch nicht** I don't know either; 4 **auch wenn** even if; 5 **wann auch** whenever; **was auch** whatever; **wo auch** wherever; **wer auch** whoever; 6 **wie dem auch sei** however that may be; 7 **lügst du auch nicht?** you're not lying, are you?

auf *preposition* ←(+DAT or +ACC) (*the dative is used when talking about position; the accusative shows movement or a change of place*) 1 on; **das Buch liegt auf dem Tisch** the book's on the table; **er hat das Buch auf den Tisch gelegt** he put the book on the table; 2 **ich war auf der Party** I was at the party; **ich gehe auf eine Party** I'm going to a party; **ich war auf der Post** I was at the post office; **er ist auf die Post gegangen** he went to the post office; 3 **auf der Straße** in the street; 4 **auf diese Art** in this way; **auf Deutsch** in German; 5 for (*indicating time or distance*); **er ist auf ein paar Tage verreist** he's gone away for a few days; 6 **auf seinen Rat hin** on his advice; 7 **auf Wiedersehen!** goodbye!
adverb 1 open; **die Tür ist auf** the door is open; **Mund auf!** open your mouth!; 2 up (*out of bed*); **auf sein** to be up; **er ist schon auf** he's already up; 3 **auf einmal** suddenly; 4 **auf einmal** at once (*at the same time*); 5 **auf und ab** up and down; 6 **sich auf und davon machen** to make off.

aufbekommen ◇ *verb* (IMPERF **bekam auf**, PERF **hat aufbekommen**) 1 to get open; 2 **Hausaufgaben aufbekommen** to be given homework.

aufbewahren *verb* (PERF **hat aufbewahrt**) to keep.

aufblasen ◇ *verb* (PRES **bläst auf**, IMPERF **blies auf**, PERF **hat aufgeblasen**) to blow up.

aufbleiben ◇ *verb* (IMPERF **blieb auf**, PERF **ist aufgeblieben**) 1 to stay open; **wie lange bleiben die Geschäfte auf?** how long do the shops stay open?; 2 to stay up (*not go to bed*).

◇ IRREGULAR VERB: *See the verb table in the centre of the dictionary*

aufbringen ◇ verb (IMPERF **brachte auf**, PERF **hat aufgebracht**) **1** to raise (money); **2** to find (patience, strength); **3** to open; **ich kann die Tür nicht aufbringen** I can't open the door; **4 jemanden aufbringen** to make somebody angry; **5 Verständnis für etwas aufbringen** to be able to understand something.

aufeinander adverb **1** one on top of the other; **die Bretter aufeinander legen** to put the planks one on top of the other; **2 aufeinander liegen** △ to lie on top of each other; **3 aufeinander folgen** △ to follow one another; **4 aufeinander warten** to wait for each other; **5 aufeinander schießen** to shoot at each other; **6 aufeinander fahren** △ to collide with each other.

Aufenthalt der (PL **die Aufenthalte**) **1** stay; **2** stop (pause in a journey); **zehn Minuten Aufenthalt haben** to stop for ten minutes.

Auffahrt die (PL **die Auffahrten**) **1** drive; **2** slip road.

auffallend adjective striking.

auffangen ◇ verb (PRES **fängt auf**, IMPERF **fing auf**, PERF **hat aufgefangen**) to catch.

aufführen verb (PERF **hat aufgeführt**) **1** to perform (a play); **2** to list (words, items); **3 sich aufführen** to behave.

Aufführung die (PL **die Aufführungen**) performance.

Aufgabe die (PL **die Aufgaben**)

1 task; **2** exercise (at school); **3** question (in a test or an exam); **4 Aufgaben** homework.

aufgeben ◇ verb (PRES **gibt auf**, IMPERF **gab auf**, PERF **hat aufgegeben**) **1** to give up; **ich gebe auf!** I give up!; **2** to post; **3** to check in (luggage); **4** to place (an advertisement, order); **5 Hausaufgaben aufgeben** to set homework.

aufgehen ◇ verb (IMPERF **ging auf**, PERF **ist aufgegangen**) **1** to open (of a door or flower, for example); **2** to come undone (of a knot or zip, for example); **3** to rise (of the sun, moon); **4** to realize; **es ist mir aufgegangen, dass ...** I've realized that ...; **5** to work out (in maths); **zehn durch drei geht nicht auf** three into ten won't go.

aufgeregt adjective excited.

aufgeschlossen adjective open-minded.

aufgrund preposition ←(+GEN) **1** because of; **2** on the strength of.

aufhaben ◇ verb (PRES **hat auf**, IMPERF **hatte auf**, PERF **hat aufgehabt**) **1** to have on (a hat); **2 den Mund aufhaben** to have your mouth open; **3 etwas aufhaben** to have homework to do; **viel aufhaben** to have a lot of homework; **4** to be open; **der Laden hat abends auf** the shop is open in the evening.

aufhalten ◇ verb (PRES **hält auf**, IMPERF **hielt auf**, PERF **hat aufgehalten**) **1** to hold open (a

△ NEW SPELLING: See page xii

aufhängen

door); **2** to hold up, to keep (*somebody from doing something*); **3 die Hand aufhalten** to hold out your hand; **4 die Augen aufhalten** to keep your eyes open; **5** to check (*inflation, an advance, unemployment*); **6 sich aufhalten** to stay; **7 sich mit etwas aufhalten** to spend your time on something.

aufhängen *verb* (PERF **hat aufgehängt**) **1** to hang up (*washing*); **2 sich aufhängen** to hang yourself.

aufheben ◊ *verb* (IMPERF **hob auf**, PERF **hat aufgehoben**) **1** to pick up (*from the ground*); **2** to keep; **3** to abolish (*a law*); **4 gut aufgehoben sein** to be well looked after.

aufheitern *verb* (PERF **hat aufgeheitert**) **1** to cheer up; **2 sich aufheitern** to brighten up (*of the weather*).

aufhören *verb* (PERF **hat aufgehört**) **1** to stop; **aufhören zu arbeiten** to stop working.

aufklären *verb* (PERF **hat aufgeklärt**) **1** to solve (*a crime*); **2** to explain (*an event, incident*); **3 ein Kind aufklären** to tell a child the facts of life; **4 sich aufklären** to be solved (*a misunderstanding or mystery*); **5 sich aufklären** to clear up; **das Wetter klärt sich auf** the weather is clearing up.

Aufkleber *der* (PL **die Aufkleber**) sticker.

auflegen *verb* (PERF **hat aufgelegt**) **1** to put on; **2** to hang up (*when*

phoning); **3** to publish; **ein Buch neu auflegen** to reprint a book.

auflösen *verb* (PERF **hat aufgelöst**) **1** to dissolve; **2** to close (*an account*); **3 sich auflösen** to dissolve; **4 sich auflösen** to break up (*of a crowd, demonstration*); **5 der Nebel hat sich aufgelöst** the fog has lifted; **6 in Tränen aufgelöst sein** to be in floods of tears.

aufmachen *verb* (PERF **hat aufgemacht**) **1** to open; **2 jemandem aufmachen** to open the door to somebody; **3** to undo (*a zip, knot*); **4 sich aufmachen** to set out.

aufmerksam *adjective* **1** attentive; **2 auf etwas aufmerksam werden** to notice something; **3 jemanden auf etwas aufmerksam machen** to draw somebody's attention to something.

aufmuntern *verb* (PERF **hat aufgemuntert**) to cheer up.

Aufnahme *die* (PL **die Aufnahmen**) **1** photograph; **2** recording; **3** admission (*to hospital, to a club*); **4** welcome.

Aufnahmeprüfung *die* (PL **die Aufnahmeprüfungen**) entrance exam.

aufnehmen ◊ *verb* (PRES **nimmt auf**, IMPERF **nahm auf**, PERF **hat aufgenommen**) **1** to receive (*guests*); **2** to take up (*an idea, activity, a theme*); **3** to admit (*to hospital, to a club*); **4** to photograph; **5** to film; **6** to record (*a song*); **7 es mit jemandem aufnehmen können**

◊ **IRREGULAR VERB:** *See the verb table in the centre of the dictionary* to be a match for somebody; **8** to take (*food, news*); **etwas gelassen aufnehmen** to take something calmly.

aufpassen *verb* (PERF **hat aufgepasst**△) **1** to pay attention; **2** to watch out; **3 auf jemanden aufpassen** to look after somebody; **4 auf etwas aufpassen** to keep an eye on something; **pass auf meine Tasche auf** keep an eye on my bag.

aufräumen *verb* (PERF **hat aufgeräumt**) to tidy up.

aufrecht *adjective* upright.

aufregen *verb* (PERF **hat aufgeregt**) **1** to excite; **2** to annoy; **3 sich aufregen** to get worked up.

aufregend *adjective* exciting.

aufs = **auf das**.

Aufsatz *der* (PL *die* **Aufsätze**) essay.

aufschieben ◇ *verb* (IMPERF **schob auf**, PERF **hat aufgeschoben**) **1** to put off (*an arrangement*); **2** to slide open.

aufschließen ◇ *verb* (IMPERF **schloss auf**△, PERF **hat aufgeschlossen**) to unlock.

Aufschnitt *der* sliced cold meat and cheese.

aufschreiben ◇ *verb* (IMPERF **schrieb auf**, PERF **hat aufgeschrieben**) to write down.

aufsehen ◇ *verb* (PRES **sieht auf**, IMPERF **sah auf**, PERF **hat aufgesehen**) to look up.

aufsetzen *verb* (PERF **hat aufgesetzt**) **1** to put on; **2** to draft; **3 sich aufsetzen** to sit up.

Aufsicht *die* **1** supervision; **2** supervisor.

Aufstand *der* (PL *die* **Aufstände**) rebellion.

aufstehen ◇ *verb* (IMPERF **stand auf**, PERF **ist aufgestanden**) **1** to get up; **2** (PERF **hat aufgestanden**) to be open.

aufstellen *verb* (PERF **hat aufgestellt**) **1** to put up; **2** to set up (*skittles, chess pieces*); **3 eine Mannschaft aufstellen** to pick a team; **4 eine Liste aufstellen** to draw up a list; **5 sich aufstellen** to line up.

auftauen *verb* (PERF **ist aufgetaut**) **1** to thaw; **2** to defrost; **die Erdbeeren sind aufgetaut** the strawberries have defrosted; **3** (PERF **hat aufgetaut**) to defrost; **ich habe die Erbeeren aufgetaut** I've defrosted the strawberries.

aufteilen *verb* (PERF **hat aufgeteilt**) to divide up.

Auftrag *der* (PL *die* **Aufträge**) **1** job; **2** order (*in business*); **etwas in Auftrag geben** to order something; **3** instructions; **einen Auftrag ausführen** to carry out an instruction; **4 im Auftrag von** on behalf of.

auftreten ◇ *verb* (PRES **tritt auf**, IMPERF **trat auf**, PERF **ist aufgetreten**) **1** to appear (*on stage*); **2** to arise (*a problem, difficulty*); **3** to behave; **4** to tread.

△ NEW SPELLING: *See page xii*

aufwachen verb (PERF ist aufgewacht) to wake up.

aufwachsen ✧ verb (PRES wächst auf, IMPERF wuchs auf, PERF ist aufgewachsen) to grow up.

aufwecken verb (PERF hat aufgeweckt) to wake up.

aufziehen ✧ verb (IMPERF zog auf, PERF hat aufgezogen) 1 to wind up (a clock or toy); 2 to draw (curtains); 3 jemanden aufziehen (informal) to tease somebody; 4 to bring up (a child).

Aufzug der (PL die Aufzüge) lift; **ich fahre mit dem Aufzug runter** I'm going down in the lift.

Auge das (PL die Augen) 1 eye; 2 unter vier Augen in private.

Augenblick der (PL die Augenblicke) moment; **im Augenblick** at the moment.

Augenbraue die (PL die Augenbrauen) eyebrow.

August der August.

aus preposition ← (+DAT) 1 out of; **er hat es aus dem Fenster geworfen** he threw it out of the window; 2 from; **aus Spanien** from Spain; **aus Erfahrung** from experience; 3 made of; **aus Holz** made of wood; 4 **aus Spaß** for fun; 5 **aus der Mode** out of fashion; 6 **aus Versehen** by mistake; 7 **aus welchem Grund?** for what reason?; 8 **aus ihr ist eine gute Rechtsanwältin geworden** she made a good lawyer; **aus ihm ist nichts geworden** he never made

anything of his life.
adverb 1 off (of a TV, radio); **das Licht ist aus** the light is off; **Licht aus!** lights out!; 2 finished; **wenn das Spiel aus ist** when the game has finished; 3 **von mir aus** as far as I'm concerned; 4 **von sich aus** of your own accord.

ausbeuten verb (PERF hat ausgebeutet) to exploit.

ausbilden verb (PERF hat ausgebildet) to train.

Ausbildung die 1 training; 2 education.

Ausdruck[1] der (PL die Ausdrücke) expression; **etwas zum Ausdruck bringen** to express something.

Ausdruck[2] der (PL die Ausdrucke) print-out.

ausdrucken verb (PERF hat ausgedruckt) to print out.

ausdrücken verb (PERF hat ausgedrückt) 1 to squeeze (oranges, lemons); 2 to express; 3 **sich ausdrücken** to express oneself.

auseinander adverb 1 apart; **etwas auseinander nehmen** △ to take something apart; **auseinander halten** △ to tell apart; 2 **auseinander gehen** △ to part; 3 **auseinander schreiben** to write as separate words; 4 **sich mit einem Problem auseinander setzen** △ to come to grips with a problem; 5 **sich mit jemandem auseinander setzen** △ to have it out with somebody.

✧ IRREGULAR VERB: See the verb table in the centre of the dictionary

Ausfahrt die (PL die Ausfahrten)
1 exit; 2 'Ausfahrt freihalten' 'keep clear'.

ausfallen ◇ verb (PRES **fällt aus**, IMPERF **fiel aus**, PERF **ist ausgefallen**)
1 to be cancelled; **etwas ausfallen lassen** to cancel something; 2 to fall out (hair); 3 to fail (an engine, brakes, a signal); 4 to break down (a machine, a car, heating); 5 to turn out; **gut ausfallen** to turn out well.

Ausflug der (PL die Ausflüge) outing, trip; **einen Ausflug machen** to go on an outing.

Ausfuhr die export.

ausführen verb (PERF **hat ausgeführt**) 1 to carry out (a plan); 2 to export (goods); 3 to take out; **er hat seine Freundin zum Essen ausgeführt** he took his girlfriend out for a meal; 4 **den Hund ausführen** to take the dog for a walk.

ausführlich adjective detailed. adverb in detail.

ausfüllen verb (PERF **hat ausgefüllt**) 1 to fill in; 2 **ihr Beruf als Lehrerin füllt sie ganz aus** teaching gives her great satisfaction.

Ausgabe die (PL die Ausgaben)
1 edition; 2 issue; 3 **Ausgaben** expenditure.

Ausgang der (PL die Ausgänge)
1 exit; 'kein Ausgang' 'no exit';
2 end, ending; 3 result (of a game, discussion).

ausgeben ◇ verb (PRES **gibt aus**, IMPERF **gab aus**, PERF **hat ausgegeben**) 1 to spend; 2 to hand

out; 3 **Fahrkarten ausgeben** to issue tickets; 4 to serve (food); 5 **sich ausgeben als** to pretend to be; 6 **einen ausgeben** (informal) to treat everybody (to a round of drinks for example).

ausgebucht adjective fully booked.

ausgehen ◇ verb (PRES **geht aus**, IMPERF **ging aus**, PERF **ist ausgegangen**) 1 to go out; 2 to run out (of supplies); 3 to end; **schlecht ausgehen** to end badly; 4 **davon ausgehen, dass ...** to assume that ...

ausgerechnet adverb
1 **ausgerechnet heute** today of all days; 2 **ausgerechnet sie** she of all people.

ausgeschlossen adjective out of the question.

ausgezeichnet adjective excellent.

aushalten ◇ verb (PRES **hält aus**, IMPERF **hielt aus**, PERF **hat ausgehalten**) 1 to stand; 2 **es ist nicht zum Aushalten** it's unbearable.

Aushilfe die (PL die Aushilfen) temporary assistant, temp.

auskennen ◇ verb (IMPERF **kannte sich aus**, PERF **hat sich ausgekannt**) 1 **sich auskennen** to know your way around; 2 **sich gut mit etwas auskennen** to know a lot about something.

auskommen ◇ verb (IMPERF **kam aus**, PERF **ist ausgekommen**) 1 to manage; **mit fünfzig Mark**

△ NEW SPELLING: See page xii

auskommen to manage on fifty marks; **2 mit jemandem gut auskommen** to get on well with somebody.

Auskunft *die* (PL *die* **Auskünfte**) 1 information; 2 information desk; 3 enquiries (*when phoning*).

auslachen *verb* (PERF **hat ausgelacht**) to laugh at.

ausladen ◇ *verb* (PRES **lädt aus**, IMPERF **lud aus**, PERF **hat ausgeladen**) 1 to unload; 2 jemanden ausladen (*informal*) to put somebody off.

Ausland *das* im Ausland abroad; ins Ausland reisen to travel abroad.

Ausländer *der* (PL *die* **Ausländer**) foreigner.

Ausländerin *die* (PL *die* **Ausländerinnen**) foreigner.

ausländisch *adjective* foreign.

Auslandsgespräch *das* (PL *die* **Auslandsgespräche**) international call.

ausleeren *verb* (PERF **hat ausgeleert**) to empty.

ausleihen ◇ *verb* (IMPERF **lieh aus**, PERF **hat ausgeliehen**) 1 to lend; 2 sich etwas ausleihen to borrow something.

ausmachen *verb* (PERF **hat ausgemacht**) 1 to turn off; 2 to put out; 3 to arrange; wir haben ausgemacht, dass wir uns heute Abend treffen we've arranged to meet up this evening; 4 das macht mir nichts aus I don't mind; macht es Ihnen etwas aus, wenn ...?

would you mind if ...?; 5 viel ausmachen to make a great difference.

Ausnahme *die* (PL *die* **Ausnahmen**) exception.

ausnutzen *verb* (PERF **hat ausgenutzt**) 1 to use; 2 to take advantage of.

auspacken *verb* (PERF **hat ausgepackt**) to unpack.

Auspuff *der* (PL *die* **Auspuffe**) exhaust.

ausrechnen *verb* (PERF **hat ausgerechnet**) to work out.

Ausrede *die* (PL *die* **Ausreden**) excuse.

ausreichend *adjective* 1 sufficient; 2 fair, pass (*as a mark at school*).

Ausreise *die* (PL *die* **Ausreisen**) departure (*from a country*).

ausrichten *verb* (PERF **hat ausgerichtet**) jemandem etwas ausrichten to tell somebody something.

Ausrufezeichen *das* (PL *die* **Ausrufezeichen**) exclamation mark.

ausruhen *verb* (PERF **hat sich ausgeruht**) sich ausruhen to have a rest.

Ausrüstung *die* equipment.

ausschalten *verb* (PERF **hat ausgeschaltet**) 1 to switch off; 2 to eliminate.

ausschneiden ◇ *verb* (IMPERF **schnitt aus**, PERF **hat ausgeschnitten**) to cut out.

◇ IRREGULAR VERB: *See the verb table in the centre of the dictionary*

Ausschuss △ der (PL die Ausschüsse) committee.

aussehen ◊ verb (PRES sieht aus, IMPERF sah aus, PERF hat ausgesehen) to look.

Aussehen das appearance.

außen adverb 1 (on the) outside; **von außen** from the outside; 2 **nach außen** outwards.

Außenminister der (PL die Außenminister) Foreign Secretary, Foreign Minister.

außer preposition ←(+DAT) 1 apart from, except (for); **alle außer ihm** everyone except (for) him; 2 out of; **außer Sicht** out of sight; **außer Betrieb** out of order; 3 **außer Haus** out; 4 **außer sich sein** to be beside yourself.
conjunction 1 except; **außer sonntags** except Sundays; 2 **außer wenn** unless.

außerdem adverb 1 as well; 2 besides.

äußerer, äußere, äußeres adjective 1 external (injury, circumstances); 2 outer (layer, circle); 3 outward (appearance, effect).

außergewöhnlich adjective unusual.

außerhalb preposition ←(+GEN) outside.
adverb **außerhalb wohnen** to live out of town.

äußerlich adjective 1 external; 2 outward (appearance).

außerordentlich adjective extraordinary.

äußerst adverb extremely.

Äußerung die (PL die Äußerungen) remark.

Aussicht die (PL die Aussichten) 1 prospect; **etwas in Aussicht haben** to have the prospect of something; **keine Aussichten auf Erfolg haben** to have no chance of success; 2 view; **ein Zimmer mit Aussicht aufs Meer** a room with a view of the sea.

Aussprache die (PL die Aussprachen) 1 pronunciation; 2 talk.

aussprechen ◊ verb (PRES spricht aus, IMPERF sprach aus, PERF hat ausgesprochen) 1 to pronounce; 2 to express; 3 **lassen Sie ihn aussprechen** let him finish (speaking); 4 **sich aussprechen** to talk; **sich mit jemandem aussprechen** to have a talk with somebody; 5 **sich gegen etwas aussprechen** to come out against something; **sich für etwas aussprechen** to come out in favour of something; 6 **sich lobend über jemanden aussprechen** to speak highly of somebody.

aussteigen ◊ verb (IMPERF stieg aus, PERF ist ausgestiegen) 1 to get out; 2 to get off.

ausstellen verb (PERF hat ausgestellt) 1 to display (in a shop); 2 to exhibit; 3 to make out (a certificate, bill); 4 to issue (a passport); 5 to switch off.

△ NEW SPELLING: See page xii

Ausstellung die (PL die Ausstellungen). exhibition.

ausstreichen ⬦ verb (IMPERF strich aus, PERF hat ausgestrichen) to cross out.

aussuchen verb (PERF hat ausgesucht) 1 to choose; 2 sich etwas aussuchen to choose something.

Austausch der exchange.

austauschen verb (PERF hat ausgetauscht) 1 to exchange; 2 to replace; 3 to substitute (a player).

Auster die (PL die Austern) oyster.

austragen ⬦ verb (PRES trägt aus, IMPERF trug aus, PERF hat ausgetragen) to deliver (post); to hold (a race).

Australien das Australia; aus Australien from Australia.

Australier der (PL die Australier) Australian.

Australierin die (PL die Australierinnen) Australian.

australisch adjective Australian.

austreten ⬦ verb (PRES tritt aus, IMPERF trat aus, PERF hat ausgetreten) 1 to stamp out (a cigarette or fire); 2 to wear out (shoes); 3 (PERF ist ausgetreten) aus einem Klub austreten to leave a club; ich trete aus I'm leaving; 4 (informal) (PERF ist ausgetreten) to go to the loo.

austrinken ⬦ verb (IMPERF trank aus, PERF hat ausgetrunken) to drink up.

Ausverkauf der (PL die Ausverkäufe) sale.

ausverkauft adjective 1 sold out; 2 ein ausverkauftes Haus a full house (at the cinema or theatre).

Auswahl die (PL die Auswahlen) choice, selection; wenig Auswahl haben to have a limited selection.

auswärts adverb 1 away (in sport); auswärts spielen to play away; 2 auswärts essen to eat out; 3 sie arbeitet auswärts she doesn't work locally.

Auswärtsspiel das (PL die Auswärtsspiele) away game.

Ausweg der (PL die Auswege) way out.

Ausweis der (PL die Ausweise) 1 identity card; 2 card (for students or members); 3 pass.

auswendig adverb by heart.

auswirken verb (PERF hat sich ausgewirkt) sich auf etwas auswirken to have an effect on something.

ausziehen ⬦ verb (IMPERF zog aus, PERF hat ausgezogen) 1 to take off (clothes); 2 to undress; 3 sich ausziehen to get undressed; 4 (PERF ist ausgezogen) to move out (move house).

Auto das (PL die Autos) car; Auto fahren to drive.

Autobahn die (PL die Autobahnen) motorway.

Autofahrer der (PL die Autofahrer) motorist.

⬦ IRREGULAR VERB: See the verb table in the centre of the dictionary

Autogramm das (PL die Autogramme) autograph.

Automat der (PL die Automaten) machine.

automatisch adjective automatic.

Autor der (PL die Autoren) author.

Autorin die (PL die Autorinnen) authoress.

Autorität die authority.

Autostopp der per Autostopp fahren to hitchhike.

Autotelefon das (PL die Autotelefone) car phone.

Autounfall der (PL die Autounfälle) car accident.

Autoverleih der (PL die Autoverleihe) car hire (firm).

Axt die (PL die Äxte) axe.

B b

Baby das (PL die Babys) baby.

Bach der (PL die Bäche) stream.

Backe die (PL die Backen) cheek.

backen ◇ verb (PRES bäckt, IMPERF backte, PERF hat gebacken) to bake.

Bäcker der (PL die Bäcker) 1 baker; 2 beim Bäcker at the baker's.

Bäckerei die (PL die Bäckereien) baker's.

Backofen der (PL die Backöfen) oven.

Backpflaume die (PL die Backpflaumen) prune.

Bad das (PL die Bäder) 1 bath; 2 bathroom; 3 pool (for swimming).

Badeanzug der (PL die Badeanzüge) swimsuit.

Badehose die (PL die Badehosen) swimming trunks.

Bademütze die (PL die Bademützen) bathing cap.

baden verb (PERF hat gebadet) 1 to have a bath; 2 to bathe (in the sea); 3 to bath (wash somebody).

Badetuch das (PL die Badetücher) bath towel.

Badewanne die (PL die Badewannen) bath (tub).

Badezimmer das (PL die Badezimmer) bathroom.

Bahn die (PL die Bahnen) 1 railway; 2 train; mit der Bahn fahren to go by train; 3 tram; 4 track (in sport); 5 lane (on a track); 6 path; auf die schiefe Bahn geraten to go off the rails.

Bahnhof der (PL die Bahnhöfe) (railway) station.

Bahnsteig der (PL die Bahnsteige) platform.

Bahnübergang der (PL die Bahnübergänge) level crossing.

bald adverb 1 soon; bis bald! see you soon!; 2 wird's bald! (informal) get a move on!; 3 almost; ich hätte bald vergessen, ihn

△ NEW SPELLING: See page xii

anzurufen I almost forgot to ring him.

Balken der (PL die Balken) beam.

Balkon der (PL die Balkons) balcony.

Ball der (PL die Bälle) 1 ball; **Ball spielen** to play ball; 2 ball; **auf dem Ball** at the ball.

Ballett das (PL die Ballette) ballet.

Balletttänzer △ der (PL die Balletttänzer) ballet dancer.

Balletttänzerin △ der (PL die Balletttänzerinnen) ballet dancer.

Ballon der (PL die Ballons) balloon.

Banane die (PL die Bananen) banana.

band SEE **binden**.

Band[1] das (PL die Bänder) 1 ribbon; 2 tape (for recording); **etwas auf Band aufnehmen** to tape something; 3 production line; **am Band arbeiten** to work on the production line; 4 **am laufenden Band** (informal) nonstop.

Band[2] der (PL die Bände) volume.

Band[3] die (PL die Bands) band.

Bank[1] die (PL die Bänke) bench.

Bank[2] die (PL die Banken) bank; **ich muss erst zur Bank gehen** I have to go to the bank first.

Bankkonto das (PL die Bankkonten) bank account.

Banknote die (PL die Banknoten) banknote.

bankrott adjective bankrupt;

bankrott gehen/machen to go bankrupt.

bar adjective (in) cash.

Bar die (PL die Bars) bar.

Bär der (PL die Bären) bear.

Bardame die (PL die Bardamen) barmaid.

barfuß adjective barefoot.

Bargeld das cash.

Barkeeper der (PL die Barkeeper) barman.

Barren der (PL die Barren) 1 bar; 2 parallel bars.

Bart der (PL die Bärte) beard.

bärtig adjective bearded.

Basel das Basle.

Basis die (PL die Basen) basis.

Bass △ der (PL die Bässe) bass.

basta exclamation and that's that!

basteln verb (PERF hat gebastelt) 1 to make (things); 2 **sie bastelt gern** she likes making things.

bat SEE **bitten**.

Batterie die (PL die Batterien) battery.

Bau der (PL die Bauten) 1 construction; **im Bau sein** to be under construction; 2 building; 3 building site; **auf dem Bau arbeiten** to work on a building site.

Bauarbeiter der (PL die Bauarbeiter) builder.

Bauch der (PL die Bäuche) stomach, belly.

◊ IRREGULAR VERB: See the verb table in the centre of the dictionary

Bauchschmerzen *plural noun* stomachache.

bauen *verb* (PERF **hat gebaut**) **1** to build; **2 einen Unfall bauen** (*informal*) to have an accident.

Bauer *der* (PL die **Bauern**) **1** farmer; **2** pawn (*in chess*).

Bäuerin *die* (PL die **Bäuerinnen**) **1** farmer; **2** farmer's wife.

Bauernhof *der* (PL die **Bauernhöfe**) farm.

Baum *der* (PL die **Bäume**) tree.

Baumwolle *die* cotton.

Bausparkasse *die* (PL die **Bausparkassen**) building society.

Baustelle *die* (PL die **Baustellen**) building site.

Bayer *der* (PL die **Bayern**) Bavarian.

Bayerin *die* (PL die **Bayerinnen**) Bavarian.

Bayern *das* Bavaria; **aus Bayern** from Bavaria.

bayrisch *adjective* Bavarian.

beabsichtigen *verb* (PERF **hat beabsichtigt**) to intend.

beachten *verb* (PERF **hat beachtet**) **1** to take notice of; **beachte ihn einfach nicht** just don't take any notice of him; **2** to observe; **3** to follow (*a rule, advice*); **4** to obey; **die Verkehrsregeln beachten** to obey traffic regulations.

Beamte *der* (PL die **Beamten**) **1** civil servant (*in Germany all public employees, such as teachers and policemen, are 'Beamte'*); **2** official.

Beamtin *die* (PL die **Beamtinnen**) **1** civil servant; **2** official.

beanspruchen *verb* (PERF **hat beansprucht**) **1** to claim (*benefit*); **2** to take up (*time, space*); **jemanden beanspruchen** to take up somebody's time; **3** to demand (*energy, attention*); **die Arbeit beansprucht sie sehr** her work is very demanding; **4** to take advantage of (*hospitality, services, help*); **ich möchte Ihre Geduld nicht zu sehr beanspruchen** I don't want to try your patience.

Beanstandung *die* (PL die **Beanstandungen**) complaint.

beantragen *verb* (PERF **hat beantragt**) to apply for.

beantworten *verb* (PERF **hat beantwortet**) to answer.

bearbeiten *verb* (PERF **hat bearbeitet**) **1** to deal with; **einen Antrag bearbeiten** to deal with an application; **2** to adapt (*a play*); **3** to treat (*wood, for example*); **er hat die Oberfläche mit Wachs bearbeitet** he's treated the surface with wax; **4** **jemanden bearbeiten, dass er etwas macht** (*informal*) to work on somebody so that he does something (*persuade*).

beaufsichtigen *verb* (PERF **hat beaufsichtigt**) to supervise.

Becher *der* (PL die **Becher**) **1** beaker, mug; **2** pot, carton (*of yoghurt, cream*).

△ NEW SPELLING: *See page xii*

Becken *das* (PL *die* **Becken**)
1 basin; 2 pool (*for swimming*);
3 pelvis.

bedanken *verb* (PERF **hat sich bedankt**) **sich bedanken** to say thank you; **vergiss nicht, dich zu bedanken** don't forget to say thank you; **ich habe mich bei ihm bedankt** I thanked him.

Bedarf *der* 1 need; 2 **bei Bedarf** if required; 3 demand; **je nach Bedarf** according to demand.

bedauerlicherweise *adverb* unfortunately.

bedauern *verb* (PERF **hat bedauert**) 1 to regret; **ich bedauere kein Wort** I don't regret a single word; 2 **ich bedauere sehr, dass du nicht kommen kannst** I'm very sorry that you can't come; **bedauere!** sorry!; 3 **jemanden bedauern** to feel sorry for somebody.

bedecken *verb* (PERF **hat bedeckt**) to cover.

bedeckt *adjective* 1 covered; 2 overcast (*weather*); **gestern war es den ganzen Tag bedeckt** it was overcast all day yesterday.

bedenken ◇ *verb* (IMPERF **bedachte**, PERF **hat bedacht**) to consider.

Bedenken *plural noun* 1 doubts; **Bedenken haben** to have doubts; 2 **ohne Bedenken** without hesitation.

bedenklich *adjective* 1 worrying; **die Situation ist sehr bedenklich** the situation is very worrying; 2 dubious; **er hat bedenkliche Mittel angewendet, um sein Ziel zu**

erreichen he's used dubious methods to achieve his aims; 3 serious.

bedeuten *verb* (PERF **hat bedeutet**) to mean.

bedeutend *adjective* 1 important; 2 considerable.

Bedeutung *die* (PL *die* **Bedeutungen**) 1 meaning; 2 importance.

bedienen *verb* (PERF **hat bedient**) 1 to serve; **hier wird man sehr schnell bedient** you get served very quickly here; 2 to operate; 3 **sich bedienen** to help oneself.

Bedienung *die* (PL *die* **Bedienungen**) 1 service;. **Bedienung inbegriffen** service included; 2 waiter, waitress; 3 shop assistant; 4 operation (*of a machine*).

Bedingung *die* (PL *die* **Bedingungen**) condition; **nur unter der Bedingung, dass du mitkommst** only on condition that you're coming with us.

bedrohen *verb* (PERF **hat bedroht**) to threaten.

Bedrohung *die* (PL *die* **Bedrohungen**) threat.

beeilen *verb* (PERF **hat sich beeilt**) **sich beeilen** to hurry (up); **beeilt euch!** hurry up!

beeindrucken *verb* (PERF **hat beeindruckt**) to impress.

beeinflussen *verb* (PERF **hat beeinflusst**) to influence.

◇ IRREGULAR VERB: *See the verb table in the centre of the dictionary*

beenden verb (PERF hat beendet) to end.

Beerdigung die (PL die Beerdigungen) funeral.

Beere die (PL die Beeren) berry.

Beet das (PL die Beete) 1 bed (of flowers); 2 patch (of vegetables).

befahl SEE **befehlen**.

Befehl der (PL die Befehle) 1 order; 2 command; **den Befehl über etwas haben** to be in command of something.

befehlen ◇ verb (PRES befiehlt, IMPERF befahl, PERF hat befohlen) 1 **jemandem etwas befehlen** to order somebody to do something; 2 to give orders.

befestigen verb (PERF hat befestigt) 1 to fix; **etwas an der Wand befestigen** to fix something to the wall; 2 to fasten.

befinden ◇ verb (IMPERF befand sich, PERF hat sich befunden) **sich befinden** to be; **sie befindet sich zur Zeit in Deutschland** she's in Germany at the moment.

befolgen verb (PERF hat befolgt) to follow.

befördern verb (PERF hat befördert) 1 to carry (people by bus or train); 2 to transport (goods by train or lorry); 3 to promote; **er ist zum Kommissar befördert worden** he's been promoted to superintendent.

befragen verb (PERF hat befragt) to question.

befreien verb (PERF hat befreit) 1 to free; 2 to exempt; **jemanden vom Wehrdienst befreien** to exempt somebody from military service; 3 **sich befreien** to free oneself.

Befreiung die liberation.

befreunden verb (PERF hat sich befreundet) **sich befreunden** to make friends.

befreundet adjective **mit jemandem befreundet sein** to be friends with somebody; **wir sind schon lange gut befreundet** we've been close friends for a long time.

befriedigen verb (PERF hat befriedigt) to satisfy.

befriedigend adjective satisfactory.

Befugnis die (PL die Befugnisse) authority.

begabt adjective gifted, talented.

Begabung die gift, talent.

begann SEE **beginnen**.

begegnen verb (PERF ist begegnet) 1 **jemandem begegnen** to meet somebody; **etwas begegnen** to meet something; 2 **sich begegnen** to meet (each other).

Begegnung die (PL die Begegnungen) meeting.

begehen ◇ verb (IMPERF beging, PERF hat begangen) to commit.

begeistern verb (PERF hat begeistert) 1 **jemanden für etwas begeistern** to fill somebody with enthusiasm for something; 2 **sich begeistern** to get enthusiastic.

△ NEW SPELLING: *See page xii*

begeistert *adjective* enthusiastic.

Begeisterung *die* enthusiasm.

Beginn *der* beginning; **zu Beginn** at the beginning.

beginnen ◇ *verb* (IMPERF **begann**, PERF **hat begonnen**) to begin, to start.

begleiten *verb* (PERF **hat begleitet**) to accompany; **er hat mich nach Hause begleitet** he took me home.

beglückwünschen *verb* (PERF **hat beglückwünscht**) to congratulate.

begonnen SEE **beginnen**.

begraben ◇ *verb* (PRES **begräbt**, IMPERF **begrub**, PERF **hat begraben**) to bury.

begreifen ◇ *verb* (IMPERF **begriff**, PERF **hat begriffen**) to understand.

Begriff *der* (PL *die* **Begriffe**)
1 concept; **davon kann ich mir keinen Begriff machen** I can't imagine that; 2 term; **ein Begriff aus der Malerei** a painting term; 3 **im Begriff sein, etwas zu tun** to be about to do something; 4 **für meine Begriffe** to my mind; 5 **schwer von Begriff** (*informal*) slow on the uptake.

Begründung *die* (PL *die* **Begründungen**) reason.

begrüßen *verb* (PERF **hat begrüßt**) 1 to greet; 2 to welcome.

Begrüßung *die* welcome.

begünstigen *verb* (PERF **hat begünstigt**) to favour.

behaglich *adjective* cosy.

behalten ◇ *verb* (PRES **behält**, IMPERF **behielt**, PERF **hat behalten**)
1 to keep; **du kannst die CD behalten** you can keep the CD; 2 to remember (*a name*).

Behälter *der* (PL *die* **Behälter**) container.

behandeln *verb* (PERF **hat behandelt**) 1 to treat; **er ist sehr schlecht behandelt worden** he's been treated very badly; **einen Patienten behandeln** to treat a patient; 2 to deal with (*a subject, question*).

Behandlung *die* (PL *die* **Behandlungen**) treatment.

behaupten *verb* (PERF **hat behauptet**) 1 to claim; 2 **sich behaupten** to assert oneself.

Behauptung *die* (PL *die* **Behauptungen**) claim.

beherrschen *verb* (PERF **hat beherrscht**) 1 to rule over (*a country, people*); 2 to control; 3 to know; 4 **sich beherrschen** to control oneself.

behilflich *adjective* **jemandem behilflich sein** to help somebody.

behindert *adjective* disabled, handicapped.

Behinderte *der/die* (PL *die* **Behinderten**) disabled person, handicapped person.

Behinderung *die* 1 obstruction; 2 handicap, disability.

Behörde *die* (PL *die* **Behörden**) authority, authorities.

◇ **IRREGULAR VERB: See the verb table in the centre of the dictionary**

behüten verb (PERF hat behütet) to protect.

bei preposition ←(+DAT) **1** near; **die Diskothek beim Bahnhof** the disco near the station; **2** at (indicating a place or time); **bei mir** at my place; **beim Arzt** at the doctor's; **bei Beginn** at the beginning; **3 bei seinen Eltern wohnen** to live with your parents; **4 bei uns in der Firma** in our firm; **bei guter Gesundheit** in good health; **5 bei einem Verlag arbeiten** to work for a publisher; **6 bei Regen** if it rains; **bei Nebel** in fog; **bei Tag** by day; **7 etwas bei sich haben** to have something on you; **8 bei Morris** c/o Morris; **9 sich bei jemandem entschuldigen** to apologize to somebody; **10 bei der hohen Miete** with the high rent; **11 beim Fahren** while driving; **beim Lesen sein** to be reading; **beim Frühstück** at breakfast; **12 bei der Ankunft** on arrival.

beibringen ◇ verb (PRES **bringt bei**, IMPERF **brachte bei**, PERF **hat beigebracht**) **jemandem etwas beibringen** to teach somebody something.

Beichte die (PL die **Beichten**) confession.

beichten verb (PERF **hat gebeichtet**) to confess.

beide adjective, pronoun **1** both; **ihr beide** both of you; **er hat seine beiden Eltern verloren** he has lost both his parents; **2 die ersten beiden** the first two; **eins von beiden** one of the two; **3 keiner von**

beiden neither (of them); **4 beides** both; **er kann beides – Klavier und Gitarre spielen** he can do both – play the piano and the guitar; **5 dreißig beide** thirty all (in tennis).

beieinander adverb together.

Beifahrer der (PL die **Beifahrer**) passenger.

Beifahrerin die (PL die **Beifahrerinnen**) passenger.

Beifall der applause.

Beil das (PL die **Beile**) axe.

Beilage die (PL die **Beilagen**) **1** supplement (to a paper); **2** side-dish; **als Beilage Reis und Spinat** served with rice and spinach.

beiläufig adjective casual.

beilegen verb (PERF **hat beigelegt**) to enclose.

beiliegen ◇ verb (PRES **liegt bei**, IMPERF **lag bei**, PERF **hat beigelegen**) to be enclosed; **ein Scheck liegt bei** please find enclosed a cheque.

beiliegend adjective enclosed.

Beileid das condolences; **jemandem sein Beileid aussprechen** to offer your condolences to somebody.

beim = bei dem.

Bein das (PL die **Beine**) leg.

beinahe adverb almost.

Beinbruch der (PL die **Beinbrüche**) broken leg; **das ist doch kein Beinbruch** (informal) it's not the end of the world.

△ NEW SPELLING: See page xii

beisammen *adverb* together.

beiseite *adverb* 1 aside; **etwas beiseite schieben** to push something aside; 2 **etwas beiseite legen** to put something by; 3 **das Geld beiseite schaffen** to hide the money away.

Beispiel *das* (PL *die* **Beispiele**) example; **zum Beispiel** for example; **mit gutem Beispiel vorangehen** to set a good example.

beispielsweise *adverb* for example.

beißen ✧ *verb* (IMPERF **biss** △, PERF **hat gebissen**) 1 to bite; 2 to sting (*of smoke, for example*); 3 **sich beißen** to clash; **die Farben beißen sich** the colours clash.

Beitrag *der* (PL *die* **Beiträge**) 1 contribution; 2 subscription; 3 premium (*insurance fee*); 4 article (*in a newspaper*).

beitragen ✧ *verb* (PRES **trägt bei**, IMPERF **trug bei**, PERF **hat beigetragen**) **zu etwas beitragen** to contribute to something.

beitreten ✧ *verb* (PRES **tritt bei**, IMPERF **trat bei**, PERF **ist beigetreten**) to join; **ich trete dem Fußballverein bei** I'm joining the football club.

bekam SEE **bekommen**.

bekämpfen *verb* (PERF **hat bekämpft**) 1 to fight; 2 **sich bekämpfen** to fight.

bekannt *adjective* 1 well known; 2 familiar; **das kommt mir bekannt vor** that seems familiar; 3 **mit jemandem bekannt sein** to know

somebody; 4 **für etwas bekannt sein** to be (well) known for something; 5 **jemanden bekannt machen** to introduce somebody; 6 **das ist mir bekannt** I know that; 7 **etwas bekannt geben/machen** to announce something; 8 **bekannt werden** to become known.

Bekannte *der/die* (PL *die* **Bekannten**) 1 acquaintance; 2 friend.

bekanntlich *adverb* **Rauchen ist bekanntlich schädlich** as you know, smoking is bad for you.

beklagen *verb* (PERF **hat sich beklagt**) **sich beklagen** to complain.

Bekleidung *die* clothes, clothing.

bekommen ✧ *verb* (IMPERF **bekam**, PERF **hat bekommen**) 1 to get; **Angst bekommen** to get frightened; 2 to catch (*a cold, the train*); 3 **ein Kind bekommen** to have a baby; 4 **was bekommen Sie?** (*in a shop*) can I help you?; (*in a restaurant*) what would you like?; 5 **was bekommen Sie dafür?** how much is it?; 6 (PERF **ist bekommen**) **fettes Essen bekommt mir nicht** fatty food doesn't agree with me; 7 (PERF **ist bekommen**) **die Ferien sind mir gut bekommen** the holiday did me good.

Belag *der* (PL *die* **Beläge**) 1 covering; 2 coating; 3 topping (*on bread*); 4 lining (*of brakes*).

belasten *verb* (PERF **hat belastet**) 1 to burden; 2 to put weight on (*foot*); 3 to pollute (*the*

✧ IRREGULAR VERB: *See the verb table in the centre of the dictionary*

atmosphere); **4** to debit (*an account*); **5** to incriminate.

belästigen *verb* (PERF hat belästigt) **1** to bother; **2** to harass.

Belastung *die* **1** strain; **2** load; **3** burden; **4** pollution.

belegen *verb* (PERF hat belegt) **1** to cover; **2** eine Scheibe Brot mit Käse belegen to put some cheese on a slice of bread; **3** to enrol for (*a course*); **4** to reserve (*a seat*); **5** den ersten Platz belegen to come first; **6** to prove (*facts*).

belegt *adjective* **1** occupied; **2** der Platz ist belegt this seat is taken; **3** ein belegtes Brot an open sandwich; **4** die Nummer ist belegt (*when phoning*) the number's engaged.

beleidigen *verb* (PERF hat beleidigt) to insult.

Beleidigung *die* (PL die Beleidigungen) insult.

Beleuchtung *die* lighting.

Belgien *das* Belgium.

Belgier *der* (PL die Belgier) Belgian.

Belgierin *die* (PL die Belgierinnen) Belgian.

belgisch *adjective* Belgian.

Belichtung *die* exposure.

beliebig *adjective* any; eine beliebige Zahl any number you like.
adverb beliebig lange as long as you like; beliebig viele as many as you like.

beliebt *adjective* popular.

Beliebtheit *die* popularity.

bellen *verb* (PERF hat gebellt) to bark.

belohnen *verb* (PERF hat belohnt) to reward.

Belohnung *die* (PL die Belohnungen) reward.

belügen *verb* (IMPERF belog, PERF hat belogen) to lie to.

bemerkbar *adjective* sich bemerkbar machen to attract attention, to become noticeable.

bemerken *verb* (PERF hat bemerkt) **1** to notice; **2** to remark; **3** nebenbei bemerkt by the way.

Bemerkung *die* (PL die Bemerkungen) remark.

bemitleiden *verb* (PERF hat bemitleidet) to pity.

bemühen *verb* (PERF hat sich bemüht) **1** sich bemühen to try; sich sehr bemühen to try hard; er bemüht sich um eine Stelle he's trying to get a job; **2** sich um jemanden bemühen to try to help somebody; **3** bitte, bemühen Sie sich nicht please don't trouble yourself.

Bemühung *die* (PL die Bemühungen) effort.

benachrichtigen *verb* (PERF hat benachrichtigt) **1** to inform; **2** to notify (*officially*).

benachteiligt *adjective* disadvantaged.

△ NEW SPELLING: *See page xii*

benehmen ◊ verb (PRES benimmt sich, IMPERF benahm sich, PERF hat sich benommen) sich benehmen to behave; benimm dich! behave yourself!

Benehmen das behaviour.

beneiden verb (PERF hat beneidet) to envy; jemanden um etwas beneiden to envy somebody something.

benoten verb (PERF hat benotet) to mark.

benutzen verb (PERF hat benutzt) to use.

Benutzer der (PL die Benutzer) user.

Benutzung die use.

Benzin das petrol.

beobachten verb (PERF hat beobachtet) to observe, to watch.

bequem adjective 1 comfortable; 2 machen Sie es sich bequem make yourself at home; 3 lazy; 4 easy; eine bequeme Lösung finden to find an easy way out.

beraten ◊ verb (PRES berät, IMPERF beriet, PERF hat beraten) 1 to advise; 2 jemanden gut/schlecht beraten to give somebody good/bad advice; 3 sich beraten lassen to get advice; 4 gut beraten sein to be well advised; 5 to discuss (a plan, matter); 6 sich über etwas beraten to discuss something.

Berater der (PL die Berater) adviser.

Beratung die (PL die Beratungen) 1 advice; 2 discussion; 3 consultation (with a doctor).

berauben verb (PERF hat beraubt) to rob.

berechnen verb (PERF hat berechnet) 1 to charge; jemandem zehn Mark für etwas berechnen to charge somebody ten marks for something; 2 jemandem zuviel berechnen to overcharge somebody; 3 to calculate.

Bereich der (PL die Bereiche) 1 area; 2 field (in a profession).

bereit adjective ready.

bereiten verb (PERF hat bereitet) 1 to make (coffee, tea); 2 to cause (trouble, difficulty); leider hat es uns Schwierigkeiten bereitet unfortunately it caused us some trouble; 3 to give (a surprise, pleasure).

bereits adverb already.

bereuen verb (PERF hat bereut) to regret.

Berg der (PL die Berge) 1 mountain; 2 hill.

bergab adverb downhill.

Bergarbeiter der (PL die Bergarbeiter) miner.

bergauf adverb uphill.

bergen ◊ verb (PRES birgt, IMPERF barg, PERF hat geborgen) to rescue.

Bergsteigen das mountaineering.

Bergsteiger der (PL die Bergsteiger) mountaineer, climber.

Bergsteigerin die (PL die Bergsteigerinnen) mountaineer, climber.

◊ IRREGULAR VERB: See the verb table in the centre of the dictionary

Bergwacht *die* mountain rescue.

Bergwerk *das* (PL *die* **Bergwerke**) mine.

Bericht *der* (PL *die* **Berichte**) report.

berichten *verb* (PERF **hat berichtet**) 1 to report; **die Zeitungen haben nichts davon berichtet** the newspapers didn't report anything about it; 2 **jemandem über etwas berichten** to tell somebody about something; **er hat mir über seine Ferien in Amerika berichtet** he told me about his holiday in America.

berücksichtigen *verb* (PERF **hat berücksichtigt**) to take into account.

Beruf *der* (PL *die* **Berufe**) 1 occupation; 2 profession; **ich bin Lehrerin von Beruf** I'm a teacher by profession; 3 trade; 4 **was sind Sie von Beruf?** what do you do for a living?

beruflich *adjective* 1 professional; 2 vocational (*training*). *adverb* 1 **beruflich erfolgreich sein** to be successful in your career; 2 **viel beruflich unterwegs sein** to be away a lot on business.

Berufsberatung *die* careers advice.

Berufsschule *die* (PL *die* **Berufsschulen**) technical college.

berufstätig *adjective* working.

Berufsverkehr *der* rush-hour traffic.

beruhigen *verb* (PERF **hat beruhigt**) 1 to calm down; 2 to reassure; 3 **sich beruhigen** to calm down.

Beruhigungsmittel *das* (PL *die* **Beruhigungsmittel**) sedative, tranquillizer.

berühmt *adjective* famous.

berühren *verb* (PERF **hat berührt**) 1 to touch; 2 to touch on (*a topic, an issue*); 3 to affect; **ihre Geschichte berührte ihn seltsam** he was strangely affected by her story; 4 **sich berühren** to touch.

besaß SEE **besitzen**.

beschädigen *verb* (PERF **hat beschädigt**) to damage.

beschaffen[1] *verb* (PERF **hat beschafft**) to get; **kannst du mir nicht einen Job beschaffen?** can't you get me a job?

beschaffen[2] *adjective* **so beschaffen sein, dass …** to be such that …

beschäftigen *verb* (PERF **hat beschäftigt**) 1 to occupy (*keep busy*); 2 to employ (*people*); 3 **sich beschäftigen** to occupy yourself; 4 **ich beschäftige mich mit den Kindern** I'm busy with the children; 5 **sich mit einem Fall beschäftigen** to deal with a case; **sein Aufsatz beschäftigt sich mit der Umweltverschmutzung** his essay deals with environmental pollution.

beschäftigt *adjective* 1 busy; 2 employed.

Beschäftigung *die* (PL *die* **Beschäftigungen**) 1 occupation; 2 activity.

Bescheid *der* (PL *die* **Bescheide**) 1 information; 2 jemandem

△ NEW SPELLING: See page xii

Bescheid sagen to let somebody know; **3 über etwas Bescheid wissen** to know about something.

bescheiden adjective modest.

Bescheinigung die (PL die Bescheinigungen) 1 certificate; **eine Bescheinigung des Arztes** a doctor's certificate; 2 (written) confirmation.

beschimpfen verb (PERF hat beschimpft) to abuse.

beschlagnahmen verb (PERF hat beschlagnahmt) to confiscate.

beschleunigen verb (PERF hat beschleunigt) 1 to speed up; 2 to accelerate; **der Lastwagen hinter uns hat plötzlich beschleunigt** the lorry behind us suddenly accelerated.

beschließen ◇ verb (IMPERF beschloss △, PERF hat beschlossen) to decide.

Beschluss △ der (PL die Beschlüsse) decision.

beschreiben ◇ verb (IMPERF beschrieb, PERF hat beschrieben) to describe.

Beschreibung die (PL die Beschreibungen) description.

beschuldigen verb (PERF hat beschuldigt) to accuse.

beschützen verb (PERF hat beschützt) to protect.

Beschwerde die (PL die Beschwerden) complaint.

beschweren verb (PERF hat beschwert) **sich beschweren** to complain; **ich habe mich bei den Nachbarn über ihn beschwert** I've complained to the neighbours about him.

beschwipst adjective tipsy.

beseitigen verb (PERF hat beseitigt) to remove.

Besen der (PL die Besen) broom.

besetzen verb (PERF hat besetzt) 1 to occupy; 2 to fill (a post, role); 3 to trim, to edge (with lace or fur).

besetzt adjective 1 occupied; 2 **besetzt sein** to be engaged (a phone, toilet); 3 taken (a table, seat); **der Platz ist besetzt** this seat is taken; 4 full (of a train, bus); **der Zug ist voll besetzt** the train is full up.

Besetztzeichen das (PL die Besetztzeichen) engaged tone.

besichtigen verb (PERF hat besichtigt) 1 to look round (a town, museum); 2 to see (sights, a house).

Besichtigung die (PL die Besichtigungen) visit.

besinnungslos adjective unconscious.

Besitz der 1 property; 2 **im Besitz einer Sache sein** to be in possession of something.

besitzen ◇ verb (IMPERF besaß, PERF hat besessen) 1 to own; **sie besitzen ein Haus in Italien** they own a house in Italy; 2 to have (talent, a quality).

Besitzer der (PL die Besitzer) owner.

◇ **IRREGULAR VERB: See the verb table in the centre of the dictionary**

Besitzerin die (PL die Besitzerinnen) owner.

besonderer, besondere, besonderes adjective 1 special; **unter besonderen Umständen** in special circumstances; 2 particular; **ohne besondere Begeisterung** without any particular enthusiasm; 3 **keine besonderen Kennzeichen** no distinguishing features.

Besonderheit die (PL die Besonderheiten) 1 special feature; 2 peculiarity.

besonders adverb particularly.

besorgen verb (PERF hat besorgt) to get; **ich kann dir Karten besorgen** I can get you tickets.

besorgt adjective worried.

besprechen ◇ verb (PRES bespricht, IMPERF besprach, PERF hat besprochen) 1 to discuss; **ich muss es erst mit meinen Eltern besprechen** I'll have to discuss it with my parents first; 2 to review (a book, film).

Besprechung die (PL die Besprechungen) 1 meeting (at work); 2 discussion; 3 review (of a film, play).

besser adjective, adverb better; **alles besser wissen** to know better.

Besserung die 1 improvement; 2 **gute Besserung!** get well soon!

beständig adjective 1 constant; 2 settled (weather).

Bestandteil der (PL die Bestandteile) component.

bestätigen verb (PERF hat bestätigt) 1 to confirm; 2 to acknowledge (receipt); 3 **sich bestätigen** to be confirmed, to prove to be true.

beste SEE **bester**.

Bestechung die (PL die Bestechungen) bribery.

Besteck das (PL die Bestecke) cutlery.

bestehen ◇ verb (IMPERF bestand, PERF hat bestanden) 1 to exist; 2 **es besteht die Gefahr, dass ...** there is a danger that ...; **noch besteht die Hoffnung, dass ...** there is still hope that ...; 3 to pass; **eine Prüfung bestehen** to pass an exam; 4 **auf etwas bestehen** to insist on something; 5 **aus etwas bestehen** to consist of something; 6 **aus etwas bestehen** to be made of something.

bestellen verb (PERF hat bestellt) 1 to order (goods); 2 to reserve (tickets); 3 to tell; **jemandem etwas bestellen** to tell somebody something; 4 **bestell ihm schöne Grüße** give him my regards; 5 **kann ich etwas bestellen?** can I take a message?; 6 to send for; **jemanden zu sich bestellen** to send for somebody.

Bestellung die (PL die Bestellungen) 1 order (for goods); 2 reservation (for tickets).

bestens adverb very well; **das hat ja bestens geklappt** that worked out very well.

△ NEW SPELLING: See page xii

bester, beste, bestes *adjective*
1 best; **sein bestes Buch** his best book; 2 **ich halte es für das Beste** △, **wenn …** I think it would be best if …; **sein Bestes tun** to do your best; 3 **einen Witz zum Besten geben** △ to tell a joke; 4 **jemanden zum Besten halten** △ to pull somebody's leg.
adverb **am besten** best; **du bleibst am besten zu Hause** you'd best stay at home; **es ist am besten, wenn wir gleich anfangen** it's best if we get started straight away.

bestimmen *verb* (PERF **hat bestimmt**) 1 to fix (*a time, price*); 2 to decide (on); **etwas allein bestimmen** to decide (on) something on your own; **er bestimmt immer, was wir machen** he always decides what we're going to do; 3 to be in charge; 4 **für jemanden bestimmt sein** to be meant for somebody; 5 **für etwas bestimmt sein** to be intended for something (*a donation for a good cause, for example*).

bestimmt *adjective* 1 certain; **zu einer bestimmten Zeit** at a certain time; 2 particular; **suchen Sie etwas Bestimmtes?** are you looking for anything in particular? 3 definite.
adverb 1 certainly, definitely; **ich komme ganz bestimmt** I'm definitely coming; 2 **er hat es bestimmt vergessen** he's bound to have forgotten; 3 **du weißt es doch bestimmt noch** surely you must remember it.

Bestimmung *die* (PL **die Bestimmungen**) regulation.

bestrafen *verb* (PERF **hat bestraft**) to punish.

bestreiten ◇ *verb* (IMPERF **bestritt**, PERF **hat bestritten**) 1 to deny; 2 to dispute; **das möchte ich nicht bestreiten** I'm not disputing it; 3 to pay for.

bestürzt *adjective* upset.

Besuch *der* (PL **die Besuche**) 1 visit; 2 attendance (*at school*); 3 **Besuch haben** to have visitors/a visitor; 4 **bei Freunden zu Besuch sein** to be staying with friends; **zu Besuch kommen** to be visiting.

besuchen *verb* (PERF **hat besucht**) 1 to visit; 2 to go to (*an exhibition, the theatre*); **die Schule besuchen** to go to school; 3 to attend (*a lecture*).

Besucher *der* (PL **die Besucher**) visitor.

Besucherin *die* (PL **die Besucherinnen**) visitor.

betätigen *verb* (PERF **hat betätigt**) 1 to operate; 2 **die Bremse betätigen** to apply the brakes; 3 **sich politisch betätigen** to be involved in politics; 4 **sich künstlerisch betätigen** to do art; 5 **sich als Reporter betätigen** to work as a reporter.

Betäubungsmittel *das* (PL **die Betäubungsmittel**) anaesthetic.

Bete *die* **Rote Bete** ▸ beetroot.

beteiligen *verb* (PERF **hat beteiligt**) 1 to give a share to; **jemanden mit**

◇ IRREGULAR VERB: *See the verb table in the centre of the dictionary*

zehn Prozent an einem Geschäft beteiligen to give somebody a ten percent share of a business; **2 sich an etwas beteiligen** to take part in something; **3 kann ich mich an eurem Spiel beteiligen?** can I join in your game?

beten verb (PERF **hat gebetet**) to pray.

Beton der concrete.

betonen verb (PERF **hat betont**) to stress.

Betonung die (PL die **Betonungen**) stress.

Betrag der (PL die **Beträge**) amount.

betragen ◇ verb (PRES **beträgt**, IMPERF **betrug**, PERF **hat betragen**) **1** to amount to, to come to; **2 sich betragen** to behave; **haben sich die Kinder gut betragen?** did the children behave well?

Betragen das behaviour.

betreffen ◇ verb (PRES **betrifft**, IMPERF **betraf**, PERF **hat betroffen**) to concern; **was mich betrifft** as far as I'm concerned.

betreten ◇ verb (PRES **betritt**, IMPERF **betrat**, PERF **hat betreten**) **1** to enter; **2 'Betreten verboten'** 'keep out', 'keep off' (*the grass, for example*).

Betrieb der (PL die **Betriebe**) **1** business, firm; **2** activity; **es war viel Betrieb** it was very busy; **3 in Betrieb sein** to be working (*of a machine*); **4 außer Betrieb sein** to be out of order; **5 eine Maschine in**

Betrieb setzen to start up a machine.

Betriebsferien plural noun firm's holiday; **'Betriebsferien'** 'closed for the holidays'.

betrinken ◇ verb (IMPERF **betrank sich**, PERF **hat sich betrunken**) **sich betrinken** to get drunk.

betrog SEE **betrügen**.

Betrug der **1** deception; **2** fraud.

betrügen ◇ verb (IMPERF **betrog**, PERF **hat betrogen**) **1** to cheat; **jemanden um tausend Mark betrügen** to cheat somebody out of a thousand marks; **2** to be unfaithful to, to cheat on; **sie hat ihren Mann betrogen** she's been unfaithful to her husband.

betrunken adjective drunk.

Bett das (PL die **Betten**) bed; **ins Bett gehen** to go to bed.

Bettbezug der (PL die **Bettbezüge**) duvet cover.

betteln verb (PERF **hat gebettelt**) to beg.

Bettlaken das (PL die **Bettlaken**) sheet.

Bettler der (PL die **Bettler**) beggar.

Bettlerin die (PL die **Bettlerinnen**) beggar.

Bettwäsche die bed linen.

Bettzeug das bedding.

beugen verb (PERF **hat gebeugt**) **1** to bend; **2** to decline, to conjugate (*in grammar*); **3 sich nach vorn beugen** to bend forwards; **sich über**

△ NEW SPELLING: See page xii

etwas beugen to bend over something; **4 sich aus dem Fenster beugen** to lean out of the window; **5 sich beugen** to submit.

Beule die (PL die **Beulen**) **1** bump; **2** lump; **3** dent.

beurteilen verb (PERF hat beurteilt) to judge.

Beutel der (PL die **Beutel**) bag.

Bevölkerung die (PL die **Bevölkerungen**) population.

bevor conjunction **1** before; **2 bevor nicht** until; **bevor er nicht unterschrieben hat** until he has signed.

bevorzugen verb (PERF hat bevorzugt) to prefer.

bewachen verb (PERF hat bewacht) to guard.

bewaffnen verb (PERF hat bewaffnet) to arm.

bewaffnet adjective armed.

bewährt adjective **1** reliable; **2** proven (method, design); **3 ein bewährtes Rezept** a well-tried recipe.

bewegen[1] verb (PERF hat bewegt) **1** to move; **2 sich bewegen** to take exercise; **3 sich bewegen** to move.

bewegen[2] ◇ verb (IMPERF **bewog**, PERF hat **bewogen**) **jemanden dazu bewegen, etwas zu tun** to persuade somebody to do something.

bewegt adjective eventful.

Bewegung die (PL die **Bewegungen**) **1** movement;

2 exercise; **3 eine Maschine in Bewegung setzen** to start (up) a machine; **4 sich in Bewegung setzen** to start to move.

Beweis der (PL die **Beweise**) **1** proof; **2 belastende Beweise** incriminating evidence; **3** token, sign.

beweisen ◇ verb (IMPERF **bewies**, PERF hat **bewiesen**) **1** to prove; **2** to show.

bewerben ◇ verb (PRES **bewirbt sich**, IMPERF **bewarb sich**, PERF hat **sich beworben**) **sich bewerben** to apply; **sich um eine Stelle bewerben** to apply for a job.

Bewerber der (PL die **Bewerber**) applicant.

Bewerberin die (PL die **Bewerberinnen**) applicant.

Bewerbung die (PL die **Bewerbungen**) application.

bewohnen verb (PERF hat bewohnt) to live in.

Bewohner der (PL die **Bewohner**) **1** resident; **2** inhabitant (of a region).

Bewohnerin die (PL die **Bewohnerinnen**) **1** resident; **2** inhabitant (of a region).

bewölkt adjective cloudy.

Bewölkung die clouds.

bewundern verb (PERF hat bewundert) to admire.

Bewunderung die admiration.

bewusst ∆ adjective **1** conscious;

◇ IRREGULAR VERB: See the verb table in the centre of the dictionary

2 deliberate; **3** sich etwas bewusst sein to be aware of something; ich war mir der Folgen bewusst I was aware of the consequences.

bewusstlos ∆ *adjective* unconscious.

Bewusstsein ∆ *das*
1 consciousness; **2** bei vollem Bewusstsein sein to be fully conscious; **3** mir kam zu(m) Bewusstsein, dass ... I realized that ...

bezahlen *verb* (PERF hat bezahlt) **1** to pay; **2** to pay for (*goods, food*); er hat das Essen bezahlt he paid for the meal.

Bezahlung *die* payment.

bezeichnend *adjective* typical.

beziehen ◇ *verb* (IMPERF bezog, PERF hat bezogen) **1** to cover; **2** das Bett frisch beziehen to put clean sheets on the bed; **3** to move into; wann kannst du die neue Wohnung beziehen? when will you be able to move into the new flat?; **4** to get (*goods, a pension*); **5** to take (*a newspaper*); **6** sich auf etwas/jemanden beziehen to refer to something/somebody; **7** es bezieht sich it's clouding over.

Beziehung *die* (PL die Beziehungen) **1** connection; **2** relationship; **3** Beziehungen contacts; Anna hat gute Beziehungen Anna has good contacts; **4** diplomatische Beziehungen diplomatic relations; **5** in dieser Beziehung in this respect; **6** eine Beziehung zu etwas

haben to be able to relate to something (*to art, pop music, for example*).

beziehungsweise *conjunction* **1** or rather; **2** respectively.

Bezirk *der* (PL die Bezirke) district.

Bezug *der* (PL die Bezüge) **1** cover (*of a cushion, duvet, etc.*); **2** connection; keinen Bezug zu etwas haben to be unable to relate to something; **3** auf etwas Bezug nehmen to refer to something; **4** in Bezug auf regarding; **5** mit Bezug auf Ihr Angebot with reference to your offer.

bezweifeln *verb* (PERF hat bezweifelt) to doubt.

BH *der* (PL die BHs) bra.

Bibel *die* (PL die Bibeln) bible; die Bibel the Bible.

Bibliothek *die* (PL die Bibliotheken) library.

biegen ◇ *verb* (IMPERF bog, PERF hat gebogen) **1** to bend; **2** sich biegen to bend; **3** (PERF ist gebogen) to turn; um die Ecke biegen to turn the corner.

Biene *die* (PL die Bienen) bee.

Bier *das* (PL die Biere) beer.

Bierdeckel *der* (PL die Bierdeckel) beer mat.

bieten ◇ *verb* (IMPERF bot, PERF hat geboten) **1** to offer; **2** to bid (*at an auction*); **3** es bietet sich die Möglichkeit there is a possibility; **4** to present (*a sight*); **5** das lasse

ich mir nicht bieten! I won't put up with it!

Bikini der (PL die Bikinis) bikini.

Bild das (PL die Bilder) 1 picture;
jemanden ins Bild setzen to put
somebody in the picture; 2 scene.

bilden verb (PERF hat gebildet) 1 to
form; 2 sich bilden to form; 3 sich
bilden to educate yourself.

Bildschirm der (PL die Bildschirme)
screen.

bildschön adjective (very)
beautiful.

Bildung die 1 formation;
2 education.

billig adjective cheap.

Billion die (PL die Billionen) billion (a
million million).

bin SEE sein.

Binde die (PL die Binden)
1 bandage; 2 sanitary towel.

binden ◇ verb (IMPERF band, PERF
hat gebunden) 1 to tie; 2 to bind (a
book); 3 to make up (a bouquet);
4 to thicken (a sauce); 5 sich
binden to commit oneself.

Bindestrich der (PL die
Bindestriche) hyphen.

Bindfaden der (PL die Bindfäden)
(piece of) string.

Bindung die (PL die Bindungen)
1 tie; 2 relationship; 3 binding (on
a ski).

Biokost die health food.

Biologie die biology.

biologisch adjective biological.

Birke die (PL die Birken) birch tree.

Birne die (PL die Birnen) 1 pear;
2 bulb.

bis preposition ←(+ACC) 1 as far as;
dieser Zug fährt nur bis Passau
this train only goes as far as Passau;
2 up to; Kinder bis zehn zahlen die
Hälfte children up to ten pay half;
bis jetzt up to now; bis zu up to;
3 until, till (with time); 4 by; bis
dahin by then; 5 bis auf except
for; alle sind durchgefallen bis auf
die zwei Mädchen everyone failed
except for the two girls; 6 bis bald!
see you soon!; 7 von München bis
Salzburg from Munich to Salzburg;
von Montag bis Freitag from
Monday to Friday; zwei bis drei
Mark two to three marks.
conjunction until, till; bis sie bleibt, bis
es dunkel wird she's staying until it
gets dark.

Bischof der (PL die Bischöfe) bishop.

bisher adverb so far.

bisherig adjective previous.

biss △ SEE beißen.

Biss △ der (PL die Bisse) bite.

bisschen △ pronoun 1 ein
bisschen a bit; ein bisschen Brot
a bit of bread; 2 kein bisschen not
a bit.

bissig adjective 1 vicious; 'Vorsicht
bissiger Hund!' 'beware of the
dog!'; 2 cutting (remark, tone).

bist SEE sein.

bitte adverb 1 please; 'möchten Sie

Kuchen?' – 'ja bitte' 'would you like some cake?' – 'yes please'; 2 you're welcome (*in reply to thanks*); 3 come in (*after a knock on the door*); 4 (*in a shop*) **bitte?** yes, please!; 5 **wie bitte?** sorry?

Bitte *die* (PL *die* **Bitten**) request.

bitten ◇ *verb* (IMPERF **bat**, PERF **hat gebeten**) to ask; **jemanden um etwas bitten** to ask somebody for something.

bitter *adjective* bitter.

blamieren *verb* (PERF **hat blamiert**) 1 to disgrace; 2 **jemanden blamieren** to embarrass somebody; 3 **sich blamieren** to make a fool of yourself.

Blase *die* (PL *die* **Blasen**) 1 bubble; 2 blister; 3 bladder.

blasen ◇ *verb* (PRES **bläst**, IMPERF **blies**, PERF **hat geblasen**) to blow.

Blasinstrument *das* (PL *die* **Blasinstrumente**) wind instrument.

Blaskapelle *die* (PL *die* **Blaskapellen**) brass band.

blass △ *adjective* pale.

Blatt *das* (PL *die* **Blätter**) 1 leaf; 2 sheet; **ein Blatt Papier** a sheet of paper; 3 page; 4 newspaper.

blau *adjective* 1 blue; **ein blau gestreiftes Kleid** a dress with blue stripes; 2 **ein blaues Auge haben** to have a black eye; 3 **ein blauer Fleck** a bruise; 4 **blau sein** (*informal*) to be tight; 5 **eine Fahrt ins Blaue** a mystery tour.

Blech *das* (PL *die* **Bleche**) 1 sheet

metal; 2 tin; 3 baking tray; 4 brass (*in music*).

Blei *das* lead.

bleiben ◇ *verb* (IMPERF **blieb**, PERF **ist geblieben**) 1 to stay, to remain; 2 to be left; 3 **bleiben Sie am Apparat** hold the line; 4 **bei etwas bleiben** to stick to something; 5 **ruhig bleiben** to keep calm; 6 **wo bleibt er so lange?** where has he got to?; 7 **etwas bleiben lassen** to not do something; **wenn du nicht mitkommen willst, dann lass es eben bleiben** if you don't want to come, then don't.

bleich *adjective* pale.

Bleichmittel *das* (PL *die* **Bleichmittel**) bleach.

bleifrei *adjective* unleaded.

Bleistift *der* (PL *die* **Bleistifte**) pencil.

Bleistiftspitzer *der* (PL *die* **Bleistiftspitzer**) pencil sharpener.

blenden *verb* (PERF **hat geblendet**) 1 to dazzle; 2 to blind.

blendend *adjective* 1 marvellous; 2 **es geht mir blendend** I feel great; **wir haben uns blendend amüsiert** we had a great time.

Blick *der* (PL *die* **Blicke**) 1 look; 2 glance; 3 **auf den ersten Blick** at first sight; 4 view; **ein Zimmer mit Blick aufs Meer** a room with a sea view.

blicken *verb* (PERF **hat geblickt**) 1 to look; 2 **sich blicken lassen** to show your face.

blieb SEE **bleiben**.

△ NEW SPELLING: *See page xii*

blies SEE **blasen**.

blind *adjective* blind.

Blinddarm *der* (PL *die* **Blinddärme**) appendix.

Blinddarmentzündung *die* (PL *die* **Blinddarmentzündungen**) appendicitis.

Blinde *der/die* (PL *die* **Blinden**) blind person, blind man/woman.

blinzeln *verb* (PERF **hat geblinzelt**) to blink.

blinken *verb* (PERF **hat geblinkt**) 1 to flash; 2 to indicate (*of a car*).

Blinker *der* (PL *die* **Blinker**) indicator.

Blitz *der* (PL *die* **Blitze**) 1 (flash of) lightning; 2 flash.

blitzen *verb* (PERF **hat geblitzt**) 1 to flash; 2 to sparkle; 3 **es hat geblitzt** there was a flash of lightning.

Block *der* (PL *die* **Blöcke**) 1 pad (*for writing on*); 2 (PL *die* **Blocks**) block (*of flats*).

Blockflöte *die* (PL *die* **Blockflöten**) recorder.

blöd *adjective* stupid.

Blödsinn *der* nonsense.

blond *adjective* blonde, fair-haired.

bloß *adverb* 1 only; **es kostet bloß fünf Mark** it's only five marks; 2 **warum hat er das bloß gemacht?** why on earth did he do it?; 3 **was mache ich bloß?** whatever shall I do?; 4 **fass das bloß nicht an!** don't touch it!
adjective 1 bare (*feet*); **mit bloßem Auge** with the naked eye; 2 mere

(*words, suspicion*); **der bloße Gedanke daran** the mere thought of it.

Blume *die* (PL *die* **Blumen**) flower.

Blumenkohl *der* cauliflower.

Bluse *die* (PL *die* **Blusen**) blouse.

Blut *das* blood.

Blutdruck *der* blood pressure.

Blüte *die* (PL *die* **Blüten**) blossom.

bluten *verb* (PERF **hat geblutet**) to bleed.

Blutprobe *die* (PL *die* **Blutproben**) blood test.

Bock *der* (PL *die* **Böcke**) 1 buck; 2 billy-goat; 3 ram; 4 **Bock auf etwas haben** (*informal*) to fancy something; 5 **einen Bock schießen** (*informal*) to make a blunder.

Bockwurst *die* (PL *die* **Bockwürste**) frankfurter.

Boden *der* (PL *die* **Böden**) 1 ground; 2 floor; 3 bottom (*of a container*); 4 loft, attic.

Bodensee *der* Lake Constance.

bog SEE **biegen**.

Bogen *der* (PL *die* **Bögen**) 1 curve; 2 arch; 3 turn (*in skiing*).

Bohne *die* (PL *die* **Bohnen**) bean.

bohren *verb* (PERF **hat gebohrt**) to drill.

Bohrer *der* (PL *die* **Bohrer**) drill.

Bohrinsel *die* (PL *die* **Bohrinseln**) oil rig.

✧ IRREGULAR VERB: See the verb table in the centre of the dictionary

Bohrmaschine die (PL die Bohrmaschinen) electric drill.

Bombe die (PL die Bomben) bomb.

Bonbon der (PL die Bonbons) sweet.

Boot das (PL die Boote) boat.

Bord¹ das (PL die Borde) shelf.

Bord² der an Bord on board; über Bord overboard.

Bordkarte die (PL die Bordkarten) boarding card.

borgen (PERF hat geborgt) 1 to borrow; 2 sich etwas borgen to borrow something; ich habe es mir von ihr geborgt I borrowed it from her; 3 jemandem etwas borgen to lend somebody something; Evi hat mir ihr Buch geborgt Evi lent me her book.

Börse die (PL die Börsen) stock exchange.

Borste die (PL die Borsten) bristle.

böse adjective 1 bad; 2 wicked; 3 naughty (child); 4 angry; böse werden to get angry; ich bin ihm böse I'm angry with him; 5 auf jemanden böse sein to be cross with somebody.

boshaft adjective malicious.

bot SEE bieten.

Bote der (PL die Boten) messenger.

Botin die (PL die Botinnen) messenger.

Botschaft die (PL die Botschaften) 1 message; 2 embassy.

Botschafter der (PL die Botschafter) ambassador.

Botschafterin die (PL die Botschafterinnen) ambassador.

Bowle die (PL die Bowlen) punch (for drinking).

boxen verb (PERF hat geboxt) 1 to box; 2 to punch.

Boxer der (PL die Boxer) boxer.

brach SEE brechen.

brachte SEE bringen.

Branche die (PL die Branchen) (line of) business.

Branchenverzeichnis das (PL die Branchenverzeichnisse) classified directory.

Brand der (PL die Brände) fire.

Brandung die surf.

brannte SEE brennen.

braten ◇ verb (PRES brät, IMPERF briet, PERF hat gebraten) 1 to fry; 2 to roast.

Braten der (PL die Braten) 1 roast; 2 joint.

Brathähnchen das (PL die Brathähnchen) roast chicken.

Bratkartoffeln plural noun fried potatoes.

Bratpfanne die (PL die Bratpfannen) frying pan.

Bratwurst die (PL die Bratwürste) fried sausage.

Brauch der (PL die Bräuche) custom.

△ NEW SPELLING: See page xii

brauchbar

brauchbar *adjective* **1** usable; **2** useful.

brauchen *verb* (PERF **hat gebraucht**) **1** need; **ich brauche eine neue Birne für meine Lampe** I need a new bulb for my light; **du brauchst nur auf den Knopf zu drücken** all you need to do is press the button; **du brauchst nicht zu gehen** you needn't go; **2 sie braucht es nur zu sagen** she only has to say; **3** to take (*time*); **wie lange brauchst du mit dem Auto?** how long does it take you by car?; **4 ich könnte es gut brauchen** I could do with it.

brauen *verb* (PERF **hat gebraut**) to brew.

Brauerei *die* (PL **die Brauereien**) brewery.

braun *adjective* **1** brown; **2 braun werden** to get a tan; **braun (gebrannt) sein** to be tanned.

Bräune *die* tan.

Brause *die* (PL **die Brausen**) fizzy drink.

Braut *die* (PL **die Bräute**) bride.

Bräutigam *der* (PL **die Bräutigame**) bridegroom.

Brautjungfer *die* (PL **die Brautjungfern**) bridesmaid.

Brautpaar *das* (PL **die Brautpaare**) bride and groom.

brav *adjective* good.

BRD *die* (*Bundesrepublik Deutschland*) FRG (*Federal Republic of Germany*).

brechen ◇ *verb* (PRES **bricht**, IMPERF **brach**, PERF **hat gebrochen**) **1** to break (*an agreement, a record*); **2 sich den Arm brechen** to break your arm; **3** to vomit; **4** (PERF **ist gebrochen**) to break; **der Ast ist gebrochen** the branch broke.

breit *adjective* **1** wide; **2** broad; **3 die breite Masse** the general public.

Breite *die* (PL **die Breiten**) width.

Bremse *die* (PL **die Bremsen**) **1** brake; **2** horsefly.

bremsen *verb* (PERF **hat gebremst**) **1** to brake; **2** to slow down (*development, production*); **3** jemanden bremsen (*informal*) to stop somebody; **er ist nicht mehr zu bremsen** there's no stopping him.

Bremslicht *das* (PL **die Bremslichter**) brake light.

Bremspedal *das* (PL **die Bremspedale**) brake pedal.

brennen ◇ *verb* (IMPERF **brannte**, PERF **hat gebrannt**) **1** to burn; **2** to be on (*of a light*); **das Licht brennen lassen** to leave the light on; **3** to sting (*of a wound or sore*); **4 das Haus brennt** the house is on fire; **es brennt!** fire!; **5 darauf brennen, etwas zu tun** to be dying to do something.

Brennnessel △ *die* (PL **die Brennnesseln**) stinging nettle.

Brennpunkt *der* (PL **die Brennpunkte**) focus.

Brett *das* (PL **die Bretter**) **1** board; **2** plank; **3** shelf.

◇ IRREGULAR VERB: *See the verb table in the centre of the dictionary*

Brezel die (PL die Brezeln) pretzel.

bricht SEE **brechen**.

Brief der (PL die Briefe) letter.

Brieffreund der (PL die Brieffreunde) pen friend.

Brieffreundin die (PL die Brieffreundinnen) pen friend.

Briefkasten der (PL die Briefkästen) 1 letterbox; 2 postbox.

Briefmarke die (PL die Briefmarken) stamp.

Brieftasche die (PL die Brieftaschen) wallet.

Briefträger der (PL die Briefträger) postman.

Briefträgerin die (PL die Briefträgerinnen) postwoman.

Briefumschlag der (PL die Briefumschläge) envelope.

Briefwechsel der correspondence.

briet SEE **braten**.

Brillant der (PL die Brillanten) diamond.

Brille die (PL die Brillen) glasses, spectacles.

bringen ◇ verb (IMPERF **brachte**, PERF **hat gebracht**) 1 to bring; 2 to take; Peter bringt dich nach Hause Peter will take you home; 3 die Kinder ins Bett bringen to put the children to bed; 4 einen Film im Fernsehen bringen to show a film on television; 5 to publish (an article); 6 to yield (interest, a profit);

7 jemanden dazu bringen, etwas zu tun to get somebody to do something; 8 mit sich bringen to entail; 9 etwas hinter sich bringen to get something over and done with; 10 es weit bringen to go far; 11 jemanden auf eine Idee bringen to give somebody an idea; 12 es zu nichts bringen to get nowhere; 13 das bringt's nicht! (informal) that's no use!

Brise die (PL die Brisen) breeze.

Brite der (PL die Briten) Briton; die Briten the British.

Britin die (PL die Britinnen) Briton.

britisch adjective British.

Brokkoli der broccoli.

Brombeere die (PL die Brombeeren) blackberry.

Brosche die (PL die Broschen) brooch.

Broschüre die (PL die Broschüren) brochure.

Brot das (PL die Brote) 1 bread; ein Brot a loaf of bread; 2 ein Brot a slice of bread.

Brötchen das (PL die Brötchen) roll.

Bruch der (PL die Brüche) 1 break; 2 fracture; 3 hernia; 4 fraction.

Bruchteil der (PL die Bruchteile) fraction.

Brücke die (PL die Brücken) bridge.

Bruder der (PL die Brüder) brother.

Brühe die (PL die Brühen) 1 broth; 2 stock (for cooking).

△ NEW SPELLING: See page xii

Brühwürfel der (PL die Brühwürfel)
stock cube.

brüllen verb (PERF hat gebrüllt) to
roar.

brummen verb (PERF hat
gebrummt) 1 to buzz; 2 to growl (of
a bear); 3 to hum (of an engine).

Brunnen der (PL die Brunnen)
1 well; 2 fountain.

Brust die (PL die Brüste) 1 chest;
2 breast.

Brustschwimmen das
breaststroke.

brutto adverb gross.

BSE das (bovine spongiforme
Enzephalopathie) BSE.

Bub der (PL die Buben) boy.

Buch das (PL die Bücher) book.

Buche die (PL die Buchen) beech.

buchen verb (PERF hat gebucht) to
book.

Bücherei die (PL die Büchereien)
library.

Bücherregal das (PL die
Bücherregale) bookcase.

Buchhalter der (PL die Buchhalter)
accountant, bookkeeper.

Buchhalterin die (PL die
Buchhalterinnen) accountant,
bookkeeper.

Buchhandlung die (PL die
Buchhandlungen) bookshop.

Büchse die (PL die Büchsen) tin,
can.

Büchsenöffner der (PL die
Büchsenöffner) tin opener.

Buchstabe der (PL die Buchstaben)
letter (of the alphabet); ein großer
Buchstabe a capital letter; ein
kleiner Buchstabe a small letter.

buchstabieren verb (PERF hat
buchstabiert) to spell.

Bucht die (PL die Buchten) bay.

bücken (PERF hat sich gebückt) sich
bücken to bend down.

Buddhismus der Buddhism.

Bude die (PL die Buden) 1 hut;
2 stall; 3 meine Bude (informal)
my room, my pad.

Büfett das (PL die Büfetts) buffet.

Bügel der (PL die Bügel) hanger.

Bügeleisen das (PL die Bügeleisen)
iron.

bügeln verb (PERF hat gebügelt) to
iron.

Bühne die (PL die Bühnen) stage.

Bulle der (PL die Bullen) 1 bull;
2 (informal) cop.

Bummel der (PL die Bummel) stroll
(around town).

bummeln verb (PERF ist
gebummelt) 1 to stroll; wir sind
durch die Stadt gebummelt we
strolled around town; 2 (PERF hat
gebummelt) to dawdle.

Bund[1] der (PL die Bünde)
1 association; 2 waistband.

Bund[2] das (PL die Bunde) bunch.

◇ IRREGULAR VERB: See the verb table in the centre of the dictionary

Bundesbürger der (PL die Bundesbürger) German citizen.

Bundeskanzler der (PL die Bundeskanzler) Federal Chancellor.

Bundesland das (PL die Bundesländer) (federal) state.

Bundesliga die (PL die Bundesligen) (German) national league.

Bundesrat der Upper House (of the German Parliament).

Bundesrepublik die Federal Republic.

Bundesstraße die (PL die Bundesstraßen) A road, major road.

Bundestag der Lower House (of the German Parliament).

Bundeswehr die (German) Army.

bunt adjective colourful.

Buntstift der (PL die Buntstifte) coloured pencil.

Burg die (PL die Burgen) castle.

Bürger der (PL die Bürger) citizen.

Bürgerin die (PL die Bürgerinnen) citizen.

Bürgermeister der (PL die Bürgermeister) mayor.

Bürgersteig der (PL die Bürgersteige) pavement.

Büro das (PL die Büros) office.

Büroklammer die (PL die Büroklammern) paper clip.

Bürste die (PL die Bürsten) brush.

bürsten verb (PERF hat gebürstet) to brush.

Bus der (PL die Busse) bus; **ich fahre mit dem Bus** I'm going by bus.

Busbahnhof der (PL die Busbahnhöfe) bus station.

Busch der (PL die Büsche) bush.

Busen der (PL die Busen) bosom.

Busfahrer der (PL die Busfahrer) bus driver.

Busfahrerin die (PL die Busfahrerinnen) bus driver.

Busfahrkarte die (PL die Busfahrkarten) bus ticket.

Bushaltestelle die (PL die Bushaltestellen) bus stop.

Bußgeld das (PL die Bußgelder) fine.

Buslinie die (PL die Buslinien) bus route.

Büstenhalter der (PL die Büstenhalter) bra.

Butter die butter.

Butterbrot das (PL die Butterbrote) sandwich, bread and butter.

bzw. = beziehungsweise.

C c

Café das (PL die Cafés) café.

Cafeteria die (PL die Cafeterias) cafeteria.

campen verb (PERF hat gecampt) to camp.

△ NEW SPELLING: See page xii

Camping das camping.

Campingkocher der (PL die Campingkocher) camping stove.

Campingplatz der (PL die Campingplätze) campsite.

CD die (PL die CDs) CD.

CD-Spieler der (PL die CD-Spieler) CD player.

Cello das (PL die Cellos) cello.

Champignon der (PL die Champignons) mushroom.

Chance die (PL die Chancen) chance.

Chaos das chaos.

chaotisch adjective chaotic.

Charakter der (PL die Charaktere) character.

charmant adjective charming.

Charterflug der (PL die Charterflüge) charter flight.

Chauvinist der (PL die Chauvinisten) chauvinist.

Chef der (PL die Chefs) 1 head (of a firm); 2 boss.

Chefin die (PL die Chefinnen) 1 head (of a firm); 2 boss.

Chemie die chemistry.

Chemiker der (PL die Chemiker) chemist.

Chemikerin die (PL die Chemikerinnen) chemist.

chemisch adjective 1 chemical; 2 chemische Reinigung dry-cleaning; dry-cleaner's.

China das China.

Chinese der (PL die Chinesen) Chinese; die Chinesen the Chinese.

Chinesin die (PL die Chinesinnen) Chinese.

chinesisch adjective Chinese.

Chipkarte die (PL die Chipkarten) smart card.

Chips plural noun crisps.

Chirurg der (PL die Chirurgen) surgeon.

Chirurgin die (PL die Chirurginnen) surgeon.

Chlor das chlorine.

Chor der (PL die Chöre) choir.

Christ der (PL die Christen) Christian.

Christin die (PL die Christinnen) Christian.

christlich adjective Christian.

Christus der Christ.

circa adverb approximately.

Clown der (PL die Clowns) clown.

Cola die (PL die Colas) Coke™.

Comic der (PL die Comics) cartoon.

Comic-Heft das (PL die Comic-Hefte) comic.

Computer der (PL die Computer) computer.

Computerspiel das (PL die Computerspiele) computer game.

Container der (PL die Container) 1 container; 2 skip.

✧ IRREGULAR VERB: See the verb table in the centre of the dictionary

Cordsamt der corduroy.

Couch die (PL die **Couchs**) sofa.

Couchtisch der (PL die **Couchtische**) coffee table.

Cousin der (PL die **Cousins**) cousin.

Cousine die (PL die **Cousinen**) cousin.

Creme die (PL die **Cremes**) 1 cream; 2 cream dessert.

Curry das 1 curry; 2 curry powder.

Currywurst die (PL die **Currywürste**) curried sausage.

Cursor der (PL die **Cursors**) cursor.

D d

da adverb 1 there; **da draußen** out there; **da drüben** over there; **da sein** to be there; **man muss pünktlich da sein** you have to be there on time; 2 **ist noch Brot da?** is there any bread left?; 3 here; **sind alle da?** is everyone here?; **da sind deine Handschuhe** here are your gloves; 4 **ist Sabine da?** is Sabine about?; 5 **von da an** from then on; 6 **ich bin wieder da** I'm back; 7 so (therefore); **der Bus war weg, da bin ich gelaufen** the bus had gone, so I walked; 8 **da kann man nichts machen** there's nothing you can do about it; 9 **da, wo die Straße nach Stuttgart abzweigt** at the turning for Stuttgart.
conjunction as, since; **da es gerade regnet** as it's raining.

dabei adverb 1 (included or next to) with it/him/her/them; **sie hatten die Kinder dabei** they had the children with them; 2 **dicht dabei** close by; 3 (referring to something already mentioned) about it; **das Wichtigste dabei** the most important thing about it; 4 at the same time; **er malte ein Bild und sang dabei** he painted a picture and sang at the same time; 5 during this; 6 **jemandem dabei helfen, etwas zu tun** to help somebody do something; 7 **was hast du dir denn dabei gedacht?** what were you thinking of?; 8 **dabei sein** △ to be there; **er ist dabei gewesen** he was there; 9 **was ist denn dabei?** so what?; 10 **dabei sein, etwas zu tun** to be just doing something; **ich war gerade dabei zu gehen** I was just about to leave; 11 **dabei bleiben** to stick with it (an opinion, for example); 12 and yet, even though.

dabeibleiben ◇ verb (IMPERF **blieb dabei**, PERF **ist dabeigeblieben**) 1 to stay on (at an organisation); 2 **er hat mit dem Training begonnen, ist aber nicht dabeigeblieben** he started training, but didn't keep it up.

dabeisein SEE **dabei**.

Dach das (PL die **Dächer**) roof.

Dachboden der (PL die **Dachböden**) loft, attic.

dachte SEE **denken**.

Dackel der (PL die **Dackel**) dachshund.

dadurch adverb 1 through it/them; **das Wasser muss dadurch**

gelaufen sein the water must have run through it; **2** as a result; **3** in this way; **ich nehme die U-Bahn, dadurch bin ich eine halbe Stunde eher da** I'll take the tube, that way I'll be there half an hour earlier.
conjunction **dadurch, dass** because.

dafür adverb **1** for it/them; **dafür kriegt man nicht viel** you won't get much for it/them; **2** instead; **wenn er schon nicht auf die Party gehen will, kann er dich dafür zum Essen einladen** if he doesn't want to go to the party he can take you for a meal instead; **3** but then (on the other hand); **4** dafür, dass considering (that); **5 ich kann nichts dafür** it's not my fault.

dagegen adverb **1** against it/them; **ich bin dagegen** I'm against it; **2** for it/them (when swapping); **3** into it; **das Auto ist dagegen gefahren** the car drove into it; **4** by comparison; **5 hast du was dagegen?** do you mind?; **6** however.

daheim adverb at home.

daher adverb **1** from there; **2** that's why.

dahin adverb **1** there; **2 bis dahin** (in the past) until then; (in the future) by then; **3 jemanden dahin bringen, dass er etwas tut** to get somebody to do something.

dahinten adverb over there.

dahinter adverb **1** behind it/them; **2 dahinter kommen** ∆ to get to the bottom of it; **ich bin endlich dahinter**

gekommen I finally got to the bottom of it.

dalassen ◇ verb (PRES **lässt da** ∆, IMPERF **ließ da**, PERF **hat dagelassen**) to leave there.

damals adverb at that time; then; **wir wohnten damals in Berlin** we were then living in Berlin.

Dame die (PL die **Damen**) **1** lady; **2** queen (in chess or cards); **3** draughts.

Damenbinde die (PL die **Damenbinden**) sanitary towel.

damit adverb **1** with it/them; **ich will damit spielen** I want to play with it; **hör auf damit!** stop it!; **2 by it**; **was meinst du damit?** what do you mean by that?; **3 damit hat es noch Zeit** there's no hurry (about that); **4** therefore, because of that; **sie hat den zweiten Satz verloren und damit das Spiel** she lost the second set and because of it the match.
conjunction so that; **ich habe es aufgeschrieben, damit du es nicht vergisst** I wrote it down so that you won't forget.

Damm der (PL die **Dämme**) **1** dam; **2** embankment.

dämmern verb (PERF **hat gedämmert**) **es dämmert** it is getting light; it is getting dark.

Dämmerung die **1** dawn; **2** dusk.

Dampf der (PL die **Dämpfe**) steam.

dampfen verb (PERF **hat gedampft**) to steam.

dämpfen verb (PERF **hat gedämpft**)

◇ IRREGULAR VERB: See the verb table in the centre of the dictionary

1 to steam (*in cooking*); 2 to muffle (*a sound*); 3 to dampen (*somebody's enthusiasm*).

Dampfer der (PL die **Dampfer**) steamer.

danach adverb 1 after it/them; 2 afterwards; **kurz danach** shortly afterwards; 3 **danach suchen** to look for it/them; 4 **danach riechen** to smell of it; 5 accordingly; 6 **es sieht danach aus** it looks like it.

Däne der (PL die **Dänen**) Dane.

daneben adverb 1 next to it/them; 2 by comparison.

Dänemark das Denmark.

Dänin die (PL die **Däninnen**) Dane.

dänisch adjective Danish.

dank preposition ←(+GEN or +DAT) thanks to.

Dank der 1 thanks; **mit Dank zurück** thanks for the loan; 2 **vielen Dank** thank you very much.

dankbar adjective 1 grateful; 2 rewarding.

danke exclamation thank you, thanks; **danke schön** thank you very much; **(nein) danke** no thank you, no thanks.

danken verb (PERF **hat gedankt**) 1 to thank; 2 **nichts zu danken** don't mention it.

dann adverb then.

daran adverb 1 on it/them; 2 **daran denken** to think of it/them; 3 **dicht daran** close to it/them; 4 **nahe daran sein, etwas zu tun** to be on

the point of doing something; 5 about it/them; **daran ist nichts zu machen** there is nothing you can do about it; 6 **es liegt daran, dass ...** it is because ...; 7 **er ist daran gestorben** he died of it.

darauf adverb 1 on it/them; 2 **darauf warten** to wait for it; 3 **darauf antworten** to reply to it; 4 after that; **kurz darauf** shortly after that; 5 **am Tag darauf** the day after; 6 **am darauf folgenden Tag** △ the following day; 7 **es kommt darauf an, ob ...** it depends whether ...

daraufhin adverb as a result.

daraus adverb 1 out of it/them, from it/them; 2 **was ist daraus geworden?** what has become of it/them? 3 **mach dir nichts daraus** don't worry about it.

darf, darfst SEE **dürfen**.

darin adverb 1 in it/them; 2 in that respect; **der Unterschied liegt darin, dass ...** the difference is that ...

Darm der (PL die **Därme**) intestine(s).

darstellen verb (PERF **hat dargestellt**) 1 to represent; 2 to portray; **dieses Gemälde stellt Szenen aus dem Bürgerkrieg dar** this painting portrays scenes from the civil war; 3 to describe; **er stellt es so dar, als sei es meine Schuld** the way he describes it, it's all my fault; 4 to play (*in the theatre*).

Darsteller der (PL die **Darsteller**) actor.

△ NEW SPELLING: See page xii

Darstellerin die (PL die Darstellerinnen) actress.

darüber adverb 1 over it/them; 2 about it; **darüber sprechen** to talk about it; 3 more; **dreißig Mark oder darüber** thirty marks or more.

darum adverb 1 round it/them; 2 **darum bitten** to ask for it; 3 that's why; **darum komme ich nicht** that's why I'm not coming; 4 **ich sorge mich darum** I worry about it; 5 **es geht darum, zu gewinnen** the main thing is to win; 6 **darum geht es nicht** that's not the point; 7 because of that; **darum, weil** because.

darunter adverb 1 under it/them; 2 **im Stock darunter** on the floor below; 3 among them; **mehrere Schüler, darunter zwei Zehnjährige** a number of pupils, among them two ten year olds; 4 less; **dreißig Mark oder darunter** thirty marks or less; 5 **was verstehen Sie darunter?** what do you understand by that?

das article (neuter) 1 the; **das Haus** the house; 2 that; **das Mädchen war es** it was that girl; **das da** that one. pronoun 1 which; that; **das Kleid, das ich im Schaufenster gesehen habe** the dress which I saw in the window; 2 **das mit der Spitze** the one with the lace; 3 who; **das Mädchen, das gegenüber wohnt** the girl who lives opposite; 4 that; **das wusste ich nicht** I didn't know that; **das geht** that's all right.

dasein SEE **da**.

Dasein das existence.

dass △ conjunction 1 that; **ich freue mich, dass …** I'm very pleased that …; 2 **ich verstehe nicht, dass Karin ihn mag** I don't understand why Karin likes him.

dasselbe pronoun the same, the same one.

Daten plural noun data.

Datenbank die (PL die Datenbanken) database.

Datenverarbeitung die data processing.

datieren verb (PERF hat datiert) to date.

Dativ der (PL die Dative) dative.

Datum das (PL die Daten) date.

Dauer die 1 duration; 2 length; 3 **für die Dauer von fünf Jahren** for (a period of) five years; 4 **von Dauer sein** to last; 5 **auf die Dauer** in the long run; **auf Dauer** permanently.

Dauerkarte die (PL die Dauerkarten) season ticket.

dauern verb (PERF hat gedauert) 1 to last; 2 **lange dauern** to take a long time; **es hat vier Wochen gedauert, bis der Brief hier ankam** it took four weeks for the letter to arrive.

dauernd adjective constant. adverb constantly.

Dauerwelle die (PL die Dauerwellen) perm.

Daumen der (PL die Daumen) thumb.

◇ IRREGULAR VERB: See the verb table in the centre of the dictionary

Daunendecke die (PL die Daunendecken) duvet.

davon adverb 1 from it/them; 2 about it; ich weiß nichts davon I don't know anything about it; 3 of it/them; die Hälfte davon half of it/them; 4 das kommt davon (informal) it serves you right; 5 was habe ich davon? what's the point?; 6 abgesehen davon apart from that.

davor adverb 1 in front of it/them; 2 beforehand; 3 Angst davor haben to be frightened of it/them; 4 kurz davor sein, etwas zu tun to be on the point of doing something.

dazu adverb 1 to it/them; 2 in addition; noch dazu in addition (to it); 3 with it; was isst du dazu? what are you having with it?; 4 ich habe keine Lust dazu I don't feel like it; 5 jemanden dazu bringen, etwas zu tun to get somebody to do something; 6 ich bin nicht dazu gekommen I didn't get round to it; 7 er ist nicht dazu bereit he's not prepared to do it.

dazugeben ◇ verb (PRES gibt dazu, IMPERF gab dazu, PERF hat dazugegeben) to add.

dazugehören verb (PERF hat dazugehört) 1 to belong to it/them; 2 to go with it/them (of accessories); alles, was dazugehört everything that goes with it.

dazukommen ◇ verb (IMPERF kam dazu, PERF ist dazugekommen) 1 to arrive; 2 to be added; 3 kommt noch etwas dazu? would you like anything else?

dazwischen adverb 1 in between; 2 between them; der Unterschied dazwischen the difference between them.

dazwischenkommen ◇ verb (PRES kommt dazwischen, IMPERF kam dazwischen, PERF ist dazwischengekommen) to crop up.

DB die (Deutsche Bundesbahn) German railways.

DDR die (Deutsche Demokratische Republik) GDR, East Germany; in der ehemaligen DDR in the former East Germany.

Debatte die (PL die Debatten) debate.

Decke die (PL die Decken) 1 blanket, cover; 2 (table)cloth; ich habe eine neue Decke aufgelegt I've put on a new tablecloth; 3 ceiling.

Deckel der (PL die Deckel) 1 lid; 2 top.

decken verb (PERF hat gedeckt) 1 to cover; 2 ein Tuch über etwas decken to spread a cloth over something; 3 den Tisch decken to lay the table; 4 jemanden decken to cover up for somebody; 5 einen Spieler decken to mark a player (in sport).

definieren verb (PERF hat definiert) to define.

dehnbar adjective elastic.

dehnen verb (PERF hat gedehnt) to stretch.

dein adjective your.

△ NEW SPELLING: See page xii

deiner, deine, deins *pronoun* yours; **meine Uhr ist kaputt, kann ich deine haben?** my watch is broken, can I take yours?

deinetwegen *adverb* 1 because of you; 2 for your sake.

deins SEE **deiner**.

deklinieren *verb* (PERF **hat dekliniert**) to decline.

Delle *die* (PL die **Dellen**) dent.

Delphin *der* (PL die **Delphine**) dolphin.

dem *article* (*dative*) 1 (to) the; 2 **es liegt auf dem Tisch** it's on the table. *pronoun* 1 him; **gib es dem** give it to him; 2 to it, to that one; 3 to whom; **der Mann, dem ich das Geld gegeben habe** the man I gave the money to; 4 which; **das Messer, mit dem ich Zwiebeln schneide** the knife that I cut onions with.

demnächst *adverb* shortly.

Demokratie *die* (PL die **Demokratien**) democracy.

demokratisch *adjective* democratic.

Demonstrant *der* (PL die **Demonstranten**) demonstrator.

Demonstrantin *die* (PL die **Demonstrantinnen**) demonstrator.

Demonstration *die* (PL die **Demonstrationen**) demonstration.

demonstrieren *verb* (PERF **hat demonstriert**) to demonstrate.

den *article* (*accusative*) 1 the; 2 **ich habe mir den Arm gebrochen** I've broken my arm.

pronoun 1 him; **kennst du den?** do you know him?; 2 it, that one; **den kannst du gerne haben** you're welcome to it; **ich nehme den** I'll take that one; 3 who(m); 4 which; **der Mantel, den ich mir gekauft habe** the coat I bought.

denen *pronoun* (*dative plural*) 1 (to) them; 2 that, (to) whom; **die Menschen, denen sie geholfen hat** the people she helped.

denkbar *adjective* conceivable.

denken ◇ *verb* (IMPERF **dachte**, PERF **hat gedacht**) 1 to think; **ich denke oft an dich** I often think of you; 2 **das kann ich mir denken** I can imagine.

Denkmal *das* (PL die **Denkmäler**) monument.

denn *conjunction* 1 because, for; 2 **mehr denn je** more than ever. *adverb* 1 **wo denn?** where?; 2 **was ist denn los?** so what's the matter?; 3 **warum denn nicht?** why ever not?; 4 **es sei denn** unless.

dennoch *conjunction* nevertheless.

deprimiert *adjective* depressed.

der *article* 1 (*masculine*) the; **der Mann** the man; 2 (*feminine and plural genitive*) of the; **die Katze der Frau** the woman's cat; **der Ball der Kinder** the children's ball; 3 (*dative*) (to) the; **ich gab es der Frau** I gave it to the woman.

pronoun 1 who; **der Mann, der hier wohnt** the man who lives here; 2 which; **der Regenschirm, der mir**

◇ IRREGULAR VERB: *See the verb table in the centre of the dictionary*

gehört the umbrella which is mine; 3 **der da** that one; 4 **him, he.**

deren *pronoun* 1 their; **die Kinder und deren Hund** the children and their dog; 2 whose; 3 of which.

derselbe *pronoun* the same, the same one.

des *article* 1 of the; **das Klingeln des Telefons** the ringing of the phone; 2 **der Ball des Jungen** the boy's ball.

deshalb *adverb* 1 therefore; 2 that's why.

desinfizieren *verb* (PERF **hat desinfiziert**) to disinfect.

dessen *pronoun* 1 his; 2 its; 3 whose; **der Junge, dessen Mutter weint** the boy whose mother is crying; 4 of which.

desto *adverb* the; **je mehr, desto besser** the more the better.

deswegen *conjunction* 1 therefore; 2 that's why.

Detektiv *der* (PL die **Detektive**) detective.

deutlich *adjective* clear. *adverb* **ich konnte ihn deutlich sehen** I could clearly see him.

deutsch *adjective* German.

Deutsch *das* German; **auf Deutsch** in German; **fließend Deutsch sprechen** to speak fluent German.

Deutsche *der/die* (PL die **Deutschen**) German; **er ist Deutscher** he's German.

Deutschland *das* Germany; **nach Deutschland** to Germany.

Devisen *plural noun* foreign currency.

Dezember *der* December; **am ersten Dezember** on the first of December; **im Dezember** in December.

Dezimalzahl *die* (PL die **Dezimalzahlen**) decimal (number).

d.h. (*das heißt*) i.e.

Dia *das* (PL die **Dias**) slide.

diagonal *adjective* diagonal.

Diagramm *das* (PL die **Diagramme**) diagram.

Dialekt *der* (PL die **Dialekte**) dialect.

Dialog *der* (PL die **Dialoge**) dialogue.

Diamant *der* (PL die **Diamanten**) diamond.

Diät *die* (PL die **Diäten**) diet; **jemanden auf Diät setzen** (*informal*) to put somebody on a diet.

dich *pronoun* 1 you; 2 yourself.

dicht *adjective* 1 thick (*fog*); 2 dense; 3 watertight; 4 airtight; 5 **er ist nicht ganz dicht** (*informal*) he's off his head. *adverb* 1 densely; 2 tightly; 3 close; **geh nicht so dicht an den Käfig** don't go so close to the cage; **dicht bei** close to.

Dichter *der* (PL die **Dichter**) poet.

Dichterin *die* (PL die **Dichterinnen**) poet.

Dichtung *die* (PL die **Dichtungen**) 1 poetry; 2 seal, washer.

△ NEW SPELLING: See page xii

dick *adjective* **1** thick; **2** swollen (*ankle, tonsils*); **3** fat (*person*).

Dickkopf *der* (PL *die* Dickköpfe) **1** stubborn person; **2** einen Dickkopf haben to be stubborn.

die *article* (*feminine and plural*) the; **die Frau** the woman; **die Bücher** the books.
pronoun (*feminine and plural*) **1** who; **die Frau, die hier wohnt** the woman who lives here; **die Frau, die ich kenne** the woman I know; **die Kinder, die ich gefragt habe** the children I asked; **2** which; **die Tasche, die ich gekauft habe** the bag I bought; **3** she, her; **4** them; **ich meine die** I mean them; **5** die da that one; (*plural*) those.

Dieb *der* (PL *die* Diebe) thief.

Diebin *die* (PL *die* Diebinnen) thief.

Diebstahl *der* (PL *die* Diebstähle) theft.

Diele *die* (PL *die* Dielen) **1** hall; **2** floorboard.

dienen *verb* (PERF hat gedient) to serve.

Dienst *der* (PL *die* Dienste) service; **Dienst haben** to work, to be on duty (*of a soldier or doctor*).

Dienstag *der* (PL *die* Dienstage) Tuesday; **am Dienstag** on Tuesday.

dienstags *adverb* on Tuesdays.

dienstfrei *adjective* **1** ein dienstfreier Tag a day off; **2** dienstfrei haben to have time off, to be off duty.

dienstlich *adverb* on business.

Dienstreise *die* (PL *die* Dienstreisen) business trip.

diese SEE dieser.

Diesel *der* diesel.

dieselbe *pronoun* the same, the same one.

dieser, diese, dieses *adjective* **1** this; **2** these; **diese Äpfel** these apples.
pronoun **1** this one; **mir gefällt dieses am besten** I like this one best; **2** these ones.

diesmal *adverb* this time.

Digitaluhr *die* (PL *die* Digitaluhren) **1** digital watch; **2** digital clock.

Diktat *das* (PL *die* Diktate) dictation.

Ding *das* (PL *die* Dinge) thing; **vor allen Dingen** above all; **das war ein Ding** (*informal*) that was quite something.

Dings *der/die/das* thingummy.

Dinosaurier *der* (PL *die* Dinosaurier) dinosaur.

Diplom *das* (PL *die* Diplome) diploma.

dir *pronoun* **1** you, to you; **sie hat es dir gegeben** she gave it to you; **ich verspreche dir, dass ...** I promise you that ...; **2 Freunde von dir** friends of yours; **3** yourself.

direkt *adjective* direct.

Direktor *der* (PL *die* Direktoren) **1** director; **2** headmaster, principal; **3** manager (*of a bank, theatre*).

Direktorin *die* (PL *die* Direktorinnen) **1** director;

⬦ IRREGULAR VERB: *See the verb table in the centre of the dictionary*

2 headmistress, principal;
3 manager (*of a bank, theatre*).

Direktübertragung die (PL die
Direktübertragungen) live
transmission.

Dirigent der (PL die Dirigenten)
conductor.

dirigieren verb (PERF hat dirigiert)
to conduct.

Diskette die (PL die Disketten)
floppy disk.

Diskothek die (PL die Diskotheken)
disco, discotheque.

Diskriminierung die
discrimination; **die Diskriminierung
von Frauen** discrimination against
women.

Diskussion die (PL die
Diskussionen) discussion; **zur
Diskussion stehen** to be under
discussion.

diskutieren verb (PERF hat
diskutiert) to discuss.

Disziplin die (PL die Disziplinen)
discipline.

DJH die (*Deutsche Jugendherberge*)
German youth hostel (association).

DM die (*Deutsche Mark*) DM,
Deutschmark.

D-Mark die (PL die D-Mark)
Deutschmark, German mark.

doch adverb 1 yes (*when you are
contradicting somebody*); '**hast du
keinen Hunger?' – 'doch!'** 'aren't
you hungry?' – 'yes, I am!'; 2 after
all; **sie hat ihn doch eingeladen** she

invited him after all; **sie ist doch
nicht gekommen** she hasn't come
after all; 3 **er hat doch meinen Brief
bekommen?** he did get my letter,
didn't he?; **sie kommt doch?** she's
coming, isn't she?; 4 anyway; **du
hörst ja doch nicht auf mich** you
won't listen to me anyway; 5 **pass
doch auf!** do be careful!
conjunction but.

Doktor der (PL die Doktoren) doctor;
den Doktor machen to do a
doctorate.

Dokument das (PL die Dokumente)
document.

Dokumentarfilm der (PL die
Dokumentarfilme) documentary.

Dokumentarsendung die (PL die
Dokumentarsendungen)
documentary (programme).

dolmetschen verb (PERF hat
gedolmetscht) to interpret.

Dolmetscher der (PL die
Dolmetscher) interpreter.

Dolmetscherin die (PL die
Dolmetscherinnen) interpreter.

Dom der (PL die Dome) cathedral.

Donau die Danube.

Donner der thunder.

donnern verb (PERF hat gedonnert)
to thunder.

Donnerstag der (PL die
Donnerstage) Thursday; **am
Donnerstag** on Thursday.

donnerstags adverb on Thursdays.

doof adjective (*informal*) stupid.

△ NEW SPELLING: See page xii

Doppel das (PL die Doppel)
1 duplicate; 2 doubles (in sport).

Doppelbett das (PL die
Doppelbetten) double bed.

Doppelfenster das (PL die
Doppelfenster) double-glazed
window; **wir haben Doppelfenster**
we've got double glazing.

Doppelhaus das (PL die
Doppelhäuser) semi-detached
house.

doppelt adjective 1 double; 2 in
doppelter Ausführung in
duplicate; 3 die doppelte Menge
twice the amount.
adverb 1 doubly; 2 twice; doppelt
so viel twice as much; sich doppelt
anstrengen to try twice as hard.

Doppelzimmer das (PL die
Doppelzimmer) double room.

Dorf das (PL die Dörfer) village.

Dorn der (PL die Dornen) thorn.

dort adverb there; dort drüben over
there.

dorther adverb from there.

dorthin adverb there; geht ihr jetzt
dorthin? are you going there now?

Dose die (PL die Dosen) tin, can.

Dosenöffner der (PL die
Dosenöffner) tin opener.

Dosis die (PL die Dosen) dose.

Dotter der (PL die Dotter) yolk.

Dozent der (PL die Dozenten)
lecturer.

Dozentin die (PL die Dozentinnen)
lecturer.

Drache der (PL die Drachen) dragon.

Drachen der (PL die Drachen) kite.

Drachenfliegen das hang-gliding.

Draht der (PL die Drähte) 1 wire; 2 er
ist auf Draht (informal) he's on the
ball.

Drama das (PL die Dramen) drama.

Dramatik die drama.

dran adverb SEE daran; 1 ich bin
dran it's my turn; wer ist dran?
whose turn is it?; 2 gut dran sein to
be well off; 3 arm dran sein to be
in a bad way; 4 spät dran sein to
be late.

drängen verb (PERF hat gedrängt)
1 to push; 2 to press, to urge
(somebody); 3 sich drängen to
crowd; die Leute drängten sich vor
der Kasse people crowded around
the box-office.

drankommen ◇ verb (IMPERF kam
dran, PERF ist drangekommen) to
have your turn; wer kommt dran?
whose turn is it?

drauf adverb SEE darauf; 1 drauf
und dran sein, etwas zu tun to be
on the point of doing something;
2 gut drauf sein (informal) to be in
a good mood.

draußen adverb outside.

Dreck der dirt.

dreckig adjective dirty, filthy.

Drehbuch das (PL die Drehbücher)
1 screenplay; 2 script.

drehen verb (PERF hat gedreht) 1 to
turn; an etwas drehen to turn

◇ IRREGULAR VERB: See the verb table in the centre of the dictionary

something; **2** to shoot (*a film*);
3 sich drehen to turn; **4 sich im
Kreis drehen** to rotate; **5 es dreht
sich um ihr Taschengeld** it's about
her pocket money.

drei *number* three.

Drei *die* (PL *die* **Dreien**) three.

Dreieck *das* (PL *die* **Dreiecke**)
triangle.

dreieckig *adjective* triangular.

dreifach *adjective* triple.

dreihundert *number* three
hundred.

dreimal *adverb* three times.

dreißig *number* thirty.

dreiviertel *number* three-quarters.

Dreiviertelstunde *die* (PL *die*
Dreiviertelstunden) three-quarters
of an hour.

dreizehn *number* thirteen.

drin *adverb* SEE **darin**; **drin sein** to
be inside.

dringend *adjective* urgent.

drinnen *adverb* **1** inside; **2** indoors.

dritt *adverb* **sie sind zu dritt** there
are three of them.

dritte SEE **dritter**.

Drittel *das* (PL *die* **Drittel**) third.

drittens *adverb* thirdly.

dritter, dritte, drittes *adjective*
third; **zum dritten Mal** for the third
time; **ein Dritter** a third person;
jeder Dritte, der mitwollte every

third person who wanted to come;
die Dritte Welt the Third World.

Droge *die* (PL *die* **Drogen**) drug.

drogenabhängig *adjective*
addicted to drugs.

Drogenabhängige *der/die* (PL *die*
Drogenabhängigen) drug addict.

Drogenabhängigkeit *die* drug
addiction.

drogensüchtig *adjective* addicted
to drugs.

Drogensüchtige *der/die* (PL *die*
Drogensüchtigen) drug addict.

Drogerie *die* (PL *die* **Drogerien**)
chemist's.

Drogist *der* (PL *die* **Drogisten**)
chemist.

Drogistin *die* (PL *die* **Drogistinnen**)
chemist.

drohen *verb* (PERF **hat gedroht**) to
threaten; **jemandem drohen** to
threaten somebody.

Drohung *die* (PL *die* **Drohungen**)
threat.

drüben *adverb* over there.

Druck *der* **1** pressure; **jemanden
unter Druck setzen** to put pressure
on somebody; **2** printing; **3** (PL *die*
Drucke) print.

drucken *verb* (PERF **hat gedruckt**) to
print.

drücken *verb* (PERF **hat gedrückt**)
1 to press; **2 an der Tür drücken** to
push the door; '**bitte drücken**'
'push'; **3** to hug; **4** to pinch (*of
shoes*); **5 die Preise drücken** to

△ NEW SPELLING: *See page xii*

force down prices; **6 sich vor etwas drücken** (*informal*) to get out of something; **du hast dich mal wieder vor dem Aufräumen gedrückt** you've got out of tidying up again.

Drucker der (PL die **Drucker**) printer.

Druckknopf der (PL die **Druckknöpfe**) press stud.

Drucksache die (PL die **Drucksachen**) printed matter.

Druckschrift die (PL die **Druckschriften**) **1** block letters; **2** type; **3** pamphlet.

Drüse die (PL die **Drüsen**) gland.

Dschungel der (PL die **Dschungel**) jungle.

du pronoun **1** you; **2 du sagen** to say 'du' (to each other); **per du sein** to be on familiar terms (*'du' is used when talking to family members, close friends, or people of your own age; otherwise 'Sie' is used*).

Dudelsack der (PL die **Dudelsäcke**) bagpipes.

Duft der (PL die **Düfte**) fragrance, scent.

duften verb (PERF **hat geduftet**) to smell; **nach Lavendel duften** to smell of lavender.

dumm adjective **1** stupid; **2 das wird mir jetzt zu dumm** (*informal*) I've had enough of it; **3 so etwas Dummes!** how annoying!; **4 der Dumme sein** to draw the short straw.

dummerweise adverb stupidly.

Dummheit die (PL die

Dummheiten) **1** stupidity; **2** stupid thing; **mach keine Dummheiten** don't do anything stupid.

Dummkopf der (PL die **Dummköpfe**) fool.

Dünger der (PL die **Dünger**) fertilizer.

dunkel adjective **1** dark; **ein dunkler Anzug** a dark suit; **2 im Dunkeln** in the dark; **3** vague (*idea*); **4** shady (*business*); **5** deep (*voice*).

Dunkelheit die darkness, dark.

dünn adjective **1** thin; **2** weak (*coffee*, *tea*).

Dunst der (PL die **Dünste**) haze.

Duo das (PL die **Duos**) duet.

durch preposition ←(+ACC) **1** through; **er ist durch das Fernsehen bekannt geworden** he's become famous through television; **2** by; **durch Boten** by courier; **3 acht durch zwei ist vier** eight divided by two is four; **4** due to. adverb **1** through; **die ganze Nacht durch** all through the night; **2 den Winter durch** throughout the winter; **3 durch und durch** completely; **4 es war acht Uhr durch** (*informal*) it was gone eight o'clock.

durcharbeiten verb (PERF **hat durchgearbeitet**) **1** to work through; **die Nacht durcharbeiten** to work through the night; **2 sich durch etwas durcharbeiten** to work your way through something.

durchaus adverb absolutely.

durchblicken verb (PERF **hat**

◇ IRREGULAR VERB: *See the verb table in the centre of the dictionary*

durchgeblickt) 1 (*informal*) to understand; 2 **durchblicken lassen, dass ...** to hint that ...

durchbrechen ◇ *verb* (PRES **bricht durch**, IMPERF **brach durch**, PERF **hat durchgebrochen**) 1 to snap, to break in two; 2 (PERF **ist durchgebrochen**) **das Brett ist durchgebrochen** the board has snapped.

durcheinander *adverb* 1 in a mess; **mein Zimmer ist durcheinander** my room is (in) a mess; 2 **die Akten durcheinander bringen** △ to muddle up the files; **Karl hat ihre Namen durcheinander gebracht** Karl got their names mixed up; 3 confused; **bring mich nicht durcheinander** don't confuse me; 4 **sie haben alle durcheinander geredet** they all talked at once.

Durcheinander *das* 1 muddle; 2 mess; **in der Wohnung herrschte ein fürchterliches Durcheinander** the flat was a terrible mess; 3 confusion; **im allgemeinen Durcheinander** in the general confusion.

durcheinanderbringen SEE **durcheinander**.

durchfahren ◇ *verb* (PRES **fährt durch**, IMPERF **fuhr durch**, PERF **ist durchgefahren**) 1 to drive through; 2 to go through; 3 **der Zug fährt (in Stuttgart) durch** the train doesn't stop (in Stuttgart).

Durchfall *der* diarrhoea.

durchfallen ◇ *verb* (PRES **fällt durch**, IMPERF **fiel durch**, PERF **ist**

durchgefallen) 1 to fall through; 2 to fail (*an exam*).

durchführen *verb* (PERF **hat durchgeführt**) to carry out.

Durchgang *der* (PL **die Durchgänge**) 1 passage; 2 **'Durchgang verboten'** 'no entry'; 3 round (*in sport*).

Durchgangsverkehr *der* through traffic.

durchgehen ◇ *verb* (IMPERF **ging durch**, PERF **ist durchgegangen**) 1 to go through; 2 (*informal*) to escape; 3 **jemandem etwas durchgehen lassen** to let somebody get away with something.

durchkommen ◇ *verb* (IMPERF **kam durch**, PERF **ist durchgekommen**) 1 to come through; 2 to get through (*on the phone, in an exam*); 3 to pull through (*after an illness*).

durchlassen ◇ *verb* (PRES **lässt durch** △, IMPERF **ließ durch**, PERF **hat durchgelassen**) 1 to let through; 2 to let in.

durchmachen *verb* (PERF **hat durchgemacht**) 1 to go through; 2 to work through (*your lunch break, for example*); 3 **wir haben die Nacht durchgemacht** we made a night of it.

Durchmesser *der* (PL **die Durchmesser**) diameter.

durchnehmen ◇ *verb* (PRES **nimmt durch**, IMPERF **nahm durch**, PERF **hat durchgenommen**) to do (*a topic at school*).

△ NEW SPELLING: See page xii

durchs = durch das.

Durchsage die (PL die Durchsagen) announcement.

Durchschnitt der (PL die Durchschnitte) average; **im Durchschnitt** on average.

durchschnittlich *adjective* average.
adverb on average.

durchsetzen verb (PERF hat durchgesetzt) **1** to carry through; **2 sich durchsetzen** to assert yourself; **3 sich durchsetzen** to catch on (*of a fashion, an idea*).

durchsichtig *adjective* transparent.

durchstreichen ✧ *verb* (IMPERF strich durch, PERF hat durchgestrichen) to cross out.

Durchzug der draught.

dürfen ✧ *verb* (PRES darf, IMPERF durfte, PERF hat gedurft *or* hat dürfen) **1** to be allowed; **sie darf das nicht** she's not allowed to do that; **er hat nicht gedurft** he wasn't allowed to; **2 Klaus hat sie im Krankenhaus besuchen dürfen** Klaus was allowed to visit her in hospital; **3 darf ich?** may I?; **4 das dürfen Sie nicht vergessen** you mustn't forget that; **du darfst es nicht alles so ernst nehmen** you mustn't take it all so seriously; **5 du darfst froh sein, dass sonst nichts passiert ist** you should be glad that nothing else happened; **das darf einfach nicht passieren** that just shouldn't happen; **das dürfte nicht schwierig sein** that shouldn't be

difficult; **6 das darf nicht wahr sein!** I don't believe it!; **7 was darf es sein?** can I help you?; **8 das dürfte der Grund sein** that's probably the reason.

durfte, durften, durftest, durftet SEE dürfen.

Dürre die (PL die Dürren) drought.

Durst der thirst; **Durst haben** to be thirsty.

durstig *adjective* thirsty.

Dusche die (PL die Duschen) shower.

duschen *verb* (PERF hat geduscht) **1** to have a shower; **2 sich duschen** to have a shower.

Düsenflugzeug das (PL die Düsenflugzeuge) jet (plane).

düster *adjective* **1** gloomy (*future, thoughts*); **2** dark.

Dutzend das (PL die Dutzende) dozen.

duzen *verb* (PERF hat geduzt) to call somebody 'du'; **wollen wir uns duzen?** shall we say 'du' to each other? (*'du' is used when talking to family members, close friends, or people of your own age*).

dynamisch *adjective* dynamic.

D-Zug der (PL die D-Züge) fast train, express.

✧ **IRREGULAR VERB: See the verb table in the centre of the dictionary**

E e

Ebbe die (PL die Ebben) low tide.

eben adjective 1 flat; 2 level.
adverb 1 just; Gabi war eben hier Gabi was just here; eben noch just now; 2 eben! exactly!

Ebene die (PL die Ebenen) 1 plain; 2 level; 3 plane (in geometry).

ebenso adverb just as; Ulla hat den Film ebenso oft gesehen wie du Ulla's seen the film just as often as you; ich habe ebenso viel Arbeit wie du I've got just as much work as you.

Echo das (PL die Echos) echo.

echt adjective real, genuine; die Kette ist aus echtem Gold the necklace is real gold.
adverb (informal) really; das ist echt gut that's really good.

Eckball der (PL die Eckbälle) corner (kick).

Ecke die (PL die Ecken) corner; um die Ecke round the corner.

eckig adjective square.

Edelstein der (PL die Edelsteine) precious stone.

EDV die (elektronische Datenverarbeitung) electronic data processing, EDP.

Efeu der (PL die Efeus) ivy.

EG die (Europäische Gemeinschaft) EC.

egal adjective 1 das ist mir egal it's all the same to me; egal wie groß no matter how big; egal, ob er es will oder nicht (it doesn't matter) whether he wants to or not.

egoistisch adjective selfish.

ehe conjunction before; ehe ich nicht weiß, was er will, mache ich nichts I won't do anything before I know what he wants.

Ehe die (PL die Ehen) marriage.

Ehefrau die (PL die Ehefrauen) wife.

ehemalig adjective former.

Ehemann der (PL die Ehemänner) husband.

Ehepaar das (PL die Ehepaare) married couple.

eher adverb 1 earlier, sooner; je eher, desto besser the sooner the better; 2 rather; eher gebe ich zu Fuß, als Geld für ein Taxi auszugeben I'd rather walk than pay for a taxi; 3 more; das ist schon eher möglich that's more likely.

Ehre die (PL die Ehren) honour.

Ehrgeiz der ambition.

ehrgeizig adjective ambitious.

ehrlich adjective honest.

Ehrlichkeit die honesty.

Ei das (PL die Eier) egg.

Eiche die (PL die Eichen) oak.

△ NEW SPELLING: See page xii

Eichhörnchen das (PL die Eichhörnchen) squirrel.

Eid der (PL die Eide) oath.

Eidechse die (PL die Eidechsen) lizard.

Eierbecher der (PL die Eierbecher) egg-cup.

Eierschale die (PL die Eierschalen) eggshell.

Eifer der eagerness.

Eifersucht die jealousy.

eifersüchtig adjective jealous; auf jemanden eifersüchtig sein to be jealous of somebody.

eifrig adjective eager.

Eigelb das (PL die Eigelb(e)) egg yolk.

eigen adjective own; sie ist erst siebzehn und hat schon ihr eigenes Auto she's only seventeen and she's already got her own car.

Eigenart die (PL die Eigenarten) peculiarity.

eigenartig adjective peculiar.

Eigenschaft die (PL die Eigenschaften) 1 quality; 2 characteristic.

eigensinnig adjective obstinate.

eigentlich adjective actual. adverb actually; eigentlich habe ich keine Lust, heute ins Kino zu gehen actually I don't fancy going to the cinema today.

Eigentum das property.

Eigentümer der (PL die Eigentümer) owner.

eignen verb (PERF hat sich geeignet) sich eignen to be suitable.

Eile die hurry.

eilen verb 1 (PERF ist geeilt) to hurry; 2 (PERF hat geeilt) to be urgent; das eilt nicht it's not urgent.

eilig adjective 1 urgent; 2 hurried; 3 es eilig haben to be in a hurry.

Eilzug der (PL die Eilzüge) fast stopping train.

Eimer der (PL die Eimer) bucket.

ein, eine, ein article a, an; ein Haus a house; eine Allergie an allergy; ein bisschen mehr a bit more; was für ein Kleid hast du gekauft? what sort of dress did you buy?
adjective 1 one; sie haben nur ein Kind they've got just one child; eines Abends one evening; 2 einer Meinung sein to be of the same opinion; 3 ein für allemal once and for all.

einander pronoun each other, one another.

Einbahnstraße die (PL die Einbahnstraßen) one-way street.

Einband der (PL die Einbände) cover.

einbauen verb (PERF hat eingebaut) 1 to fit; 2 to install.

Einbauküche die (PL die Einbauküchen) fitted kitchen.

einbiegen verb (IMPERF bog ein, PERF ist eingebogen) to turn; der Radfahrer bog langsam in die Seitenstraße ein the cyclist turned slowly down the side street.

◇ IRREGULAR VERB: See the verb table in the centre of the dictionary

einbilden verb (PERF hat sich eingebildet) 1 sich einbilden to imagine; **das bildest du dir nur ein** you're only imagining it; 2 **Till bildet sich viel ein** Till is very conceited.

Einbildung die imagination; **das ist alles nur Einbildung** it's all in the mind.

einbrechen ◇ verb (PRES **bricht ein**, IMPERF **brach ein**, PERF **ist eingebrochen**) to break in; **in unserem Haus sind Diebe eingebrochen** thieves broke into our house; **bei unseren Nachbarn ist eingebrochen worden** our neighbours have been burgled.

Einbrecher der (PL die Einbrecher) burglar.

Einbruch der (PL die Einbrüche) 1 burglary; 2 **vor Einbruch der Dunkelheit** before it gets dark; 3 **bei Einbruch der Nacht** at nightfall.

eindeutig adjective 1 clear; 2 definite (proof).

Eindruck der (PL die Eindrücke) impression.

eindrucksvoll adjective impressive.

eine SEE ein, einer.

eineinhalb number one and a half.

einer, eine, ein(e)s pronoun 1 one; **einer von uns** one of us; **wie soll das einer wissen?** how is one supposed to know?; 2 somebody; 3 **kaum einer** hardly anyone; 4 you; **das macht einen müde** it makes you tired.

einerseits adverb on the one hand; **einerseits sagt sie, dass sie kein Geld hat, andererseits kauft sie sich dauernd neue Sachen** on the one hand she claims to have no money, on the other hand she's constantly buying new things.

eines SEE einer.

einfach adjective 1 simple; 2 easy; 3 single (ticket, knot). adverb simply.

Einfachheit die simplicity.

Einfahrt die (PL die Einfahrten) 1 entrance; 2 arrival (of a train); 3 slip road (on a motorway).

Einfall der (PL die Einfälle) idea.

einfallen ◇ verb (PRES **fällt ein**, IMPERF **fiel ein**, PERF **ist eingefallen**) 1 **jemandem einfallen** to occur to somebody; 2 **ihr Name fällt mir nicht ein** I can't think of her name; 3 **was fällt dir eigentlich ein?** what do you think you're doing?; 4 **sich etwas einfallen lassen** to think of something.

Einfamilienhaus das (PL die Einfamilienhäuser) detached family house.

Einfluss △ der (PL die Einflüsse) influence.

einfrieren ◇ verb (IMPERF **fror ein**, PERF **ist eingefroren**) 1 to freeze; 2 (PERF **hat eingefroren**) to freeze (food in the freezer).

Einfuhr die (PL die Einfuhren) import.

einführen verb (PERF **hat**

△ NEW SPELLING: See page xii

eingeführt 1 to import; 2 to introduce.

Einführung die (PL die Einführungen) introduction.

Eingabe die input (of data).

eingeben ◇ verb (PRES **gibt ein**, IMPERF **gab ein**, PERF **hat eingegeben**) 1 to hand in; 2 to input, to key in.

eingebildet adjective 1 conceited; 2 imaginary (illness).

Eingeborene der/die (PL die Eingeborenen) native.

eingehen ◇ verb (IMPERF **ging ein**, PERF **ist eingegangen**) 1 to shrink (of clothes); 2 to die (of plants); 3 to arrive (of goods); 4 **auf etwas eingehen** to go into something; **sie ging näher darauf ein** she went into it in more detail; 5 **auf etwas nicht eingehen** to ignore something; 6 **auf etwas eingehen** to agree to something; **Oliver ist auf unseren Plan eingegangen** Oliver agreed to our plan; 7 **ein Risiko eingehen** to take a risk.

eingeschrieben adjective registered; **ein eingeschriebener Brief** a registered letter.

eingestellt adjective 1 **auf etwas eingestellt sein** to be prepared for something; 2 **fortschrittlich eingestellt sein** to be progressively minded.

eingewöhnen verb (PERF **hat sich eingewöhnt**) **sich eingewöhnen** to settle in.

eingießen ◇ verb (IMPERF **goss ein** △, PERF **hat eingegossen**) to pour.

Eingriff der (PL die Eingriffe) 1 intervention; 2 operation (surgical).

einheimisch adjective 1 native; 2 local.

Einheit die (PL die Einheiten) 1 unity; 2 unit (of drink, soldiers).

Einheitspreis der (PL die Einheitspreise) 1 standard price; 2 flat fare.

einholen verb (PERF **hat eingeholt**) 1 to catch up with; 2 to make up (time, a delay); 3 to buy; **einholen gehen** to go shopping.

einhundert number one hundred.

einige SEE einiger.

einigen verb (PERF **hat sich geeinigt**) **sich einigen** to come to an agreement; **sich auf etwas einigen** to agree on something.

einiger, einige, einiges adjective, pronoun 1 some; **vor einiger Zeit** some time ago; 2 several; **hier einige waren noch da** there were only a few left; 4 **einiges** quite a lot; **wir haben einiges gesehen** we saw quite a lot (of things); 5 **einiges** some things; **einiges hat uns nicht gefallen** there were some things we didn't like.

einigermaßen adverb 1 fairly; 2 fairly well; 3 **'wie geht es dir?' – 'einigermaßen'** 'how are you?' – 'so-so'.

einiges SEE einiger.

◇ IRREGULAR VERB: See the verb table in the centre of the dictionary

Einigung die agreement.

Einkauf der (PL die Einkäufe)
1 purchase; 2 shopping; Einkäufe
machen to do some shopping.

einkaufen verb (PERF hat
eingekauft) 1 to buy; ich habe
vergessen Milch einzukaufen I
forgot to buy milk; 2 to shop; wir
kaufen meist im Supermarkt ein
we usually shop at the supermarket;
einkaufen gehen to go shopping.

Einkaufsbummel der (PL die
Einkaufsbummel) shopping spree.

Einkaufswagen der (PL die
Einkaufswagen) shopping trolley.

Einkaufszentrum das (PL die
Einkaufszentren) shopping centre.

Einkommen das (PL die
Einkommen) income.

einladen ◇ verb (PRES lädt ein,
IMPERF lud ein, PERF hat eingeladen)
1 to invite; jemanden zum
Abendessen einladen to invite
somebody for dinner; 2 jemanden
ins Kino einladen to take somebody
to the cinema; 3 to treat; ich lade
euch ein I'll treat you; 4 to load
(goods).

Einladung die (PL die Einladungen)
invitation.

einleben verb (PERF hat sich
eingelebt) sich einleben to settle
down.

Einleitung die (PL die Einleitungen)
introduction.

einlösen verb (PERF hat eingelöst)
to cash.

einmal adverb 1 once (in the past);
es war einmal ... once upon a
time ...; 2 one day (in the future);
3 auf einmal suddenly; 4 auf
einmal at the same time; sie kamen
alle auf einmal they all came at the
same time; 5 nicht einmal not
even; 6 noch einmal again;
7 es geht nun einmal nicht it's just
not possible.

einmalig adjective 1 unique;
2 fantastic; 3 single, one-off
(payment).

einmischen verb (PERF hat sich
eingemischt) sich einmischen to
interfere.

einordnen verb (PERF hat
eingeordnet) 1 to put in order;
2 sich einordnen to fit in (with other
people); 3 sich einordnen to get in
lane (when driving).

einpacken verb (PERF hat
eingepackt) 1 to pack; 2 to wrap.

einreichen verb (PERF hat
eingereicht) to hand in.

Einreise die (PL die Einreisen) entry.

einreisen verb (PERF ist eingereist)
to enter a country; er reiste nach
Italien ein he entered Italy.

einrichten verb (PERF hat
eingerichtet) 1 to furnish; 2 to set
up (an organisation); 3 to arrange;
kannst du es so einrichten, dass
du vormittags da bist? can you
arrange to be here in the morning?;
4 sich einrichten to furnish your
home; 5 sich einrichten to
economize; 6 sich auf etwas

△ NEW SPELLING: See page xii

einrichten to prepare for something.

Einrichtung *die* (PL *die* **Einrichtungen**) 1 furnishing; 2 furnishings; 3 setting up; 4 institution; **staatliche Einrichtungen** state institutions.

eins *number* one; **eins zu eins** one all; **es ist eins** it's one o'clock. *pronoun* SEE **einer**. *adjective* **mir ist alles eins** it's all the same to me.

Eins *die* (PL *die* **Einsen**) one.

einsam *adjective* lonely.

einsammeln *verb* (PERF **hat eingesammelt**) to collect.

Einsatz *der* 1 use; 2 stake (*when betting*).

einschalten *verb* (PERF **hat eingeschaltet**) 1 to switch on (*a radio, TV*); 2 **sich einschalten** to intervene.

einschlafen ◊ *verb* (PRES **schläft ein**, IMPERF **schlief ein**, PERF **ist eingeschlafen**) to go to sleep.

einschließen ◊ *verb* (IMPERF **schloss ein** △, PERF **hat eingeschlossen**) 1 to lock in; 2 to include; 3 **sich einschließen** to lock yourself in.

einschließlich *preposition* ←(+GEN) including; **einschließlich der Unkosten** including expenses. *adverb* inclusive.

einschränken *verb* (PERF **hat eingeschränkt**) 1 to restrict; 2 to cut back; 3 **sich einschränken** to economize.

einschreiben ◊ *verb* (IMPERF **schrieb ein**, PERF **hat sich eingeschrieben**) 1 **sich einschreiben** to enrol (*at university*); 2 **sich einschreiben** to put your name down.

Einschreiben *das* (PL *die* **Einschreiben**) registered letter, registered parcel; **per Einschreiben** registered.

einsehen ◊ *verb* (PRES **sieht ein**, IMPERF **sah ein**, PERF **hat eingesehen**) 1 to realize; 2 to see; **das sehe ich nicht ein** I don't see why.

einseitig *adjective* one-sided.

einsenden ◊ *verb* (IMPERF **sendete ein/sandte ein**, PERF **hat eingesendet/hat eingesandt**) to send in.

einsetzen *verb* (PERF **hat eingesetzt**) 1 to put in (*a missing part*), to insert; 2 to use; **während der Weltmeisterschaft wurden Sonderzüge eingesetzt** special train were put on during the World Cup; 3 to stake (*money*); 4 to start (*of rain, snow*); 5 **sich für jemanden einsetzen** to support somebody.

Einsicht *die* 1 insight; 2 sense; 3 **zu der Einsicht kommen, dass …** to come to realize that …

einsperren *verb* (PERF **hat eingesperrt**) to lock up.

Einspruch *der* (PL *die* **Einsprüche**) objection.

◊ **IRREGULAR VERB:** *See the verb table in the centre of the dictionary*

einst *adverb* 1 once; 2 one day (*in the future*).

einstecken *verb* (PERF **hat eingesteckt**) 1 to put in (*a coin*); 2 **einen Brief einstecken** to post a letter; 3 to plug in; 4 **etwas einstecken** to put something in your pocket or bag, to take something; 5 (*informal*) to take (*insults*).

einsteigen ◇ *verb* (IMPERF **stieg ein**, PERF **ist eingestiegen**) 1 to get in; 2 to get on (*a bus or train*).

einstellen *verb* (PERF **hat eingestellt**) 1 to employ (*in a job*); 2 to adjust (*a machine*); 3 to focus (*a camera*); 4 to tune into (*a radio station*); 5 to stop; 6 **sich auf etwas einstellen** to prepare yourself for something; 7 **sich schnell auf eine neue Situation einstellen** to adjust quickly to a new situation.

Einstellung *die* (PL *die* **Einstellungen**) 1 employment; 2 adjustment; 3 stopping; 4 take (*of a film*); 5 attitude; **seine politische Einstellung** his political views.

Einstieg *der* (PL *die* **Einstiege**) entrance.

einstürzen *verb* (PERF **ist eingestürzt**) to collapse.

einstweilen *adverb* 1 for the time being; 2 meanwhile.

eintausend *number* one thousand.

einteilen *verb* (PERF **hat eingeteilt**) 1 to divide up; 2 **sich seine Zeit gut einteilen** to organize your time well.

Eintopf *der* (PL *die* **Eintöpfe**) stew.

Eintrag *der* (PL *die* **Einträge**) entry.

eintragen ◇ *verb* (PRES **trägt ein**, IMPERF **trug ein**, PERF **hat eingetragen**) 1 to enter, to write; 2 **sich eintragen** to put your name down.

einträglich *adjective* profitable.

eintreffen ◇ *verb* (PRES **trifft ein**, IMPERF **traf ein**, PERF **ist eingetroffen**) 1 to arrive; 2 to come true.

eintreten ◇ *verb* (PRES **tritt ein**, IMPERF **trat ein**, PERF **ist eingetreten**) 1 to enter; 2 **in einen Klub eintreten** to join a club; **für jemanden eintreten** to stand up for somebody.

Eintritt *der* 1 entrance; 2 admission; **'Eintritt frei'** 'admission free'.

Eintrittskarte *die* (PL *die* **Eintrittskarten**) (admission) ticket.

Eintrittspreis *der* (PL *die* **Eintrittspreise**) admission charge.

einverstanden *adjective* 1 **einverstanden sein** to agree; **einverstanden!** okay!; 2 **mit jemandem einverstanden sein** to approve of somebody.

Einwand *der* (PL *die* **Einwände**) objection.

Einwanderer *der* (PL *die* **Einwanderer**) immigrant.

Einwanderin *die* (PL *die* **Einwanderinnen**) immigrant.

einwandern *verb* (PERF **ist eingewandert**) to immigrate.

△ NEW SPELLING: *See page xii*

einweichen verb (PERF hat eingeweicht) to soak (*washing*).

einwerfen ◇ verb (PRES **wirft ein**, IMPERF **warf ein**, PERF **hat eingeworfen**) 1 to post; 2 to put in (*a coin, money*); 3 to throw in; 4 to smash.

Einwohner der (PL die **Einwohner**) inhabitant.

Einzahl die singular.

einzahlen verb (PERF hat **eingezahlt**) to pay in.

Einzel das (PL die **Einzel**) singles (*in sport*).

Einzelheit die (PL die **Einzelheiten**) detail.

Einzelkarte die (PL die **Einzelkarten**) single ticket.

Einzelkind das (PL die **Einzelkinder**) only child.

einzeln adjective 1 single; 2 individual; 3 odd (*sock, for example*). adverb 1 individually; 2 separately, one at a time; **bitte einzeln eintreten** please enter one at a time.

Einzelne △ der/die/das (PL die **Einzelnen**) 1 **der/die Einzelne** the individual; 2 **Einzelne** some; 3 **ein Einzelner/eine Einzelne/ein Einzelnes** a single one; **jeder/jede/jedes Einzelne** every single one; 4 **im Einzelnen** in detail; **ins Einzelne gehen** to go into detail.

Einzelzimmer das (PL die **Einzelzimmer**) single room.

einziehen ◇ verb (IMPERF **zog ein**, PERF **hat eingezogen**) 1 to collect (*payment*); 2 to draw in (*its feelers, claws*); 3 **den Kopf einziehen** to duck; 4 (PERF **ist eingezogen**) to move in; **wann zieht ihr in die neue Wohnung ein?** when are you moving into your new flat?; 5 (PERF **ist eingezogen**) to soak in.

einzig adjective only; **ein einziges Mal** only once.

Einzige △ der/die/das (PL die **Einzigen**) 1 **der/die/das Einzige** the only one; 2 **ein Einziger/eine Einzige/ein Einziges** a single one; **kein Einziger/keine Einzige/kein Einziges** not a single one; 3 **das Einzige, was mich stört** the only thing that bothers me.

Eis das 1 ice; 2 ice cream.

Eisbahn die (PL die **Eisbahnen**) skating rink.

Eisbär der (PL die **Eisbären**) polar bear.

Eisbecher der (PL die **Eisbecher**) ice-cream sundae.

Eisdiele die (PL die **Eisdielen**) ice-cream parlour.

Eisen das iron.

Eisenbahn die (PL die **Eisenbahnen**) railway.

eisern adjective iron.

Eishockey das ice hockey.

eisig adjective icy.

eiskalt adjective 1 ice-cold (*drink*); 2 freezing cold.

Eislaufen das ice-skating.

◇ IRREGULAR VERB: See the verb table in the centre of the dictionary

Eiswürfel der (PL die Eiswürfel) ice cube.

Eiszapfen der (PL die Eiszapfen) icicle.

eitel adjective vain.

Eitelkeit die vanity.

Eiter der pus.

Eiweiß das 1 egg-white; 2 protein.

Ekel der disgust.

ekelhaft adjective disgusting.

ekeln verb (PERF hat sich geekelt) sich vor etwas ekeln to find something disgusting.

eklig adjective disgusting.

Ekzem das (PL die Ekzeme) eczema.

Elefant der (PL die Elefanten) elephant.

elegant adjective elegant.

Elektriker der (PL die Elektriker) electrician.

elektrisch adjective electrical.

Elektrizität die electricity.

Elektroherd der (PL die Elektroherde) electric cooker.

Elektronik die electronics.

elektronisch adjective electronic.

Elektrorasierer der (PL die Elektrorasierer) electric razor.

elend adjective 1 miserable; 2 terrible.

Elend das misery.

elf number eleven.

Elfe die (PL die Elfen) fairy.

Elfmeter der (PL die Elfmeter) penalty (in soccer).

Ellbogen der (PL die Ellbogen) elbow.

Eltern plural noun parents.

Email das (PL die Emails) enamel.

E-Mail die (PL die E-Mails) E-mail.

empfahl SEE empfehlen.

Empfang der (PL die Empfänge) 1 reception; 2 receipt (of goods or a letter).

empfangen ◊ verb (PRES empfängt, IMPERF empfing, PERF hat empfangen) to receive.

Empfängnisverhütung die contraception.

Empfangsdame die (PL die Empfangsdamen) receptionist.

empfehlen ◊ verb (PRES empfiehlt, IMPERF empfahl, PERF hat empfohlen) to recommend.

empfindlich adjective 1 sensitive; 2 delicate; 3 touchy.

empfing SEE empfangen.

empfohlen SEE empfehlen.

empört adjective indignant.

Ende das (PL die Enden) 1 end; Ende April at the end of April; am Ende der Straße at the end of the road; 2 am Ende in the end; 3 ending (of a film, novel); 4 zu Ende sein to be finished, to be over; 5 Ende gut, alles gut all's well that ends well.

△ NEW SPELLING: See page xii

enden *verb* (PERF **hat geendet**) to end.

endgültig *adjective* 1 final (*consent, decision*); 2 definite.

Endivie *die* (PL *die* **Endivien**) endive.

endlich *adverb* finally, at last; **na endlich!** at last!

endlos *adjective* endless.

Endspiel *das* (PL *die* **Endspiele**) final.

Endstation *die* (PL *die* **Endstationen**) terminus.

Endung *die* (PL *die* **Endungen**) ending.

Energie *die* energy.

energisch *adjective* energetic.

eng *adjective* 1 narrow; 2 tight; 3 close; **eng befreundet sein** to be close friends.

Engel *der* (PL *die* **Engel**) angel.

England *das* England; **aus England** from England.

Engländer *der* (PL *die* **Engländer**) Englishman.

Engländerin *die* (PL *die* **Engländerinnen**) Englishwoman.

englisch *adjective* English; **auf Englisch** in English.

Enkel *der* (PL *die* **Enkel**) grandson.

Enkelin *die* (PL *die* **Enkelinnen**) granddaughter.

Enkelkind *das* (PL *die* **Enkelkinder**) grandchild.

entdecken *verb* (PERF **hat entdeckt**) to discover.

Entdeckung *die* (PL *die* **Entdeckungen**) discovery.

Ente *die* (PL *die* **Enten**) duck.

entfernen *verb* (PERF **hat entfernt**) to remove.

entfernt *adjective* 1 distant; 2 **zehn Kilometer entfernt** ten kilometres away.
adverb **entfernt verwandt sein** to be distantly related.

Entfernung *die* (PL *die* **Entfernungen**) distance.

entführen *verb* (PERF **hat entführt**) 1 to kidnap; 2 to hijack.

entgegen *preposition* ←(+DAT) contrary to.

entgegengesetzt *adjective* 1 opposite; 2 opposing (*views*).

entgegenkommen ◊ *verb* (IMPERF **kam entgegen**, PERF **ist entgegengekommen**) 1 to come towards; 2 **jemandem entgegenkommen** to come to meet somebody; 3 **jemandem auf halbem Wege entgegenkommen** to meet somebody halfway; 4 **jemandem freundlich entgegenkommen** to be accommodating towards somebody.

entgegenkommend *adjective* 1 obliging; 2 **der entgegenkommende Verkehr** the oncoming traffic.

Entgelt *das* payment.

Enthaarungsmittel *das* (PL *die*

◊ IRREGULAR VERB: *See the verb table in the centre of the dictionary*

Enthaarungsmittel) hair remover, depilatory.

enthalten ◇ *verb* (PRES **enthält**, IMPERF **enthielt**, PERF **hat enthalten**) **1** to contain; **2 sich einer Sache enthalten** to abstain from something; **sich der Stimme enthalten** to abstain; **in etwas enthalten sein** to be included in something; **im Preis enthalten** included in the price.

entkommen ◇ *verb* (IMPERF **entkam**, PERF **ist entkommen**) to escape.

entlang *preposition* ←–(+ACC *or* +DAT) along; **die Straße entlang** along the road; **am Fluss entlang** along the river.

entlanggehen ◇ *verb* (IMPERF **ging entlang**, PERF **ist entlanggegangen**) to walk along.

entlanglaufen ◇ *verb* (PRES **läuft entlang**, IMPERF **lief entlang**, PERF **ist entlanggelaufen**) to run along.

entlassen ◇ *verb* (PRES **entlässt** Δ, IMPERF **entließ**, PERF **hat entlassen**) **1** to dismiss (*from a job*); **2** to discharge (*from hospital*); **3** to release (*from prison*).

Entlassung *die* (PL *die* **Entlassungen**) **1** dismissal; **2** discharge; **3** release.

entmutigen *verb* (PERF **hat entmutigt**) to discourage.

entschädigen *verb* (PERF **hat entschädigt**) to compensate.

Entschädigung *die* compensation.

entscheiden ◇ *verb* (IMPERF **entschied**, PERF **hat entschieden**) **1** to decide (on); **2 sich entscheiden** to decide.

Entscheidung *die* (PL *die* **Entscheidungen**) decision.

entschließen ◇ *verb* (IMPERF **entschloss sich** Δ, PERF **hat sich entschlossen**) **1 sich entschließen** to decide; **2 sich anders entschließen** to change your mind; **Karl hat sich anders entschlossen** Karl has changed his mind.

entschlossen *adjective* determined.

Entschluss Δ *der* (PL *die* **Entschlüsse**) decision.

entschuldigen *verb* (PERF **hat entschuldigt**) **1** to excuse; **entschuldigen Sie bitte** excuse me; **2 sich entschuldigen** to apologize; **ich habe mich bei Michi entschuldigt** I apologized to Michi.

Entschuldigung *die* (PL *die* **Entschuldigungen**) **1** apology; **2 jemanden um Entschuldigung bitten** to apologize to somebody; **3 Entschuldigung!** sorry!; **4 Entschuldigung** (*with a question or request*) excuse me; **Entschuldigung, können Sie mir sagen, wie ich zum Bahnhof komme?** excuse me, could you tell me the way to the station?; **5** excuse.

Entsetzen *das* horror.

Δ NEW SPELLING: *See page xii*

entsetzlich adjective 1 horrible; 2 terrible.

entsetzt adjective horrified.

entspannen verb (PERF hat sich entspannt) 1 sich entspannen to relax; 2 sich entspannen to ease (of a situation).

entsprechen ✧ verb (PRES entspricht, IMPERF entsprach, PERF hat entsprochen) 1 den Anforderungen entsprechen to meet the requirements; 2 einer Sache entsprechen to correspond to something; 3 to agree with (the truth, a description); 4 to comply with (certain standards).

entsprechend adjective 1 corresponding; 2 appropriate. preposition ←(+DAT) in accordance with.

entstehen ✧ verb (IMPERF entstand, PERF ist entstanden) 1 to develop; 2 to result (of damage).

enttäuschen verb (PERF hat enttäuscht) to disappoint.

Enttäuschung die (PL die Enttäuschungen) disappointment.

entweder conjunction either; entweder heute oder morgen either today or tomorrow.

entwerten verb (PERF hat entwertet) 1 to devalue; 2 to punch (a ticket in a machine found on trains, trams, buses, and on the platform; you have to punch your ticket before each journey).

Entwerter der (PL die Entwerter) ticket-punching machine (these machines are found on trains, trams, buses, and on the platform; you have to punch your ticket before each journey).

entwickeln verb (PERF hat entwickelt) 1 to develop; 2 to display (ability, a characteristic); 3 sich entwickeln to develop.

Entwicklung die (PL die Entwicklungen) 1 development; 2 developing.

Entwicklungsland das (PL die Entwicklungsländer) developing country.

Entwurf der (PL die Entwürfe) 1 design; 2 draft.

entzückend adjective delightful.

entzünden verb (PERF hat entzündet) 1 to light (a fire, match); 2 sich entzünden to become inflamed; 3 sich entzünden to ignite.

Entzündung die (PL die Entzündungen) inflammation.

Enzian der (PL die Enziane) gentian.

Epidemie die (PL die Epidemien) epidemic.

er pronoun 1 he; 2 it; 'wo ist mein Mantel?' – 'er liegt auf dem Stuhl' 'where's my coat?' – 'it's on the chair'; 3 him (stressed); er war es it was him.

erben verb (PERF hat geerbt) to inherit.

erblich adjective hereditary.

Erbschaft die (PL die Erbschaften) inheritance.

✧ IRREGULAR VERB: See the verb table in the centre of the dictionary

Erbse die (PL die Erbsen) pea.

Erdbeben das (PL die Erdbeben) earthquake.

Erdbeere die (PL die Erdbeeren) strawberry.

Erde die 1 earth, soil; 2 ground; auf der Erde on the ground; 3 Earth; 4 earth (for electricity).

Erdgeschoss △ das (PL die Erdgeschosse) ground floor; im Erdgeschoss on the ground floor.

Erdkunde die geography.

Erdnuss △ die (PL die Erdnüsse) peanut.

ereignen verb (PERF hat sich ereignet) sich ereignen to happen.

Ereignis das (PL die Ereignisse) event.

erfahren ◇ verb (PRES erfährt, IMPERF erfuhr, PERF hat erfahren) 1 to hear, to learn; 2 to experience. adjective experienced.

Erfahrung die (PL die Erfahrungen) experience.

erfinden ◇ verb (IMPERF erfand, PERF hat erfunden) to invent.

Erfindung die (PL die Erfindungen) invention.

Erfolg der (PL die Erfolge) 1 success; Erfolg haben to be successful; 2 Erfolg versprechend △ promising; 3 viel Erfolg! good luck!

erfolglos adjective unsuccessful.

erfolgreich adjective successful.

erfolgversprechend SEE Erfolg.

erforderlich adjective necessary.

erforschen verb (PERF hat erforscht) 1 to explore; 2 to investigate.

erfreulicherweise adverb happily.

erfreut adjective pleased.

Erfrischung die (PL die Erfrischungen) refreshment.

erfüllen verb (PERF hat erfüllt) to fulfil; sich erfüllen to come true.

Ergebnis das (PL die Ergebnisse) result.

ergreifen ◇ verb (IMPERF ergriff, PERF hat ergriffen) 1 to seize, to grab; 2 to take (measures, an opportunity); 3 to take up (a job, career); 4 to move; die Nachricht von ihrem Tod hat uns tief ergriffen the news of her death moved us deeply; 5 die Flucht ergreifen to flee.

ergreifend adjective moving.

erhalten ◇ verb (PRES erhält, IMPERF erhielt, PERF hat erhalten) 1 to receive; 2 to preserve.

erhältlich adjective obtainable.

erheben ◇ verb (IMPERF erhob, PERF hat erhoben) 1 to raise; 2 to charge (a fee); 3 Protest erheben to protest; 4 sich erheben to rise up (in a rebellion).

erheblich adjective considerable.

erheitern verb (PERF hat erheitert) to amuse.

△ NEW SPELLING: See page xii

erhitzen verb (PERF hat erhitzt) to heat.

erhöhen verb (PERF hat erhöht) 1 to increase; 2 sich erhöhen to rise.

Erhöhung die (PL die Erhöhungen) increase.

erholen verb (PERF hat sich erholt) 1 sich erholen to have a rest; ich habe mich in den Ferien gut erholt I had a good rest on holiday; 2 sich von einer Krankheit erholen to recover from an illness.

erholsam adjective restful.

Erholung die rest; Iris ist zur Erholung in die Berge gefahren Iris went to the mountains for a rest.

erinnern verb (PERF hat erinnert) 1 to remind; 2 sich erinnern to remember.

Erinnerung die (PL die Erinnerungen) 1 memory; 2 souvenir.

erkälten verb (PERF hat sich erkältet) 1 sich erkälten to catch a cold; 2 erkältet sein to have a cold; Ben ist erkältet Ben has a cold.

Erkältung die (PL die Erkältungen) cold.

erkennen ◇ verb (IMPERF erkannte, PERF hat erkannt) 1 to recognize; 2 to realize.

erklären verb (PERF hat erklärt) 1 to explain; 2 to declare; 3 sich zu etwas bereit erklären to agree to something.

Erklärung die (PL die Erklärungen) 1 explanation; 2 declaration; 3 eine öffentliche Erklärung a public statement.

erkundigen verb (PERF hat sich erkundigt) 1 to enquire; 2 to ask about; Susi hat sich nach dir erkundigt Susi was asking about you.

Erkundigung die (PL die Erkundigungen) enquiry.

erlauben verb (PERF hat erlaubt) 1 to allow; jemandem etwas erlauben to allow somebody to do something; 2 sich etwas erlauben to allow yourself something; 3 sich alles erlauben to do as you please; 4 erlauben Sie mal! (informal) do you mind!

Erlaubnis die permission.

erleben verb (PERF hat erlebt) 1 to experience; 2 to have (a disappointment, an experience); eine Überraschung erleben to have a surprise; 3 er hat die Geburt seines Enkels nicht mehr erlebt he didn't live to see the birth of his grandson.

Erlebnis das (PL die Erlebnisse) experience.

erledigen verb (PERF hat erledigt) to deal with, to do.

erledigt adjective 1 settled; 2 (informal) worn out.

Erleichterung die relief.

erleiden ◇ verb (IMPERF erlitt, PERF hat erlitten) to suffer.

Erlös der (PL die Erlöse) proceeds.

◇ IRREGULAR VERB: See the verb table in the centre of the dictionary

ermäßigen *verb* (PERF hat ermäßigt) to reduce.

Ermäßigung *die* (PL die Ermäßigungen) reduction.

ermorden *verb* (PERF hat ermordet) to murder.

ermutigen *verb* (PERF hat ermutigt) to encourage.

ernähren *verb* (PERF hat ernährt) 1 to feed; 2 sich von Nudeln ernähren to live on pasta; 3 to support (*a family*).

Ernährung *die* 1 diet; eine gesunde Ernährung a healthy diet; 2 nutrition.

erneuern *verb* (PERF hat erneuert) to renew.

erneut *adjective* renewed.
adverb once again.

ernst *adjective* serious.

Ernst *der* 1 seriousness; 2 im Ernst seriously; 3 ist das dein Ernst? are you serious?

ernsthaft *adjective* serious.

ernstlich *adjective* serious.

Ernte *die* (PL die Ernten) harvest.

ernten *verb* (PERF hat geerntet) to harvest.

erobern *verb* (PERF hat erobert) to conquer.

Eroberung *die* (PL die Eroberungen) conquest.

eröffnen (PERF hat eröffnet) to open.

Eröffnung *die* (PL die Eröffnungen) opening.

erraten ◇ *verb* (PRES errät, IMPERF erriet, PERF hat erraten) to guess.

Erreger *der* (PL die Erreger) germ.

Erregung *die* excitement.

erreichen *verb* (PERF hat erreicht) 1 to reach; 2 den Zug erreichen to catch the train; 3 to achieve (*a goal, aim*); 4 Irene ist telefonisch zu erreichen Irene can be contacted by phone.

erröten *verb* (PERF ist errötet) to blush.

Ersatz *der* replacement, substitute.

Ersatzreifen *der* (PL die Ersatzreifen) spare tyre.

Ersatzteil *das* (PL die Ersatzteile) spare part.

erscheinen ◇ *verb* (IMPERF erschien, PERF ist erschienen) to appear.

erschöpft *adjective* exhausted.

erschrecken *verb* 1 (PERF hat erschreckt) to scare; 2 ◇ (PRES erschrickt, IMPERF erschrak, PERF ist erschrocken) to get a fright.

erschreckend *adjective* alarming.

erschrocken *adjective* 1 frightened; 2 startled.

ersetzen *verb* (PERF hat ersetzt) to replace; jemandem einen Schaden ersetzen to compensate somebody for damages.

Ersparnisse *plural noun* savings.

erst *adverb* 1 first; 2 erst einmal first of all; 2 only; eben erst only just; 3 not until; erst nächste Woche not

△ NEW SPELLING: See page xii

until next week; **Oma war erst zufrieden, als die ganze Familie da war** granny was not happy until all the family were there.

erstaunen verb (PERF **hat erstaunt**) to astonish.

erstaunlich adjective astonishing.

erstaunt adjective amazed; **über etwas erstaunt sein** to be amazed about something.

Erste △ der/die/das (PL die **Ersten**) **1** der/die **Erste** the first (one); **das Erste** the first (thing); **2** Dirk kam als Erster Dirk arrived first; **Marianne ging als Erste** Marianne left first; **3** als Erster/Erste etwas tun to be the first to do something; **4** als Erstes first of all; **5** fürs Erste for the time being.

erstens adverb firstly.

erster, erste, erstes adjective first; **mein erstes Rad war rot** my first bike was red; **der erste April** the first of April; **erste Hilfe** △ first aid.

erstklassig adjective first-class.

erstmals adverb for the first time.

erteilen verb (PERF **hat erteilt**) to give (advice, information).

ertragen ◇ verb (PRES **erträgt**, IMPERF **ertrug**, PERF **hat ertragen**) to bear.

ertrinken ◇ verb (IMPERF **ertrank**, PERF **ist ertrunken**) to drown.

erwachsen adjective grown-up.

Erwachsene der/die (PL die **Erwachsenen**) adult, grown-up.

Erwachsenenbildung die adult education.

erwähnen verb (PERF **hat erwähnt**) to mention.

erwarten verb (PERF **hat erwartet**) to expect.

Erwartung die (PL die **Erwartungen**) expectation.

erzählen verb (PERF **hat erzählt**) to tell.

Erzählung die (PL die **Erzählungen**) story.

Erzeugnis das (PL die **Erzeugnisse**) product.

erziehen ◇ verb (IMPERF **erzog**, PERF **hat erzogen**) **1** to bring up; **2** to educate.

Erziehung die **1** upbringing; **2** education.

es pronoun **1** it; **es regnet** it is raining; **2 es gibt** there is, there are; **3** 'wo ist das Baby?' – 'es schläft' 'where's the baby?' – 'he's/she's asleep'.

Esel der (PL die **Esel**) donkey.

essbar △ adjective edible.

essen ◇ verb (PRES **isst** △, IMPERF **aß**, PERF **hat gegessen**) to eat.

Essen das **1** meal; **2** food.

Essig der vinegar.

Essiggurke die (PL die **Essiggurken**) gherkin.

Esskastanie △ die (PL die **Esskastanien**) sweet chestnut.

◇ IRREGULAR VERB: See the verb table in the centre of the dictionary

Esszimmer △ *das* (PL *die* Esszimmer) dining room.

Etage *die* (PL *die* Etagen) floor; **in der zweiten Etage** on the second floor.

Etagenbett *das* (PL *die* Etagenbetten) bunk beds.

ethnisch *adjective* ethnic.

Etikett *das* (PL *die* Etikette) label.

Etui *das* (PL *die* Etuis) case.

etwa *adverb* 1 about; **er ist etwa so groß wie du** he's about as tall as you; 2 for example; 3 **nicht etwa, dass …** not that …; 4 **hat Klaus etwa Angst gehabt?** Klaus wasn't scared, was he?

etwas *pronoun, adverb* 1 something; 2 anything; **sonst noch etwas?** anything else?; 3 some; **etwas von dem Geld** some of the money; **noch etwas Kaffee?** (some) more coffee?; 4 a little; **nur etwas Zucker** only a little sugar; **etwas lauter singen** to sing a little louder.

EU *die* (*Europäische Union*) EU.

euch *pronoun* 1 you; **ich habe euch eingeladen** I've invited you; 2 to you; **Eva hat es euch geschenkt** Eva gave it to you; 3 (*reflexive*) yourselves.

euer *adjective* your.

Eule *die* (PL *die* Eulen) owl.

eurer, eure, eures *pronoun* yours.

Euro *der* (PL *die* Euro) (*European currency*) euro.

Europa *das* Europe.

Europäer *der* (PL *die* Europäer) European.

Europäerin *die* (PL *die* Europäerinnen) European.

europäisch *adjective* European.

evangelisch *adjective* Protestant.

eventuell *adjective* possible.
adverb possibly.

ewig *adjective* eternal.
adverb forever.

Ewigkeit *die* eternity.

Examen *das* (PL *die* Examen) examination, exam.

Exemplar *das* (PL *die* Exemplare) 1 copy; 2 specimen.

existieren *verb* (PERF hat existiert) to exist.

explodieren *verb* (PERF ist explodiert) to explode.

Explosion *die* (PL *die* Explosionen) explosion.

extra *adverb* 1 separately; 2 extra; 3 specially; 4 (*informal*) on purpose.

extrem *adjective* extreme.

F f

fabelhaft *adjective* fabulous, fantastic.

Fabrik *die* (PL *die* Fabriken) factory.

Fach *das* (PL *die* Fächer) 1 compartment; 2 drawer; 3 subject (*at school*).

△ NEW SPELLING: *See page xii*

Facharzt der (PL die **Fachärzte**) specialist.

Fachärztin die (PL die **Fachärztinnen**) specialist.

Fachfrau die (PL die **Fachfrauen**) expert.

Fachmann der (PL die **Fachleute**) expert.

Faden der (PL die **Fäden**) thread.

fähig adjective 1 capable; 2 able.

Fähigkeit die (PL die **Fähigkeiten**) ability.

Fahne die (PL die **Fahnen**) flag.

Fahrausweis der (PL die **Fahrausweise**) ticket.

Fahrbahn die (PL die **Fahrbahnen**) 1 carriageway; 2 road.

Fähre die (PL die **Fähren**) ferry.

fahren ◇ verb (PRES **fährt**, IMPERF **fuhr**, PERF **ist gefahren**) 1 to go; **mit dem Zug nach Wien fahren** to go to Vienna by train; **ich bin mit dem Auto gefahren** I went by car; 2 to drive; **Hanna ist sehr schnell gefahren** Hanna drove very fast; 3 to ride (of a cyclist); 4 to run (of a train, bus); **der Zug fährt nicht an Sonn- und Feiertagen** the train doesn't run on Sundays and public holidays; 5 to leave; **wann fahrt ihr?** when are you leaving?; 6 **was ist in sie gefahren?** (informal) what's got into her?; 7 (PERF **hat gefahren**) to drive; **er hat Doris nach Hause gefahren** he drove Doris home; **ich habe das Auto in die Garage gefahren** I drove the car into the garage.

Fahrer der (PL die **Fahrer**) driver.

Fahrerflucht die hit-and-run driving; **Fahrerflucht begehen** to be involved in a hit-and-run.

Fahrerin die (PL die **Fahrerinnen**) driver.

Fahrgast der (PL die **Fahrgäste**) passenger.

Fahrkarte die (PL die **Fahrkarten**) ticket.

Fahrkartenausgabe die ticket office.

Fahrkartenautomat der (PL die **Fahrkartenautomaten**) ticket machine.

Fahrkartenschalter der (PL die **Fahrkartenschalter**) ticket office.

fahrlässig adjective negligent.

Fahrlehrer der (PL die **Fahrlehrer**) driving instructor.

Fahrplan der (PL die **Fahrpläne**) timetable.

Fahrpreis der (PL die **Fahrpreise**) fare.

Fahrprüfung die (PL die **Fahrprüfungen**) driving test; **die Fahrprüfung machen** to take your driving test.

Fahrrad das (PL die **Fahrräder**) bicycle.

Fahrradweg der (PL die **Fahrradwege**) cycle lane.

◇ IRREGULAR VERB: See the verb table in the centre of the dictionary

Fahrschein der (PL die Fahrscheine) ticket.

Fahrschule die (PL die Fahrschulen) driving school.

Fahrstuhl der (PL die Fahrstühle) lift.

Fahrt die (PL die Fahrten) 1 journey; **gute Fahrt!** have a good journey!; 2 trip; 3 drive; 4 **in voller Fahrt** at full speed.

Fahrzeug das (PL die Fahrzeuge) vehicle.

fair adjective fair.

Faktor der (PL die Faktoren) factor.

Falke der (PL die Falken) falcon.

Fall der (PL die Fälle) 1 case; **in diesem Fall** in this case; **auf alle Fälle, auf jeden Fall** in any case; **für alle Fälle** just in case; 2 **auf jeden Fall** definitely; 3 **auf keinen Fall** on no account; 4 fall.

Falle die (PL die Fallen) trap.

fallen ◇ verb (PRES **fällt**, IMPERF **fiel**, PERF **ist gefallen**) 1 to fall; 2 **etwas fallen lassen**△ to drop something; **wir haben den Plan fallen lassen** we've dropped the idea; 3 **eine Bemerkung fallen lassen**△ to make a comment.

fallenlassen SEE fallen.

fällig adjective due.

falls conjunction 1 if; 2 in case.

Fallschirm der (PL die Fallschirme) parachute.

falsch adjective 1 wrong; **du hast ihn falsch verstanden** you got him

wrong; 2 false (teeth, etc.); 3 forged.

fälschen verb (PERF **hat gefälscht**) to forge.

Fälschung die (PL die Fälschungen) 1 fake; 2 forgery.

Falte die (PL die Falten) 1 fold; 2 crease; 3 pleat; 4 wrinkle.

falten verb (PERF **hat gefaltet**) to fold.

faltig adjective 1 wrinkled; 2 creased.

familiär adjective familiar.

Familie die (PL die Familien) family.

Familienname der (PL die Familiennamen) surname.

Fan der (PL die Fans) fan.

fand SEE finden.

fangen ◇ verb (PRES **fängt**, IMPERF **fing**, PERF **hat gefangen**) to catch.

fantastisch adjective fantastic.

Farbe die (PL die Farben) 1 colour; 2 paint; 3 dye; 4 suit (in playing cards).

farbecht adjective colour fast.

färben verb (PERF **hat gefärbt**) 1 to dye; 2 **sich die Haare färben** to dye your hair; 3 **das Sweatshirt färbt** this sweatshirt runs.

Farbfilm der (PL die Farbfilme) colour film.

farbig adjective coloured.

farblos adjective colourless.

Farbstift der (PL die Farbstifte) coloured pencil.

△ NEW SPELLING: See page xii

Farbstoff der (PL die Farbstoffe)
1 dye; 2 colouring (for food).

Farbton der (PL die Farbtöne) shade.

Fasan der (PL die Fasane) pheasant.

Fasching der (PL die Faschinge)
carnival.

Faser die (PL die Fasern) fibre.

Fass△ das (PL die Fässer) barrel; **Bier
vom Fass** draught beer.

fassen verb (PERF hat gefasst△) 1 to
grasp; 2 **einen Dieb fassen** to catch
a thief; 3 to hold (of a container);
4 to understand; 5 **nicht zu fassen**
unbelievable; 6 **sich fassen** to
compose yourself; 7 **einen
Entschluss fassen** to make a
decision; 8 **sich kurz fassen** to be
brief.

Fassung die (PL die Fassungen)
1 version; 2 composure;
3 **jemanden aus der Fassung
bringen** to throw somebody, to upset
somebody; 4 setting (for gems).

fassungslos adjective speechless.

fast adverb 1 almost; 2 **fast nie**
hardly ever.

Fastenzeit die (PL die
Fastenzeiten) Lent.

Fastnacht die carnival.

faul adjective 1 lazy; 2 rotten; 3 **eine
faule Ausrede** a lame excuse; 4 **an
der Sache ist etwas faul** (informal)
there's something fishy about it.

faulen verb (PERF ist gefault) to rot.

faulenzen verb (PERF hat
gefaulenzt) to laze about.

Faust die (PL die Fäuste) 1 fist; 2 **auf
eigene Faust** off your own bat.

Fax das (PL die Fax(e)) fax.

faxen verb (PERF hat gefaxt) to fax;
ich faxe Ihnen die Liste I'll fax you
the list.

Februar der February.

fechten ◇ verb (PRES **ficht**, IMPERF
focht, PERF **hat gefochten**) to fence.

Feder die (PL die Federn) 1 feather;
2 spring; 3 nib (of a pen).

Federball der (PL die Federbälle)
1 badminton; 2 shuttlecock.

Federmäppchen das (PL die
Federmäppchen) pencil case.

Fee die (PL die Feen) fairy.

fegen verb (PERF hat gefegt) to
sweep.

fehl adjective **fehl am Platz** out of
place.

fehlen verb (PERF hat gefehlt) 1 to
be missing; 2 to be lacking; 3 to be
absent (from school); 4 **mir fehlt die
Zeit** I haven't got the time; **es fehlt
ihnen einfach das Geld für ein
neues Auto** they simply haven't got
the money for a new car; 5 **was fehlt
dir?** what's the matter?; 6 **Rudi fehlt
mir** I miss Rudi.

Fehler der (PL die Fehler) 1 mistake;
2 fault.

Feier die (PL die Feiern) 1 party;
2 celebration.

Feierabend der (PL die
Feierabende) 1 finishing time;
2 **nach Feierabend** after work.

◇ IRREGULAR VERB: See the verb table in the centre of the dictionary

Feierlichkeiten *plural noun* festivities.

feiern *verb* (PERF **hat gefeiert**) to celebrate.

Feiertag *der* (PL *die* **Feiertage**) 1 holiday; **ein gesetzlicher Feiertag** a public holiday; 2 **am ersten Feiertag** on Christmas Day; **der zweite Feiertag** Boxing Day.

feige *adjective* cowardly; **du bist feige** you're a coward.

Feige *die* (PL *die* **Feigen**) fig.

Feigling *der* (PL *die* **Feiglinge**) coward.

Feile *die* (PL *die* **Feilen**) file.

fein *adjective* 1 fine; 2 delicate; 3 refined; 4 **sich fein machen** △ to dress up.

Feind *der* (PL *die* **Feinde**) enemy.

feindlich *adjective* hostile.

Feld *das* (PL *die* **Felder**) 1 field; 2 pitch; 3 box (*on a form*); 4 square (*on a board game*).

Fell *das* (PL *die* **Felle**) fur, skin.

Fels *der* rock.

Felsen *der* (PL *die* **Felsen**) cliff.

feminin *adjective* feminine.

Feminist *der* (PL *die* **Feministen**) feminist.

Feministin *die* (PL *die* **Feministinnen**) feminist.

Fenster *das* (PL *die* **Fenster**) window.

Fensterladen *der* (PL *die* **Fensterläden**) shutter.

Ferien *plural noun* holidays; **Ferien haben** to be on holiday.

fern *adjective* 1 distant; 2 **sich fern halten** △ to keep away; **jemanden von etwas fern halten** △ to keep somebody away from something. *adverb* far away.

Fernbedienung *die* remote control.

Ferngespräch *das* (PL *die* **Ferngespräche**) long-distance call.

fernhalten SEE **fern**.

Fernglas *das* (PL *die* **Ferngläser**) binoculars.

Fernsehapparat *der* (PL *die* **Fernsehapparate**) television set.

fernsehen ◇ *verb* (PRES **sieht fern**, IMPERF **sah fern**, PERF **hat ferngesehen**) to watch television.

Fernsehen *das* television; **im Fernsehen** on television.

Fernseher *der* (PL *die* **Fernseher**) television (set).

Fernsprecher *der* (PL *die* **Fernsprecher**) telephone.

Ferse *die* (PL *die* **Fersen**) heel.

fertig *adjective* 1 finished; **mit den Hausaufgaben fertig werden** to finish your homework; **fertig sein** to be finished; 2 **mit jemandem fertig sein** (*informal*) to be through with somebody; 3 **völlig fertig sein** to be completely worn out; 4 **mit etwas fertig werden** to cope with something (*problems, for example*); 5 ready; **das Essen ist fertig** food's ready; 6 **etwas fertig machen** △

(*prepare*) to get something ready; (*complete*) to finish something; **sich fertig machen** △ to get ready; **7 jemanden fertig machen** △ to wear somebody out, to wear somebody down; **der ständige Stress macht mich fertig** this constant stress is wearing me down; **8 es fertig bringen** △, **etwas zu tun** to bring yourself to do something; **ich bringe es einfach nicht fertig** I just can't bring myself to do it. *adverb* **fertig essen** to finish eating.

fertigbringen SEE **fertig.**

Fertiggericht *das* (PL *die* **Fertiggerichte**) ready-to-serve meal.

fertigmachen SEE **fertig.**

Fest *das* (PL *die* **Feste**) **1** party; **2** celebration; **3** festival.

fest *adjective* **1** firm; **2** fixed (*salary, address*); **3** solid; **feste Nahrung** solids; **4 fest werden** to harden. *adverb* **1 fest schlafen** to be fast asleep; **2 fest befreundet sein** to be close friends; **3 fest angestellt sein** to be in permanent employment. ◇

festbinden ◇ *verb* (IMPERF **band fest,** PERF **hat festgebunden**) to tie (up).

festhalten ◇ *verb* (PRES **hält fest,** IMPERF **hielt fest,** PERF **hat festgehalten**) **1** to hold on to; **2 sich festhalten** to hold on; **halt dich an mir fest** hold on to me.

Festigkeit *die* strength.

festlegen *verb* (PERF **hat festgelegt**) **1** to fix; **2 sich auf etwas festlegen** to commit yourself to something.

festlich *adjective* festive.

festmachen *verb* (PERF **hat festgemacht**) **1** to fix; **ich mache gleich einen Termin fest** I'll fix a date straight away; **2** to fasten.

festnehmen ◇ *verb* (PRES **nimmt fest,** IMPERF **nahm fest,** PERF **hat festgenommen**) to arrest.

feststehen ◇ *verb* (IMPERF **stand fest,** PERF **hat festgestanden**) to be certain; **eins steht fest, Daniel lade ich nicht mehr ein** one thing's certain, I'm not going to invite Daniel again.

feststellen *verb* (PERF **hat festgestellt**) **1** to establish; **2** to notice.

Fett *das* (PL *die* **Fette**) **1** fat; **2** grease.

fett *adjective* **1** fat (*person*); **2** greasy, fatty (*food*); **3** bold (*type*).

fettarm *adjective* low-fat.

fettig *adjective* greasy.

Fetzen *der* (PL *die* **Fetzen**) **1** scrap; **2** rag.

feucht *adjective* **1** damp; **2** humid.

Feuchtigkeit *die* **1** moisture; **2** humidity.

Feuer *das* **1** fire; **2 hast du Feuer?** have you got a light?

Feuerlöscher *der* (PL *die* **Feuerlöscher**) fire extinguisher.

Feuermelder *der* (PL *die* **Feuermelder**) fire alarm.

◇ **IRREGULAR VERB: See the verb table in the centre of the dictionary**

Feuertreppe die (PL die Feuertreppen) fire escape.

Feuerwehr die (PL die Feuerwehren) fire brigade.

Feuerwehrauto das (PL die Feuerwehrautos) fire engine.

Feuerwehrmann der (PL die Feuerwehrleute) fireman.

Feuerwerk das fireworks.

Feuerzeug das (PL die Feuerzeuge) lighter.

ficht SEE **fechten**.

Fieber das (high) temperature, fever; **Fieber haben** to have a temperature.

fiel SEE **fallen**.

fies adjective (informal) nasty.

Figur die (PL die Figuren) 1 figure; 2 character.

Filiale die (PL die Filialen) branch.

Film der (PL die Filme) film.

filmen verb (PERF hat gefilmt) to film.

Filter der (PL die Filter) filter.

Filzstift der (PL die Filzstifte) felt pen.

finanziell adjective financial.

finanzieren verb (PERF hat finanziert) to finance.

finden ◇ verb (IMPERF fand, PERF hat gefunden) 1 to find; 2 to think; **wie findest du das?** what do you think of it?; **findest du?** do you think so?; 3 **ich finde nichts dabei** I don't mind.

fing SEE **fangen**.

Finger der (PL die Finger) finger.

Fingernagel der (PL die Fingernägel) fingernail.

Finne die (PL die Finnen) Finn.

Finnin die (PL die Finninnen) Finn.

Finnland das Finland.

finster adjective 1 dark; **im Finstern** in the dark; 2 sinister.

Finsternis die darkness.

Firma die (PL die Firmen) firm, company.

Fisch der (PL die Fische) 1 fish; 2 Fische Pisces; **Helmut ist Fisch** Helmut is Pisces.

Fischer der (PL die Fischer) fisherman.

fit adjective fit; **er hält sich durch Jogging fit** he keeps fit by jogging.

Fitnesstraining Δ das keep fit.

fix adjective 1 quick; 2 **fix und fertig** all finished, all ready; 3 **ich bin fix und fertig** (informal) I'm shattered.

flach adjective 1 flat; 2 low; 3 shallow; **die Erdbeeren kommen in die flache Schüssel** the strawberries go into the shallow bowl.

Fläche die (PL die Flächen) 1 surface; 2 area.

flackern verb (PERF hat geflackert) to flicker.

Flagge die (PL die Flaggen) flag.

Flamme die (PL die Flammen) flame.

Flasche die (PL die Flaschen) bottle.

Flaschenöffner der (PL die Flaschenöffner) bottle opener.

flauschig adjective 1 fluffy; 2 fleecy.

Fleck der (PL die Flecken) 1 stain; 2 spot; 3 ein blauer Fleck a bruise.

fleckig adjective 1 stained; 2 blotchy (skin).

Fledermaus die (PL die Fledermäuse) bat.

Fleisch das 1 meat; 2 flesh.

Fleischer der (PL die Fleischer) butcher.

Fleischerei die (PL die Fleischereien) butcher's.

Fleiß der hard work.

fleißig adjective hard-working.

flicken verb (PERF hat geflickt) to mend.

Fliege die (PL die Fliegen) 1 fly; 2 bow tie.

fliegen ◇ verb (IMPERF flog, PERF ist geflogen) 1 to fly; 2 ich bin geflogen (informal) I fell; 3 Manfred ist geflogen (informal) Manfred has been fired; 4 (PERF hat geflogen) to fly (a plane).

fliehen ◇ verb (IMPERF floh, PERF ist geflohen) to flee.

Fliese die (PL die Fliesen) tile.

Fließband das (PL die Fließbänder) 1 conveyor belt; 2 assembly line.

fließen ◇ verb (IMPERF floss △, PERF ist geflossen) to flow.

fließend adjective 1 running;

2 fluent; fließendes Deutsch fluent German; 3 moving (traffic).

Flitterwochen plural noun honeymoon.

flitzen verb (informal) (PERF ist geflitzt) 1 to dash; 2 to whizz.

Flocke die (PL die Flocken) flake.

flog SEE fliegen.

floh SEE fliehen.

Floh der (PL die Flöhe) flee.

Flohmarkt der (PL die Flohmärkte) flea market.

floss △ SEE fließen.

Flosse die (PL die Flossen) 1 fin; 2 flipper.

Flöte die (PL die Flöten) flute.

fluchen verb (PERF hat geflucht) to curse.

Flüchtling der (PL die Flüchtlinge) refugee.

Flug der (PL die Flüge) flight.

Flugblatt das (PL die Flugblätter) pamphlet.

Flügel der (PL die Flügel) 1 wing; 2 grand piano.

Fluggast der (PL die Fluggäste) (air passenger.

Fluggesellschaft die (PL die Fluggesellschaften) airline.

Flughafen der (PL die Flughäfen) airport.

Flugplatz der (PL die Flugplätze) 1 airport; 2 airfield.

◇ IRREGULAR VERB: See the verb table in the centre of the dictionary

Flugzeug das (PL die Flugzeuge) aeroplane.

Fluor das fluoride.

Flur der (PL die Flure) 1 hall; 2 corridor.

Fluss △ der (PL die Flüsse) river.

flüssig adjective liquid.

Flüssigkeit die (PL die Flüssigkeiten) liquid.

flüstern verb (PERF hat geflüstert) to whisper.

Flut die (PL die Fluten) 1 high tide; 2 flood (of letters, complaints).

Flutlicht das floodlight.

focht SEE fechten.

Föhn △ der (PL die Föhne) hair drier.

föhnen △ verb (PERF hat geföhnt) to blow-dry.

Folge die (PL die Folgen) 1 consequence; 2 episode; 3 etwas zur Folge haben to result in something; 4 an den Folgen eines Unfalls sterben to die as the result of an accident.

folgen verb (PERF ist gefolgt) 1 to follow; daraus folgt, dass … it follows that …; ich kann dir nicht folgen I can't follow what you're saying; 2 (PERF hat gefolgt) to obey.

folgend adjective 1 following; 2 Folgendes the following.

Folgerung die (PL die Folgerungen) conclusion.

folgsam adjective obedient.

Folie die (PL die Folien) foil.

Fön™ = Föhn.

fönen = föhnen.

fordern verb (PERF hat gefordert) to demand.

fördern verb (PERF hat gefördert) 1 to promote; 2 to sponsor.

Forderung die (PL die Forderungen) 1 demand; 2 claim.

Forelle die (PL die Forellen) trout.

Form die (PL die Formen) 1 shape; 2 form; in Form sein to be on form; 3 tin (for baking).

Format das (PL die Formate) format.

formatieren verb (PERF hat formatiert) to format.

formen verb (PERF hat geformt) 1 to form; 2 sich formen to take shape.

förmlich adjective formal. adverb 1 formally; 2 jemanden förmlich zwingen, etwas zu tun to positively force somebody to do something; ich hätte förmlich schreien können I really could have screamed.

Formular das (PL die Formulare) form.

Forscher der (PL die Forscher) 1 researcher, research scientist; 2 explorer.

Forschung die (PL die Forschungen) research.

Forst der (PL die Forste) forest.

Förster der (PL die Förster) forester.

fort adverb 1 away; 2 fort sein to have gone; 3 und so fort and so on; 4 in einem fort on and on.

△ NEW SPELLING: See page xii

fortbewegen verb (PERF hat fortbewegt) 1 to move; 2 sich fortbewegen to move.

fortfahren ◇ verb (PRES fährt fort, IMPERF fuhr fort, PERF ist fortgefahren) 1 to leave; wann fährt ihr fort? when are you leaving?; 2 to continue.

fortgeschritten adjective advanced.

Fortschritt der (PL die Fortschritte) progress; Fortschritte machen to make progress.

fortsetzen verb (PERF hat fortgesetzt) to continue.

Fortsetzung die (PL die Fortsetzungen) 1 continuation; 2 instalment.

Foto das (PL die Fotos) photo.

Fotoapparat der (PL die Fotoapparate) camera.

Fotograf der (PL die Fotografen) photographer.

Fotografie die (PL die Fotografien) 1 photography; 2 photograph.

fotografieren verb (PERF hat fotografiert) 1 to photograph, to take a photograph of; 2 to take photographs.

Fotografin die (PL die Fotografinnen) photographer.

Fotokopie die (PL die Fotokopien) photocopy.

Fracht die (PL die Frachten) freight, cargo.

Frage die (PL die Fragen) question;

etwas in Frage stellen to question something; das kommt nicht in Frage that's out of the question.

Fragebogen der (PL die Fragebogen) questionnaire.

fragen verb (PERF hat gefragt) 1 to ask; 2 sich fragen to wonder.

Fragezeichen das (PL die Fragezeichen) question mark.

fraglich adjective doubtful.

Franken[1] der (PL die Franken) (Swiss) franc.

Franken[2] das Franconia.

Frankreich das France.

Franzose der (PL die Franzosen) Frenchman.

Französin die (PL die Französinnen) Frenchwoman.

französisch adjective French.

Französisch das French.

fraß SEE fressen.

Frau die (PL die Frauen) 1 woman; 2 wife; 3 Mrs, Ms ('Frau' is usually used to address both married and unmarried women).

Fräulein das (PL die Fräulein) 1 young lady; 2 Miss; Fräulein Schmidt Miss Schmidt.

frech adjective cheeky.

Frechheit die (PL die Frechheiten) 1 cheek; 2 cheeky remark.

frei adjective 1 free; 2 freelance; 3 ist dieser Platz frei? is this seat taken?; 4 ein freier Tag a day off;

◇ IRREGULAR VERB: See the verb table in the centre of the dictionary

sich frei nehmen to take a day off;
5 '**Zimmer frei**' 'vacancies'.

Freibad das (PL die **Freibäder**) open-air swimming pool.

Freie das im **Freien** in the open air.

freigebig adjective generous.

Freiheit die (PL die **Freiheiten**)
1 freedom; 2 liberty; **sich Freiheiten erlauben** to take liberties.

freimachen verb (PERF hat freigemacht) 1 to take time off;
2 **sich freimachen** to take time off.

Freistoß der (PL die **Freistöße**) free kick.

Freitag der (PL die **Freitage**) Friday.

freitags adverb on Fridays.

freiwillig adjective voluntary.

Freizeit die 1 spare time; 2 leisure.

fremd adjective 1 foreign; 2 strange;
fremde Leute strangers; **ich bin hier fremd** I'm a stranger here.

Fremde der/die (PL die **Fremden**)
1 foreigner; 2 stranger.

Fremdenverkehr der tourism.

Fremdenverkehrsbüro das (PL die **Fremdenverkehrsbüros**) tourist office.

Fremdenzimmer das (PL die **Fremdenzimmer**) room (to let).

Fremdsprache die (PL die **Fremdsprachen**) foreign language.

fressen ◇ verb (PRES **frisst** △, IMPERF **fraß**, PERF **hat gefressen**) to eat.

Freude die (PL die **Freuden**) 1 joy;
2 pleasure; **mit Freuden** with pleasure; **an etwas Freude haben** to be delighted with something;
4 **jemandem eine Freude machen** to please somebody.

freuen verb (PERF **hat sich gefreut**)
1 **sich freuen** to be pleased; **sich über etwas freuen** to be pleased about something; 2 **sich auf etwas freuen** to look forward to something.

Freund der (PL die **Freunde**)
1 friend; 2 boyfriend.

Freundin die (PL die **Freundinnen**)
1 friend; 2 girlfriend.

freundlich adjective 1 friendly;
2 kind.

freundlicherweise adverb kindly.

Freundlichkeit die friendliness.

Freundschaft die (PL die **Freundschaften**) friendship.

Frieden der peace.

Friedhof der (PL die **Friedhöfe**) cemetery.

friedlich adjective peaceful.

frieren ◇ verb (IMPERF **fror**, PERF **hat gefroren**) 1 to be cold; **frierst du?** are you cold? 2 **es friert** it's freezing, it's frosty; 3 (PERF **ist gefroren**) to freeze.

Frikadelle die (PL die **Frikadellen**) rissole.

frisch adjective fresh; **sich frisch machen** to freshen up.
adverb freshly; '**frisch gestrichen**' 'wet paint'.

△ NEW SPELLING: See page xii

Friseur der (PL die **Friseure**)
hairdresser.

Friseuse die (PL die **Friseusen**)
hairdresser.

frisieren verb (PERF hat frisiert)
1 jemanden frisieren to do
somebody's hair; 2 sich frisieren to
do your hair.

frisst △ SEE fressen.

Frisur die (PL die **Frisuren**) hairstyle,
hairdo.

froh adjective 1 happy; **frohe
Weihnachten!** happy Christmas!;
2 über etwas froh sein to be glad
about something.

fröhlich adjective cheerful.

Fröhlichkeit die cheerfulness.

fromm adjective devout.

fror SEE frieren.

Frosch der (PL die **Frösche**) frog.

Frost der (PL die **Fröste**) frost.

frostig adjective frosty.

Frottee das (PL die **Frottees**)
towelling.

Frottiertuch das (PL die
Frottiertücher) towel.

Frucht die (PL die **Früchte**) fruit.

fruchtbar adjective fertile.

Fruchtsaft der (PL die **Fruchtsäfte**)
fruit juice.

früh adjective, adverb 1 early; **von
früh auf** from an early age; 2 **heute
früh** this morning.

Frühe die **in aller Frühe** at the crack
of dawn.

früher adjective 1 earlier; 2 former.
adverb 1 earlier; 2 formerly;
3 früher war sie ganz anders she
used to be quite different; **das war
früher ein Blumengeschäft** it used
to be a florist's.

frühestens adverb at the earliest.

Frühjahr das (PL die **Frühjahre**)
spring; **im Frühjahr** in spring.

Frühling der (PL die **Frühlinge**)
spring; **im Frühling** in spring.

Frühstück das (PL die **Frühstücke**)
breakfast.

frühstücken verb (PERF hat
gefrühstückt) to have breakfast.

frühzeitig adjective early.

Fuchs der (PL die **Füchse**) fox.

fühlen verb (PERF hat gefühlt) 1 to
feel; 2 sich krank fühlen to feel ill.

fuhr SEE fahren.

führen verb (PERF hat geführt) 1 to
lead; **sie führt mit fünf Punkten** she
is five points in the lead; **unsere
Mannschaft führt** our team's
winning; 2 to run (a shop or
business); 3 to show round; 4 to
keep (a diary, list); 5 **ein
Telefongespräch führen** to make a
phone call.

Führer der (PL die **Führer**) 1 leader;
2 guide.

Führerschein der (PL die
Führerscheine) driving licence; **den
Führerschein machen** to take your
driving test.

◇ **IRREGULAR VERB: See the verb table in the centre of the dictionary**

Führung die (PL die Führungen)
1 leadership; 2 guided tour;
3 management (of a shop); 4 in
Führung in the lead.

füllen verb (PERF hat gefüllt) 1 to
fill; 2 to stuff (a turkey, peppers);
3 sich füllen to fill (up).

Füller der (PL die Füller) fountain
pen.

Füllfederhalter der (PL die
Füllfederhalter) fountain pen.

Füllung die (PL die Füllungen) filling.

Fundament das (PL die
Fundamente) foundations.

Fundbüro das (PL die Fundbüros)
lost property office.

fünf number five.

fünfhundert number five hundred.

Fünftel das (PL die Fünftel) fifth.

fünfter, fünfte, fünftes adjective
fifth.

fünfzehn number fifteen.

fünfzig number fifty.

Funke der (PL die Funken) spark.

funkeln verb (PERF hat gefunkelt)
1 to sparkle; 2 to twinkle (of a star).

funktionieren verb (PERF hat
funktioniert) to work.

für preposition ←–(+ACC) 1 for; 2 was
für ein …? what sort of … ?; 3 für
sich by yourself; jetzt habe ich das
Haus ganz für mich now I've got
the house to myself; 4 das Für und
Wider the pros and cons.

Furcht die fear.

furchtbar adjective terrible.

fürchten verb (PERF hat gefürchtet)
1 to fear; 2 sich fürchten to be
afraid; ich fürchte mich vor ihm I'm
afraid of him; ich fürchte, das geht
nicht I'm afraid that's not possible.

fürchterlich adjective dreadful.

füreinander adverb for each other.

fürs = für das.

Fürsorge die 1 care; 2 welfare;
3 (informal) social security.

Fuß der (PL die Füße) 1 foot; zu Fuß
on foot; zu Fuß gehen to walk;
2 base.

Fußball der (PL die Fußbälle)
football.

Fußballplatz der (PL die
Fußballplätze) football pitch.

Fußballspiel das (PL die
Fußballspiele) football match.

Fußballspieler der (PL die
Fußballspieler) footballer.

Fußboden der (PL die Fußböden)
floor.

Fußgänger der (PL die Fußgänger)
pedestrian.

Fußgängerzone die (PL die
Fußgängerzonen) pedestrian
precinct.

Fußweg der (PL die Fußwege)
footpath.

Futter das 1 feed; ich habe dem
Hund schon Futter gegeben I've

△ NEW SPELLING: See page xii

already given the dog his food;
2 lining (of clothes).

füttern verb (PERF **hat gefüttert**) 1 to
feed; 2 to line.

Futur das (PL die **Future**) future
(tense).

G g

gab SEE **geben**.

Gabel die (PL die **Gabeln**) fork.

gähnen verb (PERF **hat gegähnt**) to
yawn.

Galerie die (PL die **Galerien**) gallery.

galoppieren verb (PERF **ist
galoppiert**) to gallop.

Gammler der (PL die **Gammler**)
drop-out.

Gammlerin die (PL die
Gammlerinnen) drop-out.

Gang der (PL die **Gänge**) 1 walk;
2 errand; 3 corridor; 4 ein Platz am
Gang an aisle seat; 5 course (of a
meal); 6 gear (of a car); 7 in Gang
setzen to get going; 8 im Gange in
progress.

gängig adjective 1 common;
2 popular (goods).

Gans die (PL die **Gänse**) goose.

Gänseblümchen das (PL die
Gänseblümchen) daisy.

Gänsehaut die goose pimples.

ganz adjective whole; 1 ganz

Deutschland the whole of
Germany; 2 im Großen und Ganzen
on the whole; 3 eine ganze Menge
quite a lot; 4 all; mein ganzes Geld
all my money; die ganzen Leute all
the people; 5 etwas wieder ganz
machen to mend something.
adverb 1 quite; es war ganz gut it
was quite good; 2 ganz und gar
completely; 3 ganz und gar nicht
not at all.

ganztägig adjective, adverb 1 full-
time; 2 all-day; ganztägig geöffnet
open all day.

ganztags adverb 1 full time; 2 all
day.

gar adjective done, cooked.
adverb 1 gar nicht not at all; gar
nichts nothing; 2 oder gar or
even.

Garage die (PL die **Garagen**) garage.

Garantie die (PL die **Garantien**)
guarantee.

garantieren verb (PERF **hat
garantiert**) to guarantee.

Garderobe die (PL die **Garderoben**)
cloakroom; wir können die Mäntel
an der Garderobe abgeben we can
leave the coats in the cloakroom.

Gardine die (PL die **Gardinen**)
curtain.

Garn das (PL die **Garne**) thread.

Garnele die (PL die **Garnelen**)
1 shrimp; 2 prawn.

Garten der (PL die **Gärten**) garden.

Gärtner der (PL die **Gärtner**)
gardener.

◇ IRREGULAR VERB: See the verb table in the centre of the dictionary

Gärtnerin die (PL die Gärtnerinnen) gardener.

Gas das (PL die Gase) 1 gas; 2 Gas geben to accelerate.

Gasherd der (PL die Gasherde) gas cooker.

Gaspedal das (PL die Gaspedale) accelerator.

Gasse die (PL die Gassen) lane.

Gast der (PL die Gäste) 1 guest; wir haben heute Abend Gäste we've got guests tonight; 2 bei jemandem zu Gast sein to be staying with somebody.

Gastarbeiter der (PL die Gastarbeiter) foreign worker, guest worker.

Gästezimmer das (PL die Gästezimmer) 1 (hotel) room; 2 spare room.

gastfreundlich adjective hospitable.

Gastfreundschaft die hospitality.

Gastgeber der (PL die Gastgeber) host.

Gastgeberin die (PL die Gastgeberinnen) host.

Gasthaus das (PL die Gasthäuser) inn.

Gasthof der (PL die Gasthöfe) inn.

Gaststätte die (PL die Gaststätten) restaurant.

Gauner der (PL die Gauner) crook.

Gebäck das 1 pastries; 2 biscuits.

gebären ◇ verb (IMPERF gebar, PERF hat geboren) 1 to give birth to; 2 geboren werden to be born.

Gebäude das (PL die Gebäude) building.

geben ◇ verb (PRES gibt, IMPERF gab, PERF hat gegeben) 1 to give; 2 to deal (cards); 3 to teach (at school); 4 geben Sie mir bitte Frau Scheck please put me through to Mrs Scheck; 5 es gibt there is, there are; es gibt viele gute Restaurants in München there are lots of good restaurants in Munich; was gibt's im Kino? what's on at the cinema?; was gibt es zum Mittagessen? what are we having for lunch?; was gibt's Neues? what's the news?, what's new?; 7 sich geschlagen geben to admit defeat; 8 das gibt sich wieder it'll get better; 9 das gibt's doch nicht! I don't believe it!

Gebet das (PL die Gebete) prayer.

gebeten SEE bitten.

Gebiet das (PL die Gebiete) 1 area; 2 field.

gebildet adjective educated.

Gebirge das (PL die Gebirge) mountain range; im Gebirge in the mountains.

Gebiss △ das (PL die Gebisse) 1 teeth; 2 false teeth, dentures.

gebissen SEE beißen.

geblieben SEE bleiben.

geboren verb SEE gebären. adjective 1 born; 2 née; Frau Hahn, geborene Müller Mrs Hahn, née Müller.

△ NEW SPELLING: See page xii

geborgen *adjective* safe.

geboten SEE **bieten**.

gebracht SEE **bringen**.

gebraten *adjective* fried.

Gebrauch *der* (PL *die* **Gebräuche**)
1 use; **vor Gebrauch schütteln**
shake before use; 2 custom.

gebrauchen *verb* (PERF **hat
gebraucht**) to use.

Gebrauchsanweisung *die* (PL *die*
Gebrauchsanweisungen)
instructions (for use).

gebraucht *adjective* used, secondhand.

Gebrauchtwagen *der* (PL *die*
Gebrauchtwagen) second-hand
car.

gebrochen SEE **brechen**.

Gebühr *die* (PL *die* **Gebühren**) fee,
charge.

gebührenfrei *adjective* free (of
charge).

gebührenpflichtig *adjective*
1 subject to a charge; 2 **eine
gebührenpflichtige Straße** a toll
road.

gebunden SEE **binden**.

Geburt *die* (PL *die* **Geburten**) birth.

Geburtenregelung *die* birth
control.

Geburtsdatum *das* (PL *die*
Geburtsdaten) date of birth.

Geburtsort *der* (PL *die*
Geburtsorte) place of birth.

Geburtstag *der* (PL *die*
Geburtstage) birthday.

Geburtsurkunde *die* (PL *die*
Geburtsurkunden) birth certificate.

gedacht SEE **denken**.

Gedächtnis *das* (PL *die*
Gedächtnisse) memory.

Gedanke *der* (PL *die* **Gedanken**)
1 thought; **in Gedanken versunken
sein** to be lost in thought; 2 **sich
Gedanken machen** to worry;
3 **jemanden auf andere Gedanken
bringen** to take somebody's mind
off things.

gedankenlos *adjective*
thoughtless.
adverb without thinking.

Gedeck *das* (PL *die* **Gedecke**)
1 place setting; 2 set meal.

Gedicht *das* (PL *die* **Gedichte**) poem.

Geduld *die* patience.

geduldig *adjective* patient.

gedurft SEE **dürfen**.

geehrt *adjective* 1 honoured;
2 **Sehr geehrte Frau Ross** Dear
Mrs Ross.

geeignet *adjective* 1 suitable;
2 right.

Gefahr *die* (PL *die* **Gefahren**)
1 danger; **außer Gefahr** out of
danger; 2 **auf eigene Gefahr** at your
own risk; **Gefahr laufen, etwas zu
tun** to run the risk of doing
something.

gefährlich *adjective* dangerous.

gefallen[1] SEE **fallen**.

✧ IRREGULAR VERB: *See the verb table in the centre of the dictionary*

gefallen[2] ◇ *verb* (PRES **gefällt**, IMPERF **gefiel**, PERF **hat gefallen**) 1 **es gefällt mir** I like it; **es hat mir gut gefallen** I liked it a lot; 2 **sich etwas gefallen lassen** to put up with something.

Gefallen[1] *der* (PL **Gefallen**) favour.

Gefallen[2] *das* pleasure; **dir zu Gefallen** to please you.

Gefangene *der/die* (PL **die Gefangenen**) prisoner.

Gefängnis *das* (PL **die Gefängnisse**) prison.

Gefäß *das* (PL **die Gefäße**) container.

gefasst △ *adjective* 1 calm, composed; 2 **auf etwas gefasst sein** to be prepared for something.

gefiel SEE **gefallen**.

geflogen SEE **fliegen**.

geflossen SEE **fließen**.

Geflügel *das* poultry.

gefochten SEE **fechten**.

gefräßig *adjective* (*informal*) greedy.

gefrieren ◇ *verb* (IMPERF **gefror**, PERF **ist gefroren**) to freeze.

Gefrierfach *das* (PL **die Gefrierfächer**) freezer (compartment).

gefroren *adjective* frozen.

Gefühl *das* (PL **die Gefühle**) 1 feeling; 2 **etwas im Gefühl haben** to have a feel for something.

gefüllt *adjective* stuffed (*peppers, for example*).

gefunden SEE **finden**.

gegangen SEE **gehen**.

gegeben SEE **geben**.

gegebenenfalls *adverb* if need be.

gegen *preposition* ←(+ACC) 1 against; 2 **gegen die Mauer fahren** to drive into the wall; 3 **ein Mittel gegen Grippe** a cure for flu; 4 towards; **gegen Abend** towards evening; 5 **gegen vier Uhr** around four o'clock; 6 compared with; 7 versus (*in sport*).

Gegend *die* (PL **die Gegenden**) 1 area; 2 neighbourhood.

gegeneinander *adverb* against each other, against one another.

Gegenmittel *das* (PL **die Gegenmittel**) 1 remedy; 2 antidote.

Gegensatz *der* (PL **die Gegensätze**) 1 contrast; 2 opposite; 3 **im Gegensatz zu mir** unlike me.

gegenseitig *adjective* mutual. *adverb* **sich gegenseitig helfen** to help each other.

Gegenstand *der* (PL **die Gegenstände**) 1 object; 2 subject (*in grammar or of a discussion*).

Gegenteil *das* (PL **die Gegenteile**) 1 opposite; 2 **im Gegenteil** on the contrary.

gegenüber *preposition* ←(+DAT) 1 opposite; **Susi saß mir gegenüber** Susi sat opposite me; 2 compared with; 3 towards; **jemandem gegenüber freundlich sein** to be friendly towards somebody.

adverb opposite; **meine Freundin wohnt gegenüber** my friend lives opposite.

Gegenwart *die* 1 present; 2 presence.

gegessen SEE **essen**.

Gegner *der* (PL **die Gegner**) opponent.

gegrillt *adjective* grilled.

Gehackte *das* mince.

Gehalt *das* (PL **die Gehälter**) salary.

gehässig *adjective* spiteful.

geheim *adjective* secret.

Geheimnis *das* (PL **die Geheimnisse**) secret.

geheimnisvoll *adjective* mysterious.

gehen ◊ *verb* (IMPERF **ging**, PERF **ist gegangen**) 1 to go; **schlafen gehen** to go to bed; 2 to walk; 3 **über die Straße gehen** to cross the road; 4 **es geht ihr gut** she's well; **wie geht es Ihnen?** how are you?; **es geht** it's not too bad; 5 **das geht nicht** that's impossible; 6 **um etwas gehen** to be about something; **worum geht's hier?** what's it all about?; 7 **die Uhr geht falsch** the clock's wrong.

Gehirn *das* (PL **die Gehirne**) brain.

Gehirnerschütterung *die* (PL **die Gehirnerschütterungen**) concussion.

gehoben SEE **heben**.

geholfen SEE **helfen**.

Gehör *das* hearing.

gehorchen *verb* (PERF **hat gehorcht**) to obey.

gehören *verb* (PERF **hat gehört**) 1 to belong; **es gehört mir** it belongs to me; 2 **dazu gehört Mut** that takes courage; 3 **es gehört sich nicht** it isn't done.

gehorsam *adjective* obedient.

Gehsteig *der* (PL **die Gehsteige**) pavement.

Geige *die* (PL **die Geigen**) violin.

Geisel *die* (PL **die Geiseln**) hostage.

Geist *der* (PL **die Geister**) 1 mind; 2 ghost; 3 wit.

geistesabwesend *adjective* absent-minded.

Geisteskrankheit *die* (PL **die Geisteskrankheiten**) mental illness.

Geisteswissenschaften (*plural noun*) arts, humanities.

geistig *adjective* mental.

geizig *adjective* mean.

gekannt SEE **kennen**.

gekonnt SEE **können**.

Gel *das* (PL **die Gele**) gel.

Gelächter *das* (PL **die Gelächter**) laughter.

geladen SEE **laden**.

gelähmt *adjective* paralysed.

Geländer *das* (PL **die Geländer**) 1 banister(s); 2 railing(s).

gelangweilt *adjective* bored.

◊ IRREGULAR VERB: *See the verb table in the centre of the dictionary*

gelassen verb SEE **lassen**.
adjective calm.

geläufig adjective 1 common; 2 das ist mir nicht geläufig I'm not familiar with it.

gelaunt adjective gut gelaunt sein to be in a good mood.

gelb adjective yellow.

Geld das (PL die Gelder) money.

Geldautomat der (PL die Geldautomaten) cash dispenser.

Geldbörse die (PL die Geldbörsen) purse.

Geldschein der (PL die Geldscheine) banknote.

Geldstrafe die (PL die Geldstrafen) fine.

Geldwechsel der 1 bureau de change; 2 currency exchange.

gelegen SEE **liegen**.

Gelegenheit die (PL die Gelegenheiten) 1 opportunity; 2 occasion.

gelegentlich adverb occasionally.

Gelenk das (PL die Gelenke) joint.

Geliebte der/die (PL die Geliebten) lover.

geliehen SEE **leihen**.

gelingen ◇ verb (IMPERF gelang, PERF ist gelungen) to succeed; es ist mir gelungen, sie zu überreden I succeeded in persuading her.

gelten ◇ verb (PRES gilt, IMPERF galt, PERF hat gegolten) 1 to be valid; 2 to apply (of a rule); 3 jemandem

gelten to be directed at somebody; 4 sein Wort gilt viel his word is worth a lot; 5 das gilt nicht that doesn't count; 6 als etwas gelten to be regarded as something.

gelungen verb SEE **gelingen**. adjective successful.

Gemälde das (PL die Gemälde) painting.

gemein adjective mean.

Gemeinde die (PL die Gemeinden) 1 community; 2 congregation.

gemeinsam adjective 1 common; 2 joint. adverb together; gemeinsam essen to eat together.

Gemeinschaft die (PL die Gemeinschaften) community.

gemischt adjective mixed.

gemocht SEE **mögen**.

Gemüse das (PL die Gemüse) vegetables.

Gemüsehändler der (PL die Gemüsehändler) greengrocer.

gemusst △ SEE **müssen**.

gemustert adjective patterned.

gemütlich adjective 1 cosy; 2 mach es dir gemütlich make yourself comfortable.

genannt SEE **nennen**.

genau adjective 1 exact; 2 accurate (scales, description); 3 meticulous; 4 ich weiß nichts Genaues I don't know any details.
adverb 1 exactly; 2 genau genommen △ strictly speaking.

△ NEW SPELLING: See page xii

Genauigkeit *die* accuracy.

genauso *adverb* 1 just the same; 2 **genauso gut** just as good; **genauso viel** just as much, just as many; **genauso lange** just as long.

Genehmigung *die* (PL die **Genehmigungen**) 1 permission; 2 permit; 3 licence.

Generation *die* (PL die **Generationen**) generation.

generell *adjective* general.

Genetik *die* genetics.

Genf *das* Geneva.

Genfer See *der* Lake Geneva.

genial *adjective* brilliant.

Genick *das* (PL die **Genicke**) (back of the) neck.

Genie *das* (PL die **Genies**) genius.

genießbar *adjective* edible.

genießen ✧ *verb* (IMPERF **genoss**△, PERF **hat genossen**) to enjoy.

genommen SEE **nehmen**.

genug *adverb* enough.

genügen *verb* (PERF **hat genügt**) to be enough.

genügend *adjective* 1 enough; 2 sufficient.

Genuss△ *der* (PL die **Genüsse**) 1 enjoyment; 2 consumption (*of alcohol*).

geöffnet *adjective* open.

Geometrie *die* geometry.

Gepäck *das* luggage.

Gepäckausgabe *die* left-luggage office.

Gepäckaufbewahrung *die* left-luggage office.

Gepäckträger *der* (PL die **Gepäckträger**) 1 porter; 2 roof rack; 3 carrier (*on a bike*).

gerade *adjective* 1 straight; 2 etwas **gerade biegen** △ to straighten something; 3 upright; 4 eine **gerade Zahl** an even number. *adverb* 1 just; **gerade erst** only just; 2 es war nicht **gerade billig** it wasn't exactly cheap.

geradeaus *adverb* straight ahead.

geradebiegen SEE **gerade**.

gerannt SEE **rennen**.

Gerät *das* (PL die **Geräte**) 1 appliance; 2 set (*TV or radio*); 3 tool; 4 gadget; 5 die **Geräte** apparatus (*in gymnastics*).

geraten ✧ *verb* (PRES **gerät**, IMPERF **geriet**, PERF **ist geraten**) 1 to get (*somewhere, the wrong side of the road etc.*); **in etwas geraten** to get into something; **in Wut geraten** to get angry; 2 **an den Richtigen geraten** to come to the right person; 3 **gut/schlecht geraten** to turn out well/badly; 4 **nach jemandem geraten** to take after somebody.

geräuchert *adjective* smoked.

geräumig *adjective* spacious.

Geräusch *das* (PL die **Geräusche**) noise.

gerecht *adjective* 1 just; 2 fair.

✧ IRREGULAR VERB: *See the verb table in the centre of the dictionary*

Gerechtigkeit die justice.

Gerede das gossip.

Gericht das (PL die Gerichte)
1 court; 2 dish.

gerieben SEE reiben.

gering adjective 1 small (amount);
2 low (value); 3 short (time,
distance).

Gerippe das (PL die Gerippe)
skeleton.

gerissen adjective crafty.

geritten SEE reiten.

gern(e) adverb 1 gladly;
2 jemanden gern haben to like
somebody; etwas gern tun to like
doing something; ich tanze gern I
like dancing; ich hätte gerne einen
Kaffee I'd like a coffee; 3 ja, gern!
yes, I'd love to!; 4 das glaube ich
gern I can well believe that.

Gerste die barley.

Geruch der (PL die Gerüche) smell.

Gerücht das (PL die Gerüchte)
rumour.

Gerümpel das junk.

gesalzen verb SEE salzen.
adjective 1 salted; 2 gesalzene
Preise (informal) steep prices.

gesamt adjective 1 whole; 2 die
gesamten Kosten the total cost;
3 die gesamten Werke the
complete works.

Gesamtschule die (PL die
Gesamtschulen) comprehensive
school.

gesandt SEE senden.

Geschäft das (PL die Geschäfte)
1 shop; 2 business; 3 deal.

Geschäftsführer der (PL die
Geschäftsführer) manager.

Geschäftsführerin die (PL die
Geschäftsführerinnen)
manageress.

Geschäftszeiten plural noun
business hours.

geschehen ◇ verb (PRES
geschieht, IMPERF geschah, PERF ist
geschehen) to happen.

gescheit adjective clever.

Geschenk das (PL die Geschenke)
present, gift.

Geschichte die (PL die
Geschichten) 1 story; 2 history;
3 mach bloß keine große
Geschichte daraus don't make such
a thing of it.

Geschick das 1 skill; 2 fate.

geschickt adjective 1 skilful;
2 clever.

geschieden verb SEE scheiden.
adjective divorced.

geschienen SEE scheinen.

Geschirr das 1 crockery; 2 dishes.

Geschirrspülmaschine die (PL
die Geschirrspülmaschinen)
dishwasher.

Geschirrtuch das (PL die
Geschirrtücher) tea towel.

Geschlecht das (PL die
Geschlechter) 1 sex; 2 gender.

△ NEW SPELLING: See page xii

geschlossen *verb* SEE **schließen**. *adjective* closed.

Geschmack *der* (PL *die* Geschmäcke) taste.

geschmacklos *adjective* 1 tasteless; 2 **geschmacklos sein** to be in bad taste.

geschnitten SEE **schneiden**.

geschossen SEE **schießen**.

geschrieben SEE **schreiben**.

geschrien SEE **schreien**.

Geschwätz *das* talk.

geschwätzig *adjective* talkative.

Geschwindigkeit *die* (PL *die* Geschwindigkeiten) speed.

Geschwindigkeits-beschränkung *die* (PL *die* Geschwindigkeitsbeschränkungen) speed limit.

Geschwister *plural noun* brothers and sisters, siblings.

geschwommen SEE **schwimmen**.

gesellig *adjective* sociable.

Gesellschaft *die* (PL *die* Gesellschaften) 1 society; 2 company; **ich leiste dir Gesellschaft** I'll keep you company; 3 party.

gesessen SEE **sitzen**.

Gesetz *das* (PL *die* Gesetze) law.

gesetzlich *adjective* legal; **ein gesetzlicher Feiertag** a public holiday.

Gesicht *das* (PL *die* Gesichter) face.

Gesichtsausdruck *der* (facial) expression.

gesollt SEE **sollen**.

gespannt *adjective* 1 eager; 2 **auf etwas gespannt sein** to look forward eagerly to something; **auf jemanden gespannt sein** to look forward to seeing somebody; 3 **ich bin gespannt, ob …** I wonder whether …; 4 tense; **in Südafrika ist die Lage immer noch gespannt** the situation in South Africa is still tense.

Gespenst *das* (PL *die* Gespenster) ghost.

Gespräch *das* (PL *die* Gespräche) 1 conversation; 2 call (*on the phone*).

gesprächig *adjective* talkative.

gesprochen SEE **sprechen**.

gesprungen SEE **springen**.

Gestalt *die* (PL *die* Gestalten) 1 figure; 2 form.

gestanden SEE **stehen**, **gestehen**.

Geständnis *das* (PL *die* Geständnisse) confession.

gestatten *verb* (PERF **hat gestattet**) 1 to permit; 2 **nicht gestattet** prohibited; 3 **gestatten Sie?** may I?

Geste *die* (PL *die* Gesten) gesture.

gestehen ✧ *verb* (IMPERF **gestand**, PERF **hat gestanden**) to confess.

Gestell *das* (PL *die* Gestelle) 1 rack; 2 stand; 3 frame.

gestern *adverb* 1 yesterday; 2 **gestern Nacht** last night.

✧ IRREGULAR VERB: *See the verb table in the centre of the dictionary*

gestohlen SEE stehlen.

gestorben SEE sterben.

gestreift adjective striped.

gesund adjective 1 healthy; 2 wieder gesund werden to get well again; 3 Schwimmen ist gesund swimming is good for you.

Gesundheit die 1 health; 2 Gesundheit! bless you! (said after a sneeze).

gesungen SEE singen.

getan SEE tun.

Getränk das (PL die Getränke) drink.

Getränkekarte die (PL die Getränkekarten) wine list.

getrauen verb (PERF hat sich getraut) sich getrauen to dare.

Getreide das grain.

Getriebe das (PL die Getriebe) gearbox.

getrieben SEE treiben.

getroffen SEE treffen.

getrunken SEE trinken.

Getue das fuss.

geübt adjective 1 accomplished; 2 mit geübtem Auge with a practised eye.

Gewächshaus das (PL die Gewächshäuser) greenhouse.

Gewalt die 1 power; 2 force; mit Gewalt by force; 3 violence.

gewaltig adjective enormous.

gewalttätig adjective violent.

gewann SEE gewinnen.

Gewebe das (PL die Gewebe) 1 fabric; 2 tissue.

Gewehr das (PL die Gewehre) rifle, gun.

Gewerkschaft die (PL die Gewerkschaften) trade union.

gewesen SEE sein.

Gewicht das (PL die Gewichte) weight.

Gewinn der (PL die Gewinne) 1 profit; 2 winnings; 3 prize.

gewinnen ◇ verb (IMPERF gewann, PERF hat gewonnen) 1 to win; 2 to gain (time or influence); an Bedeutung gewinnen to gain in importance.

Gewinner der (PL die Gewinner) winner.

Gewinnerin die (PL die Gewinnerinnen) winner.

gewiss △ adjective certain; ein gewisser Herr Schmidt möchte Sie sprechen a Mr Schmidt would like to speak to you. adverb certainly; 'darf ich?' 'aber gewiss doch' 'may I?' 'but of course'.

Gewissen das (PL die Gewissen) conscience.

gewissenhaft adjective conscientious.

gewissermaßen adverb 1 more or less; 2 as it were.

Gewitter das (PL die Gewitter) thunderstorm.

△ NEW SPELLING: See page xii

gewöhnen *verb* (PERF hat gewöhnt) 1 jemanden an etwas gewöhnen to get somebody used to something; 2 an etwas gewöhnt sein to be used to something; 3 sich an etwas gewöhnen to get used to something.

Gewohnheit *die* (PL die Gewohnheiten) habit.

gewöhnlich *adjective* 1 usual; 2 ordinary.
adverb usually; wie gewöhnlich as usual.

gewohnt *adjective* 1 usual; 2 etwas gewohnt sein to be used to something; Renate ist es nicht gewohnt, früh aufzustehen Renate isn't used to getting up early.

gewollt SEE wollen.

gewonnen SEE gewinnen.

geworden SEE werden.

geworfen SEE werfen.

Gewürz *das* (PL die Gewürze) spice.

gewusst △ SEE wissen.

Gezeiten *plural noun* tides.

gezogen SEE ziehen.

gezwungen SEE zwingen.

gibt SEE geben.

gierig *adjective* greedy.

gießen ◇ *verb* (IMPERF goss △, PERF hat gegossen) 1 to pour; es gießt it's pouring; 2 to water; vergiss nicht, die Blumen zu gießen don't forget to water the flowers.

Gießkanne *die* (PL die Gießkannen) watering can.

Gift *das* (PL die Gifte) poison.

giftig *adjective* 1 poisonous; 2 toxic.

ging SEE gehen.

Gipfel *der* (PL die Gipfel) 1 peak, summit; 2 der Gipfel der Geschmacklosigkeit the height of bad taste.

Gips *der* plaster.

Girokonto *das* (PL die Girokonten) current account.

Giraffe *die* (PL die Giraffen) giraffe.

Gitarre *die* (PL die Gitarren) guitar.

Gitter *das* (PL die Gitter) 1 grid; 2 bars.

glänzen *verb* (PERF hat geglänzt) to shine.

glänzend *adjective* 1 shining; 2 brilliant; ein glänzender Erfolg a brilliant success.

Glas *das* (PL die Gläser) 1 glass; 2 jar.

Glasscheibe *die* (PL die Glasscheiben) pane (of glass).

glatt *adjective* 1 smooth; 2 slippery; 3 eine glatte Absage a flat refusal.
adverb 1 smoothly; 2 flatly; etwas glatt ablehnen to flatly reject something; 3 das ist glatt gelogen that's a downright lie; 4 ich habe ihren Geburtstag glatt vergessen I totally forgot about her birthday.

Glatteis *das* (black) ice.

Glatze *die* (PL die Glatzen) eine Glatze haben to be bald; eine Glatze bekommen to go bald.

◇ IRREGULAR VERB: *See the verb table in the centre of the dictionary*

glauben verb (PERF hat geglaubt)
1 to believe; **an Gott glauben** to believe in God; **2** to think; **3 nicht zu glauben!** incredible!

gleich adjective **1** same; **2** identical; **3 gleich bleibend** △ constant; **4 das ist mir gleich** it's all the same to me; **ganz gleich, wer anruft** no matter who calls.
adverb **1** the same; **2** equally; **3** immediately; **4 gleich neben** right next to; **5 er ist gleich fertig** he'll be ready in a minute.

gleichartig adjective similar.

gleichberechtigt adjective equal.

Gleichberechtigung die equality.

gleichbleibend SEE gleich.

gleichen ◇ verb (IMPERF glich, PERF hat geglichen) **1** to be like; **2 sich gleichen** to be alike.

gleichfalls adverb **1** also; **2 danke gleichfalls!** the same to you!

Gleichgewicht das balance.

gleichgültig adjective indifferent; **das ist doch gleichgültig** it's not important.

gleichzeitig adverb at the same time.

Gleis das (PL die Gleise) **1** track, line; **2** platform; **Gleis vier** platform four.

glich SEE gleichen.

Glied das (PL die Glieder) **1** limb; **2** link.

glitschig adjective slippery.

glitzern verb (PERF hat geglitzert) to glitter.

Glocke die (PL die Glocken) bell.

Glück das **1** luck; **viel Glück!** good luck!; **Glück haben** to be lucky; **zum Glück** luckily; **2** happiness.

glücklich adjective **1** lucky; **es war ein glücklicher Zufall, dass ich ihn heute in der Stadt getroffen habe** it was a lucky coincidence that I met him in town today; **2** happy.

glücklicherweise adverb luckily, fortunately.

Glückwunsch der (PL die Glückwünsche) congratulations; **herzlichen Glückwunsch zum Geburtstag!** happy birthday!

Glückwunschkarte die (PL die Glückwunschkarten) greetings card.

Glühbirne die (PL die Glühbirnen) light bulb.

glühen verb (PERF hat geglüht) to glow.

Gold das gold.

golden adjective **1** gold; **2** golden.

Goldfisch der (PL die Goldfische) goldfish.

Golf[1] der (PL die Golfe) gulf.

Golf[2] das golf.

Golfplatz der (PL die Golfplätze) golf course.

Golfschläger der (PL die Golfschläger) golf club.

goss △ SEE gießen.

Gott der (PL die Götter) god.

△ NEW SPELLING: See page xii

Gottesdienst der (PL die Gottesdienste) service.

Göttin die (PL die Göttinnen) goddess.

Grab das (PL die Gräber) grave.

graben △ verb (PRES gräbt, IMPERF grub, PERF hat gegraben) to dig.

Grad der (PL die Grade) degree.

Gramm das (PL die Gramme) gram.

Grammatik die (PL die Grammatiken) grammar.

grantig adjective grumpy.

Gras das (PL die Gräser) grass.

grässlich △ adjective horrible.

Gräte die (PL die Gräten) (fish)bone.

gratis adverb free of charge.

gratulieren verb (PERF hat gratuliert) 1 to congratulate; 2 ich habe Gabi zum Geburtstag gratuliert I wished Gabi happy birthday; 3 wir gratulieren! congratulations!

grau adjective grey.

Gräuel △ der horror.

grauen verb (PERF hat gegraut) mir graut es davor I dread it.

grauhaarig adjective grey-haired.

grausam adjective cruel.

Grausamkeit die cruelty.

graziös adjective graceful.

greifen ◇ verb (IMPERF griff, PERF hat gegriffen) 1 to take hold of; 2 to catch; 3 nach etwas greifen to

reach for something; 4 um sich greifen to spread (of fire).

grell adjective 1 glaring; 2 garish; 3 shrill.

Grenze die (PL die Grenzen) 1 border; 2 boundary; 3 limit.

grenzen verb (PERF hat gegrenzt) an etwas grenzen to border on something.

Greuel SEE Gräuel.

Grieche der (PL die Griechen) Greek.

Griechenland das Greece.

Griechin die (PL die Griechinnen) Greek.

griechisch adjective Greek.

griff SEE greifen.

Griff der (PL die Griffe) 1 grasp; 2 handle.

griffbereit adjective handy; sie hat den Korkenzieher immer griffbereit she always keeps the corkscrew handy.

Grill der (PL die Grills) 1 grill; 2 barbecue.

Grille die (PL die Grillen) cricket (the insect).

grillen verb (PERF hat gegrillt) 1 to grill; 2 to have a barbecue.

Grillfest das (PL die Grillfeste) barbecue.

grinsen verb (PERF hat gegrinst) to grin.

Grippe die (PL die Grippen) flu.

grob adjective 1 coarse; 2 rough;

◇ IRREGULAR VERB: See the verb table in the centre of the dictionary

3 rude; 4 **ein grober Fehler** a bad mistake.

Groschen der (PL die Groschen)
1 (Austrian money) groschen;
2 (informal) ten-pfennig piece;
3 **der Groschen ist gefallen** the penny's dropped.

groß adjective 1 big; 2 great; **Gisela hatte große Angst** Gisela was very frightened; 3 tall; 4 **ein großer Buchstabe** a capital letter; 5 **groß werden** to grow up; 6 **die großen Ferien** the summer holidays; 7 **im Großen und Ganzen** △ on the whole; 8 **Groß und Klein** △ young and old. adverb **was soll man da schon groß machen?** what are you supposed to do?

großartig adjective great.

Großbritannien das Great Britain.

Großbuchstabe der (PL die Großbuchstaben) capital (letter).

Größe die (PL die Größen) 1 size; 2 height; 3 greatness.

Großeltern plural noun grandparents.

großenteils adverb largely.

Großmarkt der (PL die Großmärkte) hypermarket.

Großmutter die (PL die Großmütter) grandmother.

Großstadt die (PL die Großstädte) city.

großschreiben ◇ verb (IMPERF schrieb groß, PERF hat großgeschrieben) ein Wort

großschreiben to write a word with a capital.

Großvater der (PL die Großväter) grandfather.

großzügig adjective generous.

grub SEE **graben**.

grün adjective 1 green; 2 **im Grünen** in the country; 3 **die Grünen** the Greens.

Grund der (PL die Gründe) 1 ground; 2 bottom; 3 reason; **aus diesem Grund** for this reason; 4 **im Grunde genommen** basically.

gründen verb (PERF hat gegründet) 1 to set up, to found; 2 **sich auf etwas gründen** to be based on something.

Grundlage die (PL die Grundlagen) basis.

gründlich adjective thorough.

grundsätzlich adjective
1 fundamental; 2 basic.
adverb 1 basically; 2 on principle.

Grundschule die (PL die Grundschulen) primary school.

Grundstück das (PL die Grundstücke) plot (of land).

Gruppe die (PL die Gruppen) group.

Gruß der (PL die Grüße) greeting; **einen schönen Gruß an Lars** give my regards to Lars; **mit herzlichen Grüßen** with best wishes.

grüßen verb (PERF hat gegrüßt) 1 to greet; 2 to say hello; 3 **grüß Gott!** hello; 4 **grüße Thomas von mir** give Thomas my regards; **Gisela lässt grüßen** Gisela sends her regards.

△ NEW SPELLING: See page xii

gucken verb (PERF hat geguckt) to look.

gültig adjective valid.

Gummi der (PL die Gummis) rubber.

Gummiband das (PL die Gummibänder) rubber band.

Gummistiefel der (PL die Gummistiefel) wellington (boot).

günstig adjective 1 favourable; 2 convenient.

Gurgel die (PL die Gurgeln) throat.

gurgeln verb (PERF hat gegurgelt) to gargle.

Gurke die (PL die Gurken) 1 cucumber; 2 gherkin.

Gürtel der (PL die Gürtel) belt.

Gürteltasche die (PL die Gürteltaschen) bum bag.

gut adjective 1 good; 2 guten Appetit! enjoy your meal!; 3 schon gut that's all right; also gut all right; 4 im Guten △ amicably; 5 alles Gute! all the best!
adverb 1 well; 2 gut schmecken to taste good; 3 gut zwei Stunden a good two hours; 4 uns geht's gut we're fine; ihm geht es nicht gut he's not well.

Güte die 1 goodness; du meine Güte! my goodness!; 2 quality.

Güterzug der (PL die Güterzüge) goods train.

gutgehen SEE gut.

gutmütig adjective good-natured.

Gutschein der (PL die Gutscheine) 1 voucher; 2 coupon.

Gymnasium das (PL die Gymnasien) grammar school.

Gymnastik die 1 gymnastics; 2 keep-fit (exercises).

H h

Haar das (PL die Haare) 1 hair; sich die Haare waschen to wash your hair; 2 um ein Haar (informal) very nearly.

Haarbürste die (PL die Haarbürsten) hairbrush.

haarig adjective hairy.

Haarschnitt der (PL die Haarschnitte) haircut.

Haarwaschmittel das (PL die Haarwaschmittel) shampoo.

haben ◊ verb (PRES hat, IMPERF hatte, PERF hat gehabt) 1 to have (got); 1 ich habe ein neues Auto I have (or I've got) a new car; etwas gegen jemanden haben to have something against somebody; 2 (used with another verb, like 'have' in English, to form past tenses) ich habe Werners Adresse verloren I've lost Werner's address; ich habe deine Mutter gestern angerufen I rang your mother yesterday; 3 Angst haben to be frightened; Hunger haben to be hungry; 4 heute haben wir Mittwoch it's Wednesday today; 5 die Kinder haben Ferien the children are on holiday; 6 was hat sie? what's the

◊ IRREGULAR VERB: See the verb table in the centre of the dictionary

matter with her?; **7 ich hätte gern
... ** I'd like ...; **ich hätte ihr geholfen**
I would have helped her; **8 sich
haben** (*informal*) to make a fuss.

hacken *verb* (PERF **hat gehackt**) **1** to
chop (up); **2** to peck (*of a bird*).

Hackfleisch *das* minced meat.

Hafen *der* (PL die **Häfen**) harbour.

Haferflocken *plural noun*
porridge oats.

haftbar *adjective* **für etwas haftbar
sein** to be liable for something.

haften *verb* (PERF **hat gehaftet**) **1** to
stick; **2 für etwas haften** to be
responsible for something.

Hagel *der* hail.

hageln *verb* (PERF **hat gehagelt**) to
hail.

Hagelschauer *der* (PL die
Hagelschauer) hailstorm.

Hahn *der* (PL die **Hähne**) **1** cock;
2 tap.

Hähnchen *das* (PL die **Hähnchen**)
chicken.

Hai *der* (PL die **Haie**) shark.

Haken *der* (PL die **Haken**) **1** hook;
2 tick; **3** catch; **da muss ein Haken
dran sein** there must be a catch.

halb *adjective* half; **zum halben
Preis** at half price; **halb eins** half
past twelve.

Halbfinale *das* (PL die **Halbfinale**)
semi-final.

halbieren *verb* (PERF **hat halbiert**)
to halve.

Halbkreis *der* (PL die **Halbkreise**)
semicircle.

Halbpension *die* half board.

halbtags *adverb* part-time.

halbwegs *adverb* **1** half-way;
2 more or less.

Halbzeit *die* (PL die **Halbzeiten**)
1 half; **2** half-time; **während der
Halbzeit** during half-time.

half SEE **helfen**.

Hälfte *die* (PL die **Hälften**) half; **zur
Hälfte** half.

Halle *die* (PL die **Hallen**) **1** hall;
2 foyer.

Hallenbad *das* (PL die **Hallenbäder**)
indoor swimming pool.

hallo *exclamation* hello!

Hals *der* (PL die **Hälse**) **1** neck;
2 throat; **mir tut der Hals weh** I've
got a sore throat; **3 aus vollem Hals
schreien** to shout at the top of your
voice; **4 Hals über Kopf** in a rush.

Halsband *das* (PL die **Halsbänder**)
collar.

Halsschmerzen *plural noun* sore
throat; **Paul hat Halsschmerzen**
Paul's got a sore throat.

Halstuch *das* (PL die **Halstücher**)
scarf.

halt *exclamation* stop!

Halt *der* **1** hold; **jetzt hat es einen
besseren Halt** it holds better now;
2 Halt machen △ to stop.

haltbar *adjective* **1** hard-wearing;

halten

2 durable; 3 **mindestens haltbar bis ...** best before ...

halten ◇ *verb* (PRES **hält**, IMPERF **hielt**, PERF **hat gehalten**) 1 to hold; 2 to keep; **sein Versprechen halten** to keep your promise; **warm halten** △ to keep warm; 3 to stop; **der Bus hält direkt vor seiner Haustür** the bus stops right outside his door; 4 to save (*in sport*); 5 to take (*a paper, magazine*); 6 **ich habe ihn für deinen Bruder gehalten** I took him for your brother; 7 **viel von jemandem halten** to think a lot of somebody; **jemanden für ehrlich halten** to think somebody is honest; 8 **zu jemandem halten** to stand by somebody; 9 **eine Rede halten** to make a speech; 10 **sich halten** to keep (*of milk, fruit, etc.*); 11 **sich links/rechts halten** to keep left/right; 12 **sich gut halten** to do well; 13 **sich an etwas halten** to keep to something.

Haltestelle *die* (PL **die Haltestellen**) stop.

haltmachen SEE Halt.

Haltung *die* (PL **die Haltungen**) 1 posture; 2 attitude; 3 composure.

Hammelfleisch *das* mutton.

Hammer *der* (PL **die Hämmer**) hammer.

hämmern *verb* (PERF **hat gehämmert**) to hammer.

Hamster *der* (PL **die Hamster**) hamster.

Hand *die* (PL **die Hände**) hand; **jemandem die Hand geben** to shake hands with somebody.

Handarbeit *die* (PL **die Handarbeiten**) 1 handicraft; 2 hand-made article.

Handball *der* handball.

Handbremse *die* (PL **die Handbremsen**) handbrake; **die Handbremse ziehen** to pull the handbrake.

Handbuch *das* (PL **die Handbücher**) manual.

Handel *der* 1 trade; 2 deal; 3 **in den Handel kommen** to come on the market.

handeln *verb* (PERF **hat gehandelt**) 1 to trade, to deal; 2 **mit jemandem handeln** to bargain with somebody; 3 to act; 4 **von etwas handeln** to be about something; 5 **es handelt sich um ...** it's about ...; **worum handelt es sich?** what's it about?

Handelsschule *die* (PL **die Handelsschulen**) business school, vocational college.

Handfläche *die* (PL **die Handflächen**) palm.

Handgelenk *das* (PL **die Handgelenke**) wrist.

Handgepäck *das* hand luggage.

handhaben *verb* (PERF **hat gehandhabt**) to handle.

Händler *der* (PL **die Händler**) dealer.

handlich *adjective* handy.

Handlung *die* (PL **die Handlungen**) 1 act; 2 action; 3 plot.

◇ IRREGULAR VERB: See the verb table in the centre of the dictionary

Handschellen (*plural noun*) handcuffs.

Handschrift die (PL die Handschriften) handwriting.

Handschuh der (PL die Handschuhe) glove.

Handtasche die (PL die Handtaschen) bag.

Handtuch das (PL die Handtücher) towel.

Handwerker der (PL die Handwerker) 1 craftsman; 2 workman.

Handwerkzeug das tools.

Handy das (PL die Handys) mobile (phone).

Hang der (PL die Hänge) slope.

Hängematte die (PL die Hängematten) hammock.

hängen[1] *verb* (PERF hat gehängt) 1 to hang; **Florian hat das Bild an die Wand gehängt** Florian hung the picture on the wall; **sie hängte ihren Mantel in den Schrank** she hung her coat up in the cupboard; 2 **sie haben den Wohnwagen an das Auto gehängt** they attached the caravan to the car; 3 **sich an jemanden hängen** to latch on to somebody.

hängen[2] ◇ *verb* (IMPERF hing, PERF hat gehangen) 1 to hang; **mein Bild hat immer hier gehangen** my picture used to hang here; 2 **an seinen Eltern hängen** to be attached to your parents; **sie hängt sehr an ihrer Mutter** she's very attached to her mother; 3 **an etwas**

hängen bleiben △ to catch on something, to stick to something; **ich bin mit dem Ärmel am Zaun hängen geblieben** I got my sleeve caught on the fence.

hängenbleiben SEE **hängen**[2].

Hansaplast™ das plaster.

Happen der (PL die Happen) mouthful; **ich habe heute keinen Happen gegessen** I haven't had a bite to eat all day.

Harfe die (PL die Harfen) harp.

Harke die (PL die Harken) rake.

harmlos *adjective* harmless.

hart *adjective* 1 hard; 2 harsh.

hartgekocht *adjective* hard-boiled.

Hase der (PL die Hasen) hare.

Haselnuss △ die (PL die Haselnüsse) hazelnut.

Hass △ der hatred.

hassen *verb* (PERF hat gehasst △) to hate.

hässlich △ *adjective* 1 ugly; **sie hat ein hässliches Gesicht** she's got an ugly face; 2 nasty; **das war sehr hässlich von dir** that was very nasty of you.

hast SEE **haben**.

hastig *adjective* hasty.

hat, hatte, hatten, hattest, hattet SEE **haben**.

Haube die (PL die Hauben) 1 bonnet; 2 cap.

△ NEW SPELLING: See page xii

hauen ◇ verb (PRES **haut**, IMPERF **haute**, PERF **hat gehauen**) 1 to beat; 2 to thump, to bang; 3 **sich hauen** to fight; 4 **jemanden übers Ohr hauen** (informal) to cheat somebody.

Haufen der (PL die **Haufen**) 1 heap; 2 crowd (of people); 3 **ein Haufen** (informal) heaps of; **ein Haufen Geld** heaps of money.

haufenweise adverb heaps of; **Gabi hat haufenweise CDs** Gabi has heaps of CDs.

häufig adjective frequent.

Hauptbahnhof der (PL die **Hauptbahnhöfe**) main station.

Hauptrolle die (PL die **Hauptrollen**) lead.

Hauptsache die (PL die **Hauptsachen**) main thing.

hauptsächlich adjective main. adverb mainly.

Hauptschule die secondary school.

Hauptstadt die (PL die **Hauptstädte**) capital.

Hauptstraße die (PL die **Hauptstraßen**) main road.

Hauptverkehrszeit die (PL die **Hauptverkehrszeiten**) rush hour.

Hauptwort das (PL die **Hauptwörter**) noun.

Haus das (PL die **Häuser**) 1 house; 2 **nach Hause** home; **zu Hause** at home.

Hausarbeit die (PL die **Hausarbeiten**) 1 housework; die

Kinder müssen bei der Hausarbeit helfen the children have to help with the housework; 2 homework.

Hausaufgaben plural noun homework; **hast du deine Hausaufgaben gemacht?** have you done your homework?

Hausfrau die (PL die **Hausfrauen**) housewife.

Haushalt der (PL die **Haushalte**) 1 household; 2 **den Haushalt machen** to do the housework; 3 budget.

Haushaltswarengeschäft das (PL die **Haushaltswarengeschäfte**) hardware shop.

Hausmeister der (PL die **Hausmeister**) caretaker.

Hausnummer die house number.

Hausschlüssel der (PL die **Hausschlüssel**) front-door key.

Hausschuh der (PL die **Hausschuhe**) slipper.

Haustier das (PL die **Haustiere**) pet.

Haustür die (PL die **Haustüren**) front door.

Haut die (PL die **Häute**) skin; **aus der Haut fahren** (informal) to go up the wall.

Hebamme die (PL die **Hebammen**) midwife.

Hebel der (PL die **Hebel**) lever.

heben ◇ verb (IMPERF **hob**, PERF **hat gehoben**) 1 to lift; 2 **sich heben** to rise.

Hecke die (PL die **Hecken**) hedge.

◇ IRREGULAR VERB: See the verb table in the centre of the dictionary

Heer das (PL die Heere) army.

Hefe die (PL die Hefen) yeast.

Heft das (PL die Hefte) 1 exercise book; 2 issue (of a magazine).

heften verb (PERF hat geheftet) 1 to pin; 2 to tack (by sewing); 3 to clip; 4 to staple.

heftig adjective 1 violent; 2 heavy (snow, rain).

Heftklammer die (PL die Heftklammern) staple.

Heftpflaster das (PL die Heftpflaster) sticking plaster.

Heftzwecke die (PL die Heftzwecken) drawing pin.

Heide die heath.

Heidekraut das heather.

Heidelbeere die (PL die Heidelbeeren) bilberry.

heilen verb (PERF hat geheilt) 1 to cure; 2 to heal.

heilig adjective 1 holy; 2 heilig halten to hold sacred; 3 der heilige Franz von Assisi Saint Francis of Assisi.

Heiligabend der (PL die Heiligabende) Christmas Eve.

Heilige der/die (PL die Heiligen) saint.

Heilmittel das (PL die Heilmittel) remedy.

heim adverb home.

Heim das (PL die Heime) 1 home; 2 hostel.

Heimat die (PL die Heimaten) 1 home; 2 native land.

Heimatstadt die home town.

Heimfahrt die (PL die Heimfahrten) 1 journey home; 2 way home.

heimgehen ◇ verb (IMPERF ging heim, PERF ist heimgegangen) to go home.

heimlich adjective secret. adverb secretly.

Heimspiel das (PL die Heimspiele) home game.

Heimweg der (PL die Heimwege) way home.

Heimweh das homesickness; Heimweh haben to be homesick.

Heirat die (PL die Heiraten) marriage.

heiraten verb (PERF hat geheiratet) to marry.

heiser adjective hoarse.

heiß adjective hot.

heißen ◇ verb (IMPERF hieß, PERF hat geheißen) 1 to be called; wie heißt du? what's your name?; 2 to mean; 3 das heißt that is; 4 es heißt it is said; 5 wie heißt 'dog' auf Deutsch? what's the German for 'dog'?

heiter adjective 1 bright; 2 cheerful.

heizen verb (PERF hat geheizt) 1 to heat (a room); 2 to put the heating on; 3 to have the heating on.

Heizung die heating.

hektisch adjective hectic.

Held der (PL die Helden) hero.

△ NEW SPELLING: See page xii

Heldin die (PL die Heldinnen)
heroine.

helfen ◇ verb (PRES hilft, IMPERF half,
PERF hat geholfen) 1 to help; **Lisa
hilft mir** Lisa is helping me; **2 es
hilft nichts** it's no good; **du hier
sich zu helfen wissen** to know what to
do; **ich weiß mir nicht zu helfen** I don't
know what to do.

Helfer der (PL die Helfer) 1 helper;
2 assistant.

Helferin die (PL die Helferinnen)
1 helper; 2 assistant.

hell adjective 1 light (colour);
2 bright; 3 **eine helle Stimme** a
clear voice; 4 **helles Bier** lager;
5 **da ist heller Wahnsinn**
(informal) that's sheer madness.

hellwach adjective wide awake.

Helm der (PL die Helme) helmet.

Hemd das (PL die Hemden) 1 shirt;
2 vest.

Henkel der (PL die Henkel) handle.

Henne die (PL die Hennen) hen.

her adverb 1 here; **komm her** come
here; 2 **vor jemandem her** in front
of somebody; 3 **hinter etwas her
sein** to be after something; 4 **von
der Farbe her** as far as the colour is
concerned; 5 **wo bist du her?**
where do you come from?; 6 **wo hat
Klaus das her?** where did Klaus get
it from?; 7 **her damit!** (informal)
give it to me!; 8 ago; **das ist schon
lange her** it was a long time ago; **das
ist drei Tage her** it was three days
ago.

herab adverb down.

herablassend adjective
condescending.

herabsetzen verb (PERF hat
herabgesetzt) 1 to reduce; 2 to
belittle.

heran adverb 1 **an etwas heran**
close to something, right up to
something; **bis an die Wand heran**
up to the wall; 2 **immer heran!**
come closer!

herankommen ◇ verb (IMPERF
kam heran, PERF ist
herangekommen) 1 to come near;
2 **herankommen an** to come up to;
3 **ich komme nicht heran** I can't get
at it.

herauf adverb up.

heraufkommen ◇ verb (IMPERF
kam herauf, PERF ist
heraufgekommen) to come up.

heraus adverb out.

herausbekommen ◇ verb (IMPERF
bekam heraus, PERF hat
herausbekommen) 1 to get out;
2 to find out; 3 to solve; 4 **Geld
herausbekommen** to get change.

herausfinden ◇ verb (IMPERF fand
heraus, PERF hat herausgefunden)
1 to find out; 2 to find your way out.

herausgeben ◇ verb (PRES gibt
heraus, IMPERF gab heraus, PERF hat
herausgegeben) 1 to hand over;
2 to bring out.

herauskommen ◇ verb (IMPERF
kam heraus, PERF ist
herausgekommen) to come out.

herausnehmen ◇ verb (PRES

◇ IRREGULAR VERB: See the verb table in the centre of the dictionary

nimmt heraus, IMPERF nahm heraus, PERF hat herausgenommen) **1** to take out; **sie hat ihren Lippenstift aus der Tasche herausgenommen** she took her lipstick out of the bag; **2 sich die Mandeln lassen** to have your tonsils out; **3 es sich herausnehmen, etwas zu tun** to have the nerve to do something; **du nimmst dir zu viel heraus** you're going to far.

herausstellen *verb* (PERF hat herausgestellt) **1** to put out; **2 sich herausstellen** to turn out; **es stellte sich heraus, dass ...** it turned out that ...

herausziehen ◇ *verb* (IMPERF zog heraus, PERF hat herausgezogen) to pull out.

herb *adjective* **1** sharp; **2** dry (*wine*).

herbei *adverb* over (here); **kommt herbei!** come over here!

Herberge *die* (PL *die* Herbergen) hostel.

Herbergsmutter *die* (PL *die* Herbergsmütter) warden (*in a youth hostel*).

Herbergsvater *der* (PL *die* Herbergsväter) warden (*in a youth hostel*).

herbringen ◇ *verb* (IMPERF brachte her, PERF hat hergebracht) to bring (here).

Herbst *der* (PL *die* Herbste) autumn; **im Herbst** in autumn.

Herd *der* (PL *die* Herde) cooker.

Herde *die* (PL *die* Herden) **1** herd; **2** flock.

herein *adverb* in; **herein!** come in!

hereinfallen ◇ *verb* (PRES fällt herein, IMPERF fiel herein, PERF ist hereingefallen) to be taken in; **auf einen Betrüger hereinfallen** to be taken in by a swindler.

hereinkommen ◇ *verb* (IMPERF kam herein, PERF ist hereingekommen) to come in.

hereinlassen ◇ *verb* (PRES lässt herein Δ, IMPERF ließ herein, PERF hat hereingelassen) to let in; **Max lässt mich nicht ins Zimmer herein** Max won't let me into the room.

Herfahrt *die* (PL *die* Herfahrten) **1** journey here; **2** way here.

hergeben ◇ *verb* (PRES gibt her, IMPERF gab her, PERF hat hergegeben) **1** to hand over; **gib die Tasche her!** hand over the bag!; **2** to give away; **3 sich für etwas hergeben** to get involved in something; **dazu gebe ich mich nicht her** I won't have anything to do with it.

Hering *der* (PL *die* Heringe) herring.

herkommen ◇ *verb* (IMPERF kam her, PERF ist hergekommen) to come (here); **wo kommt das her?** where does it come from?

Herkunft *die* (PL *die* Herkünfte) **1** origin; **2** background.

Heroin *das* heroin.

Herr *der* (PL *die* Herren) **1** gentleman; **2 Herr Huber** Mr Huber; **3 Sehr geehrte Herren** Dear Sirs (*in a letter*); **4 meine Herren**

Δ NEW SPELLING: *See page xii*

gentlemen!; **5** master; **6 der Herr** the Lord.

herrichten verb (PERF **hat hergerichtet**) to get ready, to prepare; **sie richtet die Betten für die Gäste her** she's getting the beds for the guests ready.

herrlich adjective marvellous.

herrschen verb (PERF **hat geherrscht**) **1** to rule; **2** to be; **es herrschte große Aufregung** there was great excitement.

herstellen verb (PERF **hat hergestellt**) to manufacture, to make; **in Deutschland hergestellt** made in Germany.

Herstellung die (PL die **Herstellungen**) manufacture, production.

herüber adverb over (here).

herum adverb **um … herum** round; **falsch herum** the wrong way round; **im Kreis herum** in a circle.

herumdrehen verb (PERF **hat herumgedreht**) **1** to turn (over or round); **2 sich herumdrehen** to turn round.

herumführen verb (PERF **hat herumgeführt**) to show around.

herumgehen ◇ verb (IMPERF **ging herum**, PERF **ist herumgegangen**) **1** to go round; **2** to walk around; **im Park herumgehen** to walk around the park; **3** to pass (of time).

herunter adverb down; **die Treppe herunter** down the stairs.

herunterfallen ◇ verb (PRES **fällt**

herunter, IMPERF **fiel herunter**, PERF **ist heruntergefallen**) **1** to fall down; **2** to fall off.

herunterkommen ◇ verb (IMPERF **kam herunter**, PERF **ist heruntergekommen**) **1** to come down; **2** (informal) to go to rack and ruin.

herunterlassen ◇ verb (PRES **lässt herunter** △, IMPERF **ließ herunter**, PERF **hat heruntergelassen**) to let down, to lower.

hervor adverb out.

hervorragend adjective outstanding.
adverb outstandingly well.

hervorrufen ◇ verb (IMPERF **rief hervor**, PERF **hat hervorgerufen**) to cause.

Herz das (PL die **Herzen**) **1** heart; **2** hearts (in cards).

Herzanfall der (PL die **Herzanfälle**) heart attack.

herzlich adjective **1** warm; **2** sincere; **3 herzlichen Dank** many thanks; **4 herzliche Grüße** best wishes; **5 herzlichen Glückwunsch!** congratulations!; **6 herzlich willkommen in Passau!** welcome to Passau!

herzlos adjective heartless.

Herzschlag der (PL die **Herzschläge**) **1** heartbeat; **2** heart failure; **er hat einen Herzschlag bekommen** he had a heart attack.

heterosexuell adjective heterosexual.

◇ IRREGULAR VERB: See the verb table in the centre of the dictionary

Heterosexuelle der/die (PL die Heterosexuellen) heterosexual.

Heu das hay.

heulen verb (PERF **hat geheult**) 1 to howl; 2 (informal) to cry.

Heuschnupfen der hay fever.

heute adverb today; **heute Abend** this evening; **heute Morgen** this morning.

heutig adjective 1 today's; 2 **in der heutigen Zeit** nowadays.

heutzutage nowadays.

Hexe die (PL die **Hexen**) witch.

Hexenschuss ∆ der lumbago.

hielt SEE **halten**.

hier adverb here.

hierher adverb here; **komm sofort hierher!** come here immediately!

hierhin adverb here.

hiesig adjective local.

hieß SEE **heißen**.

Hilfe die (PL die **Hilfen**) 1 help; 2 aid.

hilflos adjective helpless.

hilfsbereit adjective helpful.

hilft SEE **helfen**.

Himbeere die (PL die **Himbeeren**) raspberry.

Himmel der (PL die **Himmel**) 1 sky; 2 heaven.

himmlisch adjective heavenly.

hin adverb 1 there; **hin und zurück** there and back; 2 **hin und wieder** now and again; 3 **hin und her** back

and forth, to and fro; 4 **auf meinen Rat hin** on my advice; **auf Ihren Brief hin** in reply to your letter; 5 **wo ist Dominik hin?** where's Dominik gone?; 6 **es ist nicht mehr lange hin** it's not long to go; 7 **ich bin hin** (informal) I'm worn out.

hinauf adverb up; **die Straße hinauf** up the road.

hinaufgehen ◇ verb (IMPERF **ging hinauf**, PERF **ist hinaufgegangen**) to go up.

hinaus adverb 1 out; 2 **auf Jahre hinaus** for years to come.

hinausgehen ◇ verb (IMPERF **ging hinaus**, PERF **ist hinausgegangen**) 1 to go out; 2 **über etwas hinausgehen** to exceed something; 3 **das Zimmer geht nach Norden hinaus** the room faces north.

hindern verb (PERF **hat gehindert**) to stop; **jemanden daran hindern, etwas zu tun** to stop somebody from doing something.

Hindernis das (PL die **Hindernisse**) obstacle.

hinduistisch adjective Hindu.

hindurch adverb 1 through it/them; 2 **das ganze Jahr hindurch** throughout the year.

hinein adverb 1 in; 2 **in etwas hinein** into something.

hineingehen ◇ verb (IMPERF **ging hinein**, PERF **ist hineingegangen**) 1 to go in; 2 **in etwas hineingehen** to go into something.

∆ NEW SPELLING: See page xii

hinfahren ◇ verb (PRES **fährt hin**, IMPERF **fuhr hin**, PERF **ist hingefahren**) 1 to go/drive there; 2 (PERF **hat hingefahren**) to take/drive there.

Hinfahrt die (PL die **Hinfahrten**) 1 journey there, way there; 2 outward journey.

hinfallen ◇ verb (PRES **fällt hin**, IMPERF **fiel hin**, PERF **ist hingefallen**) to fall over.

hing SEE **hängen**.

hingehen ◇ verb (IMPERF **ging hin**, PERF **ist hingegangen**) 1 to go there; **wo geht ihr hin?** where are you going?; 2 to go by (of time).

hinken verb (PERF **hat/ist gehinkt**) to limp.

hinkommen ◇ verb (IMPERF **kam hin**, PERF **ist hingekommen**) 1 to get there; 2 to go; **wo kommt das Buch hin?** where does the book go?; 3 **mit etwas hinkommen** (informal) to manage (with something).

hinlegen verb (PERF **hat hingelegt**) 1 to put down; **leg die Zeitung unten hin** put the paper down there; 2 **sich hinlegen** to lie down.

hinsetzen verb (PERF **hat sich hingesetzt**) **sich hinsetzen** to sit down; **Petra setzte sich neben ihm hin** Petra sat down next to him.

hinten adverb at the back; **von hinten** from behind.

hinter preposition ←(+DAT or +ACC) 1 behind; 2 **etwas hinter sich bringen** to get something over with.

hintere SEE **hinterer**.

hintereinander adverb 1 one behind the other; 2 one after the other; **dreimal hintereinander** three times in a row.

hinterer, hintere, hinteres adjective 1 back; 2 **am hinteren Ende** at the far end.

Hintergrund der (PL die **Hintergründe**) background.

hinterher adverb afterwards.

Hintern der (PL die **Hintern**) bottom.

Hinterrad das (PL die **Hinterräder**) back wheel.

hinters = hinter das.

hinüber adverb 1 over (there), across (there); 2 **das Radio ist hinüber** (informal) the radio has had it.

hinübergehen ◇ verb (IMPERF **ging hinüber**, PERF **ist hinübergegangen**) to go over, to go across.

hinunter adverb down.

Hinweg der (PL die **Hinwege**) way there; **auf dem Hinweg** on the way there.

Hinweis der (PL die **Hinweise**) 1 hint; **das war ein deutlicher Hinweis, dass er lieber allein fährt** it was an obvious hint that he prefers to go on his own; 2 reference; 3 **Hinweise zur Bedienung** operating instructions.

hinweisen ◇ verb (IMPERF **wies hin**, PERF **hat hingewiesen**) to point; **jemanden auf etwas hinweisen** to point something out to somebody.

Hirn das (PL die **Hirne**) brain.

◇ IRREGULAR VERB: See the verb table in the centre of the dictionary

Hirsch der (PL die Hirsche) 1 deer;
2 stag; 3 venison.

historisch adjective historical.

Hitze die heat.

hitzefrei adjective hitzefrei haben
to have the day off school because of
hot weather.

Hitzewelle die (PL die Hitzewellen)
heatwave.

Hitzschlag der (PL die Hitzschläge)
heatstroke.

hob SEE heben.

Hobby das (PL die Hobbys) hobby.

hoch adjective (with endings 'hoch'
becomes 'hoher/hohe/hohes') 1 high;
der Zaun ist zu hoch the fence is
too high; ein hoher Zaun a high
fence; 2 deep (snow); 3 great (age,
weight).
adverb 1 highly; hoch begabt highly
gifted; 2 die Treppe hoch up the
stairs.

Hoch das (PL die Hochs) 1 cheer; ein
dreifaches Hoch für das
Geburtstagskind three cheers for
the birthday girl/boy; 2 high
(pressure).

hochachtungsvoll adverb
Hochachtungsvoll Yours faithfully.

hochhackig adjective high-heeled;
hochhackige Schuhe high-heeled
shoes.

Hochhaus das (PL die Hochhäuser)
high-rise building.

hochheben ◇ verb (IMPERF hob
hoch, PERF hat hochgehoben) to lift
up; sie hob das Kind hoch she lifted
up the child.

hochnäsig adjective stuck-up.

Hochschule die (PL die
Hochschulen) university, college.

Hochsprung der (PL die
Hochsprünge) high jump.

höchst adverb extremely.

höchstens adverb 1 at most;
2 except perhaps.

höchster, höchste, höchstes
adjective highest; Mount Everest
ist der der höchste Berg der Welt
Mount Everest is the highest
mountain in the world; es ist
höchste Zeit it is high time.

Höchstgeschwindigkeit die
maximum speed.

Höchsttemperatur die (PL die
Höchsttemperaturen) maximum
temperature.

Hochzeit die (PL die Hochzeiten)
wedding.

Hochzeitstag der (PL die
Hochzeitstage) 1 wedding day;
2 wedding anniversary.

Hocker der (PL die Hocker) stool.

Hockey das hockey.

Hockeyschläger der (PL die
Hockeyschläger) hockey stick.

Hof der (PL die Höfe) 1 yard; 2 farm.

hoffen verb (PERF hat gehofft) to
hope; auf etwas hoffen to hope for
something.

hoffentlich adverb hopefully;
hoffentlich nicht I hope not.

Hoffnung die (PL die Hoffnungen)
hope.

△ NEW SPELLING: See page xii

hoffnungslos *adjective* hopeless.

höflich *adjective* polite.

Höflichkeit *die* (PL *die* Höflichkeiten) politeness, courtesy.

Höhe *die* (PL *die* Höhen) 1 height; 2 das ist die Höhe! (*informal*) that's the limit!

hoher, hohe, hohes SEE hoch.

höher *adjective* 1 higher; 2 deeper.

hohl *adjective* hollow.

Höhle *die* (PL *die* Höhlen) 1 cave; 2 den.

holen *verb* (PERF hat geholt) 1 to get, to fetch; 2 jemanden holen lassen to send for somebody; 3 sich etwas holen to get something.

Holland *das* Holland.

Holländer *der* (PL *die* Holländer) Dutchman.

Holländerin *die* (PL *die* Holländerinnen) Dutchwoman.

holländisch *adjective* Dutch.

Hölle *die* (PL *die* Höllen) hell.

Holz *das* (PL *die* Hölzer) wood.

Holzkohle *die* charcoal.

homöopathisch *adjective* homeopathic.

homosexuell *adjective* homosexual.

Homosexuelle *der/die* (PL *die* Homosexuellen) homosexual.

Honig *der* (PL *die* Honige) honey.

horchen *verb* (PERF hat gehorcht) 1 to listen; 2 to eavesdrop.

hören *verb* (PERF hat gehört) 1 to hear; 2 to listen (to).

Hörer *der* (PL *die* Hörer) 1 listener; 2 receiver (*of a phone*).

Hörerin *die* (PL *die* Hörerinnen) listener.

Horizont *der* (PL *die* Horizonte) horizon.

Horn *das* (PL *die* Hörner) horn.

Horoskop *das* (PL *die* Horoskope) horoscope.

Hose *die* (PL *die* Hosen) trousers.

Hosenträger *plural noun* braces.

Hotel *das* (PL *die* Hotels) hotel.

Hotelverzeichnis *das* (PL *die* Hotelverzeichnisse) list of hotels.

hübsch *adjective* 1 pretty; 2 nice.

Hubschrauber *der* (PL *die* Hubschrauber) helicopter.

Huf *der* (PL *die* Hufe) hoof.

Hufeisen *das* (PL *die* Hufeisen) horseshoe.

Hüfte *die* (PL *die* Hüften) hip.

Hügel *der* (PL *die* Hügel) hill.

Huhn *das* (PL *die* Hühner) 1 chicken; 2 hen.

Hummel *die* (PL *die* Hummeln) bumble-bee.

Hummer *der* (PL *die* Hummer) lobster.

Humor *der* humour; Humor haben to have a sense of humour.

Hund *der* (PL *die* Hunde) dog.

✧ IRREGULAR VERB: *See the verb table in the centre of the dictionary*

Hundehütte *die* (PL *die* Hundehütten) kennel.

hundemüde *adjective* (*informal*) dog-tired.

hundert *number* a hundred, one hundred.

Hunger *der* hunger; Hunger haben to be hungry.

hungrig *adjective* hungry.

Hupe *die* (PL *die* Hupen) horn.

hurra *exclamation* hooray!

husten *verb* (PERF hat gehustet) to cough.

Husten *der* cough.

Hut *der* (PL *die* Hüte) hat.

hüten *verb* (PERF hat gehütet) 1 to look after (*a child, children*); 2 sich hüten to be on your guard; 3 sich hüten, etwas zu tun to take care not to do something.

Hütte *die* (PL *die* Hütten) hut.

hygienisch *adjective* hygienic.

hypnotisieren *verb* (PERF hat hypnotisiert) to hypnotize.

Hypothek *die* (PL *die* Hypotheken) mortgage.

hysterisch *adjective* hysterical.

I i

ich *pronoun* I.

IC-Zug *der* (PL *die* IC-Züge) (*Intercityzug*) intercity train.

ideal *adjective* ideal.

Idee *die* (PL *die* Ideen) idea.

identifizieren *verb* (PERF hat identifiziert) to identify.

identisch *adjective* identical.

Idiot *der* (PL *die* Idioten) idiot.

idiotisch *adjective* idiotic.

idyllisch *adjective* idyllic.

Igel *der* (PL *die* Igel) hedgehog.

ihm *pronoun* 1 him, to him; 2 it, to it.

ihn *pronoun* 1 him; 2 it.

ihnen *pronoun* them, to them.

ihr *pronoun* 1 you (*plural*); 2 her, to her; 3 (*standing for an object*) it, to it.
adjective 1 her; 2 its; 3 their; sie haben ihr Auto verkauft they sold their car.

Ihr *adjective* your; Ihr Sohn hat mir geschrieben your son wrote to me.

ihrer, ihre, ihr(e)s *pronoun* 1 hers; mein Rad ist rot, ihrs ist blau my bike is red, hers is blue; 2 theirs; das ist nicht ihre Katze, ihre ist

△ NEW SPELLING: *See page xii*

schwarz that's not their cat, theirs is black.

Ihrer, Ihre, Ihr(e)s *pronoun* yours; **mein Job ist nicht so interessant wie Ihrer** my job's not as interesting as yours.

ihretwegen *adverb* 1 for her sake; 2 for their sake; 3 because of her; 4 because of them.

Ihretwegen *adverb* 1 for your sake; 2 because of you.

Illusion *die* (PL *die* Illusionen) illusion.

Illustration *die* (PL *die* Illustrationen) illustration.

Illustrierte *die* (PL *die* Illustrierten) magazine.

im = in dem; **was läuft im Kino?** what's on at the cinema?; **im August** in August.

Imbiss *der* (PL *die* Imbisse) 1 snack; 2 snack bar.

Imbissstube △ *die* (PL *die* Imbissstuben) snack bar.

imitieren *verb* (PERF hat imitiert) to imitate.

immer *adverb* 1 always; 2 **immer wieder** again and again; 3 **immer mehr** more and more; **immer dunkler** darker and darker; 4 **immer noch** still; 5 **immer, wenn er anruft** every time he rings; 6 **wo/wer/wann immer** wherever/whoever/whenever; 7 **für immer** for ever.

immerhin *adverb* at least.

immerzu *adverb* all the time.

impfen *verb* (PERF hat geimpft) to vaccinate.

Impfung *die* (PL *die* Impfungen) vaccination.

imponieren *verb* (PERF hat imponiert) to impress; **jemandem imponieren** to impress somebody.

Import *der* (PL *die* Importe) import.

importieren *verb* (PERF hat importiert) to import.

imprägniert *adjective* waterproof.

imstande *adverb* **imstande sein, etwas zu tun** to be able to do something; **er ist nicht imstande, seine Hausaufgaben allein zu machen** he's not able to do his homework on his own.

in *preposition* ←(+DAT or +ACC) (*the dative is used when talking about position; the accusative shows movement towards something*) 1 in; **es ist in der Küche** it's in the kitchen; **im August** in August, this year; **ich habe es in meine Tasche gesteckt** I've put it in my bag; 3 **in die Schule gehen** to go to school; 4 **Susi ist in der Schule** Susi is at school; 5 **in diesem Jahr** this year; 6 **in sein** to be in; **der Rap ist in** rap is in.

inbegriffen *adjective* included; **Essen ist inbegriffen** food is included.

indem *conjunction* 1 while; 2 by.

Inder *der* (PL *die* Inder) Indian.

Inderin *die* (PL *die* Inderinnen) Indian.

Indianer *der* (PL *die* Indianer)

◇ IRREGULAR VERB: *See the verb table in the centre of the dictionary*

(American) Indian, native American.

Indianerin die (PL die Indianerinnen) (American) Indian, native American.

indianisch adjective (American) Indian, native American.

Indien das India.

indisch adjective Indian.

indiskutabel adjective out of the question.

individuell adjective individual.

Individuum das (PL die Individuen) individual.

Industrie die (PL die Industrien) industry.

industriell adjective industrial.

Infektion die (PL die Infektionen) infection.

Infinitiv der (PL die Infinitive) infinitive.

infizieren verb (PERF hat infiziert) 1 to infect; 2 sich bei jemandem infizieren to be infected by somebody.

infolge preposition ←(+GEN) as a result of.

infolgedessen adverb consequently.

Informatik die computer science.

Informatiker der (PL die Informatiker) computer scientist.

Informatikerin die (PL die Informatikerinnen) computer scientist.

Information die (PL die Informationen) (piece of) information.

Informationsbüro das (PL die Informationsbüros) (tourist) information office.

informieren verb (PERF hat informiert) 1 to inform; 2 informiert sein to be aware; da bist du falsch informiert you've been wrongly informed; 3 sich über etwas informieren to find out about something; ich habe mich darüber genau informieren lassen I found out all about it.

Ingenieur der (PL die Ingenieure) engineer.

Ingenieurin die (PL die Ingenieurinnen) engineer.

Ingwer der ginger.

Inhaber der (PL die Inhaber) 1 owner (of a shop); 2 holder (of an office).

Inhaberin die (PL die Inhaberinnen) 1 owner (of a shop); 2 holder (of a position).

Inhalt der (PL die Inhalte) 1 contents; den Inhalt der Dose mit etwas Wasser verdünnen dilute the contents of the tin with a little water; 2 content (of a story, film); er hat uns eine kurze Zusammenfassung des Inhalts der Geschichte gegeben he gave us a quick summary of the content of the story; 3 volume; 4 area (of a rectangle, circle, etc.).

△ NEW SPELLING: See page xii

inklusive *preposition* ←(+GEN)
including.
adverb inclusive.

innen *adverb* inside; **nach innen**
inwards.

Innenstadt *die* (PL *die* **Innenstädte**)
town centre, city centre.

Innere *das* 1 interior; 2 inside.

innerer, innere, inneres
adjective 1 inner; 2 inside;
3 internal (*injuries*).

innerhalb *preposition* ←(+GEN)
1 within; 2 during.
adverb **innerhalb von** within.

innerlich *adjective* 1 internal;
2 inner.
adverb 1 internally; 2 inwardly.

ins = **in das**; **ins Theater gehen** to go
to the theatre.

Insekt *das* (PL *die* **Insekten**) insect.

Insel *die* (PL *die* **Inseln**) island.

Inserat *das* (PL *die* **Inserate**)
advertisement.

inserieren *verb* (PERF **hat inseriert**)
to advertise.

insgesamt *adverb* in all.

Instinkt *der* (PL *die* **Instinkte**)
instinct.

instinktiv *adjective* instinctive.

Instrument *das* (PL *die*
Instrumente) instrument.

intelligent *adjective* intelligent.

Intelligenz *die* intelligence.

Intercityzug *der* (PL *die*
Intercityzüge) intercity train.

interessant *adjective* interesting.

Interesse *das* (PL *die* **Interessen**)
interest.

interessieren *verb* (PERF **hat
interessiert**) 1 to interest; 2 **sich
für etwas interessieren** to be
interested in something.

Internat *das* (PL *die* **Internate**)
boarding school.

international *adjective*
international.

Internet *das* internet.

Interview *das* (PL *die* **Interviews**)
interview.

inzwischen *adverb* in the
meantime, meanwhile.

Ire *der* (PL *die* **Iren**) Irishman; **die Iren**
the Irish.

irgend *adverb* 1 at all; **wenn irgend
möglich** if at all possible; **wenn du
irgend kannst** if you could possibly
manage it; 2 **irgend so ein Idiot**
some such idiot.

irgendein *adjective* 1 some; 2 any;
3 **irgendein anderer** someone else,
anyone else.

**irgendeiner, irgendeine,
irgendein(e)s** *pronoun* 1 any
one; '**welche möchten Sie?**' –
'**irgendeine**' 'which one would you
like?' – 'any one'; 2 somebody,
someone; 3 anybody, anyone; **hat
irgendeiner angerufen?** has
anybody phoned?

◇ IRREGULAR VERB: *See the verb table in the centre of the dictionary*

irgendetwas Δ *pronoun*
1 something; 2 anything.

irgendjemand Δ *pronoun*
1 somebody; 2 anybody, anyone.

irgendwann *adverb* 1 some time, at
some time; 2 any time, at any time.

irgendwas (*informal*) =
irgendetwas.

irgendwie *adverb* somehow.

irgendwo *adverb* 1 somewhere;
2 anywhere.

Irin *die* (PL *die* Irinnen) Irishwoman.

irisch *adjective* Irish.

Irland *das* Ireland.

ironisch *adjective* ironic.

irre *adjective* 1 mad; 2 (*informal*)
incredible, fantastic (*party, song*).
adverb **irre gut** incredibly good.

irren *verb* (PERF **ist geirrt**) 1 to
wander (about) (*when lost*); 2 (PERF
hat sich geirrt) **sich irren** to be
mistaken, to be wrong.

irrsinnig *adjective* 1 mad;
2 (*informal*) incredible.

Irrtum *der* (PL *die* Irrtümer) mistake.

Islam *der* Islam.

isst Δ SEE **essen**.

ist SEE **sein**.

Italien *das* Italy.

Italiener *der* (PL *die* Italiener)
Italian.

Italienerin *die* (PL *die*
Italienerinnen) Italian.

italienisch *adjective* Italian.

J j

ja *adverb* 1 yes; 2 **ich glaube ja** I
think so; 3 **du kommst doch, ja?**
you'll come, won't you?; **es passt
doch, ja?** it fits, doesn't it?; 4 **sag's
ihm ja nicht!** don't (you dare) tell
him, whatever you do!; **seid ja
vorsichtig!** do be careful!; 5 **es ist
ja noch früh** it's still early; **ich kann
ihn ja mal fragen, ob er mitkommen
will** I could always ask him if he
wants to come.

Jacht *die* (PL *die* Jachten) yacht.

Jacke *die* (PL *die* Jacken) 1 jacket;
2 cardigan.

Jackett *das* (PL *die* Jacketts) jacket.

Jagd *die* (PL *die* Jagden) 1 hunt;
2 hunting.

jagen *verb* (PERF **hat gejagt**) 1 to
hunt; 2 to chase; **drei Polizisten
jagten den Einbrecher, aber er
hängte sie schnell ab** three
policemen chased the burglar, but he
soon shook them off; **meine Mutter
hat mich aus dem Bett gejagt**
(*informal*) my mother chased me
out of bed; 3 **jemanden aus dem
Haus jagen** to throw somebody out
of the house; 4 **damit kannst du
mich jagen** (*informal*) I can't stand
that.

Jahr *das* (PL *die* Jahre) year; **in den
sechziger Jahren** in the sixties;

Δ NEW SPELLING: See page xii

Kinder bis zu zwölf Jahren children up to the age of twelve.

jahrelang *adverb* for years.

Jahrestag *der* (PL *die* Jahrestage) anniversary.

Jahreszeit *die* (PL *die* Jahreszeiten) season.

Jahrgang *der* (PL *die* Jahrgänge) 1 year; 2 vintage.

Jahrhundert *das* (PL *die* Jahrhunderte) century.

jährlich *adjective, adverb* yearly; zweimal jährlich twice a year.

Jahrmarkt *der* (PL *die* Jahrmärkte) fair.

Jahrtausend *das* (PL *die* Jahrtausende) millennium.

Jahrzehnt *das* (PL *die* Jahrzehnte) decade.

jähzornig *adjective* hot-tempered.

jammern *verb* (PERF hat gejammert) to moan.

Januar *der* January.

Japan *das* Japan.

Japaner *der* (PL *die* Japaner) Japanese.

Japanerin *die* (PL *die* Japanerinnen) Japanese.

japanisch *adjective* Japanese.

jawohl *adverb* 1 yes; 2 certainly.

je *adverb* 1 ever; besser denn je better than ever; 2 each; sie kosten je zwanzig Mark they are twenty marks each; 3 seit eh und je always; 4 je nach depending on.

preposition ←(+ACC) per.

conjunction 1 je mehr, desto besser the more the better; 2 je nachdem it depends.

Jeans *plural noun* jeans.

jede SEE jeder.

jedenfalls *adverb* in any case.

jeder, jede, jedes *adjective*
1 every; jedes Mal △ every time;
2 each; 3 any; ohne jeden Grund without any reason.
pronoun 1 everybody, everyone;
2 each one; 3 anybody, anyone; das kann jeder anybody can do that.

jedermann *pronoun* everybody, everyone.

jederzeit *adverb* at any time.

jedes SEE jeder.

jedesmal SEE jeder.

jedoch *adverb* however.

jemals *adverb* ever.

jemand *pronoun* 1 somebody, someone; jemand hat das für dich abgegeben somebody left this for you; 2 anybody, anyone; hat jemand angerufen? did anybody call?

jener, jene, jenes *adjective* (*used in elevated language and in literature*) 1 that; 2 those (*plural*).
pronoun 1 that one; 2 those (*plural*).

jenseits *preposition* ←(+GEN) (on) the other side of.

jetzt *adverb* now.

⬦ IRREGULAR VERB: *See the verb table in the centre of the dictionary*

Job der (PL die Jobs) job.

jobben verb (informal) (PERF hat gejobbt) to work.

joggen verb (PERF ist gejoggt) to jog.

Jogginganzug der (PL die Jogginganzüge) tracksuit.

Joghurt der (PL die Joghurt) yoghurt.

Johannisbeere die (PL die Johannisbeeren) 1 rote Johannisbeeren redcurrants; 2 schwarze Johannisbeeren blackcurrants.

Journalist der (PL die Journalisten) journalist.

Journalistin die (PL die Journalistinnen) journalist.

jubeln verb (PERF hat gejubelt) 1 to cheer; 2 Beifall jubeln to applaud.

Jubiläum das (PL die Jubiläen) 1 anniversary; 2 jubilee.

Jude der (PL die Juden) Jew.

Jüdin die (PL die Jüdinnen) Jew.

jüdisch adjective Jewish.

Jugend die youth.

Jugendherberge die (PL die Jugendherbergen) youth hostel.

Jugendklub der (PL die Jugendklubs) youth club.

Jugendliche der/die (PL die Jugendlichen) 1 young man/woman; 2 die Jugendlichen youth, young people.

Jugoslawien das Yugoslavia.

jugoslawisch adjective Yugoslavian.

Juli der July.

jung adjective 1 young; 2 Jung und Alt △ young and old.

Junge[1] der (PL die Jungen) boy.

Junge[2] das (PL die Jungen) young (animal).

Jungfrau die (PL die Jungfrauen) 1 virgin; 2 Virgo.

jüngster, jüngste, jüngstes adjective 1 youngest; 2 latest (news, developments); 3 in jüngster Zeit recently.

Juni der June.

Jury die (PL die Jurys) 1 jury; 2 judges (in sport).

Juwelier der (PL die Juweliere) jeweller.

Jux der (informal) laugh; aus Jux for a laugh.

K k

Kabel das (PL die Kabel) 1 cable; 2 wire.

Kabelfernsehen das cable television.

Kabeljau der (PL die Kabeljaus) cod.

Kabine die (PL die Kabinen) 1 cabin; 2 cubicle (for changing); 3 car (of a cable car).

Kachel die (PL die Kacheln) tile.

△ NEW SPELLING: See page xii

Käfer der (PL die **Käfer**) beetle.

Kaffee der (PL die **Kaffee(s)**) coffee; **zwei Kaffee mit Milch bitte** two white coffees please.

Kaffeekanne die (PL die **Kaffeekannen**) coffee-pot.

Käfig der (PL die **Käfige**) cage.

kahl adjective 1 bald (head); 2 bare (tree, walls).

Kaiser der (PL die **Kaiser**) emperor.

Kaiserin die (PL die **Kaiserinnen**) empress.

Kakao der (PL die **Kakao(s)**) cocoa; **zwei Kakao bitte** two cups of cocoa please.

Kakerlak der (PL die **Kakerlaken**) cockroach.

Kaktus der (PL die **Kakteen**) cactus.

Kalb das (PL die **Kälber**) 1 calf; 2 veal.

Kalbfleisch das veal.

Kalender der (PL die **Kalender**) 1 calendar; 2 diary.

Kalk der 1 lime; 2 limescale; 3 calcium.

Kalorie die (PL die **Kalorien**) calorie.

kalorienarm adjective low-calorie.

kalt adjective cold; **ist dir kalt?** are you cold?; **stell die Heizung an, den Kindern ist kalt** put on the heating, the children are cold; **abends essen wir kalt** we have a cold meal in the evening; **den Wein kalt stellen** to chill the wine.

Kälte die 1 cold; 2 coldness; 3 **fünf Grad Kälte** five degrees below zero.

kam SEE **kommen**.

Kamel das (PL die **Kamele**) camel.

Kamera die (PL die **Kameras**) camera.

Kamerad der (PL die **Kameraden**) friend.

Kameramann der (PL die **Kameramänner**) cameraman.

Kamin der (PL die **Kamine**) fireplace; **wir saßen am Kamin** we sat by the fire.

Kamm der (PL die **Kämme**) 1 comb; 2 ridge (of a mountain).

kämmen verb (PERF hat **gekämmt**) 1 to comb; 2 **sich kämmen** to comb your hair.

Kammer die (PL die **Kammern**) 1 store room; 2 chamber.

Kampf der (PL die **Kämpfe**) 1 fight; 2 contest; 3 struggle.

kämpfen verb (PERF hat **gekämpft**) to fight.

Kanada das Canada.

Kanadier der (PL die **Kanadier**) Canadian.

Kanadierin die (PL die **Kanadierinnen**) Canadian.

kanadisch adjective Canadian.

Kanal der (PL die **Kanäle**) 1 canal; 2 channel (radio, TV); 3 **der Kanal** the (English) Channel; 4 sewer, drain.

Kanalinseln plural noun Channel Islands.

◇ IRREGULAR VERB: See the verb table in the centre of the dictionary

Kanalisation *die* sewers, drains.

Kanarienvogel *der* (PL *die* Kanarienvögel) canary.

Kandidat *der* (PL *die* Kandidaten) candidate.

Kandidatin *die* (PL *die* Kandidatinnen) candidate.

Känguru Δ *das* (PL *die* Kängurus) kangaroo.

Kaninchen *das* (PL *die* Kaninchen) rabbit.

kann SEE **können**.

Kännchen *das* (PL *die* Kännchen) **1** pot; ein Kännchen Kaffee bitte a pot of coffee please; **2** jug (*of milk*).

Kanne *die* (PL *die* Kannen) **1** pot (*for coffee, tea*); **2** jug (*for water*); **3** can (*for oil*); **4** churn (*for milk*); **5** watering can.

kannst SEE **können**.

kannte SEE **kennen**.

Kante *die* (PL *die* Kanten) edge.

Kantine *die* (PL *die* Kantinen) canteen; wir essen immer in der Kantine zu Mittag we always have lunch in the canteen.

Kanu *das* (PL *die* Kanus) canoe; **Kanu fahren** to go canoeing.

Kapelle *die* (PL *die* Kapellen) chapel.

kapieren *verb* (*informal*) (PERF hat kapiert) to understand; er hat es mir schon dreimal erklärt, aber ich kapier es einfach nicht he's already explained it to me three times, but I still don't get it.

Kapital *das* capital.

Kapitalismus *der* capitalism.

Kapitän *der* (PL *die* Kapitäne) captain.

Kapitel *das* (PL *die* Kapitel) chapter.

Kappe *die* (PL *die* Kappen) cap.

kaputt *adjective* **1** broken; **2** an meinem Computer ist etwas kaputt there's something wrong with my computer; **3** ich bin kaputt (*informal*) I'm shattered.

kaputtgehen ◇ *verb* (IMPERF ging kaputt, PERF ist kaputtgegangen) **1** to break; **2** to pack up; mein Fernseher ist mitten im Fußballspiel kaputtgegangen the television packed up in the middle of the football match; **3** to wear out (*of clothing*); **4** to break up (*of a marriage or friendship*).

kaputtmachen *verb* (PERF hat kaputtgemacht) **1** to break; er macht alle seine Spielsachen kaputt he breaks all his toys; **2** to ruin (*clothes, furniture*); **3** to finish off (*a person*); die viele Arbeit macht mich ganz kaputt all this work is wearing me out; **4** sich kaputtmachen to wear yourself out.

Kapuze *die* (PL *die* Kapuzen) hood.

Karamell Δ *der* (PL *die* Karamells) caramel.

Karfreitag *der* Good Friday.

Karibik *die* die Karibik the Caribbean.

karibisch *adjective* Caribbean.

kariert *adjective* **1** check; ein

Δ NEW SPELLING: *See page xii*

karierter Rock a check skirt;
2 squared (*paper*).

Karneval der (PL die **Karnevale**)
carnival.

Karo das (PL die **Karos**) **1** square;
2 diamonds (*in cards*).

Karotte die (PL die **Karotten**) carrot.

Karriere die (PL die **Karrieren**)
career; **Karriere machen** to get to
the top.

Karte die (PL die **Karten**) **1** card; **ich
schicke euch eine Karte aus
Italien** I'll send you a card from
Italy; **2** card (*for playing*); **wir haben
den ganzen Abend Karten gespielt**
we played cards all evening;
gute/schlechte Karten haben to
have a good/bad hand; **3** ticket; **gibt
es noch Karten für das
Popfestival?** can you still get tickets
for the pop festival?; **4** menu; **5** map;
**ich kann Oberammergau nicht auf
der Karte finden** I can't find
Oberammergau on the map; **6** alles
auf eine Karte setzen** to put all your
eggs in one basket.

Kartenspiel das (PL die
Kartenspiele) **1** card game; **2** pack
of cards.

Kartoffel die (PL die **Kartoffeln**)
potato.

Kartoffelbrei der mashed
potatoes.

Karton der (PL die **Kartons**)
1 cardboard; **2** cardboard box.

Karussell das (PL die **Karussells**)
merry-go-round; **Karussell fahren**
to go on the merry-go-round.

Käse der cheese.

Käsekuchen der (PL die
Käsekuchen) cheesecake.

Kasse die (PL die **Kassen**) **1** till;
2 checkout; **an der Kasse zahlen**
pay at the checkout; **3** cash desk (*in
a bank*); **4** box-office; **Sie können
die Karten an der Kasse abholen**
you can collect the tickets from the
box office; **5** ticket office (*at a sports
stadium*); **Sie müssen sich an der
Kasse anstellen** you have to queue
at the ticket office; **6** health
insurance; **7** knapp bei Kasse sein
(*informal*) to be short of money; **gut
bei Kasse sein** (*informal*) to be in
the money.

Kassenzettel der (PL die
Kassenzettel) receipt.

Kassette die (PL die **Kassetten**)
1 cassette, tape; **ich habe den neuen
Song auf Kassette aufgenommen**
I've taped the new song; **2** box (*for
money, jewellery*).

Kassettenrekorder der (PL die
Kassettenrekorder) cassette
recorder.

kassieren verb (PERF hat kassiert)
1 to collect the money; **2** to collect
the fares; **3 wie viel hat er kassiert?**
how much did he charge you?;
4 darf ich bei Ihnen kassieren?
would you like to pay now? (*your bill
in a restaurant*); **5** (*informal*) to take
away (*a driving licence, for
example*).

Kassierer der (PL die **Kassierer**)
cashier.

◊ IRREGULAR VERB: *See the verb table in the centre of the dictionary*

Kassiererin die (PL die Kassiererinnen) cashier.

Kastanie die (PL die Kastanien) chestnut.

Kasten der (PL die Kästen) 1 box; 2 crate; **ein Kasten Bier** a crate of beer; 3 bin; 4 letter-box; 5 **was aus dem Kasten haben** (informal) to be brainy.

Katalog der (PL die Kataloge) catalogue.

Katalysator der (PL die Katalysatoren) catalytic converter.

Katastrophe die (PL die Katastrophen) catastrophe.

katastrophal adjective, adverb 1 catastrophic; 2 **sie hat katastrophal schlecht abgeschnitten** she came out terribly badly.

Kategorie die (PL die Kategorien) category.

Kater der (PL die Kater) 1 tom-cat; 2 **einen Kater haben** (informal) to have a hangover.

Kathedrale die (PL die Kathedralen) cathedral.

Katholik der (PL die Katholiken) Catholic.

Katholikin die (PL die Katholikinnen) Catholic.

katholisch adjective Catholic.

Kätzchen das (PL die Kätzchen) kitten.

Katze die (PL die Katzen) cat.

kauen verb (PERF hat gekaut) to chew.

Kauf der (PL die Käufe) 1 purchase; 2 **ein guter Kauf** a bargain; 3 **etwas in Kauf nehmen** to put up with something.

kaufen verb (PERF hat gekauft) to buy.

Käufer der (PL die Käufer) buyer.

Käuferin die (PL die Käuferinnen) buyer.

Kauffrau die (PL die Kauffrauen) businesswoman.

Kaufhaus das (PL die Kaufhäuser) department store.

Kaufmann der (PL die Kaufleute) businessman.

Kaugummi der (PL die Kaugummis) chewing gum.

kaum adverb hardly, scarcely.

kauern verb (PERF hat gekauert) to crouch.

Kaution die (PL die Kautionen) 1 deposit; 2 bail.

Kegel der (PL die Kegel) 1 cone; 2 skittle.

Kegelbahn die skittle alley.

kegeln verb (PERF hat gekegelt) to play skittles.

Kehle die (PL die Kehlen) throat.

Keim der (PL die Keime) 1 shoot; 2 germ.

kein adjective 1 no; **auf keinen Fall** on no account; 2 **ich habe keine Zeit** I haven't got any time; **er hat**

△ NEW SPELLING: See page xii

kein Geld he hasn't got any money; **3 keine zehn Minuten** less than ten minutes.

keiner, keine, kein(e)s *pronoun* **1** nobody, no one; **2** none, not one; **3 von diesen Kleidern gefällt mir keins** I don't like any of these dresses; **4 keiner von beiden** neither (of them).

keinesfalls *adverb* on no account.

keineswegs *adverb* by no means.

keinmal *adverb* not once.

keins SEE **keiner**.

Keks *der* (PL die Kekse) biscuit.

Keller *der* (PL die Keller) cellar.

Kellergeschoss△ *das* (PL die Kellergeschosse) basement.

Kellner *der* (PL die Kellner) waiter.

Kellnerin *die* (PL die Kellnerinnen) waitress.

kennen ✧ *verb* (IMPERF kannte, PERF hat gekannt) **1** to know; **2 kennen lernen**△ to get to know; **sich kennen lernen** to get to know each other; **3 kennen lernen**△ to meet; **ich habe Ulrike in London kennen gelernt** I met Ulrike in London; **wo habt ihr euch kennen gelernt?** where did you meet?

kennenlernen SEE **kennen**.

Kenntnis *die* (PL die Kenntnisse) **1** knowledge; **2 etwas zur Kenntnis nehmen** to take note of something.

Kennzeichen *das* (PL die Kennzeichen) **1** mark;

2 characteristic; **3** registration (number) (*of a vehicle*).

Kerl *der* (PL die Kerle) **1** bloke; **2 Eva ist ein netter Kerl** Eva's a nice girl.

Kern *der* (PL die Kerne) **1** pip; **2** stone (*of an apricot, peach*); **3** kernel (*of a nut*).

Kernenergie *die* nuclear power.

Kernkraftwerk *das* (PL die Kernkraftwerke) nuclear power station.

Kernwaffen *plural noun* nuclear weapons.

Kerze *die* (PL die Kerzen) candle.

Kerzenhalter *der* (PL die Kerzenhalter) candlestick.

Kessel *der* (PL die Kessel) **1** kettle; **2** boiler.

Kette *die* (PL die Ketten) chain.

Keule *die* (PL die Keulen) **1** club; **2** leg (*of lamb*); **3** drumstick (*of chicken*).

kichern *verb* (PERF hat gekichert) to giggle.

Kiefer[1] *der* (PL die Kiefer) jaw.

Kiefer[2] *die* (PL die Kiefern) pine tree.

Kieselstein *der* (PL die Kieselsteine) pebble.

Kilo *das* (PL die Kilo(s)) kilo.

Kilogramm *das* (PL die Kilogramme) kilogram.

Kilometer *der* (PL die Kilometer) kilometre.

Kind *das* (PL die Kinder) child.

✧ IRREGULAR VERB: *See the verb table in the centre of the dictionary*

Kindergarten der (PL die Kindergärten) nursery school.

Kindergeld das child benefit.

kinderleicht adjective very easy; das ist kinderleicht it's child's play.

Kindertagesstätte die (PL die Kindertagesstätten) day nursery.

Kinderwagen der (PL die Kinderwagen) pram.

Kindheit die childhood.

kindisch adjective childish.

Kinn das (PL die Kinne) chin.

Kino das (PL die Kinos) cinema.

kippen verb 1 (PERF hat gekippt) to tip; 2 (PERF ist gekippt) to topple.

Kirche die (PL die Kirchen) church.

Kirsche die (PL die Kirschen) cherry.

Kissen das (PL die Kissen) 1 cushion; 2 pillow.

Kiste die (PL die Kisten) 1 crate; 2 box.

kitzeln verb (PERF hat gekitzelt) to tickle.

kitzlig adjective ticklish.

Kiwi die (PL die Kiwis) kiwi fruit.

klagen verb (PERF hat geklagt) to complain.

Klammer die (PL die Klammern) 1 peg (for washing); 2 grip (for hair); 3 bracket.

klang SEE klingen.

Klang der (PL die Klänge) sound.

Klappe die (PL die Klappen) 1 flap;

2 clapperboard; 3 (informal) trap (mouth); halt die Klappe! shut up!

klappen verb (PERF hat geklappt) 1 nach vorne klappen to tilt forward; 2 nach hinten klappen to tip back; 3 nach oben klappen to lift up; 4 nach unten klappen to put down; 5 to work out; hoffentlich klappt es I hope it'll work out.

Klappstuhl der (PL die Klappstühle) folding chair.

klar adjective 1 clear (water, answer); klar werden △ to become clear; 2 jetzt ist mir alles klar now I understand; 3 sich klar werden △ to make up your mind; 4 sich über etwas im Klaren sein △ to realize something.
adverb clearly; na klar! (informal) of course!

klären verb (PERF hat geklärt) 1 to clarify; 2 to sort out; 3 to purify (sewage); 4 sich klären to clear (of the weather or the sky); 5 sich klären to resolve itself, to be settled.

Klarinette die (PL die Klarinetten) clarinet.

klarwerden SEE klar.

klasse adjective (informal) great, smashing.

Klasse die (PL die Klassen) 1 class; erster Klasse reisen to travel first class; 2 year; in die sechste Klasse gehen to be in year six.

Klassenarbeit die (PL die Klassenarbeiten) (written) test.

Klassenbuch das register (kept by

△ NEW SPELLING: See page xii

the teacher, it also contains notes about students' achievements).

Klassenkamerad der (PL die Klassenkameraden) class-mate.

Klassenkameradin die (PL die Klassenkameradinnen) class-mate.

Klassensprecher der (PL die Klassensprecher) class representative.

Klassensprecherin die (PL die Klassensprecherinnen) class representative.

Klassenzimmer das (PL die Klassenzimmer) classroom.

klassisch adjective classical.

Klatsch der gossip.

klatschen verb (PERF hat geklatscht) 1 to clap; jemandem Beifall klatschen to clap somebody, to applaud somebody; 2 to slap; 3 to gossip.

klauen (informal) (PERF hat geklaut) to pinch.

Klavier das (PL die Klaviere) piano.

kleben verb (PERF hat geklebt) 1 to stick; 2 to glue; 3 jemandem eine kleben (informal) to belt somebody one.

klebrig adjective sticky.

Klebstoff der (PL die Klebstoffe) glue.

Klebstreifen der (PL die Klebstreifen) sticky tape.

Klecks der (PL die Kleckse) stain.

Kleid das (PL die Kleider) 1 dress;

Uschi hat sich zwei neue Kleider gekauft Uschi bought two new dresses; 2 Kleider clothes.

Kleiderbügel der (PL die Kleiderbügel) coat hanger.

Kleiderschrank der (PL die Kleiderschränke) wardrobe.

Kleidung die clothes, clothing.

klein adjective 1 small, little; etwas klein schneiden △ to cut something up small; 2 short; Peter ist kleiner als Klaus Peter is shorter than Klaus.

Kleingeld das change.

Klempner der (PL die Klempner) plumber.

klettern verb (PERF ist geklettert) to climb.

Klima das (PL die Klimas) climate.

Klimaanlage die (PL die Klimaanlagen) air conditioning.

Klinge die (PL die Klingen) blade.

Klingel die (PL die Klingeln) bell.

klingeln verb (PERF hat geklingelt) to ring; es klingelt there's a ring at the door.

klingen △ verb (IMPERF klang, PERF hat geklungen) to sound.

Klinik die (PL die Kliniken) clinic.

Klinke die (PL die Klinken) handle.

Klippe die (PL die Klippen) rock.

Klo das (informal) (PL die Klos) loo.

klopfen verb (PERF hat geklopft) 1 to knock; 2 to beat.

△ IRREGULAR VERB: See the verb table in the centre of the dictionary

Klosett das (PL die **Klosetts**)
lavatory.

Kloster das (PL die **Kloster**)
1 monastery; 2 convent.

Klotz der (PL die **Klötze**) block.

Klub der (PL die **Klubs**) club.

klug adjective 1 clever; 2 ich werde
daraus nicht klug I don't
understand it.

Klugheit die cleverness.

Klumpen der (PL die **Klumpen**)
lump.

knabbern verb (PERF hat
geknabbert) to nibble.

Knäckebrot das (PL die
Knäckebrote) crispbread.

knacken verb (PERF hat geknackt)
to crack.

Knall der (PL die **Knalle**) bang.

knallen verb (PERF hat geknallt) 1 to
go bang; 2 (of a cork) to crack;
3 to slam (of a door); 4 to crack (of a
whip).

knapp adjective 1 scarce; 2 tight
(skirt, top); 3 knapp bei Kasse sein
to be short of money; 4 mit knapper
Mehrheit by a narrow majority;
5 just; eine knappe Stunde just
under an hour; sie haben knapp
verloren they only just lost; 6 das
war knapp (informal) that was a
close shave.

knarren verb (PERF hat geknarrt) to
creak.

Knauf der (PL die **Knäufe**) knob.

knautschen verb (PERF hat
geknautscht) 1 to crumple; 2 to
crease.

kneifen ◇ verb (IMPERF kniff, PERF
hat gekniffen) 1 to pinch;
2 (informal) to chicken out; sie hat
mal wieder gekniffen und nichts
gesagt she's chickened out yet again
and didn't say anything.

Kneipe die (PL die **Kneipen**) pub.

kneten verb (PERF hat geknetet) to
knead.

knicken verb (PERF hat geknickt)
1 to bend; 2 to fold.

Knie das (PL die **Knie**) knee.

knien verb (PERF hat gekniet) 1 to
kneel; 2 sich knien to kneel down.

kniff SEE **kneifen**.

knipsen verb (PERF hat geknipst) (to
photograph) to take a snap, to take
snaps.

Knoblauch der garlic.

Knoblauchzehe die (PL die
Knoblauchzehen) clove of garlic.

Knöchel der (PL die **Knöchel**)
1 ankle; 2 knuckle; Mario hat sich
beim Jogging den Knöchel
verstaucht Mario sprained his
ankle when jogging.

Knochen der (PL die **Knochen**) bone.

Knopf der (PL die **Knöpfe**) button.

Knoten der (PL die **Knoten**) 1 knot;
2 bun (as a hairstyle); 3 lump.

knurren verb (PERF hat geknurrt)
1 to growl; 2 to rumble; 3 to
grumble.

knusprig adjective crisp, crusty
(bread).

△ NEW SPELLING: See page xii

Koch der (PL die **Köche**) 1 cook; 2 chef.

Kochbuch das (PL die **Kochbücher**) cookery book.

kochen verb (PERF **hat gekocht**) 1 to cook; 2 to boil; **das Wasser kocht** the water's boiling.

Köchin die (PL die **Köchinnen**) cook.

Kochtopf der (PL die **Kochtöpfe**) saucepan.

Koffer der (PL die **Koffer**) suitcase.

Kofferkuli der (PL die **Kofferkulis**) baggage trolley.

Kofferraum der (PL die **Kofferräume**) boot.

Kohl der 1 cabbage; 2 (informal) rubbish; **rede keinen Kohl** don't talk rubbish.

Kohle die (PL die **Kohlen**) coal.

Kokosnuss △ die (PL die **Kokosnüsse**) coconut.

Kollege der (PL die **Kollegen**) colleague.

Kollegin die (PL die **Kolleginnen**) colleague.

Köln das Cologne.

Kölnischwasser das eau de cologne.

Kombination die (PL die **Kombinationen**) combination.

Komfort der comfort.

Komiker der (PL die **Komiker**) comedian.

komisch adjective funny.

Komma das (PL die **Kommas**) 1 comma; 2 decimal point; **zwei Komma fünf** two point five.

kommen ✧ verb (IMPERF **kam**, PERF **ist gekommen**) 1 to come; 2 to get; **wie komme ich zur U-Bahn?** how do I get to the tube station?; **kommt gut nach Hause!** have a safe journey home!; 3 **etwas kommen lassen** to send for something; 4 **wie kommst du darauf?** what gave you that idea?; 5 **hinter etwas kommen** to find out about something; 6 **zur Schule kommen** to start school; 7 to go; **die Gabeln kommen in die Schublade** the forks go in the drawer; **ins Krankenhaus kommen** to go to hospital; 8 **wer kommt zuerst?** who's first?; **du kommst an die Reihe** it's your turn; 9 **wie kommt das?** why is that?; 10 **zu etwas kommen** to acquire something; 11 **wieder zu sich kommen** to come round (after fainting or anaesthetic); 12 **dazu kommen, etwas zu tun** to get round to doing something; **ich komme einfach nicht zum Einkaufen** I just can't get round to doing the shopping; 13 **das kommt davon!** see what happens!

Kommissar der (PL die **Kommissare**) superintendent.

Kommode die (PL die **Kommoden**) chest of drawers.

Kommunismus der communism.

Kommunist der (PL die **Kommunisten**) communist.

Kommunistin die (PL die **Kommunistinnen**) communist.

✧ IRREGULAR VERB: See the verb table in the centre of the dictionary

Komödie *die* (PL *die* **Komödien**) comedy.

Kompass Δ *der* (PL *die* **Kompasse**) compass.

komplett *adjective* complete.

Kompliment *das* (PL *die* **Komplimente**) compliment.

kompliziert *adjective* complicated.

Komponist *der* (PL *die* **Komponisten**) composer.

Komponistin *die* (PL *die* **Komponistinnen**) composer.

Kompott *das* (PL *die* **Kompotte**) stewed fruit.

Kompromiss Δ *der* (PL *die* **Kompromisse**) compromise; **einen Kompromiss schließen** to compromise.

Konditorei *die* (PL *die* **Konditoreien**) patisserie, cake shop.

Kondom *das* (PL *die* **Kondome**) condom.

Konfektion *die* ready-made clothes.

Konferenz *die* (PL *die* **Konferenzen**) conference.

Konflikt *der* (PL *die* **Konflikte**) conflict.

König *der* (PL *die* **Könige**) king.

Königin *die* (PL *die* **Königinnen**) queen.

königlich *adjective* royal.

Königreich *das* (PL *die* **Königreiche**) kingdom.

Konjunktion *die* (PL *die* **Konjunktionen**) conjunction.

Konkurrent *der* (PL *die* **Konkurrenten**) competitor.

Konkurrentin *die* (PL *die* **Konkurrentinnen**) competitor.

Konkurrenz *die* competition.

können ◇ *verb* (PRES **kann**, IMPERF **konnte**, PERF **hat gekonnt**) 1 can; **kann ich Ihnen helfen?** can I help you?; **kannst du Auto fahren?** can you drive?; **kannst du Deutsch?** can you speak German?; **ich konnte nicht früher kommen** I couldn't come any earlier; **das kann ich nicht** I can't do that; 2 **etwas können** to be able to do something; **er wird es vor Dienstag nicht machen können** he won't be able to do it before Tuesday; 3 **das kann gut sein** that may well be so; **es kann sein, dass ...** it may be that...; 4 **ich kann nichts dafür** it's not my fault.

Können *das* ability.

Könner *der* (PL *die* **Könner**) expert.

könnt SEE **können**.

konnte, konnten, konntest, konntet SEE **können**.

Konserven *plural noun* tinned food.

Konsonant *der* (PL *die* **Konsonanten**) consonant.

Korsika *das* Corsica.

Kontakt *der* (PL *die* **Kontakte**) contact.

Kontaktlinse *die* (PL *die* **Kontaktlinsen**) contact lens.

Δ NEW SPELLING: *See page xii*

Kontinent der (PL die **Kontinente**) continent.

Konto das (PL die **Konten**) account.

Kontrolle die (PL die **Kontrollen**)
1 check; 2 control.

Kontrolleur der (PL die **Kontrolleure**) inspector.

kontrollieren verb (PERF hat kontrolliert) 1 to check; 2 to control.

konzentrieren verb (PERF hat konzentriert) 1 to concentrate; 2 sich konzentrieren to concentrate.

Konzert das (PL die **Konzerte**)
1 concert; 2 concerto.

Kopf der (PL die **Köpfe**) 1 head; 2 sich den Kopf zerbrechen to rack your brains; 3 seinen Kopf durchsetzen to get your own way; 4 sich den Kopf waschen to wash your hair; 5 auf dem Kopf upside down; 6 ein Kopf Salat a lettuce.

köpfen verb (PERF hat geköpft) 1 to head (in football); 2 to behead.

Kopfhörer der (PL die **Kopfhörer**) headphones.

Kopfkissen das (PL die **Kopfkissen**) pillow.

Kopfsalat der (PL die **Kopfsalate**) lettuce.

Kopfschmerzen plural noun headache.

Kopie die (PL die **Kopien**) copy.

kopieren verb (PERF hat kopiert) to copy.

Kopiergerät das (PL die **Kopiergeräte**) photocopier.

Korb der (PL die **Körbe**) 1 basket; 2 jemandem einen Korb geben to turn somebody down.

Kork der (PL die **Korke**) cork.

Korken der (PL die **Korken**) cork.

Korkenzieher der (PL die **Korkenzieher**) corkscrew.

Korn das (PL die **Körner**) corn.

Körper der (PL die **Körper**) body.

körperbehindert adjective disabled.

körperlich adjective physical.

Korrektur die (PL die **Korrekturen**) correction.

korrigieren verb (PERF hat korrigiert) to correct.

koscher adjective kosher.

Kosmetik die (PL die **Kosmetika**)
1 cosmetics; 2 beauty care.

Kost die food.

kostbar adjective precious.

kosten verb (PERF hat gekostet) 1 to cost; 2 wie viel kostet es? how much is it?; 3 to taste.

Kosten plural noun 1 cost; 2 expenses.

kostenlos adjective free (of charge).

köstlich adjective 1 delicious; 2 funny.

Kostüm das (PL die **Kostüme**)
1 suit; 2 costume.

Kotelett das (PL die **Koteletts**) chop.

◇ IRREGULAR VERB: See the verb table in the centre of the dictionary

Krabbe die (PL die Krabben) 1 crab; 2 shrimp.

krabbeln verb (PERF ist gekrabbelt) to crawl.

Krach der 1 row; 2 noise; 3 crash.

krachen verb (PERF hat gekracht) 1 to crash; 2 (PERF ist gekracht) to crack; **er ist gegen die Mauer gekracht** he crashed into the wall.

krächzen verb (PERF hat gekrächzt) to croak.

Kraft die (PL die Kräfte) 1 strength; **er hat nicht viel Kraft** he's not very strong; 2 force; **in Kraft treten** to come into force; 3 **geistige Kräfte** mental powers; 4 worker.

kräftig adjective 1 strong; 2 nourishing.
adverb 1 strongly; 2 hard; **kräftig schütteln** shake hard.

Kraftwerk das (PL die Kraftwerke) power station.

Kragen der (PL die Kragen) collar.

Krähe die (PL die Krähen) crow.

Kralle die (PL die Krallen) claw.

Kram der stuff; **mach deinen Kram allein!** (informal) do it yourself!

kramen verb (PERF hat gekramt) to rummage about.

Krampf der (PL die Krämpfe) cramp.

Kran der (PL die Kräne) crane (machine).

Kranich der (PL die Kraniche) crane (bird).

krank adjective ill, sick; **krank werden** to fall ill.

Kranke der/die (PL die Kranken) patient.

kränken verb (PERF hat gekränkt) to hurt.

Krankenhaus das (PL die Krankenhäuser) hospital; **sie haben ihn gestern ins Krankenhaus eingeliefert** he was taken to hospital yesterday.

Krankenkasse die health insurance; **bei welcher Krankenkasse sind Sie versichert?** what health insurance have you got?

Krankenpfleger der (PL die Krankenpfleger) (male) nurse.

Krankenpflegerin die (PL die Krankenpflegerinnen) nurse.

Krankenschwester die (PL die Krankenschwestern) nurse; **Ulrike ist Krankenschwester** Ulrike is a nurse.

Krankenwagen der (PL die Krankenwagen) ambulance.

Krankheit die (PL die Krankheiten) illness, disease.

kratzen verb (PERF hat gekratzt) to scratch.

Kratzer der (PL die Kratzer) scratch.

kraus adjective frizzy.

Kraut das (PL die Kräuter) 1 herb; 2 sauerkraut; 3 cabbage.

Krawall der (PL die Krawalle) 1 riot; 2 row.

Krawatte die (PL die Krawatten) tie.

kreativ adjective creative.

△ NEW SPELLING: See page xii

Krebs der (PL die Krebse) 1 crab;
2 cancer; 3 Cancer.

Kredit der (PL die Kredite) credit; auf
Kredit on credit.

Kreditkarte die (PL die
Kreditkarten) credit card.

Kreide die (PL die Kreiden) chalk.

kreieren verb (PERF hat kreiert) to
create.

Kreis der (PL die Kreise) 1 circle;
2 district.

Kreislauf der 1 cycle;
2 circulation.

Kreuz das (PL die Kreuze) 1 cross;
2 (small of the) back; 3 intersection
(of a motorway); 4 clubs (in cards).

kreuzen verb (PERF hat gekreuzt)
1 to cross; 2 sich kreuzen to cross.

Kreuzung die (PL die Kreuzungen)
1 crossroads; 2 cross (of plants,
animals).

Kreuzfahrt die (PL die
Kreuzfahrten) 1 cruise; eine
Kreuzfahrt machen to go on a
cruise; 2 crusade.

Kreuzworträtsel das (PL die
Kreuzworträtsel) crossword
(puzzle).

kriechen ◇ verb (IMPERF kroch, PERF
ist gekrochen) to crawl.

Krieg der (PL die Kriege) war.

kriegen verb (informal) (PERF hat
gekriegt) 1 to get; 2 ein Kind
kriegen to have a baby.

Krimi der (PL die Krimis) thriller.

Kriminalroman der (PL die
Kriminalromane) crime novel.

kriminell adjective criminal.

Kriminelle der/die (PL die
Kriminellen) criminal.

Krippe die (PL die Krippen)
1 manger; 2 crib; 3 crèche.

Krise die (PL die Krisen) crisis.

Kristall¹ der (PL die Kristalle) crystal.

Kristall² das (glass) crystal.

kritisch adjective critical.

kritisieren verb (PERF hat kritisiert)
1 to criticize; 2 to review.

kroch SEE kriechen.

Krokodil das (PL die Krokodile)
crocodile.

Krone die (PL die Kronen) crown.

Kröte die (PL die Kröten) toad.

Krücke die (PL die Krücken) crutch.

Krug der (PL die Krüge) 1 jug; 2 mug.

Krümel der (PL die Krümel) crumb.

krümelig adjective crumbly.

krumm adjective 1 bent; 2 crooked.

Kruste die (PL die Krusten) crust.

Küche die (PL die Küchen)
1 kitchen; 2 cooking; die
italienische Küche Italian cooking;
3 warme Küche hot food.

Kuchen der (PL die Kuchen) cake.

Kuckuck der (PL die Kuckucke)
cuckoo.

Kugel die (PL die Kugeln) 1 ball;
2 bullet; 3 sphere.

◇ **IRREGULAR VERB:** See the verb table in the centre of the dictionary

Kugelschreiber der (PL die Kugelschreiber) ballpoint pen, biro™.

Kuh die (PL die Kühe) cow.

kühl adjective cool.

kühlen verb (PERF hat gekühlt) 1 to cool, to chill; 2 to refrigerate.

Kühler der (PL die Kühler) radiator.

Kühlerhaube die (PL die Kühlerhauben) bonnet.

Kühlschrank der (PL die Kühlschränke) fridge.

Kühltruhe die (PL die Kühltruhen) freezer.

Küken das (PL die Küken) chick.

Kuli der (PL die Kulis) biro™.

Kultur die (PL die Kulturen) 1 culture; 2 civilization.

Kulturbeutel der (PL die Kulturbeutel) toilet bag.

kulturell adjective cultural.

Kummer der 1 sorrow; 2 worry; 3 trouble.

kümmern verb (PERF hat gekümmert) 1 to concern; 2 sich um jemanden kümmern to look after somebody; sich um den Garten kümmern to look after the garden; 3 sich darum kümmern, dass … to see to it that …; 4 kümmere dich um deine eigenen Angelegenheiten mind your own business.

Kunde der (PL die Kunden) 1 customer; 2 client.

kündigen verb (PERF hat gekündigt) 1 to cancel; 2 to give notice; die Firma hat ihm gekündigt the company gave him his notice; 3 seine Stellung kündigen to hand in your notice.

Kundin die (PL die Kundinnen) 1 customer; 2 client.

Kundschaft die customers.

Kunst die (PL die Künste) 1 art; 2 skill.

Künstler der (PL die Künstler) artist.

Künstlerin die (PL die Künstlerinnen) artist.

künstlerisch adjective artistic.

künstlich adjective artificial.

Kunststoff der (PL die Kunststoffe) plastic.

Kunststück das (PL die Kunststücke) 1 trick; 2 feat.

Kunstwerk das (PL die Kunstwerke) work of art.

Kupfer das copper.

Kupplung die (PL die Kupplungen) 1 clutch (of a car); 2 coupling.

Kürbis der (PL die Kürbisse) pumpkin.

Kurort der (PL die Kurorte) health resort.

Kurs der (PL die Kurse) 1 course; 2 exchange rate; 3 price (of shares).

Kurve die (PL die Kurven) 1 curve; 2 bend.

kurz adjective 1 short; vor kurzem a short time ago; 2 zu kurz kommen

△ NEW SPELLING: See page xii

to get less than your fair share, to come off badly.
adverb **1** shortly; **2** briefly; **3 kurz gesagt** in a word.

Kurzarbeit *die* short-time working.

kurzärmelig *adjective* short-sleeved.

kürzen *verb* (PERF **hat gekürzt**) **1** to shorten; **2** to cut.

kurzfristig *adjective* short-term.
adverb at short notice.

kürzlich *adverb* recently.

kurzsichtig *adjective* short-sighted.

Kurzwaren *plural noun* haberdashery.

Kusine *die* (PL *die* **Kusinen**) cousin.

Kuss △ *der* (PL *die* **Küsse**) kiss.

küssen *verb* (PERF **hat geküsst** △) **1** to kiss; **2 sich küssen** to kiss.

Küste *die* (PL *die* **Küsten**) coast.

Kuvert *das* (PL *die* **Kuverts**) envelope.

L l

Labor *das* (PL *die* **Labors**) laboratory.

Lache *die* (PL *die* **Lachen**) pool.

lächeln *verb* (PERF **hat gelächelt**) to smile.

lachen *verb* (PERF **hat gelacht**) to laugh.

lächerlich *adjective* ridiculous.

Lachs *der* (PL *die* **Lachse**) salmon.

Lack *der* (PL *die* **Lacke**) **1** varnish; **2** paint.

lackieren *verb* (PERF **hat lackiert**) **1** to varnish; **2** to spray (*with paint*).

laden ◇ *verb* (PRES **lädt**, IMPERF **lud**, PERF **hat geladen**) **1** to load; **wir haben die Möbel in den Möbelwagen geladen** we loaded the furniture into the removal van; **2 eine Batterie laden** to charge a battery; **3** to summon; **mein Bruder wurde als Zeuge geladen** my brother was summoned as a witness.

Laden *der* (PL *die* **Läden**) **1** shop; **wann macht der Laden zu?** when does the shop close?; **2** shutter; **wenn es heiß ist, lassen wir die Läden den ganzen Tag zu** when it's hot we keep the shutters closed all day.

Ladendieb *der* (PL *die* **Ladendiebe**) shoplifter.

Ladung *die* (PL *die* **Ladungen**) **1** cargo; **2** charge (*of dynamite or shot*); **3** summons; **4** load.

lag SEE **liegen**.

Lage *die* (PL *die* **Lagen**) **1** situation; **nicht in der Lage sein, etwas zu tun** not be in a position to do something; **2** layer.

Lager *das* (PL *die* **Lager**) **1** camp; **2** warehouse; **3** stock; **etwas auf Lager haben** to have something in stock; **4** stock-room; **5** bearing (*in a machine*).

lagern *verb* (PERF **hat gelagert**) **1** to store; **2** to camp.

◇ IRREGULAR VERB: *See the verb table in the centre of the dictionary*

lahm *adjective* lame.

lähmen *verb* (PERF hat gelähmt) to paralyse.

Lähmung *die* paralysis.

Laib *der* (PL die Laibe) loaf.

Laken *das* (PL die Laken) sheet.

Lakritze *die* liquorice.

Lamm *das* (PL die Lämmer) lamb.

Lampe *die* (PL die Lampen) lamp.

Lampenschirm *der* (PL die Lampenschirme) lampshade.

Land *das* (PL die Länder) 1 country; auf dem Land in the country; 2 land; 3 state (*there are 16 Länder in Germany*).

Landebahn *die* (PL die Landebahnen) runway.

landen *verb* (PERF ist gelandet) 1 to land; 2 im Krankenhaus landen (*informal*) to end up in hospital.

Landkarte *die* (PL die Landkarten) map.

Landkreis *der* (PL die Landkreise) district.

ländlich *adjective* rural.

Landschaft *die* (PL die Landschaften) 1 countryside; 2 landscape.

Landstraße *die* (PL die Landstraßen) country road.

Landtag *der* state parliament.

Landwirtschaft *die* agriculture, farming.

lang *adjective* 1 long; seit langem for a long time; 2 tall.
adverb eine Woche lang for a week.

langärmelig *adjective* long-sleeved.

lange *adverb* 1 a long time; lange nicht not for a long time; 2 so lange wie möglich as long as possible; 3 er ist lange nicht so reich he's nowhere near as rich.

Länge *die* (PL die Längen) 1 length; 2 longitude.

langen *verb* (PERF hat gelangt) 1 to be enough; das Geld langt nicht it's not enough money; mir langt's (*informal*) I've had enough; 2 to reach; nach etwas langen to reach for something; 3 jemandem eine langen (*informal*) to slap somebody's face.

Langlauf *der* cross-country (*in skiing*).

langsam *adjective, adverb* slow; die Musik geht mir langsam auf die Nerven the music is slowly getting on my nerves.

längst *adverb* 1 a long time ago; das habe ich schon längst gemacht I did it a long time ago; 2 for a long time; er weiß es schon längst he's known it for a long time; 3 längst nicht nowhere near, not nearly.

längster, längste, längstes *adjective* longest; Marion hat den längsten Aufsatz geschrieben Marion wrote the longest essay.

langweilen *verb* (PERF hat gelangweilt) 1 to bore; 2 sich langweilen to be bored.

△ NEW SPELLING: See page xii

langweilig *adjective* boring.

Lappen *der* (PL *die* **Lappen**) cloth, rag.

Laptop *der* (PL *die* **Laptops**) laptop.

Lärm *der* noise.

las SEE **lesen**.

Laser *der* (PL *die* **Laser**) laser.

Laserdrucker *der* (PL *die* **Laserdrucker**) laser printer.

lassen ◇ *verb* (PRES **lässt** △, IMPERF **ließ**, PERF **hat gelassen**) 1 to let; **jemanden schlafen lassen** to let somebody sleep; **lass uns jetzt gehen** let's go now; 2 **jemandem etwas lassen** to let somebody have something; 3 to leave; **die Kinder zu Hause lassen** to leave the children at home; **lass mich!** leave me!; 4 **jemanden warten lassen** to keep somebody waiting; 5 **etwas reparieren lassen** to have something repaired; 6 **lass das!** stop it!; 7 **die Tür lässt sich leicht öffnen** the door opens easily; **das lässt sich alles machen** that can all be arranged.

lässig *adjective* casual.

Last *die* (PL *die* **Lasten**) 1 load; 2 **jemandem zur Last fallen** to be a burden on somebody.

lästig *adjective* troublesome.

Lastwagen *der* (PL *die* **Lastwagen**) lorry, truck.

Latein *das* Latin.

Laterne *die* (PL *die* **Laternen**) 1 lantern; 2 street lamp.

Laub *das* leaves.

Lauch *der* leek(s).

Lauf *der* (PL *die* **Läufe**) 1 run; 2 course; **im Laufe der Zeit** in the course of time; **im Laufe der Jahre** over the years; 3 race; 4 barrel (*of a gun*).

Laufbahn *die* (PL *die* **Laufbahnen**) career.

laufen ◇ *verb* (PRES **läuft**, IMPERF **lief**, PERF **ist gelaufen**) 1 to run; **sie kann viel schneller laufen als ihr Bruder** she can run much faster than her brother; 2 to walk; **du kannst nach Hause laufen oder mit dem Bus fahren** you can walk home or go on the bus; 3 to be valid; 4 **Ski laufen** to ski; 5 to be on (*of a film, programme, or machine*).

laufend *adjective* 1 running; 2 current (*issue, month*); 3 **auf dem Laufenden sein** △ to be up to date; **Anita hält mich auf dem Laufenden** △ Anita keeps me up to date.
adverb continually, constantly.

Läufer *der* (PL *die* **Läufer**) 1 runner; 2 rug; 3 bishop (*in chess*).

Läuferin *die* (PL *die* **Läuferinnen**) runner.

Laufmasche *die* (PL *die* **Laufmaschen**) ladder (*in your tights*).

Laufwerk *das* (PL *die* **Laufwerke**) drive (*on a computer*).

Laune *die* (PL *die* **Launen**) mood.

launisch *adjective* moody.

◇ **IRREGULAR VERB: See the verb table in the centre of the dictionary**

Laus *die* (PL *die* **Läuse**) louse.

laut *adjective* **1** loud; **2** noisy.
adverb **1** loudly; **2** **laut lesen** to
read aloud; **3** **lauter stellen** to turn
up.
preposition ←(+GEN or +DAT)
according to.

Laut *der* (PL *die* **Laute**) sound.

lauten *verb* (PERF **hat gelautet**) **1** to
be; **2** to sound.

läuten *verb* (PERF **hat geläutet**) to
ring.

lauter *adjective* nothing but.

Lautsprecher *der* (PL *die*
Lautsprecher) (loud)speaker.

Lautstärke *die* volume.

lauwarm *adjective* lukewarm.

Lavendel *der* lavender.

Lawine *die* (PL *die* **Lawinen**)
avalanche.

leben *verb* (PERF **hat gelebt**) **1** to
live; **2** to be alive; **3** **leb wohl!**
farewell!

Leben *das* (PL *die* **Leben**) life; **am
Leben sein** to be alive; **ums Leben
kommen** to lose your life.

lebend *adjective* living.

lebendig *adjective* **1** living;
2 **lebendig sein** to be alive; **3** lively.

Lebensgefahr *die* mortal danger;
sein Vater ist in Lebensgefahr his
father is critically ill.

lebensgefährlich *adjective*
1 extremely dangerous; **2** critical;

lebensgefährlich verletzt critically
injured.

Lebenshaltungskosten *plural
noun* cost of living.

lebenslänglich *adjective* life.
adverb for life.

Lebenslauf *der* (PL *die*
Lebensläufe) CV.

Lebensmittel *plural noun* food,
groceries.

Lebensmittelgeschäft *das* (PL
die **Lebensmittelgeschäfte**)
grocer's (shop).

Lebensunterhalt *der* livelihood;
seinen Lebensunterhalt verdienen
to earn one's living.

Leber *die* (PL *die* **Lebern**) liver.

Leberfleck *der* (PL *die* **Leberflecke**)
mole.

Leberwurst *die* liver sausage.

Lebewesen *das* (PL *die*
Lebewesen) living being, living
thing.

lebhaft *adjective* **1** lively; **2** vivid
(*idea, colour*).

Lebkuchen *der* (PL *die* **Lebkuchen**)
gingerbread.

leblos *adjective* lifeless.

Leck *das* (PL *die* **Lecks**) leak.

lecken *verb* (PERF **hat geleckt**) **1** to
lick; **die Katze leckte ihre Jungen**
the cat licked the kittens; **an etwas
lecken** to lick something; **2** to leak.

lecker *adjective* delicious.

Leder *das* (PL *die* **Leder**) leather.

△ NEW SPELLING: *See page xii*

ledig *adjective* single.

lediglich *adverb* merely.

leer *adjective* empty; **leer machen** to empty.

leeren *verb* (PERF **hat geleert**) 1 to empty; 2 **ein leeres Blatt Papier** a blank sheet of paper; 3 **sich leeren** to empty.

Leerlauf *der* neutral (*gear*).

Leerung *die* (PL *die* **Leerungen**) collection.

legal *adjective* legal.

legen *verb* (PERF **hat gelegt**) 1 to put; 2 to lay; 3 **sich legen** to lie down; 4 **sich legen** to die down (*of a storm, noise*); **unsere Begeisterung hat sich gelegt** our enthusiasm has worn off.

leger *adjective, adverb* casual; **leger gekleidet sein** to be casually dressed.

Lehm *der* clay.

Lehne *die* (PL *die* **Lehnen**) 1 back (*of a chair*); 2 arm (*of a sofa or chair*).

lehnen *verb* (PERF **hat gelehnt**) 1 to lean; 2 **sich an etwas lehnen** to lean against something.

Lehrbuch *das* (PL *die* **Lehrbücher**) textbook.

lehren *verb* (PERF **hat gelehrt**) to teach.

Lehrer *der* (PL *die* **Lehrer**) 1 teacher; 2 instructor.

Lehrerin *die* (PL *die* **Lehrerinnen**) 1 teacher; 2 instructor.

Lehrerzimmer *das* (PL *die* **Lehrerzimmer**) staffroom.

Lehrling *der* (PL *die* **Lehrlinge**) 1 apprentice; 2 trainee.

Lehrplan *der* (PL *die* **Lehrpläne**) syllabus.

Lehrstelle *die* (PL *die* **Lehrstellen**) apprenticeship.

Leibwächter *der* (PL *die* **Leibwächter**) bodyguard.

Leiche *die* (PL *die* **Leichen**) (dead) body, corpse.

leicht *adjective* 1 light; 2 easy; **jemandem leicht fallen** △ to be easy for somebody; **es ist ihm nicht leicht gefallen** it wasn't easy for him; **Markus macht es sich immer leicht** Markus always takes the easy way out; 3 **ein leichter Akzent** a slight accent.

Leichtathletik *die* athletics.

leichtfallen SEE **leicht**.

Leichtsinn *der* 1 carelessness; 2 recklessness.

leichtsinnig *adjective* 1 careless; 2 reckless.

leid *adjective* **jemanden leid sein** △ to be fed up with somebody; **etwas leid sein** △ to be fed up with something.

Leid *das* 1 sorrow; 2 harm; 3 **es tut mir Leid** △ I'm sorry; **Andreas tut mir Leid** △ I feel sorry for Andreas.

leiden ◇ *verb* (IMPERF **litt**, PERF **hat gelitten**) 1 to suffer; 2 **jemanden gut leiden können** to like

◇ IRREGULAR VERB: *See the verb table in the centre of the dictionary*

somebody; **3 ich kann Erika nicht leiden** I can't stand Erika.

leider *adverb* **1** unfortunately; **2 leider ja** I'm afraid so; **leider nicht** I'm afraid not.

leihen ◇ *verb* (IMPERF **lieh**, PERF **hat geliehen**) **1** to lend; **2 sich etwas leihen** to borrow something; **ich habe mir das Buch von Alex geliehen** I borrowed the book from Alex.

Leihwagen *der* (PL **die Leihwagen**) hire car.

Leim *der* (PL **die Leime**) glue.

Leine *die* (PL **die Leinen**) **1** rope; **2** line (*for washing*); **3** lead (*for a dog*).

Leinen *das* (PL **die Leinen**) linen.

Leinwand *die* screen (*in a cinema*).

leise *adjective* quiet.
adverb **1** quietly; **2 die Musik leiser stellen** to turn the music down.

leisten *verb* (PERF **hat geleistet**) **1** to achieve; **2 jemandem Hilfe leisten** to help somebody; **3 jemandem Gesellschaft leisten** to keep somebody company; **4 sich etwas leisten** to treat yourself to something; **5 sich etwas leisten können** to be able to afford something; **ich kann mir kein neues Auto leisten** I can't afford a new car.

Leistung *die* (PL **die Leistungen**) **1** achievement; **2** performance; **3 Leistungen** payment.

leiten *verb* (PERF **hat geleitet**) **1** to lead; **2** to direct; **3** to manage, run (*a business*); **4** to conduct.

Leiter[1] *die* (PL **die Leitern**) ladder.

Leiter[2] *der* (PL **die Leiter**) **1** leader; **2** head; **3** manager; **4** director; **5** conductor (*of an orchestra or electricity*).

Leiterin *die* (PL **die Leiterinnen**) **1** leader; **2** head; **3** manageress; **4** director.

Leitung *die* (PL **die Leitungen**) **1** direction; **2** management; **3** (*phone*) line; **4** (*electric*) lead; **5** cable; **6** pipe; **7 unter der Leitung von** conducted by.

Leitungswasser *das* tap water.

Lektion *die* (PL **die Lektionen**) lesson.

lenken *verb* (PERF **hat gelenkt**) **1** to steer; **2** to guide; **3 den Verdacht auf jemanden lenken** to throw suspicion on somebody.

Lenkrad *das* (PL **die Lenkräder**) steering wheel.

Lenkstange *die* (PL **die Lenkstangen**) handlebars.

lernen *verb* (PERF **hat gelernt**) **1** to learn; **schwimmen lernen** to learn to swim; **2** to study.

lesen ◇ *verb* (PRES **liest**, IMPERF **las**, PERF **hat gelesen**) to read.

Leser *der* (PL **die Leser**) reader.

Leserin *die* (PL **die Leserinnen**) reader.

letzte SEE **letzter**.

Letzte ⚠ *der/die/das* (PL **die Letzten**) **1 der/die Letzte** the last (one); **das**

Letzte the last (thing); **2 Boris kam als Letzter** Boris arrived last.

letztens adverb **1** recently; **2** lastly.

letzter, letzte, letztes adjective **1** last; **zum letzten Mal** for the last time; **das letzte Mal** the last time; **2** latest (news, information); **3** in **letzter Zeit** recently.

leuchten verb (PERF **hat geleuchtet**) to shine.

Leuchter der (PL die **Leuchter**) candlestick.

Leuchtreklame die neon sign.

Leuchtturm der (PL die **Leuchttürme**) lighthouse.

leugnen verb (PERF **hat geleugnet**) to deny.

Leute plural noun people.

Lexikon das (PL die **Lexika**) **1** encyclopedia; **2** dictionary.

Licht das (PL die **Lichter**) light.

Lichtbild das (PL die **Lichtbilder**) photograph.

Lichtschalter der (PL die **Lichtschalter**) light switch.

Lid das (PL die **Lider**) (eye)lid.

Lidschatten der (PL die **Lidschatten**) eye shadow.

lieb adjective **1** dear; **liebe Gabi** dear Gabi; **2** nice; **das ist lieb von euch** that's nice of you; **3 jemanden lieb haben** △ to be fond of somebody; **4 es wäre mir lieber, wenn ...** I'd prefer it if ...; **5 ihr liebstes Spielzeug** her favourite toy.

Liebe die (PL die **Lieben**) love.

lieben verb (PERF **hat geliebt**) to love.

liebenswürdig adjective kind.

lieber adverb **1** rather; **2 lieber mögen** to like better; **3 lass das lieber** you'd better not do that; **4 ich trinke lieber Kaffee** I prefer coffee.

Liebesbrief der (PL die **Liebesbriefe**) love letter.

Liebeskummer der **Liebeskummer haben** to be lovesick.

liebevoll adjective loving.

liebhaben SEE lieb.

Liebling der (PL die **Lieblinge**) **1** darling; **2** favourite.

Lieblings- prefix favourite.

liebster, liebste, liebstes adjective **1** dearest; **2** favourite. adverb **am liebsten** best (of all); **ich mag Max am liebsten** I like Max best.

Lied das (PL die **Lieder**) song.

lief SEE laufen.

liefern verb (PERF **hat geliefert**) **1** to deliver; **2** to supply.

Lieferung die (PL die **Lieferungen**) delivery.

Lieferwagen der (PL die **Lieferwagen**) (delivery) van.

liegen ♦ verb (IMPERF **lag**, PERF **hat gelegen**) **1** to lie; **der Brief liegt auf dem Tisch** the letter is on the table; **es liegt viel Schnee** there's lots of snow; **2** to be, to be situated; **3 liegen bleiben** △ to stay (in bed); **er ist liegen geblieben** he didn't get

---

♦ IRREGULAR VERB: See the verb table in the centre of the dictionary

up; 4 etwas bleibt liegen
something is left behind; die Arbeit
ist liegen geblieben the job was left
undone; 5 der Schnee bleibt liegen
the snow is settling; 6 liegen
lassen △ to leave; 7 es liegt mir
nicht it doesn't suit me; 8 an etwas
liegen to be due to something;
9 das liegt an ihm it's up to him.

liegenbleiben, liegenlassen
SEE **liegen**.

Liegestuhl der (PL die **Liegestühle**)
deckchair.

Liegewagen der (PL die
Liegewagen) couchette (car).

ließ SEE **lassen**.

liest SEE **lesen**.

Lift der (PL die **Lifte**) lift.

Liga die (PL die **Ligen**) league.

lila adjective 1 purple; 2 mauve.

Limo die (PL die **Limo(s)**) = Limonade.

Limonade die (PL die **Limonaden**)
1 fizzy drink; 2 lemonade.

Limone die (PL die **Limonen**) lime.

Lineal das (PL die **Lineale**) ruler.

Linie die (PL die **Linien**) 1 line;
2 route (of a bus); Linie 6
number 6.

Linke die 1 left; zu meiner Linken
on my left; 2 left hand; 3 left side;
4 die Linke the left (in politics).

linker, linke, linkes adjective
1 left; 2 left-wing.

links adverb 1 on the left; links
fahren to drive on the left; links

abbiegen to turn left; nach links
left; von links from the left; 2 links
sein to be left-wing; 3 zwei links,
zwei rechts stricken to purl two,
knit two; 4 (clothing) inside out.

Linkshänder der (PL die
Linkshänder) left-hander.

Linkshänderin die (PL die
Linkshänderinnen) left-hander.

Linse die (PL die **Linsen**) 1 lens;
2 lentil.

Lippe die (PL die **Lippen**) lip.

Lippenstift der (PL die **Lippenstifte**)
lipstick.

Liste die (PL die **Listen**) list.

listig adjective cunning.

Liter der (PL die **Liter**) litre.

Literatur die literature.

litt SEE **leiden**.

Livesendung △ die (PL die
Livesendungen) live programme.

Lizenz die (PL die **Lizenzen**) licence.

Lkw der (PL die **Lkws**)
(Lastkraftwagen) lorry, truck.

Lob das praise.

loben verb (PERF **hat gelobt**) to
praise.

Loch das (PL die **Löcher**) hole.

Locke die (PL die **Locken**) curl.

locken verb (PERF **hat gelockt**) 1 to
tempt; 2 to curl.

locker adjective 1 loose; 2 slack
(rope); 3 relaxed (atmosphere,
person).

lockerlassen ◇ *verb* (PRES **lässt locker** Δ, IMPERF **ließ locker**, PERF **hat lockergelassen**) **nicht lockerlassen** (*informal*) not to let up.

lockig *adjective* curly.

Löffel *der* (PL **die Löffel**) **1** spoon; **2 ein Löffel Mehl** a spoonful of flour.

log SEE **lügen**.

Logik *die* logic.

logisch *adjective* **1** logical; **2 ja, logisch!** yes, of course!

Lohn *der* (PL **die Löhne**) **1** wages; **2** reward.

lohnen *verb* (PERF **hat sich gelohnt**) **sich lohnen** to be worth it.

Lokal *das* (PL **die Lokale**) **1** bar; **2** restaurant.

Lokomotive *die* (PL **die Lokomotiven**) locomotive, engine.

Lorbeerblatt *das* (PL **die Lorbeerblätter**) bay leaf.

los *adjective* **1 der Hund ist los** the dog is off the lead; **2 die Schraube ist los** the screw's loose; **3 es ist viel los** there's a lot going on; **4 etwas los sein** to be rid of something; **5 was ist los?** what's the matter? *adverb* **1 los!** go on!; **2 Achtung, fertig, los!** ready, steady, go!

Los *das* (PL **die Lose**) **1** (lottery) ticket; **2 das große Los ziehen** to hit the jackpot; **3** lot.

losbinden ◇ *verb* (IMPERF **band los**, PERF **hat losgebunden**) to untie.

löschen *verb* (PERF **hat gelöscht**) **1** to put out; **2 seinen Durst löschen** to quench your thirst; **3** to delete, to cancel; **4** to erase.

lose *adjective* loose.

lösen *verb* (PERF **hat gelöst**) **1** to solve; **2** to undo; **3 eine Fahrkarte lösen** to buy a ticket; **4 sich lösen** to come undone; **5 sich lösen** to be solved (*of a puzzle or mystery*); **sich von selbst lösen** to be resolved (*of a problem*); **6 sich in Wasser lösen** to dissolve in water.

losfahren ◇ *verb* (PRES **fährt los**, IMPERF **fuhr los**, PERF **ist losgefahren**) **1** to set off; **2** to drive off.

losgehen ◇ *verb* (IMPERF **ging los**, PERF **ist losgegangen**) **1** to set off; **2** to start; **3** to come off (*of a button*); **4** to go off (*of a bomb*); **5 auf jemanden losgehen** to go for somebody.

loslassen ◇ *verb* (PRES **lässt los** Δ, IMPERF **ließ los**, PERF **hat losgelassen**) **1** to let go of; **2** to let go.

Lösung *die* (PL **die Lösungen**) solution.

loswerden ◇ *verb* (PRES **wird los**, IMPERF **wurde los**, PERF **ist losgeworden**) to get rid of.

Lotterie *die* (PL **die Lotterien**) lottery.

Lotto *das* (PL **die Lottos**) (national) lottery.

Löwe *der* (PL **die Löwen**) **1** lion; **2** Leo.

◇ IRREGULAR VERB: *See the verb table in the centre of the dictionary*

Lücke die (PL die Lücken) gap.

Luft die (PL die Lüfte) 1 air; 2 die Luft anhalten to hold your breath; 3 in die Luft gehen (*informal*) to blow your top; 4 jemanden wie Luft behandeln to ignore somebody.

Luftballon der (PL die Luftballons) balloon.

Luftdruck der air pressure.

Luftmatratze die (PL die Luftmatratzen) air-bed.

Luftpost die airmail; per Luftpost by airmail.

Luftverschmutzung die air pollution.

Luftwaffe die air force.

Lüge die (PL die Lügen) lie.

lügen ◇ verb (IMPERF log, PERF hat gelogen) to lie.

Lügner der (PL die Lügner) liar.

Lügnerin die (PL die Lügnerinnen) liar.

Lunge die (PL die Lungen) lungs.

Lungenentzündung die pneumonia.

Lupe die (PL die Lupen) magnifying glass.

Lust die 1 pleasure; 2 Lust haben, etwas zu tun to feel like doing something; ich habe keine Lust I don't feel like it; Lust auf etwas haben to feel like something.

lustig adjective 1 jolly; 2 funny; 3 Dieter hat sich über mich lustig gemacht Dieter made fun of me.

lutschen verb (PERF hat gelutscht) to suck.

Lutscher der (PL die Lutscher) lollipop.

Luxemburg das Luxembourg.

Luxus der luxury.

M m

machen verb (PERF hat gemacht) 1 to make; 2 to do; was machst du da? what are you doing?; 3 was macht die Arbeit? how's work?; was macht Karin? how's Karin?; 4 sich an die Arbeit machen to get down to work; 5 schnell machen to hurry; 6 das macht nichts it doesn't matter; 7 das macht fünf Mark that's five marks; 8 sich nichts aus etwas machen to not be very keen on something; Roswitha macht ·i·h nichts aus Schokolade Roswitha isn't keen on chocolate.

Macht die (PL die Mächte) power; an die Macht kommen to come to power.

Mädchen das (PL die Mädchen) girl.

Made die (PL die Maden) maggot.

Mädchenname der (PL die Mädchennamen) maiden name.

mag SEE mögen.

Magazin das (PL die Magazine) magazine.

Magen der (PL die Mägen) stomach.

△ NEW SPELLING: *See page xii*

Magenschmerzen *plural noun*
stomach-ache.

mager *adjective* **1** thin; **2** lean;
3 low-fat.

Magie *die* magic.

Magnet *der* (PL die **Magneten**)
magnet.

magnetisch *adjective* magnetic.

magst SEE **mögen**.

Mahagoni *das* mahogany.

mähen *verb* (PERF hat **gemäht**) to
mow; **den Rasen mähen** to mow
the lawn.

mahlen ◇ *verb* (PERF hat **gemahlen**)
to grind.

Mahlzeit *die* (PL die **Mahlzeiten**)
meal; **Mahlzeit!** enjoy your meal!

Mai *der* May; **der Erste Mai**, May Day.

Maiglöckchen *das* (PL die
Maiglöckchen) lily of the valley.

Mais *der* maize.

Majonäse △ *die* mayonnaise.

Majoran *der* marjoram.

Makkaroni (*plural noun*) macaroni.

Makler *der* (PL die **Makler**) estate
agent.

Makrele *die* (PL die **Makrelen**)
mackerel.

mal *adverb* **1** times; **zwei mal drei**
two times three; **2** by (*with
measurements*); **3** sometime (*in the
future*); **ich möchte mal nach
Brasilien fahren** I'd like to go to
Brazil sometime; **4 schon mal**

ever; **5 ich war schon mal da** I've
been once before; **6 nicht mal** not
even; **7 komm mal her!** come here!

Mal *das* (PL die **Male**) **1** time;
nächstes Mal next time; **zum
ersten Mal** for the first time;
2 mark; **3** mole.

malen *verb* (PERF hat **gemalt**) to
paint.

Maler *der* (PL die **Maler**) painter.

Malerei *die* painting.

Malerin *die* (PL die **Malerinnen**)
painter.

Mallorca *das* Majorca.

Mama *die* (PL die **Mamas**) mum.

Mami *die* (PL die **Mamis**) mum.

man *pronoun* **1** you, one; **wie macht
man das?** how do you do it?; **man
kann ja nie wissen** one can never
tell; **2** they, people; **man sagt** they
say; **3 man hat mir gesagt** I was
told.

mancher, manche, manches
adjective **1** many a; **so manchen
Tag** many a day; **2 manche**
(*plural*) some; **an manchen Tagen**
some days.
pronoun **1** many a person;
2 manche (*plural*) some people;
3 manches some things.

manchmal *adverb* sometimes.

Mandarine *die* (PL die **Mandarinen**)
mandarin.

Mandel *die* (PL die **Mandeln**)
1 almond; **2** tonsil.

◇ IRREGULAR VERB: *See the verb table in the centre of the dictionary*

Mandelentzündung die tonsillitis.

Mangel der (PL die Mängel) 1 lack; 2 shortage; 3 defect, fault.

mangelhaft adjective 1 faulty; 2 unsatisfactory (school mark).

Manie die (PL die Manien) mania.

Manieren plural noun manners; er hat keine Manieren he's got no manners.

Mann der (PL die Männer) 1 man; 2 husband.

Männchen das (PL die Männchen) male (animal).

Mannequin das (PL die Mannequins) model.

männlich adjective 1 male; 2 manly; 3 masculine.

Mannschaft die (PL die Mannschaften) 1 team; 2 crew.

Manschette die (PL die Manschetten) cuff.

Mantel der (PL die Mäntel) coat.

Mappe die (PL die Mappen) 1 folder; 2 briefcase; 3 bag.

Märchen das (PL die Märchen) fairy tale.

Margarine die margarine.

Marienkäfer der (PL die Marienkäfer) ladybird.

Marine die (PL die Marinen) navy.

Mark die (PL die Mark) mark (the unit of German currency used before the euro).

Marke die (PL die Marken) 1 make, brand; meine Mutter fährt seit Jahren die gleiche Marke my mother has been driving the same make of car for years; Adidas ist eine führende Marke Adidas is a leading brand; 2 tag; 3 stamp (for letters); 4 coupon.

markieren verb (PERF hat markiert) 1 to mark; 2 to fake.

Markstücke das (PL die Markstücke) one-mark piece.

Markt der (PL die Märkte) market.

Marktplatz der (PL die Marktplätze) market-place.

Marmelade die (PL die Marmeladen) jam.

Marmor der marble.

Marokko das Morocco.

Marsch der (PL die Märsche) march.

März der March.

Masche die (PL die Maschen) 1 stitch; 2 mesh; 3 (informal) trick; die Masche raushaben to know how to do it; das ist die neueste Masche that's the latest thing.

Maschine die (PL die Maschinen) 1 machine; 2 plane; 3 typewriter; Maschine schreiben △ to type.

Masern plural noun measles.

Maske die (PL die Masken) mask.

maskieren verb (PERF hat sich maskiert) 1 sich maskieren to dress up; 2 sich maskieren to disguise yourself.

maß SEE messen.

Maß¹ das (PL die Maße) 1 measure; 2 measurement; 3 extent; in hohem

Maße to a high degree; **4 Maß halten** to show moderation.

Maß² die (PL die **Maß**) litre (of beer).

Masse die (PL die **Massen**) 1 mass; **eine Masse Arbeit** masses of work; 2 crowd; 3 mixture (in cooking).

massenhaft adjective masses of.

massieren verb (PERF hat massiert) to massage.

mäßig adjective moderate.

Maßnahme die (PL die **Maßnahmen**) measure.

Maßstab der (PL die **Maßstäbe**) 1 standard; 2 scale.

Mast der (PL die **Masten**) 1 mast; 2 pole; 3 pylon.

Material das (PL die **Materialien**) 1 material; 2 materials.

Mathe die (informal) maths.

Mathematik die mathematics.

Matratze die (PL die **Matratzen**) mattress.

Matrose der (PL die **Matrosen**) sailor.

Matsch der 1 mud; 2 slush.

matschig adjective 1 muddy; 2 slushy.

matt adjective 1 weak; 2 matt; 3 dull; **4 matt!** checkmate!

Matte die (PL die **Matten**) mat.

Mauer die (PL die **Mauern**) wall.

Maul das (PL die **Mäuler**) mouth; **halt's Maul!** (informal) shut up!

Maulkorb der (PL die **Maulkörbe**) muzzle.

Maulwurf der (PL die **Maulwürfe**) mole.

Maurer der (PL die **Maurer**) bricklayer.

Maus die (PL die **Mäuse**) mouse.

Mayonnaise die mayonnaise.

Mechaniker der (PL die **Mechaniker**) mechanic.

mechanisch adjective mechanical.

meckern verb (PERF hat gemeckert) 1 to bleat; 2 to grumble.

Medaille die (PL die **Medaillen**) medal.

Medien plural noun media.

Medikament das (PL die **Medikamente**) medicine, drug.

Medizin die (PL die **Medizinen**) medicine.

Meer das (PL die **Meere**) sea.

Meeresfrüchte plural noun seafood.

Meerschweinchen das (PL die **Meerschweinchen**) guinea pig.

Mehl das flour.

mehr adverb, pronoun more; **nichts mehr** no more; **nie mehr** never again.

mehrere pronoun several.

mehreres pronoun several things.

mehrfach adjective 1 multiple, many; 2 repeated. adverb several times.

◇ IRREGULAR VERB: See the verb table in the centre of the dictionary

Mehrheit *die* (PL *die* Mehrheiten) majority.

mehrmalig *adjective* repeated.

mehrmals *adverb* several times.

Mehrwertsteuer *die* value added tax.

Mehrzahl *die* 1 majority; 2 plural.

meiden ◇ *verb* (IMPERF **mied**, PERF **hat gemieden**) to avoid.

Meile *die* (PL *die* Meilen) mile.

mein *adjective* my.

meine SEE **meiner**.

meinen *verb* (PERF **hat gemeint**) 1 to think; 2 to mean; **es gut meinen** to mean well; 3 to say.

meiner, meine, mein(e)s *pronoun* mine.

meinetwegen *adverb* 1 for my sake; 2 because of me; 3 as far as I'm concerned; 'kann ich das Auto haben?' – 'meinetwegen' 'can I take the car?' – 'I don't mind'.

meins SEE **meiner**.

Meinung *die* (PL *die* Meinungen) opinion.

meist *adverb* 1 mostly; 2 usually.

meiste *adjective, pronoun* **der/die/das meiste** most; **die meisten** most; **am meisten** most, the most.

meistens *adverb* 1 mostly; 2 usually.

Meister *der* (PL *die* Meister) 1 master; 2 champion.

Meisterin *die* (PL *die* Meisterinnen) champion.

Meisterschaft *die* (PL *die* Meisterschaften) championship.

Meisterwerk *das* (PL *die* Meisterwerke) masterpiece.

melden *verb* (PERF **hat gemeldet**) 1 to report; 2 to register; 3 **sich melden** to report; (*on the phone*) to answer; (*in school*) Luise hat sich gemeldet Luise put up her hand; 4 **sich bei jemandem melden** to get in touch with somebody.

Melodie *die* (PL *die* Melodien) melody, tune.

Melone *die* (PL *die* Melonen) 1 melon; 2 bowler (hat).

Menge *die* (PL *die* Mengen) 1 quantity; **eine Menge Geld** a lot of money; 2 crowd; 3 set (*in maths*).

Mensch *der* (PL *die* Menschen) 1 human being; 2 person; **kein Mensch** nobody; **jeder Mensch** everybody; 3 **die Menschen** people; **wie viele Menschen?** how many people?; 4 (*as an exclamation*) Mensch! (*informal*) wow!, hey!; Mensch, hab ich mich geärgert! (*informal*) I was damn annoyed.

menschenleer *adjective* deserted.

Menschenverstand *der* **gesunder Menschenverstand** common sense.

Menschheit *die* mankind.

menschlich *adjective* 1 human; 2 humane.

△ NEW SPELLING: *See page xii*

Mentalität die (PL die Mentalitäten) mentality.

Menü das (PL die Menüs) 1 menu; 2 set meal.

merken verb (PERF hat gemerkt) 1 to notice; 2 sich etwas merken to remember something.

Merkmal das (PL die Merkmale) feature.

merkwürdig adjective strange, odd.

Messe die (PL die Messen) 1 mass; 2 trade fair.

messen ◇ verb (PRES misst △, IMPERF maß, PERF hat gemessen) 1 to measure; (bei jemandem) Fieber messen to take somebody's temperature; 2 sich mit jemandem messen können to be as good as somebody.

Messer das (PL die Messer) knife.

Messing das brass.

Metall das (PL die Metalle) metal.

Meter der (PL die Meter) metre.

Metermaß das (PL die Metermaße) tape measure.

Methode die (PL die Methoden) method.

metrisch adjective metric.

Metzger der (PL die Metzger) butcher.

Metzgerei die (PL die Metzgereien) butcher's (shop).

Mexiko das Mexico.

miauen verb (PERF hat miaut) to miaow.

mich pronoun 1 me; 2 myself.

mied SEE meiden.

Miete die (PL die Mieten) 1 rent; zur Miete wohnen to live in rented accommodation; 2 hire charge.

mieten verb (PERF hat gemietet) 1 to rent; 2 to hire.

Mieter der (PL die Mieter) tenant.

Mieterin die (PL die Mieterinnen) tenant.

Mietshaus das (PL die Mietshäuser) block of rented flats.

Mietvertrag der (PL die Mietverträge) lease.

Mietwagen der (PL die Mietwagen) hire car.

Mikrofon das (PL die Mikrofone) microphone.

Mikroskop das (PL die Mikroskope) microscope.

Mikrowellenherd der (PL die Mikrowellenherde) microwave oven.

Milch die milk.

mild adjective mild.

Militär das army.

militärisch adjective military.

Milliarde die (PL die Milliarden) thousand million, billion.

Millimeter der (PL die Millimeter) millimetre.

Million die (PL die Millionen) million.

◇ IRREGULAR VERB: See the verb table in the centre of the dictionary

Millionär *der* (PL *die* **Millionäre**) millionaire.

Millionärin *die* (PL *die* **Millionärinnen**) millionairess.

Minderheit *die* (PL *die* **Minderheiten**) minority.

minderjährig *adjective* under age.

mindestens *adverb* at least.

mindester, mindeste, mindestes *adjective* least. *pronoun* 1 der/die/das Mindeste △ the least; zum Mindesten △ at least; 2 nicht im Mindesten △ not in the least.

Mine *die* (PL *die* **Minen**) 1 mine; 2 lead (*in a pencil*); 3 refill (*for a ball-point*).

Mineralwasser *das* (PL *die* **Mineralwasser**) mineral water.

Minirock *der* (PL *die* **Miniröcke**) miniskirt.

Minister *der* (PL *die* **Minister**) minister.

Ministerin *die* (PL *die* **Ministerinnen**) minister.

Ministerium *das* (PL *die* **Ministerien**) ministry, department.

minus *adverb* minus.

Minute *die* (PL *die* **Minuten**) minute.

mir *pronoun* 1 me, to me; 2 myself.

mischen *verb* (PERF hat gemischt) 1 to mix; 2 die Karten mischen to shuffle the cards; 3 sich mischen to mix.

Mischung *die* (PL *die* **Mischungen**) 1 mixture; 2 blend.

miserabel *adjective* (*informal*) 1 hopeless; 2 dreadful.

missbilligen △ *verb* (PERF hat missbilligt) to disapprove.

Missbrauch △ *der* abuse.

missbrauchen △ *verb* (PERF hat missbraucht) to abuse.

Misserfolg △ *der* (PL *die* **Misserfolge**) failure.

Missgeschick △ *das* (PL *die* **Missgeschicke**) 1 misfortune; 2 mishap.

misshandeln △ *verb* (PRES hat misshandelt) to ill-treat.

misslingen △ ◇ *verb* (IMPERF misslang, PERF ist misslungen) to fail; es misslang ihr she failed.

misst △ SEE messen.

Misstrauen △ *das* 1 mistrust; 2 distrust.

misstrauen △ *verb* (PERF hat misstraut) jemandem misstrauen to mistrust somebody.

misstrauisch △ *adjective* suspicious.

Missverständnis △ *das* (PL *die* **Missverständnisse**) misunderstanding.

missverstehen △ ◇ *verb* (IMPERF missverstand, PERF hat missverstanden) to misunderstand.

Mist *der* 1 manure; 2 (*informal*) rubbish.

Mistel *die* (PL *die* **Misteln**) mistletoe.

△ NEW SPELLING: *See page xii*

mit *preposition* ←(+DAT) **1** with; **2 mit der Bahn fahren** to go by train; **3 mit sechs Jahren** at the age of six; **4 mit jemandem sprechen** to speak to somebody; **5 mit Bleistift** in pencil; **6 mit lauter Stimme** in a loud voice. *adverb* as well, too; **warst du mit dabei?** were you there too?

Mitarbeiter *der* (PL die **Mitarbeiter**) **1** colleague; **2** employee.

Mitarbeiterin *die* (PL die **Mitarbeiterinnen**) **1** colleague; **2** employee.

mitbringen ◇ *verb* (IMPERF **brachte mit**, PERF **hat mitgebracht**) to bring, to bring along; **ich bringe den Kindern Schokolade mit** I'm taking the children some chocolate.

miteinander *adverb* with each other, with one another.

Mitesser *der* (PL die **Mitesser**) blackhead.

mitfahren ◇ *verb* (PRES **fährt mit**, IMPERF **fuhr mit**, PERF **ist mitgefahren**) **1 mit jemandem mitfahren** to go with somebody; **die Kinder fahren mit uns mit** the children are coming with us; **2 bei jemandem mitfahren** to get a lift with somebody; **jemanden mitfahren lassen** to give somebody a lift.

mitgeben ◇ *verb* (PRES **gibt mit**, IMPERF **gab mit**, PERF **hat mitgegeben**) to give.

Mitglied *das* (PL die **Mitglieder**) member.

mithalten ◇ *verb* (PRES **hält mit**, IMPERF **hielt mit**, PERF **hat mitgehalten**) to keep up.

mitkommen ◇ *verb* (IMPERF **kam mit**, PERF **ist mitgekommen**) **1** to come too; **2** to keep up.

Mitleid *das* pity; **kein Mitleid mit jemandem haben** not to feel any sympathy for somebody.

mitmachen *verb* (PERF **hat mitgemacht**) **1** to join in; **hast du Lust, bei dem Spiel mitzumachen?** do you want to join in the game?; **2** to take part in; **3** to go through (*experiences, troubles*); **sie hat viel mitgemacht** she's gone through a lot.

mitnehmen ◇ *verb* (PRES **nimmt mit**, IMPERF **nahm mit**, PERF **hat mitgenommen**) **1** to take, to take along; **Anni hat die Kinder auf den Spielplatz mitgenommen** Anni has taken the children to the playground; **2** to give a lift to; **3** to affect (badly); **4 zum Mitnehmen** to take away.

Mitschüler *der* (PL die **Mitschüler**) schoolfriend.

Mitschülerin *die* (PL die **Mitschülerinnen**) schoolfriend.

mitspielen *verb* (PERF **hat mitgespielt**) **1** to play; **wer spielt bei dem Fußballspiel mit?** who's playing in the football match?; **willst du mitspielen?** do you want to join in?; **2 in einem Film mitspielen** to be in a film.

Mittag *der* (PL die **Mittage**) **1** midday; **2** lunch; **zu Mittag essen** to have lunch; **3** lunch-break.

◇ **IRREGULAR VERB:** *See the verb table in the centre of the dictionary*

Mittagessen das (PL die Mittagessen) lunch; **beim Mittagessen** at lunch.

mittags adverb 1 at lunchtime, at midday; 2 **um zwölf Uhr mittags** at noon.

Mittagspause die (PL die Mittagspausen) lunch-break.

Mitte die (PL die Mitten) 1 middle; 2 centre.

Mitteilung die (PL die Mitteilungen) 1 announcement; 2 communication.

Mittel das (PL die Mittel) 1 means; 2 **ein Mittel gegen Husten** a cough remedy; 3 **öffentliche Mittel** public funds.

Mittelalter das Middle Ages.

mittelgroß adjective medium-sized.

mittelmäßig adjective mediocre.

Mittelmeer das Mediterranean.

Mittelpunkt der (PL die Mittelpunkte) centre; **im Mittelpunkt stehen** to be the centre of attention.

Mittelstand der middle class.

Mittelstürmer der (PL die Mittelstürmer) centre-forward.

mitten adverb **mitten in/auf** in the middle of; **mitten in der Nacht** in the middle of the night.

Mitternacht die midnight.

mittlerer, mittlere, mittleres adjective 1 middle; 2 medium (quality, size); 3 average.

mittlerweile adverb 1 meanwhile; 2 by now.

Mittwoch der (PL die Mittwoche) Wednesday.

mittwochs adverb on Wednesdays.

Möbel plural noun furniture.

Möbelwagen der (PL die Möbelwagen) removal van.

Mobiltelefon das (PL die Mobiltelefone) mobile phone.

möbliert adjective furnished.

mochte, möchte SEE mögen.

Mode die (PL die Moden) fashion.

Modell das (PL die Modelle) model.

Moderator der (PL die Moderatoren) presenter (on TV).

Moderatorin die (PL die Moderatorinnen) presenter (on TV).

modern adjective modern.

modernisieren verb (PERF hat modernisiert) to modernize.

modisch adjective fashionable.

Mofa die (PL die Mofas) moped.

mogeln verb (PERF hat gemogelt) to cheat.

mögen ◇ verb (PRES **mag**, IMPERF **mochte**, PERF **hat gemocht**) 1 to like; **ich mag ihn nicht** I don't like him; **ich möchte** I'd like; **ich möchte gern wissen** I'd like to know; **möchtest du nach Hause?** would you like to go home?; 2 **lieber mögen** to prefer; **ich möchte lieber Tee** I would prefer tea; 3 **etwas nicht tun mögen** not to want to do

△ NEW SPELLING: See page xii

something; **ich mag nicht fragen** I don't want to ask; **ich mag nicht mehr** I've had enough; **4 das mag sein** maybe; **5 was mag das sein?** whatever can it be?

möglich *adjective* possible; **alles Mögliche** all sorts of things.

möglicherweise *adverb* possibly.

Möglichkeit *die* (PL *die* Möglichkeiten) possibility.

möglichst *adverb* if possible; **möglichst früh** as early as possible.

Möhre *die* (PL *die* Möhren) carrot.

Molekül *das* (PL *die* Moleküle) molecule.

Moment *der* (PL *die* Momente) moment; **im Moment** at the moment; **Moment (mal)!** just a moment!

Monat *der* (PL *die* Monate) month.

monatelang *adverb* for months.

monatlich *adjective, adverb* monthly.

Mönch *der* (PL *die* Mönche) monk.

Mond *der* (PL *die* Monde) moon.

Mondschein *der* moonlight; **im Mondschein** by moonlight.

Montag *der* (PL *die* Montage) Monday.

montags *adverb* on Mondays.

Moped *das* (PL *die* Mopeds) moped.

Moral *die* **1** moral; **2** morale; **3** morals.

moralisch *adjective* moral.

Mord *der* (PL *die* Morde) murder.

Mörder *der* (PL *die* Mörder) murderer.

Mörderin *die* (PL *die* Mörderinnen) murderer.

morgen *adverb* tomorrow; **morgen Abend** tomorrow evening.

Morgen *der* (PL *die* Morgen) morning; **am Morgen** in the morning; **heute Morgen** △ this morning; **guten Morgen!** good morning!

morgens *adverb* in the morning.

Moschee *die* (PL *die* Moscheen) mosque.

Mosel *die* (River) Moselle.

Moslem *der* (PL *die* Moslems) Muslim.

moslemisch *adjective* Muslim.

Moskau *das* Moscow.

Moslime *die* (PL *die* Moslimen) Muslim.

Motiv *das* (PL *die* Motive) **1** motive; **2** motif.

Motor *der* (PL *die* Motoren) engine, motor.

Motorrad *das* (PL *die* Motorräder) motorcycle, motorbike.

Möwe *die* (PL *die* Möwen) seagull.

Mücke *die* (PL *die* Mücken) **1** midge; **2** mosquito.

müde *adjective* tired.

Müdigkeit *die* tiredness.

Mühe *die* (PL *die* Mühen) **1** effort;

◇ IRREGULAR VERB: *See the verb table in the centre of the dictionary*

sich Mühe geben to make an effort;
2 trouble; **machen Sie sich keine
Mühe** don't go to any trouble; 3 **mit
Müh und Not** only just.

Mühle die (PL die **Mühlen**) 1 mill;
2 grinder (for coffee).

mühsam adjective laborious.

Müll der rubbish.

Müllabfuhr die refuse collection.

Mülleimer der (PL die **Mülleimer**)
rubbish bin.

Mülltonne die (PL die **Mülltonnen**)
dustbin.

Mumps der mumps.

München das Munich.

Mund der (PL die **Münder**) mouth;
halt den Mund! (informal) shut
up!

Mundharmonika die (PL die
Mundharmonikas) mouth organ.

mündlich adjective oral.

Münster das (PL die **Münster**)
cathedral.

Münze die (PL die **Münzen**) coin.

Münzfernsprecher der (PL die
Münzfernsprecher) payphone.

murmeln verb (PERF hat **gemurmelt**)
to mumble.

mürrisch adjective surly.

Muschel die (PL die **Muscheln**)
1 mussel; 2 (sea) shell;
3 mouthpiece (of a phone).

Museum das (PL die **Museen**)
museum.

Musik die music.

musikalisch adjective musical.

Musiker der (PL die **Musiker**)
musician.

Musikerin die (PL die
Musikerinnen) musician.

Muskat der nutmeg.

Muskel der (PL die **Muskeln**) muscle.

Müsli das muesli.

muss △ SEE **müssen**.

müssen ◇ verb (PRES **muss** △, IMPERF
musste △, PERF **hat gemusst** △)
1 etwas tun müssen to have to do
something; **sie muss es tun** she's
got to do it, she must do it; **muss ich?**
do I have to?; **muss das sein?** is that
necessary?; 2 **Sie müssten es mal
versuchen** you should try it; 3 **sie
müssen gleich hier sein** they'll be
here at any moment; 4 **ich muss
mal** (informal) I need (to go to) the
loo.

Muster das (PL die **Muster**)
1 pattern; 2 sample.

Mut der courage; **jemandem Mut
machen** to encourage somebody.

mutig adjective courageous.

Mutter[1] die (PL die **Mütter**) mother.

Mutter[2] die (PL die **Muttern**) nut.

Muttersprache die (PL die
Muttersprachen) mother tongue,
native language.

△ NEW SPELLING: See page xii

Muttertag *der* (PL *die* Muttertage)
Mother's Day.

Mutti *die* (PL *die* Muttis) mum.

Mütze *die* (PL *die* Mützen) cap.

MwSt. (Mehrwertsteuer) VAT.

Mythos *der* (PL *die* Mythen) myth.

N n

na *exclamation* well; na und? so
what?; na gut all right then.

Nabel *der* (PL *die* Nabel) navel.

nach *preposition* ←(+DAT) **1** to; nach
Hause gehen to go home; nach
oben up; nach hinten back; nach
rechts abbiegen to turn right;
2 after; nach Ihnen after you; zehn
nach eins ten past one; nach etwas
greifen to reach for something;
3 according to; meiner Meinung
nach in my opinion.
adverb nach und nach bit by bit,
gradually; nach wie vor still.

nachahmen *verb* (PERF hat
nachgeahmt) to imitate.

Nachbar *der* (PL *die* Nachbarn)
neighbour.

Nachbarin *die* (PL *die*
Nachbarinnen) neighbour.

Nachbarschaft *die*
neighbourhood.

nachdem *conjunction* **1** after; **2** je
nachdem it depends; je nachdem,
wie schnell du damit fertig wirst it

depends on how quicky you can
finish it.

nachdenken ◇ *verb* (IMPERF
dachte nach, PERF hat
nachgedacht) to think; über etwas
nachdenken to think about
something; ich habe lange über ihr
Angebot nachgedacht und mich
schließlich dagegen entschieden
I've thought a long time about her
offer and finally decided against it.

nachdenklich *adjective*
thoughtful.

nacheinander *adverb* one after the
other; die Bewerber kamen
nacheinander herein the
applicants came in one after the
other.

Nachfrage *die* (PL *die* Nachfragen)
demand; es besteht keine
Nachfrage there's no demand for it.

nachgehen ◇ *verb* (IMPERF ging
nach, PERF ist nachgegangen) **1** to
be slow; meine Uhr geht nach my
watch is slow; **2** jemandem
nachgehen to follow somebody;
einer Sache nachgehen to look
into something.

nachher *adverb* afterwards; erst
gehen wir ins Kino und nachher
könnten wir essen gehen we go to
the cinema first and afterwards we
could go for a meal; bis nachher!
see you later!

nachholen *verb* (PERF hat
nachgeholt) **1** to catch up on; ich
hatte Grippe und muss jetzt viel
Mathe nachholen I've had flu and
now I've got a lot of maths to catch
up on; **2** to make up for (something

missed); **3 eine Prüfung nachholen** to do an exam at a later date.

Nachtklub *der* (PL *die* **Nachtklubs**) night club.

nachkommen ◇ *verb* (IMPERF **kam nach**, PERF **ist nachgekommen**) **1** to come later, to follow; **2 ich komme nicht nach** I can't keep up; **3 einem Versprechen nachkommen** to carry out a promise; **seinen Verpflichtungen nachkommen** to meet your commitments.

nachlassen ◇ *verb* (PRES **lässt nach** Δ, IMPERF **ließ nach**, PERF **hat nachgelassen**) **1** to ease; **meine Zahnschmerzen lassen langsam nach** my toothache is getting better; **2** to let up; **sobald die Kälte nachlässt** as soon as it gets warmer; **3** to deteriorate; **4 etwas vom Preis nachlassen** to take something off the price; **jemandem zwanzig Mark nachlassen** to give somebody twenty marks off.

nachlässig *adjective* careless.

nachlaufen ◇ *verb* (PRES **läuft nach**, IMPERF **lief nach**, PERF **ist nachgelaufen**) **jemandem nachlaufen** to run after somebody; **Philipp läuft allen Mädchen nach** (*informal*) Philipp chases all the girls.

nachmachen *verb* (PERF **hat nachgemacht**) to copy.

Nachmittag *der* (PL *die* **Nachmittage**) afternoon.

nachmittags *adverb* in the afternoon.

Nachnahme *die* per **Nachnahme** cash on delivery.

Nachname *der* (PL *die* **Nachnamen**) surname.

nachprüfen *verb* (PERF **hat nachgeprüft**) to check; **er prüft nach, ob es stimmt** he's going to check if it is correct.

Nachricht *die* (PL *die* **Nachrichten**) **1** news; **ich warte noch immer auf eine Nachricht von ihm** I'm still waiting for news of him; **eine Nachricht hinterlassen** to leave a message; **2 die Nachrichten** the news; **das kam in den Nachrichten** it was on the news.

Nachrichtensprecher *der* (PL *die* **Nachrichtensprecher**) newsreader.

Nachrichtensprecherin *der* (PL *die* **Nachrichtensprecherinnen**) newsreader.

nachschlagen ◇ *verb* (PRES **schlägt nach**, IMPERF **schlug nach**, PERF **hat nachgeschlagen**) to look up.

nachsehen ◇ *verb* (PRES **sieht nach**, IMPERF **sah nach**, PERF **hat nachgesehen**) **1** to check; **sieh nach, wer da ist** go and see who's there; **2** to look up; **3 jemandem etwas nachsehen** to let somebody get away with something.

nachsitzen ◇ *verb* (IMPERF **saß nach**, PERF **hat nachgesessen**) to be in detention; **Jan muss nachsitzen** Jan has detention.

Nachspeise *die* (PL *die* **Nachspeisen**) dessert, pudding.

Δ NEW SPELLING: *See page xii*

nächste SEE nächster.

nächstens adverb shortly.

nächster, nächste, nächstes
adjective 1 next; 2 nearest; am
nächsten sein to be nearest; 3 in
nächster Nähe close by.
pronoun der/die/das Nächste △
(the) next; als Nächstes △ next.

Nacht die (PL die Nächte) night.

Nachteil der (PL die Nachteile)
disadvantage.

Nachtfalter der (PL die Nachtfalter)
moth.

Nachthemd das (PL die
Nachthemden) nightdress,
nightshirt.

Nachtigall die (PL die Nachtigallen)
nightingale.

Nachtisch der (PL die Nachtische)
dessert, pudding.

Nachtleben das nightlife.

nachträglich adjective
1 subsequent; 2 belated.
adverb 1 later; 2 belatedly.

nachts adverb at night; um zwei Uhr
nachts at two o'clock in the
morning.

Nacken der (PL die Nacken) neck.

nackt adjective 1 naked; 2 bare.

Nadel die (PL die Nadeln) 1 needle;
2 pin.

Nagel der (PL die Nägel) nail.

Nagelbürste die (PL die
Nagelbürsten) nailbrush.

Nagelfeile die (PL die Nagelfeilen)
nailfile.

Nagellack der (PL die Nagellacke)
nail varnish.

nagelneu adjective brand-new.

Nagelschere die (PL die
Nagelscheren) nail scissors.

nahe, nah adjective, adverb 1 near,
nearby; der Nahe Osten the Middle
East; nahe daran sein, etwas zu tun
to nearly do something; 2 close;
nahe bei close to; nahe verwandt
sein to be closely related;
3 jemandem nahe legen △, etwas zu
tun to urge somebody to do
something; 4 nahe liegend △
obvious.
preposition ←(+DAT) near, close to.

Nähe die 1 proximity; 2 in der Nähe
der Kirche near the church; ganz
in der Nähe nearby; 3 aus der
Nähe close up.

nahelegen, naheliegend SEE
nahe.

nähen verb (PERF hat genäht) 1 to
sew; 2 to stitch (a wound).

näher adjective 1 closer; 2 nähere
Einzelheiten further details;
3 shorter (way, road).
adverb 1 closer; näher kommen to
come closer; 2 more closely;
3 Näheres further details.

nähern verb (PERF hat sich
genähert) sich nähern to
approach.

Nähgarn das cotton.

nahm SEE nehmen.

◆ IRREGULAR VERB: See the verb table in the centre of the dictionary

Nähmaschine *die* (PL *die* Nähmaschinen) sewing machine.

Nahrung *die* food.

Naht *die* (PL *die* Nähte) seam.

Nahverkehrszug *der* (PL *die* Nahverkehrszüge) local train.

Name *der* (PL *die* Namen) name.

nämlich *adverb* 1 because; 2 namely; 3 das war nämlich ganz anders it was quite different actually.

nannte SEE nennen.

nanu *exclamation* well, well!

Narbe *die* (PL *die* Narben) scar.

Narr *der* (PL *die* Narren) fool.

Närrin *die* (PL *die* Närrinnen) fool.

Nase *die* (PL *die* Nasen) nose; die Nase voll haben (*informal*) to have had enough.

Nasenbluten *das* nosebleed.

Nashorn *das* (PL *die* Nashörner) rhinoceros.

nass △ *adjective* wet.

Nation *die* (PL *die* Nationen) nation.

Nationalhymne *die* (PL *die* Nationalhymnen) national anthem.

Nationalität *die* (PL *die* Nationalitäten) nationality.

Natur *die* 1 nature; von Natur aus by nature; 2 die freie Natur the open countryside.

natürlich *adjective* natural. *adverb* of course, naturally.

Naturschutzgebiet *das* (PL *die* Naturschutzgebiete) nature reserve.

Naturwissenschaft *die* natural science.

Nebel *der* (PL *die* Nebel) 1 fog; 2 mist.

nebelig *adjective* = neblig.

neben *preposition* ←(+DAT, or +ACC *with movement towards a place*) 1 next to; er hat neben mir gesessen he sat next to me; er hat sich neben mich gesetzt he sat down next to me; 2 apart from.

nebenan *adverb* next door.

nebenbei *adverb* 1 as well, at the same time; er liest die Zeitung und hört nebenbei Musik he reads the newspaper and listens to music at the same time; 2 on the side; nebenbei arbeite ich noch in einem Blumengeschäft I work in a florist's on the side; das mache ich so nebenbei (*informal*) that's just a sideline; 3 in passing; nebenbei bemerkt by the way.

nebeneinander *adverb* next to each other.

nebenhergehen ◇ *verb* (IMPERF ging nebenher, PERF ist nebenhergegangen) to walk alongside.

neblig *adjective* 1 foggy; 2 misty.

necken *verb* (PERF hat geneckt) to tease.

Neffe *der* (PL *die* Neffen) nephew.

negativ *adjective* negative.

Negativ *das* (PL *die* **Negative**) negative.

nehmen ◇ *verb* (PRES **nimmt**, IMPERF **nahm**, PERF **hat genommen**) 1 to take; 2 **ich nehme eine Suppe** I'll have soup; 3 **was nehmen Sie dafür?** how much do you want for it?; 4 **jemanden zu sich nehmen** to have somebody live with you; 5 **sich etwas nehmen** to help yourself; **nimm dir ein Stück Kuchen** help yourself to a piece of cake.

Neid *der* envy, jealousy.

neidisch *adjective* envious, jealous.

nein *adverb* no.

Nelke *die* (PL *die* **Nelken**) carnation.

nennen ◇ *verb* (IMPERF **nannte**, PERF **hat genannt**) 1 to call; 2 to name; 3 **ihr Name wurde nicht genannt** her name wasn't mentioned; 4 **sich nennen** to call yourself.

Nerv *der* (PL *die* **Nerven**) nerve; **Gabi geht mir auf die Nerven** Gabi gets on my nerves.

nervös *adjective* nervous.

Nervosität *die* nervousness.

Nessel *die* (PL *die* **Nesseln**) nettle.

Nest *das* (PL *die* **Nester**) 1 nest; 2 little place (*a village*).

nett *adjective* nice.

netto *adverb* net.

Netz *das* (PL *die* **Netze**) 1 net; 2 network; 3 string bag; 4 (*spider's*) web.

neu *adjective* 1 new; **wie neu** as good as new; **neue Sprachen** modern

languages; 2 **seit neuestem** recently; 3 **die neueste Mode** the latest fashion; **das Neueste** the latest news; 4 **das ist mir neu** that's news to me.
adverb 1 newly; 2 only just; **es ist neu eingetroffen** it has only just come in; 3 **etwas neu schreiben** to rewrite something.

neuartig *adjective* new; **ein neuartiger Flaschenöffner** a new kind of bottle opener.

neuerdings *adverb* recently.

Neugier *die* curiosity.

neugierig *adjective* curious, inquisitive.

Neuigkeit *die* (PL *die* **Neuigkeiten**) piece of news; **gibt es irgendwelche Neuigkeiten?** is there any news?

Neujahr *das* New Year, New Year's Day.

neulich *adverb* the other day.

neun *number* nine.

neunter, neunte, neuntes *adjective* ninth.

neunzehn *number* nineteen.

neunzig *number* ninety.

Neuseeland *das* New Zealand.

nicht *adverb* 1 not; **ich kann nicht** I can't; **Iris hat nicht angerufen** Iris didn't ring; **bitte nicht** please don't; **nicht!** don't!; **nicht berühren!** don't touch!; 2 **'ich mag das nicht'** – **'ich auch nicht'** 'I don't like it' – 'neither do I'; 3 **nicht (wahr)?** isn't he/she/it?; **du kennst ihn doch,**

nicht? you know him, don't you?;
4 gar nicht not at all; **5 nicht mehr**
no more.

Nichte *die* (PL *die* **Nichten**) niece.

Nichtraucher *der* (PL *die*
Nichtraucher) non-smoker.

nichts *pronoun* **1** nothing; **2 ich
habe nichts gewusst** I didn't know
anything; **3 nichts mehr** no more;
4 das macht nichts it doesn't
matter; **5 nichts ahnend** △
unsuspecting.

nichtsahnend SEE **nichts**.

nicken *verb* (PERF **hat genickt**) to
nod.

Nickerchen *das* (PL *die*
Nickerchen) nap; **ein Nickerchen
machen** to have a nap.

nie *adverb* never.

nieder *adjective* low.
adverb down.

Niederlage *die* (PL *die* **Niederlagen**)
defeat.

Niederlande *plural noun* die
Niederlande the Netherlands.

Niederländer *der* (PL *die*
Niederländer) Dutchman; **die
Niederländer** the Dutch.

Niederländerin *die* (PL *die*
Niederländerinnen) Dutchwoman.

niederländisch *adjective* Dutch.

niedlich *adjective* sweet.

niedrig *adjective* **1** low; **2** base.

niemals *adverb* never.

niemand *pronoun* nobody; **wir**

haben niemand *or* **niemanden
gesehen** we didn't see anybody.

Niere *die* (PL *die* **Nieren**) kidney.

nieseln *verb* (PERF **hat genieselt**) to
drizzle; **es nieselt** it's drizzling.

niesen *verb* (PERF **hat geniest**) to
sneeze.

Nilpferd *das* (PL *die* **Nilpferde**)
hippopotamus.

nimmt SEE **nehmen**.

nirgends, nirgendwo *adverb*
nowhere.

Niveau *das* (PL *die* **Niveaus**) **1** level;
2 standard.

noch *adverb* **1** still; **immer noch**
still; **2** even; **noch besser** even
better; **3 noch nicht** not yet; **noch
nie** never; **4 gerade noch** only
just; **5 wer war noch da?** who else
was there?; **was noch?** what else?;
6 noch einmal again; **7 noch ein
Bier** another beer; **noch etwas
Kaffee?** (would you like some) more
coffee?; **8 noch gestern** only
yesterday; **9 noch und noch Geld**
loads of money.
conjunction nor; **weder … noch**
neither … nor

nochmals *adverb* again.

Nominativ *der* (PL *die* **Nominative**)
nominative.

Nordamerika *das* North America.

Norden *der* north.

Nordirland *das* Northern Ireland.

nördlich *adjective* **1** northern;
2 northerly (*direction*).

△ NEW SPELLING: *See page xii*

adverb, preposition ←(+GEN)
nördlich von Wien to the north of
Vienna; **nördlich der Stadt** north of
the town.

Nordosten *der* north-east.

Nordpol *der* North Pole.

Nordsee *die* North Sea.

Nordwesten *der* north-west.

nörgeln *verb* (PERF **hat genörgelt**) to
grumble.

Norm *die* (PL **die Normen**) 1 norm;
2 standard.

normal *adjective* normal.

normalerweise *adverb* normally.

Norwegen *das* Norway.

Norweger *der* (PL **die Norweger**)
Norwegian.

Norwegerin *die* (PL **die
Norwegerinnen**) Norwegian.

norwegisch *adjective* Norwegian.

Not *die* (PL **die Nöte**) 1 need; **zur Not**
if necessary, at a pinch; **mit knapper
Not** only just; 2 hardship.

Notausgang *der* (PL **die
Notausgänge**) emergency exit.

Notdienst *der* **Notdienst haben** to
be on call.

Note *die* (PL **die Noten**) 1 note; **Noten
lesen** to read music; 2 mark.

Notfall *der* (PL **die Notfälle**)
emergency.

notfalls *adverb* if need be.

notieren *verb* (PERF **hat notiert**) to

note down; 2 **sich etwas notieren**
to make a note of something.

nötig *adjective* necessary.
adverb urgently.

Notiz *die* (PL **die Notizen**) 1 note;
2 **keine Notiz von etwas nehmen**
to take no notice of something;
3 item (*in a newspaper*).

Notizblock *der* (PL **die Notizblöcke**)
notepad.

Notizbuch *das* (PL **die Notizbücher**)
notebook.

Notlage *die* (PL **die Notlagen**) crisis.

Notruf *der* (PL **die Notrufe**)
1 emergency call; 2 emergency
number.

notwendig *adjective* necessary.

November *der* November.

nüchtern *adjective* 1 sober; **wieder
nüchtern werden** to sober up;
2 **auf nüchternen Magen** on an
empty stomach; 3 down-to-earth.

Nudeln *plural noun* 1 noodles;
2 pasta.

null *number* 1 nought; **unter null**
below zero; 2 nil; **zwei zu null** two
nil; 3 love (*in tennis*); 4 **null Fehler
haben** to have no mistakes; **ich habe
null Ahnung** (*informal*) I haven't
got a clue; 5 **in null Komma nichts**
(*informal*) in less than no time.

Null *die* (PL **die Nullen**) 1 zero,
nought; 2 failure.

numerieren = **nummerieren**.

Nummer *die* (PL **die Nummern**)
1 number; 2 issue (*of a magazine*);

◇ IRREGULAR VERB: *See the verb table in the centre of the dictionary*

3 size (of clothing); **4** act; **5 auf Nummer sicher gehen** to play safe.

nummerieren △ verb (PERF **hat nummeriert**) to number.

Nummernschild das (PL die **Nummernschilder**) number plate.

nun adverb now.
exclamation well; **nun ja ...** well, yes ...

nur adverb **1** only; **2 was sollen wir nur tun?** what on earth are we going to do?; **sie soll es nur versuchen!** just let her try!; **3 nur zu!** go ahead!

Nürnberg das Nuremberg.

Nuss △ die (PL die **Nüsse**) nut.

Nutzen der benefit; **von Nutzen sein** to be useful.

nutzen, nützen verb (PERF **hat genutzt/genützt**) **1** to use; **etwas nutzen** to take advantage of something; **2** to be no use; **3 nichts nutzen** to be no use; **das nutzt mir nichts** that won't help me; **4 das nutzt ja doch nichts** it's pointless.

nützlich adjective useful.

nutzlos adjective useless.

O o

ob conjunction **1** whether; **wissen Sie, ob heute noch ein Zug nach Freising fährt?** do you know if there is another train to Freising today?; **2 ob Alex noch anruft?** I wonder if Alex will ring; **3 und ob!** you bet!

obdachlos adjective homeless.

Obdachlose der/die (PL die **Obdachlosen**) homeless person; **die Obdachlosen** the homeless.

oben adverb **1** on top; **oben auf** on top of; **die Vase steht oben auf dem Schrank** the vase is on top of the cupboard; **2** at the top; **von oben bis unten** from top to bottom; **er hat uns von oben bis unten gemustert** he looked us up and down; **3** upstairs; **4 nach oben** up, upstairs; **er ist nach oben in sein Zimmer gegangen** he went up into his room; **geht der Fahrstuhl nach oben?** is the lift going up?; **hier oben** up here; **da oben** up there; **5** siehe above (on a page); **oben erwähnt** △ above mentioned; **6 oben ohne** (informal) topless.

obenerwähnt △ SEE oben.

Ober der (PL die **Ober**) waiter; **Herr Ober!** waiter!

oberer, obere, oberes adjective upper, top.

Oberfläche die (PL die **Oberflächen**) surface.

oberflächlich adjective superficial.

Oberhaupt das (PL die **Oberhäupter**) head.

Oberhemd das (PL die **Oberhemden**) shirt.

Oberschenkel der (PL die **Oberschenkel**) thigh.

Oberschule die (PL die **Oberschulen**) secondary school.

△ NEW SPELLING: See page xii

oberster, oberste, oberstes
adjective top.

Oberstufe die (PL die **Oberstufen**)
upper school.

Oberweite die (PL die **Oberweiten**)
chest size, bust measurement.

Objekt das (PL die **Objekte**) object.

objektiv *adjective* objective.

Objektiv das (PL die **Objektive**) lens.

Obst das fruit.

Obstbaum der (PL die **Obstbäume**)
fruit tree.

Obstsalat der (PL die **Obstsalate**)
fruit salad.

obszön *adjective* obscene.

obwohl *conjunction* although.

öde *adjective* 1 desolate; 2 dreary;
das ist so ein furchtbar öder Job
it's such terribly dull job.

oder *conjunction* 1 or; 2 **du kennst
sie doch, oder?** you know her, don't
you?

Ofen der (PL die **Öfen**) 1 oven;
2 stove; 3 heater.

offen *adjective* 1 open; **offen haben**
to be open; **Tag der offenen Tür**
open day; 2 frank; 3 vacant; **eine
offene Stelle** a vacancy; 4 **offen
bleiben** △ to stay open; 5 **offen
bleiben** △ to remain open (*of a
question, possibility*).
adverb 1 openly; 2 frankly; **offen
gesagt** frankly.

offenbar *adjective* obvious.
adverb 1 apparently; 2 **da hast du
dich offenbar geirrt** you seem to

have made a mistake; **sie hat
offenbar den Zug verpasst** she
must have missed the train.

offenbleiben SEE **offen**.

offensichtlich *adjective* obvious.

öffentlich *adjective* public.

Öffentlichkeit die public; **in aller
Öffentlichkeit** in public.

offiziell *adjective* official.

Offizier der (PL die **Offiziere**) officer.

öffnen *verb* (PERF **hat geöffnet**) to
open; **jemandem die Tür öffnen** to
open the door for somebody.

Öffner der (PL die **Öffner**) opener.

Öffnung die (PL die **Öffnungen**)
opening.

Öffnungszeiten *plural noun*
opening times.

oft *adverb* often.

öfter, öfters *adverb* quite often; **ich
habe ihn öfters mal getroffen** I
used to meet him quite often.

ohne *preposition* ←(+ACC) 1 without;
ohne mich count me out; 2 **ohne
weiteres** easily; 3 **oben ohne**
(*informal*) topless; 4 **das ist nicht
ohne** (*informal*) it's not bad.
conjunction without; **ohne zu
überlegen** without thinking.

Ohnmacht die **in Ohnmacht fallen**
to faint.

ohnmächtig *adjective*
1 unconscious; 2 **ohnmächtig
werden** to faint; **Roswitha ist
ohnmächtig** Roswitha's fainted.

◇ IRREGULAR VERB: *See the verb table in the centre of the dictionary*

Ohr das (PL die Ohren) ear.

Ohrenschmerzen plural noun earache.

Ohrring der (PL die Ohrringe) earring.

oje exclamation oh dear!

Ökoladen der (PL die Ökoläden) health-food shop.

Ökologie die ecology.

ökologisch adjective ecological.

Oktober der October.

Öl das (PL die Öle) oil.

Ölfarbe die (PL die Ölfarben) oil-paint.

Ölgemälde das (PL die Ölgemälde) oil painting.

ölig adjective oily.

Olive die (PL die Oliven) olive.

Olivenöl das (PL die Olivenöle) olive oil.

Olympiade die (PL die Olympiaden) Olympic Games; **die Olympiade findet alle vier Jahre statt** the Olympic Games take place every four years.

olympisch adjective Olympic.

Oma die (PL die Omas) granny.

Omelett das (PL die Omeletts) omelette.

Omi die (PL die Omis) granny.

Onkel der (PL die Onkel) uncle.

Opa der (PL die Opas) grandpa.

Oper die (PL die Opern) opera.

Operation die (PL die Operationen) operation.

Operationssaal der (PL die Operationssäle) operating theatre.

operieren verb (PERF hat operiert) 1 to operate on; **sich operieren lassen** to have an operation; **sie wurde am Magen operiert** she had a stomach operation; 2 to operate.

Opfer das (PL die Opfer) 1 sacrifice; 2 victim; **das Erdbeben forderte viele Opfer** the earthquake claimed many victims.

Optiker der (PL die Optiker) optician.

Optikerin die (PL die Optikerinnen) optician.

Optimist der (PL die Optimisten) optimist.

optimistisch adjective optimistic.

orange adjective orange.

Orange die (PL die Orangen) orange.

Orangensaft der (PL die Orangensäfte) orange juice.

Orchester das (PL die Orchester) orchestra.

ordentlich adjective 1 tidy; 2 respectable; 3 proper (meal, job, salary); 4 **eine ordentliche Tracht Prügel** (informal) a good hiding. adverb 1 tidily; **ordentlich schreiben** to write neatly; 2 respectably; 3 properly; 4 **ordentlich feiern** (informal) to have a really good celebration; **wir sind ordentlich nass geworden** (informal) we got soaked.

ordinär adjective vulgar.

ordnen verb (PERF hat geordnet)
1 to arrange; 2 to put in order.

Ordner der (PL die Ordner) file.

Ordnung die 1 order; **Ordnung halten** to keep order; 2 **Ordnung machen** to tidy up; **die Wohnung in Ordnung bringen** to tidy up the flat; 3 **mit der Waschmaschine ist etwas nicht in Ordnung** there's something wrong with the washing machine; 4 **etwas in Ordnung bringen** to put something right; **die Waschmaschine in Ordnung bringen** to repair the washing machine; 5 **in Ordnung!** okay!; 6 **er ist in Ordnung** he's all right.

Organ das (PL die Organe) 1 organ; 2 (informal) voice.

Organisation die (PL die Organisationen) organization.

organisch adjective organic.

organisieren verb (PERF hat organisiert) 1 to organize; 2 (informal) to get (hold of).

Orgel die (PL die Orgeln) organ.

orientieren verb (PERF hat sich orientiert) 1 **sich orientieren** to get your bearings; 2 **sich über etwas orientieren** to inform yourself about something.

Orientierung die 1 orientation; **die Orientierung verlieren** to lose your bearings; 2 **zu Ihrer Orientierung** for your information.

Orientierungssinn der sense of direction.

originell adjective original.

Orkan der (PL die Orkane) hurricane.

Ort der (PL die Orte) 1 place; **an Ort und Stelle** on the spot; 2 (small) town.

Orthografie △, **Orthographie** die spelling.

örtlich adjective local.

Ortschaft die (PL die Ortschaften) village.

Ortsgespräch das (PL die Ortsgespräche) local call.

Ossi der (informal) (PL die Ossis) East German.

Osten der east.

Osterei das (PL die Ostereier) Easter egg.

Ostern das Easter.

Österreich das Austria.

Österreicher der (PL die Österreicher) Austrian.

Österreicherin die (PL die Österreicherinnen) Austrian.

österreichisch adjective Austrian.

östlich adjective 1 eastern; 2 easterly.
adverb, preposition ←(+GEN) **östlich von Wien** to the east of Vienna; **östlich der Stadt** east of the town.

Ostsee die Baltic (Sea).

oval adjective oval.

Ozean der (PL die Ozeane) ocean.

Ozon das ozone.

Ozonschicht die ozone layer.

◇ IRREGULAR VERB: *See the verb table in the centre of the dictionary*

P p

paar *pronoun* ein paar a few; ein paar Mal △ a few times; alle paar Tage every few days.

Paar *das* (PL die Paare) 1 pair; ein Paar Schuhe a pair of shoes; 2 couple.

paarmal SEE paar.

paarweise *adjective* in pairs; die Kinder stellten sich paarweise auf the children lined up in pairs.

Päckchen *das* (PL die Päckchen) 1 package, packet; 2 small parcel.

packen *verb* (PERF hat gepackt) 1 to pack; ich muss jetzt meinen Koffer packen I must pack my case now; 2 to grab (hold of); von Furcht gepackt seized with fear.

Packung *die* (PL die Packungen) packet, pack.

Pädagoge *der* (PL die Pädagogen) 1 educationalist; 2 teacher.

pädagogisch *adjective* educational.

Paddel *das* (PL die Paddel) paddle.

Paket *das* (PL die Pakete) 1 parcel; Gabi hat mir ein Paket geschickt Gabi sent me a parcel; 2 packet; kaufe bitte ein Paket Waschpulver für mich can you please buy a packet of washing powder for me.

Palast *der* (PL die Paläste) palace.

Palme *die* (PL die Palmen) palm (tree).

Pampelmuse *die* (PL die Pampelmusen) grapefruit.

Panik *die* panic; in Panik geraten to panic.

Panne *die* (PL die Pannen) 1 breakdown; wir haben auf dem Rückweg eine Panne gehabt we had a breakdown on the way back; 2 mishap; uns ist eine Panne passiert we had a mishap.

Papa *der* (PL die Papas) daddy.

Papagei *der* (PL die Papageien) parrot.

Papier *das* (PL die Papiere) paper.

Papierkorb *der* (PL die Papierkörbe) waste-paper basket.

Papiertüte *die* (PL die Papiertüten) paper bag.

Pappe *die* (PL die Pappen) cardboard.

Paprika *der* (PL die Paprikas) 1 pepper; 2 paprika.

Papst *der* (PL die Päpste) pope.

Parabolantenne *die* (PL die Parabolantennen) satellite dish.

Paradies *das* paradise.

Paragraph *der* (PL die Paragraphen) 1 section; 2 clause.

parallel *adjective* parallel.

Pärchen *das* (PL die Pärchen) couple.

Parfüm *das* (PL die Parfüms) perfume.

Park der (PL die Parks) park.

Parkanlage die (PL die Parkanlagen) park.

parken verb (PERF hat geparkt) to park.

Parkett das (PL die Parkette) 1 (in a theatre) stalls; 2 parquet floor.

Parkhaus das (PL die Parkhäuser) multi-storey car park.

Parklücke die (PL die Parklücken) parking space.

Parkplatz der (PL die Parkplätze) 1 car park; 2 parking space.

Parkschein der (PL die Parkscheine) car-park ticket.

Parkuhr die (PL die Parkuhren) parking meter.

Parkverbot das 'Parkverbot' 'no parking'; **in der Innenstadt ist Parkverbot** you can't park in the town centre.

Parlament das (PL die Parlamente) parliament.

Parole die (PL die Parolen) slogan.

Partei die (PL die Parteien) 1 party; 2 **für jemanden Partei ergreifen** to side with somebody.

Parterre das (PL die Parterres) ground floor.

Partie die (PL die Partien) 1 part; 2 game (of tennis, chess).

Partner der (PL die Partner) partner.

Partnerin die (PL die Partnerinnen) partner.

Partnerstadt die (PL die Partnerstädte) twin town.

Party die (PL die Partys) party.

Pass △ der (PL die Pässe) 1 passport; 2 pass.

Passagier der (PL die Passagiere) passenger.

Passant der (PL die Passanten) passer-by.

Passantin die (PL die Passantinnen) passer-by.

passen (PERF hat gepasst △) 1 to fit; **jemandem passen** to fit somebody; 2 to suit; **jemandem passen** to suit somebody; **Freitag passt mir nicht** Friday doesn't suit me; **seine Art passt mir nicht** I don't like his manner; 3 **zu etwas passen** to go with something; **zu jemandem passen** to be right for somebody.

passend adjective 1 suitable; 2 matching.

passieren verb (PERF ist passiert) to happen.

passiv adjective passive.

Passiv das passive.

Passkontrolle △ die passport control.

Paste die (PL die Pasten) paste.

Pastete die (PL die Pasteten) pie.

Pate der (PL die Paten) godfather.

Patenkind das (PL die Patenkinder) godchild.

patent adjective capable, clever.

◇ IRREGULAR VERB: See the verb table in the centre of the dictionary

Patentante der (PL die Patentanten) godmother.

Patient der (PL die Patienten) patient.

Patientin die (PL die Patientinnen) patient.

Patin die (PL die Patinnen) godmother.

patschnass Δ adjective soaking wet.

pauken verb (informal) (PERF hat gepaukt) to swot.

Pauschalreise die (PL die Pauschalreisen) package tour.

Pause die (PL die Pausen) 1 break; 2 pause; 3 interval.

Pazifik der der Pazifik the Pacific (Ocean).

PC der (PL die PCs) PC.

Pech das 1 bad luck; **Pech haben** to be unlucky; 2 pitch.

Pedal das (PL die Pedale) pedal.

peinlich adjective 1 embarrassing; **es war mir sehr peinlich** I felt very embarrassed about it; 2 awkward; 3 meticulous.

Peitsche die (PL die Peitschen) whip.

Pelle die skin.

Pelz der (PL die Pelze) fur.

pendeln verb 1 (PERF ist gependelt) to commute; 2 (PERF hat gependelt) to swing.

Pendler der (PL die Pendler) commuter.

penetrant adjective 1 overpowering (odour, perfume); 2 pushy (person).

Penis der (PL die Penisse) penis.

pennen verb (informal) (PERF hat gepennt) to sleep, to kip.

Pension die (PL die Pensionen) 1 guesthouse; 2 bei voller Pension with full board; 3 pension; **eine schöne Pension haben** to get a good pension; **in Pension gehen** to retire.

pensioniert adjective retired.

per preposition ←(+ACC) 1 by; **per Luftpost** by airmail; 2 per.

perfekt adjective perfect.

Perfekt das (PL die Perfekte) perfect.

Periode die (PL die Perioden) period.

Perle die (PL die Perlen) 1 pearl; 2 bead.

Person die (PL die Personen) person; **für vier Personen** for four people; **ich für meine Person** personally.

Personal das staff, personnel.

Personenzug der (PL die Personenzüge) stopping train.

Personalausweis der (PL die Personalausweise) identity card.

persönlich adjective personal. adverb 1 personally; 2 in person.

Perücke die (PL die Perücken) wig.

Pessimist der (PL die Pessimisten) pessimist.

Δ NEW SPELLING: See page xii

pessimistisch *adjective*
pessimistic.

Petersilie *die* parsley.

Petroleum *das* paraffin.

Pfad *der* (PL *die* Pfade) path.

Pfadfinder *der* (PL *die* Pfadfinder)
(Boy) Scout.

Pfadfinderin *die* (PL *die*
Pfadfinderinnen) (Girl) Guide.

Pfand *das* (PL *die* Pfänder) 1 forfeit;
2 deposit (*on a bottle*); 3 pledge.

Pfanne *die* (PL *die* Pfannen) (frying)
pan.

Pfannkuchen *der* (PL *die*
Pfannkuchen) pancake.

Pfarrer *der* (PL *die* Pfarrer) 1 vicar;
2 priest.

Pfau *der* (PL *die* Pfauen) peacock.

Pfeffer *der* pepper.

Pfefferkorn *das* (PL *die*
Pfefferkörner) peppercorn.

Pfefferkuchen *der* gingerbread.

Pfefferminzbonbon *der* (PL *die*
Pfefferminzbonbons) mint.

Pfefferminze *die* peppermint.

Pfeffermühle *die* (PL *die*
Pfeffermühlen) peppermill.

Pfeife *die* (PL *die* Pfeifen) 1 whistle;
2 pipe.

pfeifen ◇ *verb* (IMPERF pfiff, PERF hat
gepfiffen) to whistle.

Pfeil *der* (PL *die* Pfeile) arrow.

Pfeiler *der* (PL *die* Pfeiler) 1 pillar;
2 pier.

Pfennig *der* (PL *die* Pfennige)
pfennig (*the unit of German currency
used before the euro; there were 100
pfennigs to the mark*); **ich habe
keinen Pfennig mehr** I haven't got a
penny left.

Pferd *das* (PL *die* Pferde) horse.

Pferdeschwanz *der* (PL *die*
Pferdeschwänze) ponytail.

pfiff SEE pfeifen.

Pfingsten *das* (PL *die* Pfingsten)
Whitsun.

Pfirsich *der* (PL *die* Pfirsiche) peach.

Pflanze *die* (PL *die* Pflanzen) plant.

pflanzen *verb* (PERF hat gepflanzt)
to plant.

Pflaster *das* (PL *die* Pflaster)
1 pavement; 2 plaster.

Pflaume *die* (PL *die* Pflaumen) plum.

Pflege *die* 1 care; 2 nursing; 3 **ein
Kind in Pflege nehmen** to foster a
child.

Pflegeeltern *plural noun* foster
parents.

Pflegeheim *das* (PL *die*
Pflegeheime) nursing home.

Pflegekind *das* (PL *die*
Pflegekinder) foster child.

pflegeleicht *adjective* easy-care
(*fabric*).

pflegen *verb* (PERF hat geflegt) 1 to
look after, to care for; **eine
Freundschaft pflegen** to foster a
friendship; 2 to nurse.

◇ IRREGULAR VERB: *See the verb table in the centre of the dictionary*

Pfleger der (PL die Pfleger) (male) nurse.

Pflicht die (PL die Pflichten) duty; **Pflicht sein** to be compulsory.

pflichtbewusst Δ adjective conscientious.

Pflichtfach das (PL die Pflichtfächer) compulsory subject.

pflücken verb (PERF hat gepflückt) to pick.

Pflug der (PL die Pflüge) plough.

Pforte die (PL die Pforten) gate.

Pförtner der (PL die Pförtner) porter.

Pfosten der (PL die Pfosten) post.

Pfote die (PL die Pfoten) paw.

pfui exclamation ugh!

Pfund das (PL die Pfund(e)) pound.

Pfütze die (PL die Pfützen) puddle.

Phantasie die 1 imagination; 2 Phantasien (plural) fantasies.

phantasievoll adjective imaginative.

phantastisch adjective fantastic.

Philosoph der (PL die Philosophen) philosopher.

Philosophie die (PL die Philosophien) philosophy.

Photo das (PL die Photos) photo.

Physik die physics.

Physiker der (PL die Physiker) physicist.

Physikerin die (PL die Physikerinnen) physicist.

Pickel der (PL die Pickel) spot, pimple.

Picknick das (PL die Picknicks) picnic.

Pik das spades (in cards).

pikant adjective spicy.

Pille die (PL die Pillen) pill.

Pilot der (PL die Piloten) pilot.

Pilz der (PL die Pilze) 1 mushroom; 2 fungus.

Pinguin der (PL die Pinguine) penguin.

pinkeln verb (informal) (PERF hat gepinkelt) to pee.

Pinnwand die (PL die Pinnwände) noticeboard.

Pinsel der (PL die Pinsel) brush.

Pinzette die (PL die Pinzetten) tweezers.

Pirat der (PL die Piraten) pirate.

Piste die (PL die Pisten) 1 run, piste; 2 track; 3 runway.

Pizza die (PL die Pizzas) pizza.

Pkw der (PL die Pkws) (Personenkraftwagen) car.

plagen verb (PERF hat geplagt) 1 to bother, to torment; 2 to pester; 3 sich plagen to struggle; sich in der Schule plagen to struggle at school; er muss sich plagen he has to work hard.

Plakat das (PL die Plakate) poster.

Plan der (PL die Pläne) 1 plan; 2 map.

Δ NEW SPELLING: See page xii

planen verb (PERF hat geplant) to plan.

planmäßig adjective scheduled. adverb 1 according to plan; alles läuft planmäßig everything is going according to plan; 2 on schedule; der Zug ist planmäßig abgefahren the train left on schedule.

Plastik¹ das plastic.

Plastik² die (PL die Plastiken) sculpture.

Plastiktüte die (PL die Plastiktüten) plastic bag.

platt adjective flat; platt sein (informal) to be flabbergasted.

plattdeutsch adjective low German.

Platte die (PL die Platten) 1 plate; 2 dish; kalte Platte cold meats and cheeses; 3 hotplate; 4 record; 5 board (made of wood); 6 slab (made of stone); 7 sheet (made of metal or glass); 8 top (of a table).

Plattenspieler der (PL die Plattenspieler) record player.

Platz der (PL die Plätze) 1 place; viel Platz haben to have a lot of room; Platz lassen to leave room; auf die Plätze, fertig, los! on your marks, get set, go!; 2 seat; Platz nehmen to take a seat; 3 square (in a town); 4 ground, pitch; einen Spieler vom Platz stellen to send a player off; 5 court (for tennis); 6 course (for golf).

Plätzchen das (PL die Plätzchen) 1 biscuit; 2 spot.

platzen verb (PERF ist geplatzt) 1 to burst; 2 der Plan ist geplatzt (informal) the plan fell through; 3 vor Neugier platzen to be bursting with curiosity.

plaudern verb (PERF hat geplaudert) to chat.

pleite adjective (informal) broke.

Plombe die (PL die Plomben) filling.

plombieren verb (PERF hat plombiert) to fill.

plötzlich adjective sudden. adverb suddenly.

plump adjective 1 plump; 2 clumsy.

Plural der (PL die Plurale) plural.

plus adverb plus.

Plus das 1 plus; 2 profit; 3 advantage.

PLZ = Postleitzahl.

Po der (informal) (PL die Pos) bottom.

Poesie die poetry.

Pokal der (PL die Pokale) 1 cup; 2 goblet.

Pokalspiel das (PL die Pokalspiele) cup-tie.

Pole der (PL die Polen) Pole.

Polen das Poland.

polieren verb (PERF hat poliert) to polish.

Polin die (PL die Polinnen) Pole.

Politik die 1 politics; 2 policy.

Politiker der (PL die Politiker) politician.

◇ IRREGULAR VERB: See the verb table in the centre of the dictionary

Politikerin die (PL die Politikerinnen) politician.

politisch adjective political.

Politur die (PL die Polituren) polish.

Polizei die police.

polizeilich adjective police.
adverb by the police; **sich polizeilich anmelden** to register with the police.

Polizeiwache die (PL die Polizeiwachen) police station.

Polizist der (PL die Polizisten) policeman.

Polizistin die (PL die Polizistinnen) policewoman.

polnisch adjective Polish.

Pommes frites plural noun chips, French fries.

Pony[1] das (PL die Ponys) pony.

Pony[2] der (PL die Ponys) fringe.

Popmusik die pop music.

poppig adjective bright; **Natalie hat immer poppige Socken an** Natalie always wears bright socks.

Porree der leeks; **eine Stange Porree** a leek.

Portemonnaie das = **Portmonee**.

Portier der (PL die Portiers) porter.

Portion die (PL die Portionen) portion.

Portmonee△ das (PL die Portmonees) purse.

Porto das postage.

Porträt das (PL die Porträts) portrait.

Portugal das Portugal.

Portugiese der (PL die Portugiesen) Portuguese.

Portugiesin die (PL die Portugiesinnen) Portuguese.

portugiesisch adjective Portuguese.

Posaune die (PL die Posaunen) trombone.

Post die 1 post; **mit der Post** by post; 2 post office.

Postamt das (PL die Postämter) post office.

Postbote der (PL die Postboten) postman.

Poster das (PL die Poster) poster.

Postkarte die (PL die Postkarten) postcard.

Postleitzahl die (PL die Postleitzahlen) postcode.

prächtig adjective splendid.

prahlen verb (PERF **hat geprahlt**) to boast.

praktisch adjective 1 practical; **praktische Erfahrung** practical experience; 2 handy; 3 **ein praktischer Arzt** a general practitioner.
adverb 1 practically; 2 in practice.

Praline die (PL die Pralinen) chocolate.

Präposition die (PL die Präpositionen) preposition.

Präsens das present (tense).

△ NEW SPELLING: See page xii

Präservativ das (PL die Präservative) condom.

Präsident der (PL die Präsidenten) president.

Präsidentin die (PL die Präsidentinnen) president.

Praxis die (PL die Praxen) 1 practice; 2 practical experience; 3 surgery.

Preis der (PL die Preise) 1 price; um keinen Preis not at any price; 2 prize.

Preisausschreiben das (PL die Preisausschreiben) competition.

Preiselbeere die (PL die Preiselbeeren) cranberry.

preiswert adjective reasonable, cheap.

Prellung die (PL die Prellungen) bruise.

Premierminister der (PL die Premierminister) prime minister.

Presse die press.

Priester der (PL die Priester) priest.

prima adjective (informal) brilliant.

Prinz der (PL die Prinzen) prince.

Prinzessin die (PL die Prinzessinnen) princess.

Prise die (PL die Prisen) pinch; eine Prise Salz a pinch of salt.

privat adjective private.

Privileg das (PL die Privilegien) privilege.

pro preposition ←(+ACC) per.

Probe die (PL die Proben) 1 test; jemanden auf die Probe stellen to test somebody; ein Auto Probe fahren △ to test-drive a car; 2 sample; 3 rehearsal.

probefahren SEE Probe.

probieren verb (PERF hat probiert) 1 to try; 2 to taste.

Problem das (PL die Probleme) problem.

Produkt das (PL die Produkte) product.

Produzent der (PL die Produzenten) producer.

produzieren verb (PERF hat produziert) to produce.

Profi der (PL die Profis) pro.

Profil das (PL die Profile) 1 profile; 2 tread (of a tyre).

Programm das (PL die Programme) 1 programme; 2 program (in computing); 3 channel (on TV).

programmieren verb (PERF hat programmiert) to program.

Programmierer der (PL die Programmierer) programmer.

Projekt das (PL die Projekte) project.

Promille das alcohol level; zuviel Promille haben to be over the limit.

Pronomen das (PL die Pronomen or Pronomina) pronoun.

Prospekt der (PL die Prospekte) brochure.

prost exclamation cheers!

◇ IRREGULAR VERB: See the verb table in the centre of the dictionary

Protein das (PL die Proteine)
protein.

Protest der (PL die Proteste) protest.

protestantisch adjective
Protestant.

protestieren verb (PERF hat
protestiert) to protest.

Protokoll das (PL die Protokolle)
1 minutes, transcript; 2 record (in
court); 3 protocol.

protzen verb (PERF hat geprotzt) to
show off; **Klaus protzt mit seinem
neuen Auto** Klaus is showing off
with his new car.

Proviant der provisions.

Prozent das (PL die Prozente) 1 per
cent; **zehn Prozent** ten per cent;
2 **Prozente bekommen** (informal)
to get a discount.

Prozentsatz der (PL die
Prozentsätze) percentage.

Prozess △ der (PL die Prozesse)
1 court case; **einen Prozess
gewinnen** to win a case; 2 trial;
3 process.

prüfen verb (PERF hat geprüft) 1 to
test, to examine (at school); 2 to
check; **hast du die Reifen geprüft?**
have you checked the tyres?

Prüfung die (PL die Prüfungen)
1 examination, exam; **eine Prüfung
bestehen** to pass an examination;
sie ist durch die Prüfung gefallen
she failed the exam; 2 check.

Prügel der (PL die Prügel) 1 stick;
2 **Prügel bekommen** to get a
beating.

Prügelei die (PL die Prügeleien)
fight.

prügeln verb (PERF hat geprügelt)
1 to beat; 2 **sich prügeln** to fight;
sich um etwas prügeln to fight for
something.

Psychiater der (PL die Psychiater)
psychiatrist.

Psychiaterin die (PL die
Psychiaterinnen) psychiatrist.

psychisch adjective psychological.

Psychologe der (PL die
Psychologen) psychologist.

Psychologie die psychology.

Psychologin die (PL die
Psychologinnen) psychologist.

Publikum das 1 audience, crowd;
2 public.

Pudding der (PL die Puddings)
1 blancmange; 2 pudding
(steamed).

Pudel der (PL die Pudel) poodle.

Puder der (PL die Puder) powder.

Puffmais der popcorn.

Pulli der (PL die Pullis) pullover.

Pullover der (PL die Pullover)
pullover.

Puls der (PL die Pulse) pulse.

Pult das (PL die Pulte) desk.

Pulver das (PL die Pulver) powder.

Pulverkaffee der instant coffee.

Pumpe die (PL die Pumpen) pump.

pumpen verb (PERF hat gepumpt)
1 to pump; 2 (informal) to lend;

△ NEW SPELLING: See page xii

jemandem Geld pumpen to lend somebody money; **3** (*informal*) to borrow; **sich etwas pumpen** to borrow something.

Punker *der* (PL *die* Punker) punk.

Punkerin *die* (PL *die* Punkerinnen) punk.

Punkt *der* (PL *die* Punkte) **1** dot, spot; **Punkt sechs Uhr** at six o'clock on the dot; **2** full stop; **3** point; **nach Punkten siegen** to win on points.

pünktlich *adjective* punctual.

Puppe *die* (PL *die* Puppen) **1** doll; **2** puppet.

pur *adjective* **1** pure; **2 Whisky pur** neat whisky.

Purzelbaum *der* (PL *die* Purzelbäume) somersault.

pusten *verb* (PERF hat gepustet) to blow.

Pute *die* (PL *die* Puten) turkey.

putzen *verb* (PERF hat geputzt) to clean; **putz dir die Zähne** clean your teeth; **putzen gehen** to work as a cleaner; **2 sich die Nase putzen** to blow your nose.

Putzfrau *die* (PL *die* Putzfrauen) cleaning lady, cleaner.

putzig *adjective* cute.

Puzzle *das* (PL *die* Puzzles) jigsaw (puzzle).

Pyjama *der* (PL *die* Pyjamas) pyjamas.

Pyramide *die* (PL *die* Pyramiden) pyramid.

Pyrenäen (*plural noun*) die Pyrenäen the Pyrenees.

Q q

Quadrat *das* (PL *die* Quadrate) square.

quadratisch *adjective* square.

Quadratmeter *der* (PL *die* Quadratmeter) square metre.

quaken *verb* (PERF hat gequakt) **1** to quack; **2** to croak (*of a frog*).

Qual *die* (PL *die* Qualen) **1** torment; **2** agony; **es war eine Qual, das ansehen zu müssen** it was agony to watch.

quälen *verb* (PERF hat gequält) **1** to torment; **2** to torture; **3** to pester; **4 sich quälen** to suffer; **5 sich mit etwas quälen** to struggle with something; **sich durch ein Buch quälen** to struggle (your way) through a book.

Quälgeist *der* (*informal*) (PL *die* Quälgeister) pest.

Qualifikation *die* (PL *die* Qualifikationen) qualification.

Qualität *die* (PL *die* Qualitäten) quality.

Qualle *die* (PL *die* Quallen) jellyfish.

Qualm *der* thick smoke.

qualmen *verb* (PERF hat gequalmt) to give off clouds of smoke; **sie**

✧ IRREGULAR VERB: *See the verb table in the centre of the dictionary*

qualmt wie ein Schlot (*informal*) she smokes like a chimney.

Quarantäne die quarantine.

Quark der (*curd cheese*) quark.

Quartett das (PL die Quartette) quartet.

Quartier das (PL die Quartiere) 1 accommodation; 2 quarters.

quasseln verb (*informal*) (PERF hat gequasselt) to natter.

Quatsch der (*informal*) rubbish.

quatschen verb (*informal*) (PERF hat gequatscht) to chat.

Quelle die (PL die Quellen) 1 source; 2 spring.

quer adverb 1 across; 2 crosswise; 3 diagonally; **quer gestreift** △ with diagonal stripes; 4 **quer durch** straight through.

quergestreift SEE quer.

Querstraße die (PL die Querstraßen) side street; **die erste Querstraße rechts** the first turning on the right.

quetschen verb (PERF hat gequetscht) 1 to crush; 2 to squash; 3 **ich habe mich in meine Jeans gequetscht** I squeezed into my jeans.

Quetschung die (PL die Quetschungen) bruise.

quietschen verb (PERF hat gequietscht) to squeak.

quitt adjective quits.

Quittung die (PL die Quittungen) receipt.

Quiz das (PL die Quiz) quiz.

R r

Rabatt der (PL die Rabatte) discount.

Rache die revenge.

rächen verb (PERF hat gerächt) 1 to avenge; 2 **sich an jemandem rächen** to take revenge on somebody; 3 **das wird sich rächen** you'll have to pay for it.

Rad das (PL die Räder) 1 wheel; 2 bike; **Julia ist mit dem Rad gekommen** Julia came by bike; 3 **Rad fahren** △ to cycle.

Radar der radar.

Radarschirm der (PL die Radarschirme) radar screen.

radfahren SEE Rad.

Radfahrer der (PL die Radfahrer) cyclist.

Radfahrerin die (PL die Radfahrerinnen) cyclist.

Radfahrweg der (PL die Radfahrwege) cycle lane.

radeln verb (PERF ist geradelt) to cycle; **Max ist ins Dorf geradelt** Max cycled into the village.

Radiergummi der (PL die Radiergummis) rubber.

Radieschen das (PL die Radieschen) radish.

△ NEW SPELLING: See page xii

Radio das (PL die **Radios**) radio.

radioaktiv adjective radioactive.

Radler der (PL die **Radler**) cyclist.

Radlerin die (PL die **Radlerinnen**) cyclist.

Radrennen das 1 cycle race; **Maria hat das Radrennen gewonnen** Maria won the cycle race; 2 cycle racing.

raffiniert adjective crafty.

Rahm der cream.

Rahmen der (PL die **Rahmen**) 1 frame; 2 framework; 3 limits; **im Rahmen des Möglichen** within the bounds of possibility.

rahmen verb (PERF **hat gerahmt**) to frame (a picture).

Rakete die (PL die **Raketen**) rocket.

ran (informal) SEE **heran**.

Rand der (PL die **Ränder**) 1 edge; 2 rim; **der Rand der Tasse war angeschlagen** the rim of the cup was chipped; 3 ring, mark; 4 margin (of a page); **du musst einen Rand für die Korrekturen lassen** you must leave a margin for the corrections; 5 outskirts (of a town); 6 **etwas am Rande erwähnen** to mention something in passing; 7 **am Rande der Pleite sein** to be on the verge of bankruptcy; 8 **außer Rand und Band geraten** (informal) to go wild.

Randstreifen der (PL die **Randstreifen**) hard shoulder.

Rang der (PL die **Ränge**) 1 rank; 2 (in a theatre) circle.

rannte SEE **rennen**.

rasch adjective quick.

Rasen der (PL die **Rasen**) lawn, grass.

rasen verb (PERF **ist gerast**) to tear along, to rush; **gegen eine Mauer rasen** to career into a wall.

Rasenmäher der (PL die **Rasenmäher**) lawnmower.

Rasierapparat der (PL die **Rasierapparate**) 1 shaver; 2 razor.

Rasiercreme die (PL die **Rasiercremes**) shaving cream.

rasieren verb (PERF **hat rasiert**) 1 to shave; 2 **sich rasieren** to shave.

Rasierklinge die (PL die **Rasierklingen**) razor blade.

Rasierwasser das aftershave.

Rasse die (PL die **Rassen**) 1 race; 2 breed; **ich weiß nicht, was für eine Rasse unser Hund ist** I don't know what breed our dog is.

Rassenhass △ der racial hatred.

rassisch adjective racial.

Rassismus der racism.

Rassist der (PL die **Rassisten**) racist.

Rassistin die (PL die **Rassistinnen**) racist.

rassistisch adjective racist.

rasten verb (PERF **hat gerastet**) to rest.

Rastplatz der (PL die **Rastplätze**) picnic area (on a motorway).

Raststätte die (PL die **Raststätten**) services (on a motorway).

◇ IRREGULAR VERB: See the verb table in the centre of the dictionary

Rat der 1 advice; **ein Rat** a piece of advice; **jemanden zu Rate ziehen** to ask somebody's advice; 2 **sich keinen Rat wissen** not to know what to do; 3 council.

Rate die (PL die Raten) instalment; **in monatlichen Raten abzahlen** to pay in monthly instalments.

raten ⋄ verb (PRES **rät**, IMPERF **riet**, PERF **hat geraten**) 1 **jemandem raten** to advise somebody; **was rätst du mir?** what do you advise me to do?; 2 to guess; **richtig raten** to guess right.

Rathaus das (PL die Rathäuser) town hall.

rationell adjective efficient.

ratlos adjective helpless; **Emma hat mich ratlos angesehen** Emma gave me a helpless look; **ratlos sein** not to know what to do.

ratsam adjective advisable; **es wäre ratsam, früher zu fahren** it would be advisable to leave earlier.

Ratschlag der (PL die Ratschläge) piece of advice, advice; **deine klugen Ratschläge kannst du dir sparen** you can keep your advice to yourself.

Rätsel das (PL die Rätsel) 1 puzzle; 2 mystery.

rätselhaft adjective mysterious.

Ratte die (PL die Ratten) rat.

rau △ adjective 1 rough; 2 harsh; 3 **eine raue Stimme** a husky voice; 4 **einen rauen Hals haben** to have a sore throat.

Raub der robbery.

Räuber der (PL die Räuber) robber.

Rauch der smoke.

rauchen verb (PERF hat geraucht) to smoke; **'Rauchen verboten'** 'no smoking'.

Raucher der (PL die Raucher) smoker.

Raucherin die (PL die Raucherinnen) smoker.

räuchern verb (PERF hat geräuchert) to smoke (fish, meat).

rauf (informal) SEE herauf, hinauf.

rauh adjective = rau.

Raum der (PL die Räume) 1 room; **das Haus hat sehr große Räume** the house has very big rooms; 2 space; **wir brauchen mehr Raum** we need more space; 3 **die Rakete ist im Raum explodiert** the rocket exploded in space; 4 area; **im Raum Berlin** in the area of Berlin.

räumen verb (PERF hat geräumt) 1 to clear; **das Geschirr vom Tisch räumen** to clear away the dishes; 2 **die Hemden in den Schrank räumen** to put the shirts in the cupboard; **seine Sachen beiseite räumen** to put your things to one side; **die Akten aus dem Schrank räumen** to take the files out of the cabinet; 3 to vacate.

Raumfahrt die space travel.

Raumschiff das (PL die Raumschiffe) space ship.

Raupe die (PL die Raupen) caterpillar.

raus (*informal*) SEE **heraus**, **hinaus**.

Rauschgift *das* (PL *die* Rauschgifte) drug; **Rauschgift nehmen** to take drugs.

Rauschgiftsüchtige *der/die* (PL *die* Rauschgiftsüchtigen) drug addict.

rauskriegen *verb* (*informal*) (PERF hat rausgekriegt) **1** to get out; **2 ein Geheimnis rauskriegen** to find out a secret; **3 ich kann die Aufgabe nicht rauskriegen** I can't do the exercise.

räuspern *verb* (PERF hat sich geräuspert) **sich räuspern** to clear your throat.

reagieren *verb* (PERF hat reagiert) to react.

Reaktion *die* (PL *die* Reaktionen) reaction.

realisieren *verb* (PERF hat realisiert) **1** to realize; **2** to implement.

Realschule *die* (PL *die* Realschulen) secondary school.

rebellieren *verb* (PERF hat rebelliert) to rebel.

rechnen *verb* (PERF hat gerechnet) **1** to do arithmetic; **Peter kann gut rechnen** Peter's good at arithmetic; Peter's good at figures; **2** to reckon; **mit etwas rechnen** to reckon with something; **3 er wird zu den besten Schauspielern gerechnet** he's reckoned to be one of the best actors; **4** to count; **jemanden zu seinen Freunden rechnen** to count somebody as a friend; **5 mit etwas**

rechnen to expect something; **6 auf jemanden rechnen** to count on somebody.

Rechner *der* (PL *die* Rechner) **1** calculator; **2** computer.

Rechnung *die* (PL *die* Rechnungen) **1** bill; **2** invoice; **die Rechnung liegt bei** the invoice is enclosed; **3** calculation.

recht *adjective* **1** right; **jemandem recht sein** to be all right with somebody; **wenn es dir recht ist** if it's all right with you; **2 der/die Rechte** the right man/woman; **3 das Rechte** the right thing; **etwas Rechtes** something proper; **ich habe nichts Rechtes gegessen** I haven't had a proper meal; **etwas Rechtes lernen** to learn something useful; **4** real; **ich habe keine rechte Lust** I don't really feel like it. *adverb* **1** correctly; **2** quite; **recht einfach** quite simple; **3** really; **4 recht vielen Dank** many thanks; **5 das geschieht dir recht!** (it) serves you right!; **6 man kann es nicht allen recht machen** you can't please everyone.

Recht *das* (PL *die* Rechte) **1** law; **nach deutschem Recht** under German law; **2** right; **Recht haben** △ to be right; **im Recht sein** to be in the right; **Recht bekommen** △ to be proved right; **3 jemandem Recht geben** △ to agree with somebody; **4 mit Recht** rightly; **du hast dich mit Recht beschwert** you were right to complain.

rechte SEE **rechter**.

Rechte *die* **1** right (side); **zu meiner**

◇ IRREGULAR VERB: *See the verb table in the centre of the dictionary*

Rechten on my right; **2** right hand; **3 die Rechte** the right (*in politics*).

rechteckig *adjective* rectangular.

Rechteck das (PL *die* **Rechtecke**) rectangle.

rechter, rechte, rechtes *adjective* **1** right; **auf der rechten Seite** on the right; **2** right-wing.

rechtfertigen *verb* **1** (PERF **hat gerechtfertigt**) to justify; **2 sich rechtfertigen** to justify yourself.

rechtlich *adjective* legal.

rechts *adverb* **1** on the right; **von rechts** from the right; **rechts abbiegen** to turn right; **2 rechts sein** to be right-wing; **3 zwei rechts, zwei links stricken** to knit two, purl two.

Rechtsanwalt der (PL *die* **Rechtsanwälte**) lawyer.

Rechtsanwältin die (PL *die* **Rechtsanwältinnen**) lawyer.

Rechtschreibung die spelling.

Rechtshänder der (PL *die* **Rechtshänder**) **Klaus ist Rechtshänder** Klaus is right-handed.

Rechtshänderin die (PL *die* **Rechtshänderinnen**) **Beate ist Rechtshänderin** Beate is right-handed.

rechtzeitig *adjective* timely. *adverb* in time; **wir sind gerade noch rechtzeitig angekommen** we got there just in time.

Redakteur der (PL *die* **Redakteure**) editor.

Redakteurin die (PL *die* **Redakteurinnen**) editor.

Rede die (PL *die* **Reden**) **1** speech; **eine Rede halten** to make a speech; **2 nicht der Rede wert** not worth mentioning; **davon kann keine Rede sein** it's out of the question; **jemanden zur Rede stellen** to take somebody to task.

reden *verb* (PERF **hat geredet**) **1** to talk; **2** to speak; **mit jemandem reden** to speak to somebody; **3 sie hat kein Wort geredet** she didn't say a word; **4 mir ist egal, was über mich geredet wird** I don't care what people say about me.

reduzieren *verb* (PERF **hat reduziert**) to reduce.

reflexiv *adjective* reflexive.

Reformhaus das (PL *die* **Reformhäuser**) health-food shop.

Regal das (PL *die* **Regale**) **1** shelf; **2** shelves, bookcase.

Regel die (PL *die* **Regeln**) **1** rule; **in der Regel** as a rule; **2** period (*menstruation*).

regelmäßig *adjective* regular.

regeln *verb* (PERF **hat geregelt**) **1** to regulate; **2** to direct (*the traffic*); **3** to settle (*a matter*); **wir haben die Sache so geregelt, dass ...** we've arranged things so that ...; **4 sich von selbst regeln** to sort itself out.

Regelung die (PL *die* **Regelungen**) **1** regulation; **2** settlement.

Regen der rain.

∆ NEW SPELLING: See page xii

Regenbogen der (PL die Regenbogen) rainbow.

Regenmantel der (PL die Regenmäntel) raincoat.

Regenschirm der (PL die Regenschirme) umbrella.

Regenwurm der (PL die Regenwürmer) earthworm.

regieren verb (PERF hat regiert) 1 to govern; 2 to rule, to reign.

Regierung die (PL die Regierungen) 1 government; 2 reign.

Regisseur der (PL die Regisseure) director.

Regisseurin die (PL die Regisseurinnen) director.

regnen verb (PERF hat geregnet) to rain.

regnerisch adjective rainy.

Reh das (PL die Rehe) deer.

reiben ◇ verb (IMPERF rieb, PERF hat gerieben) 1 to rub; 2 to grate.

reibungslos adjective smooth.

reich adjective rich.

Reich das (PL die Reiche) 1 empire; 2 kingdom, realm.

reichen verb (PERF hat gereicht) 1 to hand, to pass; 2 to be enough; **mit dem Geld reichen** to have enough money; 3 **bis zu etwas reichen** to reach up to something; **er reicht seinem Vater bis zur Schulter** he comes up to his father's shoulder; **die Felder reichen bis zum Wald** the fields extend as far as or go right up to the forest; 4 **mir reicht's!** (informal) I've had enough!

reichlich adjective 1 large; 2 ample (space).
adverb plenty of.

Reichtum der (PL die Reichtümer) wealth.

Reichweite die 1 reach; **außer Reichweite** out of reach; 2 range.

reif adjective 1 ripe; 2 mature.

Reifen der (PL die Reifen) 1 tyre; 2 hoop.

Reifenpanne die (PL die Reifenpannen) puncture.

Reifendruck der tyre pressure.

Reihe die (PL die Reihen) 1 row; 2 series; 3 **der Reihe nach** in turn; **außer der Reihe** out of turn; **du bist an der Reihe** it's your turn.

Reihenfolge die (PL die Reihenfolgen) order.

Reihenhaus das (PL die Reihenhäuser) terraced house.

Reim der (PL die Reime) rhyme.

reimen verb (PERF hat gereimt) 1 to rhyme; 2 **sich reimen** to rhyme.

rein[1] adjective 1 pure; 2 clean; 3 sheet (madness); 4 **etwas ins Reine schreiben** △ to make a fair copy of something; **etwas ins Reine bringen** △ to sort something out.
adverb 1 purely; 2 absolutely; **rein gar nichts** absolutely nothing.

rein[2] (informal) SEE herein, hinein.

◇ IRREGULAR VERB: See the verb table in the centre of the dictionary

reinigen *verb* (PERF hat gereinigt) to clean.

Reinigung die (PL die Reinigungen) 1 cleaning; 2 cleaner's.

Reis der rice.

Reise die (PL die Reisen) 1 journey, trip; gute Reise! have a good journey!; auf meinen Reisen on my travels; 2 voyage.

Reiseandenken das (PL die Reiseandenken) souvenir.

Reisebüro das (PL die Reisebüros) travel agency.

Reisebus der (PL die Reisebusse) coach.

Reiseführer der (PL die Reiseführer) 1 guidebook; 2 (travel) guide.

Reiseleiter der (PL die Reiseleiter) (travel) guide.

reisen *verb* (PERF ist gereist) to travel.

Reisende der/die (PL die Reisenden) traveller.

Reisepass △ der (PL die Reisepässe) passport.

Reisescheck der (PL die Reisereschecks) traveller's cheque.

Reiseziel das (PL die Reiseziele) destination.

reißen ◇ *verb* (IMPERF riss △, PERF hat gerissen) 1 to tear; 2 to snatch; 3 to pull; an etwas reißen to pull at something; 4 mit sich reißen to sweep away; 5 etwas an sich reißen to snatch something; die Macht an sich reißen to seize power; 6 Witze reißen to crack jokes; 7 sich um etwas reißen to fight for something; 8 hin und her gerissen sein to be torn; 9 (PERF ist gerissen) to tear, to break.

Reißverschluss △ der (PL die Reißverschlüsse) zip.

Reißzwecke die (PL die Reißzwecken) drawing pin.

reiten ◇ *verb* (IMPERF ritt, PERF hat/ist geritten) to ride.

Reiter der (PL die Reiter) rider.

Reiterin die (PL die Reiterinnen) rider.

Reitschule die (PL die Reitschulen) riding school.

Reiz der (PL die Reize) 1 attraction, appeal; 2 charm.

reizen *verb* (PERF hat gereizt) 1 to appeal to, to tempt; das reizt mich sehr it's very tempting; 2 to annoy; jemanden zum Zorn reizen to provoke somebody to anger; 3 to irritate (*the skin, eyes*); 4 to bid (*when playing cards*).

reizend *adjective* charming.

reizvoll *adjective* attractive.

Reklame die (PL die Reklamen) 1 advertisement, advert; für etwas Reklame machen to advertise something; 2 commercial (*on TV*).

Rekord der (PL die Rekorde) record.

Rektor der (PL die Rektoren) 1 head (*of a school*); 2 vice-chancellor (*of a university*).

Religion *die* (PL *die* **Religionen**) religion.

religiös *adjective* religious.

Rendezvous *das* (PL *die* **Rendezvous**) date.

Rennbahn *die* (PL *die* **Rennbahnen**) racetrack.

rennen ◇ *verb* (IMPERF **rannte**, PERF **ist gerannt**) to run.

Rennen *das* (PL *die* **Rennen**) race.

Rennfahrer *der* (PL *die* **Rennfahrer**) racing driver.

Rennwagen *der* (PL *die* **Rennwagen**) racing car.

renovieren *verb* (PERF **hat renoviert**) to renovate, to redecorate.

rentabel *adjective* profitable.

Rente *die* (PL *die* **Renten**) pension; **in Rente gehen** to retire.

Rentner *der* (PL *die* **Rentner**) pensioner.

Rentnerin *die* (PL *die* **Rentnerinnen**) pensioner.

Reparatur *die* (PL *die* **Reparaturen**) repair.

reparieren *verb* (PERF **hat repariert**) to repair.

Reportage *die* (PL *die* **Reportagen**) 1 report; 2 live commentary.

Reporter *der* (PL *die* **Reporter**) reporter.

Reporterin *die* (PL *die* **Reporterinnen**) reporter.

Reptil *das* (PL *die* **Reptile**) reptile.

Republik *die* (PL *die* **Republiken**) republic.

Reservat *das* (PL *die* **Reservate**) reservation.

Reserverad *das* (PL *die* **Reserveräder**) spare wheel.

reservieren *verb* (PERF **hat reserviert**) to reserve.

Reservierung *die* (PL *die* **Reservierungen**) reservation.

Respekt *der* respect.

respektieren *verb* (PERF **hat respektiert**) to respect.

Rest *der* (PL *die* **Reste**) 1 rest, remainder; 2 left-over; **zum Mittagessen gibt's die Reste** we're having the leftovers for lunch; 3 **die Reste** the remains.

Restaurant *das* (PL *die* **Restaurants**) restaurant.

restlich *adjective* remaining.

restlos *adjective* complete.

Resultat *das* (PL *die* **Resultate**) result.

retten *verb* (PERF **hat gerettet**) 1 to save, to rescue; **jemandem das Leben retten** to save somebody's life; 2 **sich retten** to escape.

Rettich *der* (PL *die* **Rettiche**) radish.

Rettung *die* rescue.

Rettungsring *der* (PL *die* **Rettungsringe**) lifebelt.

Rettungswagen *der* (PL *die* **Rettungswagen**) ambulance.

◇ IRREGULAR VERB: *See the verb table in the centre of the dictionary*

Rezept das (PL die Rezepte)
1 prescription; 2 recipe.

Rezeption die (PL die Rezeptionen)
reception; **bitte geben Sie Ihren
Schlüssel an der Rezeption ab**
please leave your key at reception.

R-Gespräch das (PL die
R-Gespräche) reverse-charge call.

Rhabarber der rhubarb.

Rhein der Rhine.

Rheuma das rheumatism.

Rhythmus der (PL die Rhythmen)
rhythm.

richten verb (PERF hat gerichtet)
1 to direct, to point (a torch,
telescope, gun); 2 **eine Frage an
jemanden richten** to put a question
to somebody; 3 to address (a letter,
remarks); 4 to prepare (a meal,
room); 5 **sich auf etwas richten** to
be directed towards something;
6 **sich nach jemandem richten** to
fit in with somebody's wishes; **sich
nach den Vorschriften richten** to
follow the rules; 7 **sich nach etwas
richten** to depend on something.

Richter der (PL die Richter) judge.

richtig adjective 1 right; 2 **das
Richtige** the right thing; **der/die
Richtige** the right man/woman;
3 real, proper.
adverb 1 correctly, right;
3 **richtig stellen**△ to put right; **die
Uhr geht richtig** the clock is right.

Richtung die (PL die Richtungen)
1 direction; 2 trend.

rieb SEE reiben.

riechen ◇ verb (IMPERF roch, PERF
hat gerochen) 1 to smell; 2 **ich
kann ihn nicht riechen** (informal)
I can't stand him.

rief SEE rufen.

Riegel der (PL die Riegel) 1 bolt;
2 **ein Riegel Schokolade** a bar of
chocolate.

Riemen der (PL die Riemen) strap.

Riese der (PL die Riesen) giant.

riesengroß adjective gigantic.

riesig adjective huge.

riet SEE raten.

Rind das (PL die Rinder) 1 ox; 2 cow;
Rinder cattle; 3 beef.

Rinde die (PL die Rinden) 1 bark;
2 rind; 3 crust.

Rindfleisch das beef.

Ring der (PL die Ringe) ring.

Ringbuch das (PL die Ringbücher)
ring binder.

Ringen das wrestling.

Rippe die (PL die Rippen) rib.

Risiko das (PL die Risiken) risk.

riskant adjective risky.

riskieren verb (PERF hat riskiert) to
risk.

riss△ SEE reißen.

Riss△ der (PL die Risse) 1 tear;
2 crack.

ritt SEE reiten.

Rivale der (PL die Rivalen) rival.

Rivalin die (PL die Rivalinnen) rival.

△ NEW SPELLING: See page xii

Robbe die (PL die **Robben**) seal.

Roboter der (PL die **Roboter**) robot.

roch SEE **riechen**.

Rock der (PL die **Röcke**) skirt.

Roggen der rye.

roh adjective **1** raw; **2** rough;
3 brutal.

Rohr das (PL die **Rohre**) **1** pipe;
2 reed; **3** cane.

Rolladen = **Rollladen**.

Rolle die (PL die **Rollen**) **1** roll;
2 reel; **3** role, part; **4** es spielt keine
Rolle it doesn't matter.

rollen verb (PERF hat **gerollt**) **1** to
roll; **2** (PERF ist **gerollt**) to roll.

Roller der (PL die **Roller**) scooter.

Rollkragen der (PL die **Rollkrägen**)
polo neck.

Rollladen ∆ der (PL die **Rollläden**)
shutter.

Rollschuh der (PL die **Rollschuhe**)
roller-skate.

Rollschuhlaufen das roller-
skating.

Rollstuhl der (PL die **Rollstühle**)
wheelchair.

Rolltreppe die (PL die **Rolltreppen**)
escalator.

Rom das Rome.

Roman der (PL die **Romane**) novel.

romantisch adjective romantic.

röntgen verb (PERF hat **geröntgt**) to
X-ray.

rosa adjective pink.

Rose die (PL die **Rosen**) rose.

Rosenkohl der (Brussels) sprouts.

Rosine die (PL die **Rosinen**) raisin.

Rosmarin der rosemary.

Rosskastanie ∆ die (PL die
Rosskastanien) horse-chestnut.

Rost der (PL die **Roste**) **1** rust;
2 grate, grill.

rosten verb (PERF ist **gerostet**) to
rust.

rösten (PERF hat **geröstet**) **1** to roast;
2 to toast.

rostig adjective rusty.

rot adjective red.

Röteln plural noun German
measles.

rothaarig adjective red-haired.

Rotkehlchen das (PL die
Rotkehlchen) robin.

Rotwein der (PL die **Rotweine**) red
wine.

rüber adverb (informal) over;
komm zu uns rüber come over to
us.

rücken verb (PERF hat **gerückt**) to
move; **kannst du ein wenig
rücken?** can you move over a bit?

Rücken der (PL die **Rücken**) **1** back;
2 spine (of a book).

Rückfahrkarte die (PL die
Rückfahrkarten) return ticket; **eine
Rückfahrkarte nach München** a
return ticket to Munich.

Rückfahrt die return journey; **auf der Rückfahrt** on the way back.

Rückgabe die (PL die **Rückgaben**) return.

rückgängig adjective **etwas rückgängig machen** to cancel something.

Rückkehr die return.

Rückreise die return journey.

Rucksack der (PL die **Rucksäcke**) rucksack.

Rückseite die (PL die **Rückseiten**) back.

Rücksicht die consideration.

rücksichtslos adjective 1 inconsiderate; **ein rücksichtsloser Fahrer** a reckless driver; 2 ruthless.

rücksichtsvoll adjective considerate.

Rücksitz der (PL die **Rücksitze**) back seat.

rückwärts adverb backwards.

Rückwärtsgang der (PL die **Rückwärtsgänge**) reverse (gear).

Rückweg der (PL die **Rückwege**) 1 way back; 2 return journey.

Rückzahlung die (PL die **Rückzahlungen**) refund, repayment.

Ruder das (PL die **Ruder**) 1 oar; 2 rudder.

Ruderboot das (PL die **Ruderboote**) rowing boat.

rudern verb (PERF **ist gerudert**) 1 to row; **ich bin über den See gerudert** I rowed across the lake; 2 (PERF **hat gerudert**) to row; **ich habe Monika über den See gerudert** I rowed Monika across the lake.

Ruf der (PL die **Rufe**) 1 call, shout; 2 reputation; 3 phone number.

rufen ◇ verb (IMPERF **rief**, PERF **hat gerufen**) to call; **den Arzt rufen** to send for the doctor.

Rufnummer die (PL die **Rufnummern**) phone number.

Ruhe die 1 silence; **Ruhe bitte!** quiet please!; 2 rest; 3 peace; **jemanden in Ruhe lassen** to leave somebody in peace; **in aller Ruhe** calmly; 4 **sich nicht aus der Ruhe bringen lassen** to not get worked up; 5 **sich zur Ruhe setzen** to retire.

ruhen verb (PERF **hat geruht**) to rest; **hier ruht …** here lies …

Ruhestand der **im Ruhestand** retired.

Ruhetag der (PL die **Ruhetage**) closing day; 'Dienstag Ruhetag' 'closed on Tuesdays'.

ruhig adjective 1 quiet; 2 peaceful; 3 calm.
adverb 1 quietly; **sich ruhig verhalten** to keep quiet; 2 calmly; **ruhig bleiben** to remain calm; 3 **sehen Sie sich ruhig um** you're welcome to look around; **du kannst es ihm ruhig sagen** it's OK, you can tell him.

Ruhm der fame.

Rührei das scrambled eggs.

△ NEW SPELLING: See page xii

rühren verb (PERF hat gerührt) 1 to move; 2 to stir; 3 sich rühren to move; 4 an etwas rühren to touch, to touch on.

Ruine die (PL die Ruinen) ruin.

ruinieren verb (PERF hat ruiniert) to ruin.

rülpsen verb (PERF hat gerülpst) to belch.

Rumänien das Romania.

rumänisch adjective Romanian.

Rummel der 1 hustle and bustle; 2 fuss; 3 fair.

Rummelplatz der (PL die Rummelplätze) fairground.

rund adjective round.
adverb about; rund um around.

Runde die (PL die Runden) 1 round; 2 lap; 3 circle, group; 4 über die Runden kommen (informal) to get by.

Rundfahrt die (PL die Rundfahrten) tour.

Rundfrage die (PL die Rundfragen) poll.

Rundfunk der radio; im Rundfunk on the radio.

rundherum adverb all around.

runter adverb (informal) SEE herunter, hinunter; runter da! get off!

runzlig adjective wrinkled.

Rüsche die (PL die Rüschen) frill.

Russe der (PL die Russen) Russian.

Rüssel der (PL die Rüssel) trunk.

Russin die (PL die Russinnen) Russian.

russisch adjective Russian.

Russland Δ das Russia.

Rüstung die (PL die Rüstungen) 1 armament; 2 arms; 3 (suit of) armour.

Rutschbahn die (PL die Rutschbahnen) slide.

rutschen verb (PERF ist gerutscht) 1 to slide; 2 to slip; 3 rutsch mal! move over!

rutschig adjective slippery.

rütteln verb (PERF hat gerüttelt) to shake; an der Tür rütteln to rattle at the door.

S s

Saal der (PL die Säle) hall.

Sabbat der (PL die Sabbate) Sabbath.

Sache die (PL die Sachen) 1 matter; das ist eine andere Sache that's a different matter; 2 business; das ist seine Sache that's his business; 3 thing; meine Sachen my things (clothing); sie räumt nie ihre Sachen weg she never puts away her things; 4 zur Sache kommen to get to the point; 5 das ist so'ne Sache (informal) it's a bit tricky.

Sachgebiet das (PL die Sachgebiete) field, area.

◆ IRREGULAR VERB: See the verb table in the centre of the dictionary

sachlich *adjective* 1 objective;
2 factual.

sächlich *adjective* neuter.

Sachsen *das* Saxony.

Sack *der* (PL die **Säcke**) 1 sack;
2 bag.

Sackgasse *die* (PL die **Sackgassen**)
cul-de-sac.

Saft *der* (PL die **Säfte**) 1 juice; 2 sap.

saftig *adjective* juicy.

Säge *die* (PL die **Sägen**) saw.

Sägemehl *das* sawdust.

sagen *verb* (PERF hat **gesagt**) 1 to
say; **man sagt, dass ...** it's said that
...; 2 **was ich noch sagen wollte** by
the way; **unter uns gesagt** between
you and me; 3 to tell; **jemandem
etwas sagen** to tell somebody
something; **sag mal** tell me; **was
sagen Sie dazu?** what do you think
about it? 4 to mean; **das hat nichts
zu sagen** it doesn't mean anything;
5 **zu jemandem Tante sagen** to call
somebody aunt; 6 **ihr Gesicht
sagte alles** it was written all over
her face.

sägen *verb* (PERF hat **gesägt**) to saw.

sagenhaft *adjective* 1 legendary;
2 (*informal*) brilliant.

sah SEE sehen.

Sahne *die* cream.

Saison *die* (PL die **Saisons**) season.

Saite *die* (PL die **Saiten**) string.

Sakko *das* (PL die **Sakkos**) jacket.

Salat *der* (PL die **Salate**) 1 lettuce;
2 salad.

Salatsoße *die* (PL die **Salatsoßen**)
salad dressing.

Salbe *die* (PL die **Salben**) ointment.

Salbei *der* sage.

salopp *adjective* casual, informal.

Salz *das* salt.

salzen *verb* (PERF hat **gesalzen**) to
salt.

salzig *adjective* salty.

Salzkartoffeln *plural noun* boiled
potatoes.

Salzwasser *das* 1 salt water;
2 salted water (*for cooking*).

Samen *der* (PL die **Samen**) 1 seed;
2 sperm, semen.

sammeln *verb* (PERF hat
gesammelt) 1 to collect; **Martin
sammelt Briefmarken** Martin
collects stamps; 2 to gather; 3 **sich
sammeln** to gather; **seine
Gedanken sammeln** to gather your
thoughts.

Sammlung *die* (PL die
Sammlungen) collection; **eine
Sammlung für einen guten Zweck**
a collection for charity.

Samstag *der* (PL die **Samstage**)
Saturday.

samstags *adverb* on Saturdays.

samt *preposition* ←(+DAT) (together)
with; **Mimi kam samt Puppen und
Katze** Mimi arrived with her dolls
and cat.

△ NEW SPELLING: *See page xii*

Samt der (PL die **Samte**) velvet.

sämtlicher, sämtliche, sämtliches adjective all the; **meine sämtlichen Bücher** all my books.

Sand der sand.

Sandale die (PL die **Sandalen**) sandal.

sandig adjective sandy.

sandte SEE **senden**.

sanft adjective gentle; **eine sanfte Stimme** a soft voice.

sang SEE **singen**.

Sänger der (PL die **Sänger**) singer.

Sängerin die (PL die **Sängerinnen**) singer.

sank SEE **sinken**.

Sardelle die (PL die **Sardellen**) anchovy.

Sardine die (PL die **Sardinen**) sardine.

Sarg der (PL die **Särge**) coffin.

Sarkasmus der sarcasm.

sarkastisch adjective sarcastic.

saß SEE **sitzen**.

Satellit der (PL die **Satelliten**) satellite.

Satellitenfernsehen das satellite television.

satt adjective 1 full (up); **bist du satt geworden?** have you had enough to eat?; **sich satt essen** to eat as much as one wants; **satt machen** to be filling; 2 **etwas satt haben** (informal) to be fed up with something.

Sattel der (PL die **Sättel**) saddle.

Satz der (PL die **Sätze**) 1 sentence; 2 set (of things or in tennis); **ein Satz Reifen** a set of tyres; 3 movement (in music); 4 rate (of tax, interest); 5 leap.

sauber adjective 1 clean; 2 neat; 3 (informal) fine (expressing irony); 4 **sauber machen**△ to clean.

Sauberkeit die cleanliness, cleanness.

saubermachen SEE **sauber**.

Sauce die (PL die **Saucen**) = **Soße**.

sauer adjective 1 sour; 2 pickled; 3 acid; **saurer Regen** acid rain; 4 **sauer sein** (informal) to be annoyed; **ich bin sauer auf Eva** I'm annoyed with Eva.

Sauerei die (informal) (PL die **Sauereien**) 1 mess; 2 disgrace, scandal; 3 obscenity.

Sauerstoff der oxygen.

saufen ◇ verb (informal) (PRES **säuft**, IMPERF **soff**, PERF **hat gesoffen**) to drink, to booze.

saugen verb (PERF **hat gesaugt**) 1 to suck; 2 to vacuum, to hoover.

Säugetier das (PL die **Säugetiere**) mammal.

Säugling der (PL die **Säuglinge**) baby, infant.

Säule die (PL die **Säulen**) column.

Säure die (PL die **Säuren**) acid.

◇ IRREGULAR VERB: See the verb table in the centre of the dictionary

Saxofon △ *das* (PL *die* **Saxofone**) saxophone.

S-Bahn *die* (PL *die* **S-Bahnen**) city and suburban railway.

schäbig *adjective* shabby.

Schach *das* chess; **Schach!** check!

Schachbrett *das* (PL *die* **Schachbretter**) chessboard.

Schachfigur *die* (PL *die* **Schachfiguren**) chess piece.

Schachtel *die* (PL *die* **Schachteln**) box.

schade *adjective* 1 **schade sein** to be a pity; **schade!** (what a) pity!; 2 **zu schade für jemanden sein** to be too good for somebody.

schaden *verb* (PERF **hat geschadet**) 1 to damage; **das hat seinem Ruf geschadet** it damaged his reputation; 2 **jemandem schaden** to harm somebody; 3 **das schadet nichts** it doesn't matter.

Schaden *der* (PL *die* **Schäden**) 1 damage; 2 disadvantage.

schädlich *adjective* harmful.

Schaf *das* (PL *die* **Schafe**) sheep.

Schäfer *der* (PL *die* **Schäfer**) shepherd.

Schäferhund *der* (PL *die* **Schäferhunde**) sheepdog.

schaffen[1] ◇ *verb* (IMPERF **schuf**, PERF **hat geschaffen**) to create; **wie geschaffen für** made for.

schaffen[2] *verb* (PERF **hat geschafft**) 1 to manage; **es schaffen, etwas zu tun** to manage to do something; 2 **eine Prüfung schaffen** to pass an exam; 3 **jemandem zu schaffen machen** to cause somebody trouble; 4 **geschafft sein** (*informal*) to be worn out.

Schaffner *der* (PL *die* **Schaffner**) 1 conductor; 2 (ticket) inspector.

Schaffnerin *die* (PL *die* **Schaffnerinnen**) 1 conductress; 2 (ticket) inspector.

Schal *der* (PL *die* **Schals**) scarf.

Schale *die* (PL *die* **Schalen**) 1 skin; 2 peel; 3 shell; 4 dish, bowl; **eine Schale Obst** a bowl of fruit.

schälen *verb* (PERF **hat geschält**) 1 to peel; **er hat ihr eine Orange geschält** he peeled an orange for her; 2 **sich schälen** to peel; **mein Rücken schält sich** my back's peeling.

Schall *der* sound.

Schallplatte *die* (PL *die* **Schallplatten**) record.

schalten *verb* (PERF **hat geschaltet**) 1 to switch; **auf etwas schalten** to turn to something; 2 to change gear; 3 **schnell schalten** (*informal*) to catch on quickly.

Schalter *der* (PL *die* **Schalter**) 1 switch; 2 counter.

Schaltjahr *das* (PL *die* **Schaltjahre**) leap year.

schämen *verb* (PERF **hat sich geschämt**) **sich schämen** to be ashamed.

Schampon *das* (PL *die* **Schampons**) shampoo.

Schande die 1 disgrace; 2 shame.

scharf adjective 1 sharp; 2 hot (food); **ein scharfer Wind** a biting wind; 3 fierce (dog, frost); 4 **scharf nachdenken** to think hard; 5 (in photography) **scharf sein** to be in focus; **scharf einstellen** to focus; 6 **scharf schießen** to fire live ammunition; 7 **scharf auf etwas sein** (informal) to be really keen on something; **sie ist scharf auf Bernd** (informal) she fancies Bernd.

Schaschlik der (PL die Schaschliks) kebab.

Schatten der (PL die Schatten) 1 shadow; 2 shade.

schattig adjective shady.

Schatz der (PL die Schätze) 1 treasure; 2 darling.

Schätzchen das (PL die Schätzchen) darling.

schätzen verb (PERF hat geschätzt) 1 to estimate; 2 to value; 3 to reckon, to guess; **schätz mal!** guess!; 4 **etwas zu schätzen wissen** to appreciate something.

Schau die (PL die Schauen) show.

schauen verb (PERF hat geschaut) to look.

Schauer der (PL die Schauer) shower.

Schauergeschichte die (PL die Schauergeschichten) horror story.

Schaufel die (PL die Schaufeln) 1 shovel; 2 dustpan.

Schaufenster das (PL die Schaufenster) shop window.

Schaukel die (PL die Schaukeln) swing.

schaukeln verb (PERF hat geschaukelt) to swing.

Schaukelstuhl der (PL die Schaukelstühle) rocking chair.

Schaum der 1 foam; 2 froth; 3 lather.

schäumen verb (PERF hat geschäumt) 1 to foam; 2 to froth (up).

Schauplatz der (PL die Schauplätze) scene.

Schauspiel das (PL die Schauspiele) 1 play; 2 spectacle.

Schauspieler der (PL die Schauspieler) actor.

Schauspielerin die (PL die Schauspielerinnen) actress.

Scheck der (PL die Schecks) cheque.

Scheckbuch das (PL die Scheckbücher) chequebook.

Scheckkarte die (PL die Scheckkarten) cheque card.

Scheibe die (PL die Scheiben) 1 pane (of a window, car); 2 slice; **eine Scheibe Schinken** a slice of ham; **die Salami in Scheiben schneiden** to slice the salami; **du könntest dir eine Scheibe von ihr abschneiden** (informal) you could take a leaf out of her book; 3 disc.

Scheibenwischer der (PL die

◇ IRREGULAR VERB: See the verb table in the centre of the dictionary

Scheibenwischer) windscreen wiper.

scheiden ◊ *verb* (IMPERF **schied**, PERF **hat geschieden**) 1 to separate; **sich scheiden lassen** to get divorced; 2 **geschieden sein** to be divorced.

Scheidung *die* (PL *die* Scheidungen) divorce.

Schein *der* (PL *die* Scheine) 1 light; 2 appearance; **etwas nur zum Schein machen** to only pretend to do something; 3 certificate; 4 note (*money*).

scheinbar *adverb* apparently.

scheinen ◊ *verb* (IMPERF **schien**, PERF **hat geschienen**) 1 to shine; 2 to seem; **mir scheint** it seems to me.

Scheinwerfer *der* (PL *die* Scheinwerfer) 1 headlamp, headlight; 2 floodlight, spotlight.

scheitern *verb* (PERF **ist gescheitert**) to fail.

Schenkel *der* (PL *die* Schenkel) thigh.

schenken *verb* (PERF **hat geschenkt**) 1 to give; **etwas geschenkt bekommen** to be given something; 2 **sich etwas schenken** to give something a miss; 3 **das ist ja geschenkt!** (*informal*) it's a gift!

Schere *die* (PL *die* Scheren) 1 (pair of) scissors; 2 shears; 3 claw (*of a crab*).

scheren *verb* (*informal*) (PERF **hat geschert**) to bother; **sich nicht um etwas scheren** not to care about

something; **scher dich um deine eigenen Angelegenheiten!** mind your own business!; **scher dich zum Teufel!** go to hell!

Scherz *der* (PL *die* Scherze) joke.

scheu *adjective* shy.

scheuern *verb* (PERF **hat gescheuert**) 1 to scrub; 2 to rub.

Scheune *die* (PL *die* Scheunen) barn.

scheußlich *adjective* horrible.

Schi *der* (PL *die* Schi(er)) = **Ski**.

Schicht *die* (PL *die* Schichten) 1 layer; 2 class; 3 shift.

schick *adjective* 1 stylish, smart; 2 (*informal*) great.

schicken *verb* (PERF **hat geschickt**) to send.

Schicksal *das* (PL *die* Schicksale) fate.

schieben ◊ *verb* (IMPERF **schob**, PERF **hat geschoben**) 1 to push; 2 **etwas auf etwas schieben** to blame something for something; **die Schuld auf jemanden schieben** to put the blame on somebody.

schied SEE **scheiden**.

Schiedsrichter *der* (PL *die* Schiedsrichter) referee, umpire.

schief *adjective* crooked; **ein schiefer Blick** a funny look. *adverb* 1 **das Bild hängt schief** the picture is not straight; 2 **schief gehen** △ to go wrong.

Schiefer *der* slate.

schiefgehen SEE **schief**.

△ NEW SPELLING: *See page xii*

schielen verb (PERF hat geschielt)
to squint.

schien SEE scheinen.

Schienbein das (PL die Schienbeine) shin.

Schiene die (PL die Schienen)
1 rail; 2 splint.

schießen ◇ verb (IMPERF schoss △, PERF hat geschossen) 1 to shoot; auf jemanden schießen to shoot at somebody; ein Tor schießen to score a goal; (PERF ist geschossen) to shoot (along); Andrea ist in die Höhe geschossen Andrea's shot up (has got a lot taller).

Schiff das (PL die Schiffe) ship.

schikanieren verb (PERF hat schikaniert) to bully.

Schikoree △ die chicory.

Schild das (PL die Schilder) 1 sign; 2 badge; 3 label.

Schildkröte die (PL die Schildkröten) 1 tortoise; 2 turtle.

Schilling der (PL die Schilling(e)) Schilling.

Schimmel der (PL die Schimmel) 1 mould; 2 white horse.

Schimpanse der (PL die Schimpansen) chimpanzee.

schimpfen verb (PERF hat geschimpft) 1 to tell off; 2 to grumble.

Schinken der (PL die Schinken) ham.

Schirm der (PL die Schirme)

1 umbrella; 2 sunshade; 3 shade (of a lamp); 4 peak (of a cap).

Schlaf der sleep.

Schlafanzug der (PL die Schlafanzüge) pyjamas.

schlafen ◇ verb (PRES schläft, IMPERF schlief, PERF hat geschlafen) 1 to sleep; 2 to be asleep; 3 schlafen gehen to go to bed.

Schlafcouch die (PL die Schlafcouchs) sofa bed.

schlaff adjective 1 slack (rope); 2 limp (handshake, body); 3 lethargic.

Schlafsaal der (PL die Schlafsäle) dormitory.

Schlafsack der (PL die Schlafsäcke) sleeping bag.

Schlafzimmer das (PL die Schlafzimmer) bedroom.

Schlafwagen der (PL die Schlafwagen) sleeper.

Schlag der (PL die Schläge) 1 blow, punch; Schläge kriegen to get a beating; 2 stroke; 3 (electric) shock; 4 Schlag auf Schlag in quick succession; auf einen Schlag all at once.

schlagen ◇ verb (PRES schlägt, IMPERF schlug, PERF hat geschlagen) 1 to hit; einen Nagel in die Wand schlagen to knock a nail into the wall; 2 to beat; 3 to bang; mit dem Kopf gegen etwas schlagen to bang your head against something; 4 to strike (of a clock); 5 to whip (cream); 6 sich schlagen to fight;

◇ IRREGULAR VERB: *See the verb table in the centre of the dictionary*

7 sich geschlagen geben to admit defeat.

Schlager der (PL die Schlager) hit.

Schläger der (PL die Schläger) 1 racket (in tennis); 2 bat (in baseball); 3 club (in golf); 4 stick (in hockey); 5 thug.

Schlägerei die (PL die Schlägereien) fight.

Schlagsahne die 1 whipping cream; 2 whipped cream.

Schlagzeile die (PL die Schlagzeilen) headline.

Schlagzeug das (PL die Schlagzeuge) drums.

Schlagzeuger der (PL die Schlagzeuger) drummer.

Schlamm der mud.

schlampen verb (PERF hat geschlampt) to be sloppy.

Schlamperei die (PL die Schlampereien) 1 sloppiness; 2 mess.

schlampig adjective sloppy.

Schlange die (PL die Schlangen) 1 snake; 2 queue; **Schlange stehen** to queue.

schlank adjective slim.

Schlankheitskur die (PL die Schlankheitskuren) diet; **eine Schlankheitskur machen** to be on a diet.

schlapp adjective worn out, tired out.

schlau adjective 1 crafty; 2 clever;

ich werde nicht schlau daraus I can't make head nor tail of it.

Schlauch der (PL die Schläuche) hose.

schlecht adjective 1 bad; **schlecht werden** to go bad; 2 **mir ist schlecht** I feel sick; 3 **jemanden schlecht machen** △ to run somebody down.
adverb 1 badly; **schlecht gelaunt** in a bad mood; 2 **es geht ihm schlecht** he's not well.

schleichen ◊ verb (IMPERF schlich, PERF ist geschlichen) 1 to creep; 2 to crawl (in traffic); 3 **sich schleichen** to creep.

Schleife die (PL die Schleifen) 1 bow; 2 loop.

Schleuder die (PL die Schleudern) 1 catapult; 2 spin-dryer.

schleudern verb (PERF hat geschleudert) 1 to hurl; 2 to spin (washing); 3 (PERF ist geschleudert) to skid.

schlich SEE schleichen.

schlicht adjective plain, simple.

schlief SEE schlafen.

schließen ◊ verb (IMPERF schloss △, PERF hat geschlossen) 1 to close, to shut; 2 to close down; 3 to lock; 4 to conclude; **aus etwas schließen, dass ...** to conclude from something that ...; 5 **einen Vertrag schließen** to enter into a contract; 6 **Freundschaft mit jemandem schließen** to make friends with somebody; 7 **sich schließen** to close.

△ NEW SPELLING: See page xii

Schließfach *das* (PL die Schließfächer) locker.

schließlich *adverb* 1 finally; 2 after all; **er hat sie schließlich doch eingeladen** he's invited her after all.

schlimm *adjective* bad.

schlimmstenfalls *adverb* if the worst comes to the worst.

Schlips *der* (PL die Schlipse) tie.

Schlitten *der* (PL die Schlitten) sledge; **Schlitten fahren gehen** to go sledging.

Schlittschuh *der* (PL die Schlittschuhe) skate; **Schlittschuh laufen** to skate.

Schlittschuhlaufen *das* ice-skating.

Schlitz *der* (PL die Schlitze) 1 slit; 2 flies (*in trousers*); 3 slot.

schloss △ SEE **schließen**.

Schloss △ *das* (PL die Schlösser) 1 lock; 2 castle.

Schluck *der* (PL die Schlucke) 1 mouthful; 2 gulp.

Schluckauf *der* hiccups.

schlucken *verb* (PERF hat geschluckt) to swallow.

schlug SEE **schlagen**.

Schlüpfer *der* (PL die Schlüpfer) knickers.

Schluss △ *der* (PL die Schlüsse) 1 end, ending; **zum Schluss** in the end; **Schluss machen** to stop; **mit jemandem Schluss machen** to finish with somebody; 2 conclusion.

Schlüssel *der* (PL die Schlüssel) 1 key; 2 spanner.

Schlussverkauf △ *der* sales.

schmal *adjective* 1 narrow; 2 thin (*face, nose*); 3 **sie ist schmäler geworden** she's lost weight.

schmecken *verb* (PERF hat geschmeckt) to taste; **die Suppe schmeckt gut** the soup tastes good; **das schmeckt mir nicht** I don't like it; **das Eis schmeckt nach Zitrone** the ice cream tastes of lemon.

schmeicheln *verb* (PERF hat geschmeichelt) to flatter; **jemandem schmeicheln** to flatter somebody.

schmeißen ✧ *verb* (*informal*) (IMPERF schmiss △, PERF hat geschmissen) to chuck; **mit etwas schmeißen** to chuck something.

schmelzen ✧ *verb* (PRES schmilzt, IMPERF schmolz, PERF ist geschmolzen) 1 to melt; **der Schnee ist geschmolzen** the snow has melted; 2 (PERF hat geschmolzen) to melt (*snow, ice*); 3 (PERF hat geschmolzen) to smelt (*ore*).

Schmerz *der* (PL die Schmerzen) 1 pain; 2 grief.

schmerzen *verb* (PERF hat geschmerzt) to hurt.

schmerzhaft *adjective* painful.

Schmerzmittel *das* (PL die Schmerzmittel) painkiller.

Schmetterling *der* (PL die Schmetterlinge) butterfly.

✧ IRREGULAR VERB: *See the verb table in the centre of the dictionary*

schmieren verb (PERF hat geschmiert) 1 to lubricate; 2 to spread {*butter, jam*}; **Brote schmieren** to spread slices of bread; **jemandem eine schmieren** (*informal*) to clout somebody; 3 to scrawl; 4 to smudge.

schmilzt SEE **schmelzen**.

Schminke die make-up.

schminken verb (PERF hat geschminkt) 1 to make up; 2 **sich schminken** to put on make-up.

schmiss △ SEE **schmeißen**.

schmolz SEE **schmelzen**.

Schmuck der 1 jewellery; 2 decoration.

schmücken verb (PERF hat geschmückt) to decorate.

schmuggeln verb (PERF hat geschmuggelt) to smuggle.

schmusen verb (PERF hat geschmust) to cuddle; **Gabi hat mit Max geschmust** Gabi cuddled Max.

Schmutz der dirt.

schmutzig adjective dirty.

Schnabel der (PL die Schnäbel) beak.

Schnalle die (PL die Schnallen) buckle.

schnarchen verb (PERF hat geschnarcht) to snore.

Schnauze die (PL die Schnauzen) 1 muzzle; **eine kalte Schnauze** a cold nose; 2 **die Schnauze halten** (*informal*) to keep your mouth shut.

schnäuzen △ (PERF hat sich geschnäuzt) **sich schnäuzen** to blow your nose.

Schnecke die (PL die Schnecken) snail.

Schnee der snow.

Schneeregen der sleet.

schneiden ✧ verb (IMPERF schnitt, PERF hat geschnitten) 1 to cut; **ich kann dir die Haare schneiden** I can cut your hair; **Evi hat sich die Haare kurz schneiden lassen** Evi had her hair cut short; **in Scheiben schneiden** to slice; 2 **sich schneiden** to cut yourself; **ich habe mich in den Finger geschnitten** I've cut my finger; 3 **sich schneiden** to intersect; 4 **Gesichter schneiden** to pull faces.

Schneider der (PL die Schneider) tailor.

Schneiderin die (PL die Schneiderinnen) dressmaker.

schneien verb (PERF hat geschneit) to snow; **es schneit** it's snowing.

schnell adjective quick, fast. adverb quickly; **mach schnell!** hurry up!

Schnelligkeit die speed.

Schnellimbiss △ der (PL die Schnellimbisse) snack bar.

schnellstens adverb as quickly as possible.

Schnellzug der (PL die Schnellzüge) express (train).

schneuzen = **schnäuzen**.

△ NEW SPELLING: See page xii

schnitt SEE **schneiden**.

Schnitt der (PL die Schnitte) 1 cut; **er hat einen tiefen Schnitt im Finger** he's got a deep cut in his finger; **das Kostüm hat einen sehr guten Schnitt** the suit is well cut; 2 cutting (of a film); 3 **im Schnitt** on average; 4 pattern.

Schnittlauch der chives.

Schnitzel das (PL die Schnitzel) 1 escalope; 2 scrap.

schnitzen verb (PERF hat geschnitzt) to carve.

Schnorchel der (PL die Schnorchel) snorkel.

schnüffeln verb (PERF hat geschnüffelt) 1 to sniff; 2 to snoop around.

Schnuller der (PL die Schnuller) dummy.

Schnupfen der (PL die Schnupfen) cold.

Schnur die (PL die Schnüre) 1 (piece of) string; 2 flex; 3 cord.

Schnurrbart der (PL die Schnurrbärte) moustache.

schnurren verb (PERF hat geschnurrt) to purr.

Schnürsenkel der (PL die Schnürsenkel) shoelace.

schob SEE **schieben**.

Schock der (PL die Schocks) shock.

schockieren verb (PERF hat schockiert) to shock.

Schokolade die (PL die Schokoladen) chocolate.

schon adverb 1 already ('schon' is often not translated); **schon wieder** again; **schon oft** often; **du wirst schon sehen** you'll see; **ja schon, aber …** well yes, but …; **nun geh schon!** go on then!; 2 yet; **hast du sie schon gesehen?** have you seen her yet?; **du weißt schon** you know; 3 even; **4 komm schon!** come on!; 5 **schon deshalb** for that reason alone; 6 **das ist schon möglich** that's quite possible; 7 **er war schon mal da** he's been there before.

schön adjective 1 beautiful; 2 nice; **schönes Wochenende!** have a nice weekend!; 3 good; **na schön** all right then; 4 **schönen Dank** thank you very much; **schöne Grüße** best wishes.

schonen verb (PERF hat geschont) 1 to look after; 2 **sich schonen** to take things easy.

Schönheit die (PL die Schönheiten) beauty.

Schornstein der (PL die Schornsteine) chimney, funnel.

schoss △ SEE **schießen**.

Schoß der (PL die Schöße) lap.

Schotte der (PL die Schotten) Scot, Scotsman.

Schottin die (PL die Schottinnen) Scot, Scotswoman.

schottisch adjective Scottish.

Schottland das Scotland.

schräg adjective 1 diagonal;

✧ **IRREGULAR VERB: See the verb table in the centre of the dictionary**

2 sloping.
adverb etwas schräg halten to tilt
something; etwas schräg stellen
to put something at an angle.

Schrank der (PL die Schränke)
1 cupboard; 2 wardrobe.

Schranke die (PL die Schranken)
barrier.

Schraube die (PL die Schrauben)
screw.

schrauben *verb* (PERF hat
geschraubt) to screw.

Schraubenschlüssel der (PL die
Schraubenschlüssel) spanner.

Schraubenzieher der (PL die
Schraubenzieher) screwdriver.

Schreck der (PL die Schrecke) fright;
jemandem einen Schreck einjagen to give
somebody a fright; ich habe einen
Schreck bekommen I got a fright.

schrecklich *adjective* terrible.

Schrei der (PL die Schreie) 1 cry,
shout; 2 scream; 3 der letzte
Schrei (*informal*) the latest thing.

schreiben ◇ *verb* (IMPERF schrieb,
PERF hat geschrieben) 1 to write;
David hat mir einen Brief
geschrieben David wrote a letter to
me; einen Test schreiben to do a
test; 2 to spell; wie schreibt man
das? how is it spelt?; 3 to type.

Schreibmaschine die (PL die
Schreibmaschinen) typewriter.

Schreibpapier das writing paper.

Schreibtisch der (PL die
Schreibtische) desk.

Schreibwaren *plural noun*
stationery.

schreien ◇ *verb* (IMPERF schrie, PERF
hat geschrien) 1 to cry, to shout;
das Baby schreit the baby's crying;
2 to scream; vor Lachen schreien to
scream with laughter; zum Schreien
sein (*informal*) to be a scream.

Schreiner der (PL die Schreiner)
joiner.

schrie SEE schreien.

schrieb SEE schreiben.

Schrift die (PL die Schriften)
1 writing; 2 type; 3 script.

schriftlich *adjective* written.
adverb in writing; das lasse ich mir
schriftlich geben I'll get that in
writing; jemanden schriftlich
einladen to send somebody a
written invitation.

Schriftsteller der (PL die
Schriftsteller) writer.

Schriftstellerin die (PL die
Schriftstellerinnen) writer.

Schritt der (PL die Schritte) step.

schrumpfen *verb* (PERF ist
geschrumpft) 1 to shrink; 2 to
shrivel.

Schublade die (PL die Schubladen)
drawer.

schubsen *verb* (PERF hat
geschubst) to shove.

schüchtern *adjective* shy.

schuf SEE schaffen.

△ NEW SPELLING: See page xii

Schuh der (PL die Schuhe) shoe.

Schuhgröße die (PL die Schuhgrößen) shoe size.

Schularbeiten plural noun homework.

Schulaufgaben plural noun homework.

Schulbuch das (PL die Schulbücher) schoolbook.

Schuld die (PL die Schulden) 1 blame; **Schuld haben** △ to be to blame; **jemandem Schuld geben** to blame somebody; **2 fault; es war seine Schuld** it was his fault; **3 guilt; 4 debt; Schulden haben** to be in debt; **Schulden machen** to get into debt.

schuld adjective **schuld sein** to be to blame; **du bist schuld daran** it's your fault.

schulden verb (PERF hat geschuldet) to owe.

schuldig adjective 1 guilty; 2 jemandem etwas schuldig sein to owe somebody something.

Schule die (PL die Schulen) school.

schulen verb (PERF hat geschult) to train.

Schüler der (PL die Schüler) pupil, student.

Schülerin die (PL die Schülerinnen) pupil, student.

Schulferien plural noun school holidays.

schulfrei adjective **ein schulfreier Tag** a day off school; **wir haben heute schulfrei** there's no school today.

Schulfreund der (PL die Schulfreunde) schoolfriend.

Schulfreundin die (PL die Schulfreundinnen) schoolfriend.

Schulhof der (PL die Schulhöfe) playground.

Schulstunde die (PL die Schulstunden) period.

Schultasche die (PL die Schultaschen) schoolbag.

Schulter die (PL die Schultern) shoulder.

schummeln verb (PERF hat geschummelt) to cheat.

Schuppe die (PL die Schuppen) 1 scale; 2 Schuppen dandruff.

Schuppen der (PL die Schuppen) shed.

Schürze die (PL die Schürzen) apron.

Schuss △ der (PL die Schüsse) 1 shot; 2 dash (of brandy, vinegar); 3 schuss (in skiing).

Schüssel die (PL die Schüsseln) bowl, dish.

Schuster der (PL die Schuster) shoemaker.

schütten verb (PERF hat geschüttet) 1 to pour; es schüttet (informal) it's pouring (down); 2 to tip; 3 to spill.

schütteln verb (PERF hat geschüttelt) 1 to shake; 2 sich

◇ IRREGULAR VERB: See the verb table in the centre of the dictionary

schütteln to shake yourself; **sich vor Ekel schütteln** to shudder.

Schutz der 1 protection; 2 shelter.

Schütze der (PL die Schützen) 1 marksman; 2 Sagittarius; **Daniel ist Schütze** Daniel's Sagittarius.

schützen verb (PERF hat geschützt) 1 to protect; **die meisten Cremes schützen die Haut gegen Sonnenbrand** most creams protect the skin from sunburn; 2 gesetzlich geschützt registered (as a trademark).

schwach adjective 1 weak; 2 poor (performance, memory).

Schwäche die (PL die Schwächen) weakness.

schwachsinnig adjective idiotic.

Schwager der (PL die Schwäger) brother-in-law.

Schwägerin die (PL die Schwägerinnen) sister-in-law.

Schwalbe die (PL die Schwalben) swallow.

schwamm SEE schwimmen.

Schwamm der (PL die Schwämme) sponge.

Schwan der (PL die Schwäne) swan.

schwanger adjective pregnant.

schwanken verb (PERF hat geschwankt) 1 to sway; 2 to fluctuate; 3 to waver; 4 (PERF ist geschwankt) to stagger.

Schwanz der (PL die Schwänze) tail.

schwänzen verb (PERF hat geschwänzt) to skip, to skive off; **die Schule schwänzen** to play truant.

Schwarm der (PL die Schwärme) swarm.

schwarz adjective, adverb 1 black; **schwarz gekleidet** dressed in black; **ein schwarz gestreiftes Kleid** a dress with black stripes; **das habe ich schwarz auf weiß** I have it in black and white; 2 ins Schwarze treffen to hit the nail on the head, to score a bull's eye; 3 schwarz sehen△ to be pessimistic; 4 etwas schwarz machen to do something illegally.

Schwarze der/die (PL die Schwarzen) black.

schwarzsehen SEE schwarz.

Schwarzwald der Black Forest.

schwätzen verb (PERF hat geschwätzt) to chatter.

Schwede der (PL die Schweden) Swede.

Schweden das Sweden.

Schwedin die (PL die Schwedinnen) Swede.

schwedisch adjective Swedish.

schweigen ◇ verb (IMPERF schwieg, PERF hat geschwiegen) to be silent; **ganz zu schweigen von …** not to mention …

Schwein das (PL die Schweine) 1 pig; 2 pork; 3 du Schwein! (informal) you swine!; Schwein haben (informal) to be lucky.

Schweinefleisch das pork.

Schweiß *der* sweat.

Schweiz *die* **die Schweiz** Switzerland.

Schweizer *der* (PL *die* **Schweizer**) Swiss.

Schweizerin *die* (PL *die* **Schweizerinnen**) Swiss.

schweizerisch *adjective* Swiss.

schwer *adjective* 1 heavy; **zwei Pfund schwer sein** to weigh two pounds; 2 difficult; 3 serious. *adverb* 1 heavily; 2 seriously; **schwer krank** seriously ill; 3 **schwer arbeiten** to work hard; **jemandem schwer fallen** △ to be hard for somebody; 4 **sich mit etwas schwer tun** △ to have difficulty with something.

schwerfallen SEE **schwer**.

schwerhörig *adjective* hard of hearing.

Schwert *das* (PL *die* **Schwerter**) sword.

schwertun SEE **schwer**.

Schwester *die* (PL *die* **Schwestern**) sister.

schwieg SEE **schweigen**.

Schwiegereltern *plural noun* parents-in-law.

Schwiegermutter *die* (PL *die* **Schwiegermütter**) mother-in-law.

Schwiegersohn *der* (PL *die* **Schwiegersöhne**) son-in-law.

Schwiegertochter *die* (PL *die* **Schwiegertöchter**) daughter-in-law.

Schwiegervater *der* (PL *die* **Schwiegerväter**) father-in-law.

schwierig *adjective* difficult.

Schwierigkeit *die* (PL *die* **Schwierigkeiten**) difficulty.

Schwimmbad *das* (PL *die* **Schwimmbäder**) swimming baths.

Schwimmbecken *das* (PL *die* **Schwimmbecken**) swimming pool.

schwimmen ✧ *verb* (IMPERF **schwamm**, PERF **ist/hat geschwommen**) 1 to swim; 2 to float.

Schwimmweste *die* (PL *die* **Schwimmwesten**) life-jacket.

schwindlig *adjective* dizzy; **mir ist schwindlig** I feel dizzy.

Schwips *der* (PL *die* **Schwipse**) **einen Schwips haben** to be tipsy.

schwitzen *verb* (PERF **hat geschwitzt**) to sweat.

schwören ✧ *verb* (IMPERF **schwor**, PERF **hat geschworen**) to swear.

schwul *adjective* gay.

schwül *adjective* close.

Schwule *der* (PL *die* **Schwulen**) gay.

Schwung *der* (PL *die* **Schwünge**) 1 swing; 2 drive; **die Party in Schwung bringen** to get the party going.

sechs *number* six.

sechste, sechste, sechstes *adjective* sixth.

sechzehn *number* sixteen.

sechzig *number* sixty.

✧ IRREGULAR VERB: *See the verb table in the centre of the dictionary*

See¹ der (PL die Seen) lake.

See² die sea.

Seehund der (PL die Seehunde) seal.

seekrank adjective seasick.

Seele die (PL die Seelen) soul.

Seemann der (PL die Seeleute) seaman, sailor.

Seetang der seaweed.

Segel das (PL die Segel) sail.

Segelboot das (PL die Segelboote) sailing boat.

Segelfliegen das gliding.

Segelflugzeug das (PL die Segelflugzeuge) glider.

segeln verb (PERF ist gesegelt) to sail.

sehen ◇ verb (PRES sieht, IMPERF sah, PERF hat gesehen) 1 to see; jemanden wieder sehen △ to see somebody again; mal sehen, ob ... let's see if ...; 2 to look; 3 eine Fernsehsendung sehen to watch a television programme; 4 gut/schlecht sehen to have good/bad eyesight; 5 nach jemandem sehen to look after somebody.

sehenswert adjective worth seeing.

Sehenswürdigkeiten plural noun sights.

Sehnsucht die longing; Sehnsucht nach jemandem haben to long to see somebody.

sehr adverb 1 very; sehr gut very good; 2 danke sehr thank you very much; 3 ich habe Karin sehr gern I like Karin a lot; 4 Sehr geehrte Frau Huber Dear Mrs Huber.

seid SEE sein.

Seide die (PL die Seiden) silk.

Seife die (PL die Seifen) soap.

Seil das (PL die Seile) 1 rope; 2 cable.

Seilbahn die (PL die Seilbahnen) cable railway.

sein¹ ◇ verb (PRES ist, IMPERF war, PERF ist gewesen) 1 to be; wir sind in der Küche we're in the kitchen; Rosi ist krank Rosi is ill; mir ist schlecht I feel sick; mir ist kalt I'm cold; 2 sie ist Lehrerin she's a teacher; 3 es ist drei Uhr it's three o'clock; Karl ist aus München Karl's from Munich; es war viel zu tun there was a lot to be done; 4 aus Seide sein to be made of silk; 5 etwas sein lassen △ to stop something; lass das sein! stop it!; 6 es sei denn, dass ... unless ...; 7 (used with certain verbs to form past tenses) ich bin nach Berlin gefahren I went to Berlin; wir sind kurz vor acht nach Hause gekommen we got home shortly before eight o'clock; er ist abgeholt worden he's been collected.

sein² adjective 1 his; 2 (of a thing or animal) its; der Hund ist in seiner Hütte the dog is in its kennel; 3 (after the pronoun 'man') your, one's; wenn man sich seine Eltern aussuchen könnte if you could choose your parents.

△ NEW SPELLING: See page xii

seiner, seine, sein(e)s *pronoun*
1 his; **das ist nicht meine CD, das
ist seine** it's not my CD, it's his; **du
kannst seins nehmen** you can take
his; 2 (*after the pronoun 'man'*) your
own, one's own; **das Seine tun** to
do one's share.

seinetwegen *adverb* 1 for his sake;
2 because of him; 3 on his account.

seinlassen SEE **sein**.

seins SEE **seiner**.

seit *preposition* ✧ (+DAT),
conjunction 1 since; **seit etwa einer
Woche** since about a week; **seit du
hier wohnst** since you've been
living here; **seit wann?** since
when?; 2 **ich bin seit zwei Wochen
hier** I've been here for two weeks;
seit einiger Zeit for some time.

seitdem *adverb* since then; **ich
habe sie seitdem nicht mehr
gesehen** I haven't seen her since.
conjunction since.

Seite *die* (PL *die* **Seiten**) 1 side; **auf
der einen Seite** on the one hand;
2 page; **das steht auf Seite zwanzig**
it's on page twenty.

Seitenstechen *das* stich; **ich habe
Seitenstechen** I've got a stitch.

Seitenstraße *die* (PL *die*
Seitenstraßen) side street.

seither *adverb* since then.

Sekretärin *die* (PL *die*
Sekretärinnen) secretary.

Sekt *der* (PL *die* **Sekte**) sparkling
wine.

Sekte *die* (PL *die* **Sekten**) sect.

Sekunde *die* (PL *die* **Sekunden**)
second.

selbst *pronoun* 1 **ich selbst** I
myself; **er selbst** he himself; **wir
selbst** we ourselves; **Sie selbst** you
yourself, you yourselves; 2 **von
selbst** by itself; 3 **sie schneidet
sich die Haare selbst** she cuts her
own hair; 4 on one's own; **ich kann
es selbst machen** I can do it on my
own; 5 **selbst gemacht** ✧ homemade.
adverb even; **selbst wenn** even if.

selbständig = **selbstständig**.

Selbstbedienung *die* self-service.

selbstbewusst ✧ *adjective* self-
confident.

Selbstbewusstsein ✧ *das*
self-confidence.

selbstgemacht SEE **selbst**.

Selbstmord *der* (PL *die*
Selbstmorde) suicide; **Selbstmord
begehen** to commit suicide.

selbstständig ✧ *adjective*
1 independent; 2 self-employed;
sich selbstständig machen to set
up on your own.

selbstverständlich *adjective*
natural; **etwas für
selbstverständlich halten** to take
something for granted; **das ist
selbstverständlich** it goes without
saying.
adverb naturally, of course; **wir
haben ihn selbstverständlich auf
die Party eingeladen** of course we
invited him to the party.

✧ IRREGULAR VERB: *See the verb table in the centre of the dictionary*

selten *adjective* rare.
adverb rarely.

seltsam *adjective* strange, odd.

Semester *das* (PL *die* **Semester**)
semester, term.

Semikolon *das* (PL *die* **Semikolons**)
semicolon.

Semmel *die* (PL *die* **Semmeln**) roll.

senden *verb* (PERF **hat gesendet**)
1 to send; **etwas an jemanden
senden** to send something to
somebody; 2 to broadcast; **seine
Rede wird in ersten Programm
gesendet** his speech will be
broadcast on channel one; 3 to
transmit.

Sendung *die* (PL *die* **Sendungen**)
1 programme; 2 consignment.

Senf *der* (PL *die* **Senfe**) mustard.

Senior *der* (PL *die* **Senioren**)
1 senior; 2 **Senioren** senior
citizens.

sensationell *adjective* sensational.

sensibel *adjective* sensitive.

September *der* September.

Serie *die* (PL *die* **Serien**) 1 series;
2 serial.

Service[1] *das* (PL *die* **Service**) set (*of
china, for example*).

Service[2] *der* service; **das Essen im
Hotel ist gut, aber der Service ist
furchtbar** the food in the hotel is
good but the service is appalling.

servieren *verb* (PERF **hat serviert**) to
serve.

Serviette *die* (PL *die* **Servietten**)
napkin.

Sessel *der* (PL *die* **Sessel**) armchair.

Sessellift *der* (PL *die* **Sessellifte**)
chair-lift.

setzen *verb* (PERF **hat gesetzt**) 1 to
put; **ein Komma setzen** to put a
comma; **vergiss nicht, deinen
Namen auf die Liste zu setzen**
don't forget to put your name on the
list; 2 to move (*a counter in games*);
3 **auf etwas setzen** to bet on
something; **auf ein Pferd setzen** to
back a horse; **sich setzen** to sit
down; **sich auf einen Stuhl setzen**
to sit down on a chair.

seufzen *verb* (PERF **hat geseufzt**) to
sigh.

Seufzer *der* (PL *die* **Seufzer**) sigh.

Sex *der* sex.

Sexismus *der* sexism.

sexistisch *adjective* sexist.

sexuell *adjective* sexual.

Shampoo *das* (PL *die* **Shampoos**)
shampoo.

sich *pronoun* 1 (*with 'er/sie/es'*)
himself/herself/itself; **sie hat sich
eingeschlossen** she locked herself
in; 2 (*with plural 'sie'*) themselves;
3 (*with 'Sie'*) yourself, yourselves
(*plural*); 4 each other, one another;
sich kennen to know each other;
Petra und Werner lieben sich Petra
and Werner love each other; 5 (*not
translated with certain verbs*) **sich
freuen** to be pleased; **sich wundern**
to be surprised; 6 **Anita wäscht sich**

△ NEW SPELLING: *See page xii*

die Haare Anita is washing her hair; sich den Arm brechen to break your arm; **7** sich gut verkaufen to sell well; **8** von sich aus of your own accord.

sicher *adjective* **1** safe; **2** certain; bist du sicher? are you sure? *adverb* **1** safely; **2** certainly, surely; sicher! certainly!

Sicherheit *die* **1** safety; zur Sicherheit for safety's sake; schnallen Sie sich zur Ihrer eigenen Sicherheit an fasten your seat belt for your own safety; etwas in Sicherheit bringen to rescue something; in Sicherheit sein to be safe; **2** security; die Sicherheit der Arbeitsplätze job security; **3** certainty; mit Sicherheit! certainly! (*as a reply*).

Sicherheitsgurt *der* (PL die Sicherheitsgurte) seatbelt.

Sicherheitsnadel *die* (PL die Sicherheitsnadeln) safety pin.

sicherlich *adverb* certainly.

sichern *verb* (PERF hat gesichert) to secure; jemandem etwas sichern to secure something for somebody.

Sicherung *die* (PL die Sicherungen) **1** fuse; die Sicherung is durchgebrannt the fuse has blown; **2** safeguard; die Sicherung der Arbeitsplätze safeguarding jobs; **3** safety catch.

Sicht *die* **1** view; ich hatte eine gute Sicht auf den See I had a good view of the lake; auf lange Sicht in the long term; **2** aus meiner Sicht as I

see it; **3** visibility; gute/schlechte Sicht good/poor visibility.

sichtbar *adjective* visible.

sie *pronoun* **1** she; **2** her; ich kenne sie I know her; **3** it; so eine hübsche Bluse, war sie teuer? what a pretty blouse, was it expensive?; **4** they; sie sind in der Küche they're in the kitchen; **5** them; ich habe sie gestern abgeschickt I posted them yesterday.

Sie *pronoun* you; kommen Sie herein! come in!

Sieb *das* (PL die Siebe) **1** sieve; **2** strainer.

sieben *number* seven.

siebter, siebte, siebtes *adjective* seventh.

siebzehn *number* seventeen.

siebzig *number* seventy.

Siedlung *die* (PL die Siedlungen) **1** (housing) estate; **2** settlement.

Sieg *der* (PL die Siege) victory, win.

Siegel *das* (PL die Siegel) seal.

siegen *verb* (PERF hat gesiegt) to win.

Sieger *der* (PL die Sieger) winner.

Siegerin *die* (PL die Siegerinnen) winner.

sieht SEE sehen.

Silbe *die* (PL die Silben) syllable.

Silber *das* silver.

silbern *adjective* silver.

✦ IRREGULAR VERB: See the verb table in the centre of the dictionary

Silvester *das* New Year's Eve.

sind SEE **sein**.

Sinfonie *die* (PL *die* Sinfonien) symphony.

singen ◇ *verb* (IMPERF **sang**, PERF **hat gesungen**) to sing.

sinken ◇ *verb* (IMPERF **sank**, PERF **ist gesunken**) 1 to sink; 2 to go down.

Sinn *der* (PL *die* Sinne) 1 sense; 2 meaning; 3 point; **das hat keinen Sinn** there's no point.

sinnlos *adjective* pointless.

sinnvoll *adjective* 1 sensible; 2 meaningful.

Situation *die* (PL *die* Situationen) situation.

Sitz *der* (PL *die* Sitze) 1 seat; 2 fit (*of clothes*).

sitzen ◇ *verb* (IMPERF **saß**, PERF **hat gesessen**) 1 to sit; **sitzen bleiben**△ to remain seated; 2 **sitzen bleiben**△ to have to repeat a year, to stay down (*at school*); 3 **er sitzt** (*informal*) he's in jail; 4 **jemanden sitzen lassen**△ to leave somebody in the lurch; 5 to fit (*of clothes*); **der Mantel sitzt gut** the coat fits well.

Sitzplatz *der* (PL *die* Sitzplätze) seat.

Sitzung *die* (PL *die* Sitzungen) 1 meeting; 2 session.

Sizilien *das* Sicily.

Skandal *der* (PL *die* Skandale) scandal.

Skandinavien *das* Scandinavia.

skandinavisch *adjective* Scandinavian.

Skelett *das* (PL *die* Skelette) skeleton.

Ski *der* (PL *die* Ski(er)) ski; **Ski fahren/laufen** to ski.

Skifahren *das* skiing.

Skifahrer *der* (PL *die* Skifahrer) skier.

Skifahrerin *die* (PL *die* Skifahrerinnen) skier.

Skilaufen *das* skiing.

Skiläufer *der* (PL *die* Skiläufer) skier.

Skiläuferin *die* (PL *die* Skiläuferinnen) skier.

Skilehrer *der* (PL *die* Skilehrer) ski instructor.

Skizze *die* (PL *die* Skizzen) sketch.

Skorpion *der* (PL *die* Skorpione) 1 scorpion; 2 Scorpio.

Skulptur *die* (PL *die* Skulpturen) sculpture.

Slip *der* (PL *die* Slips) briefs, pants.

Slowake *der* (PL *die* Slowaken) Slovak.

Slowakei *die* Slovakia.

Slowakin *die* (PL *die* Slowakinnen) Slovak.

slowakisch *adjective* Slovak.

Smoking *der* (PL *die* Smokings) dinner jacket.

so *adverb* 1 so; **nicht so viel** not so much; **und so weiter** and so on; 2 like this, like that; **so nicht** not like

△ NEW SPELLING: See page xii

that; **3** as; **so bald wie** as soon as; **4** such; **so ein Zufall!** what a coincidence!; **5 das kriegst du so** (*informal*) you get it for nothing; **6 so um zwanzig Mark** (*informal*) about twenty marks.
conjunction **so dass** so that.
exclamation right!, well!; **so?** really?

sobald *conjunction* as soon as.

Socke *die* (PL *die* **Socken**) sock.

Sofa *das* (PL *die* **Sofas**) sofa.

sofort *adverb* immediately.

sogar *adverb* even.

sogleich *adverb* at once.

Sohle *die* (PL *die* **Sohlen**) sole.

Sohn *der* (PL *die* **Söhne**) son.

solange *conjunction* as long as.

solch *pronoun* such; **solch einer/eine/eins** one like that, somebody like that.

solcher, solche, solches
adjective, pronoun **1** such; **ich habe solche Angst** I'm so frightened; **2 ein solcher Mann** a man like that; **eine solche Frage** a question like that; **ein solches Haus** a house like that; **3 solche** (*plural*) those; **solche wie die** people like that.

Soldat *der* (PL *die* **Soldaten**) soldier.

solide *adjective* **1** solid; **2** respectable.

Solist *der* (PL *die* **Solisten**) soloist.

Solistin *die* (PL *die* **Solistinnen**) soloist.

sollen ◇ *verb* (PRES **soll**, IMPERF **sollte**, PERF **hat gesollt**) **1** should; **sollte es regnen** if it should rain; **2** to be supposed to; **was soll das heißen?** what's that supposed to mean?; **3 sagen Sie ihr, sie soll anrufen** tell her to ring; **4 was soll ich machen?** what shall I do?; **soll ich?** shall I?; **5 was soll's!** so what!

sollte, sollten, solltest, solltet
SEE **sollen**.

Sommer *der* (PL *die* **Sommer**) summer.

sommerlich *adjective* summery, summer.

Sommersprossen *plural noun* freckles.

Sonderangebot *das* (PL *die* **Sonderangebote**) special offer; **im Sonderangebot** on special offer.

sonderbar *adjective* strange, odd.

sondern *conjunction* but; **nicht nur ..., sondern auch ...** not only ..., but also ...

Song *der* (PL *die* **Songs**) song.

Sonnabend *der* (PL *die* **Sonnabende**) Saturday.

sonnabends *adverb* on Saturdays.

Sonne *die* (PL *die* **Sonnen**) sun.

sonnen *verb* (PERF **hat sich gesonnt**) **sich sonnen** to sun yourself.

Sonnenaufgang *der* sunrise.

Sonnenbrand *der* sunburn.

Sonnenbrille *die* (PL *die* **Sonnenbrillen**) sunglasses.

◇ IRREGULAR VERB: *See the verb table in the centre of the dictionary*

Sonnencreme *die* (PL *die* **Sonnencremes**) suntan lotion.

Sonnenenergie *die* solar energy.

Sonnenmilch *die* suntan lotion.

Sonnenöl *das* suntan oil.

Sonnenschein *der* sunshine.

Sonnenstich *der* sunstroke.

sonnig *adjective* sunny.

Sonntag *der* (PL *die* **Sonntage**) Sunday.

sonntags *adverb* on Sundays.

sonst *adverb* 1 usually; 2 else; **wer sonst?** who else?; **was sonst?** what else?; 3 **sonst noch etwas?** anything else?; **sonst noch jemand?** anybody else?; 4 **sonst wo** △ somewhere; **es kann sonst wo sein** it could be anywhere; 5 otherwise; **geh jetzt, sonst verpasst du den Bus** go now, otherwise you'll miss the bus.

sonstwo SEE **sonst**.

sooft *conjunction* whenever.

Sorge *die* (PL *die* **Sorgen**) worry; **sich Sorgen machen** to worry.

sorgen *verb* (PERF **hat gesorgt**) 1 **für etwas sorgen** to take care of something; **für die Musik sorgen** to see to the music; **für jemanden sorgen** to look after somebody; 2 **dafür sorgen, dass ...** to make sure that ...; 3 **sich sorgen** to worry; **ich sorge mich um meine Eltern** I worry about my parents.

sorgfältig *adjective* careful.

Sorte *die* (PL *die* **Sorten**) 1 kind; 2 brand.

Soße *die* (PL *die* **Soßen**) 1 sauce; 2 gravy; 3 dressing.

Souvenir *das* (PL *die* **Souvenirs**) souvenir.

soviel *conjunction* as far as; **soviel ich weiß** as far as I know.
adverb SEE **viel**.

soweit *conjunction* as far as; **soweit ich weiß, ist er in Ferien** as far as I know, he's on holiday.
adverb SEE **weit**.

sowenig SEE **wenig**.

sowie *conjunction* 1 as well as; 2 as soon as.

sowieso *adverb* anyway.

sowohl *adverb* **sowohl ... als auch ...** both ... and ...; **sowohl er wie auch sein Freund** both he and his friend.

sozial *adjective* social.

Sozialarbeiter *der* (PL *die* **Sozialarbeiter**) social worker.

Sozialarbeiterin *die* (PL *die* **Sozialarbeiterinnen**) social worker.

Sozialhilfe *die* social security.

Sozialismus *der* socialism.

sozialistisch *adjective* socialist.

Sozialkunde *die* social studies.

Sozialwohnung *die* (PL *die* **Sozialwohnungen**) council flat.

Soziologie *die* sociology.

sozusagen *adverb* so to speak.

△ NEW SPELLING: *See page xii*

Spalte die (PL die Spalten) 1 crack; 2 column (in text).

spalten verb (PERF hat gespalten) to split.

Spanien das Spain.

Spanier der (PL die Spanier) Spaniard.

Spanierin die (PL die Spanierinnen) Spaniard.

spanisch adjective Spanish.

spann SEE spinnen

spannend adjective exciting.

Spannung die (PL die Spannungen) 1 tension; 2 suspense (in a film or novel, for example); 3 voltage.

sparen verb (PERF hat gespart) to 1 to save; auf etwas sparen to save up for something; 2 sich etwas sparen not to bother with something; sich die Mühe sparen to save yourself the trouble; 3 an etwas sparen to economize on something.

Spargel der asparagus.

Sparkasse die savings bank.

sparsam adjective 1 economical; 2 thrifty.

Spaß der (PL die Späße) 1 fun; zum/aus Spaß for fun; das macht Spaß it's fun; Segeln macht mir keinen Spaß I don't like sailing; 2 viel Spaß! have a good time!; 3 joke; er macht nur Spaß he's only joking.

spät adjective, adverb late; zu spät

kommen to be late; wie spät ist es? what time is it?

Spaten der (PL die Spaten) spade.

später adjective later.

spätestens adverb at the latest.

Spatz der (PL die Spatzen) sparrow.

spazieren verb (PERF ist spaziert) 1 to stroll; 2 spazieren gehen △ to go for a walk; hast du Lust, spazieren zu gehen? would you like to go for a walk?

spazierengehen SEE spazieren

Spaziergang der (PL die Spaziergänge) walk; einen Spaziergang machen to go for a walk.

Speck der bacon.

Speiche die (PL die Speichen) spoke.

Speicher der (PL die Speicher) 1 loft, attic; 2 memory (in computing).

speichern verb (PERF hat gespeichert) 1 to store; 2 to save (in computing).

Speise die (PL die Speisen) 1 food; 2 dish.

Speisekarte die (PL die Speisekarten) menu.

Speisesaal der (PL die Speisesäle) 1 dining hall; 2 dining room.

Speisewagen der (PL die Speisewagen) dining car.

Spende die (PL die Spenden) donation.

◇ IRREGULAR VERB: See the verb table in the centre of the dictionary

spenden verb (PERF hat gespendet)
1 to donate; 2 to give.

spendieren verb (PERF hat
spendiert) jemandem etwas
spendieren to treat somebody to
something.

Sperre die (PL die Sperren)
1 barrier; 2 ban.

sperren verb (PERF hat gesperrt)
1 to close; 2 to block (an entrance,
access); 3 den Strom sperren to cut
off the electricity; 4 einen Scheck
sperren to stop a cheque; 5 ein Tier
in einen Käfig sperren to shut an
animal (up) in a cage.

Spezialität die (PL die
Spezialitäten) speciality.

speziell adjective special.

Spiegel der (PL die Spiegel) mirror.

Spiegelbild das (PL die
Spiegelbilder) reflection.

Spiegelei das (PL die Spiegeleier)
fried egg.

spiegeln verb (PERF hat gespiegelt)
1 to reflect; 2 sich spiegeln to be
reflected.

Spiel das (PL die Spiele) 1 game;
2 ein Spiel Karten a pack of cards;
3 es steht viel auf dem Spiel there's
a lot at stake.

spielen verb (PERF hat gespielt) 1 to
play; wir spielen morgen Tennis
we're going to play tennis tomorrow;
2 to gamble; 3 to act; das Stück war
gut gespielt the play was well
acted; 4 der Film spielt in Rom the
film is set in Rome.

spielend adverb easily.

Spieler der (PL die Spieler) 1 player;
2 gambler.

Spielerin die (PL die Spielerinnen)
1 player; 2 gambler.

Spielfeld das (PL die Spielfelder)
pitch, field.

Spielhalle die (PL die Spielhallen)
amusement arcade.

Spielplatz der (PL die Spielplätze)
playground.

Spielverderber der (PL die
Spielverderber) spoilsport.

Spielverderberin die (PL die
Spielverderberinnen) spoilsport.

Spielwaren plural noun toys.

Spielzeug das 1 toy; 2 toys.

Spinat der spinach.

Spinne die (PL die Spinnen) spider.

spinnen ◇ verb (IMPERF spann, PERF
hat gesponnen) 1 to spin; 2 du
spinnst! (informal) you're mad!

Spinnennetz das (PL die
Spinnennetze) cobweb.

Spion der (PL die Spione) spy.

Spionage die spying, espionage.

spionieren verb (PERF hat
spioniert) to spy.

Spirituosen plural noun spirits
(alcohol).

spitz adjective pointed.

Spitze die (PL die Spitzen) 1 point;
2 top; Schalke liegt jetzt an der
Spitze Schalke is top of the league

△ NEW SPELLING: See page xii

at the moment; **3** peak; **von hier kann man die schneebedeckten Spitzen sehen** you can see the snow-covered peaks from here; **4** front; **an der Spitze liegen** to be in the lead; **5** lace; **6 Spitze sein** (*informal*) to be great.

spitzen *verb* (PERF **hat gespitzt**) **1** to sharpen; **2 sich auf etwas spitzen** (*informal*) to look forward to something.

Spitzname *der* (PL *die* **Spitznamen**) nickname.

Splitter *der* (PL *die* **Splitter**) splinter.

sponsern *verb* (PERF **hat gesponsert**) to sponsor.

Sport *der* sport.

Sporthalle *die* (PL *die* **Sporthallen**) sports hall.

Sportler *der* (PL *die* **Sportler**) sportsman.

Sportlerin *die* (PL *die* **Sportlerinnen**) sportswoman.

sportlich *adjective* **1** sporting; **2** sporty.

Sportplatz *der* (PL *die* **Sportplätze**) sports field, sports ground.

Sportschuh *der* (PL *die* **Sportschuhe**) trainer.

Sportverein *der* (PL *die* **Sportvereine**) sports club.

Sportwagen *der* (PL *die* **Sportwagen**) **1** sports car; **2** pushchair.

Sportzentrum *das* (PL *die* **Sportzentren**) sports centre.

spotten *verb* (PERF **hat gespottet**) to mock.

sprach SEE **sprechen**.

Sprache *die* (PL *die* **Sprachen**) **1** language; **2** speech; **etwas zur Sprache bringen** to bring something up.

sprachlos *adjective* speechless.

sprang SEE **springen**.

sprechen ◇ *verb* (PRES **spricht**, IMPERF **sprach**, PERF **hat gesprochen**) **1** to speak; **Deutsch sprechen** to speak German; **mit wem spreche ich?** who's speaking? (*on the phone*); **jemanden sprechen** to speak to somebody; **2 Frau Hahn ist nicht zu sprechen** Mrs Hahn is not available; **3** to talk; **mit jemandem über etwas sprechen** to talk to somebody about something; **4** to say (*a word, sentence*).

Sprecher *der* (PL *die* **Sprecher**) **1** spokesman; **2** (*on TV*) announcer; **3** (*in a film*) narrator; **4** speaker.

Sprecherin *die* (PL *die* **Sprecherinnen**) **1** spokeswoman; **2** (*on TV*) announcer; **3** (*in a film*) narrator; **4** speaker.

Sprechstunde *die* (PL *die* **Sprechstunden**) surgery.

spricht SEE **sprechen**.

Sprichwort *das* (PL *die* **Sprichwörter**) proverb.

springen ◇ *verb* (IMPERF **sprang**, PERF **ist gesprungen**) **1** to jump;

◇ IRREGULAR VERB: *See the verb table in the centre of the dictionary*

2 to bounce (*of a ball*); 3 to dive; 4 to crack.

Spritze die (PL die **Spritzen**)
1 syringe; 2 injection; 3 hose.

spritzen verb (PERF hat **gespritzt**)
1 to inject; 2 to splash; **du hast mich nass gespritzt** you've splashed me; 3 to spray; 4 to spit (*of fat*); 5 (PERF **ist gespritzt**) to splash up.

Sprudel der (PL die **Sprudel**)
sparkling mineral water.

sprühen verb (PERF hat **gesprüht**)
1 to spray; 2 to sparkle (*of eyes*); 3 (PERF **ist gesprüht**) to fly (*of sparks*); **die Funken sind in alle Richtungen gesprüht** sparks flew in all directions.

Sprung der (PL die **Sprünge**)
1 jump; 2 dive; 3 crack (*in china, glass*).

Sprungbrett das (PL die **Sprungbretter**) diving board.

spucken verb (PERF hat **gespuckt**)
to spit.

Spülbecken das (PL die **Spülbecken**) sink.

spülen verb (PERF hat **gespült**) 1 to rinse; 2 to wash up; 3 to flush.

Spülmaschine die (PL die **Spülmaschinen**) dishwasher.

Spülmittel das (PL die **Spülmittel**) washing-up liquid.

Spur die (PL die **Spuren**) 1 track; **auf der falschen Spur sein** to be on the wrong track; **jemandem auf die Spur kommen** to get on to somebody;

2 lane; **in der Spur bleiben** to keep in lane; 3 trail; 4 trace.

spüren verb (PERF hat **gespürt**) 1 to feel; 2 to sense.

Staat der (PL die **Staaten**) state.

staatlich adjective state; **eine staatliche Schule** a state school.
adverb by the state.

Staatsangehörigkeit die (PL die **Staatsangehörigkeiten**) nationality.

stabil adjective 1 stable; 2 sturdy.

stach SEE **stechen**.

Stachel der (PL die **Stacheln**)
1 spine; 2 spike; 3 sting.

Stachelbeere die (PL die **Stachelbeeren**) gooseberry.

Stacheldraht der barbed wire.

Stadion das (PL die **Stadien**)
stadium.

Stadium das (PL die **Stadien**) stage.

Stadt die (PL die **Städte**) town, city.

städtisch adjective 1 urban; 2 municipal.

Stadtmitte die town centre.

Stadtplan der (PL die **Stadtpläne**)
street map.

Stadtrand der outskirts (of town); **am Stadtrand** on the outskirts.

Stadtrundfahrt die (PL die **Stadtrundfahrten**) sightseeing tour (*of a town*).

Stadtteil der (PL die **Stadtteile**)
district.

stahl SEE **stehlen**.

△ NEW SPELLING: See page xii

Stahl der steel.

Stall der (PL die Ställe) 1 stable; 2 cowshed; 3 pigsty.

Stamm der (PL die Stämme) 1 trunk; 2 tribe; 3 stem (of a word).

stammen verb (PERF hat gestammt) aus Deutschland stammen to come from Germany.

Stammgast der (PL die Stammgäste) regular customer (in a pub or restaurant).

stand SEE stehen.

Stand der (PL die Stände) 1 state; etwas auf den neuesten Stand bringen to bring something up to date; 2 score (in a game); 3 stall; 4 level.

ständig adjective constant.

Standort der (PL die Standorte) position, location; von ihrem Standort aus konnte sie nichts sehen she couldn't see anything from where she was standing.

Stange die (PL die Stangen) 1 bar; 2 pole.

stank SEE stinken.

starb SEE sterben.

stark adjective 1 strong; 2 heavy (rain, traffic); 3 severe (frost, pain); 4 (informal) great; das ist stark! that's great!

Stärke die (PL die Stärken) 1 strength; 2 starch.

starrsinnig adjective obstinate.

Start der (PL die Starts) 1 start; 2 take-off.

Startbahn die (PL die Startbahnen) runway.

starten verb (PERF ist gestartet) 1 (of a plane) to take off; 2 (PERF hat gestartet) to start, to launch (a campaign).

Station die (PL die Stationen) 1 station; 2 stop; Station machen to stop over; 3 ward.

statt conjunction, preposition ←(+GEN) instead of; statt zu arbeiten instead of working; sie ging statt ihrer Schwester she went instead of her sister.

stattdessen △ conjunction instead.

stattfinden ◇ verb (IMPERF fand statt, PERF hat stattgefunden) to take place.

Stau der (PL die Staus) 1 congestion; 2 traffic jam.

Staub der dust.

staubig adjective dusty.

staubsaugen verb (PERF hat staubgesaugt) to vacuum.

Staubsauger der (PL die Staubsauger) vacuum cleaner.

staunen verb (PERF hat gestaunt) to be amazed.

stechen ◇ verb (PRES sticht, IMPERF stach, PERF hat gestochen) 1 to prick; sich in den Finger stechen to prick your finger; 2 to sting, to bite (of an insect); 3 mit etwas in etwas stechen to jab something into something.

◇ IRREGULAR VERB: See the verb table in the centre of the dictionary

Steckdose die (PL die Steckdosen) socket.

stecken verb (PERF hat gesteckt) 1 to put; du musst die Münze in den Schlitz stecken put the coin into the slot; 2 to pin; 3 wo steckt er? where is he?; 4 stecken bleiben△ to get stuck; den Schlüssel stecken lassen△ to leave the key in the lock.

Stecker der (PL die Stecker) plug.

Stecknadel die (PL die Stecknadeln) pin.

stehen ◇ verb (IMPERF stand, PERF hat gestanden) 1 to stand; 2 to be; es steht zwei zu zwei the score is two all; wie steht's? what's the score?; 3 to have stopped (of a clock or a machine); 4 es steht schlecht um ihn he's in a bad way; na, wie steht's? how are you?; 5 stehen bleiben△ to stop; die Uhr ist stehen geblieben the clock has stopped; 6 in der Zeitung steht, dass … it says in the paper that …; 7 jemandem (gut) stehen to suit somebody; 8 zu jemandem stehen to stand by somebody; 9 sich gut stehen to be on good terms; 10 zum Stehen kommen to come to a standstill.

stehenbleiben SEE stehen.

stehlen ◇ verb (PRES stiehlt, IMPERF stahl, PERF hat gestohlen) to steal.

steif adjective stiff.

steigen verb (IMPERF stieg, PERF ist gestiegen) 1 to climb; auf eine Leiter steigen to climb up a ladder; auf ein Fahrrad steigen to get on a bike; in den Bus steigen to get on the bus; 2 to rise.

steil adjective steep.

Stein der (PL die Steine) stone.

Steinbock der (PL die Steinböcke) 1 ibex; 2 Capricorn; Petra ist Steinbock Petra's Capricorn.

Stelle die (PL die Stellen) 1 place; an deiner Stelle in your place; 2 job; 3 authority; 4 auf der Stelle immediately.

stellen verb (PERF hat gestellt) 1 to put; 2 to set (a watch, task); 3 zur Verfügung stellen to provide; 4 lauter stellen to turn up; leiser stellen to turn down; die Heizung höher stellen to turn the heating up; 5 sich krank stellen to pretend to be ill; 6 sich stellen to give yourself up; 7 die Kinder stellten sich an die Wand the children stood against the wall.

Stellenanzeige die (PL die Stellenanzeigen) job advertisement.

Stellung die (PL die Stellungen) position.

Stempel der (PL die Stempel) 1 stamp; 2 postmark.

stempeln verb (PERF hat gestempelt) to stamp.

Steppdecke die (PL die Steppdecken) quilt.

sterben ◇ verb (PRES stirbt, IMPERF starb, PERF ist gestorben) to die.

Stereoanlage die (PL die Stereoanlagen) stereo (system).

△ NEW SPELLING: See page xii

Stern der (PL die Sterne) star.

Sternzeichen das (PL die Sternzeichen) star sign; **was ist dein Sternzeichen?** what star sign are you?

Steuer[1] das (PL die Steuer) 1 (steering) wheel; 2 helm.

Steuer[2] die (PL die Steuern) tax.

steuern verb (PERF hat gesteuert) 1 to steer; 2 to control; 3 (PERF ist gesteuert) to head.

Stewardess △ die (PL die Stewardessen) stewardess, air hostess.

Stich der (PL die Stiche) 1 prick; 2 stab; 3 sting, bite (of an insect); 4 stitch; 5 trick (when playing cards); 6 engraving; 7 **jemanden im Stich lassen** to leave somebody in the lurch.

sticht SEE stechen.

sticken verb (PERF hat gestickt) to embroider.

Stickstoff der nitrogen.

Stiefbruder der (PL die Stiefbrüder) stepbrother.

Stiefel der (PL die Stiefel) boot.

Stiefkind das (PL die Stiefkinder) stepchild.

Stiefmutter die (PL die Stiefmütter) stepmother.

Stiefschwester die (PL die Stiefschwestern) stepsister.

Stiefvater der (PL die Stiefväter) stepfather.

stieg SEE steigen.

stiehlt SEE stehlen.

Stiel der (PL die Stiele) 1 handle; 2 stem.

Stier der (PL die Stiere) 1 bull; 2 Taurus; **Andrea ist Stier** Andrea's Taurus.

stieß SEE stoßen.

Stift der (PL die Stifte) 1 pencil; 2 crayon; 3 tack (nail).

Stil der (PL die Stile) style.

still adjective 1 quiet; 2 still.

stillen verb (PERF hat gestillt) 1 to quench; 2 to breast-feed.

stillhalten ◇ verb (PRES hält still, IMPERF hielt still, PERF hat stillgehalten) to keep still.

Stimme die (PL die Stimmen) 1 voice; 2 vote.

stimmen verb (PERF hat gestimmt) 1 to be right; **stimmt das?** is that right?; 2 to vote; 3 to tune.

Stimmung die (PL die Stimmungen) 1 mood; 2 atmosphere.

stinken ◇ verb (IMPERF stank, PERF hat gestunken) to smell, to stink.

Stipendium das (PL die Stipendien) 1 scholarship; 2 grant.

stirbt SEE sterben.

Stirn die (PL die Stirnen) forehead.

Stock[1] der (PL die Stöcke) stick.

Stock[2] der (PL die Stock) floor.

Stockwerk das (PL die Stockwerke) floor.

◇ IRREGULAR VERB: See the verb table in the centre of the dictionary

Stoff der (PL die Stoffe) 1 material, fabric; 2 substance.

stöhnen verb (PERF hat gestöhnt) to groan.

stolpern verb (PERF ist gestolpert) 1 to stumble; 2 to trip; **ich bin über einen Stein gestolpert** I tripped on a stone.

stolz adjective proud.

stoppen verb (PERF hat gestoppt) to stop.

Stöpsel der (PL die Stöpsel) 1 plug; 2 stopper.

stören verb (PERF hat gestört) 1 to disturb; 2 to bother; **das stört mich nicht** that doesn't bother me; 3 **stört es Sie, wenn ich das Fenster aufmache?** do you mind if I open the window?; **der Empfang ist gestört** there's interference (on a TV).

Störung die (PL die Störungen) 1 disturbance, interruption; **entschuldigen Sie die Störung** I'm sorry to bother you; 2 interference; **eine technische Störung** a technical fault.

Stoß der (PL die Stöße) 1 push; 2 pile; **ein Stoß Handtücher** a pile of towels.

stoßen ◇ verb (PRES stößt, IMPERF stieß, PERF hat gestoßen) 1 to push; 2 to kick; 3 **sich den Kopf stoßen** to hit your head; **ich habe mir den Kopf an dem Balken gestoßen** I hit my head on the beam; **sich stoßen** to bump yourself; 4 **sich an etwas stoßen** to object to something;

5 (PERF **ist gestoßen**) **gegen etwas stoßen** to bump into something; 6 (PERF **ist gestoßen**) **auf etwas stoßen** to come across something.

Stoßstange die (PL die Stoßstangen) bumper.

Stoßzeit die (PL die Stoßzeiten) rush hour.

stottern verb (PERF hat gestottert) to stutter.

Strafe die (PL die Strafen) 1 punishment; 2 fine; 3 penalty.

Straftat die (PL die Straftaten) crime.

Strahl der (PL die Strahlen) 1 ray, beam; 2 jet.

strahlen verb (PERF hat gestrahlt) 1 to shine; 2 to beam.

Strand der (PL die Strände) beach.

Straße die (PL die Straßen) street, road; **in welcher Straße ist der Supermarkt?** which street is the supermarket in?; **über die Straße gehen** to cross the road; **jemanden auf die Straße setzen** (informal) to give somebody the sack; **mein Wirt hat mich einfach auf die Straße gesetzt** (informal) my landlord just turned me out (of a flat or room).

Straßenbahn die (PL die Straßenbahnen) tram; **mit der Straßenbahn fahren** to go by tram.

Strauch der (PL die Sträucher) bush.

Strauß[1] der (PL die Sträuße) bunch of flowers, bouquet.

Strauß[2] der (PL die Strauße) ostrich.

Streber der (PL die Streber) swot.

Strecke die (PL die Strecken)
1 distance; 2 route; 3 line (rail).

strecken verb (PERF hat gestreckt)
1 to stretch (your arms, legs); 2 sich
strecken to stretch.

Streich der (PL die Streiche) trick.

streicheln verb (PERF hat
gestreichelt) to stroke.

streichen ⬦ verb (IMPERF strich,
PERF hat gestrichen) 1 to paint;
'frisch gestrichen' 'wet paint'; 2 to
spread (with butter); 3 to delete;
4 to cancel (a flight); 5 jemandem
über den Kopf streichen to stroke
somebody's head.

Streichholz das (PL die
Streichhölzer) match.

Streifen der (PL die Streifen)
1 stripe; 2 strip.

Streik der (PL die Streiks) strike.

streiken verb (PERF hat gestreikt) to
strike.

Streit der (PL die Streite) quarrel,
argument.

streiten ⬦ verb (IMPERF stritt, PERF
hat gestritten) 1 to quarrel, to
argue; 2 sich streiten to quarrel, to
argue.

streng adjective strict.

Stress △ der stress.

stressig adjective stressful.

streuen verb (PERF hat gestreut)
1 to spread; die Straßen streuen to
grit the roads; 2 to sprinkle.

strich SEE streichen.

Strich der (PL die Striche) 1 line;
2 stroke.

Strichpunkt der (PL die
Strichpunkte) semicolon.

stricken verb (PERF hat gestrickt) to
knit.

Strickjacke die (PL die
Strickjacken) cardigan.

stritt SEE streiten.

Stroh das straw.

Strohhalm der (PL die Strohhalme)
straw (for drinking).

Strom der (PL die Ströme) 1 river;
2 stream (of people or blood); es
regnet in Strömen it's pouring with
rain; 3 current.

strömen verb (PERF ist geströmt) to
stream.

Strömung die (PL die Strömungen)
current.

Strumpf der (PL die Strümpfe)
1 stocking; 2 sock.

Strumpfhose die (PL die
Strumpfhosen) tights.

Stube die (PL die Stuben) room.

Stück das (PL die Stücke) 1 piece;
2 item; eine Mark das Stück one
mark each; 3 play.

Stückchen das (PL die Stückchen)
little piece.

Student der (PL die Studenten)
student.

Studentin die (PL die Studentinnen)
student.

⬦ IRREGULAR VERB: See the verb table in the centre of the dictionary

studieren verb (PERF hat studiert) to study; **Horst studiert Mathematik** Horst is studying mathematics.

Studium das (PL die Studien) studies.

Stufe die (PL die Stufen) 1 step; **'Vorsicht Stufe'** 'mind the step'; 2 stage (of development).

Stuhl der (PL die Stühle) chair.

stumm adjective 1 dumb; 2 silent.

stumpf adjective 1 blunt; 2 dull; 3 **ein stumpfer Winkel** an obtuse angle.

Stunde die (PL die Stunden) 1 hour; 2 lesson.

stundenlang adverb for hours.

Stundenplan der (PL die Stundenpläne) timetable.

stündlich adjective hourly.

stur adjective stubborn.

Sturm der (PL die Stürme) storm.

stürmisch adjective stormy.

Sturz der (PL die Stürze) 1 fall; 2 overthrow.

stürzen verb (PERF ist gestürzt) 1 to fall; 2 to rush (into a room); 3 (PERF hat gestürzt) to overthrow; 4 (PERF hat sich gestürzt) er hat sich aus dem Fenster gestürzt he threw himself out of the window; **sich auf jemanden stürzen** to pounce on somebody.

Sturzhelm der (PL die Sturzhelme) crash helmet.

stützen verb (PERF hat gestützt) to support; **sich auf jemanden stützen** to lean on somebody.

Subjekt das (PL die Subjekte) subject.

Substantiv das (PL die Substantive) noun.

subventionieren verb (PERF hat subventioniert) to subsidize.

Suche die (PL die Suchen) search.

suchen verb (PERF hat gesucht) 1 to look for; **'Zimmer gesucht'** 'room wanted'; 2 to search.

süchtig adjective addicted.

Süchtige der/die (PL die Süchtigen) addict.

Südafrika das South Africa.

Südamerika das South America.

Süden der south.

südlich adjective 1 southern; 2 southerly. adverb, preposition ←(+GEN) **südlich von Wien** south of Vienna; **südlich der Stadt** to the south of the town.

Südosten der south-east.

Südpol der South Pole.

Südwesten der south-west.

Summe die (PL die Summen) sum.

summen verb (PERF hat gesummt) 1 to hum; 2 to buzz.

super adjective (informal) great.

Supermarkt der (PL die Supermärkte) supermarket.

Suppe die (PL die Suppen) soup.

△ NEW SPELLING: See page xii

surfen *verb* (PERF hat gesurft) to surf.

süß *adjective* sweet.

Süßigkeit *die* (PL die Süßigkeiten) sweet.

sympathisch *adjective* likeable.

Synagoge *die* (PL die Synagogen) synagogue.

synthetisch *adjective* synthetic.

System *das* (PL die Systeme) system.

Szene *die* (PL die Szenen) scene.

T t

Tabak *der* (PL die Tabake) tobacco.

Tabelle *die* (PL die Tabellen) table.

Tablett *das* (PL die Tabletts) tray.

Tablette *die* (PL die Tabletten) tablet.

Tafel *die* (PL die Tafeln) 1 board, blackboard; **ein Wort an die Tafel schreiben** to write a word on the blackboard; 2 **eine Tafel Schokolade** a bar of chocolate.

Tag *der* (PL die Tage) day; **guten Tag** hello; **am Tag** in the daytime.

Tagebuch *das* (PL die Tagebücher) diary.

tagelang *adverb* for days.

Tagesanbruch *der* dawn.

Tageskarte *die* (PL die Tageskarten) 1 today's menu; 2 day ticket.

Tageslicht *das* daylight.

Tageslichtprojektor *der* (PL die Tageslichtprojektoren) overhead projector.

Tagesmutter *die* (PL die Tagesmütter) childminder.

Tagesschau *die* (PL die Tagesschauen) news (on television).

Tageszeitung *die* (PL die Tageszeitungen) daily paper.

täglich *adverb, adjective* daily; **zweimal täglich** twice a day.

tagsüber *adverb* during the day.

Taille *die* (PL die Taillen) waist.

Takt *der* (PL die Takte) 1 tact; 2 time; **im Takt** in time to the music; 3 rhythm.

taktlos *adjective* tactless.

taktvoll *adjective* tactful.

Tal *das* (PL die Täler) valley.

Talent *das* (PL die Talente) talent.

Tampon *der* (PL die Tampons) tampon.

Tank *der* (PL die Tanks) tank.

tanken *verb* (PERF hat getankt) to fill up (with petrol), to get petrol.

Tankstelle *die* (PL die Tankstellen) petrol station.

Tankwart *der* (PL die Tankwarte) petrol-pump attendant.

Tanne *die* (PL die Tannen) fir.

Tannenbaum *der* (PL die Tannenbäume) 1 fir tree; 2 Christmas tree.

⬦ IRREGULAR VERB: See the verb table in the centre of the dictionary

Tante die (PL die Tanten) aunt.

Tanz der (PL die Tänze) dance.

tanzen verb (PERF hat getanzt) to dance.

Tänzer der (PL die Tänzer) dancer.

Tänzerin die (PL die Tänzerinnen) dancer.

Tapete die (PL die Tapeten) wallpaper.

tapezieren verb (PERF hat tapeziert) to (wall)paper.

tapfer adjective brave.

Tarif der (PL die Tarife) 1 tariff; 2 rate.

Tasche die (PL die Taschen) 1 bag; 2 pocket; **er hat es aus eigener Tasche bezahlt** he paid for it out of his own pocket; **Max hat mir fünf Euro aus der Tasche gezogen** (informal) Max wangled five euro out of me.

Taschenbuch das (PL die Taschenbücher) paperback.

Taschendieb der (PL die Taschendiebe) pickpocket.

Taschengeld das pocket money.

Taschenlampe die (PL die Taschenlampen) torch.

Taschenmesser das (PL die Taschenmesser) penknife.

Taschenrechner der (PL die Taschenrechner) pocket calculator.

Taschentuch das (PL die Taschentücher) handkerchief.

Tasse die (PL die Tassen) cup.

Tastatur die (PL die Tastaturen) keyboard.

Taste die (PL die Tasten) 1 key; 2 button (on a phone or a machine).

tasten verb (PERF hat getastet) 1 to feel; 2 **sich tasten** to feel your way.

tat SEE **tun**.

Tat die (PL die Taten) 1 action; 2 **eine gute Tat** a good deed; 3 crime; 4 **in der Tat** indeed.

Täter der (PL die Täter) 1 culprit; 2 offender.

Täterin die (PL die Täterinnen) 1 culprit; 2 offender.

Tätigkeit die (PL die Tätigkeiten) 1 activity; 2 job.

Tätowierung die (PL die Tätowierungen) tattoo.

Tatsache die (PL die Tatsachen) fact.

tatsächlich adjective actual. adverb 1 actually; 2 really.

Tau¹ der dew.

Tau² das (PL die Taue) rope.

taub adjective deaf.

Taube die (PL die Tauben) 1 pigeon; 2 dove.

tauchen verb (PERF hat getaucht) 1 to dip; 2 (PERF hat/ist getaucht) ('ist getaucht' is used when movement is described) to dive.

Taucher der (PL die Taucher) diver.

Taucherin die (PL die Taucherinnen) diver.

tauen verb (PERF **ist getaut**) 1 to melt; 2 **es taut** it's thawing.

Taufe die (PL die **Taufen**) christening.

taufen verb (PERF **hat getauft**) 1 to christen; 2 to baptize.

taugen verb (PERF **hat getaugt**) **nichts taugen** to be no good.

tauschen verb (PERF **hat getauscht**) to exchange, to swap.

tausend number a thousand.

Taxi das (PL die **Taxis**) taxi.

Taxifahrer der (PL die **Taxifahrer**) taxi driver.

Taxifahrerin die (PL die **Taxifahrerinnen**) taxi driver.

Taxistand der (PL die **Taxistände**) taxi rank.

Technik die (PL die **Techniken**) 1 technology; 2 technique.

Techniker der (PL die **Techniker**) technician.

Technikerin die (PL die **Technikerinnen**) technician.

technisch adjective 1 technical; 2 technological.

Technologie die technology.

technologisch adjective technological.

Teddybär der (PL die **Teddybären**) teddy bear.

Tee der (PL die **Tee(s)**) tea; **Tee mit Zitrone** lemon tea.

Teebeutel der (PL die **Teebeutel**) tea bag.

Teekanne die (PL die **Teekannen**) teapot.

Teelöffel der (PL die **Teelöffel**) teaspoon.

Teenager der (PL die **Teenager**) teenager.

Teich der (PL die **Teiche**) pond.

Teig der (PL die **Teige**) 1 dough; 2 pastry; 3 mixture.

Teigwaren plural noun pasta.

Teil[1] der (PL die **Teile**) 1 part; **der zweite Teil** the second part; **zum größten Teil** for the most part; **zum Teil** partly; 3 share; **mein Teil am Gewinn** my share of the profit.

Teil[2] das (PL die **Teile**) 1 spare part; 2 part (of a car, machine); 3 unit (of furniture).

teilen verb (PERF **hat geteilt**) 1 to divide; 2 **sich etwas mit jemandem teilen** to share something with somebody.

teilnehmen ◇ verb (PRES **nimmt teil**, IMPERF **nahm teil**, PERF **hat teilgenommen**) **an etwas teilnehmen** to take part in something.

Teilnehmer der (PL die **Teilnehmer**) 1 participant; 2 competitor.

Teilnehmerin die (PL die **Teilnehmerinnen**) 1 participant; 2 competitor.

teils adverb partly.

Teilung die (PL die **Teilungen**) division.

◇ IF REGULAR VERB: See the verb table in the centre of the dictionary

Teilzeitarbeit *die* part-time work.

Telefax *das* (PL die Telefax(e)) fax.

Telefon *das* (PL die Telefone) telephone.

Telefonanruf *der* (PL die Telefonanrufe) phone call.

Telefonbuch *das* (PL die Telefonbücher) telephone directory, phone book.

Telefongespräch *das* (PL die Telefongespräche) telephone call.

Telefonhörer *der* (PL die Telefonhörer) receiver.

telefonieren *verb* (PERF hat telefoniert) to telephone, to make a phone call.

telefonisch *adjective* telephone. *adverb* by telephone; **er ist telefonisch nicht erreichbar** he can't be contacted by phone.

Telefonkarte *die* (PL die Telefonkarten) phone card.

Telefonnummer *die* (PL die Telefonnummern) telephone number.

Telefonzelle *die* (PL die Telefonzellen) phone box, call box.

Teller *der* (PL die Teller) plate.

Temperatur *die* (PL die Temperaturen) temperature.

Tempo *das* (PL die Tempos) speed; **Tempo Tempo!** (*informal*) hurry up!

Tendenz *die* (PL die Tendenzen) 1 trend; 2 tendency.

tendieren *verb* (PERF hat tendiert) **zu etwas tendieren** to tend towards something.

Tennis *das* tennis.

Tennisplatz *der* (PL die Tennisplätze) tennis court.

Tennisschläger *der* (PL die Tennisschläger) tennis racket.

Tennisspieler *der* (PL die Tennisspieler) tennis player.

Tennisspielerin *die* (PL die Tennisspielerinnen) tennis player.

Teppich *der* (PL die Teppiche) 1 carpet; 2 rug.

Termin *der* (PL die Termine) 1 date; **einen Termin vereinbaren** to fix a date; 2 appointment; 3 **der letzte Termin** the deadline.

Terminal[1] *der* (PL die Terminals) terminal.

Terminal[2] *das* (PL die Terminals) (computer) terminal.

Terrasse *die* (PL die Terrassen) terrace.

Terror *der* terror.

Terrorismus *der* terrorism.

Terrorist *der* (PL die Terroristen) terrorist.

Terroristin *die* (PL die Terroristinnen) terrorist.

Tesafilm™ *der* Sellotape™.

Test *der* (PL die Tests) test.

testen *verb* (PERF hat getestet) to test.

△ NEW SPELLING: *See page xii*

teuer *adjective* expensive; **wie teuer?** how much?

Teufel *der* (PL *die* **Teufel**) devil.

Text *der* (PL *die* **Texte**) 1 text;
2 lyrics; 3 caption.

Textverarbeitung *die* word processing.

Theater *das* (PL *die* **Theater**)
1 theatre; 2 (*informal*) fuss.

Theaterstück *das* (PL *die* **Theaterstücke**) play.

Theke *die* (PL *die* **Theken**) 1 bar;
2 counter.

Thema *das* (PL *die* **Themen**) subject, topic.

Themse *die* Thames.

theoretisch *adjective* theoretical.
adverb in theory.

Theorie *die* (PL *die* **Theorien**) theory.

Therapie *die* (PL *die* **Therapien**) therapy.

Thermometer *das* (PL *die* **Thermometer**) thermometer.

Thron *der* (PL *die* **Throne**) throne.

Thunfisch *der* (PL *die* **Thunfische**) tuna.

Thymian *der* thyme.

tief *adjective* 1 deep; 2 low.

Tiefe *die* (PL *die* **Tiefen**) depth.

Tiefgarage *die* (PL *die* **Tiefgaragen**) underground car park.

Tiefkühlfach *das* (PL *die* **Tiefkühlfächer**) freezer compartment.

Tiefkühlkost *die* frozen food.

Tiefkühltruhe *die* (PL *die* **Tiefkühltruhen**) freezer.

Tiefsttemperatur *die* (PL *die* **Tiefsttemperaturen**) minimum temperature.

Tier *das* (PL *die* **Tiere**) animal.

Tierarzt *der* (PL *die* **Tierärzte**) vet.

Tierärztin *die* (PL *die* **Tierärztinnen**) vet.

Tiergarten *der* (PL *die* **Tiergärten**) zoo.

Tierkreis *der* zodiac.

Tiger *der* (PL *die* **Tiger**) tiger.

Tinte *die* (PL *die* **Tinten**) ink.

Tintenfisch *der* (PL *die* **Tintenfische**) 1 octopus; 2 squid.

Tipp △ *der* (PL *die* **Tipps**) tip.

tippen *verb* (PERF hat **getippt**) 1 to type; 2 to tap; 3 **auf etwas tippen** to bet on something; **ich tippe auf ihn** I'm tipping him to win; **im Lotto tippen** to do the lottery.

Tisch *der* (PL *die* **Tische**) 1 table;
2 **nach Tisch** after the meal.

Tischdecke *die* (PL *die* **Tischdecken**) tablecloth.

Tischler *der* (PL *die* **Tischler**) joiner, carpenter.

Tischtennis *das* table tennis.

Tischtuch *das* (PL *die* **Tischtücher**) tablecloth.

Titel *der* (PL *die* **Titel**) title.

Toast *der* (PL *die* **Toasts**) toast.

◇ IRREGULAR VERB: *See the verb table in the centre of the dictionary*

toben verb (PERF hat getobt) 1 to rage; 2 to go mad; 3 to charge about.

Tochter die (PL die Töchter) daughter.

Tod der (PL die Tode) death.

Todesstrafe die death penalty.

tödlich adjective 1 fatal; 2 deadly.

todmüde adjective dead tired.

todschick adjective trendy.

Toilette die (PL die Toiletten) toilet; auf die Toilette gehen to go to the toilet.

Toilettenpapier das toilet paper.

toll adjective (informal) brilliant.

Tollwut die rabies.

Tomate die (PL die Tomaten) tomato.

Tomatenmark das tomato purée.

Ton[1] der (PL die Töne) 1 sound; er hat keinen Ton gesagt he didn't make a sound; 2 große Töne spucken (informal) to talk big; 3 tone; einen frechen Ton anschlagen to adopt a cheeky tone; 4 note; 5 shade (of colour); 6 stress (in pronunciation).

Ton[2] der clay.

Tonband das (PL die Tonbänder) tape.

Tonbandgerät das (PL die Tonbandgeräte) tape recorder.

Tonne die (PL die Tonnen) 1 barrel; 2 bin (for rubbish); 3 tonne, ton.

Topf der (PL die Töpfe) 1 pot; 2 pan.

Töpferei die (PL die Töpfereien) pottery.

Tor das (PL die Tore) 1 gate; 2 goal.

Torte die (PL die Torten) 1 gateau; 2 cake.

Torwart der (PL die Torwarte) goalkeeper.

tot adjective dead.

total adjective complete. adverb completely; du bist total verrückt you're totally mad.

Tote der/die (PL die Toten) 1 dead man/woman; die Toten the dead; 2 fatality.

töten verb (PERF hat getötet) to kill.

totlachen verb (informal) (PERF hat sich totgelacht) sich totlachen to laugh your head off.

Tour die (PL die Touren) 1 tour; 2 trip; 3 auf diese Tour (informal) in this way.

Tourismus der tourism.

Tourist der (PL die Touristen) tourist.

Touristin die (PL die Touristinnen) tourist.

Tournee die (PL die Tournees) tour.

traben verb (PERF ist getrabt) to trot.

Tradition die (PL die Traditionen) tradition.

traditionell adjective traditional.

traf SEE **treffen**.

tragbar adjective 1 portable; 2 wearable.

tragen ◇ verb (PRES trägt, IMPERF trug, PERF hat getragen) 1 to carry; 2 to wear; sie trug ein weißes Kleid she wore a white dress; man trägt

△ NEW SPELLING: See page xii

wieder kurz short skirts are in fashion again; **3** to bear; **die Verantwortung für etwas tragen** to be responsible for something; **4** to support; **die Organisation trägt sich selbst** the organization is self-supporting.

Träger der (PL die **Träger**) **1** porter; **2** bearer (of a name, title); **3** strap (of a dress); **4** girder.

Tragetasche die (PL die **Tragetaschen**) carrier bag.

tragisch adjective tragic.

Tragödie die (PL die **Tragödien**) tragedy.

Trainer der (PL die **Trainer**) coach, trainer.

trainieren verb (PERF hat **trainiert**) **1** to coach; **2** to train.

Training das training.

Trainingsanzug der (PL die **Trainingsanzüge**) tracksuit.

Traktor der (PL die **Traktoren**) tractor.

trampen verb (PERF ist **getrampt**) to hitchhike.

Tramper der (PL die **Tramper**) hitchhiker.

Tramperin die (PL die **Tramperinnen**) hitchhiker.

Träne die (PL die **Tränen**) tear.

trank SEE **trinken**.

Transport der (PL die **Transporte**) **1** transport; **2** consignment.

transportieren verb (PERF hat **transportiert**) to transport.

trat SEE **treten**.

Traube die (PL die **Trauben**) grape.

trauen verb (PERF hat **getraut**) **1** to trust; **jemandem trauen** to trust somebody; **2** sich trauen to dare; **Ich trau mich nicht** I don't dare; **3** to marry.

Trauer die **1** grief; **2** mourning.

Traum der (PL die **Träume**) dream.

träumen verb (PERF hat **geträumt**) to dream.

traumhaft adjective fabulous.

traurig adjective sad.

Traurigkeit die sadness.

Trauung die (PL die **Trauungen**) wedding.

treffen ◊ verb (PRES **trifft**, IMPERF **traf**, PERF hat **getroffen**) **1** to hit; **2** to meet; **3** to make (arrangements, a decision); **4** sich mit jemandem treffen to meet somebody; **5** sich gut treffen to be convenient; **6** (PERF ist **getroffen**) auf etwas treffen to meet with (resistance, difficulties).

Treffen das (PL die **Treffen**) meeting.

Treffer der (PL die **Treffer**) **1** hit; **2** winner; **3** goal.

Treffpunkt der (PL die **Treffpunkte**) meeting place.

treiben ◊ verb (IMPERF **trieb**, PERF hat **getrieben**) **1** to drive; **2** to do; **viel Sport treiben** to do a lot of sport;

◊ IRREGULAR VERB: See the verb table in the centre of the dictionary

Handel treiben to trade;
3 jemanden zur Eile treiben to
hurry somebody up; 4 Unsinn
treiben to mess about; 5 (PERF ist
getrieben) to drift.

Treibhaus das (PL die Treibhäuser)
hothouse.

Treibhauseffekt der greenhouse
effect.

Treibstoff der fuel.

trennen verb (PERF hat getrennt)
1 to separate; 2 to divide (words,
parts of a room); 3 sich trennen to
separate; wir haben uns getrennt
we've separated; Jutta hat sich von
ihm getrennt Jutta has left him;
4 sich von etwas trennen to part
with something.

Trennung die (PL die Trennungen)
1 separation; 2 division.

Treppe die (PL die Treppen) stairs;
eine Treppe a flight of stairs.

Treppenhaus das stairwell; im
Treppenhaus on the stairs.

treten ◊ verb (PRES tritt, IMPERF trat,
PERF ist getreten) 1 to step; 2 to
tread; 3 to kick; 4 mit jemandem in
Verbindung treten to get in touch
with somebody.

treu adjective faithful.

Tribüne die (PL die Tribünen)
1 stand (in a stadium); 2 platform.

Trick der (PL die Tricks) trick.

Trickfilm der (PL die Trickfilme)
cartoon.

trieb SEE treiben.

trifft SEE treffen.

Trimm-dich-Pfad der (PL die
Trimm-dich-Pfade) keep-fit trail.

trimmen verb (PERF hat getrimmt)
1 to trim; 2 sich trimmen to keep
fit.

trinken ◊ verb (IMPERF trank, PERF
hat getrunken) to drink.

Trinkgeld das (PL die Trinkgelder)
tip.

Trinkwasser das drinking water.

tritt SEE treten.

Tritt der (PL die Tritte) 1 step; 2 kick.

Triumph der (PL die Triumphe)
triumph.

trocken adjective dry.

trocknen verb (PERF hat
getrocknet) to dry.

Trockner der (PL die Trockner) drier.

Trödel der (informal) junk.

Trödelmarkt der (PL die
Trödelmärkte) flea market.

Trommel die (PL die Trommeln)
drum.

trommeln verb (PERF hat
getrommelt) to drum.

Trompete die (PL die Trompeten)
trumpet.

Tropen (plural noun) die Tropen
the tropics.

tropfen verb (PERF hat getropft) to
drip.

Tropfen der (PL die Tropfen) drop.

△ NEW SPELLING: See page xii

Trophäe die (PL die Trophäen) trophy.

tropisch adjective tropical.

trösten verb (PERF hat getröstet) to console, to comfort.

trotz preposition ←(+GEN) despite, in spite of.

trotzdem adverb nevertheless.

trüb adjective 1 dull, dismal; 2 cloudy (liquid).

trübsinnig adjective gloomy.

trug SEE **tragen**.

Truhe die (PL die Truhen) chest.

Trümmer plural noun ruins.

Trumpf der (PL die Trümpfe) 1 trump (card); 2 trumps.

Trunkenheit die drunkenness; **Trunkenheit am Steuer** drink-driving.

Truppen plural noun troops.

Truthahn der (PL die Truthähne) turkey.

Tscheche der (PL die Tschechen) Czech.

Tschechin die (PL die Tschechinnen) Czech.

tschechisch adjective Czech.

Tschechische Republik die Czech Republic.

tschüss △ exclamation bye!

T-Shirt das (PL die T-Shirts) T-shirt.

Tube die (PL die Tuben) tube.

Tuberkulose die tuberculosis.

Tuch das (PL die Tücher) 1 cloth; 2 scarf.

tüchtig adjective 1 competent; 2 big.

Tulpe die (PL die Tulpen) tulip.

Tumor der (PL die Tumoren) tumour.

tun ◇ verb (PRES tut, IMPERF tat, PERF hat getan) 1 to do; **das tut man nicht** it isn't done; **das tut's** (informal) that'll do; 2 to put; **die Butter in den Kühlschrank tun** to put the butter in the fridge; 3 to pretend; **er tut nur so** he's only pretending; 4 to act; **freundlich tun** to act friendly; 5 **jemandem etwas tun** to hurt somebody; 6 **mit jemandem etwas zu tun haben** to have dealings with somebody; **das hat nichts damit zu tun** it's got nothing to do with it; 7 **das tut nichts** it doesn't matter; **es hat sich viel getan** lots has happened.

Tunfisch △ der (PL die Tunfische) tuna.

Tunesien das Tunisia.

Tunesier der (PL die Tunesier) Tunisian.

Tunesierin die (PL die Tunesierinnen) Tunisian.

tunesisch adjective Tunisian.

Tunnel der (PL die Tunnel) tunnel.

tupfen verb (PERF hat getupft) to dab.

Tupfen der (PL die Tupfen) dot.

Tür die (PL die Türen) door.

Türke der (PL die Türken) Turk.

◇ IRREGULAR VERB: See the verb table in the centre of the dictionary

Türkei *die* Turkey.

Türkin *die* (PL *die* **Türkinnen**) Turk.

türkis *adjective* turquoise.

türkisch *adjective* Turkish.

Turm *der* (PL *die* **Türme**) 1 tower;
2 steeple; 3 rook, castle (*in chess*).

turnen *verb* (PERF **hat geturnt**) to do
gymnastics.

Turnen *das* 1 gymnastics;
2 physical education, PE.

Turnhalle *die* (PL *die* **Turnhallen**)
gymnasium, gym.

Turnier *das* (PL *die* **Turniere**)
tournament.

Turnschuh *der* (PL *die* **Turnschuhe**)
1 trainer; 2 gym shoe.

Turnverein *der* (PL *die* **Turnvereine**)
gymnastics club.

tuscheln *verb* (PERF **hat getuschelt**)
to whisper.

tut SEE **tun**.

Tüte *die* (PL *die* **Tüten**) bag.

Typ *der* (PL *die* **Typen**) 1 type;
2 (*informal*) bloke.

typisch *adjective* typical.

U u

U-Bahn *die* (PL *die* **U-Bahnen**)
underground.

übel *adjective* 1 bad; 2 **mir ist übel**
I feel sick; 3 **etwas übel nehmen** Δ
to take offence at something;
jemandem etwas übel nehmen Δ to
hold something against somebody.

Übelkeit *die* nausea.

übelnehmen SEE **übel**.

üben *verb* (PERF **hat geübt**) to
practise.

über *preposition* ←(+DAT, *or* +ACC *with
movement towards a place*) 1 over;
über Weihnachten over Christmas;
2 above; **er wohnt über uns** he lives
above us; **fünf Grad über Null** five
degrees above zero; 3 about; **über
etwas schreiben** to write about
something; 4 for; **ein Scheck über
hundert Mark** a cheque for one
hundred marks; 5 across (*a field, the
street*); 6 **über Frankfurt fahren** to
go via Frankfurt; 7 **über die Straße
gehen** to cross the road.
adverb 1 **über und über** over and
over; 2 **jemandem über sein** to be
better than somebody; 3 **über sein**
(*informal*) to be left over;
4 **jemandem ist etwas über**
(*informal*) somebody is fed up with
something; 5 **etwas über haben** Δ
(*informal*) to be fed up with
something; **Nudeln habe ich über**
I'm getting fed up with pasta.

überall adverb everywhere.

Überblick die (PL die Überblicke)
1 einen guten Überblick über
etwas haben to have a good view of
something; 2 overall view; den
Überblick verlieren to lose track of
things; 3 summary.

überblicken verb (PERF hat
überblickt) 1 to overlook; 2 to
assess.

Überdruss △ der bis zum
Überdruss ad nauseam.

übereinander adverb 1 one on top
of the other; 2 übereinander
sprechen to talk about each other.

übereinstimmen verb (PERF hat
übereingestimmt) to agree.

überempfindlich adjective
hypersensitive.

überfahren ◇ verb (PRES
überfährt, IMPERF überfuhr, PERF hat
überfahren) to run over; das Kind ist
von einem Auto überfahren
worden the child was run over by a
car.

Überfahrt die (PL die Überfahrten)
crossing.

Überfall der (PL die Überfälle)
1 attack; 2 raid.

überfallen verb (PRES überfällt,
IMPERF überfiel, PERF hat überfallen)
1 to attack, to mug; 2 to raid;
3 jemanden mit Fragen überfallen
to bombard somebody with
questions.

überfällig adjective overdue.

überflüssig adjective superfluous.

Überführung die (PL die
Überführungen) 1 transfer;
2 flyover; 3 footbridge.

überfüllt adjective 1 crowded;
2 oversubscribed.

Übergang der (PL die Übergänge)
1 crossing; 2 transition.

übergeben ◇ verb (PRES übergibt,
IMPERF übergab, PERF hat
übergeben) 1 to hand over; 2 sich
übergeben to be sick.

überhaben SEE über.

überhaupt adverb 1 in general;
2 anyway; was will er überhaupt?
what does he want anyway?;
3 überhaupt nicht not at all;
überhaupt nichts nothing at all;
überhaupt keine Zeit haben to
have no time at all.

überholen verb (PERF hat überholt)
1 to overtake; 2 to overhaul.

überholt adjective out-of-date.

überlassen ◇ verb (PRES
überlässt △ IMPERF überließ, PERF
hat überlassen) 1 jemandem etwas
überlassen to let somebody have
something; 2 etwas jemandem
überlassen to leave something up
to somebody (a decision, for
example); das bleibt dir
überlassen it's up to you.

überlaufen ◇ verb (PRES läuft über,
IMPERF lief über, PERF ist
übergelaufen) to overflow.

überleben verb (PERF hat überlebt)
to survive.

überlegen[1] verb (PERF hat

◇ IRREGULAR VERB: See the verb table in the centre of the dictionary

überlegt) 1 to think; **sich etwas überlegen** to think something over; **ohne zu überlegen** without thinking; 2 **ich habe es mir anders überlegt** I've changed my mind.

überlegen² adjective 1 superior; **jemandem überlegen sein** to be superior to somebody; 2 convincing (victory).

überm = über dem.

übermäßig adjective excessive.

übermorgen adverb the day after tomorrow.

übernächster, übernächste, übernächstes adjective next but one; **übernächstes Jahr** the year after next.

übernachten verb (PERF hat **übernachtet**) to stay the night; **bei jemandem übernachten** to stay the night at somebody's house.

übernehmen ◇ verb (PRES **übernimmt**, IMPERF **übernahm**, PERF hat **übernommen**) 1 to take over; 2 to take on; 3 **sich übernehmen** to take on too much.

überqueren verb (PERF hat **überquert**) to cross.

überraschen verb (PERF hat **überrascht**) to surprise.

Überraschung die (PL die **Überraschungen**) surprise.

überreden verb (PERF hat **überredet**) to persuade.

übers = über das.

Überschrift die (PL die **Überschriften**) heading.

überschüssig adjective surplus.

überschütten verb (PERF hat **überschüttet**) **jemanden mit etwas überschütten** to shower somebody with something.

Überschwemmung die (PL die **Überschwemmungen**) flood.

übersehen¹ ◇ verb (PRES **übersieht**, IMPERF **übersah**, PERF hat **übersehen**) 1 to overlook; **einen Fehler übersehen** to overlook a mistake; 2 to assess (consequences, damages).

übersehen² ◇ verb (PRES **sieht sich über**, IMPERF **sah sich über**, PERF hat **sich übergesehen**) **sich etwas übersehen** to get fed up of seeing something.

übersetzen verb (PERF hat **übersetzt**) to translate.

Übersetzer der (PL die **Übersetzer**) translator.

Übersetzerin die (PL die **Übersetzerinnen**) translator.

Übersetzung die (PL die **Übersetzungen**) translation.

Übersicht die 1 overall view; 2 summary.

überspringen ◇ verb (IMPERF **übersprang**, PERF hat **übersprungen**) 1 to jump (over); 2 to skip (a chapter).

überstehen ◇ verb (IMPERF **überstand**, PERF hat **überstanden**) 1 to get over; 2 to survive.

△ NEW SPELLING: See page xii

Überstunden *plural noun*
overtime; **Überstunden machen** to
work overtime.

übertragen ◇ *verb* (PRES
überträgt, IMPERF **übertrug**, PERF **hat
übertragen**) 1 to transfer; 2 to
transmit; 3 to broadcast; 4 **etwas
ins Reine übertragen** to make a fair
copy of something; 5 **sich auf
jemanden übertragen** to
communicate itself to somebody (*of
enthusiasm or nervousness*).

Übertragung *die* (PL *die*
Übertragungen) 1 broadcast;
2 transmission.

übertreiben ◇ *verb* (IMPERF
übertrieb, PERF **hat übertrieben**)
1 to exaggerate; 2 to overdo.

Übertreibung *die* (PL *die*
Übertreibungen) exaggeration.

überwältigend *adjective*
overwhelming.

überweisen ◇ *verb* (IMPERF
überwies, PERF **hat überwiesen**)
1 to transfer; 2 to refer (*a patient*).

überzeugen *verb* (PERF **hat
überzeugt**) 1 to convince; 2 **sich
selbst überzeugen** to satisfy
yourself.

überzeugend *adjective*
convincing.

Überzeugung *die* (PL *die*
Überzeugungen) conviction.

überziehen[1] ◇ *verb* (IMPERF **zog
über**, PERF **hat übergezogen**) to put
on (*a cardigan, jacket*).

überziehen[2] ◇ *verb* (IMPERF

überzog, PERF **hat überzogen**) 1 to
overdraw; 2 to cover (*with icing, for
example*).

üblich *adjective* usual.

übrig *adjective* 1 remaining; 2 **übrig
sein** to be left over; 3 **etwas übrig
lassen** △ to leave something (over);
4 **uns blieb nichts anderes übrig**
we had no other choice; 5 **alles
Übrige** the rest; **die Übrigen** the
others; 6 **im Übrigen** besides.

übrigens *adverb* by the way.

übriglassen SEE **übrig**.

Übung *die* (PL *die* **Übungen**)
1 exercise; 2 practice; **aus der
Übung sein** to be out of practice.

Ufer *das* (PL *die* **Ufer**) 1 bank (*of a
river*); 2 shore.

Uhr *die* (PL *die* **Uhren**) 1 clock;
2 watch; 3 (*in time phrases*) **es ist
ein Uhr** it's one o'clock; **wie viel Uhr
ist es?** what's the time?; **um
sechzehn Uhr** at four o'clock (*in the
afternoon*).

Uhrzeiger *der* (PL *die* **Uhrzeiger**)
hand (*of a clock or watch*).

Uhrzeigersinn *der* **im
Uhrzeigersinn** clockwise;
entgegen dem Uhrzeigersinn anti-
clockwise.

Uhrzeit *die* time; **jemanden nach
der Uhrzeit fragen** to ask
somebody the time.

ulkig *adjective* funny.

um *preposition* ←(+ACC) 1 round,
around; **um das Haus herum**
around the house; 2 at; **um fünf Uhr**

◇ IRREGULAR VERB: *See the verb table in the centre of the dictionary*

at five o'clock; **3** around (about); **4** for; **um etwas bitten** to ask for something; **um seinetwillen** for his sake; **5 sich um jemanden sorgen** to worry about somebody; **6** by (*indicating difference*); **um vieles besser** better by far; **um so besser** so much the better.

adverb **1** about, around; **um die dreihundert Mark herum** about three hundred marks; **um Weihnachten** around Christmas; **2 um sein** (*informal*) to be over.

conjunction **um zu** (in order) to; **er ist noch zu klein, um in die Schule zu gehen** he's too young to go to school.

umarmen *verb* (PERF **hat umarmt**) to hug.

Umbau *der* (PL *die* **Umbauten**) **1** renovation; **2** conversion.

umbinden ◇ *verb* (IMPERF **band um**, PERF **hat umgebunden**) to put on.

umblättern *verb* (PERF **hat umgeblättert**) to turn over.

umbringen ◇ *verb* (IMPERF **brachte um**, PERF **hat umgebracht**) to kill.

umdrehen *verb* (PERF **hat umgedreht**) **1** to turn (round); **2 sich umdrehen** to turn round, to turn over.

umfallen ◇ *verb* (PRES **fällt um**, IMPERF **fiel um**, PERF **ist umgefallen**) to fall down.

Umfrage *die* (PL *die* **Umfragen**) survey.

umgänglich *adjective* sociable.

Umgangsformen *plural noun* manners.

Umgangssprache *die* slang, colloquial language.

umgeben ◇ *verb* (PRES **umgibt**, IMPERF **umgab**, PERF **hat umgeben**) to surround.

Umgebung *die* (PL *die* **Umgebungen**) **1** surroundings; **2** neighbourhood.

umgehen[1] ◇ *verb* (IMPERF **ging um**, PERF **ist umgegangen**) **1** to go round (*of a rumour, an illness*); **2 mit jemandem streng umgehen** to treat somebody strictly; **3 er kann mit Geld nicht umgehen** he can't handle money; **mit seinen Sachen sorgfältig umgehen** to handle one's things carefully.

umgehen[2] ◇ *verb* (IMPERF **umging**, PERF **hat umgangen**) to avoid.

umgekehrt *adjective* **1** opposite; **2** reverse (*order*); **3 es war umgekehrt** it was the other way round.

adverb **1 und umgekehrt** and vice versa; **2** the other way round; **warum machst du es nicht umgekehrt?** why don't you do it the other way round?

umkehren *verb* (PERF **ist umgekehrt**) **1** to turn back; **nach zehn Minuten sind wir wieder umgekehrt** ten minutes later we turned back again; **2** to turn round (*a picture, book*); **3** to turn inside out (*a bag, for example*); **4 sie hat das ganze Zimmer umgekehrt**

△ NEW SPELLING: *See page xii*

(*informal*) she turned the whole room upside down.

Umkleidekabine die (PL die **Umkleidekabinen**) changing cubicle.

Umkleideraum der (PL die **Umkleideräume**) changing room.

umkommen ◇ verb (IMPERF **kam um**, PERF **ist umgekommen**) to be killed.

Umlaut der (PL die **Umlaute**) umlaut.

umlegen verb (PERF hat **umgelegt**) 1 to put on (*a scarf*); 2 to transfer (*a patient, call*); 3 **jemanden umlegen** (*informal*) to bump somebody off.

Umleitung die (PL die **Umleitungen**) diversion.

umrechnen verb (PERF hat **umgerechnet**) to convert.

Umrechnung die conversion.

Umrechnungskurs der exchange rate.

Umriss △ der (PL die **Umrisse**) outline.

umrühren verb (PERF hat **umgerührt**) to stir.

ums = um das.

umschalten verb (PERF hat **umgeschaltet**) 1 to turn over; **vom ersten aufs zweite Programm umschalten** to turn from channel one to channel two; 2 **auf Rot umschalten** to change to red.

Umschlag der (PL die **Umschläge**) 1 envelope; 2 cover.

umsehen ◇ verb (PRES **sieht sich**

um, IMPERF **sah sich um**, PERF **hat sich umgesehen**) **sich umsehen** to look round.

umso △ adverb **umso besser** all the better; **je mehr, umso besser** the more the better.

umsonst adverb 1 in vain; 2 free, for nothing.

Umstand der (PL die **Umstände**) 1 circumstance; 2 **unter Umständen** possibly; 3 **jemandem Umstände machen** to put somebody to trouble; **das macht gar keine Umstände** it's no trouble at all; 4 **in anderen Umständen sein** to be pregnant.

umständlich adjective 1 laborious; 2 complicated.

umsteigen ◇ verb (IMPERF **stieg um**, PERF **ist umgestiegen**) to change.

umstellen[1] verb (PERF hat **umgestellt**) 1 to rearrange; 2 to reset; 3 to change over; 4 **sich umstellen** to adjust.

umstellen[2] ◇ verb (PERF hat **umstellt**) to surround.

Umtausch der exchange.

umtauschen verb (PERF hat **umgetauscht**) to change, to exchange.

Umweg der (PL die **Umwege**) detour.

Umwelt die environment.

umweltfreundlich adjective environmentally friendly.

Umweltschützer der (PL die **Umweltschützer**) environmentalist.

◇ IRREGULAR VERB: *See the verb table in the centre of the dictionary*

Umweltverschmutzung *die* pollution.

umwerfen ◇ *verb* (PRES **wirft um**, IMPERF **warf um**, PERF **hat umgeworfen**) 1 to knock over; 2 to upset (*a plan*); **das hat mich umgeworfen** it's thrown me.

umwerfend *adjective* fantastic.

umziehen ◇ *verb* (IMPERF **zog um**, PERF **ist umgezogen**) 1 to move; **sie ziehen nächste Woche um** they're moving next week; 2 (PERF **hat umgezogen**) to change; 3 (PERF **hat sich umgezogen**) **sich umziehen** to get changed.

Umzug *der* (PL *die* **Umzüge**) move.

unabhängig *adjective* independent.

Unabhängigkeit *die* independence.

unangenehm *adjective* 1 unpleasant; 2 embarrassing (*question, situation*).

unartig *adjective* naughty.

unbedeutend *adjective* insignificant. *adverb* slightly.

unbedingt *adjective* absolute. *adverb* really; **ich muss ihn unbedingt sprechen** I really must talk to him; **nicht unbedingt** not necessarily.

unbefriedigend *adjective* unsatisfactory.

unbefriedigt *adjective* unsatisfied.

unbehaglich *adjective* 1 uncomfortable; 2 uneasy.

unbekannt *adjective* unknown.

unbeliebt *adjective* unpopular.

unbequem *adjective* uncomfortable.

unbestimmt *adjective* 1 indefinite; **auf unbestimmte Zeit** for an indefinite period; 2 uncertain. *adverb* vaguely; **etwas unbestimmt lassen** to leave something open.

unbewusst △ *adjective* unconscious.

und *conjunction* and; **und so weiter** and so on; **na und?** so what?

undankbar *adjective* ungrateful.

undeutlich *adjective* unclear.

undicht *adjective* leaking, leaky; **eine undichte Stelle** a leak.

uneben *adjective* uneven.

unempfindlich *adjective* 1 hard-wearing, easy-care; 2 immune; **gegen Kälte unempfindlich sein** not to feel the cold.

unentbehrlich *adjective* indispensable.

unentschieden *adjective* undecided; **unentschieden spielen** to draw.

unerträglich *adjective* unbearable.

unerwartet *adjective* unexpected.

unfähig *adjective* 1 incompetent; 2 **unfähig sein, etwas zu tun** to be incapable of doing something.

△ NEW SPELLING: See page xii

unfair *adjective* unfair.

Unfall der (PL die **Unfälle**) accident.

unfreundlich *adjective* unfriendly.

Unfug der 1 nonsense; 2 mischief; **Unfug machen** to get up to mischief.

Ungar der (PL die **Ungarn**) Hungarian.

Ungarin die (PL die **Ungarinnen**) Hungarian.

ungarisch *adjective* Hungarian.

Ungarn das Hungary.

Ungeduld die impatience.

ungeduldig *adjective* impatient.

ungeeignet *adjective* unsuitable.

ungefähr *adjective* approximate. *adverb* approximately, about.

ungefährlich *adjective* safe, harmless.

ungeheuer *adjective* enormous.

Ungeheuer das (PL die **Ungeheuer**) monster.

ungehorsam *adjective* disobedient.

ungelegen *adjective* inconvenient.

ungemütlich *adjective* uncomfortable.

ungenau *adjective* 1 inaccurate; 2 vague.

ungenießbar *adjective* 1 inedible; 2 undrinkable; 3 **Bernd ist heute aber ungenießbar** (*informal*) Bernd is quite unbearable today.

ungenügend *adjective* 1 insufficient; 2 unsatisfactory (*mark at school*).

ungerade *adjective* **eine ungerade Zahl** an odd number.

ungerecht *adjective* unjust.

ungern *adverb* reluctantly.

ungeschickt *adjective* clumsy.

ungesund *adjective* unhealthy.

ungewöhnlich *adjective* unusual.

Ungeziefer das vermin.

ungezwungen *adjective* 1 informal; 2 natural.

unglaublich *adjective* incredible.

Unglück das (PL die **Unglücke**) 1 accident; 2 misfortune; 3 bad luck; **das bringt Unglück** that's unlucky.

unglücklich *adjective* 1 unhappy; 2 unfortunate.

unglücklicherweise *adverb* unfortunately.

unheilbar *adjective* incurable.

unheimlich *adjective* eerie. *adverb* 1 eerily; 2 (*informal*) incredibly; **unheimlich viel** an incredible amount.

unhöflich *adjective* impolite.

Uniform die (PL die **Uniformen**) uniform.

uninteressant *adjective* uninteresting.

Universität die (PL die **Universitäten**) university.

Unkenntnis die ignorance.

✧ IRREGULAR VERB: *See the verb table in the centre of the dictionary*

unklar *adjective* unclear.

Unkosten *plural noun* expenses.

Unkraut *das* weed.

unmodern *adjective* old-fashioned.

unleserlich *adjective* illegible.

unlogisch *adjective* illogical.

unmittelbar *adjective* immediate, direct.

unmöglich *adjective* impossible.

Unmöglichkeit *die* impossibility.

unnötig *adjective* unnecessary.

unordentlich *adjective* untidy.

Unordnung *die* 1 disorder; 2 mess.

unpraktisch *adjective* impractical.

unpünktlich *adjective* unpunctual; **unpünktlich sein** to be late.

unrecht *adjective* wrong; **jemandem unrecht tun** to do somebody an injustice.

Unrecht *das* 1 wrong; **zu Unrecht** wrongly; **Unrecht haben** Δ to be wrong; 2 **jemandem Unrecht geben** Δ to disagree with somebody.

unregelmäßig *adjective* irregular.

unreif *adjective* 1 unripe; 2 immature.

Unruhe *die* (PL **die Unruhen**) 1 restlessness; 2 agitation; 3 **Unruhen** unrest.

Unruhestifter *der* (PL **die Unruhestifter**) troublemaker.

unruhig *adjective* restless.

uns *pronoun* 1 us; **gib es uns** give it

to us; **sie kommen mit uns** they're coming with us; 2 ourselves; **wir waschen uns die Hände** we are washing our hands; 3 each other; **wir kennen uns** we know each other.

unschuldig *adjective* innocent.

unser our.

unserer, unsere, unser(e)s *pronoun* ours.

unsertwegen *adverb* 1 for our sake; 2 because of us; 3 as far as we're concerned.

unsicher *adjective* 1 uncertain; 2 insecure.
adverb unsteadily.

unsichtbar *adjective* invisible.

Unsinn *der* nonsense.

unsrer SEE **unserer**.

unsympathisch *adjective* unpleasant; **Tobias ist mir unsympathisch** I don't like Tobias.

unten *adverb* 1 at the bottom; 2 underneath; 3 downstairs; **hier unten** down here; **nach unten** down.

unter *preposition* ←(+DAT or +ACC *with movement towards a place*) 1 under, below; 2 **unter anderem** among other things; 3 **unter sich** by themselves; **unter uns gesagt** between ourselves; 4 **unter der Woche** during the week.

Unterbewusstsein Δ *das* subconscious.

unterbrechen ◇ *verb* (PRES **unterbricht**, IMPERF **unterbrach**, PERF **hat unterbrochen**) to interrupt.

Δ NEW SPELLING: See page xii

Unterbrechung die (PL die Unterbrechungen) interruption.

unterbringen ◇ verb (IMPERF brachte unter, PERF hat untergebracht) 1 to put; 2 to put up (a guest).

untere SEE unterer.

untereinander adverb 1 among ourselves/yourselves/themselves; 2 one below the other.

unterer, untere, unteres adjective lower.

Unterführung die (PL die Unterführungen) subway.

untergehen ◇ verb (IMPERF ging unter, PERF ist untergegangen) 1 to set (of the sun); 2 to sink, to drown; 3 to come to an end.

Untergrundbahn die (PL die Untergrundbahnen) underground.

unterhalb preposition ←(+GEN) below.

unterhalten ◇ verb (PRES unterhält, IMPERF unterhielt, PERF hat unterhalten) 1 to support; 2 to run (a hotel, leisure centre); 3 to entertain; 4 sich über etwas unterhalten to talk about something; 5 sich unterhalten to enjoy yourself.

unterhaltsam adjective entertaining.

Unterhaltung die (PL die Unterhaltungen) 1 conversation; 2 entertainment.

Unterhemd das (PL die Unterhemden) vest.

Unterhose die (PL die Unterhosen) underpants.

Unterkunft die (PL die Unterkünfte) accommodation.

Unterlagen plural noun documents, papers.

Untermieter der (PL die Untermieter) lodger.

Untermieterin die (PL die Untermieterinnen) lodger.

unternehmen ◇ verb (PRES unternimmt, IMPERF unternahm, PERF hat unternommen) 1 to undertake; 2 nichts unternehmen to do nothing; was unternehmt ihr heute? what are you doing today?

Unternehmen das (PL die Unternehmen) 1 enterprise; 2 concern.

Unterricht der 1 lessons; heute haben wir keinen Unterricht we've got no lessons today; 2 teaching.

unterrichten verb (PERF hat unterrichtet) 1 to teach; 2 to inform; 3 sich unterrichten to inform yourself.

Unterrichtsfach das (PL die Unterrichtsfächer) subject.

Unterrock der (PL die Unterröcke) slip.

unterscheiden ◇ verb (IMPERF unterschied, PERF hat unterschieden) 1 to distinguish, to tell apart; 2 sich unterscheiden to differ.

Unterschied der (PL die Unterschiede) difference.

◇ IRREGULAR VERB: See the verb table in the centre of the dictionary

unterschiedlich *adjective* different; **das ist unterschiedlich** it varies.

unterschreiben ◊ *verb* (IMPERF **unterschrieb**, PERF **hat unterschrieben**) to sign.

Unterschrift *die* (PL *die* **Unterschriften**) signature.

unterster, unterste, unterstes *adjective* bottom, lowest.

unterstreichen ◊ *verb* (IMPERF **unterstrich**, PERF **hat unterstrichen**) to underline.

unterstützen *verb* (PERF **hat unterstützt**) to support.

Unterstützung *die* support.

untersuchen *verb* (PERF **hat untersucht**) 1 to examine; 2 to investigate.

Untersuchung *die* (PL *die* **Untersuchungen**) 1 examination, check-up; 2 investigation.

Untertasse *die* (PL *die* **Untertassen**) saucer.

Untertitel *der* (PL *die* **Untertitel**) subtitle.

Unterwäsche *die* underwear.

unterwegs *adverb* on the way; **den ganzen Tag unterwegs sein** to be out all day.

untreu *adjective* 1 unfaithful; 2 disloyal.

ununterbrochen *adjective* uninterrupted.

unverbleit *adjective* unleaded.

unvergleichlich *adjective* incomparable.

unverheiratet *adjective* unmarried.

unverkäuflich *adjective* not for sale; **ein unverkäufliches Muster** a free sample.

unverschämt *adjective* impertinent.

unverständlich *adjective* incomprehensible.

unvorsichtig *adjective* careless.

unwahr *adjective* untrue.

unwahrscheinlich *adjective* 1 unlikely; 2 incredible. *adverb* (*informal*) incredibly; **unwahrscheinlich schön** incredibly beautiful.

Unwetter *das* storm.

unwichtig *adjective* unimportant.

unzählig *adjective* countless.

unzerbrechlich *adjective* unbreakable.

unzertrennlich *adjective* inseparable.

unzufrieden *adjective* dissatisfied.

üppig *adjective* lavish.

uralt *adjective* ancient.

Urenkel *der* (PL *die* **Urenkel**) great-grandson; **die Urenkel** the great-grandchildren.

Urenkelin *die* (PL *die* **Urenkelinnen**) great-granddaughter.

△ NEW SPELLING: See page xii

Urkunde die (PL die Urkunden) certificate.

Urlaub der (PL die Urlaube) holiday; **Urlaub haben** to be on holiday; **auf/im Urlaub** on holiday.

Urlauber der (PL die Urlauber) holidaymaker.

Ursache die (PL die Ursachen) cause; **keine Ursache!** don't mention it!

Urprung der (PL die Ursprünge) origin.

ursprünglich adjective original. adverb originally.

Urteil das (PL die Urteile) 1 judgement; 2 opinion; 3 verdict.

urteilen verb (PERF hat geurteilt) to judge.

Urwald der (PL die Urwälder) jungle.

USA plural noun USA.

usw. (und so weiter) etc.

V v

vage adjective vague.

Vagina die (PL die Vaginen) vagina.

Valentinstag der Valentine's Day.

Vanille die vanilla.

Vase die (PL die Vasen) vase.

Vater der (PL die Väter) father.

Vaterunser das Lord's Prayer.

Vati der (PL die Vatis) dad.

Veganer der (PL die Veganer) vegan.

Vegetarier der (PL die Vegetarier) vegetarian.

Vegetarierin die (PL die Vegetarierinnen) vegetarian.

vegetarisch adjective vegetarian.

Veilchen das (PL die Veilchen) violet.

Vene die (PL die Venen) vein.

Ventil das (PL die Ventile) valve.

Ventilator der (PL die Ventilatoren) fan.

verabreden verb (PERF hat verabredet) 1 to arrange; **was habt ihr verabredet?** what did you arrange?; **mit jemandem verabredet sein** to have arranged to meet somebody; 2 **sich mit jemandem verabreden** to arrange to meet somebody; **ich habe mich mit Oliver zum Tennis verabredet** I've arranged to play tennis with Oliver.

Verabredung die (PL die Verabredungen) 1 appointment; 2 date; 3 arrangement.

verabschieden verb (PERF hat verabschiedet) 1 to say goodbye to; 2 **sich verabschieden** to say goodbye.

Verachtung die contempt.

verallgemeinern verb (PERF hat verallgemeinert) to generalize.

veralten verb (PERF ist veraltet) to become obsolete.

veränderlich adjective changeable.

✧ IRREGULAR VERB: See the verb table in the centre of the dictionary

verändern *verb* (PERF hat verändert) 1 to change; 2 sich verändern to change.

Veränderung *die* (PL die Veränderungen) change.

veranstalten *verb* (PERF hat veranstaltet) to organize.

Veranstalter *der* (PL die Veranstalter) organizer.

Veranstaltung *die* (PL die Veranstaltungen) event.

verantwortlich *adjective* responsible.

Verantwortung *die* responsibility.

verantwortungsbewusst △ *adjective* responsible.

verantwortungslos *adjective* irresponsible.

verarbeiten *verb* (PERF hat verarbeitet) 1 to process; etwas zu etwas verarbeiten to make something into something; 2 to digest (*food, information*).

verärgern *verb* (PERF hat verärgert) to annoy.

Verb *das* (PL die Verben) verb.

verband SEE verbinden.

Verband *der* (PL die Verbände) 1 association; sich zu einem Verband zusammenschließen to form an association; 2 bandage, dressing; einen Verband anlegen to apply a dressing.

verbergen ◇ *verb* (PRES verbirgt, IMPERF verbarg, PERF hat verborgen) 1 to hide; 2 sich verbergen to hide.

verbessern *verb* (PERF hat verbessert) 1 to improve; 2 to correct; 3 sich verbessern to improve.

Verbesserung *die* (PL die Verbesserungen) 1 improvement; 2 correction.

verbiegen ◇ *verb* (IMPERF verbog, PERF hat verbogen) 1 to bend; 2 sich verbiegen to bend.

verbieten ◇ *verb* (IMPERF verbot, PERF hat verboten) 1 to forbid; sie hat ihm verboten, das Haus zu betreten she forbade him to enter the house; meine Eltern verbieten mir, am Abend wegzugehen my parents don't allow me to go out in the evening; 2 to ban.

verbilligt *adjective* reduced.

verbinden ◇ *verb* (IMPERF verband, PERF hat verbunden) 1 to connect, to join; 2 to combine; 3 to bandage, to dress (*a wound*); jemandem die Augen verbinden to blindfold somebody; 4 jemanden verbinden to put somebody through (*on the phone*); ich verbinde I'm putting you through.

verbindlich *adjective* 1 friendly; 2 binding (*agreement, decision*).

Verbindung *die* (PL die Verbindungen) 1 connection; 2 gute Verbindungen haben to have good contacts; sich mit jemandem in Verbindung setzen to get in touch with somebody; 3 combination; 4 eine chemische Verbindung a chemical compound.

verbirgt SEE verbergen.

△ NEW SPELLING: See page xi■

verbleit *adjective* leaded.

verblüffen *verb* (PERF **hat verblüfft**) to amaze.

verbog SEE **verbiegen**.

verbogen *adjective* hidden.

verbot SEE **verbieten**.

Verbot *das* (PL *die* **Verbote**) ban.

verboten *adjective* forbidden; **'Rauchen verboten'** 'no smoking'.

verbracht, verbrachte SEE **verbringen**.

verbrannt, verbrannte SEE **verbrennen**.

Verbrauch *der* consumption.

verbrauchen *verb* (PERF **hat verbraucht**) to use, to use up; **die Waschmaschine verbraucht nicht viel Strom** the washing machine doesn't use up much electricity.

Verbraucher *der* (PL *die* **Verbraucher**) consumer.

Verbrechen *das* (PL *die* **Verbrechen**) crime.

Verbrecher *der* (PL *die* **Verbrecher**) criminal.

verbreiten *verb* (PERF **hat verbreitet**) 1 to spread; **eine Krankheit verbreiten** to spread an illness; 2 **eine Meldung über den Rundfunk verbreiten** to broadcast a message; 3 **sich verbreiten** to spread; **die Neuigkeit hat sich schnell verbreitet** the news spread quickly.

verbreitet *adjective* widespread.

verbrennen ◇ *verb* (IMPERF **verbrannte**, PERF **ist verbrannt**) 1 to burn; 2 (PERF **hat verbrannt**) to burn (*rubbish, leaves*); 3 to cremate; 4 **sich die Hand verbrennen** to burn your hand.

verbringen ◇ *verb* (IMPERF **verbrachte**, PERF **hat verbracht**) to spend; **wir haben schöne Ferien in Bayern verbracht** we spent a nice holiday in Bavaria.

verbunden SEE **verbinden**.

Verdacht *der* suspicion.

verdächtig *adjective* suspicious.

verdächtigen *verb* (PERF **hat verdächtigt**) to suspect.

verdammt *adjective, adverb* (*informal*) damned; **verdammt!** damn!

verdarb SEE **verderben**.

Verdauung *die* digestion.

verderben ◇ *verb* (PRES **verdirbt**, IMPERF **verdarb**, PERF **hat verdorben**) 1 to spoil, to ruin; **das hat mir den Abend verdorben** it ruined the evening for me; **ich habe mir den Magen verdorben** I have an upset stomach; 2 **es sich mit jemandem verderben** to get into somebody's bad books; 3 (PERF **ist verdorben**) to go off; **die Milch verdirbt, wenn du sie nicht in den Kühlschrank stellst** the milk will go off if you don't put it in the fridge.

verdienen *verb* (PERF **hat verdient**) 1 to earn; 2 to deserve.

◇ IRREGULAR VERB: *See the verb table in the centre of the dictionary*

Verdienst der (PL die Verdienste)
1 salary; 2 achievement.

verdirbt SEE verderben.

verdoppeln verb (PERF hat
verdoppelt) 1 to double; 2 sich
verdoppeln to double.

verdorben SEE verderben.

verdünnen verb (PERF hat
verdünnt) to dilute.

verehren verb (PERF hat verehrt) to
worship.

Verehrer der (PL die Verehrer)
admirer.

Verehrerin die (PL die
Verehrerinnen) admirer.

Verein der (PL die Vereine) 1 society;
2 organization; 3 club.

vereinbaren verb (PERF hat
vereinbart) to arrange.

Vereinbarung die (PL die
Vereinbarungen) 1 agreement;
2 arrangement.

vereinfachen verb (PERF hat
vereinfacht) to simplify.

vereinigen verb (PERF hat vereinigt)
to unite; ein Land wieder
vereinigen △ to reunify a country.

Vereinigte Staaten plural noun
United States.

Vereinigung die (PL die
Vereinigungen) organization.

verfahren ◇ verb (PRES verfährt,
IMPERF verfuhr, PERF ist verfahren)
1 to proceed; 2 ich habe mich
verfahren I've lost my way.

verfallen ◇ verb (PRES verfällt,
IMPERF verfiel, PERF ist verfallen) 1 to
decay; 2 to expire (of a passport or
ticket).

Verfassung die (PL die
Verfassungen) 1 constitution;
2 state (of a person).

verfaulen verb (PERF ist verfault) to
rot.

verfiel SEE verfallen.

verfolgen verb (PERF hat verfolgt)
1 to follow; 2 to persecute.

Verfolgung die (PL die
Verfolgungen) 1 pursuit, hunt;
2 persecution.

verfügbar adjective available.

Verfügung die jemandem etwas
zur Verfügung stellen to put
something at somebody's disposal;
jemandem zur Verfügung stehen
to be at somebody's disposal.

verfuhr SEE verfahren.

verführen verb (PERF hat verführt)
1 to tempt; 2 to seduce.

Verführung die (PL die
Verführungen) 1 temptation;
2 seduction.

vergab SEE vergeben.

vergangen verb SEE vergehen.
adjective last.

Vergangenheit die 1 past; 2 past
tense.

vergaß SEE vergessen.

vergeben ◇ verb (PRES vergibt,
IMPERF vergab, PERF hat vergeben)
1 to forgive; jemandem etwas
vergeben to forgive somebody for

△ NEW SPELLING: See page xii

something; **2** to give away, to award;
3 vergeben sein to be taken; **das
Zimmer ist schon vergeben** the
room's already taken.

vergeblich *adverb* in vain.

vergehen ◇ *verb* (IMPERF **verging**,
PERF **ist vergangen**) to pass.

vergessen ◇ *verb* (PRES **vergisst**△,
IMPERF **vergaß**, PERF **hat vergessen**)
to forget.

vergesslich △ *adjective* forgetful.

vergewaltigen *verb* (PERF **hat
vergewaltigt**) to rape.

Vergewaltigung *die* (PL *die*
Vergewaltigungen) rape.

vergibt SEE **vergeben**

vergiften *verb* (PERF **hat vergiftet**)
to poison.

verging SEE **vergehen**

vergisst △ SEE **vergessen**

Vergleich *der* (PL *die* **Vergleiche**)
comparison.

vergleichen ◇ *verb* (IMPERF
verglich, PERF **hat verglichen**) to
compare.

Vergnügen *das* (PL *die* **Vergnügen**)
pleasure; **viel Vergnügen!** have
fun!

vergnügt *adjective* cheerful.

vergrößern *verb* (PERF **hat
vergrößert**) **1** to enlarge; **2** to
increase; **3** to magnify; **4** to extend
(*a room, building*); **5 sich
vergrößern** to expand, to grow
bigger.

Vergrößerung *die* (PL *die*
Vergrößerungen) **1** expansion;
2 enlargement (*of a photograph*).

verhaften *verb* (PERF **hat verhaftet**)
to arrest; **er ist verhaftet worden** he
was arrested.

verhalten ◇ *verb* (PRES **verhält
sich**, IMPERF **verhielt sich**, PERF **hat
sich verhalten**) **sich verhalten** to
behave.

Verhalten *das* behaviour.

Verhältnis *das* (PL *die* **Verhältnisse**)
1 relationship; **sie hat ein gutes
Verhältnis zu ihren Eltern** she has a
good relationship with her parents;
2 affair; **Gabi hat ein Verhältnis mit
einem verheirateten Mann** Gabi is
having an affair with a married man;
3 ratio (*in maths*); **4 in keinem
Verhältnis zu etwas stehen** to be
out of all proportion to something;
5 Verhältnisse conditions; **über
seine Verhältnisse leben** to live
beyond your means.

verhältnismäßig *adverb*
relatively.

verhandeln *verb* (PERF **hat
verhandelt**) to negotiate; **über
etwas verhandeln** to negotiate
something.

Verhandlung *die* (PL *die*
Verhandlungen) **1** negotiation;
2 hearing; **3** trial.

verhauen *verb* (PERF **hat verhauen**)
1 to beat up; **2 die Prüfung
verhauen** (*informal*) to make a
mess of the exam.

verheimlichen *verb* (PERF **hat
verheimlicht**) to keep secret.

◇ IRREGULAR VERB: *See the verb table in the centre of the dictionary*

verheiratet *adjective* married.

verhielt SEE **verhalten**.

verhindern *verb* (PERF hat verhindert) 1 to prevent; 2 verhindert sein to be unable to make it; Petra ist verhindert Petra won't be able to make it.

verhungern *verb* (PERF ist verhungert) to starve.

Verhütungsmittel *das* (PL die Verhütungsmittel) contraceptive.

verirren *verb* (PERF hat sich verirrt) sich verirren to get lost.

verkam SEE **verkommen**.

Verkauf *der* (PL die Verkäufe) sale; zum Verkauf for sale.

verkaufen *verb* (PERF hat verkauft) to sell; zu verkaufen for sale.

Verkäufer *der* (PL die Verkäufer) 1 seller; 2 sales assistant.

Verkäuferin *die* (PL die Verkäuferinnen) 1 seller; 2 sales assistant.

Verkehr *der* traffic.

Verkehrsampel *die* (PL die Verkehrsampeln) traffic lights.

Verkehrsamt *das* (PL die Verkehrsämter) tourist office.

Verkehrsunfall *der* (PL die Verkehrsunfälle) road accident.

Verkehrszeichen *das* (PL die Verkehrszeichen) traffic sign, road sign.

verkehrt *adjective* 1 wrong;

2 verkehrt herum inside out, the wrong way round.

verklagen *verb* (PERF hat verklagt) to sue.

verkleiden *verb* (PERF hat sich verkleidet) sich verkleiden to dress up.

Verkleidung *die* (PL die Verkleidungen) disguise, fancy dress.

verkommen◇ *verb* (IMPERF verkam, PERF ist verkommen) 1 to go off (of food); 2 to become dilapidated (of a house); 3 to go to the bad.

verkratzt *adjective* scratched.

Verlag *der* (PL die Verlage) publisher's.

verlangen *verb* (PERF hat verlangt) 1 to ask for, to require; am Telefon verlangt werden to be wanted on the phone; 2 to demand; 3 to charge.

verlängern *verb* (PERF hat verlängert) 1 to extend; 2 to lengthen; 3 to renew (a passport, driving licence).

Verlängerung *die* (PL die Verlängerungen) 1 extension; 2 renewal; 3 extra time (in sport).

verlassen¹◇ *verb* (PRES verlässt△, IMPERF verließ, PERF hat verlassen) 1 to leave; jemanden verlassen to leave somebody; 2 sich auf etwas verlassen to rely on something; du kannst dich auf ihn verlassen you can rely on him.

verlassen² *adjective* deserted.

△ NEW SPELLING: See page xii

verlaufen ◊ *verb* (PRES **verläuft**, IMPERF **verlief**, PERF **ist verlaufen**) 1 to go; **es ist gut verlaufen** it went well; 2 **sich verlaufen** to lose your way; 3 **die Menge verlief sich schnell** the crowd quickly dispersed.

verlegen[1] *adjective* embarrassed.

verlegen[2] *verb* (PERF **hat verlegt**) 1 to mislay; 2 to postpone; 3 to publish; 4 to lay (*a carpet, cable*).

Verlegenheit *die* embarrassment.

Verleih *der* (PL **die Verleihe**) 1 renting out, hiring out; 2 rental firm, hire shop.

verleihen ◊ *verb* (IMPERF **verlieh**, PERF **hat verliehen**) 1 to hire out; 2 to lend; 3 to award.

verlernen *verb* (PERF **hat verlernt**) to forget.

verletzen *verb* (PERF **hat verletzt**) 1 to injure; 2 to hurt; 3 to violate (*a law*); 4 **sich verletzen** to hurt yourself.

Verletzte *der/die* (PL **die Verletzten**) 1 injured person; 2 casualty.

Verletzung *die* (PL **die Verletzungen**) injury.

verlieben *verb* (PERF **hat sich verliebt**) **sich verlieben** to fall in love.

verlief SEE **verlaufen**.

verlieh SEE **verleihen**.

verlieren ◊ *verb* (IMPERF **verlor**, PERF **hat verloren**) to lose.

verließ SEE **verlassen**.

verloben *verb* (PERF **hat sich**

verlobt) **sich verloben** to get engaged.

Verlobte *der/die* (PL **die Verlobten**) fiancé, fiancée.

Verlobung *die* (PL **die Verlobungen**) engagement.

verlor, verloren SEE **verlieren**.

Verlosung *die* (PL **die Verlosungen**) prize draw.

Verlust *der* (PL **die Verluste**) loss.

vermeiden ◊ *verb* (IMPERF **vermied**, PERF **hat vermieden**) to avoid.

vermieten *verb* (PERF **hat vermietet**) 1 to rent out, to hire out; 2 to let; **Zimmer zu vermieten** rooms to let.

Vermieter *der* (PL **die Vermieter**) landlord.

Vermieterin *die* (PL **die Vermieterinnen**) landlady.

vermissen *verb* (PERF **hat vermisst** Δ) to miss.

Vermittlung *die* (PL **die Vermittlungen**) 1 arrangement; 2 agency; 3 switchboard; 4 telephone exchange; 5 mediation.

Vermögen *das* (PL **die Vermögen**) fortune.

vermuten *verb* (PERF **hat vermutet**) to suspect.

vermutlich *adjective* probable. *adverb* probably.

vernichten *verb* (PERF **hat vernichtet**) 1 to destroy; 2 to exterminate.

◊ IRREGULAR VERB: *See the verb table in the centre of the dictionary*

Vernunft *die* reason.

vernünftig *adjective* sensible.

verpacken *verb* (PERF **hat verpackt**) 1 to pack; 2 to wrap up.

Verpackung *die* (PL *die* **Verpackungen**) packaging.

verpassen *verb* (PERF **hat verpasst** △) to miss.

Verpflegung *die* food; **Unterkunft und Verpflegung** board and lodging.

verpflichten *verb* (PERF **hat verpflichtet**) 1 **sich verpflichten** to promise; 2 **sich vertraglich verpflichten** to sign a contract; 3 **verpflichtet sein, etwas zu tun** to be obliged to do something; **jemandem zu Dank verpflichtet sein** to be obliged to somebody; 4 **verpflichtend** binding.

Verpflichtung *die* (PL *die* **Verpflichtungen**) 1 obligation; 2 commitment.

verprügeln *verb* (PERF **hat verprügelt**) to beat up.

verraten ◊ *verb* (PRES **verrät**, IMPERF **verriet**, PERF **hat verraten**) 1 to betray; 2 to give away; 3 to tell; 4 **sich verraten** to give yourself away.

verrechnen *verb* (PERF **hat sich verrechnet**) **sich verrechnen** to make a mistake.

verregnet *adjective* rainy.

verreisen *verb* (PERF **ist verreist**) to go away; **verreist sein** to be away.

verriet SEE **verraten**.

verrosten *verb* (PERF **ist verrostet**) to rust.

verrostet *adjective* rusty.

verrückt *adjective* mad, crazy.

Verrückte *der/die* (PL *die* **Verrückten**) maniac.

versagen *verb* (PERF **hat versagt**) to fail.

versammeln *verb* (PERF **hat versammelt**) 1 to assemble; 2 **sich versammeln** to assemble.

Versammlung *die* (PL *die* **Versammlungen**) meeting.

versäumen *verb* (PERF **hat versäumt**) to miss; **es versäumen, etwas zu tun** to fail to do something.

verschenken *verb* (PERF **hat verschenkt**) to give away.

verschieben ◊ *verb* (IMPERF **verschob**, PERF **hat verschoben**) to postpone.

verschieden *adjective* 1 different; 2 various.

verschlafen ◊ *verb* (PRES **verschläft**, IMPERF **verschlief**, PERF **hat verschlafen**) 1 to oversleep; 2 to sleep through (*the day*); 3 to miss (*a date, the train*).

verschlechtern *verb* (PERF **hat verschlechtert**) 1 to make worse; 2 **sich verschlechtern** to get worse.

verschlief SEE **verschlafen**.

verschließen ◊ *verb* (IMPERF **verschloss** △, PERF **hat verschlossen**) 1 to close (*a tin,*

△ NEW SPELLING: *See page xii*

package); **2** to lock (*a door, drawer*).

verschlimmern *verb* (PERF **hat verschlimmert**) **1** to make worse; **2 sich verschlimmern** to get worse.

verschloss SEE **verschließen**.

verschlucken *verb* (PERF **hat verschluckt**) **1** to swallow; **2 sich verschlucken** to choke.

Verschluss *der* (PL *die* **Verschlüsse**) **1** fastener, clasp; **2** top (*of a bottle*).

verschmutzen *verb* (PERF **hat verschmutzt**) to soil; **die Umwelt verschmutzen** to pollute the environment.

Verschmutzung *die* pollution.

verschob SEE **verschieben**.

verschreiben *verb* (IMPERF **verschrieb**, PERF **hat verschrieben**) **1** to prescribe; **2 sich verschreiben** to make a mistake.

verschütten *verb* (PERF **hat verschüttet**) to spill.

verschwand SEE **verschwinden**.

verschwenden *verb* (PERF **hat verschwendet**) to waste.

Verschwendung *die* waste.

verschwinden *verb* (IMPERF **verschwand**, PERF **ist verschwunden**) to disappear.

Versehen *das* (PL *die* **Versehen**) oversight; **aus Versehen** by mistake.

versehentlich *adverb* by mistake.

versetzen *verb* (PERF **hat versetzt**) **1** to move, to transfer (*a person*);

2 to move up (*into the next class at school*); **3** jemanden versetzen to stand somebody up; **4** jemandem einen Schreck versetzen to give somebody a fright; **jemandem einen Tritt versetzen** to kick somebody; **5 sich in jemandes Lage versetzen** to put yourself in somebody's position.

versichern *verb* (PERF **hat versichert**) **1** to insure; **2** to assert; **jemandem versichern, dass ...** to assure somebody that ...

Versicherung *die* (PL *die* **Versicherungen**) **1** insurance; **2** assurance.

versöhnen *verb* (PERF **hat sich versöhnt**) **sich versöhnen** to make up; **sich mit jemandem versöhnen** to make it up with somebody.

versorgen *verb* (PERF **hat versorgt**) **1** to supply; **2** to provide for; **3** to look after.

verspäten *verb* (PERF **hat sich verspätet**) **sich verspäten** to be late.

Verspätung *die* lateness, delay; **Verspätung haben** to be late.

versprechen ◊ *verb* (PRES **verspricht**, IMPERF **versprach**, PERF **hat versprochen**) **1** to promise; **2 sich viel von etwas versprechen** to have high hopes of something; **3 sich versprechen** to make a slip of the tongue.

Versprechen *das* (PL *die* **Versprechen**) promise.

verstand SEE **verstehen**.

◊ IRREGULAR VERB: *See the verb table in the centre of the dictionary*

Verstand der 1 mind; **den Verstand verlieren** to go out of your mind; 2 reason.

verstanden SEE **verstehen**.

verständigen verb (PERF **hat verständigt**) 1 to notify; 2 **sich verständigen** to communicate, to make yourself understood; 3 **sich über etwas verständigen** to agree on something.

verständlich adjective 1 understandable; **jemandem etwas verständlich machen** to make something clear to somebody; 2 comprehensible.

Verständigung die 1 communication; 2 notification.

Verstärker der (PL die **Verstärker**) amplifier.

verstauchen verb (PERF **hat verstaucht**) to sprain; **sich den Fuß verstauchen** to sprain your ankle.

Versteck das (PL die **Verstecke**) hiding place.

verstecken verb (PERF **hat versteckt**) 1 to hide; 2 **sich verstecken** to hide.

verstehen ◇ verb (IMPERF **verstand**, PERF **hat verstanden**) 1 to understand; **etwas falsch verstehen** to misunderstand something; 2 **sich gut verstehen** to get on well; 3 **das versteht sich von selbst** that goes without saying.

verstellbar adjective adjustable.

verstellen verb (PERF **hat verstellt**) 1 to adjust; 2 to block; 3 to disguise; 4 **sich verstellen** to pretend.

verstimmt adjective 1 out of tune; 2 peeved; 3 **ein verstimmter Magen** an upset stomach.

Versuch der (PL die **Versuche**) 1 attempt; 2 experiment.

versuchen verb (PERF **hat versucht**) to try.

verteidigen verb (PERF **hat verteidigt**) to defend.

Verteidiger der (PL die **Verteidiger**) 1 defender; 2 defence counsel.

Verteidigung die defence.

verteilen verb (PERF **hat verteilt**) to distribute.

Vertrag der (PL die **Verträge**) 1 contract; 2 treaty.

vertragen ◇ verb (PRES **verträgt**, IMPERF **vertrug**, PERF **hat vertragen**) 1 to stand, to take; 2 **ich vertrage keinen Kaffee** coffee disagrees with me; 3 **sich vertragen** to get on; **sich wieder vertragen** to make it up.

vertrat SEE **vertreten**.

vertrauen verb (PERF **hat vertraut**) to trust.

Vertrauen das trust; **im Vertrauen** in confidence.

vertraulich adjective 1 confidential; 2 familiar.

vertreten ◇ verb (PRES **vertritt**, IMPERF **vertrat**, PERF **hat vertreten**) 1 to stand in for; 2 to represent; 3 **eine Meinung vertreten** to hold an opinion; 4 **sich die Beine vertreten** to stretch your legs.

△ NEW SPELLING: *See page xii*

Vertreter der (PL die **Vertreter**)
1 representative; 2 deputy.

Vertreterin die (PL die
Vertreterinnen) 1 representative;
2 deputy.

vertritt SEE **vertreten**.

vertrug SEE **vertragen**.

verunglücken verb (PERF ist
verunglückt) to have an accident.

verursachen verb (PERF hat
verursacht) to cause.

verurteilen verb (PERF hat
verurteilt) 1 to sentence; 2 to
condemn.

Verwaltung die (PL die
Verwaltungen) administration.

verwandt adjective related.

Verwandte der/die (PL die
Verwandten) relative.

Verwandtschaft die relatives.

verwechseln verb (PERF hat
verwechselt) to mix up, to confuse;
**jemanden mit jemandem
verwechseln** to mistake somebody
for somebody.

verwenden verb (PERF hat
verwendet) to use.

Verwendung die use.

verwickelt adjective complicated.

verwirren verb (PERF hat verwirrt)
1 to confuse; 2 to tangle up.

verwirrt adjective confused.

verwöhnen verb (PERF hat
verwöhnt) to spoil.

verwunden verb (PERF hat
verwundet) to wound.

Verwundete der/die (PL die
Verwundeten) casualty, injured
person.

Verwundung die (PL die
Verwundungen) injury, wound.

verzählen verb (PERF hat sich
verzählt) sich **verzählen** to
miscount.

Verzeichnis das (PL die
Verzeichnisse) 1 list; 2 index.

verzeihen verb (IMPERF **verzieh**, PERF
hat **verziehen**) to forgive; **verzeihen
Sie, können Sie mir sagen ...?**
excuse me, could you tell me ...?

Verzeihung die forgiveness;
jemanden um Verzeihung bitten to
apologize to somebody;
Verzeihung! sorry!

verzieh, verziehen SEE **verzeihen**.

verzichten verb (PERF hat
verzichtet) 1 to do without; **ich
verzichte auf deine Hilfe** I can do
without your help; **2 auf etwas
verzichten** to give up something
(smoking or your share of
something); to relinquish something
(a right or privilege).

verzögern verb (PERF hat
verzögert) 1 to delay; 2 sich
verzögern to be delayed.

Verzögerung die (PL die
Verzögerungen) delay.

verzollen verb (PERF hat verzollt) to
pay duty on; **haben Sie etwas zu**

◇ IRREGULAR VERB: See the verb table in the centre of the dictionary

verzollen? have you anything to declare?

verzweifeln verb (PERF ist verzweifelt) to despair.

verzweifelt adjective desperate.

Verzweiflung die despair.

Vetter der (PL die Vettern) cousin.

Video das (PL die Videos) video.

Videokamera die (PL die Videokameras) video camera.

Videokassette die (PL die Videokassetten) video cassette.

Videorekorder der (PL die Videorekorder) video recorder.

Videospiel das (PL die Videospiele) video game.

Videothek die (PL die Videotheken) video shop.

Vieh das cattle.

viel adjective, pronoun 1 a lot of; **Erika hat viel Arbeit** Erika's got a lot of work; 2 **viele** (plural) many, a lot of; **viele Leute** many people; 3 much, a lot; **wie viel?** how much?, how many?; **zu viel** too much; **vielen Dank** thank you very much; **viel Spaß!** have fun!; **viel Glück!** good luck!; 4 **das viele Geld** all that money.
adverb 1 much, a lot; **viel weniger** much less; **so viel wie möglich** as much as possible; **sie redet viel** she talks a lot; 2 **viel zu groß** far too big, much too big; **das dauert viel zu lange** it'll take far too long.

vielleicht adverb perhaps.

vielmals adverb **danke vielmals** thanks a lot.

vier number four.

Viereck das (PL die Vierecke) 1 rectangle; 2 square.

viereckig adjective 1 rectangular; 2 square.

vierte SEE **vierter**.

Viertel das (PL die Viertel) quarter; **es ist Viertel vor acht** it's quarter to eight.

viertel adjective quarter; **wir treffen uns um viertel acht**△ we'll meet at quarter past seven; **um drei viertel acht**△ at quarter to eight.

Viertelstunde die (PL die Viertelstunden) quarter of an hour.

vierter, vierte, viertes adjective fourth.

vierzehn number fourteen.

vierzig number forty.

Villa die (PL die Villen) villa.

virtuell adjective virtual; **virtuelle Realität** virtual reality.

Virus das (PL die Viren) virus.

visuell adjective visual.

Visum das (PL die Visa) visa.

Vitamin das (PL die Vitamine) vitamin.

Vogel der (PL die Vögel) bird.

Vokabel die (PL die Vokabeln) word; **Vokabeln** vocabulary.

Vokal der (PL die Vokale) vowel.

Volk das (PL die Völker) people.

△ NEW SPELLING: See page xii

Volkshochschule die adult education centre; **ein Kurs an der Volkshochschule** an adult education class.

Volkslied das (PL die **Volkslieder**) folk song.

Volkswirtschaft die economics.

voll adjective 1 full; **ein Korb voll Äpfel** a basket full of apples; **die volle Wahrheit** the whole truth; 2 **etwas voll machen**△ to fill something up; **voll tanken**△ to fill up with petrol.
adverb 1 fully, completely; **voll und ganz** completely; 2 **jemanden nicht für voll nehmen** (informal) not to take somebody seriously.

völlig adjective complete.
adverb completely.

vollkommen adjective 1 perfect; 2 complete.
adverb completely.

Vollkornbrot das wholemeal bread.

vollmachen SEE voll.

Vollpension die full board.

vollständig adjective complete.

volltanken SEE voll.

vom = von dem.

von preposition ←(+DAT) 1 from; **von heute an** from today; **von hier bis ... from here to ...;** 2 of; **eine Freundin von mir** a friend of mine; 3 about; **Peter hat mir von dem neuen Haus erzählt** Peter told me about the new house; 4 by; **ein**

Theaterstück von Brecht a play by Brecht; 5 **von mir aus** I don't mind.

voneinander adverb from each other; **sie sind voneinander abhängig** they depend on each other.

vor preposition ←(+DAT or +ACC with movement towards a place) 1 in front of; 2 before; **Manfred war vor euch da** Manfred arrived before you; **kurz vor der Ampel** shortly before the lights; 3 with; **vor Angst zittern** to tremble with fear; 4 (with clock time) **zehn vor fünf** ten to five; 5 ago; **vor zwei Jahren** two years ago; 6 **sich vor jemandem fürchten** to be frightened of somebody; 7 **vor allen Dingen** above all; 8 **vor sich hin summen** to hum to yourself.
adverb forward; **vor und zurück** backwards and forwards.

voraus adverb 1 ahead; 2 **im Voraus**△ in advance.

vorausgehen ◇ verb (IMPERF ging voraus, PERF ist vorausgegangen) 1 to go on ahead; 2 to precede.

voraussetzen verb (PERF hat vorausgesetzt) 1 to take for granted; 2 to require; 3 **vorausgesetzt, dass ...** provided that ...

Voraussetzung die (PL die **Voraussetzungen**) 1 condition; 2 assumption.

vorbei adverb 1 past; 2 over; **vorbei sein** to be over.

vorbeifahren ◇ verb (PRES **fährt vorbei,** IMPERF **fuhr vorbei,** PERF **ist**

◇ IRREGULAR VERB: See the verb table in the centre of the dictionary

vorbeigefahren) to drive past, to pass.

vorbeigehen ◇ *verb* (IMPERF **ging vorbei**, PERF **ist vorbeigegangen**) 1 to go past, to pass; 2 to drop in; **ich gehe bei Anne vorbei** I'll drop in on Anne.

vorbeikommen ◇ *verb* (IMPERF **kam vorbei**, PERF **ist vorbeigekommen**) 1 to pass; 2 to get past; 3 to drop in.

vorbereiten *verb* (PERF **hat vorbereitet**) 1 to prepare; 2 **sich vorbereiten** to prepare.

Vorbereitung *die* (PL *die* **Vorbereitungen**) preparation.

vorbeugen *verb* (PERF **hat vorgebeugt**) 1 to prevent; 2 **sich vorbeugen** to lean forward.

Vorbild *das* (PL *die* **Vorbilder**) example.

vorderer, vordere, vorderes *adjective* front.

Vorderseite *die* front.

vorderster, vorderste, vorderstes *adjective* front.

Vorfahrt *die* right of way; 'Vorfahrt beachten/gewähren' 'give way'.

Vorfall *der* (PL *die* **Vorfälle**) incident.

Vorführung *die* (PL *die* **Vorführungen**) 1 performance; 2 demonstration.

Vorgänger *der* (PL *die* **Vorgänger**) predecessor.

Vorgängerin *die* (PL *die* **Vorgängerinnen**) predecessor.

vorgehen ◇ *verb* (IMPERF **ging vor**, PERF **ist vorgegangen**) 1 to go on ahead; 2 to go forward; 3 to proceed; 4 **die Uhr geht vor** the clock is fast; 5 **was geht hier vor?** what's going on here?

vorgestern *adverb* the day before yesterday.

vorhaben ◇ *verb* (PRES **hat vor**, IMPERF **hatte vor**, PERF **hat vorgehabt**) 1 to intend; 2 **etwas vorhaben** to have something planned.

Vorhang *der* (PL *die* **Vorhänge**) curtain.

vorher *adverb* beforehand, before.

Vorhersage *die* (PL *die* **Vorhersagen**) 1 forecast; 2 prediction.

vorhin *adverb* just now.

voriger, vorige, voriges *adjective* last.

vorkommen ◇ *verb* (IMPERF **kam vor**, PERF **ist vorgekommen**) 1 to happen; 2 to occur; 3 to come forward; 4 to come out (*from behind somewhere*); 5 to seem; **jemandem bekannt vorkommen** to seem familiar to somebody; 6 **sich alt vorkommen** to feel old.

vorlesen ◇ *verb* (PRES **liest vor**, IMPERF **las vor**, PERF **hat vorgelesen**) 1 to read (out); 2 **jemandem vorlesen** to read to somebody.

vorletzter, vorletzte, vorletztes *adjective* last but one; **vorletztes Jahr** the year before last.

△ NEW SPELLING: See page xii

Vormittag der (PL die **Vormittage**) morning.

vormittags adverb in the morning.

vorn adverb 1 at the front; **nach vorn** to the front; 2 **von vorn** from the beginning; **wieder von vorn anfangen** to start again at the beginning; **da vorn** over there.

Vorname der (PL die **Vornamen**) first name.

vorne = **vorn**.

vornehm adjective 1 elegant; 2 distinguished.

vornehmen ◇ verb (PRES **nimmt vor**, IMPERF **nahm vor**, PERF **hat vorgenommen**) 1 to carry out; 2 **sich vornehmen, etwas zu tun** to plan to do something.

Vorort der (PL die **Vororte**) suburb.

Vorrat der (PL die **Vorräte**) supply, stock.

Vorsatz der (PL die **Vorsätze**) intention.

Vorschau die 1 preview; 2 trailer (of a film).

Vorschlag der (PL die **Vorschläge**) suggestion.

vorschlagen ◇ verb (PRES **schlägt vor**, IMPERF **schlug vor**, PERF **hat vorgeschlagen**) to suggest.

Vorschrift die (PL die **Vorschriften**) 1 regulation; 2 instruction.

Vorschule die (PL die **Vorschulen**) infant school.

vorsehen ◇ verb (PRES **sieht sich vor**, IMPERF **sah sich vor**, PERF **hat**

sich **vorgesehen**) **sich vorsehen** to be careful.

Vorsicht die care; **Vorsicht!** careful!; (on a sign) caution!

vorsichtig adjective careful.

vorsichtshalber adverb to be on the safe side.

Vorspeise die (PL die **Vorspeisen**) starter.

Vorsprung der (PL die **Vorsprünge**) 1 ledge (of a rock); 2 lead (over somebody).

vorstellen verb (PERF **hat vorgestellt**) 1 to introduce; **darf ich Ihnen Herrn Schulz vorstellen?** may I introduce Mr Schulz?; 2 **die Uhr vorstellen** to put the clock forward; 3 **sich vorstellen** to introduce yourself; 4 **sich beim Personalchef vorstellen** to go for an interview with the personnel manager; 5 **sich etwas vorstellen** to imagine something; **stell dir vor!** can you imagine!

Vorstellung die (PL die **Vorstellungen**) 1 performance; 2 introduction; 3 interview (for a job); 4 idea; 5 imagination.

Vorteil der (PL die **Vorteile**) advantage.

Vortrag der (PL die **Vorträge**) talk.

vorüber adverb **vorüber sein** to be over.

vorübergehend adjective temporary.
adverb temporarily.

◇ IRREGULAR VERB: See the verb table in the centre of the dictionary

Vorurteil das (PL die **Vorurteile**) prejudice.

Vorwahl die (PL die **Vorwahlen**) dialling code.

vorwärts adverb forward(s).

vorwiegend adverb predominantly.

Vorwurf der (PL die **Vorwürfe**) reproach; **jemandem Vorwürfe machen** to reproach somebody.

vorzeigen verb (PERF hat **vorgezeigt**) to show.

vorziehen ◇ verb (PRES **zieht vor**, IMPERF **zog vor**, PERF hat **vorgezogen**) 1 to prefer; 2 to pull up (a chair); 3 **den Vorhang vorziehen** to draw the curtain.

vorzüglich adjective excellent.

vulgär adjective vulgar.

Vulkan der (PL die **Vulkane**) volcano.

W w

Waage die (PL die **Waagen**) 1 scales; 2 Libra; **Gabi ist Waage** Gabi's Libra.

waagerecht adjective horizontal.

wach adjective awake; **wach sein** to be awake; **wach werden** to wake up.

Wache die (PL die **Wachen**) 1 guard; 2 (police) station.

Wachhund der (PL die **Wachhunde**) guard dog.

Wachs das wax.

wachsen ◇ verb (PRES **wächst**, IMPERF **wuchs**, PERF **ist gewachsen**) to grow.

Wachstum das growth.

wackelig adjective wobbly.

wackeln verb (PERF hat **gewackelt**) to wobble.

Wade die (PL die **Waden**) calf.

Waffe die (PL die **Waffen**) weapon.

Waffel die (PL die **Waffeln**) waffle.

wagen verb (PERF hat **gewagt**) 1 to risk; 2 **es wagen, etwas zu tun** to dare to do something; **sich nicht irgendwohin wagen** not dare to go somewhere.

Wagen der (PL die **Wagen**) 1 car; **nimmst du den Wagen?** are you going by car?; 2 carriage (of a train); 3 cart.

Wagenheber der (PL die **Wagenheber**) jack.

Wahl die (PL die **Wahlen**) 1 choice; **er hat die Wahl** it's his choice; 2 election; **die nächsten Wahlen sind im Herbst** the next election is in autumn.

wählen verb (PERF hat **gewählt**) 1 to choose; **zwischen zwei Möglichkeiten wählen** to choose between two possibilities; 2 **haben Sie schon gewählt?** are you ready to order? (in a restaurant); 3 to elect; 4 to vote; **wählt Schröder!** vote for Schröder!; 5 to dial; **ich muss die falsche Nummer gewählt**

△ NEW SPELLING: See page xii

haben I must have dialled the wrong number.

Wahlfach das (PL die Wahlfächer) optional subject, option.

Wahnsinn der madness.

wahnsinnig adjective 1 mad; **wahnsinnig werden** to go mad; 2 **wahnsinnigen Durst haben** to be terribly thirsty; **der Film war wahnsinnig gut** the film was incredibly good.

wahr adjective 1 true; 2 **du kommst doch, nicht wahr?** you're coming, aren't you?

während preposition ←(+GEN) during.
conjunction 1 while; 2 whereas.

Wahrheit die (PL die Wahrheiten) truth.

Wahrsager der (PL die Wahrsager) fortune-teller.

Wahrsagerin die (PL die Wahrsagerinnen) fortune-teller.

wahrscheinlich adjective probable, likely.
adverb probably.

Währung die (PL die Währungen) currency.

Waise die (PL die Waisen) orphan.

Wal der (PL die Wale) whale.

Wald der (PL die Wälder) wood, forest.

Waliser der (PL die Waliser) Welshman.

Waliserin die (PL die Waliserinnen) Welshwoman.

walisisch adjective Welsh.

Walkman™ der (PL die Walkmen) walkman™.

Walnuss△ die (PL die Walnüsse) walnut.

Wand die (PL die Wände) wall.

wandern verb (PERF ist gewandert) 1 to hike; 2 to go walking.

Wanderung die (PL die Wanderungen) 1 hike; 2 walking tour.

wann adverb when.

Wanne die (PL die Wannen) 1 tub; 2 bath.

war SEE sein.

warb SEE werben.

Ware die (PL die Waren) 1 article; 2 **Waren** goods.

waren SEE sein.

Warenhaus das (PL die Warenhäuser) department store.

warf SEE werfen.

warm adjective warm; **eine warme Mahlzeit** a hot meal; **das Essen warm machen** to heat up the food.

Wärme die warmth.

wärmen verb (PERF hat gewärmt) to warm, to heat.

Warndreieck das (PL die Warndreiecke) warning triangle.

warnen verb (PERF hat gewarnt) to warn; **jemanden vor etwas warnen** to warn somebody of something.

◇ IRREGULAR VERB: See the verb table in the centre of the dictionary

Warnung die (PL die **Warnungen**) warning.

warst, wart SEE **sein**.

Warteliste die (PL die **Wartelisten**) waiting list.

warten verb (PERF hat **gewartet**) 1 to wait; **auf jemanden warten** to wait for somebody; 2 **auf sich warten lassen** to take your time.

Wärter der (PL die **Wärter**) 1 keeper; 2 attendant; 3 warder.

Warteraum der (PL die **Warteräume**) waiting room.

Wärterin die (PL die **Wärterinnen**) 1 keeper; 2 attendant; 3 warder.

Wartezeit die; **eine Stunde Wartezeit** an hour's wait.

Wartezimmer das (PL die **Wartezimmer**) waiting room.

warum adverb why.

was pronoun 1 what; **was für ein/eine ...?** what kind of ...?; **was für ein Fahrrad hast du?** what kind of bike do you have?; **was für ein Glück!** what luck!; **was kostet das?** how much is it?; 2 that; **alles, was wir brauchen** all (that) we need; **alles, was du willst** all (that) you want; 3 (short for 'etwas') something; **heute gibt's was Gutes im Fernsehen** there's something good on television today; 4 (short for 'etwas' in questions and negatives) anything; **hast du was für mich?** have you got anything for me?

Waschbecken das (PL die **Waschbecken**) washbasin.

Wäsche die 1 washing; 2 underwear.

waschen ◊ verb (PRES **wäscht**, IMPERF **wusch**, PERF hat **gewaschen**) 1 to wash; 2 **sich waschen** to have a wash; **sich die Hände waschen** to wash your hands.

Wäscherei die (PL die **Wäschereien**) laundry.

Waschlappen der (PL die **Waschlappen**) flannel.

Waschmaschine die (PL die **Waschmaschinen**) washing machine.

Waschsalon der (PL die **Waschsalons**) launderette.

Waschpulver das (PL die **Waschpulver**) washing powder.

Wasser das water.

wasserdicht adjective waterproof.

Wasserfall der (PL die **Wasserfälle**) waterfall.

Wasserfarbe die (PL die **Wasserfarben**) watercolour.

Wasserhahn der (PL die **Wasserhähne**) tap.

Wassermann der Aquarius; **Lisa ist Wassermann** Lisa's Aquarius.

Wasserskifahren das water-skiing.

Watte die cotton wool.

wattiert adjective padded.

WC das (PL die **WCs**) WC, toilet.

weben verb (PERF hat **gewebt**) to weave.

△ NEW SPELLING: See page xii

Wechselkurs der (PL die Wechselkurse) exchange rate.

wechseln verb (PERF hat gewechselt) 1 to change; **kannst du mir zehn Mark wechseln?** have you got change for ten marks?; 2 to exchange (*glances, letters*).

Wechselstube die (PL die Wechselstuben) bureau de change.

wecken verb (PERF hat geweckt) to wake (up).

Wecker der (PL die Wecker) alarm clock; **Max geht mir auf den Wecker** (*informal*) Max gets on my nerves.

weder conjunction **weder ... noch** neither ... nor.

weg adverb 1 away; **geh weg!** go away!; **Hände weg!** hands off!; 2 gone; **der Ring ist weg** the ring's gone; **Heidi ist schon weg** Heidi's already gone.

Weg der (PL die Wege) 1 way; **auf dem Weg nach Hause** on the way home; 2 path; 3 **sich auf den Weg machen** to set off; 4 **im Weg sein** to be in the way.

wegen preposition ←(+GEN) because of.

wegfahren ◇ verb (PRES **fährt weg**, IMPERF **fuhr weg**, PERF **ist weggefahren**) 1 to leave; **sie fahren gerade weg** they are leaving just now; 2 (PERF **hat weggefahren**) to drive away (*a car or things*).

weggehen ◇ verb (IMPERF **ging weg**, PERF **ist weggegangen**) 1 to go away; 2 to leave; 3 to go out; **wir gehen heute Abend weg** we're going out tonight; 4 to come out (*of a stain*).

weglassen ◇ verb (PRES **lässt weg** △, IMPERF **ließ weg**, PERF **hat weggelassen**) 1 to let go; 2 to leave out.

weglaufen ◇ verb (PRES **läuft weg**, IMPERF **lief weg**, PERF **ist weggelaufen**) to run away.

weglegen verb (PERF hat **weggelegt**) 1 to put down; 2 to put away.

wegmachen verb (PERF hat **weggemacht**) to get rid of (*a stain or wart, for example*).

wegmüssen ◇ verb (*informal*) (PRES **muss weg** △, IMPERF **musste weg** △, PERF **hat weggemusst** △) to have to go.

wegnehmen ◇ verb (PRES **nimmt weg**, IMPERF **nahm weg**, PERF **hat weggenommen**) to take away.

wegräumen verb (PERF hat **weggeräumt**) to clear away.

wegschicken verb (PERF hat **weggeschickt**) 1 to send away; 2 to send off.

wegtun ◇ verb (IMPERF **tat weg**, PERF **hat weggetan**) to put away.

Wegweiser der (PL die Wegweiser) signpost.

wegwerfen ◇ verb (PRES **wirft weg**, IMPERF **warf weg**, PERF **hat weggeworfen**) to throw away.

◇ IRREGULAR VERB: *See the verb table in the centre of the dictionary*

weh *adjective* 1 sore; 2 **oh weh!** oh dear!; 3 **es tut weh** it hurts.

wehen *verb* (PERF **hat geweht**) to blow.

Wehrdienst *der* military service.

wehren *verb* (PERF **hat sich gewehrt**) **sich wehren** to defend yourself.

wehrlos *adjective* defenceless.

wehtun △ ◇ *verb* (PRES **tut weh**, IMPERF **tat weh**, PERF **hat wehgetan**) 1 to hurt; **mein Arm tut weh** my arm hurts; **jemandem wehtun** to hurt somebody; 2 **sich wehtun** to hurt yourself.

Weibchen *das* (PL *die* **Weibchen**) female.

weiblich *a.ljective* 1 female; 2 feminine (*noun*).

weich *adjective* soft.

Weide *die* (PL *die* **Weiden**) 1 willow; 2 pasture.

weigern *verb* (PERF **hat sich geweigert**) **sich weigern** to refuse.

Weihnachten *das* (PL *die* **Weihnachten**) Christmas; **Frohe Weihnachten!** Merry Christmas!

Weihnachtslied *das* (PL *die* **Weihnachtslieder**) Christmas carol.

Weihnachtsmann *der* (PL *die* **Weihnachtsmänner**) Father Christmas.

Weihnachtstag *der* (PL *die* **Weihnachtstage**) Christmas Day; **zweiter Weihnachtstag** Boxing Day.

weil *conjunction* because.

Weile *die* while.

Wein *der* (PL *die* **Weine**) wine.

Weinberg *der* (PL *die* **Weinberge**) vineyard.

Weinbergschnecke *die* (PL *die* **Weinbergschnecken**) snail.

Weinbrand *der* brandy.

weinen *verb* (PERF **hat geweint**) to cry.

Weinkarte *die* (PL *die* **Weinkarten**) wine list.

Weinkeller *der* (PL *die* **Weinkeller**) wine cellar.

Weinstube *die* (PL *die* **Weinstuben**) wine bar.

Weintraube *die* (PL *die* **Weintrauben**) grape.

weise *adjective* wise.

Weise *die* (PL *die* **Weisen**) way; **auf diese Weise** in this way.

Weisheit *die* (PL *die* **Weisheiten**) wisdom.

weiß[1] SEE **wissen**.

weiß[2] *adjective* white.

Weißwein *der* (PL *die* **Weißweine**) white wine.

weit *adjective, adverb* 1 wide, loose (*clothes*); 2 long; **eine weite Reise** a long journey; 3 far; **wie weit ist es?** how far is it?; **ist es noch weit?** is it much further?; **so weit wie möglich** as far as possible; **bei weitem** by far; **von weitem** from a distance; 5 **ich bin so weit** I'm ready; 6 **weit verbreitet**

△ NEW SPELLING: See page xii

widespread; **7 zu weit gehen** to go ➤too far.

weiten verb (PERF **hat sich geweitet**) **sich weiten** to stretch.

weiter adjective, adverb **1** further; **2** in addition; **3 etwas weiter tun** to go on doing something; **weiter nichts** nothing else; **weiter niemand** nobody else; **4 und so weiter** and so on.

weiterer, weitere, weiteres adjective **1** further; **2 ohne weiteres** just like that, easily; **3 bis auf weiteres** for the time being.

weiterfahren ◇ verb (PRES **fährt weiter**, IMPERF **fuhr weiter**, PERF **ist weitergefahren**) to go on.

weitergehen ◇ verb (IMPERF **ging weiter**, PERF **ist weitergegangen**) to go on.

weiterhin adverb **1** still; **2** in future; **3 etwas weiterhin tun** to go on doing something.

weitermachen verb (PERF **hat weitergemacht**) to carry on.

Weitsprung der long jump.

Weizen der wheat.

welcher, welche, welches adjective which; **welches Kleid?** which dress?; **um welche Zeit?** at what time?
pronoun **1** which (one); **2** some; **brauchst du Briefmarken? ich habe welche** do you need stamps? I've got some; **3** any; **hast du welche?** have you got any?

Welle die (PL die **Wellen**) wave.

Wellensittich der (PL die **Wellensittiche**) budgerigar.

wellig adjective wavy.

Welt die (PL die **Welten**) world; **auf der ganzen Welt** in the whole world.

Weltall das universe.

Weltkrieg der (PL die **Weltkriege**) world war.

Weltmeister der (PL die **Weltmeister**) world champion.

Weltmeisterin die (PL die **Weltmeisterinnen**) world champion.

Weltmeisterschaft die (PL die **Weltmeisterschaften**) **1** world championship; **2 die Weltmeisterschaft** (football) the World Cup.

Weltraum der space.

wem pronoun to whom; **wem hat er das Geld gegeben?** who did he give the money to?

wen pronoun whom, who; **wen hast du eingeladen?** who did you invite?

Wende die **1** change; **2** reunification (of Germany).

wenig pronoun, adjective **1** little; **zu wenig** too little, not enough; **2 wenige** few; **in wenigen Wochen** in a few weeks.
adverb little; **so wenig wie möglich** as little as possible.

weniger pronoun, adjective less, fewer; **sie hat weniger Geschenke bekommen** she got fewer presents;

◇ IRREGULAR VERB: *See the verb table in the centre of the dictionary*

immer weniger Geld less and less money; **immer weniger Häuser** fewer and fewer houses. *adverb, conjunction* less; **zehn weniger fünf** ten minus five.

wenigste SEE wenigster.

wenigstens *adverb* at least.

wenigster, wenigste, wenigstes *adjective, pronoun* least; **am wenigsten** least; **sein Geschenk hat mir am wenigsten gefallen** I liked his present least.

wenn *conjunction* 1 when; **wenn ich in München bin, schreibe ich dir** I'll write to you when I'm in Munich; **immer, wenn** whenever; 2 if; **wenn es regnet** if it rains; 3 **außer wenn** unless.

wer *pronoun* who.

werben ◇ *verb* (PRES **wirbt,** IMPERF **warb,** PERF **hat geworben**) 1 to advertise; 2 to recruit (*members*).

Werbespot *der* (PL *die* **Werbespots**) advert, commercial.

Werbung *die* 1 advertising; **in der Werbung arbeiten** to work in advertising; 2 advert; **im Fernsehen kommt viel Werbung** there are many adverts on television; **Werbung für etwas machen** to advertise something.

werden ◇ *verb* (PRES **wird,** IMPERF **wurde,** PERF **ist geworden**) 1 to become; **Arzt werden** to become a doctor; 2 **müde werden** to get tired; **alt werden** to get old; **mir wird kalt** I'm getting cold; 3 **mir wurde schlecht** I felt sick; **blass werden**

to turn pale; 4 **wach werden** to wake up; 5 (*used to form the future tense*) will, shall; **sie wird anrufen** she'll ring; **sie wird gleich da sein** she'll be here in a minute; 6 (*used to form the passive*) to be; **gerufen werden** to be called; **er wurde gefragt** he was asked; 7 (*used to form the conditional*) **sie würde kommen** she would come; **ich würde gern kommen, aber …** I'd like to come but …

werfen ◇ *verb* (PRES **wirft,** IMPERF **warf,** PERF **hat geworfen**) to throw.

Werk *das* (PL *die* **Werke**) 1 work; 2 works (*a factory*).

Werken *das* handicraft.

Werkstatt *die* (PL *die* **Werkstätten**) workshop.

Werktag *der* (PL *die* **Werktage**) weekday.

werktags *adverb* on weekdays.

Werkzeug *das* (PL *die* **Werkzeuge**) tool.

wert *adjective* **viel wert sein** to be worth a lot; **nichts wert sein** to be worthless.

Wert *der* (PL *die* **Werte**) 1 value; **im Wert von hundert Mark** worth one hundred marks; 2 **auf etwas Wert legen** to attach importance to something; 3 **es hat doch keinen Wert** there's no point.

wertlos *adjective* worthless.

wertvoll *adjective* valuable.

Wesen *das* (PL *die* **Wesen**) 1 nature, manner; 2 creature.

△ NEW SPELLING: *See page xii*

wesentlich *adjective* essential; **im Wesentlichen**△ essentially.
adverb considerably.

weshalb *adverb* why.

Wespe *die* (PL *die* **Wespen**) wasp.

wessen *pronoun* whose.

Wessi *der* (*informal*) (PL *die* **Wessis**) West German.

Weste *die* (PL *die* **Westen**) waistcoat.

Westen *der* west.

Westinder *der* (PL *die* **Westinder**) West Indian.

Westinderin *die* (PL *die* **Westinderinnen**) West Indian.

westlich *adjective* 1 western;
2 westerly.
adverb, preposition ←(+GEN)
westlich von Wien west of Vienna;
westlich der Stadt to the west of the town.

weswegen *adverb* why.

Wettbewerb *der* (PL *die* **Wettbewerbe**) competition, contest.

Wette *die* (PL *die* **Wetten**) bet; **mit jemandem um die Wette laufen** to race somebody.

wetten *verb* (PERF **hat gewettet**) to bet; **mit jemandem um etwas wetten** to bet somebody something.

Wetter *das* weather.

Wetterbericht *der* (PL *die* **Wetterberichte**) weather report.

Wettervorhersage *die* weather forecast.

Wettkampf *der* (PL *die* **Wettkämpfe**) contest.

Wettlauf *der* race.

wichtig *adjective* important.

wickeln *verb* (PERF **hat gewickelt**)
1 to wind; **2 ein Kind wickeln** to change a baby.

Widder *der* (PL *die* **Widder**) 1 ram;
2 Aries; **Jan ist Widder** Jan's Aries.

widerlich *adjective* disgusting.

widersprechen ◇ *verb* (PRES **widerspricht**, IMPERF **widersprach**, PERF **hat widersprochen**) to contradict.

Widerspruch *der* (PL *die* **Widersprüche**) contradiction.

Widerstand *der* resistance.

widerstehen ◇ *verb* (IMPERF **widerstand**, PERF **hat widerstanden**) to resist.

widmen *verb* (PERF **hat gewidmet**)
1 to dedicate; 2 to devote; **3 sich einer Sache widmen** to devote yourself to something.

wie *adverb* 1 how; **wie geht's?** how are you?; **wie viel?**△ how much?, how many?; **um wie viel**△ **Uhr kommst du?** (at) what time are you coming?;
2 **wie ist Ihr Name?** what is your name?; **wie ist das Wetter?** what's the weather like?; **3 wie bitte?** sorry?
conjunction 1 as; **so schnell wie möglich** as quickly as possible;
2 like; **wie du** like you; **3 wie zum Beispiel** such as.

wieder *adverb* 1 again; **sie ist**

◇ IRREGULAR VERB: *See the verb table in the centre of the dictionary*

wieder da she's back again;
2 jemanden wieder erkennen△ to recognize somebody; **etwas wieder finden**△ to find something (again); **etwas wieder verwerten**△ to recycle something.

wiederbekommen ◇ verb (IMPERF **bekam wieder**, PERF **hat wiederbekommen**) to get back.

wiedererkennen SEE wieder.

wiederfinden SEE wieder.

wiederholen verb (PERF **hat wiederholt**) 1 to repeat; 2 to revise (work at school); 3 **sich wiederholen** to recur; **er hat sich wiederholt** he's repeated himself.

Wiederholung die (PL die **Wiederholungen**) 1 repetition; 2 repeat; 3 revision (at school).

Wiederhören das auf **Wiederhören!** (said on the phone) goodbye!

wiederkommen ◇ verb (IMPERF **kam wieder**, PERF **hat wiedergekommen**) 1 to come back; 2 to come again.

wiedersehen SEE sehen.

Wiedersehen das (PL die **Wiedersehen**) 1 reunion; 2 auf **Wiedersehen!** goodbye!

wiedervereinigen SEE vereinigen.

Wiedervereinigung die reunification.

wiederverwerten SEE wieder.

Wiege die (PL die **Wiegen**) cradle.

wiegen ◇ verb (IMPERF **wog**, PERF **hat gewogen**) to weigh.

Wiegenlied das (PL die **Wiegenlieder**) lullaby.

Wien das Vienna.

Wiese die (PL die **Wiesen**) meadow.

wieso adverb why.

wieviel SEE wie.

wievielmal adverb how often.

wievielter, wievielte, wievieltes adjective 1 which; 2 die wievielte Querstraße ist das von hier aus? how many roads is that from here?; der Wievielte ist heute? what's the date today?

wild adjective wild.

Wildleder das suede.

Wildpark der (PL die **Wildparks**) wildlife park.

will SEE wollen.

Wille der will; seinen Willen durchsetzen to get your own way.

willkommen adjective welcome.

willst SEE wollen.

Wimper die (PL die **Wimpern**) eyelash.

Wimperntusche die (PL die **Wimperntuschen**) mascara.

Wind der (PL die **Winde**) wind.

Windel die (PL die **Windeln**) nappy.

Windhund der (PL die **Windhunde**) greyhound.

windig adjective windy.

△ NEW SPELLING: See page xii

Windmühle die (PL die Windmühlen) windmill.

Windpocken plural noun chickenpox.

Windschutzscheibe die (PL die Windschutzscheiben) windscreen.

Winkel der (PL die Winkel) 1 angle; 2 corner.

winken verb (PERF hat gewinkt) to wave.

Winter der (PL die Winter) winter.

winzig adjective tiny.

wir pronoun we; **wir sind es** it's us; **wir alle** all of us.

Wirbelsäule die (PL die Wirbelsäulen) spine.

wirbt SEE werben.

wird SEE werden.

wirft SEE werfen.

wirken verb (PERF hat gewirkt) 1 to have an effect; 2 **gegen etwas wirken** to be effective against something; 3 to seem (sad, happy).

wirklich adjective real. adverb really.

Wirklichkeit die reality.

wirksam adjective effective.

Wirkung die (PL die Wirkungen) effect.

wirst SEE werden.

Wirt der (PL die Wirte) landlord.

Wirtin die (PL die Wirtinnen) landlady.

Wirtschaft die (PL die Wirtschaften) 1 economy; 2 pub.

wirtschaftlich adjective economic.

Wirtshaus das (PL die Wirtshäuser) pub.

wischen verb (PERF hat gewischt) to wipe.

wissen ◇ verb (PRES weiß, IMPERF wusste △, PERF hat gewusst △) to know; **ich weiß, dass er in London wohnt** I know he lives in London; **ich wüsste gern …** I'd like to know …; **von etwas wissen** to know about something; **weißt du was?** you know what?

Wissen das knowledge.

Wissenschaft die (PL die Wissenschaften) science.

Wissenschaftler der (PL die Wissenschaftler) scientist.

Wissenschaftlerin die (PL die Wissenschaftlerinnen) scientist.

wissenschaftlich adjective scientific.

Witwe die (PL die Witwen) widow.

Witwer der (PL die Witwer) widower.

Witz der (PL die Witze) joke.

witzig adjective funny.

wo adverb where; **wo seid ihr gewesen?** where have you been?; **in München, wo Markus seit einem Jahr lebt** in Munich, where Markus has been living for a year; **wo immer** wherever. conjunction 1 seeing that;

◇ IRREGULAR VERB: *See the verb table in the centre of the dictionary*

2. although; jetzt ist sie mir böse, wo ich doch so nett zu ihr war now she's angry with me, although I've been so nice to her.

woanders *adverb* elsewhere.

Woche die (PL die **Wochen**) week.

Wochenende das (PL die **Wochenenden**) weekend.

wochenlang *adverb* for weeks.

Wochentag der (PL die **Wochentage**) weekday.

wochentags *adverb* on weekdays.

wöchentlich *adjective* weekly.

wofür *adverb* what ... for; wofür brauchst du das Geld? what do you need the money for?

wog SEE **wiegen**.

woher *adverb* where ... from; woher ist er? where does he come from?; woher weißt du das? how do you know?

wohin *adverb* where ... (to); wohin geht ihr? where are you going?

wohl *adverb* 1 well; sich wohl fühlen to feel well; ich fühle mich heute nicht wohl I don't feel well today; 2 sich wohl fühlen to be happy; Anni fühlt sich in London wohl Anni is happy in London; 3 jemandem wohl tun△ to do somebody good; 4 probably; er hat den Zug wohl verpasst he probably missed the train; du bist wohl verrückt! you must be mad!; 5 wohl kaum hardly.

Wohl das 1 welfare, well-being; 2 zu seinem Wohl for his benefit; 3 zum Wohl! cheers!

wohlhabend *adjective* well-off.

wohltun SEE **wohl**.

wohnen *verb* (PERF hat gewohnt) 1 to live; 2 to stay (*for a short time*).

Wohngemeinschaft die (PL die **Wohngemeinschaften**) people sharing a flat/house; wir wohnen in einer Wohngemeinschaft we share a flat.

wohnhaft *adjective* resident.

Wohnheim das (PL die **Wohnheime**) 1 hostel; 2 home (*for old people*).

Wohnort der (PL die **Wohnorte**) place of residence.

Wohnsitz der (PL die **Wohnsitze**) place of residence.

Wohnung die (PL die **Wohnungen**) flat.

Wohnwagen der (PL die **Wohnwagen**) caravan.

Wohnzimmer das (PL die **Wohnzimmer**) living room.

Wolf der (PL die **Wölfe**) wolf.

Wolke die (PL die **Wolken**) cloud.

Wolkenkratzer der (PL die **Wolkenkratzer**) skyscraper.

wolkig *adjective* cloudy.

Wolldecke die (PL die **Wolldecken**) blanket.

Wolle die wool.

wollen ◇ *verb* (PRES will, IMPERF wollte, PERF hat gewollt) 1 to want; Anne will einen Hund Anne wants a

△ NEW SPELLING: *See page xii*

dog; **ich will nach Hause** I want to go home; **2 sie wollte gerade gehen** she was just about to go; **3 ganz wie du willst** as you like.

womit *adverb* **1** what ... with; **womit hast du das gewaschen?** what did you wash it with?; **2** with which.

womöglich *adverb* possibly.

wonach *adverb* **1** what ... for; **wonach suchst du?** what are you looking for?; **wonach riecht es?** what does it smell of?; **2** after which, according to which; **eine Regelung, wonach wir eine Stunde mehr arbeiten müssen** a rule according to which we have to work an extra hour.

woran *adverb* what ... of; **1 woran denkst du?** what are you thinking of?; **woran hast du ihn erkannt?** how did you recognize him?; **2** on which, of which; **nichts, woran man sich verletzen könnte** nothing you could hurt yourself on.

worauf *adverb* **1** what ... on, what ... for; **worauf hast du die Vase gestellt?** what did you put the vase on?; **worauf wartet ihr?** what are you waiting for?; **2** on which, for which; **das Regal, worauf das Radio steht** the shelf the radio is on; **das Einzige, worauf ich mich freue** the only thing I'm looking forward to.

woraus *adverb* **1** what ... from, what ... of; **woraus ist das?** what's it made of?; **2** from which; **es gibt nichts, woraus wir trinken können** there isn't anything we can drink out of.

worin *adverb* **1** what ... in, in what; **2** in which; **die Punkte, worin ich mit dir übereinstimme** the points I agree with you on.

Wort *das* (PL die **Worte/Wörter**) word; **mir fehlen die Worte** I'm lost for words; **ich habe heute zwanzig neue Wörter gelernt** I've learnt twenty new words today.

Wörterbuch *das* (PL die **Wörterbücher**) dictionary.

wörtlich *adjective* word for word.

Wortschatz *der* vocabulary.

Wortspiel *das* (PL die **Wortspiele**) pun.

worüber *adverb* **1** what ... over, what ... about; **worüber lacht ihr?** what are you laughing about?; **2** over which, about which.

worum *adverb* **1** about what; **worum geht es?** what's it about?; **worum hat sie dich gebeten?** what did she ask you for?; **2** for which; **3** round which.

wovon *adverb* **1** what ... from, what ... about; **wovon redet ihr?** what are you talking about?; **2** from which, about which; **der Geruch, wovon mir schlecht geworden ist** the smell which made me feel sick.

wovor *adverb* **1** what ... of; **wovor hast du Angst?** what are you frightened of?; **2** in front of what; **3** of which; **4** in front of which; **der Turm, wovor wir stehen** the tower we are standing in front of.

wozu *adverb* **1** what ... for, why; **wozu brauchst du das?** what do

---

⬦ IRREGULAR VERB: *See the verb table in the centre of the dictionary*

you need it for?; **wozu?** what for?; 2 to which, for which; **wozu ich dir raten würde** which I would advise.

Wrack das (PL die **Wracks**) wreck.

wuchs SEE **wachsen**.

Wuchs der growth.

wund adjective sore.

Wunde die (PL die **Wunden**) wound.

Wunder das (PL die **Wunder**) miracle; **kein Wunder!** no wonder!

wunderbar adjective wonderful.

wundern verb (PERF **hat sich gewundert**) **sich wundern** to be surprised.

wunderschön adjective beautiful.

wundervoll adjective wonderful.

Wunsch der (PL die **Wünsche**) wish; **auf Wunsch** on request; **haben Sie sonst noch einen Wunsch?** will there be anything else?

wünschen verb (PERF **hat gewünscht**) 1 to wish; **ich wünsche dir alles Gute zum Geburtstag** I wish you a happy birthday; **ich wünschte, ich könnte ...** I wish I could ...; **was wünschen Sie?** can I help you?; 2 **sich etwas wünschen** to want something.

wünschenswert adjective desirable.

wurde, würde, wurden, würden, wurdest, würdest, wurdet, würdet SEE **werden**.

Wurf der (PL die **Würfe**) throw.

Würfel der (PL die **Würfel**) 1 dice (in games); 2 cube.

würfeln verb (PERF **hat gewürfelt**) to throw the dice.

Wurm der (PL die **Würmer**) worm.

Wurst die (PL die **Würste**) 1 sausage; 2 **das ist mir Wurst** (informal) I couldn't care less.

Würstchen das (PL die **Würstchen**) (little) sausage.

Wurzel die (PL die **Wurzeln**) root.

würzen verb (PERF **hat gewürzt**) to season.

würzig adjective spicy.

wusch SEE **waschen**.

wusste Δ SEE **wissen**.

Wüste die (PL die **Wüsten**) desert.

Wut die rage; **eine Wut auf jemanden haben** to be furious with somebody.

wütend adjective furious.

X x

x-beliebig adjective (informal) any; **eine x-beliebige Zahl** any number (you like).

x-mal adverb (informal) umpteen times; **zum x-ten Mal** for the umpteenth time.

Xylophon das (PL die **Xylophone**) xylophone.

Y y

Yoga das yoga.

Ypsilon das (PL die **Ypsilons**) Y.

Z z

zaghaft adjective 1 timid;
2 tentative.

zäh adjective tough.

Zahl die (PL die **Zahlen**) 1 number;
2 figure.

zahlen verb (PERF hat gezahlt) 1 to
pay; **hast du schon gezahlt?** have
you paid?; 2 to pay for; **bitte zahlen!**
the bill please!

zählen verb (PERF hat gezählt) 1 to
count; **auf jemanden zählen** to
count on somebody; **jemanden zu
seinen Freunden zählen** to count
somebody among your friends;
2 **zählen zu** to be one of.

Zähler der (PL die **Zähler**) meter.

zahlreich adjective numerous.

Zahlung die (PL die **Zahlungen**)
payment.

Zählung die (PL die **Zählungen**)
1 count; 2 census.

zahm adjective tame.

Zahn der (PL die **Zähne**) tooth.

Zahnarzt der (PL die **Zahnärzte**)
dentist.

Zahnärztin die (PL die
Zahnärztinnen) dentist.

Zahnbürste die (PL die
Zahnbürsten) toothbrush.

Zahnfleisch das gums.

Zahnpasta die (PL die **Zahnpasten**)
toothpaste.

Zahnschmerzen plural noun
toothache.

Zange die (PL die **Zangen**) pliers.

zanken verb (PERF hat sich gezankt)
sich zanken to squabble.

zappeln verb (PERF hat gezappelt)
1 to wriggle; 2 to fidget.

zart adjective 1 delicate, soft;
2 gentle; 3 tender.

zärtlich adjective affectionate.

Zauber der 1 magic; 2 spell.

Zauberer der (PL die **Zauberer**)
magician, conjurer.

zauberhaft adjective enchanting.

zaubern verb (PERF hat gezaubert)
to do magic.

Zaun der (PL die **Zäune**) fence.

z.B. (zum Beispiel) e.g.

Zebra das (PL die **Zebras**) zebra.

Zebrastreifen der (PL die
Zebrastreifen) zebra crossing.

Zeh der (PL die **Zehen**) toe.

Zehe die (PL die **Zehen**) 1 toe;
2 clove (of garlic).

◇ IRREGULAR VERB: See the verb table in the centre of the dictionary

zehn *number* ten.

Zehntel *das* (PL *die* **Zehntel**) tenth.

zehnter, zehnte, zehntes *adjective* tenth.

Zeichen *das* (PL *die* **Zeichen**)
1 sign; 2 signal.

zeichnen *verb* (PERF **hat gezeichnet**) to draw.

Zeichnung *die* (PL *die* **Zeichnungen**) drawing.

Zeigefinger *der* (PL *die* **Zeigefinger**) index finger.

zeigen *verb* (PERF **hat gezeigt**) 1 to show; **Peter hat uns sein neues Auto gezeigt** Peter showed us his new car; 2 to point; **auf jemanden zeigen** to point at somebody; 3 **sich zeigen** to appear; 4 **es hat sich gezeigt, dass ...** it has become clear that ...; **es wird sich zeigen** time will tell.

Zeiger *der* (PL *die* **Zeiger**) hand.

Zeile *die* (PL *die* **Zeilen**) line.

Zeit *die* (PL *die* **Zeiten**) 1 time; **sich Zeit lassen** to take your time; **ich habe keine Zeit mehr** I haven't got any more time; **eine Zeit lang**△ for a time; 2 **es hat Zeit** there's no hurry; **die erste Zeit** at first; **in nächster Zeit** in the near future.

Zeitalter *das* (PL *die* **Zeitalter**) age.

Zeitlang *die* SEE **Zeit**.

Zeitlupe *die* slow motion; **in Zeitlupe** in slow motion.

Zeitraum *der* (PL *die* **Zeiträume**) period.

Zeitschrift *die* (PL *die* **Zeitschriften**) magazine.

Zeitung *die* (PL *die* **Zeitungen**) newspaper.

Zeitverschwendung *die* waste of time.

zeitweise *adverb* at times.

Zeitungshändler *der* (PL *die* **Zeitungshändler**) newsagent.

Zelle *die* (PL *die* **Zellen**) 1 cell; 2 booth.

Zelt *das* (PL *die* **Zelte**) tent.

zelten *verb* (PERF **hat gezeltet**) to camp.

Zeltplatz *der* (PL *die* **Zeltplätze**) campsite.

Zement *der* cement.

Zentimeter *der* (PL *die* **Zentimeter**) centimetre.

Zentimetermaß *das* (PL *die* **Zentimetermaße**) tape measure.

zentral *adjective* central.

Zentrale *die* (PL *die* **Zentralen**) 1 central office, head office; 2 headquarters; 3 (telephone) exchange, switchboard.

Zentralheizung *die* central heating.

Zentrum *das* (PL *die* **Zentren**) centre.

zerbrechen ◊ *verb* (PRES **zerbricht**, IMPERF **zerbrach**, PERF **hat zerbrochen**) 1 to break; **Irene hat meine Vase zerbrochen** Irene broke my vase; 2 (PERF **ist zerbrochen**) to break; **die**

△ NEW SPELLING: See page xii

Untertasse ist zerbrochen the saucer broke.

zerbrechlich adjective fragile.

Zeremonie die (PL die Zeremonien) ceremony.

zerreißen ◊ verb (IMPERF zerriss △, PERF hat zerrissen) 1 to tear; **sie hat sich das Kleid zerrissen** she tore her dress; 2 to tear up; **Anna hat seinen Brief zerrissen** Anna tore up his letter; 3 (PERF ist zerrissen) to tear; **das Hemd ist in der Wäsche zerrissen** the shirt got torn in the washing.

zerschlagen ◊ verb (PRES zerschlägt, IMPERF zerschlug, PERF hat zerschlagen) 1 to smash, to smash up; 2 **sich zerschlagen** to fall through (of plans); **meine Hoffnungen haben sich zerschlagen** my hopes were dashed.

zerschneiden ◊ verb (IMPERF zerschnitt, PERF hat zerschnitten) to cut, to cut up.

zerstören verb (PERF hat zerstört) to destroy.

Zerstörung die destruction.

zerstreuen verb (PERF hat zerstreut) 1 to scatter; 2 **jemanden zerstreuen** to entertain somebody; 3 **sich zerstreuen** to take your mind off things; 4 **die Menge hat sich zerstreut** the crowd's dispersed.

zerstreut adjective absent-minded.

Zettel der (PL die Zettel) 1 piece of paper; 2 note; 3 leaflet.

Zeug das (informal) 1 stuff; 2 things, gear; 3 **dummes Zeug** nonsense.

Zeuge der (PL die Zeugen) witness.

Zeugin die (PL die Zeuginnen) witness.

Zeugnis das (PL die Zeugnisse) 1 certificate; 2 report (at school).

Zickzack der (PL die Zickzacke) zigzag; **im Zickzack laufen** to zigzag.

Ziege die (PL die Ziegen) goat.

Ziegel der (PL die Ziegel) 1 brick; 2 tile.

ziehen ◊ verb (IMPERF zog, PERF hat gezogen) 1 to pull; **an etwas ziehen** to pull on something; **einen Zahn ziehen** to pull out a tooth; 2 to draw; **einen Strich ziehen** to draw a line; **eine Niete ziehen** to draw a blank; 3 **die Bremse ziehen** to put on the brakes; 4 to grow (vegetables, flowers); 5 **sich ziehen** to run (of a path, road); 6 (PERF ist gezogen) to move; **sie sind nach Berlin gezogen** they've moved to Berlin.

Ziel das (PL die Ziele) 1 destination; 2 goal, aim; 3 finish (in sport).

zielen verb (PERF hat gezielt) to aim; **auf etwas zielen** to aim at something.

Zielscheibe die (PL die Zielscheiben) target.

ziemlich adjective fair.
adverb 1 quite; **ziemlich viel** quite a lot; 2 fairly; **ihre Eltern haben ein**

◊ IRREGULAR VERB: See the verb table in the centre of the dictionary

ziemlich großes Haus her parents have a fairly large house.

zierlich adjective dainty.

Ziffer die (PL die **Ziffern**) figure.

Zifferblatt das (PL die **Zifferblätter**) face, dial.

zig adjective (informal) umpteen.

Zigarette die (PL die **Zigaretten**) cigarette.

Zigarre die (PL die **Zigarren**) cigar.

Zigeuner der (PL die **Zigeuner**) gypsy.

Zigeunerin die (PL die **Zigeunerinnen**) gypsy.

Zimmer das (PL die **Zimmer**) room; **Zimmer mit Frühstück** bed and breakfast; **'Zimmer frei'** 'vacancies'.

Zimmermädchen das (PL die **Zimmermädchen**) chambermaid.

Zimt der cinnamon.

Zink das zinc.

zirka adverb about.

Zirkel der (PL die **Zirkel**) pair of compasses.

Zirkus der (PL die **Zirkusse**) circus.

zischen verb (PERF hat gezischt) to hiss.

Zitat das (PL die **Zitate**) quotation.

zitieren verb (PERF hat zitiert) to quote.

Zitrone die (PL die **Zitronen**) lemon.

Zitronensaft der (PL die **Zitronensäfte**) lemon juice.

zittern verb (PERF hat gezittert) to tremble; **vor Kälte zittern** to shiver.

Zivildienst der community service.

Zivilisation die (PL die **Zivilisationen**) civilization.

zog SEE ziehen.

zögern verb (PERF hat gezögert) to hesitate.

Zoll der (PL die **Zölle**) 1 customs; **am Zoll** at customs; 2 duty; **Zoll auf etwas bezahlen** to pay duty on something.

Zollbeamte der (PL die **Zollbeamten**) customs officer.

Zollbeamtin die (PL die **Zollbeamtinnen**) customs officer.

zollfrei adjective duty-free.

Zollkontrolle die (PL die **Zollkontrollen**) customs check.

Zone die (PL die **Zonen**) zone.

Zoo der (PL die **Zoos**) Zoo.

Zoomobjektiv das (PL die **Zoomobjektive**) zoom lens.

Zopf der (PL die **Zöpfe**) plait.

Zorn der anger.

zornig adjective angry.

zu preposition ←(+DAT) 1 to; **ich gehe zum Arzt** I'm going to the doctor's; **zu einer Party eingeladen sein** to be invited to a party; **zum Fenster hin** towards the window; **er kam zu dieser Tür herein** he came in through this door; 3 with; **das passt nicht zu meinem Mantel** it doesn't go with

my coat; **es gab Wein zum Käse** there was wine with the cheese; **4 at; zu Weihnachten** at Christmas; **zu Hause** at home; **5 zu etwas werden** to turn into something; **6 zu diesem Zweck** for this purpose; **was schenkst du Karin zum Geburtstag?** what are you giving Karin for her birthday?; **zum Spaß** for fun; **zum ersten Mal** for the first time; **7 sich zu etwas äußern** to comment on something; **Papier zum Schreiben** paper to write on; **8 nett zu jemandem sein** to be nice to somebody; **9 sie waren zu zweit** there were two of them; **eine Marke zu achtzig Pfennig** an 80-pfennig stamp; **es steht drei zu zwei** the score is 3–2; **10 zu Fuß** on foot.
adverb **1 too; zu groß** too big; **2 closed; zu haben**△ to be closed; **Tür zu!** (*informal*) shut the door!; **3 zu sein**△ to be closed; **alle Läden sind zu gewesen** the shops were all closed; **4 towards** (*indicating direction*); **5 mach zu!** (*informal*) hurry up!
conjunction to; **nichts zu essen** nothing to eat; **zu verkaufen** for sale.

zuallererst *adverb* first of all.

zuallerletzt *adverb* last of all.

Zubehör *das* accessories.

zubereiten *verb* (PERF **hat zubereitet**) to prepare; **sie bereitet das Essen zu** she's preparing the meal.

zubinden ◇ *verb* (IMPERF **band zu**,

PERF **hat zugebunden**) to tie, to tie up.

zubringen ◇ *verb* (IMPERF **brachte zu**, PERF **hat zugebracht**) to spend; **sie bringt viel Zeit bei ihrem Freund zu** she spends a lot of time with her boyfriend.

Zucchini *plural noun* courgettes.

züchten *verb* (PERF **hat gezüchtet**) to breed.

zucken *verb* (PERF **hat gezuckt**) to twitch.

Zucker *der* sugar.

Zuckerguss△ *der* icing.

zuckerkrank *adjective* diabetic.

zudecken *verb* (PERF **hat zugedeckt**) **1** to cover up, to cover; **2** to tuck up (*in bed*).

zueinander *adverb* **1** to one another; **lieb zueinander sein** to be nice to one another; **2** together; **zueinander passen** to go together; **zueinander halten**△ to stick together.

zuerst *adverb* **1** first; **2** at first.

Zufahrt *die* (PL *die* **Zufahrten**) **1** access; **2** drive(way).

Zufall *der* (PL *die* **Zufälle**) **1** chance; **durch Zufall** by chance; **2** coincidence; **so ein komischer Zufall** such a strange coincidence; **per Zufall traf ich ihn in der U-Bahn** I happened to meet him on the tube.

zufällig *adjective* chance; **das war rein zufällig** it was purely by chance.
adverb by chance, **kannst du mir zufällig zehn Mark leihen?** could

◇ IRREGULAR VERB: See the verb table in the centre of the dictionary

you lend me ten marks by any chance?

zufrieden adjective 1 content; 2 satisfied; mit etwas zufrieden sein to be satisfied with something. adverb jemanden zufrieden lassen Δ to leave somebody in peace; jemanden zufrieden stellen Δ to satisfy somebody.

zufriedenlassen, zufriedenstellen SEE zufrieden.

Zug der (PL die Züge) 1 train; 2 procession; 3 characteristic, trait; 4 move (in games); 5 swig (when drinking); 6 drag (when smoking); 7 in einem Zug in one go.

Zugabe die (PL die Zugaben) 1 free gift; 2 encore.

Zugang der (PL die Zugänge) access.

zugeben ◇ verb (PRES gibt zu, IMPERF gab zu, PERF hat zugegeben) 1 to add; 2 to admit.

zugehen ◇ verb (IMPERF ging zu, PERF ist zugegangen) 1 to close, to shut; die Tür geht nicht zu the door won't shut; 2 auf etwas zugehen to go towards something; auf jemanden zugehen to walk up to somebody; 3 jemandem zugehen to be sent to somebody; 4 auf der Party ging es lustig zu the party was good fun; 5 dem Ende zugehen to be nearing the end.

zügig adjective quick.

zugreifen ◇ verb (IMPERF griff zu, PERF hat zugegriffen) 1 to grab it/them; 2 to help yourself; 3 to lend a hand.

zugunsten preposition ←(+GEN) in favour of.

zuhaben SEE zu.

Zuhause das home.

zuhören verb (PERF hat zugehört) to listen.

Zuhörer der (PL die Zuhörer) listener.

Zuhörerin die (PL die Zuhörerinnen) listener.

zukommen ◇ verb (IMPERF kam zu, PERF ist zugekommen) 1 auf jemanden zukommen to come up to somebody; nächstes Jahr kommt eine Menge Arbeit auf mich zu I'm in for a lot of work next year; 2 jemandem etwas zukommen lassen to give somebody something; 3 etwas auf sich zukommen lassen to take things as they come.

Zukunft die future.

zukünftig adjective future.

zulassen ◇ verb (PRES lässt zu Δ, IMPERF ließ zu, PERF hat zugelassen) 1 to allow; 2 to register (a car); 3 to leave closed.

Zulassung die (PL die Zulassungen) 1 registration; 2 admission.

zuletzt adverb 1 last; 2 in the end.

zum = zu dem; 1 etwas zum Lesen something to read; 2 spätestens zum fünften März by 5 March at the latest; 3 er hat es zum Fenster hinausgeworfen he threw it out of the window.

Δ NEW SPELLING: See page xii

zumachen verb (PERF hat zugemacht) 1 to close, to shut; 2 to fasten.

zumindest adverb at least.

zunächst adverb 1 first (of all); 2 at first.

Zuname der (PL die Zunamen) surname.

zunehmen ◇ verb (PRES nimmt zu, IMPERF nahm zu, PERF hat zugenommen) 1 to increase; 2 to put on weight.

Zunge die (PL die Zungen) tongue.

zur = zu der.

zurechtkommen ◇ verb (IMPERF kam zurecht, PERF ist zurechtgekommen) to cope, to manage.

zurechtlegen verb (PERF hat zurechtgelegt) 1 to put out ready; 2 sich eine Ausrede zurechtlegen to think up an excuse.

zurück adverb 1 back; 2 Hamburg, hin und zurück a return to Hamburg.

zurückbekommen ◇ verb (IMPERF bekam zurück, PERF hat zurückbekommen) to get back; zehn Pfennig zurückbekommen to get 10 pfennigs change.

zurückbringen ◇ verb (IMPERF brachte zurück, PERF hat zurückgebracht) 1 to bring back; 2 to take back.

zurückfahren ◇ verb (PRES fährt zurück, IMPERF fuhr zurück, PERF ist zurückgefahren) 1 to go back; 2 to drive back; 3 (PERF hat zurückgefahren) to drive back; jemanden zurückfahren to drive somebody back.

zurückgeben ◇ verb (PRES gibt zurück, IMPERF gab zurück, PERF hat zurückgegeben) to give back.

zurückgehen ◇ verb (IMPERF ging zurück, PERF ist zurückgegangen) 1 to go back; zurückgehen auf to go back to; 2 to go down; 3 to decrease.

zurückhalten ◇ verb (PRES hält zurück, IMPERF hielt zurück, PERF hat zurückgehalten) 1 to hold back; 2 sich zurückhalten to restrain yourself.

zurückkommen ◇ verb (IMPERF kam zurück, PERF ist zurückgekommen) 1 to come back; 2 to get back.

zurücklassen ◇ verb (PRES lässt zurück △, IMPERF ließ zurück, PERF hat zurückgelassen) to leave behind.

zurücklegen verb (PERF hat zurückgelegt) 1 to put back; 2 to keep, to put aside; 3 Geld für etwas zurücklegen to put money by for something; 4 to cover (a distance); 5 sich zurücklegen to lie back.

zurücknehmen ◇ verb (PRES nimmt zurück, IMPERF nahm zurück, PERF hat zurückgenommen) to take back.

zurückrufen ◇ verb (IMPERF rief zurück, PERF hat zurückgerufen) to call back.

zurücktreten ◇ verb (PRES tritt zurück, IMPERF trat zurück, PERF ist

◇ IRREGULAR VERB: See the verb table in the centre of the dictionary

zurückgetreten) 1 to step back; 2 to resign.

zurückzahlen verb (PERF hat zurückgezahlt) to pay back.

zurückziehen ◇ verb (IMPERF zog zurück, PERF hat zurückgezogen) 1 to draw back; 2 to withdraw (*an offer*); 3 sich zurückziehen to withdraw, to retire.

zurzeit △ adverb at the moment.

Zusage die (PL die Zusagen) acceptance.

zusammen adverb 1 together; zusammen sein to be together; 2 altogether.

Zusammenarbeit die co-operation.

zusammenarbeiten verb (PERF hat zusammengearbeitet) to co-operate.

zusammenbleiben ◇ verb (IMPERF blieb zusammen, PERF ist zusammengeblieben) to stay together.

zusammenbrechen ◇ verb (PRES bricht zusammen, IMPERF brach zusammen, PERF ist zusammengebrochen) to collapse.

zusammenfassen verb (PERF hat zusammengefasst △) to summarize.

Zusammenfassung die (PL die Zusammenfassungen) summary.

zusammenhalten ◇ verb (PRES hält zusammen, IMPERF hielt zusammen, PERF hat zusammengehalten) 1 to hold together; 2 to keep together; 3 die Kinder haben zusammengehalten the children stuck together.

Zusammenhang der (PL die Zusammenhänge) 1 context; 2 connection.

zusammenkommen ◇ verb (IMPERF kam zusammen, PERF ist zusammengekommen) 1 to meet; 2 to accumulate.

Zusammenkunft die (PL die Zusammenkünfte) meeting.

zusammenlegen verb (PERF hat zusammengelegt) 1 to put together; 2 to fold up; 3 to club together.

zusammennehmen ◇ verb (PRES nimmt zusammen, IMPERF nahm zusammen, PERF hat zusammengenommen) 1 to gather up; 2 to summon up, to collect; 3 sich zusammennehmen to pull yourself together.

zusammenpassen verb (PERF hat zusammengepasst △) 1 to match; 2 to be well matched (*of people*); 3 to fit together.

Zusammensein das get-together.

Zusammenstoß der (PL die Zusammenstöße) collision, crash.

zusammenstoßen ◇ verb (PRES stößt zusammen, IMPERF stieß zusammen, PERF ist zusammengestoßen) to collide, to crash.

zusammenzählen verb (PERF hat zusammengezählt) to add up.

△ NEW SPELLING: See page xii

zusätzlich *adjective* additional, extra.
adverb in addition, extra.

zuschauen *verb* (PERF hat zugeschaut) to watch.

Zuschauer *der* (PL die Zuschauer) 1 spectator; 2 viewer; 3 die Zuschauer the audience.

Zuschauerin *die* (PL die Zuschauerinnen) 1 spectator; 2 viewer.

Zuschlag *der* (PL die Zuschläge) 1 surcharge; 2 supplement.

Zuschuss △ *der* (PL die Zuschüsse) 1 contribution; 2 grant.

zusehen ◇ *verb* (PRES sieht zu, IMPERF sah zu, PERF hat zugesehen) 1 to watch; 2 zusehen, dass ... to see (to it) that ...

zusein SEE zu.

zusenden *verb* (PERF hat zugesendet) to send; jemandem etwas zusenden to send something to somebody.

Zustand *der* (PL die Zustände) 1 condition; 2 state.

zustande *adverb* zustande bringen to bring about; zustande kommen to come about.

zuständig *adjective* responsible.

Zustellung *die* (PL die Zustellungen) delivery.

zustimmen *verb* (PERF hat zugestimmt) to agree.

Zustimmung *die* (PL die Zustimmungen) 1 agreement; 2 approval.

zustoßen ◇ *verb* (PRES stößt zu, IMPERF stieß zu, PERF ist zugestoßen) to happen.

Zutat *die* (PL die Zutaten) ingredient.

zutreffen ◇ *verb* (PRES trifft zu, IMPERF traf zu, PERF hat zugetroffen) auf etwas zutreffen to apply to something.

Zutritt *der* entry; Zutritt haben to have access.

zuverlässig *adjective* reliable.

zuviel SEE viel.

zuvor *adverb* 1 before; der Tag zuvor the day before; 2 first.

zuwenig SEE wenig.

zuzahlen *verb* (PERF hat zugezahlt) to pay extra.

zuziehen ◇ *verb* (IMPERF zog zu, PERF hat zugezogen) 1 to pull tight; 2 to draw (*curtains*); 3 to call in (*an expert etc.*); 4 (PERF ist zugezogen) to move into an area; 5 sich eine Verletzung zuziehen to sustain an injury; sich eine Erkältung zuziehen to catch a cold.

zuzüglich *preposition* ←(+GEN) plus.

zwang SEE zwingen.

Zwang *der* (PL die Zwänge) 1 compulsion; 2 urge; 3 obligation.

zwängen *verb* (PERF hat gezwängt) to squeeze.

zwanglos *adjective* casual, informal.

◇ IRREGULAR VERB: *See the verb table in the centre of the dictionary*

zwar *adverb* 1 admittedly; 2 **ich war zwar dabei, habe aber nichts gesehen** I was there, but I didn't see anything; 3 **und zwar** to be exact.

Zweck *der* (PL die Zwecke) 1 purpose; 2 point; **es hat keinen Zweck** there's no point.

zwecklos *adjective* pointless.

zwei *number* two.

zweideutig *adjective* ambiguous.

zweifach *adjective* twice.

Zweifel *der* (PL die Zweifel) doubt.

zweifelhaft *adjective* 1 doubtful; 2 dubious.

zweifellos *adverb* undoubtedly.

zweifeln *verb* (PERF hat gezweifelt) to doubt; **an etwas zweifeln** to doubt something.

Zweig *der* (PL die Zweige) branch.

zweihundert *number* two hundred.

zweimal *adverb* twice.

zweisprachig *adjective* bilingual.

zweit *adverb* **zu zweit** in twos; **wir sind zu zweit** there are two of us.

zweite SEE **zweiter**.

zweitens *adverb* secondly.

zweiter, zweite, zweites *adjective* second; **Mario kam als Zweiter** Mario was the second to arrive.

Zwerg *der* (PL die Zwerge) dwarf.

Zwiebel *die* (PL die Zwiebeln) 1 onion; 2 bulb.

Zwilling *der* (PL die Zwillinge) 1 twin; 2 **Zwillinge** Gemini; **Markus ist Zwilling** Markus is Gemini.

zwingen ◇ *verb* (IMPERF zwang, PERF hat gezwungen) 1 to force; 2 **sich zwingen** to force yourself.

zwinkern *verb* (PERF hat gezwinkert) to wink.

zwischen *preposition* ←(+DAT, or +ACC *with movement towards a place*) 1 between; 2 among (*a crowd*).

zwischendurch *adverb* 1 in between; 2 now and again.

Zwischenfall *der* (PL die Zwischenfälle) incident.

Zwischenlandung *die* (PL die Zwischenlandungen) stop-over.

Zwischenraum *der* (PL die Zwischenräume) gap, space.

Zwischenzeit *die* **in der Zwischenzeit** in the meantime.

zwo *number* two.

zwölf *number* twelve.

zwoter, zwote, zwotes *adjective* second.

△ NEW SPELLING: *See page xii.*

VERB TABLES AND FORMS

On the following pages you will find forms for a regular German verb **machen** followed by the forms for a reflexive verb **sich waschen** and then the forms for the twelve most important irregular verbs in alphabetical order: **dürfen, essen, fahren, gehen, haben, kommen, können, müssen, sein, sollen, werden, wissen.**

After these are given the main forms for other irregular verbs. Note that the forms for separable verbs such as **aufstehen** are not given as they can be looked up under the base form (**stehen**).

machen
to do *or* to make

Imperative	Past participle
mach!	hat gemacht
macht!	
machen Sie!	

Present

ich mache
du machst
er* macht
wir machen
ihr macht
sie machen

Present subjunctive

ich mache
du machest
er mache
wir machen
ihr machet
sie machen

Perfect

ich habe gemacht
du hast gemacht
er hat gemacht
wir haben gemacht
ihr habt gemacht
sie haben gemacht

Imperfect

ich machte
du machtest
er machte
wir machten
ihr machtet
sie machten

Future

ich werde machen
du wirst machen
er wird machen
wir werden machen
ihr werdet machen
sie werden machen

Conditional

ich würde machen
du würdest machen
er würde machen
wir würden machen
ihr würdet machen
sie würden machen

* er *should be read as* er/sie/es

2

sich waschen
to wash (oneself)

Imperative	**Past participle**
wasch dich!	hat sich
wascht euch!	gewaschen
waschen Sie sich!	

Present

ich wasche mich
du wäschst dich
er wäscht sich
wir waschen uns
ihr wascht euch
sie waschen sich

Perfect

ich habe mich gewaschen
du hast dich gewaschen
er hat sich gewaschen
wir haben uns gewaschen
ihr habt euch gewaschen
sie haben sich gewaschen

Future

ich werde mich waschen
du wirst dich waschen
er wird sich waschen
wir werden uns waschen
ihr werdet euch waschen
sie werden sich waschen

Present subjunctive

ich wasche mich
du waschest dich
er wasche sich
wir waschen uns
ihr waschet euch
sie waschen sich

Imperfect

ich wusch mich
du wuschst dich
er wusch sich
wir wuschen uns
ihr wuscht euch
sie wuschen sich

Conditional

ich würde mich waschen
du würdest dich waschen
er würde sich waschen
wir würden uns waschen
ihr würdet euch waschen
sie würden sich waschen

Note: New German spellings are
used throughout this verb table.
For a general note on the
German spelling reform see
page xii.

dürfen
to be allowed

Imperative
—

Past participle
hat gedurft

Present
ich darf
du darfst
er darf
wir dürfen
ihr dürft
sie dürfen

Present subjunctive
ich dürfe
du dürfest
er dürfe
wir dürfen
ihr dürfet
sie dürfen

Perfect
ich habe gedurft
du hast gedurft
er hat gedurft
wir haben gedurft
ihr habt gedurft
sie haben gedurft

Imperfect
ich durfte
du durftest
er durfte
wir durften
ihr durftet
sie durften

Future
ich werde dürfen
du wirst dürfen
er wird dürfen
wir werden dürfen
ihr werdet dürfen
sie werden dürfen

Conditional
ich würde dürfen
du würdest dürfen
er würde dürfen
wir würden dürfen
ihr würdet dürfen
sie würden dürfen

4

Imperative	Past participle	**essen**
iss!	hat gegessen	to eat
esst!		
essen Sie!		

Present	Present subjunctive
ich esse	ich esse
du isst	du essest
er isst	er esse
wir essen	wir essen
ihr esst	ihr esset
sie essen	sie essen

Perfect	Imperfect
ich habe gegessen	ich aß
du hast gegessen	du aßest
er hat gegessen	er aß
wir haben gegessen	wir aßen
ihr habt gegessen	ihr aßt
sie haben gegessen	sie aßen

Future	Conditional
ich werde essen	ich würde essen
du wirst essen	du würdest essen
er wird essen	er würde essen
wir werden essen	wir würden essen
ihr werdet essen	ihr würdet essen
sie werden essen	sie würden essen

fahren
to drive *or* to go

Imperative	Past participle
fahr!	ist gefahren
fahrt!	
fahren Sie!	

Present

ich fahre
du fährst
er fährt
wir fahren
ihr fahrt
sie fahren

Present subjunctive

ich fahre
du fahrest
er fahre
wir fahren
ihr fahret
sie fahren

Perfect

ich bin gefahren
du bist gefahren
er ist gefahren
wir sind gefahren
ihr seid gefahren
sie sind gefahren

Imperfect

ich fuhr
du fuhrst
er fuhr
wir fuhren
ihr fuhrt
sie fuhren

Future

ich werde fahren
du wirst fahren
er wird fahren
wir werden fahren
ihr werdet fahren
sie werden fahren

Conditional

ich würde fahren
du würdest fahren
er würde fahren
wir würden fahren
ihr würdet fahren
sie würden fahren

6

Imperative	Past participle	**gehen**
geh!	ist gegangen	to go
geht!		
gehen Sie!		

Present

ich gehe
du gehst
er geht
wir gehen
ihr geht
sie gehen

Perfect

ich bin gegangen
du bist gegangen
er ist gegangen
wir sind gegangen
ihr seid gegangen
sie sind gegangen

Future

ich werde gehen
du wirst gehen
er wird gehen
wir werden gehen
ihr werdet gehen
sie werden gehen

Present subjunctive

ich gehe
du gehest
er gehe
wir gehen
ihr gehet
sie gehen

Imperfect

ich ging
du gingst
er ging
wir gingen
ihr gingt
sie gingen

Conditional

ich würde gehen
du würdest gehen
er würde gehen
wir würden gehen
ihr würdet gehen
sie würden gehen

haben
to have

Imperative
hab!
habt!
haben Sie!

Past participle
hat gehabt

Present
ich habe
du hast
er hat
wir haben
ihr habt
sie haben

Present subjunctive
ich habe
du habest
er habe
wir haben
ihr habet
sie haben

Perfect
ich habe gehabt
du hast gehabt
er hat gehabt
wir haben gehabt
ihr habt gehabt
sie haben gehabt

Imperfect
ich hatte
du hattest
er hatte
wir hatten
ihr hattet
sie hatten

Future
ich werde haben
du wirst haben
er wird haben
wir werden haben
ihr werdet haben
sie werden haben

Imperfect subjunctive
ich hätte
du hättest
er hätte
wir hätten
ihr hättet
sie hätten

Conditional
ich würde haben
du würdest haben
er würde haben
wir würden haben
ihr würdet haben
sie würden haben

Imperative	**Past participle**	**kommen**
komm!	ist gekommen	to come
kommt!		
kommen Sie!		

Present

ich komme
du kommst
er kommt
wir kommen
ihr kommt
sie kommen

Perfect

ich bin gekommen
du bist gekommen
er ist gekommen
wir sind gekommen
ihr seid gekommen
sie sind gekommen

Future

ich werde kommen
du wirst kommen
er wird kommen
wir werden kommen
ihr werdet kommen
sie werden kommen

Present subjunctive

ich komme
du kommest
er komme
wir kommen
ihr kommet
sie kommen

Imperfect

ich kam
du kamst
er kam
wir kamen
ihr kamt
sie kamen

Conditional

ich würde kommen
du würdest kommen
er würde kommen
wir würden kommen
ihr würdet kommen
sie würden kommen

können
can *or* to be able to

Imperative	Past participle
—	hat gekonnt *or* hätte können

Present
ich kann
du kannst
er kann
wir können
ihr könnt
sie können

Perfect
ich habe gekonnt
du hast gekonnt
er hat gekonnt
wir haben gekonnt
ihr habt gekonnt
sie haben gekonnt

Future
ich werde können
du wirst können
er wird können
wir werden können
ihr werdet können
sie werden können

Present subjunctive
ich könne
du könnest
er könne
wir können
ihr könnet
sie können

Imperfect
ich konnte
du konntest
er konnte
wir konnten
ihr konntet
sie konnten

Imperfect subjunctive
ich könnte
du könntest
er könnte
wir könnten
ihr könntet
sie könnten

Conditional
ich würde können
du würdest können
er würde können
wir würden können
ihr würdet können
sie würden können

10

Imperative	Past participle	**müssen**
—	hat gemusst *or* hätte müssen	must *or* to have to

Present
ich muss
du musst
er muss
wir müssen
ihr müsst
sie müssen

Perfect
ich habe gemusst
du hast gemusst
er hat gemusst
wir haben gemusst
ihr habt gemusst
sie haben gemusst

Future
ich werde müssen
du wirst müssen
er wird müssen
wir werden müssen
ihr werdet müssen
sie werden müssen

Present subjunctive
ich müsse
du müssest
er müsse
wir müssen
ihr müsset
sie müssen

Imperfect
ich musste
du musstest
er musste
wir mussten
ihr musstet
sie mussten

Imperfect subjunctive
ich müsste
du müsstest
er müsste
wir müssten
ihr müsstet
sie müssten

Conditional
ich würde müssen
du würdest müssen
er würde müssen
wir würden müssen
ihr würdet müssen
sie würden müssen

sein
to be

Imperative	Past participle
sei!	ist gewesen
seid!	
seien Sie!	

Present
ich bin
du bist
er ist
wir sind
ihr seid
sie sind

Perfect
ich bin gewesen
du bist gewesen
er ist gewesen
wir sind gewesen
ihr seid gewesen
sie sind gewesen

Future
ich werde sein
du wirst sein
er wird sein
wir werden sein
ihr werdet sein
sie werden sein

Present subjunctive
ich sei
du sei(e)st
er sei
wir seien
ihr seiet
sie seien

Imperfect
ich war
du warst
er war
wir waren
ihr wart
sie waren

Imperfect subjunctive
ich wäre
du wär(e)st
er wäre
wir wären
ihr wär(e)t
sie wären

Conditional
ich würde sein
du würdest sein
er würde sein
wir würden sein
ihr würdet sein
sie würden sein

Imperative	Past participle	**sollen**
—	hat gesollt	should

Present

ich soll
du sollst
er soll
wir sollen
ihr sollt
sie sollen

Perfect

ich habe gesollt
du hast gesollt
er hat gesollt
wir haben gesollt
ihr habt gesollt
sie haben gesollt

Future

ich werde sollen
du wirst sollen
er wird sollen
wir werden sollen
ihr werdet sollen
sie werden sollen

Present subjunctive

ich solle
du sollest
er solle
wir sollen
ihr sollet
sie sollen

Imperfect

ich sollte
du solltest
er sollte
wir sollten
ihr solltet
sie sollten

Imperfect subjunctive

ich sollte
du solltest
er sollte
wir sollten
ihr solltet
sie sollten

Conditional

ich würde sollen
du würdest sollen
er würde sollen
wir würden sollen
ihr würdet sollen
sie würden sollen

werden
to become *or* to get

Imperative
werde!
werdet!
werden Sie!

Past participle
ist geworden

Present	Present subjunctive
ich werde	ich werde
du wirst	du werdest
er wird	er werde
wir werden	wir werden
ihr werdet	ihr werdet
sie werden	sie werden

Perfect	Imperfect
ich bin geworden	ich wurde
du bist geworden	du wurdest
er ist geworden	er wurde
wir sind geworden	wir wurden
ihr seid geworden	ihr wurdet
sie sind geworden	sie wurden

Future	Conditional
ich werde werden	ich würde werden
du wirst werden	du würdest werden
er wird werden	er würde werden
wir werden werden	wir würden werden
ihr werdet werden	ihr würdet werden
sie werden werden	sie würden werden

14

Imperative	Past participle	**wissen**
wisse!	hat gewusst	to know
wisst!		
wissen Sie!		

Present

ich weiß
du weißt
er weiß
wir wissen
ihr wisst
sie wissen

Present subjunctive

ich wisse
du wissest
er wisse
wir wissen
ihr wisset
sie wissen

Perfect

ich habe gewusst
du hast gewusst
er hat gewusst
wir haben gewusst
ihr habt gewusst
sie haben gewusst

Imperfect

ich wusste
du wusstest
er wusste
wir wussten
ihr wusstet
sie wussten

Future

ich werde wissen
du wirst wissen
er wird wissen
wir werden wissen
ihr werdet wissen
sie werden wissen

Conditional

ich würde wissen
du würdest wissen
er würde wissen
wir würden wissen
ihr würdet wissen
sie würden wissen

German irregular verb forms

This list shows the main forms of other irregular verbs.

Infinitive	Present ich, du, er/sie/es	Imperfect er/sie/es	Perfect er/sie/es
bekommen	bekomme, bekommst, bekommt	bekam	hat bekommen
bergen	berge, birgst, birgt	barg	hat geborgen
besitzen	besitze, besitzt, besitzt	besaß	hat besessen
betrügen	betrüge, betrügst, betrügt	betrog	hat betrogen
biegen	biege, biegst, biegt	bog	hat *or* ist gebogen
bieten	biete, bietest, bietet	bot	hat geboten
binden	binde, bindest, bindet	band	hat gebunden
bitten	bitte, bittest, bittet	bat	hat gebeten
blasen	blase, bläst, bläst	blies	hat geblasen
bleiben	bleibe, bleibst, bleibt	blieb	ist geblieben
braten	brate, brätst, brät	briet	hat gebraten
brechen	breche, brichst, bricht	brach	hat *or* ist gebrochen
brennen	brenne, brennst, brennt	brannte	hat gebrannt
bringen	bringe, bringst, bringt	brachte	hat gebracht
denken	denke, denkst, denkt	dachte	hat gedacht
dürfen	darf, darfst, darf	durfte	hat gedurft
einladen	lade ein, lädst ein, lädt ein	lud ein	hat eingeladen
empfangen	empfange, empfängst, empfängt	empfing	hat empfangen
empfehlen	empfehle, empfiehlst, empfiehlt	empfahl	hat empfohlen
entscheiden	entscheide, entscheidest, entscheidet	entschied	hat entschieden

Infinitive	Present ich, du, er/sie/es	Imperfect er/sie/es	Perfect er/sie/es
erfahren	erfahre, erfährst, erfährt	erfuhr	hat erfahren
erfinden	erfinde, erfindest, erfindet	erfand	hat erfunden
erschrecken	erschrecke, erschrickst, erschrickt	erschrak	ist erschrocken
ertrinken	ertrinke, ertrinkst, ertrinkt	ertrank	ist ertrunken
essen	esse, isst, isst	aß	hat gegessen
fahren	fahre, fährst, fährt	fuhr	ist or hat gefahren
fallen	falle, fällst, fällt	fiel	ist gefallen
fangen	fange, fängst, fängt	fing	hat gefangen
fechten	fechte, fichtst, ficht	focht	hat gefochten
finden	finde, findest, findet	fand	hat gefunden
fliegen	fliege, fliegst, fliegt	flog	ist or hat geflogen
fliehen	fliehe, fliehst, flieht	floh	ist geflohen
fließen	fließe, fließt, fließt	floss	ist geflossen
fressen	fresse, frisst, frisst	fraß	hat gefressen
frieren	friere, frierst, friert	fror	hat or ist gefroren
geben	gebe, gibst, gibt	gab	hat gegeben
gefallen	gefalle, gefällst, gefällt	gefiel	hat gefallen
gehen	gehe, gehst, geht	ging	ist gegangen
gelingen	es gelingt mir/dir/ihm/ ihr/ihm	gelang	ist gelungen
gelten	gelte, giltst, gilt	galt	hat gegolten
genießen	genieße, genießt, genießt	genoss	hat genossen
geraten	gerate, gerätst, gerät	geriet	ist geraten
geschehen	es geschieht	geschah	ist geschehen
gewinnen	gewinne, gewinnst, gewinnt	gewann	hat gewonnen
gießen	gieße, gießt, gießt	goss	hat gegossen
gleichen	gleiche, gleichst, gleicht	glich	hat geglichen
graben	grabe, gräbst, gräbt	grub	hat gegraben
greifen	greife, greifst, greift	griff	hat gegriffen

Infinitive	Present ich, du, er/sie/es	Imperfect er/sie/es	Perfect er/sie/es
haben	habe, hast, hat	hatte	hat gehabt
halten	halte, hältst, hält	hielt	hat gehalten
hängen	hänge, hängst, hängt	hing	hat gehangen
heben	hebe, hebst, hebt	hob	hat gehoben
heißen	heiße, heißt, heißt	hieß	hat geheißen
helfen	helfe, hilfst, hilft	half	hat geholfen
hinweisen	weise hin, weist hin, weist hin	wies hin	hat hingewiesen
kennen	kenne, kennst, kennt	kannte	hat gekannt
klingen	klinge, klingst, klingt	klang	hat geklungen
kneifen	kneife, kneifst, kneift	kniff	hat gekniffen
kommen	komme, kommst, kommt	kam	ist gekommen
können	kann, kannst, kann	konnte	hat gekonnt
kriechen	krieche, kriechst, kriecht	kroch	ist gekrochen
lassen	lasse, lässt, lässt	ließ	hat gelassen
laufen	laufe, läufst, läuft	lief	ist gelaufen
leiden	leide, leidest, leidet	litt	hat gelitten
leihen	leihe, leihst, leiht	lieh	hat geliehen
lesen	lese, liest, liest	las	hat gelesen
liegen	liege, liegst, liegt	lag	hat gelegen
lügen	lüge, lügst, lügt	log	hat gelogen
mahlen	mahle, mahlst, mahlt	mahlte	hat gemahlen
meiden	meide, meidest, meidet	mied	hat gemieden
messen	messe, mißt, mißt	maß	hat gemessen
misslingen Δ	misslinge, misslingst, misslingt	misslang	ist misslungen
mögen	mag, magst, mag	mochte	hat gemocht
müssen	muss, musst, muss	musste	hat gemusst

Infinitive	Present ich, du, er/sie/es	Imperfect er/sie/es	Perfect er/sie/es
nehmen	nehme, nimmst, nimmt	nahm	hat genommen
nennen	nenne, nennst, nennt	nannte	hat genannt
pfeifen	pfeife, pfeifst, pfeift	pfiff	hat gepfiffen
raten	rate, rätst, rät	riet	hat geraten
reiben	reibe, reibst, reibt	rieb	hat gerieben
reißen	reiße, reißt, reißt	riss	hat or ist gerissen
reiten	reite, reitest, reitet	ritt	hat or ist geritten
rennen	renne, rennst, rennt	rannte	ist gerannt
riechen	rieche, riechst, riecht	roch	hat gerochen
rufen	rufe, rufst, ruft	rief	hat gerufen
saufen	saufe, säufst, säuft	soff	hat gesoffen
schaffen	schaffe, schaffst, schafft	schuf	hat geschaffen
scheiden	scheide, scheidest, scheidet	schied	hat or ist geschieden
scheinen	scheine, scheinst, scheint	schien	hat geschienen
schieben	schiebe, schiebst, schiebt	schob	hat geschoben
schießen	schieße, schießt, schießt	schoss	hat or ist geschossen
schlafen	schlafe, schläfst, schläft	schlief	hat geschlafen
schlagen	schlage, schlägst, schlägt	schlug	hat geschlagen
schleichen	schleiche, schleichst, schleicht	schlich	ist geschlichen
schließen	schließe, schließt, schließt	schloss	hat geschlossen
schmeißen	schmeiße, schmeißt, schmeißt	schmiss	hat geschmissen
schmelzen	schmelze, schmilzt, schmilzt	schmolz	ist geschmolzen
schneiden	schneide, schneidest, schneidet	schnitt	hat geschnitten

Infinitive	Present ich, du, er/sie/es	Imperfect er/sie/es	Perfect er/sie/es
schreiben	schreibe, schreibst, schreibt	schrieb	hat geschrieben
schreien	schreie, schreist, schreit	schrie	hat geschrien
schweigen	schweige, schweigst, schweigt	schwieg	hat geschwiegen
schwimmen	schwimme, schwimmst, schwimmt	schwamm	ist *or* hat geschwommen
schwören	schwöre, schwörst, schwört	schwor	hat geschworen
sehen	sehe, siehst, sieht	sah	hat gesehen
sein	bin, bist, ist	war	ist gewesen
singen	singe, singst, singt	sang	hat gesungen
sinken	sinke, sinkst, sinkt	sank	ist gesunken
sitzen	sitze, sitzt, sitzt	saß	hat gesessen
sollen	soll, sollst, soll	sollte	hat gesollt
spinnen	spinne, spinnst, spinnt	spann	hat gesponnen
sprechen	spreche, sprichst, spricht	sprach	hat gesprochen
springen	springe, springst, springt	sprang	ist gesprungen
stechen	steche, stichst, sticht	stach	hat gestochen
stehen	stehe, stehst, steht	stand	hat gestanden
stehlen	stehle, stiehlst, stiehlt	stahl	hat gestohlen
steigen	steige, steigst, steigt	stieg	ist gestiegen
sterben	sterbe, stirbst, stirbt	starb	ist gestorben
stinken	stinke, stinkst, stinkt	stank	hat gestunken
stoßen	stoße, stößt, stößt	stieß	hat *or* ist gestoßen
streichen	streiche, streichst, streicht	strich	hat gestrichen
streiten	streite, streitest, streitet	stritt	hat gestritten
tragen	trage, trägst, trägt	trug	hat getragen
treffen	treffe, triffst, trifft	traf	hat getroffen
treiben	treibe, treibst, treibt	trieb	hat getrieben
treten	trete, trittst, tritt	trat	hat *or* ist getreten
trinken	trinke, trinkst, trinkt	trank	hat getrunken
tun	tue, tust, tut	tat	hat getan

Infinitive	Present ich, du, er/sie/es	Imperfect er/sie/es	Perfect er/sie/es
überweisen	überweise, überweist, überweist	überwies	hat überwiesen
umziehen	ziehe um, ziehst um, zieht um	zog um	ist *or* hat umgezogen
verbieten	verbiete, verbietest, verbietet	verbot	hat verboten
verderben	verderbe, verdirbst, verdirbt	verdarb	hat *or* ist verdorben
vergessen	vergesse, vergißt, vergißt	vergaß	hat vergessen
verlieren	verliere, verlierst, verliert	verlor	hat verloren
verschwinden	verschwinde, verschwindest, verschwindet	verschwand	ist verschwunden
verstehen	verstehe, verstehst, versteht	verstand	hat verstanden
verzeihen	verzeihe, verzeihst, verzeiht	verzieh	hat verziehen
wachsen	wachse, wächst, wächst	wuchs	ist gewachsen
waschen	wasche, wäscht, wäscht	wusch	hat gewaschen
werben	werbe, wirbst, wirbt	warb	hat geworben
werden	werde, wirst, wird	wurde	ist geworden
werfen	werfe, wirfst, wirft	warf	hat geworfen
wiegen	wiege, wiegst, wiegt	wog	hat gewogen
wissen	weiß, weißt, weiß	wusste	hat gewusst
wollen	will, willst, will	wollte	hat gewollt
ziehen	ziehe, ziehst, zieht	zog	hat *or* ist gezogen
zwingen	zwinge, zwingst, zwingt	zwang	hat gezwungen

Note: New German spellings are used throughout this verb table. For a general note on the German spelling reform see page xii.

A a

a *indefinite article* 1 (*before a noun which is masculine in German*) ein; **a tree** ein Baum; 2 (*before a noun which is feminine in German*) eine; **a story** eine Geschichte; 3 (*before a noun which is neuter in German*) ein; **a dress** ein Kleid; 4 **not a** kein; **the party was not a success** die Party war kein Erfolg; **he didn't say a word** er hat kein Wort gesagt; 5 **six marks a kilo** sechs Mark das Kilo; 6 **fifty kilometres an hour** fünfzig Stundenkilometer; 7 **three times a day** dreimal täglich.

abandon *verb* 1 aufgeben ◊ SEP; **they abandoned the plan** sie gaben den Plan auf; 2 verlassen ◊; **they abandoned the city** sie verließen die Stadt.

abbey *noun* Abtei *die* (PL *die* Abteien).

abbreviation *noun* Abkürzung *die* (PL *die* Abkürzungen).

ability *noun* Fähigkeit *die* (PL *die* Fähigkeiten); **to have the ability to do something** etwas tun können.

about *preposition* 1 über (+ACC); **a film about space** ein Film über den Weltraum; **to talk about something/somebody** über etwas/jemanden reden; **what is she talking about?** worüber redet sie?; 2 um (+ACC); **to be about something** um etwas gehen; **what's it about?** worum geht es?; 3 **to know about something** von etwas ←(DAT) wissen; **she didn't know about the party** sie wusste nichts von der Party; **he knows nothing about it** er weiß nichts davon; 4 **to think about something/somebody** an etwas/jemanden ←(ACC) denken; **I'm thinking about you** ich denke an dich.

adverb 1 (*approximately*) ungefähr; **about sixty people** ungefähr sechzig Leute; **in about a week** in ungefähr einer Woche; 2 (*when talking about time*) gegen; **about three o'clock** gegen drei Uhr; 3 **to be about to do something** gerade etwas tun wollen; **I was (just) about to leave** ich wollte gerade gehen.

above *preposition* 1 über (+DAT); **the lamp above the table** die Lampe über dem Tisch; 2 **above all** vor allem.

abroad *adverb* im Ausland; **to live abroad** im Ausland leben; **to go abroad** ins Ausland fahren.

absent *adjective* abwesend; **to be absent from school** in der Schule fehlen.

absent-minded *adjective* zerstreut.

absolute *adjective* absolut; **an absolute disaster** eine absolute Katastrophe.

absolutely *adverb* 1 wirklich; **it's absolutely dreadful** das ist wirklich furchtbar; 2 völlig; **you're**

△ NEW SPELLING: *See page xii*

absolutely right du hast völlig recht.

abuse noun **1** Missbrauch △ der; **drug abuse** Missbrauch von Drogen; **2** (insults) Beschimpfungen (plural).
verb **1 to abuse somebody** jemanden missbrauchen; **2** (to insult) beschimpfen.

accelerator noun Gaspedal das (PL die Gaspedale).

accent noun Akzent der (PL die Akzente); **to speak with a German accent** mit deutschem Akzent sprechen.

accept verb annehmen ◇ SEP; **he accepted the invitation** er nahm die Einladung an.

acceptable adjective annehmbar.

access noun Zugang der.
verb **to access data** auf Daten zugreifen.

accessory noun **1** Zubehörteil das; **accessories** Zubehör das; **2 accessories** (fashion items) Accessoires (plural).

accident noun **1** Unfall der (PL die Unfälle); **to have an accident** einen Unfall haben; **road accident** der Verkehrsunfall; **car accident** der Autounfall; **2** Zufall der (PL die Zufälle); **by accident** zufällig; **I found it by accident** ich habe es zufällig gefunden.

accidental adjective zufällig; **an accidental discovery** eine zufällige Entdeckung.

accidentally adverb **1** (without meaning to) versehentlich; **I accidentally threw it away** ich habe es versehentlich weggeworfen; **2** (by chance) zufällig; **I accidentally discovered that ...** ich habe zufällig herausgefunden, dass ...

accommodation noun Unterkunft die; **accommodation is free** Unterkunft ist kostenlos; **I'm looking for accommodation** (when looking for a room) ich suche ein Zimmer.

according in phrase **according to** laut (+DAT); **according to Sophie** laut Sophie.

accordion noun Akkordeon das (PL die Akkordeons).

account noun **1** (in a bank, shop, or post office) Konto das (PL die Konten); **bank account** das Bankkonto; **to open an account** ein Konto eröffnen; **I have fifty pounds in my account** ich habe fünfzig Pfund auf meinem Konto; **2** (an explanation) Darstellung die (PL die Darstellungen); **I want to hear his account of what happened** ich möchte seine Darstellung der Ereignisse hören; **3 on account of** wegen (+GEN); **4 to take something into account** etwas berücksichtigen.

accountant noun Buchhalter der (PL die Buchhalter), Buchhalterin die (PL die Buchhalterinnen); **she's an accountant** sie ist Buchhalterin.

accurate adjective genau.

accurately adverb genau.

◇ IRREGULAR VERB: See the verb table in the centre of the dictionary

accuse verb beschuldigen; **she accused me of stealing her pen** sie beschuldigte mich, ihren Kugelschreiber gestohlen zu haben.

ace noun Ass △ das (PL die Asse); **the ace of hearts** das Herzass.
adjective klasse (informal); **he's an ace drummer** er spielt klasse Schlagzeug.

achieve verb 1 leisten; **she's achieved a great deal** sie hat eine Menge geleistet; 2 erreichen (an aim); **he achieved what he wanted** er hat erreicht, was er wollte.

achievement noun Leistung die (PL die Leistungen); **it's a great achievement** das ist eine große Leistung.

acid noun Säure die (PL die Säuren).

acne noun Akne die.

across preposition 1 (over to the other side of) über (+ACC); **to run across the road** über die Straße laufen; **we walked across the park** wir sind durch den Park gegangen; 2 (on the other side of) auf der anderen Seite (+GEN); **he lives across the river** er wohnt auf der anderen Seite des Flusses; 3 **they live across the street** sie wohnen gegenüber.

act noun (deed) Tat die (PL die Taten).
verb (in a play or film) spielen; **to act the part of the hero** die Rolle des Helden spielen.

action noun 1 Handlung die (PL die Handlungen); 2 **to take action** etwas unternehmen.

active adjective aktiv.

activity noun Aktivität die (PL die Aktivitäten).

actor noun Schauspieler der (PL die Schauspieler).

actress noun Schauspielerin die (PL die Schauspielerinnen).

actual adjective **what were his actual words?** was genau hat er gesagt?; **in actual fact** eigentlich.

actually adverb 1 (in fact, as it happens) eigentlich; **actually, I've changed my mind** ich habe mich eigentlich anders entschlossen; 2 (really and truly) wirklich; **did she actually say that?** hat sie das wirklich gesagt?

ad noun 1 (on TV) Werbespot der (PL die Werbespots); 2 (in a newspaper) Anzeige die (PL die Anzeigen); **to put an ad in the paper** eine Anzeige in die Zeitung setzen; **the small ads** die Kleinanzeigen.

AD (Anno Domini) n.Chr. (nach Christus); **in 400 AD** 400 n.Chr.

adapt verb 1 **to adapt something** (a book or film) etwas bearbeiten; 2 **to adapt to** sich anpassen SEP (+DAT); **she's adapted to her new surroundings** sie hat sich der neuen Umgebung angepasst.

adaptor noun 1 Adapter der (PL die Adapter); 2 (for two plugs) Doppelstecker der (PL die Doppelstecker).

add verb 1 hinzufügen SEP; **to add an introduction to something** etwas ←(DAT) eine Einleitung hinzufügen; 2 dazugeben ◇ SEP; **add three eggs** geben Sie drei Eier dazu.

● **to add up** zusammenzählen SEP

△ NEW SPELLING: See page xi

addict noun 1 (*drug addict*) Süchtige der/die (PL die Süchtigen); 2 she's a telly addict sie ist fernsehsüchtig; he's a football addict er hat die Fußballsucht.

addicted adjective 1 to become addicted to drugs drogensüchtig werden; 2 he's addicted to football Fußball ist bei ihm zur Sucht geworden; 3 I'm addicted to sweets ich bin nach Süßigkeiten süchtig.

addition noun 1 (*adding up*) Addition die; 2 in addition außerdem; 3 in addition to zusätzlich zu (+DAT).

additional adjective zusätzlich.

additive noun Zusatz der (PL die Zusätze).

address noun Adresse die (PL die Adressen); do you know his address? weißt du seine Adresse?; to change address die Adresse wechseln.

address book noun Adressbuch △ das (PL die Adressbücher).

adhesive noun Klebstoff der. adjective **adhesive tape** der Klebstreifen.

adjective noun Adjektiv das (PL die Adjektive).

adjust verb 1 to adjust something etwas einstellen SEP; he adjusted the set er stellte das Gerät ein; to adjust the distance auf die richtige Entfernung einstellen; 2 to adjust

to something sich an etwas ←(ACC) gewöhnen.

adjustable adjective verstellbar.

administration noun Verwaltung die.

admiration noun Bewunderung die.

admire verb bewundern.

admission noun Eintritt der; 'admission free' 'Eintritt frei'.

admit verb 1 (confess, concede) zugeben ◇ SEP; she admits she lied sie gibt zu, dass sie gelogen hat; 2 (allow to enter) hereinlassen ◇ SEP; to admit somebody to a restaurant jemanden in ein Restaurant hereinlassen; 3 to be admitted to hospital ins Krankenhaus eingeliefert werden.

adolescence noun Jugend die.

adolescent noun Jugendliche der/die (PL die Jugendlichen).

adopt verb adoptieren.

adopted adjective adoptiert.

adoption noun Adoption die (PL die Adoptionen).

adore verb lieben.

adult noun Erwachsene der/die (PL die Erwachsenen). adjective **the adult population** Erwachsene (plural).

Adult Education noun Erwachsenenbildung die.

advance noun Fortschritt der (PL die Fortschritte); advances in

technology technologische Fortschritte.
verb **1** (*make progress*) Fortschritte machen; **2** (*move forward*) (*of a group or an army*) vorrücken SEP (PERF sein).

advanced *adjective* fortgeschritten (*student, age*).

advantage *noun* **1** Vorteil *der* (PL die Vorteile); **there are several advantages** es gibt verschiedene Vorteile; **2 to take advantage of something** etwas ausnutzen SEP; **I always take advantage of the sales to buy myself some shoes** ich nutze immer den Ausverkauf aus, um mir Schuhe zu kaufen; **3 to take advantage of somebody** (*unfairly*) jemanden ausnutzen SEP.

Advent *noun* Advent *der*.

adventure *noun* Abenteuer *das* (PL die Abenteuer).

adverb *noun* Adverb *das* (PL die Adverbien).

advert, advertisement *noun* **1** (*at the cinema or on television*) Werbespot *der* (PL die Werbespots); **2** (*in a newspaper for a job, article for sale, etc.*) Anzeige *die* (PL die Anzeigen); **she answered a job advertisement** sie meldete sich auf eine Stellenanzeige.

advertise *verb* **to advertise something in the newspaper** (*in the small ads*) etwas in der Zeitung inserieren; **I saw a bike advertised in the paper** ich habe ein Rad in der Zeitung inseriert gesehen.

advertising *noun* Werbung *die*.

advice *noun* Rat *der*; **to ask somebody's advice** jemanden um Rat fragen; **a piece of advice** ein Ratschlag.

advise *verb* raten ✧ (+DAT) **to advise somebody to do something** jemandem raten, etwas zu tun; **I advised him to stop** ich riet ihm anzuhalten; **I advised her not to buy the car** ich habe ihr geraten, das Auto nicht zu kaufen.

aerial *noun* Antenne *die* (PL die Antennen).

aerobics *noun* Aerobic *das*; **to do aerobics** Aerobic machen.

aeroplane *noun* Flugzeug *das* (PL die Flugzeuge).

aerosol *noun* **an aerosol can** eine Spraydose.

affair *noun* **1** Angelegenheit *die* (PL die Angelegenheiten); **international affairs** internationale Angelegenheiten; **current affairs** die Tagespolitik; **2 love affair** *das* Liebesverhältnis.

affect *verb* beeinflussen.

affectionate *adjective* liebevoll.

afford *verb* **to be able to afford something** ←(DAT) etwas leisten können; **we can't afford to go out much** wir können es uns nicht leisten, oft auszugehen; **I can't afford a new bike** ich kann mir kein neues Rad leisten.

afraid *adjective* **1 to be afraid of something** Angst vor etwas ←(DAT) haben; **she's afraid of dogs** sie hat vor Hunden Angst; **2 I'm afraid I**

△ NEW SPELLING: **See page x**

can't help you ich kann dir leider
nicht helfen; **I'm afraid so** leider ja;
I'm afraid not leider nicht.

Africa noun Afrika das; **to Africa**
nach Afrika.

African noun Afrikaner der (PL die
Afrikaner), Afrikanerin die (PL die
Afrikanerinnen).
adjective afrikanisch; **she is
African** sie ist Afrikanerin.

after preposition, adverb **1** nach
(+DAT); **after 10 o'clock** nach zehn
Uhr; **after lunch** nach dem
Mittagessen; **after school** nach der
Schule; **2 the day after tomorrow**
übermorgen; **soon after** kurz
danach; **3 to run after somebody**
jemandem hinterherlaufen ◇ SEP.
conjunction nachdem; **after I'd
finished my homework** nachdem
ich meine Hausaufgaben gemacht
hatte.

after all adverb schließlich; **after
all, she's only six** sie ist schließlich
erst sechs.

afternoon noun **1** Nachmittag der
(PL die Nachmittage); **in the
afternoon** am Nachmittag; **every
afternoon** jeden Nachmittag; **2 this
afternoon** heute Nachmittag; **on
Sunday afternoon** am
Sonntagnachmittag; **3 on Saturday
afternoons** samstagsnachmittags;
at four o' clock in the afternoon
um vier Uhr nachmittags.

after-shave noun
Rasierwasser das.

afterwards adverb danach; **shortly
afterwards** kurz danach.

again adverb **1** wieder; **she's ill
again** sie ist wieder krank; **2 I saw
her again yesterday** ich habe sie
gestern wieder gesehen; **3 never
again!** nie wieder!; **again and
again** immer wieder; **4** (one more
time) noch einmal; **try again**
versuche es noch einmal; **you should
ask her again** du solltest sie noch
einmal fragen.

against preposition gegen (+ACC);
against the wall gegen die Wand;
to lean against the wall sich gegen
die Wand lehnen; **I'm against the
idea** ich bin gegen die Idee.

age noun **1** Alter das; **at the age of
fifty** im Alter von fünfzig; **she's the
same age as me** sie ist genauso alt
wie ich; **to be under age**
minderjährig sein; **2 I haven't seen
Johnny for ages** ich habe Johnny
schon ewig nicht mehr gesehen; **I
haven't been to London for ages**
ich bin schon ewig nicht mehr in
London gewesen.

agent noun Vertreter der (PL die
Vertreter); **an estate agent** ein
Immobilienmakler; **a travel agent's**
ein Reisebüro.

aggressive adjective aggressiv.

ago adverb vor (+DAT); **an hour ago**
vor einer Stunde; **three days ago**
vor drei Tagen; **a long time ago** vor
langer Zeit; **not long ago** vor
kurzem; **how long ago was it?** wie
lange ist das her?

agree verb **1 to agree with
somebody** mit jemandem
übereinstimmen SEP; **I agree with**

◇ **IRREGULAR VERB: See the verb table in the centre of the dictionary**

Laura ich stimme mit Laura überein; **2 I agree** ich bin der gleichen Meinung; **I don't agree** ich bin anderer Meinung; **3 to agree that …** zugeben ◊ SEP, dass …; **I agree that it's too late now** ich gebe zu, dass es jetzt zu spät ist; **4 to agree to something** mit etwas einverstanden sein; **Steve's agreed to help me** Steve war damit einverstanden, mir zu helfen; **5 coffee doesn't agree with me** Kaffee bekommt mir nicht.

agreement noun **1** (*when sharing an opinion*) Übereinstimmung die; **2** (*contract*) Abkommen das (PL die Abkommen).

agriculture noun Landwirtschaft die.

ahead adverb **1 go ahead!** bitte!; **2 straight ahead** geradeaus; **keep going straight ahead until you get to the crossroads** gehen Sie immer geradeaus bis zur Kreuzung; **3 our team was ten points ahead** unsere Mannschaft hatte zehn Punkte Vorsprung; **4 ahead of time** früher als geplant; **5 the people ahead of me** die Leute vor mir.

aid noun **1** Hilfe die; **aid to developing countries** die Entwicklungshilfe; **2 in aid of** zugunsten (+GEN); **in aid of the homeless** zugunsten der Obdachlosen.

Aids noun Aids das; **to have Aids** Aids haben.

aim noun **1** Ziel das (PL die Ziele); **their aim is to control pollution** ihr Ziel

ist es, die Verschmutzung unter Kontrolle zu bringen.
verb **1 to aim to do something** beabsichtigen, etwas zu tun; **we're aiming to finish it today** wir beabsichtigen, es heute fertig zu machen; **2 the campaign is aimed at young people** die Kampagne ist auf junge Leute abgezielt.

air noun **1** Luft die; **in the open air** im Freien; **to go out for a breath of air** frische Luft schöpfen gehen; **2 to travel by air** fliegen ◊ (PERF sein).

air-conditioned adjective klimatisiert.

air conditioning noun Klimaanlage die.

Air Force noun Luftwaffe die.

air hostess noun Stewardess △ die (PL die Stewardessen); **she's an air hostess** sie ist Stewardess.

airline noun Fluggesellschaft die (PL die Fluggesellschaften).

airmail noun **by airmail** per Luftpost.

airport noun Flughafen der (PL die Flughäfen).

alarm noun Alarm der (PL die Alarme); **fire alarm** der Feuermelder; **burglar alarm** die Alarmanlage.

alarm clock noun Wecker der (PL die Wecker).

album noun Album das (PL die Alben).

alcohol noun Alkohol der.

△ NEW SPELLING: See page xii

alcoholic noun Alkoholiker der (PL die Alkoholiker), Alkoholikerin die (PL die Alkoholikerinnen).
adjective alkoholisch.

A levels noun Abitur das (Students who want to go on to university do the Abitur at the end of secondary school; they are examined in four subjects).

alike adjective 1 gleich; 2 they're all alike sie sind alle gleich; 3 to look alike sich ←(DAT) ähnlich sehen; the two brothers look alike die beiden Brüder sehen sich ähnlich.

alive adjective 1 to be alive leben; to stay alive am Leben bleiben; 2 (lively) lebendig.

all adjective 1 (with a singular noun) ganz; all the time die ganze Zeit; all day den ganzen Tag; 2 (with a plural noun) alle; all the knives alle Messer; all our friends alle unsere Freunde.
pronoun 1 (everything) alles; they've eaten it all sie haben alles aufgegessen; 2 (everybody) alle; all of us wir alle; they're all there sie sind alle da; 3 not at all gar nicht.
adverb 1 ganz; all alone ganz allein; 2 three all drei zu drei.

all along adverb die ganze Zeit; I knew it all along ich habe es die ganze Zeit gewusst.

allergic adjective allergisch; to be allergic to something gegen etwas ←(ACC) allergisch sein.

allow verb 1 to allow somebody to do something jemandem erlauben, etwas zu tun; the teacher allowed them to go home der Lehrer

erlaubte ihnen, nach Hause zu gehen; 2 to be allowed to dürfen ◇; I'm not allowed to go to the cinema during the week ich darf während der Woche nicht ins Kino gehen.

all right adverb 1 (yes) ist gut, okay (informal); 'come round to my house around six' – 'all right' 'komm um sechs bei mir vorbei' – 'okay'; 2 (fine) in Ordnung, okay (informal); is everything all right? ist alles okay?; she's all right now sie ist jetzt okay; it's all right by me das geht in Ordnung; is it all right if I come later? geht es in Ordnung, wenn ich später komme?; 3 (not bad) gut, okay (informal); the meal was all right das Essen war okay; 4 'how are you?' – 'all right' 'wie geht's dir?' – 'mir geht's gut'.

almost adverb fast; almost every day fast jeden Tag; almost everybody fast alle.

alone adjective 1 allein; he lives alone er lebt allein; 2 leave me alone! lass mich in Ruhe!

along preposition 1 entlang (+ACC, or +DAT); there are trees all along the river den ganzen Fluss entlang stehen Bäume; to go for a walk along the beach am Strand entlang spazieren gehen; 2 (there is often no direct translation for 'along', so the sentence has to be expressed differently) she lives along the road from me sie wohnt in der gleichen Straße wie ich; I'll bring it along ich bringe es mit.

◇ IRREGULAR VERB: See the verb table in the centre of the dictionary

aloud adverb laut; **to read something aloud** etwas vorlesen ◇ SEP.

alphabet noun Alphabet das (PL die Alphabete).

Alps plural noun **the Alps** die Alpen.

already adverb schon; **they've already left** sie sind schon weggefahren; **it's six o'clock already** es ist schon sechs Uhr.

Alsatian noun Schäferhund der (PL die Schäferhunde).

also adverb auch; **I've also invited Karen** ich habe Karen auch eingeladen.

alternative noun 1 Alternative die (PL die Alternativen); **there are several alternatives** es gibt mehrere Alternativen; 2 **we have no alternative** wir haben keine andere Wahl.
adjective anderer/andere/anderes (masculine/feminine/neuter); **to find an alternative solution** eine andere Lösung finden.

alternative medicine noun Alternativmedizin die.

although conjunction obwohl; **although she's ill, she wants to help us** obwohl sie krank ist, will sie uns helfen.

altogether adverb 1 insgesamt; **I've spent thirty pounds altogether** insgesamt habe ich dreißig Pfund ausgegeben; 2 (completely) ganz; **I'm not altogether convinced** ich bin nicht ganz überzeugt.

always adverb immer; **I always leave at five** ich gehe immer um fünf weg.

am verb SEE be.

a.m. abbreviation vormittags; **at 8 a.m.** um acht Uhr morgens.

amateur noun 1 Amateur der (PL die Amateure); 2 **amateur dramatics** das Laientheater.

amaze verb erstaunen; **what amazes me is...** was mich erstaunt, ist...

amazed adjective erstaunt; **I was amazed to see her** ich war erstaunt, sie zu sehen.

amazing adjective 1 (terrific) fantastisch △; **they've got an amazing house** sie haben ein fantastisches Haus; 2 (extraordinary) erstaunlich; **she has an amazing number of friends** sie hat erstaunlich viele Freunde.

ambition noun Ehrgeiz der.

ambitious adjective ehrgeizig.

ambulance noun Krankenwagen der (PL die Krankenwagen).

America noun Amerika das; **in America** in Amerika; **to America** nach Amerika.

American noun Amerikaner der (PL die Amerikaner), Amerikanerin die (PL die Amerikanerinnen).
adjective amerikanisch; **she's American** sie ist Amerikanerin.

among, amongst preposition 1 unter (+DAT); **I found it amongst my books** ich habe das unter

meinen Büchern gefunden;
amongst other things unter
anderem; **2** (*between*) **among
yourselves** untereinander.

amount *noun* **1** Menge *die* (PL *die*
Mengen); **a huge amount of work**
eine Menge Arbeit; **2** (*of money*)
Betrag *der* (PL *die* Beträge); **a large
amount of money** ein sehr hoher
Betrag.

amp *noun* (*amplifier*)
Verstärker *der* (PL *die* Verstärker).

amplifier *noun* Verstärker *der* (PL
die Verstärker).

amuse *verb* amüsieren.

amusement arcade *noun*
Spielhalle *die* (PL *die* Spielhallen).

amusing *adjective* amüsant.

an *article* SEE **a**.

anchovy *noun* Sardelle *die* (PL *die*
Sardellen).

ancient *adjective* **1** alt; **ancient
Greece** *das* alte Griechenland;
2 (*very old*) uralt; **an ancient pair of
jeans** uralte Jeans.

and *conjunction* **1** und; **Rosie and I**
Rosie und ich; **girls and boys**
Mädchen und Jungen; **2 louder and
louder** immer lauter; **3 try and
come** versuche zu kommen.

angel *noun* Engel *der* (PL *die* Engel).

anger *noun* Zorn *der*.

angle *noun* Winkel *der* (PL *die*
Winkel).

angrily *adverb* wütend.

angry *adjective* **to be angry** böse
sein; **she was angry with me** sie
war böse auf mich; **to get angry**
böse werden.

animal *noun* Tier *das* (PL *die* Tiere).

ankle *noun* Knöchel *der* (PL *die*
Knöchel).

anniversary *noun* **1** Jahrestag *der*
(PL *die* Jahrestage); **2 our wedding
anniversary** unser Hochzeitstag.

annoy *verb* **to be annoyed** verärgert
sein; **to get annoyed with
somebody** sich über jemanden
ärgern; **she got annoyed about it**
sie hat sich darüber geärgert.

annoying *adjective* ärgerlich.

annual *adjective* jährlich.

anorak *noun* Anorak *der* (PL *die*
Anoraks).

anorexia *noun* Magersucht *die*.

another *adjective* **1** (*additional*)
noch ein/noch eine/noch ein;
would you like another cup of tea?
möchtest du noch eine Tasse Tee?;
we need another three chairs wir
brauchen noch drei Stühle;
2 (*different*) ein anderer/eine
andere/ein anderes; **we saw
another film** wir haben einen
anderen Film gesehen; **3** in another
two years in zwei weiteren Jahren.

answer *noun* **1** Antwort *die* (PL *die*
Antworten); **the right answer** die
richtige Antwort; **the wrong answer**
die falsche Antwort; **the answer
to a problem** die Lösung eines
Problems.
verb **1** antworten (+DAT); **why don't
you answer him?** warum

◇ **IRREGULAR VERB: See the verb table in the centre of the dictionary**

antwortest du ihm nicht?;
2 beantworten (*a letter, a question*);
he hasn't answered our letter er
hat unseren Brief nicht beantwortet.

answering machine *noun*
Anrufbeantworter *der* (PL *die*
Anrufbeantworter).

anthem *noun* **the national anthem**
die Nationalhymne.

antibiotic *noun* Antibiotikum *das*
(PL *die* Antibiotika).

antique *noun* **antiques**
Antiquitäten (*plural*).
adjective antik; **an antique table**
ein antiker Tisch.

antique shop *noun*
Antiquitätengeschäft *das* (PL *die*
Antiquitätengeschäfte).

anxious *adjective* **1** (*worried*)
besorgt; **2** (*keen*) **she was anxious
to see him** sie wollte ihn unbedingt
sehen.

anxiously *adverb* ängstlich.

any *adjective* **1** irgendein; **if they had
any plan** wenn sie irgendeinen Plan
hätten; **2** (*with plural nouns*)
irgendwelche; **if they had any plans**
wenn sie irgendwelche Pläne hätten;
3 (*in questions 'any' is often not
translated*) **have you got any
stamps?** haben Sie Briefmarken?;
have we got any milk? haben wir
Milch?; **4 not any** kein; **they
haven't made any plans** sie haben
keine Pläne gemacht; **we haven't
got any milk** wir haben keine Milch;
5 (*no matter which*) jeder
beliebige/jede beliebige/jedes

beliebige; **you can have any colour**
du kannst jede beliebige Farbe
haben.
pronoun **1** (*in questions, replacing
the noun*) welcher/welche/welches;
(*replacing a plural noun*) welche;
**I need some flour, have you got
any?** ich brauche Mehl, hast du
welches?; **2 not any** keiner/keine/
keins; (*replacing a plural noun*)
keine; **I don't want any** ich will
keins haben; **there aren't any** es gibt
keine; **3** (*no matter which one*)
irgendein; **'which chair can I take?'
– 'take any of them'** 'welchen
Stuhl kann ich nehmen?' – 'nimm
irgendeinen'.
adverb **1** (*in questions*) noch; **would
you like any more?** möchtest du
noch etwas?; **2** (*with negatives*) **I
can't see him any more** ich kann
ihn nicht mehr sehen.

anybody, anyone *pronoun* **1** (*in
questions*) jemand; **does anybody
want some tea?** möchte jemand
Tee?; **is anybody in?** ist
irgendjemand da?; **2 not anybody**
niemand; **there isn't anybody in the
office** niemand ist im Büro;
3 (*absolutely anybody*) jeder;
anybody can do it das kann jeder.

anyhow *adverb* SEE anyway.

anyone *pronoun* SEE anybody.

anything *pronoun* **1** (*in questions*)
irgendetwas △; **is there anything I
can do to help?** kann ich irgendwie
helfen?; **2 not anything** nichts;
there isn't anything on the table
auf dem Tisch liegt nichts;
3 (*anything at all*) alles; **I'll do**

△ NEW SPELLING: *See page xii*

anything to help him ich werde alles tun, um ihm zu helfen.

anyway, anyhow *adverb*
1 jedenfalls; **anyway, I'll ring you before I leave** jedenfalls ruf ich dich an, bevor ich fahre; **2** sowieso.

anywhere *adverb* **1** (*in questions*) irgendwo; **have you seen my keys anywhere?** hast du meine Schlüssel irgendwo gesehen?; **2** *not anywhere* nirgends; **I can't find my keys anywhere** ich kann meine Schlüssel nirgends finden; **3** (*to any place*) irgendwohin; **are you going anywhere tomorrow?** fahrt ihr morgen irgendwohin?; **put your cases down anywhere** stell deine Koffer irgendwohin; **4** (*in any place*) überall; **you can get that anywhere** das kann man überall kriegen.

apart *adjective, adverb* **1** (*separate*) auseinander; **they've been apart for some time** sie sind schon lange auseinander; **2 to be two metres apart** zwei Meter auseinander liegen; **3** *apart from* außer (+DAT); **apart from my brother everybody was there** außer meinem Bruder waren alle da.

apologize *verb* sich entschuldigen; **he apologized for his mistake** er enschuldigte sich für seinen Fehler; **he apologized to Sam** er hat sich bei Sam entschuldigt.

apology *noun* Entschuldigung die (PL die Entschuldigungen).

apostrophe *noun* Apostroph der (PL die Apostrophe).

apparent *adjective* offensichtlich.

apparently *adverb* offensichtlich.

appeal *noun* Appell der (PL die Appelle).
verb **1 to appeal for something** um etwas ←(ACC) bitten ◇; **2 to appeal to somebody** sich an jemanden wenden ◇; **horror films don't appeal to me** Horrorfilme sind nicht mein Geschmack.

appear *verb* **1** erscheinen ◇ (PERF sein); **Mick appeared at breakfast** Mick erschien zum Frühstück; **2 to appear on television** im Fernsehen auftreten ◇ SEP (PERF sein); **3** (*seem*) scheinen ◇; **it appears that somebody has stolen the key** es scheint, dass jemand den Schlüssel gestohlen hat.

appendicitis *noun* Blinddarmentzündung die.

appetite *noun* Appetit der; **it'll spoil your appetite** das verdirbt dir den Appetit.

applaud *verb* Beifall klatschen.

applause *noun* Beifall der.

apple *noun* Apfel der (PL die Äpfel).

apple tree *noun* Apfelbaum der (PL die Apfelbäume).

applicant *noun* Bewerber der (PL die Bewerber), Bewerberin die (PL die Bewerberinnen).

application *noun* Bewerbung die (PL die Bewerbungen).

application form *noun* (*for a job*) Bewerbungsformular das (PL die Bewerbungsformulare).

◇ IRREGULAR VERB: *See the verb table in the centre of the dictionary*

apply verb 1 to apply for a job sich um eine Stellung bewerben ◇; 2 to apply for university sich um einen Studienplatz bewerben ◇; 3 to apply for a passport einen Pass beantragen; 4 to apply to zutreffen ◇ SEP auf (+ACC); that doesn't apply to students das trifft nicht auf Studenten zu.

appointment noun Termin der (PL die Termine); to make a dental appointment einen Termin mit dem Zahnarzt vereinbaren; I've got a hair appointment at four ich bin um vier beim Friseur angemeldet.

appreciate verb I appreciate your advice ich bin dir für deinen Rat dankbar; I'd appreciate it if you could tidy up afterwards es wäre nett von dir, wenn du danach aufräumen würdest.

apprentice noun Lehrling der (PL die Lehrlinge).

apprenticeship noun Lehre die (PL die Lehren).

approve verb to approve of something mit etwas ←(DAT) einverstanden sein; they don't approve of her friends sie sind nicht mit ihren Freunden einverstanden.

approximate adjective ungefähr.

approximately adverb ungefähr; approximately fifty people ungefähr fünfzig Personen.

apricot noun Aprikose die (PL die Aprikosen).

April noun April der; in April im April.

April Fool noun (trick) Aprilscherz der (PL die Aprilscherze); April fool! April, April!

April Fool's Day noun der erste April.

apron noun Schürze die (PL die Schürzen).

Aquarius noun Wassermann der; Sharon's Aquarius Sharon ist Wassermann.

archaeologist noun Archäologe der (PL die Archäologen), Archäologin die (PL die Archäologinnen); she's an archaeologist sie ist Archäologin.

archaeology noun Archäologie die.

architect noun Architekt der (PL die Architekten), Architektin die (PL die Architektinnen); he's an architect er ist Architekt.

architecture noun Architektur die.

are verb SEE **be**.

area noun 1 (part of a town, a region) Gegend die (PL die Gegenden); a nice area eine nette Gegend; in the Leeds area in der Gegend von Leeds; 2 picnic area der Picknickplatz.

argue verb sich streiten ◇; to argue about something sich über etwas ←(ACC) streiten; they're arguing about the result sie streiten sich über das Ergebnis.

argument noun Streit der (PL die Streite); to get into an argument with somebody mit jemandem in

Streit geraten ◇; **to have an argument** sich streiten ◇.

Aries noun Widder der; **Pauline's Aries** Pauline ist Widder.

arm noun Arm der (PL die Arme); **arm in arm** Arm in Arm; **to break your arm** sich ←(DAT) den Arm brechen.

armchair noun Sessel der (PL die Sessel).

armed adjective bewaffnet.

army noun 1 Heer das (PL die Heere); 2 (profession) Militär das; **to join the army** zum Militär gehen.

around preposition, adverb 1 (with time of day) gegen (+ACC); **we'll be there around ten** wir werden gegen zehn da sein; 2 (with ages or at 'ounts) etwa; **she's around fifteen** sie ist etwa fünfzehn; **we need around six kilos** wir brauchen etwa sechs Kilo; 3 (with dates) um (+ACC); **around 10 August** um den 10. August; 4 (surrounding) um … herum; **the countryside around Edinburgh** die Landschaft um Edinburgh herum; 5 (near) **is there a post office around here?** gibt es hier in der Gegend eine Post?; **is Phil around?** ist Phil da?

arrange verb to arrange something etwas vereinbaren; **we've arranged to go to the cinema on Saturday** wir haben vereinbart, am Samstag ins Kino zu gehen.

arrest noun **to be under arrest** verhaftet sein.
verb verhaften.

◇ **IRREGULAR VERB: See the verb table in the centre of the dictionary.**

arrival noun Ankunft die (PL die Ankünfte).

arrive verb ankommen ◇ SEP (PERF sein); **they arrived at 3 p.m.** sie kamen um fünfzehn Uhr an.

art noun 1 Kunst die (PL die Künste); **modern art** moderne Kunst; 2 (school subject) Kunsterziehung die.

art gallery noun Kunstgalerie die (PL die Kunstgalerien).

article noun 1 (in a newspaper or magazine) Artikel der (PL die Artikel); 2 (object) Stück das (PL die Stücke).

artificial adjective künstlich.

artist noun Künstler der (PL die Künstler), Künstlerin die (PL die Künstlerinnen); **he's an artist** er ist Künstler.

artistic adjective künstlerisch.

art school noun Kunsthochschule die (PL die Kunsthochschulen).

as conjunction, adverb 1 wie; **as you know** wie du weißt; **as usual** wie üblich; **as I told you** wie ich dir gesagt habe; 2 (because) da; **as there was no bus, we took a taxi** da es keinen Bus gab, nahmen wir ein Taxi; 3 **as … as** so … wie; **he's as tall as his brother** er ist so groß wie sein Bruder; **come as quickly as possible** komm so schnell wie möglich; 4 **as much … as** so viel … wie; **you have as much time as I do** du hast so viel Zeit wie ich; 5 **as many … as** so viele … wie; **we have**

as many problems as he does wir haben so viele Probleme wie er; **6 as long as** vorausgesetzt; **we'll go tomorrow, as long as it's a nice day** wir gehen morgen, vorausgesetzt es ist schönes Wetter; **7 for as long as** solange; **you can stay for as long as you like** du kannst bleiben, solange du willst; **8 as soon as possible** so bald wie möglich; **9 to work as** arbeiten als; **he works as a waiter in the evenings** abends arbeitet er als Kellner; **as well** auch.

ash noun **1** Asche die (PL die Aschen); **2** (tree) Esche die (PL die Eschen).

ashamed adjective **to be ashamed of something** sich über etwas ←(ACC) schämen; **you should be ashamed of yourself!** du solltest dich schämen!

ashtray noun Aschenbecher der (PL die Aschenbecher).

Asia noun Asien das; **in Asia** in Asien.

ask verb **1** fragen; **to ask somebody something** jemanden nach etwas ←(DAT) fragen; **I asked him the way** ich fragte ihn nach dem Weg; **2 to ask something** um etwas ←(ACC) bitten; **to ask somebody a favour** jemanden um einen Gefallen bitten; **to ask somebody to do something** jemanden bitten, etwas zu tun; **ask Danny to give you a hand** bitte Danny, dir zu helfen; **3 to ask somebody a question** jemandem eine Frage stellen; **I asked him a few questions** ich habe ihn ein paar Fragen gestellt; **4** einladen ◆ SEP;

they've asked us to a party sie haben uns auf eine Party eingeladen; **Paul's asked Janie out on Friday** Paul hat Janie Freitag eingeladen; **5 to ask for** verlangen; **how much are they asking for the car?** wieviel verlangen sie für das Auto?

asparagus noun Spargel der (PL die Spargel).

aspirin noun Aspirin das.

assembly noun (at school) Morgenandacht die (PL die Morgenandachten).

assignment noun (at school) Aufgabe die (PL die Aufgaben).

assistance noun Hilfe die.

assistant noun **1** Helfer der (PL die Helfer), Helferin die (PL die Helferinnen); **2** (in school) Assistent der (PL die Assistenten), Assistentin die (PL die Assistentinnen); **3 shop assistant** der Verkäufer, die Verkäuferin.

association noun Verband der (PL die Verbände).

assorted adjective gemischt.

assortment noun Auswahl die.

assume verb annehmen ◆ SEP; **I assume** ich nehme an.

asthma noun Asthma das.

astrology noun Astrologie die.

astronaut noun Astronaut der (PL die Astronauten), Astronautin die (PL die Astronautinnen).

astronomy noun Astronomie die.

△ NEW SPELLING: See page xii

at preposition 1 in (+DAT); **at school** in der Schule; **at my office** in meinem Büro; **at the supermarket** im Supermarkt; **2 an** (+DAT); **at the station** am Bahnhof; **at the bus stop** an der Bushaltestelle; **3 bei** (+DAT); **at the dentist** beim Zahnarzt; **at discussions** bei Besprechungen; **at Emma's** bei Emma; **she's at her brother's this evening** sie ist heute Abend bei ihrem Bruder; **at the hairdresser's** beim Friseur; **4 at a party** auf einer Party; **5 at home** zu Hause; **6** (talking about the time) um; **at eight o'clock** um acht Uhr; **7 at night** nachts; **at Christmas** zu Weihnachten; **at the weekend** am Wochenende; **8 at last** endlich; **she's found a job at last** sie hat endlich einen Job gefunden.

athlete noun Athlet der (PL die Athleten), Athletin die (PL die Athletinnen).

athletic adjective sportlich.

athletics noun Leichtathletik die.

Atlantic noun **the Atlantic** (Ocean) der Atlantik.

atlas noun Atlas der (PL die Atlanten).

atmosphere noun Atmosphäre die (PL die Atmosphären).

attach verb befestigen.

attached adjective (emotionally) **to be attached to somebody/ something** an jemandem/ etwas ←(DAT) hängen ◇.

attack noun Angriff der (PL die Angriffe).
verb 1 angreifen ◇ SEP; 2 (mug or raid) überfallen ◇.

attempt noun Versuch der (PL die Versuche); **at the first attempt** beim ersten Versuch.
verb **to attempt to do something** versuchen, etwas zu tun.

attend verb teilnehmen ◇ SEP an (+DAT); **to attend a meeting** an einer Besprechung teilnehmen; **to attend an evening class** einen Abendkurs besuchen.

attention noun
1 Aufmerksamkeit die; **to pay attention** aufpassen SEP; **I wasn't paying attention** ich habe nicht aufgepasst; **2 he wasn't paying attention to the teacher** er hörte dem Lehrer nicht zu.

attic noun Dachboden der (PL die Dachböden); **in the attic** auf dem Dachboden.

attitude noun 1 (way of thinking) Einstellung die; 2 (way of acting) Haltung die.

attract verb anziehen ◇ SEP.

attraction noun 1 Anziehung die; 2 (a thing that attracts) Attraktion die (PL die Attraktionen); **the whale was a big attraction** der Wal war eine große Attraktion.

attractive adjective attraktiv.

aubergine noun Aubergine die (PL die Auberginen).

audience noun Publikum das; **the television audience** die Fernsehzuschauer (plural).

◇ IRREGULAR VERB: See the verb table in the centre of the dictionary

August noun August der; **in August** im August.

aunt, auntie noun Tante die (PL die Tanten).

au pair noun Aupairmädchen △ das (PL die Aupairmädchen); **I'm looking for a job as an au pair** ich suche eine Aupair-Stelle.

Australia noun Australien das; **to Australia** nach Australien.

Australian noun Australier der (PL die Australier), Australierin die (PL die Australierinnen). adjective australisch; **she's Australian** sie ist Australierin.

Austria noun Österreich das; **in Austria** in Österreich.

Austrian noun Österreicher der (PL die Österreicher), Österreicherin die (PL die Österreicherinnen). adjective österreichisch; **he's Austrian** er ist Österreicher.

author noun Autor der (PL die Autoren), Autorin die (PL die Autorinnen).

autograph noun Autogramm das (PL die Autogramme).

automatic adjective automatisch.

automatically adverb automatisch.

autumn noun Herbst der (PL die Herbste); **in autumn** im Herbst.

available adjective (on sale) erhältlich.

average noun Durchschnitt der (PL die Durchschnitte); **on average** im Durchschnitt; **above average** über

dem Durchschnitt. adjective durchschnittlich; **the average height** die durchschnittliche Größe.

avocado noun Avocado die (PL die Avocados).

avoid verb 1 vermeiden ◇; **to avoid doing something** es vermeiden, etwas zu tun; **I avoid speaking to him** ich vermeide es, mit ihm zu reden; 2 (keep away from somebody or a place) meiden ◇; **she avoids me** sie meidet mich.

awake adjective **to be awake** wach sein; **are you still awake?** bist du noch wach?

award noun Preis der (PL die Preise); **to win an award** einen Preis gewinnen.

aware adjective **to be aware of a problem** sich ←(DAT) eines Problems bewusst sein; **I'm aware of the danger** ich bin mir der Gefahr bewusst; **as far as I'm aware** soweit ich weiß.

away adverb 1 **to be away** nicht da sein; **I'll be away next week** ich bin nächste Woche nicht da; 2 **to go away** verreisen (PERF sein); **Laura's gone away for a week** Laura ist auf eine Woche verreist; **go away!** geh weg!; 3 **to run away** weglaufen ◇ SEP (PERF sein); **the thieves ran away** die Diebe liefen weg; 4 **the school is two kilometres away** die Schule ist zwei Kilometer entfernt; **how far away is it?** wie weit entfernt ist es?; **not far away** nicht weit entfernt; 5 **to put something away** etwas wegräumen SEP; **I'm just putting my**

books away ich räume gerade meine Bücher weg; **6 to give something away** etwas weggeben ◇ SEP; *(as a present)* etwas verschenken; **she's given away all her cassettes** sie hat alle ihre Kassetten verschenkt.

awful *adjective* furchtbar; **the film was awful** der Film war furchtbar; **I feel awful** *(ill)* ich fühle mich furchtbar; **I feel awful about it** es ist mir furchtbar unangenehm; **an awful lot of mistakes** furchtbar viele Fehler.

awkward *adjective* **1** schwierig; **it's an awkward situation** das ist eine schwierige Situation; **it's a bit awkward** das ist ein bisschen schwierig; **an awkward child** ein schwieriges Kind; **2 an awkward question** eine peinliche Frage.

B b

baby *noun* Baby *das* (PL die Babys).

babysit *verb* babysitten.

babysitter *noun* Babysitter *der* (PL die Babysitter).

babysitting *noun* Babysitten *das*.

back *noun* **1** *(of a person or animal)* Rücken *der* (PL die Rücken); **he did it behind my back** er hat es hinter meinem Rücken getan; **2** *(of a piece of paper, cheque, or building)* Rückseite *die* (PL die Rückseiten); **on the back** auf der Rückseite; **3 the**

back of your hand der Handrücken; **4 at the back** hinten; **at the back of the room** hinten im Zimmer; **we sat at the back** wir saßen hinten; **a garden at the back of the house** ein Garten hinter dem Haus; **5** *(of a chair or sofa)* Rückenlehne *die* (PL die Rückenlehnen); **6** *(in football or hockey)* Verteidiger *der* (PL die Verteidiger); **left back** *der* Linksverteidiger.

adjective **1 the back seat** *(of a car)* der Rücksitz; **2 the back door** die Hintertür; **the back garden** der Garten hinter dem Haus.

adverb **1** zurück; **there and back** hin und zurück; **to go back** *(on foot)* zurückgehen ◇ SEP *(PERF sein)* *(in a vehicle)* zurückfahren ◇ SEP *(PERF sein)*; **2 to come back** zurückkommen ◇ SEP *(PERF sein)*; **they've come back from Italy** sie sind aus Italien zurückgekommen; **I'll be back at 8 o'clock** ich bin um acht Uhr zurück; **Sue's not back yet** Sue ist noch nicht zurück; **3 to phone back** zurückrufen ◇ SEP; **I'll ring back later** ich rufe dich später zurück; **4 to give something back to somebody** jemandem etwas zurückgeben ◇ SEP; **give it back!** gib es zurück!

verb *(bet on)* setzen auf (+ACC).

- **to back up** *(computing)* sichern; **to back up a file** eine Sicherungsdatei machen.

- **to back somebody up** jemanden unterstützen.

backache *noun* Rückenschmerzen *(plural)*.

◇ IRREGULAR VERB: See the verb table in the centre of the dictionary

background noun 1 (of a person) Verhältnisse (plural); she comes from a poor background sie kommt aus ärmlichen Verhältnissen; 2 (in a picture, view, or situation) Hintergrund der (PL die Hintergründe); background noise Hintergrundgeräusche (plural); 3 (to events or problems) Hintergründe (plural).

backing noun 1 (on sticky-back plastic, for example) Verstärkung die (PL die Verstärkungen); 2 (moral support) Unterstützung die; 3 (in music) Begleitung die; a backing group eine Begleitband.

backpack noun Rucksack der (PL die Rucksäcke).
verb to go backpacking trampen (PERF sein).

back seat noun Rücksitz der (PL die Rücksitze).

backstroke noun Rückenschwimmen das.

back to front adverb verkehrt herum; your jumper's back to front du hast deinen Pullover verkehrt herum an.

backup noun 1 (support) Unterstützung die; 2 (in computing) Sicherungskopie die (PL die Sicherungskopien); a backup disk eine Sicherungsdiskette.

backwards adverb 1 rückwärts; 2 to lean backwards sich nach hinten lehnen; to fall backwards nach hinten fallen.

bacon noun Speck der; bacon and eggs Eier mit Speck.

bad adjective 1 (not good) schlecht; a bad idea eine schlechte Idee; a bad meal ein schlechtes Essen; his new film's not bad sein neuer Film ist nicht schlecht; it's bad for your health das ist ungesund; I'm bad at physics ich bin schlecht in Physik; 2 (serious) schlimm; a bad mistake ein schlimmer Fehler; a bad cold eine schlimme Erkältung; 3 a bad accident ein schwerer Unfall; 4 (rotten) schlecht; to go bad schlecht werden; 5 a bad apple ein fauler Apfel; 6 bad language Kraftausdrücke (plural); ★ too bad! schade!, so ein Pech!

badge noun Abzeichen das (PL die Abzeichen).

badly adverb 1 (poorly) schlecht; he writes badly er schreibt schlecht; I slept badly ich habe schlecht geschlafen; 2 (seriously) schwer; they were badly injured sie waren schwer verletzt; 3 (very much) dringend; to need something badly etwas dringend brauchen.

bad-mannered adjective to be bad-mannered schlechte Manieren haben.

badminton noun Badminton das.

bad-tempered adjective schlecht gelaunt △; a bad-tempered old man ein schlecht gelaunter alter Mann.

bag noun 1 Tasche die (PL die Taschen); 2 (made of paper or plastic) Tüte die (PL die Tüten).

△ NEW SPELLING: See page xii

baggage *noun* Gepäck *das*.

bagpipes *plural noun* Dudelsack *der*.

bags *plural noun* Gepäck *das*; **to pack your bags** sein Gepäck packen; ★ **to have bags under your eyes** Ringe unter den Augen haben (*informal*).

bake *verb* **1** backen; **to bake a cake** einen Kuchen backen; **2 to bake vegetables** Gemüse backen.

baked *adjective* (*fish or fruit*) überbacken; **baked apples** Bratäpfel; **2 a baked potato** eine (in der Schale) gebackene Kartoffel.

baked beans *plural noun* Bohnen in Tomatensoße.

baker *noun* Bäcker *der* (PL die Bäcker); **to go to the baker's** zum Bäcker gehen.

balance *noun* **1** Gleichgewicht *das*; **to lose your balance** das Gleichgewicht verlieren; **2** (*in a bank account*) Kontostand *der*.

balanced *adjective* ausgeglichen.

balcony *noun* Balkon *der* (PL die Balkons).

bald *adjective* **1** kahl; **2** (*of a person*) kahlköpfig; **to go bald** eine Glatze bekommen.

ball *noun* **1** (*for tennis, football, or golf*) Ball *der* (PL die Bälle); **2** (*for billiards, croquet*) Kugel *die* (PL die Kugeln); **3** (*of string or wool*) Knäuel *das* (PL die Knäuel).

ballet *noun* Ballett *das* (PL die Ballette).

ballet dancer *noun* Balletttänzer △ *der* (PL die Balletttänzer); Balletttänzerin △ *die* (PL die Balletttänzerinnen).

balloon *noun* **1** Luftballon *der* (PL die Luftballons); **2** (*hot-air*) Ballon *der* (PL die Ballons).

ballpoint (pen) *noun* Kugelschreiber *der* (PL die Kugelschreiber).

ban *noun* **1** Verbot *das* (PL die Verbote); **a ban on smoking** ein Rauchverbot.
verb verbieten ◇; **to ban someone from smoking** jemandem verbieten zu rauchen.

banana *noun* **1** Banane *die* (PL die Bananen); **2 a banana yoghurt** ein Bananenjoghurt.

band *noun* **1** (*playing music*) Band *die* (PL die Bands); **rock band** die Rockband; **brass band** die Blaskapelle; **2 rubber band** das Gummiband.

bandage *noun* Verband *der* (PL die Verbände).
verb verbinden ◇.

bang *noun* (*noise*) Knall *der* (PL die Knalle).
verb **1** (*hit, knock*) schlagen ◇; **he banged his fist on the table** er hat mit der Faust auf den Tisch geschlagen; **to bang on the door** gegen die Tür schlagen; **2 I banged my head on the door** ich habe mir den Kopf an der Tür gestoßen; **3 to bang into something** gegen etwas ←(ACC) knallen; **4** (*shut loudly*) zuknallen SEP; **he banged the door**

er knallte die Tür zu.
exclamation peng!

bank *noun* 1 (*for money*) Bank *die* (PL *die* Banken); **I'm going to the bank** ich gehe auf die Bank; 2 (*of a river or lake*) Ufer *das* (PL *die* Ufer).

bank account *noun* Bankkonto *das* (PL *die* Bankkonten).

bank balance *noun* Kontostand *der* (PL *die* Kontostände).

bank card *noun* Scheckkarte *die* (PL *die* Scheckkarten).

bank holiday *noun* gesetzliche Feiertag *der* (PL *die* gesetzlichen Feiertage).

banknote *noun* Geldschein *der* (PL *die* Geldscheine).

bank statement *noun* Kontoauszug *der* (PL *die* Kontoauszüge).

bar *noun* 1 (*selling drinks*) Bar *die* (PL *die* Bars); **Janet works in a bar** Janet arbeitet in einer Bar; 2 (*counter*) Theke *die* (PL *die* Theken); **on the bar** auf der Theke; 3 **a bar of chocolate** eine Tafel Schokolade; 4 **a bar of soap** ein Stück Seife; 5 (*made of wood or metal*) Stange *die* (PL *die* Stangen); **an iron bar** eine Eisenstange; 6 (*in music*) Takt *der* (PL *die* Takte).

barbecue *noun* 1 (*apparatus*) Grill *der* (PL *die* Grills); 2 (*party*) Grillfest *das* (PL *die* Grillfeste). *verb* **to barbecue a chicken** ein Hühnchen grillen; **barbecued chicken** gegrilltes Hühnchen.

bare *adjective* nackt.

barefoot *adjective* **to be barefoot** barfuß sein; **to walk barefoot** barfuß gehen.

bargain *noun* (*a good buy*) gute Kauf *der* (PL *die* guten Käufe); **I got a bargain** ich habe einen guten Kauf gemacht; **it's a bargain!** ein guter Kauf!

bark *noun* 1 (*of a tree*) Rinde *die* (PL *die* Rinden); 2 (*of a dog*) Bellen *das*. *verb* bellen.

barmaid *noun* Bardame *die* (PL *die* Bardamen).

barman *noun* Barkeeper *der* (PL *die* Barkeeper).

barn *noun* Scheune *die* (PL *die* Scheunen).

barrel *noun* Fass △ *das* (PL *die* Fässer).

barrier *noun* Absperrung *die* (PL *die* Absperrungen).

base *noun* (*bottom part*) Fuß *der* (PL *die* Füße).

baseball *noun* Baseball *der*.

based *adjective* 1 **to be based on** basieren auf (+DAT); **the film is based on a true story** der Film basiert auf einer wahren Geschichte; 2 **to be based in** wohnen in (+DAT); **he's based in Bristol** er wohnt in Bristol.

basement *noun* Kellergeschoss △ *das* (PL *die* Kellergeschosse).

△ NEW SPELLING: See page xii

bash noun 1 Schlag der (PL die Schläge); 2 I'll have a bash ich probier's mal.
verb I bashed my head ich habe mir den Kopf angehauen.

basic adjective 1 grundlegend, Grund-; **basic knowledge** Grundkenntnisse (plural); **her basic salary** ihr Grundgehalt; 2 **the basic problem** das Hauptproblem; 3 (not luxurious) einfach.

basically adverb 1 grundsätzlich; **it's basically all right** grundsätzlich ist es okay; 2 **basically, I don't want to come** eigentlich will ich nicht kommen.

basics plural noun **the basics** das Wesentliche.

basin noun Becken das (PL die Becken).

basis noun 1 Basis die; 2 **on a regular basis** regelmäßig.

basket noun Korb der (PL die Körbe); **a basket of apples** ein Korb Äpfel; **waste-paper basket** der Papierkorb.

basketball noun Basketball der.

bass noun 1 Bass △ der (PL die Bässe); 2 **double bass** der Kontrabass △.

bass guitar noun Bassgitarre △ die (PL die Bassgitarren).

bassoon noun Fagott das (PL die Fagotte).

bat noun 1 (for games) Schläger der (PL die Schläger); 2 (animal) Fledermaus die (PL die Fledermäuse).

bath noun 1 Bad das (PL die Bäder); **to have a bath** baden; 2 (tub) Badewanne die (PL die Badewannen).

bathroom noun Badezimmer das (PL die Badezimmer).

baths plural noun Badeanstalt die (PL die Badeanstalten).

bath towel noun Badetuch das (PL die Badetücher).

batter noun Teig der (PL die Teige); **fish in batter** ausgebackener Fisch.

battery noun Batterie die (PL die Batterien).

battle noun 1 (in war) Schlacht die (PL die Schlachten); 2 (contest) Kampf der (PL die Kämpfe).

Bavaria noun Bayern das.

bay noun Bucht die (PL die Buchten).

BC (before Christ) v.Chr. (vor Christus).

be verb 1 sein ✧ (PERF sein); **Melanie is in the kitchen** Melanie ist in der Küche; **where is the butter?** wo ist die Butter?; **I'm tired** ich bin müde; **when we were in Germany** als wir in Deutschland waren; 2 (with jobs and professions) sein ✧ (PERF sein); **she's a teacher** sie ist Lehrerin; **he's a taxi driver** er ist Taxifahrer; 3 (in clock times, days of the week, dates, and age) sein ✧ (PERF sein); **it's three o'clock** es ist drei Uhr; **it's half past five** es ist halb sechs; **what day is it today?** welcher Tag ist heute?; **it's Tuesday today** heute ist Dienstag; **it's the twentieth of May** heute ist der zwanzigste Mai; **what's**

✧ IRREGULAR VERB: See the verb table in the centre of the dictionary

the date today? der Wievielte ist heute?; **how old are you?** wie alt bist du?; **I'm fifteen** ich bin fünfzehn; 4 (*cold, hot, ill*) sein ✧ (PERF *sein*); **I'm hot** mir ist heiß; **I'm cold** mir ist kalt; **to be ill** krank sein; 5 (*weather*) sein ✧ (PERF *sein*); **it's cold today** heute ist es kalt; **it's a nice day** es ist schönes Wetter; **it's raining** es regnet; 6 **I'm hungry** ich habe Hunger; **it's thirsty** sie hat Durst; 7 (*saying how much something costs*) kosten; **how much are the bananas?** wie viel kosten die Bananen?; 8 (*go, come, or visit*) sein ✧ (PERF *sein*); **I've never been to Berlin** ich bin noch nie in Berlin gewesen; **have you been to England before?** bist du schon einmal in England gewesen?; **has the postman been?** war der Briefträger schon da?; 9 (*forming the passive*) werden ✧ (PERF *sein*); **to be loved** geliebt werden; **he has been promoted** er ist befördert worden; 10 **there is/are** es gibt; **are there any shops near here?** gibt es hier in der Nähe Geschäfte?

beach *noun* Strand *der* (PL die Strände); **to go to the beach** zum Strand gehen; **on the beach** am Strand.

bead *noun* Perle *die* (PL die Perlen).

beam *noun* 1 (*of light*) Strahl *der* (PL die Strahlen); 2 (*for a roof*) Balken *der* (PL die Balken).

bean *noun* Bohne *die* (PL die Bohnen); **green beans** grüne Bohnen.

bear *noun* Bär *der* (PL die Bären). *verb* 1 ertragen ✧; **I can't bear the idea** ich kann den Gedanken nicht ertragen; 2 **to bear something in mind** an etwas ◆–(ACC) denken; **I'll bear it in mind** ich denke daran.

beard *noun* Bart *der* (PL die Bärte).

bearded *adjective* bärtig.

bearings *plural noun* **to get one's bearings** sich orientieren.

beast *noun* 1 (*animal*) Tier *das* (PL die Tiere); 2 **you beast!** du Biest!

beat *noun* (*in music*) Takt *der*. *verb* 1 schlagen ✧; (*defeat*) **we beat them!** wir haben sie geschlagen; 2 **you can't beat a good meal** es geht doch nichts über ein gutes Essen.

● **to beat somebody up** jemanden verprügeln.

beautiful *adjective* schön.

beauty *noun* 1 Schönheit *die* (PL die Schönheiten); 2 **the beauty of it is that …** das Schöne daran ist, dass …

because *conjunction* 1 weil; **because it's cold** weil es kalt ist; 2 **because of** wegen (+GEN); **because of the accident** wegen des Unfalls; **because of you** deinetwegen.

become *verb* werden ✧ (PERF *sein*); **she's become a painter** sie ist Malerin geworden.

bed *noun* 1 Bett *das* (PL die Betten); **double bed** das Doppelbett; **in bed** im Bett; **to go to bed** ins Bett gehen; 2 (*flower bed*) Beet *das* (PL die Beete).

bedclothes *plural noun*
Bettwäsche *die*.

bedding *noun* Bettzeug *das*.

bedroom *noun* Schlafzimmer *das*
(PL *die* Schlafzimmer); **bedroom
furniture** Schlafzimmermöbel
(*plural*); **my bedroom window**
mein Schlafzimmerfenster.

bedside table *noun* Nachttisch
der.

bedsit, bedsitter *noun* möblierte
Zimmer *das* (PL *die* möblierten
Zimmer).

bedspread *noun* Tagesdecke *die*
(PL *die* Tagesdecken).

bedtime *noun* Schlafenszeit *die*; **at
bedtime** vor dem Schlafengehen.

bee *noun* Biene *die* (PL *die* Bienen).

beech *noun* Buche *die* (PL *die*
Buchen).

beef *noun* Rindfleisch *das*; **we had
roast beef** wir haben Rinderbraten
gegessen.

beefburger *noun* Hamburger *der*
(PL *die* Hamburger).

beer *noun* Bier *das* (PL *die* Biere);
two beers please zwei Bier bitte;
beer can die Bierdose.

beetle *noun* Käfer *der* (PL *die* Käfer).

beetroot *noun* Rote Bete △ *die*.

before *preposition* 1 vor (+DAT);
before Monday vor Montag; **he left
before me** er ist vor mir gegangen;
the day before the wedding am Tag
vor der Hochzeit; **the day before**
am Tag zuvor; **the day before**

yesterday vorgestern; **the week
before** in der Woche zuvor;
3 (*already*) schon einmal; **I've seen
him before somewhere** ich habe
ihn schon einmal irgendwo gesehen;
I had seen the film before ich hatte
den Film schon einmal gesehen.
conjunction bevor; **I closed the
windows before leaving** (or before
I left) ich habe die Fenster
zugemacht, bevor ich wegging;
before the train leaves bevor der
Zug abfährt; **oh, before I forget ...**
bevor ich es vergesse ...

beforehand *adverb* (*ahead of time*)
vorher; **phone beforehand** rufe
vorher an.

beg *verb* 1 betteln; **to beg for money**
um Geld betteln; 2 (*ask*) bitten ✧;
he begged her not to say anything
er bat sie, nichts zu sagen; 3 **I beg
your pardon** entschuldigen Sie
bitte.

begin *verb* anfangen ✧ SEP,
beginnen ✧; **the meeting begins at
ten** die Besprechung fängt um zehn
an; **the words beginning with P** die
Wörter, die mit P anfangen; **to begin
to do something** anfangen, etwas
zu tun; beginnen, etwas zu tun; **I'm
beginning to understand why ...**
ich beginne zu verstehen, warum ...

beginner *noun* Anfänger *der* (PL *die*
Anfänger), Anfängerin *die* (PL *die*
Anfängerinnen).

beginning *noun* Anfang *der* (PL *die*
Anfänge); **at the beginning** am
Anfang; **at the beginning of the
holidays** am Anfang der Ferien.

✧ IRREGULAR VERB: *See the verb table in the centre of the dictionary*

behave verb 1 sich benehmen ◇; he behaved badly er hat sich schlecht benommen; 2 to behave oneself sich benehmen ◇; behave yourself! benimm dich!

behaviour noun Benehmen das.

behind noun Hintern der (informal) (PL die Hintern). preposition, adverb 1 hinter (+DAT, or +ACC when there is movement towards a place); behind the sofa hinter dem Sofa; behind them hinter ihnen; the car behind das Auto hinter ihnen/uns; 2 to leave something behind (belongings) etwas vergessen.

beige adjective beige.

Belgian noun Belgier der (PL die Belgier), Belgierin die (PL die Belgierinnen).
adjective belgisch; he's Belgian er ist Belgier.

Belgium noun Belgien das; to Belgium nach Belgien.

belief noun Glaube der (PL die Glauben); his political beliefs seine politische Überzeugung.

believe verb 1 glauben; I believe so ich glaube schon; they believed what I said sie glaubten, was ich sagte; I don't believe you das glaube ich dir nicht; 2 to believe in something an etwas ←(ACC) glauben; to believe in God an Gott glauben.

bell noun 1 (in a church) Glocke die (PL die Glocken); 2 (on a door) Klingel die (PL die Klingeln); to ring the bell klingeln; 3 (for a cat or toy)

Glöckchen das (PL die Glöckchen);
★ that name rings a bell der Name sagt mir etwas (literally: says something to me).

belong verb 1 to belong to gehören (+DAT); that belongs to my mother das gehört meiner Mutter; 2 to belong to a club einem Klub angehören; 3 (go) gehören; where does this vase belong? wo gehört diese Vase hin?

belongings plural noun Sachen (plural); all my belongings alle meine Sachen.

below preposition unter (+DAT, or +ACC when there is movement towards a place); below the window unter dem Fenster; the flat below yours die Wohnung unter dir.
adverb 1 (further down) unten; he called from below er rief von unten; 2 the flat below die Wohnung darunter.

belt noun Gürtel der (PL die Gürtel).

bench noun Bank die (PL die Bänke).

bend noun 1 (in a road) Kurve die (PL die Kurven); 2 (in a river) Biegung die (PL die Biegungen).
verb 1 (make a bend in) biegen ◇ (a pipe or wire), beugen (your knee, arm, or head); 2 (curve) eine Biegung machen; 3 to bend down sich bücken.

beneath preposition unter (+DAT).

benefit noun 1 Vorteil der (PL die Vorteile); 2 unemployment benefit die Arbeitslosenunterstützung.

bent adjective verbogen.

△ NEW SPELLING: See page xii

beret noun Baskenmütze die (PL die Baskenmützen).

beside preposition (next to) neben (+DAT, or +ACC when there is movement towards a place); **she was sitting beside me** sie saß neben mir; **she sat down beside me** sie hat sich neben mich gesetzt; ★ **that's beside the point** das hat nichts damit zu tun.

besides adverb (anyway) außerdem; **besides, it's too late** außerdem ist es zu spät; (as well) **four dogs, and six cats besides** vier Hunde und außerdem sechs Katzen.

best adjective 1 bester/beste/bestes; **she's my best friend** sie ist meine beste Freundin; 2 **she's the best at tennis** im Tennis ist sie die Beste; **it's best to wait** das Beste ist zu warten.
adverb neben; **he plays best** er spielt am besten; **I like Munich best** München gefällt mir am besten; **best of all** alles am besten; **I like grapes best** ich mag Weintrauben am liebsten; ★ **all the best!** alles Gute!; ★ **to make the best of it** das Beste daraus machen; ★ **to do your best** sein Bestes tun; **I did my best to help her** ich habe mein Bestes getan, um ihr zu helfen.

bet noun Wette die (PL die Wetten).
verb wetten; **to bet on a horse** auf ein Pferd wetten; **I bet you he'll forget** ich wette mit dir, dass er es vergisst.

better adjective, adverb 1 besser; **she's found a better flat** sie hat eine bessere Wohnung gefunden; 2 **it works better than the other one** dieser geht besser als der andere; **even better** noch besser; **it's even better than before** das ist noch besser als vorher; 3 (less ill) **I'm better** es geht mir besser; **he's a bit better today** es geht ihm heute ein bisschen besser; **I feel better** ich fühle mich besser; 4 **to get better** besser werden; **my German is getting better** mein Deutsch wird besser; 5 **so much the better** umso besser; **the sooner the better** je eher, desto besser.
adverb **it's better to phone at once** es wäre besser, sofort anzurufen; **he'd better not go** er sollte besser nicht gehen; **I'd better go now** ich gehe jetzt besser.

better off adjective 1 (richer) besser gestellt; **they're better off than us** sie sind besser gestellt als wir; 2 (more comfortable) **to be better off** besser dran sein; **you'd be better off in bed** du wärst im Bett besser dran.

between preposition 1 zwischen (+DAT, or +ACC when there is movement towards a place); **between London and Dover** zwischen London und Dover; **between Monday and Friday** zwischen Montag und Freitag; 2 (sharing) unter (+DAT); **between ourselves** unter uns; **between the two of them** unter sich.

beyond preposition 1 (in space)

◊ **IRREGULAR VERB: See the verb table in the centre of the dictionary**

jenseits (+GEN); **beyond the border**
jenseits der Grenze; **2** (*in time*) nach
(+DAT); **beyond midnight** nach
Mitternacht; **3 it's beyond me!** das
ist mir unverständlich.

bicycle *noun* Fahrrad *das* (PL die
Fahrräder); **she rides a bicycle** sie
fährt Rad.

big *adjective* groß; **a big house** ein
großes Haus; **my big sister** meine
große Schwester; **a big mistake** ein
großer Fehler; **it's too big for me**
das ist mir zu groß.

big toe *noun* große Zehe *die* (PL die
großen Zehen).

bike *noun* Rad *das* (PL die Räder); **by
bike** mit dem Rad.

bilingual *adjective* zweisprachig.

bill *noun* Rechnung *die* (PL die
Rechnungen); **can we have the bill,
please?** die Rechnung bitte.

billiards *noun* Billard *das*; **to play
billiards** Billard spielen.

bin *noun* Mülleimer *der* (PL die
Mülleimer).

biochemistry *noun*
Biochemie *die*.

biology *noun* Biologie *die*.

bird *noun* Vogel *der* (PL die Vögel).

bird sanctuary *noun*
Vogelschutzgebiet *das* (PL die
Vogelschutzgebiete).

Biro™ *noun* Kugelschreiber *der* (PL
die Kugelschreiber).

birth *noun* Geburt *die* (PL die
Geburten).

birth certificate *noun*
Geburtsurkunde *die* (PL die
Geburtsurkunden).

birthday *noun* Geburtstag *der* (PL
die Geburtstage); **happy birthday!**
herzlichen Glückwunsch zum
Geburtstag!

birthday party *noun*
Geburtstagsfeier *die* (PL die
Geburtstagsfeiern).

biscuit *noun* Keks *der* (PL die
Kekse).

bit *noun* **1** (*piece*) Stückchen *das*; **a
bit of chocolate** ein Stückchen
Schokolade; **2** (*a small amount*) **a
bit of** ein bisschen △; **a bit of sugar**
ein bisschen Zucker, **3** (*in a book,
film, etc.*) Teil *der* (PL die Teile); **this
bit is brilliant** dieser Teil ist
glänzend; **4 a bit** ein bisschen △; **a
bit too early** ein bisschen zu früh;
wait a bit! warte ein bisschen !;
5 he's a bit of a show-off er ist ein
ziemlicher Angeber; **6 bit by bit**
nach und nach.

bite *noun* **1** (*snack*) Happen *der* (PL
die Happen); **we'll just have a bite
before we go** wir essen noch einen
kleinen Happen, bevor wir gehen;
2 (*from an insect*) Stich *der* (PL die
Stiche); **mosquito bite** der
Mückenstich; **3** (*from a dog*)
Biss △ *der* (PL die Bisse).
verb **1** (*person or dog*) beißen ◇;
2 (*insect*) stechen ◇.

bitter *adjective* (*taste*) bitter.

black *adjective* **1** schwarz; **my black
jacket** meine schwarze Jacke; **2 a
black man** ein Schwarzer; **a black
woman** eine Schwarze.

△ NEW SPELLING: *See page xii*

blackberry noun Brombeere die
(PL die Brombeeren).

blackbird noun Amsel die (PL die
Amseln).

blackboard noun Tafel die (PL die
Tafeln).

blackcurrant noun schwarze
Johannisbeere die (PL die schwarzen
Johannisbeeren).

blame noun Schuld die; **to take the
blame for something** die Schuld für
etwas ←(ACC) auf sich ←(ACC) nehmen;
to put the blame on somebody die
Schuld auf jemanden schieben.
verb **to blame somebody for
something** jemandem die Schuld
an etwas ←(DAT) geben; **they blamed
him for the accident** sie haben ihm
die Schuld an dem Unfall gegeben;
she is to blame for it sie ist daran
schuld; **I blame the parents** ich
gebe den Eltern Schuld; **I don't
blame you** ich kann es dir nicht
verdenken.

blank noun Lücke die (PL die
Lücken).
adjective **1** (page) leer; (tape or
disk) unbespielt; **2 blank cheque**
der Blankoscheck.

blanket noun Decke die (PL die
Decken).

blaze noun Feuer das (PL die Feuer).
verb brennen ◇.

bleach noun Bleichmittel das (PL
die Bleichmittel).

bleed verb bluten; **my nose is
bleeding** meine Nase blutet.

blend verb mischen.

blender noun Mixer der (PL die
Mixer).

bless verb segnen; **bless you!** (after
a sneeze) Gesundheit!

blind noun (in a window) Rollo das
(PL die Rollos).
adjective blind.

blister noun Blase die (PL die
Blasen).

block noun (a building or buildings)
Block der (PL die Blocks); **block of
flats** der Wohnblock; **office block**
das Bürohaus; **to drive round the
block** um den Block fahren.
verb **1** sperren (an exit or a road);
2 the sink's blocked das
Spülbecken ist verstopft.

blonde adjective blond.

blood noun Blut das.

blood test noun Blutprobe die (PL
die Blutproben).

blouse noun Bluse die (PL die
Blusen).

blow noun Schlag der (PL die
Schläge).
verb **1** (a person) blasen ◇; **2** (the
wind) wehen; **3 the bomb blew the
bridge to pieces** die Bombe hat die
Brücke in die Luft gesprengt; **4 to
blow your nose** sich ←(DAT) die Nase
putzen.
● **to blow something out** etwas
ausblasen ◇ SEP.
● **to blow up** (explode) explodieren
(PERF sein).
● **to blow something up** (a tyre or
balloon) etwas aufblasen ◇ SEP;
(with explosives) etwas sprengen.

◇ IRREGULAR VERB: See the verb table in the centre of the dictionary

blow-dry noun Föhnen das Δ; a cut and blow-dry Schneiden und Föhnen.

blue adjective blau; blue eyes blaue Augen.

blunder noun Fehler der (PL die Fehler).

blunt adjective 1 (a knife, pencil, or scissors) stumpf; 2 (a person or question) direkt.

blush verb erröten (PERF sein).

board noun 1 (plank, notice board, game) Brett das (PL die Bretter); chess board das Schachbrett; 2 (blackboard) Tafel die (PL die Tafeln); 3 (accommodation in a hotel) full board die Vollpension; half board die Halbpension; board and lodging Unterkunft und Verpflegung.

boarder noun (in a school) Internatsschüler der (PL die Internatsschüler), Internatsschülerin die (PL die Internatsschülerinnen).

board game noun Brettspiel das (PL die Brettspiele).

boarding noun (on a plane, train) Einsteigen das.

boarding card noun Bordkarte die (PL die Bordkarten).

boarding school noun Internat das (PL die Internate).

boast verb prahlen; he was boasting about his new bike er prahlte mit seinem neuen Rad.

boat noun 1 Boot das (PL die Boote); rowing boat das Ruderboot; 2 (larger boat) Schiff das (PL die Schiffe); to go by boat mit dem Schiff fahren.

body noun 1 Körper der (PL die Körper); 2 (corpse) Leiche die (PL die Leichen).

bodybuilding noun Bodybuilding das.

bodyguard noun Leibwächter der (PL die Leibwächter).

boil noun 1 to bring the water to the boil das Wasser zum Kochen bringen; 2 (swelling) Furunkel der (PL die Furunkel).
verb 1 kochen; the water's boiling das Wasser kocht; to boil vegetables Gemüse kochen; 2 (put the kettle on) to boil some water Wasser aufsetzen SEP

● to boil over überkochen SEP (PERF sein).

boiled egg noun gekochte Ei das (PL die gekochten Eier).

boiled potato noun Salzkartoffel die (PL die Salzkartoffeln).

boiler noun (for central heating) Heizkessel der (PL die Heizkessel).

boiling adjective (water) kochend; 2 it's boiling hot today heute ist es wahnsinnig heiß.

bolt noun (on a door) Riegel der (PL die Riegel).
verb 1 (lock) verriegeln; 2 (gobble down) runterschlingen ◇ SEP (informal).

bomb noun Bombe die (PL die Bomben).
verb bombardieren.

bombing noun 1 (in war) Bombardierung die (PL die Bombardierungen); 2 (a terrorist attack) Bombenattentat das (PL die Bombenattentate).

bone noun 1 Knochen der (PL die Knochen); 2 (of a fish) Gräte die (PL die Gräten).

bonfire noun Feuer das (PL die Feuer).

book noun 1 Buch das (PL die Bücher); **a book about dinosaurs** ein Buch über Dinosaurier; **my biology book** mein Biologiebuch; 2 (of stamps, tickets) Heft das (PL die Hefte); 3 **exercise book** das Heft; **cheque book** das Scheckbuch.
verb 1 buchen (holiday, flight); 2 bestellen (a table, theatre, or cinema tickets); **I booked a table for 8 p.m.** ich habe einen Tisch für zwanzig Uhr bestellt.

bookcase noun Bücherregal das (PL die Bücherregale).

booking noun (for a flight or a holiday, for example) Buchung die (PL die Buchungen).

booking office noun 1 (at a train station) Fahrkartenschalter der (PL die Fahrkartenschalter); 2 (in a theatre or cinema) Kasse die (PL die Kassen).

booklet noun Broschüre die (PL die Broschüren).

bookshelf noun Bücherregal das (PL die Bücherregale).

bookshop noun Buchhandlung die (PL die Buchhandlungen).

boot noun 1 Stiefel der (PL die Stiefel); 2 (for football, walking, climbing, or skiing) Schuh der (PL die Schuhe); **football boots** Fußballschuhe; 3 (of a car) Kofferraum der (PL die Kofferräume).

border noun (between countries) Grenze die (PL die Grenzen); **at the border** an der Grenze.

bore noun 1 (a boring person) langweilige Mensch der (PL die langweiligen Menschen); 2 (a nuisance) **what a bore!** wie ärgerlich!

bored adjective **to be bored** sich langweilen; **I'm bored** ich langweile mich.

boring adjective langweilig.

born adjective geboren; **to be born** geboren werden; **she was born in Germany** sie ist in Deutschland geboren.

borrow verb sich ←(DAT) borgen; **can I borrow your bike?** kann ich mir dein Rad borgen; **to borrow something from somebody** sich etwas von jemandem borgen; **I borrowed some money from Dad** ich habe mir Geld von Vati geborgt.

boss noun Chef der (PL die Chefs), Chefin die (PL die Chefinnen).

bossy adjective herrisch.

◇ IRREGULAR VERB: See the verb table in the centre of the dictionary

both *pronoun* beide; **they both came** sie kamen beide; **both my sisters were there** meine beiden Schwestern waren da; **both of us** wir beide; **they are both sold** beide sind verkauft.

adverb **both at home and at school** sowohl zu Hause als auch in der Schule; **both in summer and in winter** sowohl im Sommer als auch im Winter.

bother *noun* (*minor trouble*) Ärger *der*; **I've had a lot of bother with the car** ich hatte viel Ärger mit dem Auto; **2 if it isn't too much bother** wenn es nicht zuviel Mühe macht; **it's no bother** das ist kein Problem; **the children were no bother** die Kinder waren kein Problem; **without any bother** ohne irgendwelche Schwierigkeiten.

verb **1** (*disturb*) stören; **I'm sorry to bother you** es tut mir leid, dich zu stören; **2** (*worry*) stören; **what's bothering you?** was stört dich?; **it doesn't bother me at all** das stört mich überhaupt nicht; **3** (*take trouble*) **don't bother to write** du brauchst nicht zu schreiben; **she didn't even bother to wait** sie hat nicht einmal gewartet; **don't bother!** lass es! (*informal*); **I can't be bothered** ich habe keine Lust.

bottle *noun* Flasche *die* (PL *die* Flaschen).

bottle bank *noun* Altglascontainer *der* (PL *die* Altglascontainer).

bottle opener *noun* Flaschenöffner *der* (PL *die* Flaschenöffner).

bottom *noun* **1** (*of a bag, bottle, hole, or stretch of water*) Boden *der* (PL *die* Böden); **at the bottom of the lake** am Boden des Sees; **2** (*of a hill or building*) Fuß *der* (PL *die* Füße); **at the bottom of the tower** am Fuß des Turms; **3** (*of a garden, street, list*) Ende *das* (PL *die* Enden); **at the bottom of the street** am Ende der Straße; **4 at the bottom of the page** unten auf der Seite; **5** (*buttocks*) Hintern *der* (*informal*) (PL *die* Hintern).

adjective **1** unterster/unterste/ unterstes; **the bottom shelf** das unterste Regal; **2 the bottom flat** die Wohnung im Erdgeschoss.

bounce *verb* (*jump*) springen ❖ (PERF *sein*).

bouncer *noun* Rausschmeißer *der* (PL *die* Rausschmeißer).

bound *adjective* (*certain*) **he's bound to be late** er kommt ganz bestimmt zu spät; **that was bound to happen** das musste ja kommen.

bow *noun* **1** (*in a shoelace or ribbon*) Schleife *die* (PL *die* Schleifen); **2** (*for a violin or with arrows*) Bogen *der* (PL *die* Bogen); **with bow and arrow** mit Pfeil und Bogen.

bowl *noun* **1** (*large, for salad, mixing, or washing up*) Schüssel *die* (PL *die* Schüsseln); **2** (*smaller*) Schale *die* (PL *die* Schalen).

bowler *noun* (*in cricket*) Werfer *der* (PL *die* Werfer), Werferin *die* (PL *die* Werferinnen).

bowling *noun* (*tenpin*) Bowling *das*; **to go bowling** bowlen gehen.

△ NEW SPELLING: *See page xii*

bow tie noun Fliege die (PL die Fliegen).

box noun 1 Schachtel die (PL die Schachteln); **a box of chocolates** eine Schachtel Pralinen; **2 cardboard box** der Karton; **3** (on a form) Kästchen das (PL die Kästchen).

boxer noun Boxer der (PL die Boxer).

boxing noun 1 Boxen das; **2 boxing match** der Boxkampf.

Boxing Day noun zweite Weihnachtsfeiertag der.

boy noun Junge der (PL die Jungen); **a little boy** ein kleiner Junge.

boyfriend noun Freund der (PL die Freunde).

bra noun BH der (PL die BHs).

brace noun (for teeth) Spange die (PL die Spangen).

bracelet noun Armband das (PL die Armbänder).

bracket noun Klammer die (PL die Klammern); **in brackets** in Klammern.

brain noun Gehirn das (PL die Gehirne).

brainwave noun Geistesblitz der (PL die Geistesblitze).

brake noun Bremse die (PL die Bremsen).
verb bremsen.

branch noun 1 (of a tree) Ast der (PL die Äste); **2** (of a shop) Filiale die (PL die Filialen); **3** (of a bank) Zweigstelle die (PL die Zweigstellen).

brand noun Marke die (PL die Marken).

brand new adjective nagelneu.

brass noun 1 (metal) Messing das; **2** (in an orchestra) **the brass** das Blech.

brass band noun Blaskapelle die (PL die Blaskapellen).

brave adjective tapfer.

bread noun Brot das (PL die Brote); **a slice of bread** eine Scheibe Brot; **a piece of bread and butter** ein Butterbrot.

break noun 1 (a short rest or at school) Pause die (PL die Pausen); **ten minutes' break** eine Pause von zehn Minuten; **to take a break** Pause machen; **at break** in der Pause; **2 the Christmas break** die Weihnachtsferien (plural).
verb 1 zerbrechen ✧, kaputtmachen SEP (informal); **he broke a glass** er hat ein Glas zerbrochen; **don't break the doll** mach die Puppe nicht kaputt; **2** (get damaged) zerbrechen ✧ (PERF sein), kaputtgehen ✧ SEP (informal) (PERF sein); **the glass broke** das Glas zerbrach; **the eggs broke** die Eier sind kaputtgegangen; **3 to break your arm** sich ←(DAT) den Arm brechen; **4** brechen ✧ (rules, promise); **to break one's promise** sein Versprechen brechen; **5 to break the record** den Rekord brechen ✧; **6 to break the news that …** melden, dass …
● **to break down** 1 (car) eine Panne haben; **the car broke down** das

Auto hatte eine Panne; **2** (*talks, negotiations*) scheitern (PERF *sein*).
● **to break in** einbrechen ◇ SEP (PERF *sein*).
● **to break up 1** (*couple*) sich trennen; **2** (*crowd*) sich auflösen SEP; **3 we break up on Thursday** die Ferien fangen Donnerstag an.

breakdown *noun* **1** (*of a vehicle*) Panne *die* (PL *die* Pannen); **we had a breakdown on the motorway** wir hatten eine Panne auf der Autobahn; **2** (*in talks or negotiations*) Scheitern *das*; **3** (*a nervous collapse*) Zusammenbruch *der* (PL *die* Zusammenbrüche); **to have a nervous breakdown** einen Nervenzusammenbruch haben.

breakfast *noun* Frühstück *das* (PL *die* Frühstücke); **we have breakfast at eight** wir frühstücken um acht Uhr.

break-in *noun* Einbruch *der* (PL *die* Einbrüche).

breast *noun* Brust *die* (PL *die* Brüste).

breath *noun* Atem *der*; **out of breath** außer Atem; **to hold your breath** den Atem anhalten; **to get your breath back** wieder zu Atem kommen; **to take a deep breath** tief einatmen.

breathe *verb* atmen.

breed *noun* (*of animal*) Rasse *die* (PL *die* Rassen).

breeze *noun* Brise *die* (PL *die* Brisen).

brew *verb* **1** brauen (*beer*); **2** aufbrühen SEP (*tea*); **the tea's brewing** der Tee zieht noch.

brick *noun* Ziegel *der* (PL *die* Ziegel); **a brick wall** eine Ziegelmauer.

bride *noun* Braut *die* (PL *die* Bräute); **the bride and groom** das Brautpaar.

bridegroom *noun* Bräutigam *der* (PL *die* Bräutigame).

bridesmaid *noun* Brautjungfer *die* (PL *die* Brautjungfern).

bridge *noun* **1** (*over a river*) Brücke *die* (PL *die* Brücken); **2** (*card game*) Bridge *das*.

brief *adjective* kurz.

briefcase *noun* Aktentasche *die* (PL *die* Aktentaschen).

briefly *adverb* kurz.

briefs *plural noun* Slip *der* (PL *die* Slips).

bright *adjective* **1** (*colour*) leuchtend; **bright green socks** leuchtend grüne Socken; **2** (*eyes, sunshine*) strahlend; **3** (*light*) hell; **4** (*clever*) intelligent; **she's not very bright** sie ist nicht sehr intelligent; ★ **to look on the bright side** die Sache positiv sehen (*literally: to see things positively*).

brilliant *adjective* **1** (*very clever*) glänzend; **he's a brilliant surgeon** er ist ein glänzender Chirurg; **2** (*wonderful*) toll; **the party was brilliant!** die Party war toll!

bring *verb* **1** mitbringen ◇ SEP; **he brought a present** er brachte ein Geschenk mit; **bring your camera**

△ NEW SPELLING: See page xii

bring deinen Fotoapparat mit; **2** (*to a place*) bringen ◇; **she's bringing the children home** sie bringt die Kinder nach Hause.

● **to bring somebody up** jemanden großziehen ◇ SEP; **he was brought up by his aunt** er wurde von seiner Tante großgezogen.

Britain *noun* Großbritannien *das*; **to Britain** nach Großbritannien.

British *plural noun* **the British** die Briten.
adjective **1** britisch; **the British Isles** die Britischen Inseln; **2 he's British** er ist Brite; **she's British** sie ist Britin.

broad *adjective* **1** (*wide*) breit; **2** (*extensive*) weit.

broad bean *noun* dicke Bohne *die* (PL die dicken Bohnen).

broadcast *noun* Sendung *die* (PL die Sendungen).
verb senden.

broccoli *noun* Brokkoli *der* (PL die Brokkoli).

brochure *noun* Broschüre *die* (PL die Broschüren) .

broke *adjective* **to be broke** pleite sein (*informal*).

broken *adjective* zerbrochen, kaputt (*informal*); **the window's broken** das Fenster ist kaputt; **to have a broken leg** ein gebrochenes Bein haben.

bronchitis *noun* Bronchitis *die*.

brooch *noun* Brosche *die* (PL die Broschen).

brother *noun* Bruder *der* (PL die Brüder); **my mother's brother** der Bruder meiner Mutter.

brother-in-law *noun* Schwager *der* (PL die Schwäger).

brown *adjective* braun; **my brown shoes** meine braunen Schuhe; **light brown** hellbraun; **dark brown** dunkelbraun; **to go brown** (*suntanned*) braun werden.

brown bread *noun* Mischbrot *das* (PL die Mischbrote).

bruise *noun* **1** (*on a person*) blaue Fleck *der* (PL die blauen Flecken); **2** (*on fruit*) Druckstelle *die* (PL die Druckstellen).

brush *noun* **1** (*for your hair, clothes, nails, or shoes*) Bürste *die* (PL die Bürsten); **my hair brush** meine Haarbürste; **2** (*for sweeping*) Besen *der* (PL die Besen); **3** (*for paint*) Pinsel *der* (PL die Pinsel). *verb* **1** bürsten; **to brush your hair** sich ←(DAT) die Haare bürsten; **I brushed my hair** ich habe mir die Haare gebürstet; **2 to brush your teeth** sich ←(DAT) die Zähne putzen.

Brussels *noun* Brüssel *das*.

Brussels sprout *noun* Rosenkohl *der*; **he likes Brussels sprouts** er mag Rosenkohl.

bubble *noun* Blase *die* (PL die Blasen).

bubble bath *noun* Badeschaum *der*.

bucket *noun* Eimer *der* (PL die Eimer).

◇ **IRREGULAR VERB: See the verb table in the centre of the dictionary**

buckle noun Schnalle die (PL die Schnallen).

Buddhism noun Buddhismus der.

Buddhist noun Buddhist der (PL die Buddhisten), Buddhistin die (PL die Buddhistinnen).

budget noun Budget das (PL die Budgets).

buffet car noun Speisewagen der (PL die Speisewagen).

bug noun 1 (insect) Wanze die (PL die Wanzen); 2 (germ) Bazillus der (PL die Bazillen); **a stomach bug** eine Magengrippe; **3 a computer bug** ein Programmierfehler.

build verb bauen.

builder noun Bauarbeiter der (PL die Bauarbeiter).

building noun Gebäude das (PL die Gebäude).

building site noun Baustelle die (PL die Baustellen).

built-up adjective 1 bebaut; 2 **built-up area** das Wohngebiet.

bulb noun 1 (lightbulb) Birne die (PL die Birnen); 2 (flower bulb) Zwiebel die (PL die Zwiebeln).

bull noun Bulle der (PL die Bullen).

bullet noun Kugel die (PL die Kugeln).

bulletin noun 1 (written) Bulletin das (PL die Bulletins); 2 (on TV, radio) news bulletin die Kurzmeldung.

bully noun 1 (in school) Rabauke der (PL die Rabauken);

2 (adult) Tyrann der (PL die Tyrannen).
verb schikanieren.

bum noun Hintern der (informal) (PL die Hintern).

bump noun 1 (on a surface) Unebenheit die (PL die Unebenheiten); **there are lots of bumps in the road** die Straße hat viele Unebenheiten; 2 (swelling) Beule die (PL die Beulen); **a bump on the head** eine Beule am Kopf; 3 (jolt) Stoß der (PL die Stöße); 4 (noise) Bums der (PL die Bumse).
verb 1 (bang) stoßen ◇; **I bumped my head** ich habe mir den Kopf gestoßen; **to bump into something** gegen etwas ←(ACC) stoßen; **2 to bump into somebody** (meet by chance) jemanden zufällig treffen.

bumper noun Stoßstange die (PL die Stoßstangen).

bumpy adjective holperig.

bun noun 1 (for a burger) Brötchen das (PL die Brötchen), Semmel die (PL die Semmeln); 2 (sweet) süße Brötchen das (PL die süßen Brötchen), süße Semmel die (PL die süßen Semmeln).

bunch noun 1 (of flowers) Strauß der (PL die Sträuße); 2 (of carrots, radishes, or keys) Bund das (PL die Bunde); **3 a bunch of grapes** eine ganze Weintraube.

bundle noun Bündel das (PL die Bündel).

bunk noun 1 (on a boat) Koje die (PL die Kojen); 2 (on a train) Bett das (PL die Betten).

△ NEW SPELLING: See page xii

bunk beds plural noun
Etagenbett das (singular).

burger noun Hamburger der (PL die
Hamburger).

burglar noun Einbrecher der (PL die
Einbrecher).

burglar alarm noun
Alarmanlage die (PL die
Alarmanlagen).

burglary noun Einbruch der (PL die
Einbrüche).

burn noun 1 (on the skin)
Verbrennung die (PL die
Verbrennungen); 2 (on fabric,
object) Brandstelle die (PL die
Brandstellen).
verb 1 verbrennen✧; she burnt his
letters sie hat seine Briefe
verbrannt; 2 (fire, candle)
brennen✧; 3 (injure)
verbrennen✧; to burn yourself
sich verbrennen; you'll burn your
fingers! du verbrennst dir die
Finger!; 4 (cake, meat, etc.)
anbrennen✧ SEP; Mum's burnt the
cake Mutti hat den Kuchen
anbrennen lassen.

burnt adjective 1 (papers, rubbish)
verbrannt; 2 (cake, meat, etc.)
angebrannt.

burst verb 1 platzen lassen (a
balloon); the tyre has burst der
Reifen ist geplatzt; 2 to burst out
laughing in Lachen ausbrechen✧
SEP (PERF sein); to burst into tears in
Tränen ausbrechen✧ SEP (PERF
sein); 3 to burst into flames in
Flammen aufgehen✧ SEP (PERF
sein).

bury verb 1 begraben✧ (a dead
person); 2 vergraben✧ (a treasure
or a bone).

bus noun Bus der (PL die Busse); on
the bus im Bus; by bus mit dem
Bus.

bus driver noun Busfahrer der (PL
die Busfahrer), Busfahrerin die (PL
die Busfahrerinnen).

bush noun Busch der (PL die
Büsche).

business noun 1 (commercial
dealings) Geschäfte (plural);
business is bad die Geschäfte
gehen schlecht; he's in Leeds on
business er ist geschäftlich in
Leeds; 2 (a line of business or
profession) Branche die (PL die
Branchen); he's in the insurance
business er ist in der
Versicherungsbranche; 3 (firm or
company) Betrieb der (PL die
Betriebe); small businesses kleine
Betriebe; 4 (personal concern)
Angelegenheit die (PL die
Angelegenheiten); mind your own
business! kümmere dich um deine
eigenen Angelegenheiten!

businessman noun
Geschäftsmann der (PL die
Geschäftsleute).

business trip noun
Geschäftsreise die (PL die
Geschäftsreisen).

businesswoman noun
Geschäftsfrau die (PL die
Geschäftsfrauen).

bus pass noun Zeitkarte die (PL die
Zeitkarten).

✧ IRREGULAR VERB: See the verb table in the centre of the dictionary

bus route noun Buslinie die (PL die Buslinien).

bus shelter noun Wartehäuschen das (PL die Wartehäuschen).

bus station noun Busbahnhof der (PL die Busbahnhöfe).

bus stop noun Bushaltestelle die (PL die Bushaltestellen).

bus ticket noun Busfahrkarte die (PL die Busfahrkarten).

busy adjective 1 beschäftigt; he's busy er ist beschäftigt; she was busy packing sie war mit Packen beschäftigt; 2 to have a busy day viel zu tun haben; 3 the shops were busy die Läden waren sehr voll; 4 (phone) besetzt.

but conjunction 1 aber; small but strong klein aber stark; 2 (after a negative statement) sondern; not Thursday but Friday nicht Donnerstag, sondern Freitag; not only … but also nicht nur … sondern auch.
preposition 1 außer (+DAT); everyone but Winston alle außer Winston; anything but that! nur das nicht!; 2 the last but one der/die/das Vorletzte.

butcher noun 1 Fleischer der (PL die Fleischer), Metzger der (PL die Metzger); he's a butcher er ist Fleischer, er ist Metzger; 2 the butcher's die Fleischerei, die Metzgerei.

butter noun Butter die.
verb buttern.

butterfly noun Schmetterling der (PL die Schmetterlinge).

button noun Knopf der (PL die Knöpfe).

buttonhole noun Knopfloch das (PL die Knopflöcher).

buy noun Kauf der (PL die Käufe); a bad buy ein schlechter Kauf.
verb kaufen; I bought the tickets ich habe die Karten gekauft; to buy something for somebody jemandem etwas kaufen; Sarah bought him a sweater Sarah hat ihm einen Pullover gekauft.

buzz verb (a fly or bee) summen.

buzzer noun Summer der (PL die Summer).

by preposition 1 von (+DAT); I was bitten by a dog ich bin von einem Hund gebissen worden; by Mozart von Mozart; 2 by mistake versehentlich; 3 (travel) mit (+DAT); to come by bus mit dem Bus kommen; to go by train mit dem Zug fahren; by bike mit dem Rad; 4 (near) an (+DAT); by the sea am Meer; the stop by the school die Haltestelle an der Schule; 5 (before) bis; it'll be ready by Monday es wird bis Montag fertig sein; I'll be back by four ich bin bis vier Uhr zurück; 6 by now inzwischen; 7 by yourself ganz allein; I was by myself in the house ich war ganz allein im Haus; she did it by herself sie hat es ganz allein gemacht; 8 by the way übrigens; 9 to go by vorbeigehen ◊ SEP (PERF sein).

bye exclamation tschüs! (informal).

△ NEW SPELLING: See page xii

C c

cab noun **1** Taxi das (PL die Taxis); **to call a cab** ein Taxi rufen; **2** (on a lorry) Führerhaus das (PL die Führerhäuser).

cabbage noun Kohl der.

café noun Café das (PL die Cafés).

cage noun Käfig der (PL die Käfige).

cake noun Kuchen der (PL die Kuchen); **would you like a piece of cake?** möchtest du ein Stück Kuchen?

calculate verb berechnen.

calculation noun Rechnung die (PL die Rechnungen).

calculator noun Taschenrechner der (PL die Taschenrechner).

calendar noun Kalender der (PL die Kalender).

calf noun **1** (animal) Kalb das (PL die Kälber); **2** (of your leg) Wade die (PL die Waden).

call noun (telephone) Anruf der (PL die Anrufe); **I had several calls this morning** ich erhielt heute Morgen mehrere Anrufe; **thank you for your call** danke für deinen Anruf; **a phone call** ein Telefonanruf. verb **1** rufen◇; **to call a taxi** ein Taxi rufen; **to call the doctor** einen Arzt rufen; **they called the police** sie riefen die Polizei; **2** (phone)

anrufen◇ SEP; **call me later** ruf mich später an; **thank you for calling** danke für deinen Anruf; **I'll call you back later** ich rufe dich später zurück; **3** nennen◇; **they've called the baby Julie** sie haben das Baby Julie genannt; **4 to be called heißen◇**; **her brother is called Dan** ihr Bruder heißt Dan; **what's he called?** wie heißt er?

call box noun Telefonzelle die (PL die Telefonzellen).

calm adjective ruhig. verb beruhigen.
- **to calm down** sich beruhigen; **he's calmed down a bit** er hat sich etwas beruhigt.
- **to calm somebody down** jemanden beruhigen; **I tried to calm her down** ich habe versucht, sie zu beruhigen.

calmly adverb ruhig.

camcorder noun Camcorder der (PL die Camcorder).

camera noun **1** Fotoapparat der (PL die Fotoapparate); **2** (film or video camera) Kamera die (PL die Kameras).

camp noun Lager das (PL die Lager). verb campen, zelten.

camper van noun Camper der (PL die Camper).

camping noun Camping das; **to go camping** zelten; **we're going camping in Bavaria this summer** diesen Sommer zelten wir in Bayern.

campsite noun Campingplatz der (PL die Campingplätze).

can[1] noun **1** Dose die (PL die Dosen);

a can of tomatoes eine Dose Tomaten; **2** (*for petrol or oil*) Kanister *der* (PL die Kanister).

can² *verb* **1** können ◇; **I can't be there before ten** ich kann vor zehn Uhr nicht da sein; **can you open the door, please?** kannst du die Tür bitte aufmachen?; **can I help you?** kann ich Ihnen helfen?; **they couldn't come** sie konnten nicht kommen; **you could have told me** das hättest du mir wirklich sagen können; **I can't see him** ich kann ihn nicht sehen; **I can't remember it** ich kann mich nicht daran erinnern; **she can't drive** sich kann nicht Auto fahren; **2** (*be allowed*) dürfen ◇; **you can't smoke here** Sie dürfen hier nicht rauchen.

Canada *noun* Kanada *das*; **to Canada** nach Kanada.

Canadian *noun* Kanadier *der* (PL die Kanadier), Kanadierin *die* (PL die Kanadierinnen).
adjective kanadisch; **he is Canadian** er ist Kanadier.

canal *noun* Kanal *der* (PL die Kanäle).

cancel *verb* absagen SEP; **the concert's been cancelled** das Konzert ist abgesagt worden.

cancer *noun* Krebs *der*; **to have lung cancer** Lungenkrebs haben.

Cancer *noun* Krebs *der* (PL die Krebse); **I'm Cancer** ich bin Krebs.

candidate *noun* Kandidat *der* (PL die Kandidaten), Kandidatin *die* (PL die Kandidatinnen).

candle *noun* Kerze *die* (PL die Kerzen).

candlestick *noun* Kerzenhalter *der* (PL die Kerzenhalter).

canned *adjective* in Dosen; **canned tomatoes** Tomaten in Dosen.

canoe *noun* Kanu *das* (PL die Kanus).

canoeing *noun* **to go canoeing** Kanu fahren ◇; **I like canoeing** ich fahre gerne Kanu.

can-opener *noun* Dosenöffner *der* (PL die Dosenöffner).

canteen *noun* Kantine *die* (PL die Kantinen).

canvas *noun* **1** (*of a tent or bag*) Segeltuch *das*; **2** (*for painting on*) Leinwand *die*.

cap *noun* **1** (*hat*) Kappe *die* (PL die Kappen); **baseball cap** die Baseballkappe; **2** (*on a bottle or tube*) Verschluss △ *der* (PL die Verschlüsse).

capable *adjective* fähig.

capital *noun* **1** (*city*) Hauptstadt *die* (PL die Hauptstädte); **Berlin is the capital of Germany** Berlin ist die Hauptstadt von Deutschland; **2** (*letter*) Großbuchstabe *der* (PL die Großbuchstaben); **in capitals** mit Großbuchstaben.

capitalism *noun* Kapitalismus *der*.

△ NEW SPELLING: *See page xii*

Capricorn noun Steinbock der (PL die Steinböcke); **Linda's Capricorn** Linda ist Steinbock.

captain noun Kapitän der (PL die Kapitäne).

car noun Auto das (PL die Autos); **to park the car** das Auto einparken; **we're going by car** wir fahren mit dem Auto; **car crash** der Autounfall.

caramel noun Karamell △ der (PL die Karamells).

caravan noun Wohnwagen der (PL die Wohnwagen).

card noun Karte die (PL die Karten); **card game** das Kartenspiel; **to have a game of cards** Karten spielen.

cardboard noun Pappe die.

cardigan noun Strickjacke die (PL die Strickjacken).

cardphone noun Kartentelefon das (PL die Kartentelefone).

care noun 1 Vorsicht die; **to take care crossing the road** vorsichtig beim Überqueren der Straße sein; **take care!** (be careful) sei vorsichtig!; (when saying goodbye) mach's gut!; 2 **to take care to do something** aufpassen SEP, dass man etwas tut; **to take care of somebody** auf jemanden aufpassen.
verb 1 **to care about something** sich um etwas ←(ACC) kümmern; **she cares about the environment** sie kümmert sich um die Umwelt; 2 **she doesn't care** es ist ihr egal; **I couldn't care less!** das ist mir völlig egal!

careful adjective vorsichtig; **a careful driver** ein vorsichtiger Fahrer, eine vorsichtige Fahrerin; **be careful!** sei vorsichtig!

carefully adverb 1 sorgfältig; **to read the instructions carefully** die Anweisungen sorgfältig lesen; 2 vorsichtig; **she put the vase down carefully** sie stellte die Vase vorsichtig hin; **drive carefully!** fahr vorsichtig!; 3 **listen carefully!** hören Sie gut zu!

careless adjective 1 **he's very careless** er ist sehr nachlässig; **this is careless work** das ist eine nachlässige Arbeit; 2 **a careless mistake** ein Flüchtigkeitsfehler; 3 **a careless driver** ein leichtsinniger Fahrer.

car ferry noun Autofähre die (PL die Autofähren).

car hire noun Autovermietung die.

Caribbean noun **the Caribbean (islands)** die Karibik (singular).

carnation noun Nelke die (PL die Nelken).

carnival noun Karneval der (PL die Karnevale).

car park noun Parkplatz der (PL die Parkplätze); (multi-storey) Parkhaus das (PL die Parkhäuser).

carpenter noun Tischler der (PL die Tischler).

carpentry noun Tischlerhandwerk das.

carpet noun Teppich der (PL die Teppiche).

◇ **IRREGULAR VERB: See the verb table in the centre of the dictionary**

car phone noun Autotelefon das (PL die Autotelefone).

car radio noun Autoradio das (PL die Autoradios).

carriage noun (of a train) Abteil das (PL die Abteile).

carrier bag noun Tragetasche die (PL die Tragetaschen).

carrot noun Karotte die (PL die Karotten), Möhre die (PL die Möhren).

carry verb tragen; she was carrying a case sie trug einen Koffer.
● to carry on weitermachen SEP; they carried on working sie machten ihre Arbeit weiter.

carrycot noun Babytragetasche die (PL die Babytragetaschen).

carsick adjective he gets carsick ihm wird beim Autofahren schlecht.

carton noun 1 (of cream or yoghurt) Becher der (PL die Becher); 2 (of milk or orange) Tüte die (PL die Tüten).

cartoon noun 1 (a film) Zeichentrickfilm der (PL die Zeichentrickfilme); 2 (a comic strip) Cartoon der (PL die Cartoons); 3 (a drawing) Karikatur die (PL die Karikaturen).

cartridge noun (for a pen) Patrone die (PL die Patronen).

case¹ noun 1 (suitcase) Koffer der (PL die Koffer); to pack a case einen Koffer packen; 2 (a large wooden box) Kiste die (PL die Kisten); 3 (for spectacles or small things) Etui das (PL die Etuis).

case² noun 1 Fall der (PL die Fälle); in that case in dem Fall; that's not the case das ist nicht der Fall; in case of fire bei Feuer; 2 in case falls; in case he comes falls er kommt; 3 just in case für alle Fälle; 4 in any case sowieso; in any case, it's too late es ist sowieso zu spät.

cash noun 1 (money in general) Geld das; I haven't any cash on me ich habe kein Geld dabei; 2 (money rather than a cheque) Bargeld das; to pay in cash bar zahlen; £50 in cash fünfzig Pfund in bar.

cash card noun Bankkarte die (PL die Bankkarten).

cash desk noun Kasse die (PL die Kassen); to pay at the cash desk an der Kasse zahlen.

cash dispenser noun Geldautomat der (PL die Geldautomaten).

cashier noun Kassierer der (PL die Kassierer), Kassiererin die (PL die Kassiererinnen).

cash point noun Geldautomat der (PL die Geldautomaten).

cassette noun Kassette die (PL die Kassetten).

cassette recorder noun Kassettenrekorder der (PL die Kassettenrekorder).

cast noun (of a play) Besetzung die.

castle noun 1 Burg die (PL die Burgen); 2 (in chess) Turm der (PL die Türme).

casual adjective zwanglos.

△ NEW SPELLING: See page xii

casualty noun 1 (in an accident) Verletzte der/die (PL die Verletzten); 2 (hospital department) Unfallstation die (PL die Unfallstationen); he's in casualty er ist auf der Unfallstation.

cat noun Katze die (PL die Katzen); (tomcat) Kater der (PL die Kater); ★ it's raining cats and dogs es regnet in Strömen (literally: it's raining in streams).

catalogue noun Katalog der (PL die Kataloge).

catastrophe noun Katastrophe die (PL die Katastrophen).

catch noun 1 (on a door) Schnapper der (PL die Schnapper); 2 (a drawback) Haken der (PL die Haken); where's the catch? wo ist der Haken? verb 1 fangen ◇; Tom caught the ball Tom hat den Ball gefangen; she caught a fish sie hat einen Fisch gefangen; catch me! fang mich!; 2 to catch somebody doing something jemanden bei etwas ←(DAT) erwischen; he was caught stealing money er wurde beim Geldstehlen erwischt; 3 (be in time for) noch erreichen; did Tim catch his plane? hat Tim sein Flugzeug noch erreicht?; 4 (become ill with) bekommen ◇; she's caught chickenpox sie hat die Windpocken bekommen; 5 verstehen ◇ (what somebody says); I didn't catch your name ich habe Ihren Namen nicht verstanden.
● to catch up with somebody jemanden einholen SEP.

catering noun 1 (trade) Gastronomie die; 2 who's doing the catering? wer liefert das Essen und die Getränke?

cathedral noun Kathedrale die (PL die Kathedralen); Cologne cathedral der Kölner Dom.

Catholic noun Katholik der (PL die Katholiken), Katholikin die (PL die Katholikinnen). adjective katholisch.

cattle plural noun Vieh das.

cauliflower noun Blumenkohl der; cauliflower cheese der Blumenkohlauflauf.

cause noun 1 Ursache die (PL die Ursachen); the cause of the accident die Unfallursache; 2 for a good cause für eine gute Sache. verb verursachen; to cause difficulties Schwierigkeiten verursachen.

cave noun Höhle die (PL die Höhlen).

caving noun Höhlenforschung die; to go caving auf Höhlenforschung gehen.

CD noun CD die (PL die CDs).

CD player noun CD-Spieler der (PL die CD-Spieler).

CD-ROM noun CD-ROM die (PL die CD-ROMs).

ceiling noun Decke die (PL die Decken); on the ceiling an der Decke.

◇ **IRREGULAR VERB:** See the verb table in the centre of the dictionary

celebrate verb feiern; he's celebrating his birthday er feiert seinen Geburtstag.

celebrity noun Berühmtheit die (PL die Berühmtheiten).

celery noun Sellerie der (PL die Sellerie).

cell noun Zelle die (PL die Zellen).

cellar noun Keller der (PL die Keller).

cello noun Cello das (PL die Cellos); to play the cello Cello spielen.

cement noun Zement der.

cemetery noun Friedhof der (PL die Friedhöfe).

centigrade adjective Celsius; ten degrees centigrade zehn Grad Celsius.

centimetre noun Zentimeter der (PL die Zentimeter).

central adjective 1 zentral; the office is very central das Büro ist sehr zentral gelegen; 2 in central London im Zentrum von London.

central heating noun Zentralheizung die.

centre noun Zentrum das (PL die Zentren); in the centre of im Zentrum von (+DAT); in the town centre im Stadtzentrum; a shopping centre ein Einkaufszentrum.

century noun Jahrhundert das (PL die Jahrhunderte); in the twentieth century im zwanzigsten Jahrhundert.

cereal noun breakfast cereal Frühstücksflocken (plural).

certain adjective 1 (definite) bestimmt; a certain number of eine bestimmte Zahl von (+DAT); 2 (confident) sicher; to be certain sich ←(DAT) sicher sein; are you certain of the address? bist du dir der Adresse sicher? I'm absolutely certain ich bin mir ganz sicher; to be certain that ... sicher sein, dass ...; 3 nobody knows for certain niemand weiß es genau.

certainly adverb bestimmt; certainly not bestimmt nicht.

certificate noun
1 Bescheinigung die (PL die Bescheinigungen); 2 birth certificate die Geburtsurkunde; 3 (at school) Zeugnis das (PL die Zeugnisse).

chain Kette die (PL die Ketten).

chair noun 1 (upright) Stuhl der (PL die Stühle); a kitchen chair ein Küchenstuhl; 2 (with arms) Sessel der (PL die Sessel).

chair lift noun Sessellift der (PL die Sessellifte).

chalet noun 1 (in the mountains) Chalet das (PL die Chalets); 2 (in a holiday camp) Ferienhaus das (PL die Ferienhäuser).

challenge noun Herausforderung die (PL die Herausforderungen).

champion noun Meister der (PL die Meister), Meisterin die (PL die Meisterinnen); the world slalom champion der Weltmeister im Slalom, die Weltmeisterin im Slalom.

△ NEW SPELLING: See page xii

chance noun 1 (*opportunity*)
Gelegenheit die (PL die
Gelegenheiten); **to have the chance
to do something** die Gelegenheit
haben, etwas zu tun; **if you have the
chance to go to New York** wenn
du die Gelegenheit hast, nach New
York zu fahren; **I had no chance to
speak to him** ich hatte keine
Gelegenheit, mit ihm zu reden;
2 (*likelihood*) Aussicht die (PL die
Aussichten); **he's got no chance of
winning** er hat keine Aussicht zu
gewinnen; 3 (*luck*) Zufall der; **by chance**
zufällig; **do you have her address,
by any chance?** hast du zufällig ihre
Adresse?

change noun 1 (*from one thing to
another*) Änderung die (PL die
Änderungen); **a change of address**
eine Adressenänderung; **there's
been a change of plan** der Plan ist
geändert worden; 2 (*alteration*)
Veränderung die (PL die
Veränderungen); **they've made
some changes to the house** sie
haben im Haus ein paar
Veränderungen vorgenommen; **a
change in the weather** eine
Wetterveränderung; 3 (*for the sake
of variety*) **for a change, we could
go to a restaurant** zur Abwechslung
könnten wir in ein Restaurant gehen;
**it makes a change from
hamburgers** das ist mal etwas
anderes als Hamburger; **a change of
clothes** etwas anderes zum
Anziehen; 4 (*cash*)
Wechselgeld das; **I haven't any
change** ich habe kein Wechselgeld.
verb 1 (*make different*) ändern; **you
can't change her** du kannst sie nicht

ändern; **to change your address**
seine Adresse ändern; 2 (*become
different*) sich verändern; **Liz has
changed a lot** Liz hat sich sehr
verändert; 3 (*transform completely*)
verwandeln; **the prince changed
into a frog** der Prinz hat sich in
einen Frosch verwandelt;
4 (*exchange in a shop*) umtauschen
SEP; **just change it for a larger size**
tauschen Sie es einfach gegen eine
größere Größe um; 5 (*change
clothes*) sich umziehen ◇ SEP;
Mike's just changing Mike zieht
sich gerade um; 6 (*switch from one
train or bus to another*)
umsteigen ◇ SEP (PERF sein); **we
changed trains at Crewe** wir sind
in Crewe umgestiegen; 7 (*switch one
thing for another*) wechseln; **I want
to change my job** ich möchte meine
Stellung wechseln; **they changed
places** sie haben die Plätze
gewechselt; 8 **to change your mind**
sich anders entschließen ◇.

changing room noun (*for sport or
swimming*) Umkleideraum der (PL
die Umkleideräume).

channel noun 1 (*on TV*) Kanal der
(PL die Kanäle); **to change channels**
auf einen anderen Kanal schalten;
2 **the Channel** der Kanal.

Channel Tunnel noun
Eurotunnel der.

chaos noun Chaos das; **it was
chaos!** das war ein Chaos!

chapel noun Kapelle die (PL die
Kapellen).

◇ **IRREGULAR VERB: See the verb table in the centre of the dictionary**

chapter noun Kapitel das (PL die Kapitel); **in chapter two** im zweiten Kapitel.

character noun 1 (personality) Charakter der; 2 (somebody in a book) Charakter der (PL die Charaktere); 3 (part in a play or film) Rolle die (PL die Rollen); **the main character** die Hauptrolle.

charcoal noun 1 (for burning) Holzkohle die; 2 (for drawing) Kohlestift der (PL die Kohlestifte).

charge noun 1 (what you pay) Gebühr die (PL die Gebühren); **a booking charge** Buchungskosten (plural); **an extra or additional charge** eine zusätzliche Gebühr; **there's no charge** das ist kostenlos; **to be in charge** für etwas ←(ACC) verantwortlich sein; **who's in charge of the children?** wer ist für die Kinder verantwortlich?; **to be on a charge of theft** wegen Diebstahls angeklagt sein.
verb 1 (ask to pay) berechnen; **they charge us fifteen pounds an hour** sie berechnen uns fünfzehn Pfund pro Stunde; **they didn't charge for delivery** sie haben die Lieferung nicht berechnet; **we won't charge you for it** wir berechnen Ihnen nichts dafür; 2 **to charge somebody with something** jemanden wegen etwas ←(GEN) anklagen SEP.

charity noun Wohltätigkeitsverein der (PL die Wohltätigkeitsvereine).

charming adjective reizend.

chart noun 1 (table) Tabelle die (PL die Tabellen); 2 **the weather chart** die Wetterkarte; 3 **the charts** die Hitparade.

charter flight noun Charterflug der (PL die Charterflüge).

chase noun Verfolgungsjagd die (PL die Verfolgungsjagden); **a car chase** eine Verfolgungsjagd im Auto.
verb jagen.

chat noun Plauderei die (PL die Plaudereien); **to have a chat with somebody** mit jemandem plaudern.

chat show noun Talkshow die (PL die Talkshows).

chatter verb 1 (talk) schwatzen; 2 **my teeth were chattering** ich habe mit den Zähnen geklappert.

cheap adjective billig; **cheap shoes** billige Schuhe; **that's very cheap** das ist sehr billig.

cheaply adverb billig; **to eat cheaply** billig essen.

cheap-rate adjective verbilligt; **a cheap-rate phone call** ein Gespräch zum Spartarif.

cheat noun 1 Betrüger der (PL die Betrüger), Betrügerin die (PL die Betrügerinnen); 2 (in games) Mogler der (PL die Mogler), Moglerin die (PL die Moglerinnen).
verb 1 betrügen ◇; 2 (in games) mogeln.

check noun 1 (in a factory or at a border control) Kontrolle die (PL die Kontrollen); **passport check** die

△ NEW SPELLING: See page xii

Passkontrolle; **2** (*in chess*) **check!**
Schach!

verb **1** (*make sure*) prüfen; **he
checked their statements** er prüfte
ihre Aussage; **2** (*make sure by
looking*) nachsehen ◇ SEP; **to check
the time** nachsehen, wie viel Uhr es
ist; **check they're all back** sieh
nach, ob alle wieder da sind;
3 (*inspect*) kontrollieren; **to check
the tickets** die Fahrkarten
kontrollieren.

check in *verb* (*for a flight*)
einchecken SEP.

check-in *noun*
Abfertigungsschalter *der* (PL *die*
Abfertigungsschalter).

checkout *noun* Kasse *die* (PL *die*
Kassen); **at the checkout** an der
Kasse.

check-up *noun* Untersuchung *die*
(PL *die* Untersuchungen).

cheek *noun* **1** (*part of face*)
Backe *die* (PL *die* Backen); **2** (*nerve*)
Frechheit *die*; **what a cheek!** so
eine Frechheit!

cheer *noun* **1** **three cheers for
Tom!** ein dreifaches Hurra für
Tom!; **2** (*when drinking*) **cheers!**
prost!

verb (*shout hurray*) Hurra
schreien ◇.

● **to cheer somebody up** jemanden
aufmuntern SEP; **your visits always
cheer me up** dein Besuch muntert
mich immer auf; **cheer up!** Kopf
hoch!

cheerful *adjective* fröhlich.

cheese *noun* Käse *der*; **a cheese
sandwich** ein Käsebrot.

chef *noun* Koch *der* (PL *die* Köche),
Köchin *die* (PL *die* Köchinnen).

chemist *noun* **1** (*in a pharmacy*)
Apotheker *der* (PL *die* Apotheker),
Apothekerin *die* (PL *die*
Apothekerinnen); **2** **chemist's**
(*dispensing*) Apotheke *die* (PL *die*
Apotheken); **at the chemist's** in der
Apotheke; **3** (*scientist*)
Chemiker *der* (PL *die* Chemiker),
Chemikerin *die* (PL *die*
Chemikerinnen).

chemistry *noun* Chemie *die*.

cheque *noun* Scheck *der* (PL *die*
Schecks); **to pay by cheque** mit
Scheck bezahlen; **to write a cheque**
einen Scheck austellen.

cheque book *noun*
Scheckbuch *das* (PL *die*
Scheckbücher).

cherry *noun* Kirsche *die* (PL *die*
Kirschen).

chess *noun* Schach *das*; **to play
chess** Schach spielen.

chessboard *noun*
Schachbrett *das* (PL *die*
Schachbretter).

chest *noun* **1** (*part of the body*)
Brust *die* (PL *die* Brüste); **2** (*box*)
Truhe *die* (PL *die* Truhen); **3** **a chest
of drawers** eine Kommode.

chestnut *noun* Esskastanie △ *die*
(PL *die* Esskastanien).

chestnut tree *noun* **1** (*horse-
chestnut*) Rosskastanie △ *die* (PL *die*
Rosskastanien); **2** (*sweet chestnut*)

◇ IRREGULAR VERB: *See the verb table in the centre of the dictionary.*

Edelkastanie die (PL die Edelkastanien).

chew verb kauen.

chewing gum noun Kaugummi der (PL die Kaugummis).

chicken noun Huhn das (PL die Hühner; roast chicken das Brathähnchen; chicken breast die Hühnerbrust.

chickenpox noun Windpocken (plural).

child noun Kind das (PL die Kinder); when I was a child ... als Kind ...

childish adjective kindisch.

childminder noun Tagesmutter die (PL die Tagesmütter).

chill noun 1 Kälte die; 2 to have a chill eine Erkältung haben.

chilled adjective gekühlt.

chilli noun Chili der.

chimney noun Schornstein der (PL die Schornsteine).

chimpanzee noun Schimpanse der (PL die Schimpansen).

chin noun Kinn das (PL die Kinne).

china noun Porzellan das; china bowl die Porzellanschüssel.

China noun China das.

Chinese noun 1 the Chinese (people) die Chinesen; 2 (language) Chinesisch das. adjective 1 chinesisch; a Chinese-man ein Chinese; a Chinese

woman eine Chinesin; 2 to have a Chinese meal chinesisch essen.

chip noun 1 (fried potato) chips Pommes frites (plural); fish and chips ausgebackener Fisch mit Pommes frites; 2 (microchip) Chip der (PL die Chips); 3 (in glass or china) angeschlagene Stelle die (PL die angeschlagenen Stellen).

chipped adjective angeschlagen.

chocolate noun 1 Schokolade die; a box of chocolates eine Schachtel Pralinen; 2 chocolate ice cream das Schokoladeneis; 3 a cup of hot chocolate eine Tasse Kakao.

choice noun 1 Wahl die (PL die Wahlen); to make a good choice eine gute Wahl treffen; 2 (variety) Auswahl die; you have a choice of two flights du hast zwei Flüge zur Auswahl.

choir noun Chor der (PL die Chöre).

choke noun (on a car) Choke der (PL die Chokes). verb (by yourself) sich verschlucken; she choked on a bone sie hat sich an einer Gräte verschluckt.

choose verb 1 wählen; you chose well du hast gut gewählt; it's hard to choose from all these colours es ist schwer, unter allen diesen Farben zu wählen; 2 (select from a group of things) sich ←(DAT) aussuchen SEP; Cathy chose the red skirt Cathy suchte sich den roten Rock aus.

chop noun Kotelett das (PL die Koteletts); a pork chop ein

Schweinekotelett.
verb hacken.

chord *noun* Akkord der (PL die
Akkorde).

chorus *noun* 1 (*when you all join in
the song*) Refrain der (PL die
Refrains); 2 (*a group of singers*)
Chor der (PL die Chöre).

Christ *noun* Christus der.

christening *noun* Taufe die (PL die
Taufen).

Christian *noun* Christ der (PL die
Christen), Christin die (PL die
Christinnen).
adjective christlich.

Christian name *noun*
Vorname der (PL die Vornamen).

Christmas *noun* Weihnachten das
(PL die Weihnachten); **at Christmas**
zu Weihnachten; **what did you get
for Christmas?** was hast du zu
Weihnachten bekommen?; **Happy
Christmas!** Frohe Weihnachten!

Christmas card *noun*
Weihnachtskarte die (PL die
Weihnachtskarten).

Christmas carol *noun*
Weihnachtslied das (PL die
Weihnachtslieder).

Christmas cracker *noun*
Knallbonbon der (PL die
Knallbonbons).

Christmas Day *noun* erste
Weihnachtstag der.

Christmas Eve *noun*
Heiligabend der; **on Christmas Eve**
Heiligabend.

Christmas present *noun*
Weihnachtsgeschenk das (PL die
Weihnachtsgeschenke).

Christmas tree *noun*
Weihnachtsbaum der (PL die
Weihnachtsbäume).

church *noun* Kirche die (PL die
Kirchen); **to go to church** in die
Kirche gehen.

chute *noun* (*in a swimming pool or
playground*) Rutsche die (PL die
Rutschen).

cider *noun* Apfelwein der (PL die
Apfelweine).

cigar *noun* Zigarre die (PL die
Zigarren).

cigarette *noun* Zigarette die (PL die
Zigaretten).

cinema *noun* Kino das (PL die
Kinos); **to go to the cinema** ins
Kino gehen.

circle *noun* Kreis der (PL die Kreise);
to sit in a circle im Kreis sitzen; **to
go round in circles** sich im Kreis
drehen.

circus *noun* Zirkus der (PL die
Zirkusse).

citizen *noun* Bürger der (PL die
Bürger), Bürgerin die (PL die
Bürgerinnen).

city *noun* Stadt die (PL die Städte);
the city of Berlin die Stadt Berlin.

city centre *noun*
Stadtzentrum das (PL die
Stadtzentren); **in the city centre** im
Stadtzentrum.

◈ IRREGULAR VERB: *See the verb table in the centre of the dictionary*

civilization noun Zivilisation die (PL die Zivilisationen).

civil servant noun Beamte der (PL die Beamten), Beamtin die (PL die Beamtinnen); **she's a civil servant** sie ist Beamtin.

claim verb behaupten; **he claims to know who ...** er behauptet zu wissen, wer ...

clap verb 1 klatschen; **everyone clapped** alle klatschten; **2 to clap your hands** in die Hände klatschen.

clarinet noun Klarinette die (PL die Klarinetten); **to play the clarinet** Klarinette spielen.

clash noun (between two groups) Zusammenstoß der (PL die Zusammenstöße).
verb 1 (rival groups) zusammenstoßen ◇ SEP; 2 (colours) sich beißen ◇; **the curtains clash with the wallpaper** die Vorhänge beißen sich mit der Tapete.

class noun 1 (a group of students or pupils) Klasse die (PL die Klassen); **she's in my class** sie geht in meine Klasse; **2** (a lesson) Stunde die (PL die Stunden); **history class** die Geschichtsstunde; **in class** im Unterricht; **3** (category) Klasse die (PL die Klassen); **social class** die gesellschaftliche Klasse.

classical adjective klassisch; **classical music** die klassische Musik.

classroom noun Klassenzimmer das (PL die Klassenzimmer).

clay noun Ton der.

clean adjective sauber; **a clean shirt** ein sauberes Hemd; **my hands are clean** ich habe saubere Hände.
verb 1 putzen; **I cleaned the windows** ich habe die Fenster geputzt; **2 to clean your teeth** sich ←(DAT) die Zähne putzen; **I'm going to clean my teeth** ich putze mir jetzt die Zähne.

cleaner noun 1 (cleaning lady) Putzfrau die (PL die Putzfrauen); **2** (in a public place) Reinigungskraft die (PL die Reinigungskräfte); **3 dry cleaner's** die chemische Reinigung.

cleaning noun **to do the cleaning** putzen.

cleanser noun 1 (for the house) Reinigungsmittel das (PL die Reinigungsmittel); **2** (for your face) Reinigungsmilch die.

clear adjective 1 (that you can see through) klar; **clear water** klares Wasser; **2** (cloudless) klar; **3** (easy to understand) klar; **clear instructions** klare Anweisungen; **is that clear?** ist das klar? (informal); **to make something clear** etwas klarmachen.
verb 1 räumen; **have you cleared your stuff out of your room?** hast du deine Sachen aus deinem Zimmer geräumt?; **2 can I clear the table?** kann ich den Tisch abräumen SEP?; **3 to clear your throat** sich räuspern.
• **to clear up 1** (tidy up) aufräumen SEP; **2** (the weather) sich aufklären SEP; **the weather's clearing up a bit**

△ NEW SPELLING: See page xii

das Wetter klärt sich ein bisschen auf.

clearly adverb 1 (to think, speak, or hear) deutlich; 2 (obviously) eindeutig; **she was clearly better** sie war eindeutig besser.

clementine noun Klementine die (PL die Klementinen).

clever adjective 1 klug; **their children are all very clever** ihre Kinder sind alle sehr klug; 2 (ingenious) clever; **a clever idea** eine clevere Idee.

cliff noun Klippe die (PL die Klippen).

climate noun Klima das (PL die Klimas).

climb verb 1 (the stairs, a hill) hinaufgehen ◇ SEP (PERF sein); **to climb a mountain** auf einen Berg steigen ◇ (PERF sein); 2 (a wall, tree, or rock) klettern (PERF sein) auf (+ACC); **to climb a tree** auf einen Baum klettern.

climber noun Bergsteiger der (PL die Bergsteiger), Bergsteigerin die (PL die Bergsteigerinnen).

climbing noun Bergsteigen das; **they go climbing in Italy** sie gehen in Italien bergsteigen.

clinic noun Klinik die (PL die Kliniken).

clip noun 1 (from a film) Ausschnitt der (PL die Ausschnitte); 2 (for your hair) Klammer die (PL die Klammern).

cloakroom noun (for coats) Garderobe die (PL die Garderoben).

clock noun 1 Uhr die (PL die Uhren); **to put the clocks forward an hour** die Uhr eine Stunde vorstellen; **to put the clocks back** die Uhr zurückstellen; 2 **an alarm clock** ein Wecker.

close[1] adjective, adverb 1 (result) knapp; 2 (friend, connection) eng; 3 (relation or acquaintance) nahe; 4 (near) in der Nähe; **the station's very close** der Bahnhof ist ganz in der Nähe; **she lives close by** sie wohnt in der Nähe; 5 **close to** nahe, nah (informal) (+DAT); **close to the cinema** nahe am Kino; **not very close** nicht sehr nah.

close[2] noun Ende das; **at the close** am Ende.
verb 1 zumachen SEP, schließen ◇; **close your eyes!** mach die Augen zu!; **she closed the door** sie machte die Tür zu; **the post office closes at six** die Post macht um sechs zu, die Post schließt um sechs.

closed adjective geschlossen; **'closed on Mondays'** 'Montags geschlossen'.

closing date noun **the closing date for entries** (for a competition) der Einsendeschluss ∆; (for a sporting event) der Meldeschluss ∆.

closing time noun 1 Ladenschluss ∆ der; 2 (of a pub) Polizeistunde die.

cloth noun 1 (for drying up and polishing) Tuch das (PL die Tücher); 2 (for the floor) Lappen der (PL die

◇ IRREGULAR VERB: See the verb table in the centre of the dictionary

Lappen); 3 (*fabric*) Stoff der (PL die Stoffe).

clothes *plural noun* 1 Kleider (*plural*); 2 **to put your clothes on** sich anziehen ◇ SEP; **to take your clothes off** sich ausziehen ◇ SEP; **to change your clothes** sich umziehen ◇ SEP.

clothes peg *noun* Wäscheklammer die (PL die Wäscheklammern).

clothing *noun* Kleidung die.

cloud *noun* Wolke die (PL die Wolken).

cloudy *adjective* bewölkt.

clown *noun* Clown der (PL die Clowns).

club *noun* 1 (*association, for tennis-players, golfers*) Klub der (PL die Klubs); (*for footballers*) Verein der (PL die Vereine); **a football club** ein Fußballverein; 2 (*in cards*) Kreuz das (PL die Kreuze); **the four of clubs** die Kreuz-Vier; 3 (*golfing iron*) Schläger der (PL die Schläger).

clue *noun* 1 Anhaltspunkt der (PL die Anhaltspunkte); **they have a few clues** sie haben ein paar Anhaltspunkte; 2 (*in a crossword*) Frage die (PL die Fragen); ★ **I haven't a clue** ich habe keine Ahnung.

clumsy *adjective* ungeschickt.

clutch *noun* (*in a car*) Kupplung die (PL die Kupplungen). *verb* **to clutch something** etwas festhalten ◇ SEP.

coach *noun* 1 (*bus*) Bus der (PL die Busse); **on the coach** im Bus; **to travel by coach** mit dem Bus fahren; 2 (*sports trainer*) Trainer der (PL die Trainer), Trainerin die (PL die Trainerinnen); 3 (*railway carriage*) Wagen der (PL die Wagen).

coach station *noun* Busbahnhof der (PL die Busbahnhöfe).

coach trip *noun* Busausflug der (PL die Busausflüge); **to go on a coach trip** einen Busausflug machen.

coal *noun* Kohle die (PL die Kohlen).

coarse *adjective* grob.

coast *noun* Küste die (PL die Küsten); **on the east coast** an der Ostküste.

coat *noun* 1 Mantel der (PL die Mäntel); 2 **coat of paint** der Anstrich.

coat hanger *noun* Kleiderbügel der (PL die Kleiderbügel).

cock *noun* Hahn der (PL die Hähne).

cocoa *noun* Kakao der.

coconut *noun* Kokosnuss △ die (PL die Kokosnüsse).

cod *noun* Kabeljau der (PL die Kabeljaue).

code *noun* 1 (*in law*) Gesetzbuch das; **the highway code** die Straßenverkehrsordnung; 2 **the dialling code for Hull** die Vorwahl für Hull.

coffee *noun* Kaffee der (PL die Kaffees); **a cup of coffee** eine Tasse

△ NEW SPELLING: See page xii

Kaffee; **a black coffee, please** einen Kaffee ohne Milch bitte; **a white coffee, please** einen Kaffee mit Milch bitte.

coffee break *noun* Kaffeepause *die* (PL *die* Kaffeepausen).

coffee cup *noun* Kaffeetasse *die* (PL *die* Kaffeetassen).

coffee machine *noun* Kaffeemaschine *die* (PL *die* Kaffeemaschinen).

coin *noun* 1 Münze *die* (PL *die* Münzen); **she collects old coins** sie sammelt alte Münzen; 2 **a pound coin** ein Einpfundstück.

coincidence *noun* Zufall *der* (PL *die* Zufälle).

Coke™ *noun* Cola *die*; **two Cokes™ please** zwei Cola bitte.

cold *noun* 1 (*cold weather*) Kälte *die*; **to be out in the cold** draußen in der Kälte sein; 2 (*illness*) Schnupfen *der* (PL *die* Schnupfen), Erkältung *die* (PL *die* Erkältungen); **to have a cold** Schnupfen haben; **Carol's got a cold** Carol hat Schnupfen; **a bad cold** eine schlimme Erkältung.
adjective 1 kalt; **your hands are cold** du hast kalte Hände; **cold milk** kalte Milch; 2 (*weather, temperature*) **it's cold today** heute ist es kalt; 3 (*feeling*) **I'm cold** mir ist kalt.

collapse *verb* 1 (*a roof or wall*) einstürzen SEP (PERF *sein*); 2 (*a person*) zusammenbrechen ✧ SEP (PERF *sein*); **he collapsed in his**

office er brach in seinem Büro zusammen.

collar *noun* 1 (*on a garment*) Kragen *der* (PL *die* Kragen); 2 (*for an animal*) Halsband *das* (PL *die* Halsbänder).

colleague *noun* Kollege *der* (PL *die* Kollegen), Kollegin *die* (PL *die* Kolleginnen).

collect *verb* 1 (*as a hobby*) sammeln; **do you collect stamps?** sammelst du Briefmarken?; 2 (*fetch*) abholen SEP; **she collects the children from school** sie holt die Kinder von der Schule ab; 3 **to collect up the exercise books** die Hefte einsammeln SEP.

collection *noun* (*of stamps, CDs, money, etc.*) Sammlung *die* (PL *die* Sammlungen).

college *noun* 1 (*for higher education*) Hochschule *die* (PL *die* Hochschulen); **to go to college** studieren; 2 (*a school*) College *das* (PL *die* Colleges).

Cologne *noun* Köln *das*.

colour *noun* Farbe *die* (PL *die* Farben); **what colour is it?** welche Farbe hat es?; **do you have it in a different colour?** haben Sie es in einer anderen Farbe?
verb 1 (*with paints or crayons*) anmalen SEP; **to colour something red** etwas rot anmalen; 2 (*with dye*) färben.

colour film *noun* Farbfilm *der* (PL *die* Farbfilme).

colourful *adjective* bunt.

✧ IRREGULAR VERB: See the verb table in the centre of the dictionary

column noun 1 (of a building) Säule die (PL die Säulen); 2 (on a page) Spalte die (PL die Spalten).

comb noun Kamm der (PL die Kämme).
verb kämmen; **to comb your hair** sich ←(DAT) die Haare kämmen; **I'll just comb my hair** ich kämme mir nur die Haare.

come verb 1 kommen ◇ (PERF sein); **come quick! komm schnell!; come here! komm mal her!;** Nick came by car Nick kam mit dem Auto; **can you come over for a coffee?** kannst du auf eine Tasse Kaffee kommen ?; **did Jess come to school yesterday?** war Jess gestern in der Schule?; 2 (arrive) **coming!** ich komme schon!; **the bus is coming** der Bus kommt gerade; **come along! komm schon!**
● **to come back** zurückkommen ◇ SEP (PERF sein); **he's coming back to collect us** er kommt zurück, um uns abzuholen.
● **to come down** herunterkommen ◇ SEP (PERF sein).
● **to come for** (collect) abholen SEP; **my father's coming for me** mein Vater holt mich ab.
● **to come in** hereinkommen ◇ SEP (PERF sein); **come in!** herein!; **she came into the kitchen** sie kam in die Küche.
● **to come off** (a button) abgehen ◇ SEP (PERF sein).
● **to come out** herauskommen ◇ SEP (PERF sein); **they came out when I called** als ich rief, kamen sie heraus; **the new CD's coming**

out soon die neue CD kommt bald heraus.
● **to come up** heraufkommen ◇ SEP (PERF sein); **can you come up a moment?** kannst du eine Sekunde heraufkommen?
● **to come up to somebody** auf jemanden zukommen ◇ SEP (PERF sein).

comedian noun Komiker der (PL die Komiker), Komikerin die (PL die Komikerinnen).

comedy noun Komödie die (PL die Komödien), Komikerin die (PL die Komikerinnen).

comfortable adjective 1 bequem; **this chair's really comfortable** dieser Sessel ist wirklich bequem; 2 **to feel comfortable** (a person) sich wohl fühlen.

comfortably adverb bequem.

comic noun (magazine) Comic-Heft das (PL die Comic-Hefte).

comic strip noun Comic der (PL die Comics).

comma noun Komma das (PL die Kommas).

comment noun (remark) Bemerkung die (PL die Bemerkungen); **he made some rude comments about my friends** er hat ein paar unhöfliche Bemerkungen über meine Freunde gemacht.

commentary noun Reportage die (PL die Reportagen); **the commentary on the soccer match** die Reportage über das Fußballspiel.

commentator noun Reporter der (PL die Reporter), Reporterin die (PL

△ NEW SPELLING: See page xii

die Reporterinnen); **sports
commentator** *der* Sportreporter.

commercial *noun* Werbespot *der*
(PL *die* Werbespots).
adjective kommerziell.

committee *noun* Ausschuss △ *der*
(PL *die* Ausschüsse).

common *adjective* 1 häufig; **it's a
common problem** das Problem
kommt häufig vor; 2 **in common**
gemeinsam; **they have nothing in
common** sie haben nichts
gemeinsam.

common sense *noun* gesunde
Menschenverstand *der*.

communication *noun*
Verständigung *die*.

communion *noun* (*in a Catholic
church*) Kommunion *die*; (*in a
Protestant church*) Abendmahl *das*.

communism *noun*
Kommunismus *der*.

community *noun*
Gemeinschaft *die* (PL *die*
Gemeinschaften); **the European
Community** die Europäische
Gemeinschaft.

commute *verb* **to commute
between Oxford and London**
zwischen Oxford und London
pendeln (PERF *sein*).

commuter *noun* Pendler *der* (PL *die*
Pendler), Pendlerin *die* (PL *die*
Pendlerinnen).

compact disc *noun*
Compactdisc △ *die* (PL *die*
Compactdiscs).

compact disc player *noun*
Compactdisc Spieler △ *der* (PL *die*
Compactdisc Spieler).

company *noun* 1 (*business*)
Gesellschaft *die* (PL *die*
Gesellschaften); **an airline
company** eine Fluggesellschaft;
she's set up a company sie hat eine
Firma gegründet; 2 (*group*)
Truppe *die* (PL *die* Truppen); **a
theatre company** eine
Theatertruppe; 3 **to keep
somebody company** jemandem
Gesellschaft leisten; **the dog keeps
me company** der Hund leistet mir
Gesellschaft.

compare *verb* vergleichen ✧; **if you
compare the German phrase with
the English** wenn man den
deutschen mit dem englischen
Ausdruck vergleicht; **our house is
small compared with yours** unser
Haus ist klein verglichen mit eurem.

compass *noun* Kompass △ *der* (PL
die Kompasse).

compatible *adjective* 1 zueinander
passend; 2 (*in computing*)
kompatibel.

compete *verb* 1 **to compete in
something** (*race, event*) an etwas
◄(DAT) teilnehmen ✧ SEP; 2 **to
compete with each other**
miteinander konkurrieren; 3 **to
compete for something** um etwas
◄(ACC) kämpfen; **thirty people are
competing for one job** dreißig Leute
kämpfen um eine Stelle.

competent *adjective* fähig.

✧ IRREGULAR VERB: *See the verb table in the centre of the dictionary*

competition noun 1 (a contest) Wettbewerb der (PL die Wettbewerbe); 2 (in a magazine) Preisausschreiben das (PL die Preisausschreiben).

competitor noun Konkurrent der (PL die Konkurrenten), Konkurrentin die (PL die Konkurrentinnen).

complain verb sich beschweren; **we complained about the meals** wir haben uns über das Essen beschwert.

complete adjective 1 (whole) vollständig; **the complete collection** die vollständige Sammlung; 2 (absolute) völlig; **a complete idiot** ein völliger Idiot (informal).
verb (to finish) beenden.

completely adverb völlig.

complexion noun Teint der (PL die Teints).

complicated adjective kompliziert.

compliment noun Kompliment das (PL die Komplimente); **to pay somebody a compliment** jemandem ein Kompliment machen.

composer noun Komponist der (PL die Komponisten), Komponistin die (PL die Komponistinnen).

comprehensive school noun Gemeinschaftsschule die (PL die Gemeinschaftsschulen).

compulsory adjective 1 obligatorisch; 2 (at school) **compulsory subject** das Pflichtfach.

computer noun Computer der (PL die Computer); **to work on a computer** mit einem Computer arbeiten; **to have something on computer** etwas im Computer gespeichert haben.

computer engineer noun Computeringenieur der (PL die Computeringenieure), Computeringenieurin die (PL die Computeringenieurinnen).

computer game noun Computerspiel das (PL die Computerspiele).

computer programmer noun Programmierer der (PL die Programmierer), Programmiererin die (PL die Programmiererinnen).

computer science noun Informatik die.

computing noun Computertechnik die.

concentrate verb sich konzentrieren; **I can't concentrate** ich kann mich nicht konzentrieren; **I was concentrating on the film** ich konzentrierte mich auf den Film.

concentration noun Konzentration die.

concern verb (to affect) betreffen ◇; **this doesn't concern you** das betrifft Sie nicht; **as far as I'm concerned** was mich betrifft.

concert noun 1 Konzert das (PL die Konzerte); **to go to a concert** ins Konzert gehen; 2 **concert ticket** die Konzertkarte.

conclusion noun Schluss △ der (PL die Schlüsse).

△ NEW SPELLING: See page xii

concrete noun Beton der; concrete floor der Betonboden.

condemn verb verurteilen; to condemn somebody to death jemanden zum Tode verurteilen.

condition noun 1 Zustand der (PL die Zustände); in good condition in gutem Zustand; weather conditions die Wetterlage; 2 (something you insist on) Bedingung die (PL die Bedingungen); on condition that you let me pay unter der Bedingung, dass du mich zahlen lässt.

conditioner noun (for your hair) Spülung die (PL die Spülungen).

condom noun Kondom das (PL die Kondome).

conduct noun Benehmen das. verb dirigieren (an orchestra or a piece of music).

conductor noun (of an orchestra) Dirigent der (PL die Dirigenten), Dirigentin die (PL die Dirigentinnen).

cone noun 1 (for ice-cream) Eistüte die (PL die Eistüten); 2 (for traffic) Kegel der (PL die Kegel).

conference noun Konferenz die (PL die Konferenzen).

confess verb gestehen ◇.

confession noun Geständnis das (PL die Geständnisse).

confidence noun 1 (self-confidence) Selbstvertrauen das; to be lacking in confidence kein Selbstvertrauen haben; 2 (faith in somebody else) Vertrauen das; to

have confidence in somebody zu jemandem Vertrauen haben.

confident adjective 1 (sure of yourself) selbstbewusst △; 2 (sure that something will happen) zuversichtlich.

confirm verb bestätigen; he confirmed the date er bestätigte das Datum.

confused adjective 1 wirr; a confused story eine wirre Geschichte; 2 durcheinander; I'm confused about the holiday plans ich bin mit den Ferienplänen durcheinander; now I'm completely confused jetzt bin ich völlig durcheinander.

confusing adjective verwirrend; the instructions are confusing die Anweisungen sind verwirrend.

confusion noun Verwirrung die.

congratulate verb gratulieren; I congratulated Tim on passing his exam ich gratulierte Tim zur bestandenen Prüfung.

congratulations plural noun Glückwünsche (plural); congratulations on the baby! herzlichen Glückwunsch zum Baby!

connect verb (to plug in to the mains) anschließen ◇ SEP (a dishwasher or TV, for example).

connection noun 1 (between two ideas or events) Zusammenhang der (PL die Zusammenhänge); there's no connection between his letter and my decision es besteht kein Zusammenhang zwischen seinem Brief und meiner Entscheidung; **2** (*between trains, planes, on phone, and electrical*) Anschluss △ *der* (PL *die* Anschlüsse); **Sally missed her connection** Sally hat ihren Anschluss verpasst.

conscience *noun* Gewissen *das*; **to have a guilty conscience** ein schlechtes Gewissen haben.

conservation (*of nature*) Schutz *der*; **environmental conservation** *der* Umweltschutz.

conservative *noun* Konservative *der/die* (PL *die* Konservativen). *adjective* konservativ.

conservatory *noun* Wintergarten *der* (PL *die* Wintergärten).

consider *verb* **1** sich ←(DAT) überlegen; (*a suggestion or idea*) **all things considered** alles in allem; **2** (*think about (doing)*) erwägen ◇; **we are considering buying a flat** wir erwägen, eine Wohnung zu kaufen.

considerate *adjective* rücksichtsvoll.

considering *preposition* wenn man bedenkt; **considering her age** wenn man ihr Alter bedenkt; **considering he did it all himself** wenn man bedenkt, dass er es ganz allein gemacht hat.

consist *verb* **to consist of** bestehen ◇ aus (+DAT).

constant *adjective* ständig.

construct *verb* bauen.

consumer *noun* Verbraucher *der* (PL *die* Verbraucher), Verbraucherin *die* (PL *die* Verbraucherinnen).

contact *noun* Kontakt *der* (PL *die* Kontakte); **to be in contact with somebody** mit jemandem in Kontakt sein; **we've lost contact** wir haben den Kontakt verloren; **Rob has contacts in the music business** Rob hat Kontakte zur Musikindustrie. *verb* sich in Verbindung setzen mit (+DAT); **I'll contact you tomorrow** ich setze mich morgen mit dir in Verbindung.

contact lens *noun* Kontaktlinse *die* (PL *die* Kontaktlinsen).

contain *verb* enthalten ◇.

container *noun* Behälter *der* (PL *die* Behälter).

contemporary *adjective* **1** (*around today*) zeitgenössisch; **2** (*modern*) modern.

contents *plural noun* Inhalt *der*; **the contents of my suitcase** der Inhalt meines Koffers.

contest *noun* Wettbewerb *der* (PL *die* Wettbewerbe).

contestant *noun* Teilnehmer *der* (PL *die* Teilnehmer), Teilnehmerin *die* (PL *die* Teilnehmerinnen).

continent *noun* Kontinent *der* (PL *die* Kontinente).

continue *verb* **1** fortsetzen SEP; **we continued (with) our journey** wir setzten unsere Reise fort; **2** to

continue to do something etwas weiter tun; **Jill continued talking** Jill redete weiter; **3 'to be continued'** 'Fortsetzung folgt'.

continuous *adjective* ununterbrochen.

contraceptive *noun* Verhütungsmittel *das* (PL *die* Verhütungsmittel).

contract *noun* Vertrag *der* (PL *die* Verträge).

contradict *verb* widersprechen ◊ (+DAT).

contradiction *noun* Widerspruch *der* (PL *die* Widersprüche).

contrary *noun* Gegenteil *das*; **on the contrary** im Gegenteil.

contrast *noun* Kontrast *der* (PL *die* Kontraste).

contribute *verb* beisteuern SEP (*money*).

contribution *noun* (*to charity or an appeal*) Spende *die* (PL *die* Spenden).

control *noun* (*of a crowd or animals*) Kontrolle *die*; **the police are in control of the situation** die Polizei hat die Situation unter Kontrolle; **keep your dogs under control** halten Sie Ihre Hunde unter Kontrolle; **everything's under control** alles ist unter Kontrolle; **to get out of control** außer Kontrolle geraten.
verb **to control yourself** sich beherrschen.

convenient *adjective* **1** praktisch; **frozen food is very convenient** Tiefkühlkost ist sehr praktisch; **2** **to be convenient for somebody** jemandem passen; **whenever's convenient for you** wann immer es dir passt.

conventional *adjective* konventionell.

conversation *noun* Gespräch *das* (PL *die* Gespräche).

convert *verb* **1** umwandeln SEP; **2** (*adapt a building*) umbauen SEP; **we're going to convert the garage into a workshop** wir wollen die Garage zu einer Werkstatt umbauen.

convince *verb* überzeugen; **I'm convinced he's wrong** ich bin davon überzeugt, dass er sich irrt.

convincing *adjective* überzeugend.

cook *noun* Koch *der* (PL *die* Köche), Köchin *die* (PL *die* Köchinnen).
verb **1** kochen; **who's cooking tonight?** wer kocht heute Abend?; **I like cooking** ich koche gern; **to cook vegetables and pasta** Gemüse und Nudeln kochen; **cook the cabbage for five minutes** lass den Kohl fünf Minuten kochen; **2** (*prepare food or a meal*) machen; **Fran's busy cooking supper** Fran macht gerade Abendessen; **how do you cook duck?** wie macht man Ente?; **3** (*boil*) kochen; (*fry or roast*) braten ◊; **the potatoes are cooking** die Kartoffeln kochen; **the sausages are cooking** die Würstchen braten.

cooker *noun* Herd *der* (PL *die* Herde); **electric cooker** der

◊ IRREGULAR VERB: See the verb table in the centre of the dictionary

Elektroherd; **gas cooker** der Gasherd.

cookery noun Kochen das.

cookery book noun Kochbuch das (PL die Kochbücher).

cooking noun 1 (preparing food) Kochen das; **cooking is fun** Kochen macht Spaß; **who's doing the cooking?** wer kocht?; 2 (food) Küche die; **Italian cooking** die italienische Küche.

cool noun 1 (coldness) Kühle die; 2 (calm) **to lose one's cool** durchdrehen SEP (PERF sein) (informal); **don't lose your cool!** dreh nicht durch!; **he kept his cool** er blieb gelassen.
adjective 1 (cold) kühl; **it's cool inside** es ist kühl drinnen; 2 (laid back) gelassen; **to stay cool** gelassen bleiben (PERF sein).
verb abkühlen SEP (PERF sein).

cop noun Polizist der (PL die Polizisten).

cope verb zurechtkommen ◊ SEP (PERF sein); **she copes well** sie kommt gut zurecht; **to cope with the children** mit den Kindern zurechtkommen; **she's had a lot to cope with** sie musste mit viel zurechtkommen.

copy noun 1 (photocopy) Kopie die (PL die Kopien); 2 (of a book) Exemplar das (PL die Exemplare).
verb 1 (imitate) kopieren; 2 (make a copy of) abschreiben ◊ SEP; **I copied (down) the address** ich habe die Adresse abgeschrieben; (in an exam) **to copy from somebody** bei jemandem abschreiben.

cord noun (for a blind, for example) Schnur die (PL die Schnüre).

cordless telephone noun schnurlose Telefon das (PL die schnurlosen Telefone).

core noun (of an apple or a pear) Kerngehäuse das (PL die Kerngehäuse).

cork noun 1 (in a bottle) Korken der (PL die Korken); 2 (material) Kork der.

corkscrew noun Korkenzieher der (PL die Korkenzieher).

corn noun 1 (wheat) Korn das; 2 (sweetcorn) Mais der.

corner noun 1 Ecke die (PL die Ecken); **at the corner of the street** an der Straßenecke; **it's just round the corner** es ist gleich um die Ecke; 2 (of mouth, eye) Winkel der (PL die Winkel); **out of the corner of your eye** aus dem Augenwinkel heraus; 3 (bend in the road) Kurve die (PL die Kurven); 4 (in football) Eckball der (PL die Eckbälle).

corpse noun Leiche die (PL die Leichen).

correct adjective 1 richtig; **the correct answer** die richtige Antwort; 2 **yes, that's correct** ja, das stimmt.
verb 1 verbessern; 2 (teacher) korrigieren; **the teacher has already corrected our homework**

△ NEW SPELLING: See page xii

der Lehrer hat unsere Hausaufgaben schon korrigiert.

correction noun Verbesserung die (PL die Verbesserungen).

corridor noun Korridor der (PL die Korridore).

cosmetics plural noun Kosmetik die.

cost noun 1 Kosten (plural); **the cost of living** die Lebenshaltungskosten (plural); 2 **the cost of a new computer** der Preis für einen neuen Computer. verb kosten; **how much does it cost?** was kostet es?; **the tickets cost £10** die Karten kosten zehn Pfund; **it costs too much** das ist zu teuer.

costume noun Kostüm das (PL die Kostüme).

cosy adjective (a room) gemütlich.

cot noun Kinderbett das (PL die Kinderbetten).

cottage noun Häuschen das (PL die Häuschen).

cotton noun 1 (fabric) Baumwolle die; **cotton shirt** das Baumwollhemd; 2 (thread) Nähgarn das (PL die Nähgarne).

cotton wool noun Watte die.

couch noun Couch die (PL die Couchs).

cough noun Husten der; **a nasty cough** ein schlimmer Husten; **to have a cough** Husten haben. verb husten.

could verb 1 (the past tense of können is used to translate 'was able to') **I couldn't open it** ich konnte es nicht aufmachen; **they couldn't come** sie konnten nicht kommen; **she did all she could** sie hat getan, was sie konnte; **he couldn't drive** er konnte nicht Auto fahren; **she couldn't see anything** sie konnte überhaupt nichts sehen; 2 (the past tense of dürfen is used to translate 'was allowed to') **they couldn't smoke there** sie durften da nicht rauchen; 3 (might) (the subjunctive of können is used to translate a wish or suggestion) **could I speak to David?** könnte ich David sprechen?; **you could try phoning** du könntest versuchen anzurufen; **if he could pay** wenn er zahlen könnte; **he could be right** er könnte recht haben.

count verb 1 (reckon up) zählen; **I counted my money** ich habe mein Geld gezählt; 2 (include) mitzählen SEP; **thirty-five not counting the children** fünfunddreißig, die Kinder nicht mitgezählt.

counter noun 1 (in a shop) Ladentisch der (PL die Ladentische); 2 (in a post office or bank) Schalter der (PL die Schalter); 3 (in a bar or café) Theke die (PL die Theken); 4 (for board games) Spielmarke die (PL die Spielmarken).

country noun 1 (Germany, England, etc.) Land das (PL die Länder); **a foreign country** ein fremdes Land; **from another country** aus einem anderen Land; 2 (not town)

◆ IRREGULAR VERB: See the verb table in the centre of the dictionary

Land *das*; **in the country** auf dem Land; **country road** *die* Landstraße.

country dancing *noun* Volkstanz *der*.

countryside *noun* 1 (*not town*) Land *das*; 2 (*scenery*) Landschaft *die*.

county *noun* Grafschaft *die* (PL *die* Grafschaften).

couple *noun* 1 (*a pair*) Paar *das* (PL *die* Paare); 2 **a couple of** ein paar; **a couple of times** ein paar Mal; **I've got a couple of things to do** ich habe ein paar Sachen zu tun.

courage *noun* Mut *der*.

course *noun* 1 (*lessons*) Kurs *der* (PL *die* Kurse); **computer course** *der* Computerkurs; **to go on a course** einen Kurs machen; 2 (*part of a meal*) Gang *der* (PL *die* Gänge); **the main course** *der* Hauptgang; 3 **golf course** *der* Golfplatz; 4 **of course** natürlich; **yes, of course!** ja, natürlich!; **he's forgotten, of course** er hat es natürlich vergessen.

court *noun* 1 (*for playing sports*) Platz *der* (PL *die* Plätze); 2 (*lawcourt*) Gericht *das*; **to go to court** vor Gericht gehen.

cousin *noun* Vetter *der* (PL *die* Vettern), Kusine *die* (PL *die* Kusinen); **my cousin Sonia** meine Kusine Sonia.

cover *noun* 1 (*of a book*) Einband *der* (PL *die* Einbände); 2 (*for a duvet or cushion*) Bezug *der* (PL *die* Bezüge).

verb 1 (*to cover up*) zudecken SEP; **he covered her with a blanket** er hat sie mit einer Decke zugedeckt; 2 **he was covered in spots** er war völlig verpickelt; **the room was covered in dust** das Zimmer war völlig verstaubt; 3 (*with leaves, snow, or for protection*) bedecken; **the ground was covered with snow** der Boden war mit Schnee bedeckt; 4 (*with fabric*) beziehen ✧.

cow *noun* Kuh *die* (PL *die* Kühe); **mad cow disease** *der* Rinderwahn.

coward *noun* Feigling *der* (PL *die* Feiglinge).

cowboy *noun* Cowboy *der* (PL *die* Cowboys).

crack *noun* 1 (*in a glass or cup*) Sprung *der* (PL *die* Sprünge); 2 (*in wood or a wall*) Riss *der* (PL *die* Risse); 3 (*a cracking noise*) Knack *der* (PL *die* Knacke). *verb* 1 (*to make a crack in*) anschlagen ✧ SEP; 2 (*to break*) zerbrechen ✧; 3 (*to make a noise*) (*a twig*) knacken.

cracker *noun* 1 (*biscuit*) Cracker *der* (PL *die* Cracker); 2 (*Christmas cracker*) Knallbonbon *der* (PL *die* Knallbonbons).

craft *noun* (*at school*) Werken *das*.

cramp *noun* Krampf *der* (PL *die* Krämpfe); **to have cramp in your leg** einen Krampf im Bein haben.

crash *noun* 1 (*an accident*) Unfall *der* (PL *die* Unfälle); **car crash** *der* Autounfall; 2 (*a noise*) Krachen *das*.

△ NEW SPELLING: *See page xii*

verb 1 (*a plane*) abstürzen SEP (PERF *sein*); **the plane crashed** das Flugzeug ist abgestürzt; 2 (*have a collision in a car*) einen Unfall haben; 3 **to crash into something** gegen etwas ←(ACC) krachen (PERF *sein*); **the car crashed into a tree** das Auto krachte gegen einen Baum.

crash course *noun* Schnellkurs *der* (PL die Schnellkurse).

crash helmet *noun* Sturzhelm *der* (PL die Sturzhelme).

crate *noun* Kiste *die* (PL die Kisten).

crawl *noun* (*in swimming*) Kraul *das*.
verb 1 (*a person*) kriechen ✧ (PERF *sein*); (*a baby*) krabbeln (PERF *sein*); 2 (*cars in a jam*) im Schneckentempo fahren ✧ (PERF *sein*); **we were crawling along** wir fuhren im Schneckentempo.

crayon *noun* 1 (*wax*) Wachsstift *der* (PL die Wachsstifte); 2 (*coloured pencil*) Buntstift *der* (PL die Buntstifte).

craze *noun* Mode *die*; **the craze for rollerskates** die Inlinermode.

crazy *adjective* verrückt; **to be crazy for something** verrückt auf etwas ←(ACC) sein.

cream *noun* Sahne *die*; **strawberries and cream** Erdbeeren mit Sahne.

cream cheese *noun* Frischkäse *der*.

creased *adjective* zerknittert.

creative *adjective* kreativ.

creature *noun* Geschöpf *das* (PL die Geschöpfe).

credit *noun* Kredit *der*; **to buy something on credit** etwas auf Kredit kaufen.

credit card *noun* Kreditkarte *die* (PL die Kreditkarten).

cress *noun* Kresse *die*.

crew *noun* 1 (*on a ship or plane*) Besatzung *die*; 2 **camera crew** Kamerateam; 3 (*in water sports*) Mannschaft *die* (PL die Mannschaften).

crew cut *noun* Bürstenschnitt (PL die Bürstenschnitte).

cricket *noun* 1 (*game*) Kricket; **to play cricket** Kricket spielen 2 (*insect*) Grille *die* (PL die Gril

cricket bat *noun* Kricketschläger *der*.

crime *noun* 1 Verbrechen *da* Verbrechen); **theft is a crime** Diebstahl ist ein Verbrechen; 2 (*criminality*) Kriminalität **fight crime** die Kriminalität bekämpfen.

criminal *noun* Kriminelle (PL die Kriminellen).
adjective kriminell.

crisis *noun* Krise *die* (PL

crisp *noun* Chip *der* (PL die **a packet of potato crisps** Kartoffelchips.
adjective 1 (*biscuit*) knuspr 2 (*apple*) knackig.

✧ IRREGULAR VERB: *See the verb table in the centre of the dictionary*

criticism noun Kritik die (PL die Kritiken).

criticize verb kritisieren.

crocodile noun Krokodil das (PL die Krokodile).

crook noun (criminal) Schwindler der (PL die Schwindler).

crop noun Ernte die.

cross noun Kreuz das (PL die Kreuze).
adjective ärgerlich; **she was very cross** sie war sehr ärgerlich; **I'm cross with you** ich bin sehr ärgerlich auf dich.
verb 1 (to cross over) überqueren; **to cross the road** die Straße überqueren; 2 **to cross your legs** die Beine übereinanderschlagen ◆ SEP; 3 (to cross each other) sich kreuzen; **the two roads cross here** die beiden Straßen kreuzen sich hier.
● **to cross out** ausstreichen ◆ SEP.

cross-Channel adjective **a cross-Channel ferry** eine Fähre über den Kanal.

cross-country noun 1 Cross der; 2 **cross-country skiing** der Langlauf.

crossing noun 1 (from one place to another) Überquerung die (PL die Überquerungen); 2 (a sea journey) Überfahrt die (PL die Überfahrten); **Channel crossing** die Überfahrt über den Kanal; 3 **pedestrian crossing** der Fußgängerübergang; **level crossing** der Bahnübergang.

crossroads noun Kreuzung die (PL die Kreuzungen); **at the crossroads** an der Kreuzung.

crossword noun Kreuzworträtsel das (PL die Kreuzworträtsel); **to do the crossword** ein Kreuzworträtsel machen.

crow noun Krähe die (PL die Krähen).
verb (a cock) krähen.

crowd noun 1 Menschenmenge die (PL die Menschenmengen); **in the crowd** in der Menschenmenge; 2 (spectators) **a crowd of five thousand** fünftausend Zuschauer (plural).
verb **to crowd into** or **onto something** sich in etwas ←(ACC) drängen; **we all crowded into the train** wir drängten uns alle in den Zug.

crowded adjective überfüllt.

crown noun Krone die (PL die Kronen).

crude adjective 1 (rough and ready) primitiv; 2 (vulgar) ordinär.

cruel adjective grausam.

crumb noun Krümel der (PL die Krümel).

crumpled adjective zerknittert.

crunchy adjective knusprig.

crush verb zerquetschen.

crust noun Kruste die (PL die Krusten).

crusty adjective knusprig.

△ NEW SPELLING: See page xii

crutch noun Krücke die (PL die Krücken); **to be on crutches** an Krücken gehen.

cry noun Schrei der (PL die Schreie). verb 1 (weep) weinen; 2 (call out) schreien ◇.

cub noun 1 (animal) Junge das (PL die Jungen); 2 (boy scout) Wölfling der (PL die Wölflinge).

cube noun Würfel der (PL die Würfel); **ice cube** der Eiswürfel.

cubic adjective (in measurements) Kubik-; **three cubic metres** drei Kubikmeter.

cubicle noun 1 (in a changing room) Kabine die; 2 (in a public lavatory) Toilette die (PL die Toiletten).

cuckoo noun Kuckuck der (PL die Kuckucke).

cucumber noun Gurke die (PL die Gurken).

cuddle noun **to give somebody a cuddle** jemanden in den Arm nehmen. verb schmusen.

cue noun (billiards, pool, snooker) Queue das (PL die Queues).

cuff noun (on a shirt) Manschette die (PL die Manschetten).

cul-de-sac noun Sackgasse die (PL die Sackgassen).

culture noun Kultur die (PL die Kulturen).

cunning adjective listig.

cup noun 1 (for drinking) Tasse die (PL die Tassen); **a cup of tea** eine Tasse Tee; 2 (a trophy) Pokal der (PL die Pokale).

cupboard noun Schrank der (PL die Schränke); **in the kitchen cupboard** im Küchenschrank.

cup tie noun Pokalspiel das (PL die Pokalspiele).

cure noun Heilmittel das (PL die Heilmittel). verb heilen.

curiosity noun Neugier die.

curious adjective neugierig.

curl noun Locke die (PL die Locken). verb 1 locken (hair); 2 (of hair) sich locken.

currant noun Korinthe die (PL die Korinthen).

currency noun Währung die (PL die Währungen); **the Japanese currency** die japanische Währung; **foreign currencies** Devisen (plural).

current noun 1 (electricity) Strom der; 2 (in water or air) Strömung die (PL die Strömungen). adjective aktuell.

current affairs noun Tagespolitik die.

curriculum noun Lehrplan der (PL die Lehrpläne).

curry noun Curry das; **vegetable curry** das Gemüse in Currysoße.

curtain noun Vorhang der (PL die Vorhänge).

cushion noun Kissen das (PL die Kissen).

◇ IRREGULAR VERB: *See the verb table in the centre of the dictionary*

custard noun Vanillesoße die (PL die Vanillesoßen).

custom noun Brauch der (PL die Bräuche).

customer noun Kunde der (PL die Kunden), Kundin die (PL die Kundinnen).

customs plural noun Zoll der; **to go through customs** durch den Zoll gehen.

customs hall noun Zollabfertigung die.

customs officer noun Zollbeamte der (PL die Zollbeamten), Zollbeamtin die (PL die Zollbeamtinnen).

cut noun 1 (injury) Schnittwunde die (PL die Schnittwunden); 2 (haircut) Schnitt der (PL die Schnitte). verb 1 schneiden ◇; **can you cut the bread please?** kannst du bitte Brot schneiden?; **you'll cut yourself!** du schneidest dich!; **Kevin's cut his finger** Kevin hat sich in den Finger geschnitten; 2 **to cut the grass** den Rasen mähen; 3 **to get your hair cut** sich ←(DAT) die Haare schneiden lassen; **I had my hair cut** ich habe mir die Haare schneiden lassen; 4 **to cut prices** die Preise senken.

● **to cut down** 1 fällen (a tree); 2 **to cut down on cigarettes** seinen Zigarettenkonsum einschränken SEP.

● **to cut out something** 1 etwas ausschneiden ◇ SEP (a shape, a newspaper article); 2 etwas streichen ◇ (sugar, fatty food, holidays, for example).

● **to cut something up** etwas zerschneiden ◇ (food).

cutlery noun Besteck das (PL die Bestecke).

CV noun Lebenslauf der (PL die Lebensläufe).

cycle noun (bike) Rad das (PL die Räder). verb Rad fahren ◇ Δ (PERF sein); **do you like cycling?** fährst du gerne Rad?; **we cycle to school** wir fahren mit dem Rad zur Schule.

cycle lane noun Fahrradspur die (PL die Fahrradspuren).

cycle race noun Radrennen das (PL die Radrennen).

cycling noun Radfahren das.

cycling shorts noun Radlerhose die (PL die Radlerhosen).

cyclist noun Radfahrer der (PL die Radfahrer), Radfahrerin die (PL die Radfahrerinnen).

D d

dad noun Vati der (PL die Vatis).

daffodil noun Osterglocke die (PL die Osterglocken).

daily adjective täglich.

dairy products plural noun Milchprodukte (plural).

daisy noun Gänseblümchen das (PL die Gänseblümchen).

damage noun Schaden der (PL die Schäden); **to do a lot of damage** großen Schaden anrichten.
verb beschädigen.

damn noun **I don't give a damn** das ist mir piepegal (informal).
exclamation **damn!** verdammt!

damp adjective feucht.
noun Feuchtigkeit die.

dance noun Tanz der (PL die Tänze); **a folk dance** ein Volkstanz.
verb tanzen; **I like dancing** ich tanze gerne.

dancer noun Tänzer der (PL die Tänzer), Tänzerin die (PL die Tänzerinnen).

dancing noun Tanzen das.

dancing class noun Tanzstunde die (PL die Tanzstunden); **to go to dancing classes** in die Tanzstunde gehen.

dandruff noun Schuppen (plural).

danger noun Gefahr die (PL die Gefahren); **to be in danger** in Gefahr sein.

dangerous adjective gefährlich; **it's dangerous to drive too fast** es ist gefährlich, zu schnell zu fahren.

Danish noun Dänisch das.
adjective dänisch; **he's Danish** er ist Däne; **she's Danish** sie ist Dänin.

dare verb **1** wagen; **to dare to do something** es wagen, etwas zu tun; **I didn't dare suggest it** ich habe es nicht gewagt, das vorzuschlagen; **2 don't you dare tell her I'm here!** unterseh dich, ihr zu sagen, dass ich da bin!; **3 I dare you!** trau dich!; **I**

dare you to tell him! sag's ihm, trau dich doch!

daring adjective gewagt; **that was a bit daring** das war etwas gewagt.

dark noun **in the dark** im Dunkeln; **after dark** nach Einbruch der Dunkelheit; **to be afraid of the dark** Angst im Dunkeln haben.
adjective **1** (colour) dunkel (adjectives ending in -el drop the e when followed by a vowel, which means that dunkel becomes dunkler/dunkle/dunkles); **a dark colour** eine dunkle Farbe; **it gets dark around five** es wird gegen fünf dunkel; **2 a dark blue skirt** ein dunkelblauer Rock; **she has dark brown hair** sie hat dunkelbraune Haare.

darkness noun Dunkelheit die; **in darkness** in der Dunkelheit.

darling noun Liebling der (PL die Lieblinge); **see you later, darling!** bis später, Liebling!

dart noun **1** Wurfpfeil der (PL die Wurfpfeile); **2** (game) **darts** Darts das; **to play darts** Darts spielen.

data plural noun Daten (plural).

database noun Datenbank die (PL die Datenbanken).

date noun **1** Datum das (PL die Daten); **what's the date today?** welches Datum haben wir heute?; **the date of the meeting** das Datum für das Treffen; **what date is he coming?** wann kommt er?; **2** Termin der (PL die Termine); **the**

◊ **IRREGULAR VERB: See the verb table in the centre of the dictionary**

last date for payment der letzte
Zahlungstermin; **3 out of date**
ungültig; **my passport's out of date**
mein Pass ist ungültig; **4** (*fruit*)
Dattel *die* (PL *die* Datteln).

date of birth *noun*
Geburtsdatum *das* (PL *die*
Geburtsdaten).

daughter *noun* Tochter *die* (PL *die*
Töchter); **Tina's daughter** Tinas
Tochter.

daughter-in-law *noun*
Schwiegertochter *die* (PL *die*
Schwiegertöchter).

dawn *noun* Morgendämmerung *die*
(PL *die* Morgendämmerungen).

day *noun* **1** Tag *der* (PL *die* Tage);
three days later drei Tage später; **a
few days ago** vor ein paar Tagen;
the day I went to London an dem
Tag, an dem ich nach London
gefahren bin; **we spent the day in
London** wir haben den Tag in
London verbracht; **it rained all day**
es hat den ganzen Tag geregnet; **the
day after** am Tag danach; **the day
after the wedding** am Tag nach der
Hochzeit; **the day before** am Tag
davor; **the day before the wedding**
am Tag vor der Hochzeit; **2 the day
after tomorrow** übermorgen; **my
sister's arriving the day after
tomorrow** meine Schwester kommt
übermorgen an; **3 the day before
yesterday** vorgestern; **my brother
arrived the day before yesterday**
mein Bruder kam vorgestern an;
4 during the day tagsüber.

dead *adjective* tot; **her father's
dead** ihr Vater ist tot.

adverb (*really*) irre (*informal*); **he's
dead nice** er ist irre nett; **it was
dead good** es war irre gut; **it was
dead easy** es war kinderleicht;
you're dead right du hast völlig
Recht; **she arrived dead on time** sie
kam auf die Minute pünktlich an.

deadline *noun* letzte Termin *der*
(PL *die* letzten Termine).

deaf *adjective* taub.

deafening *adjective*
ohrenbetäubend.

deal *noun* **1** (*involving money*)
Geschäft *das* (PL *die* Geschäfte); **it's
a good deal** das ist ein gutes
Geschäft; **2** (*agreement*)
Vereinbarung *die* (PL *die*
Vereinbarungen); **to make a deal
with somebody** mit jemandem eine
Vereinbarung treffen; **it's a deal!**
abgemacht!; **3 a great deal of** viel;
I don't have a great deal of time
ich habe nicht viel Zeit.
verb (*in cards*) geben; **it's you to
deal** du gibst.

● **to deal with something** sich um
etwas ←(ACC) kümmern; **Linda deals
with the accounts** Linda kümmert
sich um die Buchführung; **I'll deal
with it as soon as possible** ich
kümmere mich so schnell wie
möglich darum.

dear *adjective* **1** lieb; **Dear Franz**
Lieber Franz; **Dear Mr Smith** Sehr
geehrter Herr Smith; **2** (*expensive*)
teuer.

death *noun* Tod *der*; **after his
father's death** nach dem Tod seines
Vaters; **three deaths** drei

Todesfälle; ★ **I was bored to death** ich habe mich zu Tode gelangweilt; ★ **I'm sick to death of it** ich habe es gründlich satt.

death penalty noun Todesstrafe die.

debate noun Debatte die (PL die Debatten).
verb debattieren.

debt noun (money owed) Schulden (plural); **to get into debt** in Schulden geraten.

decaffeinated adjective koffeinfrei.

deceive verb betrügen◇.

December noun Dezember der (PL die Dezember); **in December** im Dezember.

decent adjective anständig; **a decent salary** ein anständiges Gehalt; **a decent meal** ein anständiges Essen.

decide verb 1 entscheiden◇; **to decide on something** sich für etwas ←(ACC) entscheiden; **he's decided against buying a new car** er hat sich entschieden, kein neues Auto zu kaufen; 2 **to decide to do something** sich entschließen◇, etwas zu tun; **they've decided to buy a house** sie haben sich entschlossen, ein Haus zu kaufen.

decimal adjective Dezimal-; **decimal number** die Dezimalzahl.

decimal point noun Komma das (PL die Kommas).

decision noun Entscheidung die (PL die Entscheidungen); **to make a**

decision eine Entscheidung treffen.

deckchair noun Liegestuhl der (PL die Liegestühle).

declare verb 1 erklären; 2 (at customs) **nothing to declare** nichts zu verzollen.

decorate verb 1 schmücken; **to decorate the Christmas tree** den Weihnachtsbaum schmücken; 2 (with paint) streichen◇; (with wallpaper) tapezieren; **we're decorating the kitchen this weekend** wir streichen dieses Wochenende die Küche.

decoration noun Verzierung die (PL die Verzierungen); **Christmas decorations** der Weihnachtsschmuck.

deep adjective tief; **a deep feeling of gratitude** ein tiefes Dankbarkeitsgefühl; **how deep is the swimming pool?** wie tief ist das Schwimmbecken?; **a hole two metres deep** ein zwei Meter tiefes Loch.

deep freeze noun Tiefkühltruhe die (PL die Tiefkühltruhen); (upright) Tiefkühlschrank der (PL die Tiefkühlschränke).

deeply adverb tief.

deer noun 1 Hirsch der (PL die Hirsche); 2 (roe deer) Reh das (PL die Rehe).

defeat noun Niederlage die (PL die Niederlagen).
verb schlagen◇.

defence noun Verteidigung die.

◇ IRREGULAR VERB: See the verb table in the centre of the dictionary

defend *verb* verteidigen.

defender *noun* Verteidiger der (PL die Verteidiger), Verteidigerin die (PL die Verteidigerinnen).

definite *adjective* 1 eindeutig; a definite improvement eine eindeutige Besserung; 2 (*certain*) sicher; it's not definite yet es ist noch nicht sicher; 3 (*exact*) klar; a definite answer eine klare Antwort.

definitely *adverb* 1 (*when giving your opinion about something*) eindeutig; your German is definitely better than mine dein Deutsch ist eindeutig besser als meins; 2 (*without doubt*) bestimmt; she's definitely going to be there sie wird bestimmt dort sein; I'm definitely not coming ich komme ganz bestimmt nicht; 3 'are you sure you like this one better?' – 'definitely!' 'gefällt dir diese wirklich besser?' – 'klar!' (*informal*).

degree *noun* 1 Grad der (PL die Grade); thirty degrees dreißig Grad; 2 a university degree ein akademischer Grad.

delay *noun* Verspätung die (PL die Verspätungen); a two-hour delay eine zweistündige Verspätung.
verb 1 (*hold up*) aufhalten ◇ SEP; she was delayed in the office sie ist im Büro aufgehalten worden; 2 (*train, plane*) to be delayed Verspätung haben; the flight was delayed by bad weather der Flug hatte wegen des schlechten Wetters Verspätung; 3 (*postpone*) aufschieben ◇ SEP; the decision has been delayed until Thursday die

Entscheidung wurde bis Donnerstag aufgeschoben.

delete *verb* 1 streichen ◇; 2 (*in computing*) löschen.

deliberate *adjective* absichtlich.

deliberately *adverb* absichtlich; she did it deliberately sie hat das absichtlich getan.

delicate *adjective* 1 (*fabric, health*) zart; 2 (*situation, question*) heikel; 3 (*taste, smell*) fein.

delicatessen *noun* Feinkostgeschäft das (PL die Feinkostgeschäfte).

delicious *adjective* köstlich.

delighted *adjective* hocherfreut; to be delighted begeistert sein; they're delighted with their new flat sie sind von ihrer neuen Wohnung begeistert; I'm delighted that you can come ich freue mich sehr, dass ihr kommen könnt.

deliver *verb* 1 liefern; they're delivering the washing machine tomorrow die Waschmaschine wird morgen geliefert; 2 (*mail, newspapers*) zustellen SEP.

delivery *noun* 1 Lieferung die (PL die Lieferungen); 2 (*of mail, newspapers*) Zustellung die (PL die Zustellungen).

demand *noun* Nachfrage die (PL die Nachfragen); much in demand sehr gefragt.
verb verlangen.

demo *noun* (*protest*) Demo die (*informal*) (PL die Demos).

△ NEW SPELLING: See page xii

democracy noun Demokratie die
(PL die Demokratien).

democratic adjective
demokratisch.

demonstrate verb 1 (a machine,
product, or technique) vorführen SEP;
2 (protest) demonstrieren; **to
demonstrate against something**
gegen etwas ←(ACC) demonstrieren.

demonstration noun 1 (of a
machine, product, or technique)
Vorführung die (PL die
Vorführungen); 2 (protest)
Demonstration die (PL die
Demonstrationen).

demonstrator noun
Demonstrant der (PL die
Demonstranten), Demonstrantin
die (PL die Demonstrantinnen).

denim noun Jeansstoff der (PL die
Jeansstoffe); **a denim jacket** eine
Jeansjacke.

Denmark noun Dänemark das.

dental adjective 1 Zahn-; **dental
floss** die Zahnseide; **dental hygiene**
die Zahnpflege; 2 **to have a dental
appointment** beim Zahnarzt
angemeldet sein.

dentist noun Zahnarzt der (PL die
Zahnärzte), Zahnärztin die (PL die
Zahnärztinnen); **my mum's a
dentist** meine Mutter ist
Zahnärztin.

deny verb bestreiten ◊.

deodorant noun Deodorant das
(PL die Deodorants).

depart verb 1 (set out on a journey)
abreisen SEP (PERF sein); 2 (train,
coach) abfahren ◊ SEP (PERF sein);
3 (plane) abfliegen ◊ SEP (PERF sein).

department noun 1 (in a shop,
firm, or hospital) Abteilung die (PL
die Abteilungen); **the men's
department** die Herrenabteilung;
2 (of a university) Seminar das (PL
die Seminare); **the history
department** das Seminar für
Geschichte; 3 (in school)
Fachbereich der (PL die
Fachbereiche).

department store noun
Kaufhaus das (PL die Kaufhäuser).

departure noun 1 (of a person)
Abreise die; 2 (of a car, train)
Abfahrt die; 3 (of a plane)
Abflug der.

departure lounge noun
Abflughalle die (PL die
Abflughallen).

depend verb **1 to depend on**
abhängen ◊ SEP von (+DAT); **it
depends on the price** das hängt
vom Preis ab; **it depends on what
you want** das hängt davon ab, was
du willst; 2 **it depends** es kommt
darauf an.

deposit noun 1 (when renting or
hiring) Kaution die (PL die
Kautionen); 2 (when booking a
holiday or hotel room)
Anzahlung die (PL die Anzahlungen);
to pay a deposit eine Anzahlung
leisten; 3 (on a bottle) Pfand das.

depressed adjective deprimiert.

depressing adjective
deprimierend.

◊ IRREGULAR VERB: See the verb table in the centre of the dictionary

depth noun Tiefe die.

deputy noun Stellvertreter der (PL die Stellvertreter), Stellvertreterin die (PL die Stellvertreterinnen).

describe verb beschreiben ◇.

description noun Beschreibung die (PL die Beschreibungen).

desert noun Wüste die (PL die Wüsten).

desert island noun verlassene Insel die (PL die verlassenen Inseln).

deserve verb verdienen.

design noun 1 Konstruktion die (PL die Konstruktionen); **the design of the plane** die Flugzeugkonstruktion; 2 (artistic design) Design das (PL die Designs); **modern design** modernes Design; 3 (pattern) Muster das (PL die Muster); **a floral design** ein Blumenmuster; 4 (sketch) Entwurf der (PL die Entwürfe).
verb 1 konstruieren (a machine, plane, system); 2 entwerfen ◇ (costumes, fabric, scenery).

designer noun Designer der (PL die Designer), Designerin die (PL die Designerinnen).

desk noun 1 (in an office or at home) Schreibtisch der (PL die Schreibtische); 2 (pupil's) Pult das (PL die Pulte); 3 **the reception desk** die Rezeption; **the information desk** die Auskunft.

despair noun Verzweiflung die.
verb **to despair of doing**

something alle Hoffnung aufgeben ◇ SEP, etwas zu tun.

desperate adjective 1 verzweifelt; **a desperate attempt** ein verzweifelter Versuch; 2 **to be desperate to do something** etwas dringend tun müssen; **I'm desperate to speak to you** ich muss dich dringend sprechen; **to be desperate for something** etwas dringend brauchen.

dessert noun Nachtisch der (PL die Nachtische); **what's for dessert?** was gibt's zum Nachtisch?

destination noun Ziel das (PL die Ziele).

destroy verb zerstören.

destruction noun Zerstörung die.

detached house noun Einzelhaus das (PL die Einzelhäuser).

detail noun Einzelheit die (PL die Einzelheiten).

detailed adjective ausführlich.

detective noun 1 (in the police) Kriminalbeamte der (PL die Kriminalbeamten), Kriminalbeamtin die (PL die Kriminalbeamtinnen); 2 **private detective** der Detektiv, die Detektivin.

detective story noun Detektivgeschichte die (PL die Detektivgeschichten).

detention noun 1 (at school) Nachsitzen das; 2 (in prison) Haft die.

△ NEW SPELLING: See page xii

detergent noun Waschmittel das
(PL die Waschmittel).

determined adjective
entschlossen; **he's determined to
leave** er ist fest entschlossen zu
gehen.

detour noun Umweg der (PL die
Umwege).

develop verb 1 entwickeln; **to get a
film developed** einen Film
entwickeln lassen; 2 sich
entwickeln; **how children develop**
wie Kinder sich entwickeln.

developing country noun
Entwicklungsland das (PL die
Entwicklungsländer).

development noun
Entwicklung die (PL die
Entwicklungen).

devil noun Teufel der (PL die Teufel).

devoted adjective treu.

diabetes noun
Zuckerkrankheit die.

diabetic noun Diabetiker der (PL die
Diabetiker), Diabetikerin die (PL die
Diabetikerinnen).
adjective zuckerkrank; **to be
diabetic** zuckerkrank sein.

diagonal adjective diagonal.

diagram noun Diagramm das (PL
die Diagramme).

dial verb wählen; **I dialled the wrong
number** ich habe die falsche
Nummer gewählt.

dialling tone noun
Freizeichen das.

dialogue noun Dialog der (PL die
Dialoge).

diamond noun 1 Diamant der (PL
die Diamanten); (gemstone)
Brillant der (PL die Brillanten); 2 (in
cards) Karo das; **the jack of
diamonds** der Karobube; 3 (shape)
Raute die (PL die Rauten).

diarrhoea noun Durchfall der.

diary noun 1 (for appointments)
Terminkalender der (PL die
Terminkalender); 2 Tagebuch das
(PL die Tagebücher); **to keep a diary**
ein Tagebuch führen.

dice noun Würfel der (PL die Würfel);
to throw the dice würfeln.

dictation noun Diktat das (PL die
Diktate).

dictionary noun Wörterbuch das
(PL die Wörterbücher).

did verb SEE do.

die verb 1 sterben ◇ (PERF sein); **my
grannie died in January** meine
Oma starb im Januar; 2 **to be dying
to do something** darauf brennen,
etwas zu tun; **I'm dying to meet her**
ich brenne darauf, sie kennen zu
lernen.

diesel noun 1 Dieselöl das; 2 **diesel
engine** der Dieselmotor; **diesel car**
der Diesel.

diet noun 1 Ernährung die; **a
healthy diet** eine gesunde
Ernährung; 2 (slimming or special)
Diät die (PL die Diäten); **to be on a
diet** Diät machen.

◇ **IRREGULAR VERB: See the verb table in the centre of the dictionary**

difference noun 1 Unterschied der (PL die Unterschiede); **I can't see any difference between the two** ich finde, es besteht kein Unterschied zwischen den beiden; **what's the difference between ...?** was ist der Unterschied zwischen ...?; 2 **it makes a difference** es ist ein Unterschied; **it makes no difference** es ist egal; **it makes no difference what I say** es ist egal, was ich sage.

different adjective 1 verschieden; **the two sisters are very different** die beiden Schwestern sind sehr verschieden; 2 **to be different from** anders sein als; **she's very different from her sister** sie ist ganz anders als ihre Schwester; 2 (separate) anderer/andere/anderes; **she reads a different book every day** sie liest jeden Tag ein anderes Buch.

difficult adjective schwer; **it's really difficult** es ist sehr schwer; **he finds it difficult** es fällt ihm schwer.

difficulty noun Schwierigkeit die (PL die Schwierigkeiten); **to have difficulty doing something** Schwierigkeiten haben, etwas zu tun; **I had difficulty finding your house** ich hatte Schwierigkeiten, dein Haus zu finden.

dig verb graben ◇; **to dig a hole** ein Loch graben.

digital adjective digital; **digital watch** die Digitaluhr; **digital recording** die Digitalaufnahme.

din noun Lärm der; **stop making such a din!** hör auf, so einen Lärm zu machen!

dinghy noun 1 **sailing dinghy** das Dingi; 2 **rubber dinghy** das Schlauchboot.

dining room noun Esszimmer △ das (PL die Esszimmer); **in the dining room** im Esszimmer.

dinner noun 1 (evening) Abendessen das (PL die Abendessen); **to invite somebody to dinner** jemanden zum Abendessen einladen; 2 (midday) Mittagessen das (PL die Mittagessen); **to have school dinner** in der Schulkantine zu Mittag essen.

dinner party noun Abendessen das (PL die Abendessen).

dinner time noun Essenszeit die.

dinosaur noun Dinosaurier der (PL die Dinosaurier).

diploma noun Diplom das (PL die Diplome).

direct adjective direkt.
verb 1 **to direct a film or a play** bei einem Film oder einem Theaterstück Regie führen; 2 regeln (traffic).

direction noun 1 Richtung die (PL die Richtungen); **to go in the other direction** in die andere Richtung gehen; 2 **to ask somebody for directions** jemanden nach dem Weg fragen; 3 **directions for use** die Gebrauchsanweisung (singular).

director noun 1 (of a company) Direktor der (PL die Direktoren), Direktorin die (PL die Direktorinnen); 2 (of a programme, play, or film) Regisseur der (PL die Regisseure), Regisseurin die (PL die Regisseurinnen).

directory noun Telefonbuch das (PL die Telefonbücher); **he's ex-directory** seine Nummer steht nicht im Telefonbuch.

dirt noun Schmutz der.

dirty adjective schmutzig; **my hands are dirty** ich habe schmutzige Hände; **to get something dirty** etwas schmutzig machen; **you'll get your dress dirty** du machst dir das Kleid schmutzig; **to get dirty** schmutzig werden; **the curtains get dirty quickly** die Vorhänge werden sehr schnell schmutzig.

disabled adjective behindert; **disabled people** Behinderte (plural);

disadvantage noun 1 Nachteil der (PL die Nachteile); 2 **to be at a disadvantage** im Nachteil sein.

disagree verb 1 **I disagree** ich bin anderer Meinung; 2 **to disagree with somebody** mit jemandem nicht übereinstimmen SEP; **I disagree with James** ich stimme mit James nicht überein.

disappear verb verschwinden ◇ (PERF sein).

disappearance noun Verschwinden das.

disappointed adjective enttäuscht; **I'm disappointed with my marks** ich bin über meine Noten enttäuscht.

disappointment noun Enttäuschung die (PL die Enttäuschungen).

disaster noun Katastrophe die (PL die Katastrophen); **it was a complete disaster** es war eine komplette Katastrophe.

disastrous adjective katastrophal.

disc noun 1 **compact disc** die Compact disc; 2 **tax disc** (for a vehicle) die Steuerplakette; 3 **slipped disc** der Bandscheibenvorfall.

discipline noun Disziplin die.

disc-jockey noun Diskjockey der (PL die Diskjockeys).

disco noun 1 Diskoparty die (PL die Diskopartys); **they're having a disco** sie machen eine Diskoparty; 2 (club) Disko die (PL die Diskos); **to go to a disco** in eine Disko gehen.

discount noun Rabatt der (PL die Rabatte).

discover verb entdecken.

discovery noun Entdeckung die (PL die Entdeckungen).

discreet adjective diskret.

discrimination noun Diskriminierung die; **discrimination against women** die Diskriminierung von Frauen; **racial discrimination** die Rassendiskriminierung.

discuss verb **to discuss something** etwas besprechen ◇; **we'll discuss the problem tomorrow** wir besprechen das Problem morgen;

◇ IRREGULAR VERB: See the verb table in the centre of the dictionary

I'm going to discuss it with Phil ich werde es mit Phil besprechen.

discussion noun Gespräch das (PL die Gespräche).

disease noun Krankheit die (PL die Krankheiten).

disguise noun Verkleidung die (PL die Verkleidungen); **to be in disguise** verkleidet sein. verb verkleiden; **disguised as a woman** als Frau verkleidet.

disgust noun Ekel der.

disgusted adjective 1 (filled with indignation) empört; 2 (nauseated) angeekelt.

disgusting adjective eklig.

dish noun 1 Schüssel die (PL die Schüsseln); **a large white dish** eine große weiße Schüssel; **satellite dish** die Satellitenschüssel; 2 (type of food) Gericht das (PL die Gerichte); **risotto is my favourite dish** Risotto ist mein Lieblingsgericht; 3 (crockery) **the dishes** das Geschirr; **to do the dishes** Geschirr spülen.

dishonest adjective unehrlich.

dishonesty noun Unehrlichkeit die.

dishwasher noun Geschirrspülmaschine die (PL die Geschirrspülmaschinen).

disinfectant noun Desinfektionsmittel das.

disk noun Diskette die (PL die Disketten); **floppy disk** die Diskette; **hard disk** die Festplatte.

diskette noun Diskette die (PL die Disketten).

dismiss verb entlassen ❖ (an employee).

disobedient adjective ungehorsam.

display noun 1 Ausstellung die (PL die Ausstellungen); **handicrafts display** die Handarbeitsausstellung; **to be on display** ausgestellt sein; 2 **window display** die Auslage; 3 **firework display** das Feuerwerk. verb ausstellen SEP.

disposable adjective Wegwerf-; **disposable towel** das Wegwerfhandtuch.

disqualify verb disqualifizieren.

dissolve verb auflösen SEP.

distance noun Entfernung die (PL die Entfernungen); **from this distance** aus dieser Entfernung; **from a distance** von weitem; **in the distance** in der Ferne; **it's within walking distance** es ist zu Fuß erreichbar.

distant adjective fern.

distinct adjective deutlich.

distinctly adverb 1 deutlich; 2 **it's distinctly odd** es ist äußerst komisch.

distract verb ablenken SEP.

distribute verb verteilen.

district noun 1 (of a town) Stadtteil der (PL die Stadtteile); **a poor district of Berlin** ein ärmlicher Stadtteil von Berlin; 2 (in the country) Gebiet das (PL die Gebiete).

△ NEW SPELLING: See page xii

disturb verb stören; **sorry to disturb you** Entschuldigung, dass ich störe.

dive noun Kopfsprung der (PL die Kopfsprünge).
verb 1 einen Kopfsprung machen; 2 (swim underwater) tauchen (PERF sein).

diver noun 1 (underwater) Taucher der (PL die Taucher), Taucherin die (PL die Taucherinnen); 2 (from a diving board) Springer der (PL die Springer), Springerin die (PL die Springerinnen).

diversion noun (of traffic) Umleitung die (PL die Umleitungen).

divide verb teilen.

diving noun 1 (underwater) Tauchen das; 2 (from a diving board) Kopfspringen das.

diving board noun Sprungbrett das (PL die Sprungbretter).

division noun 1 Teilung die (PL die Teilungen); 2 (in maths) Division die (PL die Divisionen); 3 (sports league) Liga die (PL die Ligen).

divorce noun Scheidung die (PL die Scheidungen).

divorced adjective geschieden.

DIY noun 1 Heimwerken das; 2 to do DIY heimwerken; 3 DIY shop der Baumarkt (PL die Baumärkte).

dizzy adjective I feel dizzy mir ist schwindlig.

DJ noun DJ der (PL die DJs).

do verb 1 tun ✧, machen; what are you doing? was machst du?; I'm doing my homework ich mache meine Hausaufgaben; what have you done with the hammer? was hast du mit dem Hammer gemacht?; can you do me a favour? kannst du mir einen Gefallen tun?; do as I say tu was ich sage; 2 she's doing the cleaning sie putzt; I'll do the washing up ich wasche ab; I must do the shopping ich muss einkaufen gehen; 3 (in questions) do you like it? gefällt es dir?; when does the film start? wann fängt der Film an?; how do you open the door? wie macht man die Tür auf?; do you know him? kennst du ihn?; 4 (in negative sentences) I don't like mushrooms ich mag keine Pilze; Rosie doesn't like spinach Rosie mag keinen Spinat; you didn't shut the door du hast die Tür nicht zugemacht; it doesn't matter das macht nichts; 5 (when it refers back to another verb, 'do' is not translated) 'do you live here?' – 'yes, I do' 'wohnst du hier?' – 'ja'; she has more money than I do sie hat mehr Geld als ich; 'I live in Oxford' – 'so do I' 'ich wohne in Oxford' – 'ich auch'; 'I didn't phone Gemma' – 'neither did I' 'ich habe Gemma nicht angerufen' – 'ich auch nicht'; 6 don't you?, doesn't he?, etc. nicht wahr?; you know Helen, don't you? du kennst Helen, nicht wahr?; she left on Thursday, didn't she? sie ist Donnerstag abgefahren, nicht

✧ IRREGULAR VERB: See the verb table in the centre of the dictionary

wahr?; **7** that'll do das reicht; **it'll
do like that** das geht so.

● **to do something up 1** etwas
zubinden ◇ SEP (*shoes*); **2** etwas
zumachen SEP (*a cardigan, jacket*);
3 etwas renovieren (*a house*).

● **to do without something** ohne etwas
←(ACC) auskommen ◇ SEP (PERF *sein*);
we can do without knives wir
können ohne Messer auskommen.

doctor *noun* Arzt *der* (PL *die* Ärzte,
Ärztin *die* (PL *die* Ärztinnen); **her
mother's a doctor** ihre Mutter ist
Ärztin.

documentary *noun*
Dokumentarfilm *der* (PL *die*
Dokumentarfilme).

dog *noun* Hund *der* (PL *die* Hunde).

do-it-yourself *noun*
Heimwerken *das*.

dole *noun* Stempelgeld *das*; **to be
on the dole** stempeln gehen
(*informal*).

doll *noun* Puppe *die* (PL *die* Puppen).

dollar *noun* Dollar *der* (PL *die*
Dollars).

domino *noun* **1** Dominostein *der*
(PL *die* Dominosteine); **2** (*game*)
dominoes Domino *das*; **to play
dominoes** Domino spielen.

donkey *noun* Esel *der* (PL *die* Esel).

don't SEE do.

door *noun* Tür *die* (PL *die* Türen); **to
open the door** die Tür aufmachen;
to shut the door die Tür zumachen.

doorbell *noun* Türklingel *die* (PL *die*
Türklingeln); **to ring the doorbell**
klingeln.

dot *noun* **1** Punkt *der* (PL *die* Punkte);
at ten on the dot Punkt zehn Uhr;
2 (*small dot on fabric*)
Pünktchen *das* (PL *die* Pünktchen).

double *adjective, adverb* **1** doppelt;
a double helping eine doppelte
Portion; **double the size** doppelt so
groß; **double the time** doppelt so
viel Zeit; **at double the price** zum
doppelten Preis; **2 double room** *das*
Doppelzimmer; **3 double bed** *das*
Doppelbett.

double bass *noun*
Kontrabass △ *der* (PL *die*
Kontrabässe).

double-decker bus *noun*
Doppeldeckerbus *der* (PL *die*
Doppeldeckerbusse).

doubles *noun* (*in tennis*)
Doppel *das* (PL *die* Doppel).

doubt *noun* Zweifel *der* (PL *die*
Zweifel); **there's no doubt about it**
es besteht kein Zweifel daran; **I have
my doubts** ich habe gewisse
Zweifel.
verb ● **to doubt something** etwas
bezweifeln; **I doubt it** das bezweifle
ich; **I doubt that …** ich bezweifle,
dass …; **I doubt they'll buy it** ich
bezweifle, dass sie es kaufen.

doubtful *adjective* **1** fraglich; **it's
doubtful** es ist fraglich; **2 to be
doubtful about doing something**
Bedenken haben, ob man etwas tun
soll; **I'm doubtful about inviting
them together** ich habe Bedenken,
ob ich sie zusammen einladen soll.

△ NEW SPELLING: *See page xii*

dough noun Teig der.

doughnut noun Krapfen der (PL die Krapfen).

down adverb, preposition 1 unten; he's down in the cellar er ist unten im Keller; it's down there es ist da unten; 2 down the road (nearby) in der Nähe; there's a chemist's just down the road eine Apotheke ist ganz in der Nähe; 3 to go down nach unten gehen; I went down to open the door ich bin nach unten gegangen, um die Tür aufzumachen; to walk down the street die Straße entlanggehen ◇ SEP (PERF sein); to run down the stairs die Treppe runterrennen SEP (PERF sein) (informal); 4 to come down herunterkommen ◇ SEP (PERF sein); she came down into the kitchen sie kam in die Küche herunter; 5 to sit down sich setzen; she sat down on the chair sie setzte sich auf den Stuhl; 6 to write something down etwas aufschreiben ◇ SEP.

downstairs adverb 1 unten; she's downstairs sie ist unten; 2 (with movement) nach unten; to go downstairs nach unten gehen; 3 im Erdgeschoss △; the flat downstairs die Wohnung im Erdgeschoss.

dozen noun Dutzend das (PL die Dutzende).

drag noun 1 what a drag! so'n Mist! (informal); 2 what a drag she is! Mann, ist die langweilig! (informal). verb schleppen.

drama noun 1 (play) Drama das (PL die Dramen); he made a big drama out of it er hat ein großes Drama daraus gemacht (informal); 2 (dramatic nature) Dramatik die.

dramatic adjective dramatisch.

draught noun Luftzug der; there's a draught in here hier zieht es.

draughts noun Damespiel das; to play draughts Dame spielen.

draw noun 1 (in a match) Unentschieden das; to end in a draw mit einem Unentschieden enden; 2 (lottery) Ziehung die (PL die Ziehungen). verb 1 zeichnen; she can draw really well sie kann wirklich sehr gut zeichnen; 2 to draw the curtains (open) die Vorhänge aufziehen ◇ SEP; (close) die Vorhänge zuziehen ◇ SEP; 3 (in a match) unentschieden spielen; we drew three all wir haben drei zu drei unentschieden gespielt.

drawer noun Schublade die (PL die Schubladen).

drawing noun Zeichnung die (PL die Zeichnungen).

drawing pin noun Reißzwecke die (PL die Reißzwecken).

dreadful adjective furchtbar.

dreadfully adverb furchtbar; I'm dreadfully late ich habe mich furchtbar verspätet; I'm dreadfully sorry es tut mir furchtbar Leid.

dream noun Traum der (PL die Träume); to have a dream einen Traum haben. verb träumen; to dream about something von etwas ←(DAT) träumen.

◇ IRREGULAR VERB: See the verb table in the centre of the dictionary

dress noun Kleid das (PL die Kleider).
verb to dress a child ein Kind anziehen ◇ SEP.
● to dress up sich verkleiden; to dress up as a vampire sich als Vampir verkleiden.

dressed adjective 1 angezogen; is Tom dressed yet? ist Tom schon angezogen?; 2 she was dressed in black trousers and a yellow shirt sie trug schwarze Hosen und ein gelbes Hemd; 3 to get dressed sich anziehen ◇ SEP; I got dressed quickly ich zog mich schnell an.

dressing gown noun Morgenrock der (PL die Morgenröcke).

dressing table noun Frisierkommode die (PL die Frisierkommoden).

drier noun hair drier der Föhn △; tumble drier der Wäschetrockner.

drill noun Bohrer der (PL die Bohrer).

drink noun Getränk das (PL die Getränke); 1 to have a drink etwas trinken; would you like a drink of water? möchtest du etwas Wasser trinken?; 2 (an alcoholic drink) Drink der (PL die Drinks); they've invited us round for drinks sie haben uns auf einen Drink eingeladen; let's have a drink! trinken wir einen! (informal).
verb trinken ◇; he drank a glass of water er trank ein Glas Wasser.

drive noun 1 to go for a drive eine Autofahrt machen; 2 (in front of a house) Einfahrt die (PL die Einfahrten).

verb 1 fahren ◇ (PERF sein); she drives very fast sie fährt sehr schnell; to drive a car Auto fahren; I'd like to learn to drive ich möchte Autofahren lernen; can you drive? kannst du Auto fahren?; 2 we drove to Berlin wir sind mit dem Auto nach Berlin gefahren; 3 to drive somebody (to a place) jemanden (irgendwohin) fahren (PERF haben); Mum drove me to the station Mutti hat mich zum Bahnhof gefahren; to drive somebody home jemanden nach Hause fahren; ★ she drives me mad! sie macht mich verrückt!

driver noun 1 Fahrer der (PL die Fahrer), Fahrerin die (PL die Fahrerinnen); 2 (of a locomotive) Führer der (PL die Führer), Führerin die (PL die Führerinnen).

driving instructor noun Fahrlehrer der (PL die Fahrlehrer), Fahrlehrerin die (PL die Fahrlehrerinnen).

driving lesson noun Fahrstunde die (PL die Fahrstunden).

driving licence noun Führerschein der.

driving test noun Fahrprüfung die; to take your driving test die Fahrprüfung machen; Jenny's passed her driving test Jenny hat den Führerschein gemacht.

drop noun Tropfen der (PL die Tropfen).
verb 1 to drop something etwas fallen lassen; I dropped my glasses

△ NEW SPELLING: See page xii

ich habe meine Brille fallen lassen; **2 drop it!** lass das!; **3 I'm going to drop history next year** nächstes Jahr lege ich Geschichte ab; **4** absetzen SEP (*a person*); **could you drop me at the station?** könntest du mich am Bahnhof absetzen?

drug noun **1** (*medicine*) Medikament *das* (PL die Medikamente); **2** (*illegal*) **drugs** Drogen (*plural*).

drug abuse noun Drogenmissbrauch △ *der*.

drug addict noun Drogenabhängige *der/die* (PL die Drogenabhängigen).

drug addiction noun Drogenabhängigkeit *die*.

drum noun **1** Trommel *die* (PL die Trommeln); **2 drums** das Schlagzeug; **to play drums** Schlagzeug spielen.

drummer noun Schlagzeuger *der* (PL die Schlagzeuger).

drunk noun Betrunkene *der/die* (PL die Betrunkenen). adjective betrunken; **to get drunk** sich betrinken ◇.

dry adjective trocken. verb **1** trocknen; **to let something dry** etwas trocknen lassen; **to dry your hair** sich ←(DAT) die Haare trocknen; **to dry the washing** die Wäsche trocknen; **2 to dry your hands** sich ←(DAT) die Hände abtrocknen SEP; **I dried my feet** ich trocknete mir die Füße ab; **to dry the dishes** das Geschirr abtrocknen .

dry cleaner's noun chemische Reinigung *die*.

dryer noun SEE **drier**.

dubbed adjective **a dubbed film** ein synchronisierter Film.

duck noun Ente *die* (PL die Enten).

due adjective, adverb **1 to be due to do something** etwas tun müssen; **Paul's due back soon** Paul muss bald zurück sein; **we're due to leave on Thursday** wir müssen Donnerstag abfahren; **2 due to** wegen (+GEN); **due to bad weather** wegen schlechten Wetters.

dull adjective **1 dull weather** trübes Wetter; **it's a dull day today** heute ist ein trüber Tag; **2** (*boring*) langweilig.

dumb adjective **1** stumm; **2** (*stupid*) dumm; **he asked some dumb questions** er hat ein paar dumme Fragen gestellt.

dump verb **1** abladen ◇ SEP (*rubbish*); **2** (*put down*) hinwerfen ◇ SEP; **he dumped it in the rubbish** er hat es in den Müll geworfen; **3** abschieben ◇ SEP (*a person*) (*informal*); **she's dumped her boyfriend** sie hat ihren Freund abgeschoben.

dungarees plural noun Latzhose *die* (PL die Latzhosen).

during preposition während (+GEN); **during the night** während der Nacht; **I saw her during the holidays** ich habe sie während der Ferien gesehen.

◇ IRREGULAR VERB: *See the verb table in the centre of the dictionary.*

dust noun Staub der.
verb 1 abstauben SEP (furniture, objects); 2 (in a room) Staub wischen; **she's dusting** sie wischt Staub.

dustbin noun Mülltonne die (PL die Mülltonnen).

dustman noun Müllmann der (PL die Müllmänner).

dusty adjective staubig.

Dutch noun 1 (language) Holländisch das; 2 **the Dutch** (people) die Holländer.
adjective holländisch; **he's Dutch** er ist Holländer; **she's Dutch** sie ist Holländerin.

duty noun 1 Pflicht die (PL die Pflichten); **to have a duty to do something** die Pflicht haben, etwas zu tun; **you have a duty to inform us** du hast die Pflicht, uns zu benachrichtigen; 2 **to be on duty** Dienst haben; **to be on night duty** Nachtdienst haben; **I'm off duty tonight** ich habe heute Abend keinen Dienst.

duty-free adjective zollfrei; **duty-free shop** der Dutyfreeshop; **duty-free goods** zollfreie Waren (plural).

duvet noun Federbett das (PL die Federbetten).

duvet cover noun Bettbezug der (PL die Bettbezüge).

dye noun Farbe die (PL die Farben). verb färben; **to dye your hair** sich ←(DAT) die Haare färben; **I'm going to have my hair dyed pink** ich lasse mir die Haare rosa färben.

dynamic adjective dynamisch.

dyslexia noun Legasthenie die.

dyslexic adjective legasthenisch; **to be dyslexic** Legastheniker sein, Legasthenikerin sein.

E e

each adjective, pronoun
1 jeder/jede/jedes; **each Sunday** jeden Sonntag; **each time** jedes Mal; **at the beginning of each year** am Anfang jedes Jahres; **we each have an invitation** jeder von uns hat eine Einladung; **my sisters each have a computer** meine Schwestern haben alle einen Computer; **she gave us an apple each** sie hat jedem von uns einen Apfel gegeben; **each of you** jeder von euch/jede von euch; **we each got a present** jeder Einzelne hat ein Geschenk bekommen; 2 **the tickets cost ten pounds each** die Karten kosten je zehn Pfund; **£5 each** (per person) fünf Pfund pro Person; (per item) fünf Pfund pro Stück.

each other pronoun ('each other' is usually translated using a reflexive pronoun) **they love each other** sie lieben sich; **we know each other** wir kennen uns; **do you see each other often?** seht ihr euch oft?

ear noun Ohr das (PL die Ohren).

earache noun **to have earache** Ohrenschmerzen haben.

△ NEW SPELLING: See page xii

earlier adverb 1 (a while ago) vor kurzem; **your brother phoned earlier** dein Bruder hat vor kurzem angerufen; 2 (not as late) früher; **we should have started earlier** wir hätten früher anfangen sollen.

early adverb 1 (in the morning) früh; **to get up early** früh aufstehen; **it's too early** es ist zu früh; 2 (for an appointment) **to be early** früh dran sein; **we're early, the train doesn't leave until ten** wir sind früh dran, der Zug fährt erst um zehn Uhr ab. adjective 1 (one of the first) **in the early months** während der ersten Monate; **I'm getting the early train** ich nehme den früheren Zug; 2 **to have an early lunch** früh zu Mittag essen; **Jan's having an early night** Jan geht früh zu Bett; 3 **in the early afternoon** am frühen Nachmittag; **in the early hours** in den frühen Morgenstunden.

earn verb verdienen; **Richard earns four pounds an hour** Richard verdient vier Pfund die Stunde.

earring noun Ohrring der (PL die Ohrringe).

earth noun Erde die; **life on earth** das Leben auf der Erde; ★ **what on earth are you doing?** was in aller Welt machst du da?

easily adverb leicht; **he's easily the best** er ist mit Abstand der Beste.

east noun Osten der; **in the east** im Osten. adjective, adverb östlich, Ost-; **the east side** die Ostseite; **an east**

wind ein Ostwind; **east of Munich** östlich von München.

Easter noun Ostern das (PL die Ostern); **they're coming at Easter** sie kommen zu Ostern; **Happy Easter** Frohe Ostern.

Easter Day noun Ostersonntag der (PL die Ostersonntage).

Easter egg noun Osterei das (PL die Ostereier).

Eastern Europe noun Osteuropa das.

easy adjective leicht; **it's easy!** das ist leicht!; **it was easy to decide** es war leicht zu entscheiden.

eat verb 1 essen ✧; **he was eating a banana** er aß eine Banane; **we're going to have something to eat** wir essen jetzt etwas; 2 **to eat your breakfast** frühstücken.

EC noun EG die (Europäische Gemeinschaft).

ecological adjective ökologisch.

ecology noun Ökologie die.

economical adjective sparsam.

economics noun Wirtschaftswissenschaften (plural).

economy noun Wirtschaft die.

edge noun 1 Kante die (PL die Kanten); **the edge of the table** die Tischkante; 2 (of a road, sheet of paper, or cliff) Rand der (PL die Ränder); **at the edge of the forest** am Waldrand.

editor noun 1 (of a newspaper or magazine) Chefredakteur der (PL

✦ IRREGULAR VERB: See the verb table in the centre of the dictionary

educate verb erziehen ◇

education noun Ausbildung die.

effect noun 1 Wirkung die (Pl.die Wirkungen); the effect of the explosion was horrific die Wirkung der Explosion war entsetzlich; 2 to have an effect on something eine Auswirkung auf etwas →(ACC) haben; it had a good effect on the whole family es hatte eine gute Auswirkung auf die ganze Familie; 3 (in a film) Effekt der (Pl.die Effekte); special effects besondere Effekte.

efficient adjective 1 (person) tüchtig; 2 (machine or organization) leistungsfähig.

effort noun 1 Mühe die (Pl.die Mühen); 2 to make an effort sich bemühen; Toya made an effort to help us Toya hat sich bemüht, uns zu helfen; he didn't even make the effort to apologize er hat sich nicht einmal die Mühe gemacht, sich zu entschuldigen.

e.g. abbreviation z.B. (zum Beispiel)

egg noun Ei das (Pl.die Eier); a fried egg ein Spiegelei; a hard-boiled egg ein hart gekochtes Ei.

egg-cup noun Eierbecher der (Pl.die Eierbecher).

eggshell noun Eierschale die (Pl.die Eierschalen).

egg-white noun Eiweiß das (Pl.die Eiweiße).

egg-yolk noun Eigelb das (Pl.die Eigelbe).

eight number acht; Maya's eight Maya ist acht; at eight o'clock um acht Uhr.

eighteen number achtzehn; Jason's eighteen Jason ist achtzehn.

eighth number achter/achte/achtes; on the eighth of July am achten.

eighty number achtzig; eighty-five fünfundachtzig.

either pronoun 1 (one or the other) einer von beiden/eine von beiden/eines von beiden (or them); I don't like either (of them) ich mag keinen von beiden/keine von beiden/keins von beiden; take either (of them) nimm einen von beiden/eine von beiden (or them); 2 (both) beide (plural); either is possible beide sind möglich; on either side auf beiden Seiten.
conjunction 1 either ... or ... or entweder ... oder; either Susie or Judy entweder Susie oder Judy; 2 either ... or (with a negative) weder ... or or; he didn't ring either Sam or noch; he didn't ring either Sam or Emma er hat weder Sam noch Emma angerufen; 3 I don't know them either ich kenne sie auch nicht.

elastic noun Gummiband das (Pl. die Gummibänder).

elastic band noun Gummiband das (Pl.die Gummibänder).

△ NEW SPELLING: See page xii

elbow

elbow noun Ellbogen der (Pl. die Ellbogen).

elder adjective älterer/ältere/älteres; **her elder brother** ihr älterer Bruder.

elderly adjective alt; **the elderly** ältere Menschen (plural).

eldest adjective ältester/älteste/ältestes; **her eldest brother** ihr ältester Bruder.

elect verb wählen; **she has been elected** sie ist gewählt worden.

election noun Wahl die (Pl. die Wahlen); **in the election** bei den Wahlen.

electric adjective elektrisch.

electrical adjective elektrisch; **electrical equipment** Elektrogeräte (plural).

electrician noun Elektriker der (Pl. die Elektriker), Elektrikerin die (Pl. die Elektrikerinnen).

electricity noun Strom der, die Elektrizität.

electronic adjective elektronisch.

electronics noun Elektronik die.

elephant noun Elefant der (Pl. die Elefanten).

eleven number elf; **Josh is eleven** Josh ist elf; **at eleven o'clock** um elf Uhr; **a football eleven** eine Fußballelf.

eleventh number elfter/elfte/elftes; **the eleventh of May** der elfte Mai; **on the eleventh floor** im elften Stock.

else adverb 1 (in addition) sonst; **who else?** wer sonst?; **did you see anyone else?** hast du sonst noch jemanden gesehen?; **nothing else** sonst nichts; **I don't want anything else** ich will sonst nichts; 2 **would you like something else?** möchten Sie sonst noch etwas?; 3 (instead or different) anderer/andere/anderes; **somebody else** jemand anders; **somewhere else** irgendwo anders; **everyone else** alle anderen; **something else** etwas anderes; 4 **or else** sonst; **hurry up, or else we'll be late** beeil dich, sonst kommen wir zu spät.

e-mail noun E-Mail die (Pl. die E-Mails).

embarrassed adjective verlegen; **he was very embarrassed** er war ganz verlegen.

embarrassing adjective peinlich.

emergency noun Notfall der (Pl. die Notfälle).

emergency exit noun Notausgang der (Pl. die Notausgänge).

emotion noun Gefühl das (Pl. die Gefühle).

emotional adjective 1 (person) emotionsgeladen; 2 (speech or occasion) emphatisch.

emphasize verb betonen; **he emphasized that it was voluntary** er betonte, dass es freiwillig war.

employ verb 1 (have working for you) beschäftigen; 2 (take on a worker) einstellen see

◆ IRREGULAR VERB: See the verb table in the centre of the dictionary.

employee *noun* Angestellte *der/die* (PL *die* Angestellten).

employer *noun* Arbeitgeber *der* (PL *die* Arbeitgeber), Arbeitgeberin *die* (PL *die* Arbeitgeberinnen).

employment *noun* Arbeit *die*.

empty *adjective* leer; **an empty bottle** eine leere Flasche. *verb* 1 (*empty out*) ausleeren SEP; 2 (*pour*) schütten.

enclose *verb* (*in a letter*) beilegen SEP; **please find enclosed a cheque** ein Scheck liegt bei.

encourage *verb* ermutigen; **to encourage somebody to do something** jemanden dazu ermutigen, etwas zu tun; **Mum encouraged me to try again** Mutti hat mich dazu ermutigt, es noch einmal zu versuchen.

encouragement *noun* Ermutigung *die* (PL *die* Ermutigungen).

encouraging *adjective* ermutigend.

encyclopedia *noun* Lexikon *das* (PL *die* Lexika).

end *noun* 1 Ende *das* (PL *die* Enden); **'The End'** 'Ende'; **at the end of the film** am Ende des Films; **by the end of the lesson** als die Stunde zu Ende war; **in the end I went home** schließlich bin ich nach Hause gegangen; **Sally's coming at the end of June** Sally kommt Ende Juni; **I read to the end of the page** ich habe die Seite zu Ende gelesen; **hold the other end** halte das andere Ende fest; **at the end of the street** am Ende der Straße; 2 (*in sports*) Spielfeldhälfte *die* (PL *die* Spielfeldhälften); **to change ends** die Seiten wechseln. *verb* 1 (*to put an end to*) beenden; **they've ended the strike** sie haben den Streik beendet; 2 (*to come to an end*) enden; **the day ended with a meal** der Tag endete mit einem Essen.

● **to end up** 1 **to end up doing something** am Ende etwas tun; **we ended up taking a taxi** am Ende haben wir ein Taxi genommen; 2 **to end up somewhere** irgendwo landen (PERF sein) (*informal*); **Rob ended up in Berlin** Rob ist in Berlin gelandet.

ending *noun* 1 Ende *das* (PL *die* Enden); 2 (*in grammar*) Endung *die* (PL *die* Endungen).

endless *adjective* endlos (*day or journey, for example*).

enemy *noun* Feind *der* (PL *die* Feinde); **to make enemies** sich ←(DAT) Feinde machen.

energetic *adjective* energiegeladen.

energy *noun* Energie *die*.

engaged *adjective* 1 (*to be married*) verlobt; **they're engaged** sie sind verlobt; **to get engaged** sich verloben; 2 (*a phone or toilet*) besetzt; **it's engaged, I'll ring later** es ist besetzt, ich rufe später an.

engagement *noun* (*to marry*) Verlobung *die* (PL *die* Verlobungen).

△ NEW SPELLING: *See page xii*

engagement ring *noun*
Verlobungsring *der* (PL die
Verlobungsringe).

engine *noun* 1 (*in a car*) Motor *der*
(PL die Motoren); 2 (*pulling a train*)
Lokomotive *die* (PL die
Lokomotiven).

engineer *noun* 1 (*who comes for
repairs*) Techniker *der* (PL die
Techniker), Technikerin *die* (PL die
Technikerinnen); 2 (*who builds
roads and bridges*) Ingenieur *der* (PL
die Ingenieure), Ingenieurin *die* (PL
die Ingenieurinnen).

England *noun* England *das*; I'm
from England ich bin Engländer,
ich bin Engländerin.

English *noun* 1 (*the language*)
Englisch *das*; do you speak
English? sprechen Sie Englisch?; he
answered in English er hat auf
Englisch geantwortet; 2 (*the people*)
the English die Engländer.
adjective 1 (*of or from England*)
englisch; the English team die
englische Mannschaft; he's English
er ist Engländer; she's English sie
ist Engländerin; 2 an English
lesson eine Englischstunde; our
English teacher unser
Englischlehrer.

English Channel *noun* the
English Channel der Ärmelkanal.

Englishman *noun* Engländer *der*
(PL die Engländer).

Englishwoman *noun*
Engländerin *die* (PL die
Engländerinnen).

enjoy *verb* 1 did you enjoy the
party? hat dir die Party gefallen?; we

really enjoyed the concert das
Konzert hat uns wirklich gut
gefallen; 2 to enjoy doing
something etwas gerne machen ◇; I
enjoy reading ich lese gerne; do you
enjoy living in York? wohnst du
gerne in York?; 3 to enjoy oneself
sich gut amüsieren; we really
enjoyed ourselves wir haben uns
richtig gut amüsiert; enjoy
yourselves! viel Vergnügen!; did
you enjoy yourself? hast du dich
gut amüsiert?

enjoyable *adjective* nett.

enormous *adjective* riesig.

enough *adverb, adjective, pronoun*
1 genug; there's enough for
everyone es gibt genug für alle; big
enough groß genug; have we got
enough bread? haben wir genug
Brot?; 2 that's enough das reicht.

enrol *verb* sich anmelden SEP; I want
to enrol on the course ich möchte
mich zu dem Kurs anmelden.

enter *verb* 1 (*to go inside*) gehen ◇
(PERF *sein*) (+ACC) (*a room or a
building*); we all entered the
church wir gingen alle in die
Kirche; 2 (*in computing*)
eingeben ◇ SEP; 3 to enter for sich
anmelden SEP zu (+DAT) (*an exam or
a race*); to enter for a competition
an einem Preisausschreiben
teilnehmen ◇ SEP.

entertain *verb* 1 (*to keep amused*)
unterhalten ◇; 2 (*to have people
round*) Gäste haben ◇; they don't
entertain much sie haben selten
Gäste.

entertainment noun (fun)
Unterhaltung die; **there wasn't
much entertainment in the
evenings** abends wurde wenig
Unterhaltung geboten.

enthusiasm noun
Begeisterung die.

enthusiast noun 1 Enthusiast der
(PL die Enthusiasten), Enthusiastin
die (PL die Enthusiastinnen); 2 (for
sports) Fan der (PL die Fans); **he's a
rugby enthusiast** er ist ein
Rugbyfan.

enthusiastic adjective begeistert.

entire adjective ganz; **the entire
class** die ganze Klasse.

entirely adverb ganz.

entrance noun 1 (fee) Eintritt der;
2 (way in) Eingang der (PL die
Eingänge).

entry noun 1 (way in) Eingang der
(PL die Eingänge); (for cars)
Einfahrt die (PL die Einfahrten);
2 'no entry' 'Zutritt verboten'; (to
cars) 'Einfahrt verboten'.

entry phone noun
Sprechanlage die (PL die
Sprechanlagen).

envelope noun Briefumschlag der
(PL die Briefumschläge).

environment noun Umwelt die.

environmental adjective Umwelt-;
environmental pollution die
Umweltverschmutzung.

environment-friendly adjective
umweltfreundlich.

epidemic noun Epidemie die (PL
die Epidemien).

epileptic adjective epileptisch.

episode noun 1 (an event)
Episode die (PL die Episoden);
2 (on TV or radio) Folge die (PL die
Folgen).

equal adjective gleich; **milk and
water in equal quantities** gleich
viel Milch und Wasser.
verb gleichen ◇ (+DAT).

equality noun
Gleichberechtigung die.

equally adverb (to share)
gleichmäßig; **we divided it equally**
wir haben es gleichmäßig verteilt.

equator noun Äquator der.

equip verb ausrüsten SEP; **well
equipped for the hike** für die
Wanderung gut ausgerüstet;
equipped with rucksacks mit
Rucksäcken ausgerüstet.

equipment noun 1 (for sport)
Ausrüstung die (PL die
Ausrüstungen); 2 Ausstattung die
(PL die Ausstattungen); **laboratory
equipment** die Laborausstattung;
3 (something needed for an activity)
Geräte (plural); **recording
equipment** Aufnahmegeräte.

error noun 1 (in spelling, typing, on
a computer, or in maths) Fehler der
(PL die Fehler); **spelling error** der
Schreibfehler; 2 (wrong opinion)
Irrtum der (PL die Irrtümer).

error message noun
Fehlermeldung die (PL die
Fehlermeldungen).

△ NEW SPELLING: *See page xii*

escalator noun Rolltreppe die (PL die Rolltreppen).

escape noun (from prison) Ausbruch der (PL die Ausbrüche). verb 1 (from prison) ausbrechen ◇ SEP (PERF sein); 2 entkommen ◇ (PERF sein); **to escape from somebody** jemandem entkommen.

especially adverb besonders.

essay noun Aufsatz der (PL die Aufsätze); **an essay on German reunification** ein Aufsatz über die deutsche Wiedervereinigung.

essential adjective unbedingt erforderlich; **it's essential to reply quickly** es ist unbedingt erforderlich, sofort zu antworten.

estate noun 1 (a housing estate) Wohnsiedlung die (PL die Wohnsiedlungen); 2 (a big house and grounds) Landsitz der (PL die Landsitze).

estate agent noun Immobilienmakler der (PL die Immobilienmakler).

estate car noun Kombiwagen der (PL die Kombiwagen).

estimate noun 1 (a quote for work) Kostenvoranschlag der (PL die Kostenvoranschläge); 2 (a rough guess) Schätzung die (PL die Schätzungen). verb schätzen.

etc. abbreviation usw. (und so weiter).

ethnic adjective ethnisch; **an ethnic minority** eine ethnische Minderheit.

EU noun EU die (Europäische Union).

euro noun Euro der (PL die Euro).

Europe noun Europa das.

European noun Europäer der (PL die Europäer), Europäerin die (PL die Europäerinnen). adjective europäisch.

European Union noun Europäische Union die.

even[1] adverb 1 sogar; **even Lisa is coming** sogar Lisa kommt; 2 **not even** nicht einmal; **I don't like animals, not even dogs** ich mag keine Tiere, nicht einmal Hunde; 3 **without even asking** ohne wenigstens zu fragen; 4 **even if** selbst wenn; **even if they arrive late** selbst wenn sie spät ankommen; 5 (with a comparison) (sogar) noch; **even bigger** sogar noch größer; **even faster** noch schneller; **even better than** sogar noch besser als; **the song is even better than their last one** das Lied ist sogar noch besser als ihr letztes; 6 **even so** trotzdem; **even so, we had a good time** trotzdem haben wir uns amüsiert.

even[2] adjective 1 (surface or layer) eben; 2 (number) gerade; **six is an even number** sechs ist eine gerade Zahl; 3 (equal) gleich (distance, value); **the score is even** die Punktzahl ist gleich; 4 **to get even with somebody** es jemandem heimzahlen.

evening noun 1 Abend der (PL die Abende); **in the evening** am Abend; **this evening** heute Abend;

◇ IRREGULAR VERB: See the verb table in the centre of the dictionary

tomorrow evening morgen Abend; **on Monday evening** am Montagabend; **every Thursday evening** jeden Donnerstagabend; **the evening before** am Abend zuvor; **the evening meal** das Abendessen; **2 at six o'clock in the evening** um sechs Uhr abends; **the other evening** neulich abends; **I work in the evening(s)** ich arbeite abends.

evening class *noun* Abendkurs *der* (PL die Abendkurse).

event *noun* **1** (*a happening*) Ereignis *das* (PL die Ereignisse); **2** (*in athletics*) Disziplin *die* (PL die Disziplinen).

eventually *adverb* schließlich.

ever *adverb* **1** (*at any time*) je; **have you ever noticed that?** hast du das je bemerkt?; **more than ever** denn je; **colder than ever** kälter denn je; **he drove more slowly than ever** er fuhr langsamer als je zuvor; **2 not ever** nie; **nobody ever came** es kam nie jemand; **hardly ever** fast nie; **3** (*always*) immer; **as cheerful as ever** so vergnügt wie immer; **the same as ever** so wie immer; **4 ever since** seitdem; **and it's been raining ever since** und seitdem regnet es.

every *adjective* **1** jeder/jede/jedes; **every house has a garden** jedes Haus hat einen Garten; **every day** jeden Tag; **every Monday** jeden Montag; **every time** jedes Mal; **2 every few days** alle paar Tage; **every ten kilometres** alle zehn Kilometer; **3 every one** jeder

Einzelne/jede Einzelne/jedes Einzelne A; **I've seen every one of his films** ich habe jeden Einzelnen seiner Filme gesehen; **4 every now and then** ab und zu.

everybody, everyone *pronoun* **1** alle (*plural*); **everybody knows that …** alle wissen, dass …; **everyone else** alle anderen; **2** (*each one*) jeder; **not everybody can afford it** das kann sich nicht jeder leisten.

everything *pronoun* alles; **everything is ready** es ist alles fertig; **everything's fine** alles ist okay (*informal*); **everything else** alles andere; **he gets everything he wants** er bekommt alles, was er will.

everywhere *adverb* **1** überall; **there was dirt everywhere**, überall war Dreck; **she went everywhere** sie ist überall hingegangen; **everywhere else** sonst überall; **2 everywhere she went** wohin sie auch ging.

evidently *adverb* offensichtlich.

exact *adjective* genau; **the exact fare** das genaue Fahrgeld; **it 's the exact opposite** das ist genau das Gegenteil.

exactly *adverb* genau; **they're exactly the right age** sie sind genau im richtigen Alter; **yes, exactly!** ja, genau!

exaggerate *verb* übertreiben ✧.

exaggeration *noun* Übertreibung *die* (PL die Übertreibungen).

exam noun Prüfung die (PL die Prüfungen); **history exam** die Geschichtsprüfung; **to sit an exam** eine Prüfung machen; **to pass an exam** eine Prüfung bestehen; **to fail an exam** durch eine Prüfung fallen.

examination noun Prüfung die (PL die Prüfungen).

examine verb 1 (at school or university) prüfen; 2 (at the doctor's) untersuchen.

examiner noun Prüfer der (PL die Prüfer), Prüferin die (PL die Prüferinnen).

example noun Beispiel das (PL die Beispiele); **for example** zum Beispiel; **to set a good example** ein gutes Beispiel geben.

excellent adjective ausgezeichnet.

except preposition 1 außer (+DAT); **every day except Tuesday** täglich außer Dienstag; **we play except when it rains** wir spielen, außer wenn es regnet; **except in March** außer März; 2 **except for** außer (+DAT); **except for the children** außer den Kindern.

exception noun Ausnahme die (PL die Ausnahmen); **without exception** ohne Ausnahme; **with the exception of** mit Ausnahme von (+DAT).

exchange noun 1 Austausch der; **the students are coming to London on an exchange** die Studenten kommen im Austausch nach London; **exchange student** der Austauschstudent, die Austauschstudentin; **an exchange of**

pupils ein Schüleraustausch; 2 **in exchange for his help** für seine Hilfe.
verb umtauschen SEP; **can I exchange this shirt for a smaller one?** kann ich dieses Hemd gegen ein kleineres umtauschen?

exchange rate noun Wechselkurs der (PL die Wechselkurse).

excite verb 1 (thrill) begeistern; 2 (agitate) aufregen SEP.

excited adjective 1 aufgeregt; **the children are excited** die Kinder sind aufgeregt; **the dogs get excited when they hear the car** die Hunde sind aufgeregt, wenn sie das Auto hören; 2 (annoyed or angry) **to get excited** sich aufregen SEP.

exciting adjective aufregend; **a very exciting film** ein sehr aufregender Film.

exclamation mark noun Ausrufezeichen das (PL die Ausrufezeichen).

excursion noun Ausflug der (PL die Ausflüge).

excuse noun Entschuldigung die (PL die Entschuldigungen).
verb (apologizing) **excuse me!** Entschuldigung!

exercise noun 1 Übung die (PL die Übungen); **a maths exercise** eine Übung in Mathe; 2 **physical exercise** körperliche Bewegung; **to get exercise** Bewegung haben.

exercise bike noun Heimtrainer der (PL die Heimtrainer).

◇ IRREGULAR VERB: See the verb table in the centre of the dictionary

exercise book noun Heft das (PL die Hefte); **my German exercise book** mein Deutschheft.

exhausted adjective erschöpft.

exhaust fumes noun Abgase (plural).

exhaust (pipe) noun Auspuff der (PL die Auspuffe).

exhibition noun Ausstellung die (PL die Ausstellungen); **the Dürer exhibition** die Dürer-Ausstellung.

exist verb existieren.

exit noun 1 Ausgang der (PL die Ausgänge); 2 (from a motorway) Ausfahrt die (PL die Ausfahrten).

expect verb 1 erwarten (guests or a baby); **we're expecting thirty visitors** wir erwarten dreißig Besucher; 2 (require something) **to expect somebody to do something** von jemandem erwarten, dass er etwas tut; 3 rechnen mit (+DAT) (something to happen); **I didn't expect that** damit habe ich nicht gerechnet; **I didn't expect it at all** damit habe ich überhaupt nicht gerechnet; 4 (suppose) glauben; **I expect she'll bring her boyfriend** ich glaube, sie bringt ihren Freund mit; **yes, I expect so** ich glaube ja.

expel verb **to be expelled** (from school) von der Schule verwiesen werden.

expensive adjective teuer; **those shoes are too expensive for me** diese Schuhe sind mir zu teuer; **the most expensive CDs** die teuersten CDs.

experience noun 1 Erfahrung die (PL die Erfahrungen); 2 (an event) Erlebnis das (PL die Erlebnisse).

experienced adjective erfahren.

experiment noun Experiment das (PL die Experimente); **to do an experiment** ein Experiment machen.

expert noun Experte der (PL die Experten), Expertin die (PL die Expertinnen); **he's a computer expert** er ist ein Computerexperte.

expire verb ablaufen ✧ SEP (PERF sein).

explain verb erklären.

explanation noun Erklärung die (PL die Erklärungen).

explode verb explodieren (PERF sein).

explore verb erforschen.

explosion noun Explosion die (PL die Explosionen).

exposure noun (of a film) Belichtung die; **a 24-exposure film** ein Film mit 24 Aufnahmen.

express noun (train) Schnellzug der (PL die Schnellzüge). verb 1 ausdrücken SEP; 2 **to express yourself** sich ausdrücken.

expression noun Ausdruck der (PL die Ausdrücke).

extension noun 1 (to a house) Anbau der (PL die Anbauten); 2 (telephone) Apparat der (PL die Apparate); **can I have extension 2347 please?** bitte verbinden Sie mich mit Apparat 2347 (note that in

*spoken German telephone numbers
are usually broken down into groups
of two figures*); **3** (*electrical*)
Verlängerung *die* (PL *die*
Verlängerungen).

extension number *noun*
Apparatnummer *die* (PL *die*
Apparatnummern).

exterior *adjective*
äußerer/äußere/äußeres.

extinguish *verb* **1** löschen (*a fire*);
2 to extinguish a cigarette eine
Zigarette ausmachen SEP.

extinguisher *noun*
Feuerlöscher *der* (PL *die*
Feuerlöscher).

extra *adjective* **1** zusätzlich, extra
(*informal*) (*extra never has an
ending*); **extra homework**
zusätzliche Hausaufgaben; **wine is
extra** Wein ist extra; **you have to
pay extra** das wird extra berechnet;
2 at no extra charge ohne
Aufschlag.
adverb **1** besonders; **he was
extra careful** er war besonders
vorsichtig; **2** extra large extragroß.

extraordinary *adjective*
außerordentlich.

extra time *noun* (*in football*)
Verlängerung *die* (PL *die*
Verlängerungen); **to go into extra
time** in die Verlängerung gehen.

extravagant *adjective*
verschwenderisch (*person*).

extreme *noun* Extrem *das* (PL *die*
Extreme); **to go from one extreme
to another** von einem Extrem ins

andere fallen.
adjective extrem.

extremely *adverb* äußerst;
extremely fast äußerst schnell.

eye *noun* Auge *das* (PL *die* Augen);
a girl with blue eyes ein Mädchen
mit blauen Augen; **shut your eyes!**
mach die Augen zu!; ★ **to keep an
eye on something** auf etwas ←(ACC)
aufpassen SEP.

eyebrow *noun* Augenbraue *die* (PL
die Augenbrauen).

eyelash *noun* Augenwimper *die* (PL
die Augenwimpern).

eyelid *noun* Augenlid *das* (PL *die*
Augenlider).

eyeliner *noun* Eyeliner *der* (PL *die*
Eyeliner).

eye shadow *noun* Lidschatten *der*
(PL *die* Lidschatten).

eyesight *noun* **to have good
eyesight** gute Augen haben; **to
have bad eyesight** schlechte Augen
haben.

F f

fabric *noun* (*cloth*) Stoff *der* (PL *die*
Stoffe).

fabulous *adjective* phantastisch.

face *noun* **1** (*of a person*)
Gesicht *das* (PL *die* Gesichter); **to
pull a face** ein Gesicht machen;
2 (*of a clock or watch*)
Zifferblatt *das* (PL *die* Zifferblätter).

◇ **IRREGULAR VERB: See the verb table in the centre of the dictionary**

verb 1 gegenüberstehen ✧ SEP (PERF *sein*) (+DAT); **she was facing him** sie stand ihm gegenüber; **2 the house faces the park** das Haus ist gegenüber dem Park; **3** (*to stand the idea of*) verkraften; **I can't face going back** ich kann es nicht verkraften zurückzugehen; **4** to **face up to something** sich etwas ←(+DAT) stellen.

facilities plural noun **1 the school has good sports facilities** die Schule hat gute Sportanlagen; **2 the flat has no cooking facilities** die Wohnung hat keine Kochgelegenheit.

fact noun Tatsache die (PL die Tatsachen); **the fact is that ...** Tatsache ist, dass ...; **in fact** tatsächlich; **is that a fact?** Tatsache?

factory noun Fabrik die (PL die Fabriken).

fade verb **1** (*fabric*) verbleichen ✧ (PERF *sein*); **faded jeans** ausgeblichene Jeans; **2** (*a colour or memory*) verblassen (PERF *sein*); **the colours have faded** die Farben sind verblasst.

fail verb **1** nicht bestehen ✧ (*a test or an exam*); **I failed my driving test** ich habe meine Fahrprüfung nicht bestanden; **2** (*in a test or an exam*) durchfallen ✧ SEP (PERF *sein*); **three students failed** drei Studenten sind durchgefallen; **3** to **fail to do something** etwas nicht tun; **he failed to inform us** er hat uns nicht benachrichtigt; ★ **without fail** auf

jeden Fall; **ring me without fail** ruf mich auf jeden Fall an.

faint adjective **1** (*slight*) leicht; **a faint smell of gas** ein leichter Gasgeruch; **I haven't the faintest idea** ich habe keine blasse Ahnung (*informal*); **2** (*voice or sound*) leise. verb ohnmächtig werden; **Lisa fainted** Lisa wurde ohnmächtig.

fair noun Jahrmarkt der (PL die Jahrmärkte). adjective **1** (*not unfair*) gerecht; **2** (*hair*) blond; **he's fair-haired** er ist blond; **3** (*skin*) hell; **fair-skinned** hellhäutig; **4** (*fairly good*) ganz gut (*chance, condition, or performance*); **5** (*weather*) schön; **if it's fair tomorrow** wenn es morgen schön ist.

fairground noun Jahrmarkt der (PL die Jahrmärkte).

fairly adverb (*quite*) ziemlich.

fairy noun Fee die (PL die Feen).

fairy tale noun Märchen das (PL die Märchen).

faith noun **1** (*trust*) Vertrauen das; **to have faith in somebody** Vertrauen zu jemandem haben; **2** (*religious belief*) Glaube der (PL die Glauben).

faithful adjective treu; **to be faithful to somebody** jemandem treu sein.

faithfully adverb **Yours faithfully** Hochachtungsvoll.

fake noun Imitation die (PL die Imitationen); **the diamonds were fakes** die Brillanten waren eine Imitation; **2** (*a painting or money*)

△ NEW SPELLING: See page xii

Fälschung die (PL die Fälschungen).
adjective gefälscht; **a fake passport**
ein gefälschter Pass.

fall noun Fall der (PL die Fälle); **to
have a fall** stürzen (PERF sein).
verb 1 fallen ◇ (PERF sein); **mind,
you'll fall** pass auf, dass du nicht
hinfällst; **Tony fell off his bike** Tony
ist vom Rad gefallen; **she fell down
the stairs** sie ist die Treppe
heruntergefallen; (of temperature,
prices) sinken ◇ (PERF sein).

false adjective falsch; **a false alarm**
ein falscher Alarm.

fame noun Ruhm der.

familiar adjective bekannt; **his face
is familiar** sein Gesicht kommt mir
bekannt vor.

family noun Familie die (PL die
Familien); **a family of six** eine
sechsköpfige Familie; **Ben's one of
the family** Ben gehört zur Familie;
the Morris family Familie Morris.

famous adjective berühmt.

fan noun 1 (a supporter) Fan der (PL
die Fans); **Will's a Chelsea fan** Will
ist ein Fan von Chelsea; 2 (electric,
for cooling) Ventilator der (PL die
Ventilatoren); 3 (hand-held)
Fächer der (PL die Fächer).

fanatic noun Fanatiker der (PL die
Fanatiker), Fanatikerin die (PL die
Fanatikerinnen).

fancy noun **to take somebody's
fancy** jemandem gefallen ◇; **the
picture took his fancy** das Bild hat
es ihm angetan.
adjective (equipment) ausgefallen.

verb 1 (to want) (**do you**) **fancy a
coffee?** hast du Lust auf einen
Kaffee?; **do you fancy going to the
cinema?** hast du Lust, ins Kino zu
gehen?; 2 **I really fancy him** ich mag
ihn wirklich sehr gern; 3 (just) **fancy
that!** stell dir vor!; **fancy you being
here!** na so was, dich hier zu
treffen!

fancy dress noun **in fancy dress**
verkleidet; **fancy-dress party** das
Kostümfest.

fantastic adjective fantastisch Δ;
really? that's fantastic! wirklich?
das ist ja fantastisch!; **a fantastic
holiday** fantastische Ferien.

far adverb, adjective 1 weit; **it's not
far** es ist nicht weit; **is it far to
Carlisle?** ist Carlisle weit von hier?;
how far is it to Bristol? wie weit ist
es bis nach Bristol?; 2 **he took us as
far as Newport** er hat uns bis
Newport mitgenommen; 3 **by far**
bei weitem; **the prettiest by far** die
bei weitem das hübscheste; 4 (much)
viel; **far better** viel besser; **far
faster** viel schneller; **far too many
people** viel zu viele Leute; 5 **so far**
bis jetzt; **so far everything's going
well** bis jetzt läuft alles gut; 6 **as far
as I know** soweit ich weiß.

fare noun 1 (on a bus, train, or the
underground) Fahrpreis der (PL
die Fahrpreise); 2 (on a plane)
Flugpreis der (PL die Flugpreise);
half fare der halbe Fahrpreis; **full
fare** der volle Fahrpreis.

farm noun Bauernhof der (PL die
Bauernhöfe).

◇ IRREGULAR VERB: See the verb table in the centre of the dictionary

farmer noun Bauer der (PL die Bauern), Bäuerin die (PL die Bäuerinnen).

fascinating adjective faszinierend.

fashion noun Mode die (PL die Moden); **in fashion** in Mode; **to go out of fashion** aus der Mode kommen.

fashionable adjective modisch.

fashion model noun Mannequin das (PL die Mannequins).

fashion show noun Modenschau die (PL die Modenschauen).

fast adjective 1 schnell; **a fast car** ein schnelles Auto; 2 (of a clock or watch) **to be fast** vorgehen ◇ SEP (PERF sein); **my watch is fast** meine Uhr geht vor; **you're ten minutes fast** deine Uhr geht zehn Minuten vor.
adverb 1 schnell; **he swims fast** er schwimmt schnell; 2 **to be fast asleep** fest schlafen.

fat noun Fett das (PL die Fette).
adjective 1 (meat) fett; 2 (person) dick, fett (informal); **a fat man** ein dicker Mann; **to get fat** fett werden (informal).

father noun Vater der (PL die Väter); **my father's office** das Büro von meinem Vater.

Father Christmas noun der Weihnachtsmann.

father-in-law noun Schwiegervater der (PL die Schwiegerväter).

fault noun 1 (when you are responsible) Schuld die; **it's Stephen's fault** Stephen ist Schuld; **it's not my fault** es ist nicht meine Schuld; 2 (in tennis) **double fault** der Doppelfehler.

favour noun 1 (a kindness) Gefallen der (PL die Gefallen); **to do somebody a favour** jemandem einen Gefallen tun; **can you do me a favour?** kannst du mir einen Gefallen tun?; **to ask a favour of somebody** jemanden um einen Gefallen bitten; 2 **to be in favour of something** für etwas ←(ACC) sein.

favourite adjective Lieblings-; **my favourite band** meine Lieblingsband.

fax noun Fax das (PL die Faxe).
verb faxen.

fear noun Angst die (PL die Ängste).
verb fürchten.

feather noun Feder die (PL die Federn).

feature noun 1 (of your face) Gesichtszug der (PL die Gesichtszüge); **to have delicate features** feine Gesichtszüge haben; 2 (of a car or a machine) Merkmal das (PL die Merkmale).

February noun Februar der; **in February** im Februar.

fed up adjective 1 **I'm fed up** ich habe die Nase voll (informal); **he's fed up with her** er hat die Nase voll von ihr; 2 **to be fed up with something** etwas ←(ACC) satt haben (informal); **I'm fed up with working**

△ NEW SPELLING: See page xii

every day ich habe es satt, jeden Tag zu arbeiten.

feed verb füttern; **have you fed the dog?** hast du den Hund gefüttert?

feel verb 1 sich fühlen; **I don't feel well** ich fühle mich nicht gut; 2 spüren; **I didn't feel a thing** ich habe nichts gespürt; 3 **I feel tired** ich bin müde; **I feel cold** mir ist kalt; 4 **to feel afraid** Angst haben; **to feel thirsty** Durst haben; 5 **to feel like doing something** Lust haben, etwas zu tun; **I feel like going to the cinema** ich habe Lust, ins Kino zu gehen; 6 (touch) fühlen; 7 (to the touch) sich anfühlen SEP; **to feel soft** sich weich anfühlen.

feeling noun 1 Gefühl das (PL die Gefühle); **to show your feelings** seine Gefühle zeigen; **a dizzy feeling** ein Schwindelgefühl; **I have the feeling James doesn't like me** ich habe das Gefühl, dass James mich nicht mag; 2 **to hurt somebody's feelings** jemanden verletzen.

felt-tip (pen) noun Filzstift der (PL die Filzstifte).

female noun (animal) Weibchen das (PL die Weibchen).
adjective weiblich.

feminine adjective weiblich.

feminist noun Feministin die (PL die Feministinnen), Feminist der (PL die Feministen).
adjective feministisch.

fence noun Zaun der (PL die Zäune).

ferry noun Fähre die (PL die Fähren).

festival noun (of films, art, or music) Festspiele (plural).

fetch verb 1 (collect) abholen SEP; **Tom's fetching the children** Tom holt die Kinder ab; 2 holen; **fetch me the other knife** hol mir das andere Messer.

fever noun Fieber das.

few adjective, pronoun 1 wenige; **few people know that** ... wenige Leute wissen, dass ...; 2 **a few** (several) ein paar (ein paar never changes); **a few weeks** ein paar Wochen; **in a few minutes** in ein paar Minuten; **have you got any tomatoes? we want a few for the salad** haben Sie Tomaten? wir brauchen ein paar für den Salat; 3 **quite a few** eine ganze Menge; **there were quite a few questions** es gab eine ganze Menge Fragen.

fewer adjective weniger; **there are fewer mosquitoes this year** dieses Jahr gibt es weniger Mücken.

field noun 1 (with grass or crops) Feld das (PL die Felder); **a field of wheat** ein Kornfeld; 2 (for sport) Spielfeld das (PL die Spielfelder).

fierce adjective 1 wild (animal or person); 2 heftig (storm or battle).

fifteen number fünfzehn.

fifth number fünfter/fünfte/fünftes; **the fifth of January** der fünfte Januar; **on the fifth floor** im fünften Stock.

fifty number fünfzig.

◊ IRREGULAR VERB: See the verb table in the centre of the dictionary

fight noun 1 (a scuffle) Schlägerei die (PL die Schlägereien); 2 (in boxing or against illness) Kampf der (PL die Kämpfe).
verb 1 (to have a fight) sich prügeln; **they were fighting** sie haben sich geprügelt; 2 (to quarrel) sich streiten ◇; **they're always fighting** sie streiten sich immer; 3 (struggle against) kämpfen gegen (+ACC) (poverty or a disease).

figure noun 1 (number) Zahl die (PL die Zahlen); **a four-figure number** eine vierstellige Zahl; 2 (body shape) Figur die; **good for your figure** gut für die Figur; 3 (a person) Gestalt die (PL die Gestalten).
verb **to figure something out** etwas herausfinden ◇ SEP (the answer or reason).

file noun 1 (for records of a person or case) Akte die (PL die Akten); 2 (ring binder or folder) Ordner der (PL die Ordner); 3 (on a computer) Datei die (PL die Dateien); 4 **a nail file** eine Nagelfeile.
verb 1 ablegen SEP (a form); 2 **to file your nails** sich ← (DAT) die Nägel feilen.

fill verb 1 füllen (a container); **she filled my glass** sie füllte mein Glas; 2 **to be filled with people** voller Menschen sein; **filled with smoke** voller Rauch.
• **to fill in** ausfüllen SEP (a form).

film noun (in a cinema and for a camera) Film der (PL die Filme); **shall we go and see the new film about Freud?** wollen wir uns den neuen Film über Freud ansehen?; **to make a film** einen Film drehen; **a**

24-exposure colour film ein Farbfilm mit 24 Aufnahmen.

film star noun Filmstar der (PL die Filmstars).

filter noun Filter der (PL die Filter).

filthy adjective dreckig.

final noun (in sport) Endspiel das (PL die Endspiele).
adjective letzter/letzte/letztes; **the final instalment** die letzte Folge; **the final result** das Endergebnis.

finally adverb schließlich.

find verb finden ◇; **did you find your passport?** hast du deinen Pass gefunden?; **I can't find my keys** ich kann meine Schlüssel nicht finden.
• **to find out** 1 (to enquire) sich informieren; **I don't know, I'll find out** das weiß ich nicht, ich werde mich informieren; 2 **to find something out** etwas ← (ACC) herausfinden ◇ SEP (the facts or an answer); **when she found out the truth** als sie die Wahrheit herausfand.

fine noun Bußgeld das (PL die Bußgelder) (for parking or speeding).
adjective 1 (in good health) gut; **'how are you?'** – **'fine, thanks'** 'wie geht's?' – 'danke, gut'; **I'm fine** mir geht es gut; 2 (convenient) in Ordnung; **ten o'clock? yes, that's fine** zehn Uhr? ja, in Ordnung!; **Friday will be fine** Freitag geht in Ordnung; 3 (sunny) schön; (weather or day) **if it's fine** wenn es schön ist; **in fine weather** bei schönem Wetter; 4 (not coarse or thick) fein.

△ NEW SPELLING: See page xii

finely adverb fein (*chopped or grated*).

finger noun Finger der (PL die Finger); ★ **I'll keep my fingers crossed for you** ich drücke dir den Daumen.

fingernail noun Fingernagel der (PL die Fingernägel).

finish noun 1 (*end*) Schluss △ der (PL die Schlüsse); 2 (*in a race*) Ziel das (PL die Ziele).
verb 1 beenden (*a conversation or quarrel*); **to finish a discussion** ein Gespräch beenden; **to be finished with something** mit etwas ←(DAT) fertig sein (*work or a project*); **have you finished your homework?** bist du mit den Hausaufgaben fertig?; **wait, I haven't finished!** warte, ich bin noch nicht fertig!; 2 (*to finish off*) **to finish doing something** etwas zu Ende tun; **have you finished (reading) the letter?** hast du den Brief zu Ende gelesen?; **he hasn't yet finished (writing) the report** er hat den Bericht noch nicht zu Ende geschrieben; 3 (*come to an end*) zu Ende sein, aus sein △ (*informal*) (*a meeting or performance*); **the film finishes at ten o'clock** der Film ist um zehn Uhr zu Ende; **when does school finish?** wann ist die Schule aus?
● **to finish with** (*complete your use of*) nicht mehr brauchen; **when you've finished with these clothes, give them back to me** wenn du die Sachen nicht mehr brauchst, gib sie mir zurück; **have you finished with**
the computer? brauchen Sie den Computer noch?

Finland noun Finnland das.

Finnish noun (*the language*) Finnisch das.
adjective finnisch; **he's Finnish** er ist Finne; **she's Finnish** sie ist Finnin.

fire noun 1 (*in a grate*) Kaminfeuer das (PL die Kaminfeuer); **to light the fire** das Feuer im Kamin anmachen; 2 (*accidental*) Feuer das (PL die Feuer); **to catch fire** (*fabric, furnishings*) Feuer fangen; 3 (*in a building or forest*) Brand der (PL die Brände); **to set fire to a factory** eine Fabrik in Brand stecken; 4 **to be on fire** brennen ◇.
verb 1 (*with a gun*) schießen ◇; **to fire at somebody** auf jemanden schießen; 2 abfeuern SEP (*a gun*).

fire alarm noun Feuermelder der (PL die Feuermelder).

fire brigade noun Feuerwehr die.

fire engine noun Feuerwehrauto das (PL die Feuerwehrautos).

fire escape noun Feuertreppe die (PL die Feuertreppen).

fire extinguisher noun Feuerlöscher der (PL die Feuerlöscher).

firefighter noun Feuerwehrmann der (PL die Feuerwehrleute).

fireplace noun Kamin der (PL die Kamine).

◇ IRREGULAR VERB: See the verb table in the centre of the dictionary

fire station noun Feuerwache die (PL die Feuerwachen).

firework noun Feuerwerkskörper der (PL die Feuerwerkskörper); **firework display** das Feuerwerk.

firm noun (business) Firma die (PL die Firmen).
adjective **1** fest; **2** (strict) streng.

first adjective erster/erste/erstes; **the first of May** der erste Mai; **for the first time** zum ersten Mal; **I was the first to arrive** ich kam als Erster/Erste an; **Susan was first** Susan war die Erste; **to come first in the 100 metres** beim Hundertmeterlauf Erster/Erste werden.
adverb **1** (to begin with) zuerst; **first, I'm going to make some tea** zuerst mache ich Tee; **2** at first zuerst; **at first he was shy** er war zuerst schüchtern.

first aid noun erste Hilfe Δ die.

first class adjective (ticket, carriage, or hotel) erster Klasse (goes after the noun); **a first-class hotel** ein Hotel erster Klasse; **he always travels first class** er reist immer erster Klasse; **a first-class compartment** ein Erste-Klasse-Abteil.

first floor noun erste Stock der; **on the first floor** im ersten Stock.

first name noun Vorname der (PL die Vornamen).

fir tree noun Tanne die (PL die Tannen).

fish noun Fisch der (PL die Fische).
verb fischen; (with a rod) angeln.

fish and chips noun ausgebackener Fisch mit Pommes frites.

fishing noun Fischen das; (with a rod) Angeln das; **to go fishing** fischen/angeln gehen.

fishing rod noun Angel die (PL die Angeln).

fishing tackle noun Angelgeräte (plural).

fist noun Faust die (PL die Fäuste).

fit noun **1** (of rage) Anfall der (PL die Anfälle); **your dad'll have a fit when he sees your hair** dein Vater kriegt bestimmt einen Anfall, wenn er deine Haare sieht; **2** an epileptic fit ein epileptischer Anfall.
adjective (healthy) fit; **I feel really fit** ich fühle mich richtig fit; **to keep fit** fit bleiben.
verb **1** (be the right size for) (of shoes or a garment) passen (+DAT); **this skirt doesn't fit me** der Rock passt mir nicht; **2** (be able to be put into) passen in (+ACC); **will my cases all fit in the car?** passen meine Koffer alle in das Auto?; **the key doesn't fit in the lock** der Schlüssel passt nicht ins Schloss; **3** (install) einbauen SEP.

fitted carpet noun Teppichboden der (PL die Teppichböden).

fitted kitchen noun Einbauküche die (PL die Einbauküchen).

five number fünf; **it's five o'clock** es ist fünf Uhr.

fix verb 1 (repair) reparieren; **Mum's fixed the computer** Mutti hat den Computer repariert; 2 (decide on) festlegen ◇ SEP; **to fix a date** einen Termin festlegen; 3 machen (a meal); **I'll fix supper** ich mache Abendessen.

fizzy adjective sprudelnd; **fizzy water** das Sprudelwasser.

flag noun Fahne die (PL die Fahnen).

flame noun Flamme die (PL die Flammen).

flan noun Torte die (PL die Torten); **fruit flan** die Obsttorte.

flap verb (of a bird) **to flap its wings** mit den Flügeln schlagen ◇.

flash noun (of a camera) Blitz der (PL die Blitze); **flash of lightning** der Blitz.
verb 1 (a light) aufleuchten SEP; (repeatedly) blinken; 2 **to flash by** or **past** vorbeiflitzen SEP (informal).

flat noun Wohnung die (PL die Wohnungen); **a third-floor flat** eine Wohnung im dritten Stock.
adjective 1 flach; **flat shoes** flache Schuhe; **a flat landscape** eine flache Landschaft; 2 **a flat tyre** ein platter Reifen.

flatmate noun Mitbewohner der (PL die Mitbewohner), Mitbewohnerin die (PL die Mitbewohnerinnen).

flavour noun 1 Geschmack der (PL die Geschmäcke); **the sauce has a bitter flavour** die Soße hat einen bitteren Geschmack; **strawberry flavour** Erdbeergeschmack; 2 (of drinks, coffee, or tea) Aroma das (PL die Aromen).
verb abschmecken SEP; **vanilla-flavoured** mit Vanillegeschmack.

flea noun Floh der (PL die Flöhe).

flight noun 1 Flug der (PL die Flüge); **the flight was delayed** der Flug hatte Verspätung; **charter flight** der Charterflug; **the flight from Munich to London takes an hour and a half** die Flugzeit von München nach London beträgt eineinhalb Stunden; 2 **flight of stairs** die Treppe.

flipper noun Flosse die (PL die Flossen).

flirt verb flirten.

float verb 1 (on water) treiben ◇; 2 (in the air) schweben.

flood noun 1 (of water) Überschwemmung die (PL die Überschwemmungen); 2 **to be in floods of tears** in Tränen aufgelöst sein; 3 (of letters or complaints) Flut die.
verb überschwemmen.

floodlight noun Flutlicht das.

floor noun 1 Boden der (PL die Böden); **your glasses are on the floor** deine Brille liegt auf dem Boden; 2 **to sweep the floor** ausfegen SEP; **to sweep the kitchen floor** die Küche ausfegen; 3 (a storey) Stock der (PL die Stock); **on the second floor** im zweiten Stock.

floppy disk noun Diskette die (PL die Disketten).

◇ **IRREGULAR VERB: See the verb table in the centre of the dictionary**

florist noun Blumenhändler der (PL die Blumenhändler), Blumenhändlerin die (PL die Blumenhändlerinnen).

flour noun Mehl das.

flower noun Blume die (PL die Blumen); **bunch of flowers** der Blumenstrauß.
verb blühen.

flu noun Grippe die (PL die Grippen); **to have flu** die Grippe haben.

fluent adjective **she speaks fluent Italian** sie spricht fließend Italienisch.

fluently adverb fließend.

flute noun Flöte die (PL die Flöten); **to play the flute** Flöte spielen.

fly noun Fliege die (PL die Fliegen).
verb 1 fliegen ◇ (PERF sein); **we flew to Berlin** wir sind nach Berlin geflogen; 2 steigen lassen (a kite); 3 fliegen ◇ (PERF haben) (a plane or helicopter); 4 (to pass quickly) schnell vergehen ◇ (PERF sein).

foam noun 1 (foam rubber) Schaumgummi der; **foam mattress** die Schaumgummimatratze; 2 (on a drink) Schaum der.

fog noun Nebel der.

foggy adjective neblig.

foil noun (kitchen foil) Alufolie die.

fold noun 1 (in fabric or skin) Falte die (PL die Falten); 2 (in paper) Kniff der (PL die Kniffe).
verb falten; **to fold something up** etwas zusammenfalten SEP.

folder noun Mappe die (PL die Mappen).

follow verb 1 folgen (PERF sein) (+DAT); **follow me!** folgen Sie mir!; 2 **do you follow me?** verstehst du, was ich meine?

following adjective folgend; **the following evening** am folgenden Abend.

fond adjective **to be fond of somebody** jemanden gern haben; **I'm very fond of him** ich habe ihn sehr gern.

food noun 1 Essen das; **I have to buy some food** ich muss noch etwas zu essen einkaufen; 2 **I like German food** ich mag die deutsche Küche; 3 (stocks) Lebensmittel (plural); **we bought food for the holiday** wir haben Lebensmittel für die Ferien eingekauft.

fool noun Dummkopf der (PL die Dummköpfe).

foot noun Fuß der (PL die Füße); **Lucy came on foot** Lucy ist zu Fuß gekommen.

football noun Fußball der (PL die Fußbälle); **to play football** Fußball spielen.

footballer noun Fußballspieler der (PL die Fußballspieler), Fußballspielerin die (PL die Fußballspielerinnen).

footpath noun Fußweg der (PL die Fußwege).

for preposition 1 für (+ACC); **a present for my mother** ein Geschenk für

△ NEW SPELLING: See page xii

meine Mutter; **what's it for?** wofür ist das? 2 (*for a particular occasion or event*) zu (+DAT); **sausages for lunch** Würstchen zum Mittagessen; **Sam got a bike for Christmas** Sam hat ein Rad zu Weihnachten bekommen; **what for?** wozu?; 3 (*time expressions in the past but continuing in the present*) seit (+DAT); **I've been waiting here for an hour** (*and I'm still waiting*) ich warte hier seit einer Stunde; **my brother's been living in Berlin for three years** (*and he still lives there*) mein Bruder wohnt seit drei Jahren in Berlin; 4 (*time expressions in the past or the future*) für; **I studied French for six years** (*but I no longer do*) ich habe sechs Jahre lang Französisch gelernt; **I'll be away for four days** ich werde vier Tage nicht da sein; 5 (*with a price*) für (+ACC); **I sold my bike for fifty pounds** ich habe mein Rad für fünfzig Pfund verkauft; 6 **what's the German for 'bee'?** wie heißt 'bee' auf Deutsch?

forbid *verb* verbieten ◇; **to forbid somebody to do something** jemandem verbieten, etwas zu tun.

forbidden *adjective* verboten.

force *noun* Kraft *die* (PL die Kräfte). *verb* zwingen ◇; **to force somebody to do something** jemanden zwingen, etwas zu tun.

forecast *noun* Vorhersage *die* (PL die Vorhersagen).

forehead *noun* Stirn *die* (PL die Stirnen).

foreign *adjective* 1 ausländisch; **in a**

foreign country im Ausland; **from a foreign country** aus dem Ausland; 2 **foreign language** *die* Fremdsprache.

foreigner *noun* Ausländer *der* (PL die Ausländer), Ausländerin *die* (PL die Ausländerinnen).

forest *noun* Wald *der* (PL die Wälder).

forever *adverb* 1 immer; **I'd like to stay here forever** ich möchte immer hier bleiben; 2 (*non-stop*) ständig; **he's forever asking questions** er fragt ständig.

forget *verb* vergessen ◇; **to forget about something** etwas vergessen; **we've forgotten the bread** wir haben Brot vergessen; **to forget to do something** vergessen, etwas zu tun; **I forgot to phone** ich habe vergessen anzurufen.

forgive *verb* verzeihen ◇ (+DAT); **to forgive somebody** jemandem verzeihen; **I forgave him** ich habe ihm verziehen; **to forgive somebody for doing something** jemandem verzeihen, dass er/sie etwas getan hat; **I forgave her for losing my ring** ich habe ihr verziehen, dass sie meinen Ring verloren hat.

fork *noun* Gabel *die* (PL die Gabeln).

form *noun* 1 Formular *das* (PL die Formulare); **to fill in a form** ein Formular ausfüllen; 2 (*shape or kind*) Form *die* (PL die Formen); **in the form of** in Form von; **to be on form** gut in Form sein; 3 (*in school*)

◇ IRREGULAR VERB: *See the verb table in the centre of the dictionary*

Klasse *die* (PL *die* Klassen).
verb bilden.

formal *adjective* formell (*invitation, event*).

format *noun* Format *das* (PL *die* Formate).

former *adjective* ehemalig; **a former pupil** ein ehemaliger Schüler, eine ehemalige Schülerin.

fortnight *noun* vierzehn Tage (*plural*); **we're going to Spain for a fortnight** wir fahren vierzehn Tage nach Spanien.

fortunately *adverb* glücklicherweise.

forty *number* vierzig.

forward *noun* (*in sport*) Stürmer *der* (PL *die* Stürmer). *adverb* (*to the front*) nach vorn; **to move forward** vorrücken SEP (PERF *sein*); **a seat further forward** ein Platz weiter vorn.

foster child *noun* Pflegekind *das* (PL *die* Pflegekinder).

foul *noun* (*in sport*) Foul *das* (PL *die* Fouls). *adjective* scheußlich; **the weather's foul** das Wetter ist scheußlich.

fountain *noun* Brunnen *der* (PL *die* Brunnen).

fountain pen *noun* Füllfederhalter *der* (PL *die* Füllfederhalter).

four *number* vier; **it's four o'clock** es ist vier Uhr; ★ **on all fours** auf allen vieren.

fourteen *number* vierzehn.

fourth *number* vierter/vierte/viertes; **the fourth of July** der vierte Juli; **on the fourth floor** im vierten Stock.

fox *noun* Fuchs *der* (PL *die* Füchse).

frame *noun* **1** Rahmen *der* (PL *die* Rahmen); **2** (*of spectacles*) Gestell *das* (PL *die* Gestelle).

franc *noun* **1** Franc *der* (PL *die* Francs); **a fifty-franc note** ein Fünfzig-Franc-Schein; **2** (*Swiss*) Franken *der* (PL *die* Franken).

France *noun* Frankreich *das*; **to France** nach Frankreich.

frantic *adjective* **1** (*very upset*) **to be frantic** außer sich ←(DAT) sein; **I was frantic with worry** ich war außer mir vor Sorge; **2** (*desperate*) hektisch (*effort or search*).

freckle *noun* Sommersprosse *die* (PL *die* Sommersprossen).

free *adjective* **1** (*when you don't pay*) kostenlos; **a free ride** eine kostenlose Fahrt; **a free ticket** eine Freikarte; **2** (*without charge*) umsonst; **to do something for free** etwas umsonst machen; **3** (*not occupied*) frei; **are you free on Thursday?** sind Sie am Donnerstag frei?; **4** sugar-free** ohne Zucker; **lead-free** bleifrei. *verb* befreien.

freedom *noun* Freiheit *die*.

free gift *noun* Werbegeschenk *das* (PL *die* Werbegeschenke).

freeze *verb* **1** (*in a freezer*) einfrieren ◇ SEP; **to freeze raspberries** Himbeeren einfrieren

2 (*in cold weather*) frieren ◇; **it's freezing** es friert; 3 (*become covered with ice*) zufrieren ◇ SEP (PERF *sein*); **the pond is frozen** der Teich ist zugefroren.

freezer *noun* Gefrierschrank *der* (PL *die* Gefrierschränke).

freezing *noun* **below freezing** unter Null; **three degrees above freezing** drei Grad über Null.
adjective 1 **I'm freezing** ich friere sehr; 2 **it's freezing outside** es ist eiskalt draußen.

French *noun* 1 (*the language*) Französisch *das*; 2 (*the people*) **the French** die Franzosen.
adjective 1 französisch; **Jean-Marc is French** Jean-Marc ist Franzose; 2 (*teacher or lesson*) Französisch-; **the French class** der Französischunterricht.

French bean *noun* grüne Bohne *die* (PL *die* grünen Bohnen).

French dressing *noun* Vinaigrette *die*.

French fries *plural noun* Pommes frites (*plural*).

Frenchman *noun* Franzose *der* (PL *die* Franzosen).

French window *noun* Verandatür *die* (PL *die* Verandatüren).

Frenchwoman *noun* Französin *die* (PL *die* Französinnen).

fresh *adjective* frisch; **fresh eggs** frische Eier; **I'm going out for some fresh air** ich gehe ein bisschen frische Luft schnappen.

Friday *noun* 1 Freitag *der* (PL *die* Freitage); **next Friday** nächsten Freitag; **last Friday** letzten Freitag; **on Friday** (am) Freitag; **I'll phone you on Friday evening** ich rufe dich Freitagabend an; **every Friday** jeden Freitag; **Good Friday** Karfreitag; 2 **on Fridays** freitags; **closed on Fridays** freitags geschlossen.

fridge *noun* Kühlschrank *der* (PL *die* Kühlschränke); **put it in the fridge** stell es in den Kühlschrank.

friend *noun* 1 Freund *der* (PL *die* Freunde), Freundin *die* (PL *die* Freundinnen); **a friend of mine** ein Freund von mir; 2 **to make friends** sich anfreunden; **he made friends with Danny** er hat sich mit Danny angefreundet; **he is friends with Danny** er ist mit Danny befreundet.

friendly *adjective* freundlich.

fries *plural noun* Pommes frites (*plural*).

fright *noun* 1 Schreck *der* (PL *die* Schrecke); **to have** *or* **get a fright** einen Schreck bekommen; 2 **you gave me a fright!** du hast mich erschreckt!

frighten *verb* 1 (*of an explosion or shot*) erschrecken; 2 (*scare or threaten*) **to frighten somebody** jemandem Angst machen.

frightened *adjective* **to be frightened** Angst haben; **Martin's frightened of snakes** Martin hat Angst vor Schlangen.

frightening *adjective* beängstigend.

✧ IRREGULAR VERB: *See the verb table in the centre of the dictionary*

fringe noun 1 (*hairstyle*) Pony der (PL die Ponys); 2 (*on clothes or a curtain*) Fransen (*plural*).

frog noun Frosch der (PL die Frösche).

from preposition 1 von (+DAT); **ten metres from the cinema** zehn Meter vom Kino; **a letter from Tom** ein Brief von Tom; **from Monday to Friday** von Montag bis Freitag; **from now on** von jetzt an; 2 aus (+DAT); **he comes from Dublin** er kommt aus Dublin; **the train from London** der Zug aus London; 3 **from seven o'clock onwards** ab sieben Uhr; **from then on** von da ab.

front noun 1 (*of a building*) Vorderfront die (PL die Vorderfronten); (*of a cupboard, card, or envelope*) Vorderseite die (PL die Vorderseiten); 2 (*of a garment or in an interior*) Vorderteil das (PL die Vorderteile); 3 (*at the seaside*) Strandpromenade die (PL die Strandpromenaden); 4 (*of a car*) **to sit in (the) front** vorne sitzen; 5 (*of a train or queue*) vordere Ende das; 6 (*of a procession or in a race*) Spitze die; 7 **in/at the front** vorne; **in/at the front of** vorne in (+DAT, or +ACC *with movement towards a place*); **there are still seats at the front of the train** es gibt noch Plätze vorne im Zug; **we got on at the front of the train** wir sind vorne in den Zug eingestiegen; 8 **in front of** vor (+DAT, or +ACC *with movement towards a place*); **in front of the TV** vor dem Fernseher; **in front of me** vor mir. adjective 1 vorderer/vordere/

vorderes; **in the front rows** in den vorderen Reihen; 2 Vorder-; **front seat** (*of a car*) der Vordersitz; **front wheel** das Vorderrad.

front door noun Haustür die (PL die Haustüren).

frontier noun Grenze die (PL die Grenzen).

frost noun Frost der.

frosty adjective frostig.

frown verb die Stirn runzeln; **he frowned at us** er runzelte die Stirn.

frozen adjective (*in a freezer*) tiefgekühlt; **a frozen pizza** eine tiefgekühlte Pizza.

fruit noun 1 (*a single fruit or type of fruit*) Frucht die (PL die Früchte); 2 (*various fruits*) Obst das; **we bought cheese and fruit** wir haben Käse und Obst gekauft.

fruit juice noun Fruchtsaft der (PL die Fruchtsäfte).

fruit machine noun Spielautomat der (PL die Spielautomaten).

fruit salad noun Obstsalat der (PL die Obstsalate).

frustrated adjective frustriert.

fry verb braten ◇; **we fried fish** wir haben Fisch gebraten; **fried potatoes** Bratkartoffeln; **fried egg** das Spiegelei.

frying pan noun Bratpfanne die (PL die Bratpfannen).

fuel noun (*for a car*) Kraftstoff der.

△ NEW SPELLING: *See page xii*

full *adjective* 1 voll; **the glass is full** das Glas ist voll; **I'm full** ich bin voll (*informal*); 2 **full of** voller (+GEN); **the train was full of tourists** der Zug war voller Touristen; 3 **at full speed** in voller Fahrt; 4 **to write something out in full** etwas voll ausschreiben.

full stop *noun* Punkt der (PL die Punkte).

full-time *adjective* **a full-time job** eine Ganztagsstelle.

fully *adverb* voll.

fun *noun* 1 Spaß der; **have fun!** viel Spaß!; **we had fun catching the ponies** wir hatten Spaß daran, die Ponys einzufangen; **skiing is fun** Skifahren macht Spaß; **I do it for fun** ich mache es aus Spaß; 2 **to have fun** sich amüsieren; ★ **to make fun of somebody** sich über jemanden lustig machen.

funds *plural noun* Geldmittel (*plural*).

funeral *noun* Beerdigung die (PL die Beerdigungen).

funfair *noun* Jahrmarkt der (PL die Jahrmärkte).

funny *adjective* 1 (*amusing*) lustig; **he's so funny** er ist so lustig; **a funny story** eine lustige Geschichte; 2 (*strange*) komisch; **a funny noise** ein komisches Geräusch; **that's funny, I'm sure I paid** das ist komisch, ich bin mir sicher, dass ich gezahlt habe.

fur *noun* 1 (*on an animal*) Fell das (PL die Felle); 2 (*for a coat*) Pelz der (PL die Pelze); **fur coat** der Pelzmantel.

furious *adjective* wütend; **she was furious with Steve** sie war wütend auf Steve.

furniture *noun* Möbel (*plural*); **to buy some furniture** Möbel kaufen; **piece of furniture** das Möbelstück.

further *adverb* weiter; **further than the station** weiter als der Bahnhof; **ten kilometres further on** zehn Kilometer weiter; **further off** weiter entfernt; **further forward** weiter vorn; **further back** weiter hinten.

fuse *noun* Sicherung die (PL die Sicherungen).

fuss *noun* Theater das; **to make a fuss** ein Theater machen; **to make a big fuss about the bill** ein großes Theater um die Rechnung machen.

fussy *adjective* **to be fussy about something** wählerisch in etwas ←(DAT) sein (*food, for example*).

future *noun* Zukunft die; **in future** in Zukunft.

G g

gadget *noun* Gerät das (PL die Geräte).

gain *verb* 1 gewinnen ◇; **in order to gain time** um Zeit zu gewinnen; 2 profitieren; **to gain by something** von etwas profitieren.

◇ IRREGULAR VERB: *See the verb table in the centre of the dictionary*

gale noun Sturm der (PL die Stürme).

gallery noun Galerie die (PL die Galerien).

gamble verb spielen (for money).

game noun 1 Spiel das (PL die Spiele); **game of chance** das Glücksspiel; **board game** das Brettspiel; 2 **to have a game of cards** eine Partie Karten spielen; 3 **to have a game of football** Fußball spielen; 4 **games** (at school) Sport der.

gang noun Bande die (PL die Banden); **all the gang were there** die ganze Bande war da.

gap noun 1 (hole) Lücke die (PL die Lücken); 2 (in time) Pause die (PL die Pausen); **a two-hour gap** eine zweistündige Pause; 3 **age gap** der Altersunterschied.

garage noun 1 (for keeping your car) Garage die (PL die Garagen); 2 (for repairing cars) Autowerkstatt die (PL die Autowerkstätten); 3 (for petrol) Tankstelle die (PL die Tankstellen).

garden noun Garten der (PL die Gärten).

gardener noun Gärtner der (PL die Gärtner), Gärtnerin die (PL die Gärtnerinnen).

gardening noun Gartenarbeit die.

garlic noun Knoblauch der.

garment noun Kleidungsstück das (PL die Kleidungsstücke).

gas noun Gas das.

gas cooker noun Gasherd der (PL die Gasherde).

gas fire noun Gasofen der (PL die Gasöfen).

gas meter noun Gaszähler der (PL die Gaszähler).

gate noun 1 (in garden) Pforte die (PL die Pforten); 2 (in field) Gatter das (PL die Gatter); 3 (at an airport) Flugsteig der (PL die Flugsteige).

gather verb 1 (of people) sich versammeln; 2 sammeln (fruit, vegetables, flowers); 3 **as far as I can gather** soweit ich weiß.

gay adjective (homosexual) schwul (informal).

gaze verb **to gaze at something** etwas anstarren SEP.

gear noun 1 (in a car) Gang der (PL die Gänge); **to change gear** schalten; 2 (equipment) Ausrüstung die; **camping gear** die Campingausrüstung; 3 (things) Sachen (plural); **I've left all my gear at Gary's** ich habe alle meine Sachen bei Gary gelassen.

gear lever noun Schalthebel der (PL die Schalthebel).

gel noun Gel das (PL die Gele).

Gemini noun Zwillinge (plural); **Steph's Gemini** Steph ist Zwilling.

gender noun (of a word) Geschlecht das (PL die Geschlechter); **what is the gender of 'Haus'?** welches Geschlecht hat 'Haus'?

△ NEW SPELLING: See page xii

general noun General der (PL die Generäle).
adjective allgemein; **in general** im Allgemeinen; **the general election** die allgemeinen Wahlen.

general knowledge noun Allgemeinwissen das.

generally adverb im Allgemeinen △.

generation noun Generation die (PL die Generationen).

generous adjective großzügig.

genetics noun Genetik die.

Geneva noun Genf das; **Lake Geneva** der Genfer See.

genius noun Genie das (PL die Genies); **Lisa, you're a genius!** Lisa, du bis ein Genie!

gentle adjective sanft.

gentleman noun Herr der (PL die Herren); **ladies and gentlemen!** meine Damen und Herren!

gently adverb sanft.

gents noun (lavatory) Herrentoilette die (PL die Herrentoiletten); (on a sign) 'Gents' 'Herren'; **where's the gents?** wo ist die Toilette?

genuine adjective 1 (real, authentic) echt; **a genuine diamond** ein echter Brillant; 2 aufrichtig (person); **she's very genuine** sie ist sehr aufrichtig.

geography noun Geographie die; (at school) Erdkunde die.

germ noun 1 Keim der (PL die Keime); 2 (causing a cold) **germs** Bazillen (plural).

German noun (person) 1 Deutsche der/die (PL die Deutschen); 2 (language) Deutsch das; **in German** auf Deutsch.
adjective deutsch; **he is German** er ist Deutscher; **she is German** sie ist Deutsche; **our German teacher** unser Deutschlehrer, unsere Deutschlehrerin.

Germany Deutschland das; **to Germany** nach Deutschland; **from Germany** aus Deutschland.

get verb 1 (obtain, receive) bekommen ◇, kriegen (informal); **I got a bike for my birthday** ich habe ein Rad zum Geburtstag bekommen; **Fred got the job** Fred hat die Stelle bekommen; **she got a shock** sie hat einen Schreck gekriegt; **I got a good mark for my German homework** ich habe eine gute Note für meine Deutschhausaufgaben gekriegt; 2 **he's got lots of money** er hat viel Geld; **she's got long hair** sie hat lange Haare; **I've got a headache** ich habe Kopfschmerzen; 3 (fetch) holen; **I'll get some bread** ich hole Brot; **I'll get your bag for you** ich hole dir deine Tasche; 4 **to have got to do something** etwas tun müssen ◇; **I've got to phone before midday** ich muss vor Mittag anrufen; 5 **to get (to) somewhere** irgendwo ankommen ◇ SEP (PERF sein); **when I got to London** als ich in London ankam; **we got here this morning** wir sind heute Morgen angekommen; **what time did they get there?** wann sind sie angekommen?; 6 (become) werden ◇ (PERF sein); **it's getting**

◇ **IRREGULAR VERB: See the verb table in the centre of the dictionary**

late es wird spät; **it's getting dark** es wird dunkel; **7 to get something done** etwas machen lassen ◇; **I'm getting my hair cut today** ich lasse mir heute die Haare schneiden.

● **to get back** zurückkommen ◇ SEP (PERF *sein*); **Mum gets back at six** Mutti kommt um sechs zurück.

● **to get something back** etwas zurückbekommen ◇ SEP, etwas zurückkriegen SEP (*informal*); **did you get your books back?** hast du deine Bücher zurückbekommen?

● **to get into something** (*a vehicle*) in etwas ←(ACC) einsteigen ◇ SEP (PERF *sein*); **he got into the car** er ist ins Auto eingestiegen.

● **to get off something** (*a vehicle*) aus etwas ←(DAT) aussteigen ◇ SEP (PERF *sein*); **I got off the train at Banbury** ich bin in Banbury aus dem Zug ausgestiegen.

● **to get on: how's Amanda getting on?** wie geht's Amanda?

● **to get on something** (*a vehicle*) in etwas ←(ACC) einsteigen ◇ SEP (PERF *sein*); **she got on the train at Reading** sie ist in Reading in den Zug eingestiegen.

● **to get on with somebody** sich mit jemandem verstehen ◇; **she doesn't get on with her brother** sie versteht sich nicht mit ihrem Bruder.

● **to get out of something** (*a vehicle*) aus etwas ←(DAT) aussteigen ◇ SEP (PERF *sein*); **Laura got out of the car** Laura ist aus dem Auto ausgestiegen.

● **to get together** sich wieder sehen ◇ SEP Δ; **we must get together soon** wir müssen uns bald mal wieder sehen.

● **to get up** aufstehen ◇ SEP (PERF *sein*); **I get up at seven** ich stehe um sieben auf.

ghost *noun* Geist *der* (PL *die* Geister).

gift *noun* **1** Geschenk *das* (PL *die* Geschenke); **a Christmas gift** ein Weihnachtsgeschenk; **2** Begabung *die*; **to have a gift for something** für etwas ←(ACC) begabt sein; **Jo has a real gift for languages** Jo ist richtig sprachbegabt.

gigantic *adjective* riesig.

gin *noun* Gin *der* (PL *die* Gins).

ginger *noun* Ingwer *der* (PL *die* Ingwer).

girl *noun* Mädchen *das* (PL *die* Mädchen); **three boys and four girls** drei Jungen und vier Mädchen; **when I was a little girl I had …** als kleines Mädchen hatte ich …

girlfriend *noun* Freundin *die* (PL *die* Freundinnen).

give *verb* **1** geben ◇; **to give something to somebody** jemandem etwas geben; **I'll give you my address** ich gebe dir meine Adresse; **give me the key** gib mir den Schlüssel; **Yasmin's dad gave her the money** Yasmins Vater hat ihr das Geld gegeben; **2** (*give as a gift*) schenken; **to give somebody a present** jemandem etwas schenken.

● **to give something away** etwas weggeben ◇ SEP; **she's given away all her books** sie hat alle ihre Bücher weggegeben.

Δ NEW SPELLING: *See page xii*

- **to give something back to somebody** jemandem etwas zurückgeben ✧ SEP; **I gave her back the keys** ich habe ihr die Schlüssel zurückgegeben.

- **to give in** nachgeben ✧ SEP; **my mum said no but she gave in in the end** meine Mutti hat nein gesagt, aber schließlich hat sie nachgegeben.

- **to give up** aufgeben ✧ SEP; **I give up!** ich gebe auf!

- **to give up doing something** etwas aufgeben ✧SEP; **she's given up smoking** sie hat das Rauchen aufgegeben.

glad adjective froh; **I'm glad to hear he's better** ich bin froh, dass es ihm besser geht; **I'm glad to be back** ich bin froh, dass ich wieder zurück bin.

glass noun Glas das (PL die Gläser); **a glass of water** ein Glas Wasser; **a glass table** ein Glastisch.

glasses plural noun Brille die (PL die Brillen); **to wear glasses** eine Brille tragen.

glove noun Handschuh der (PL die Handschuhe); **a pair of gloves** ein Paar Handschuhe.

glove compartment noun Handschuhfach das (PL die Handschuhfächer).

glue noun Klebstoff der (PL die Klebstoffe).

go noun 1 (in a game) whose go is it? wer ist dran?; **it's my go** ich bin dran; 2 **to have a go at doing something** versuchen, etwas zu tun; **I'll have a go at mending it** ich versuche, es zu reparieren.

verb 1 (on foot) gehen ✧ (PERF sein); **to go to school** in die Schule gehen; **Mark's gone to the dentist's** Mark ist zum Zahnarzt gegangen; **to go shopping** einkaufen gehen; 2 (in a vehicle) fahren ✧ (PERF sein); **we're going to London** wir fahren nach London; **we're planning to go early** wir wollen früh fahren; **to go on holiday** in die Ferien fahren; 3 (by plane) fliegen ✧ (PERF sein); 4 **to go for a walk** spazieren gehen △ ✧ SEP (PERF sein); 5 (with another verb) **I'm going to do it** ich werde es tun; **I'm going to make some tea** ich mache Tee; **he was going to phone you** er wollte dich anrufen; 6 (leave) gehen ✧ (PERF sein); **Pauline's already gone** Pauline ist schon gegangen; 7 (on a journey) abfahren ✧ SEP (PERF sein); **when does the train go?** wann fährt der Zug ab?; 8 (turn out) verlaufen ✧ (PERF sein) (event); **how did your evening go?** wie ist dein Abend verlaufen?; **the party went well** die Party war gut.

- **to go away** 1 weggehen ✧ SEP (PERF sein); **go away!** geh weg!; 2 (on holiday) verreisen ✧ (PERF sein).

- **to go back** 1 zurückgehen ✧ SEP (PERF sein); **I'm going back to Germany in March** ich gehe im März nach Deutschland zurück; **I'm not going back there again!** ich gehe da nicht wieder zurück!; 2 **I went back home** ich bin nach Hause gegangen.

- **to go down** 1 hinuntergehen ✧ SEP (PERF sein); **she's gone down to the kitchen** sie ist in die Küche

✧ **IRREGULAR VERB: See the verb table in the centre of the dictionary**

hinuntergegangen; **to go down the stairs** die Treppe hinuntergehen; **2** (*price, temperature*) fallen ◇ (PERF *sein*); **3** (*tyre, balloon, airbed*) Luft verlieren ◇.

● **to go in** hineingehen ◇ SEP (PERF *sein*); **he went in and shut the door** er ist hineingegangen und hat die Tür zugemacht.

● **to go into 1** (*person*) gehen in (+ACC) (PERF *sein*); **Fran went into the kitchen** Fran ging in die Küche; **2** (*object*) passen in (+ACC); **this book won't go into my bag** dieses Buch passt nicht in meine Tasche.

● **to go off 1** (*bomb*) hochgehen ◇ SEP (PERF *sein*); **2** (*alarm clock*) klingeln; **my alarm clock went off at six** mein Wecker hat um sechs geklingelt; **3** (*fire or burglar alarm*) losgehen ◇ SEP (PERF *sein*); **the fire alarm went off** der Feuermelder ging los.

● **to go on 1** what's going on? was ist los?; **2 to go on doing something** weiter etwas tun; **she went on talking** sie hat weiter geredet; **3 to go on about something** stundenlang von etwas ←(DAT) reden; **he's always going on about his dog** er redet stundenlang von seinem Hund.

● **to go out 1** (*for an evening*) ausgehen ◇ SEP weggehen ◇ SEP (PERF *sein*) (*informal*); **we're going out tonight** wir gehen heute Abend aus; **2** (*leave*) **she went out of the kitchen** sie ist aus der Küche gegangen; **3 to go out with somebody** mit jemandem gehen ◇ (PERF *sein*) (*informal*); **she's going out with my brother** sie geht mit

meinem Bruder; **4** (*light, fire*) ausgehen ◇ SEP (PERF *sein*); **the light went out** das Licht ist ausgegangen.

● **to go past something** an etwas ←(DAT) vorbeigehen ◇ SEP; **we went past your house** wir sind an eurem Haus vorbeigegangen.

● **to go round: to go round to somebody's house** jemanden besuchen; **we went round to Fred's last night** wir haben gestern Abend Fred besucht.

● **to go round something 1** um etwas ←(ACC) herumgehen ◇ SEP (PERF *sein*) (*building, park, garden*); **2** besichtigen (*museum, monument*).

● **to go through 1** the train goes through Cologne der Zug fährt durch Köln; **2 to go through a room** durch ein Zimmer gehen; **3** (*search*) durchsuchen.

● **to go up 1** (*person*) hinaufgehen ◇ SEP (PERF *sein*); **she's gone up to her room** sie ist in ihr Zimmer hinaufgegangen; **to go up the stairs** die Treppe hinaufgehen; **2** (*prices*) steigen ◇ (PERF *sein*); **the price of petrol has gone up** der Benzinpreise sind gestiegen.

goal noun Tor das (PL die Tore); **to score a goal** ein Tor schießen.

goalkeeper noun Torwart der (PL die Torwarte).

goat noun Ziege die (PL die Ziegen).

god noun Gott der (PL die Götter).

God noun Gott der; **to believe in God** an Gott glauben.

△ NEW SPELLING: *See page xii*

godchild noun Patenkind das (PL die Patenkinder).

goddaughter noun Patentochter die (PL die Patentöchter).

goddess noun Göttin die (PL die Göttinnen).

godfather noun Pate der (PL die Paten).

godmother noun Patin die (PL die Patinnen).

godson noun Patensohn der (PL die Patensöhne).

gold noun Gold das; **a gold bracelet** ein Goldarmband.

goldfish noun Goldfisch der (PL die Goldfische).

golf noun Golf das; **to play golf** Golf spielen.

golf club noun 1 (place) Golfklub der (PL die Golfklubs); 2 (iron) Golfschläger der (PL die Golfschläger).

golf course noun Golfplatz der (PL die Golfplätze).

good adjective 1 gut; **she's a good teacher** sie ist eine gute Lehrerin; **the cherries are very good** die Kirschen sind sehr gut; 2 **to be good for you** gesund sein; **tomatoes are good for you** Tomaten sind gesund; 3 **good at** gut in (+DAT); **she's good at maths** sie ist gut in Mathe; **he's good at drawing** er ist gut im Zeichnen; 4 (well-behaved) brav; **be good!** sei brav!; 5 (kind) nett; **she's been very good to me** sie ist sehr nett zu mir gewesen; 6 for

good endgültig; **I've stopped smoking for good** ich habe das Rauchen endgültig aufgegeben.

good afternoon exclamation guten Tag!

goodbye exclamation auf Wiedersehen!

good evening exclamation guten Abend!

Good Friday noun Karfreitag der (PL die Karfreitage).

good-looking adjective gut aussehend △.

good morning exclamation guten Morgen!

goodness exclamation meine Güte!; **for goodness sake!** um Himmels willen!

good night exclamation gute Nacht!

goods plural noun Waren (plural).

goods train noun Güterzug der (PL die Güterzüge).

goose noun Gans die (PL die Gänse).

gorgeous adjective herrlich; **it's a gorgeous day** es ist ein herrlicher Tag.

gorilla noun Gorilla der (PL die Gorillas).

gosh exclamation Mensch!

gossip noun 1 (person) Klatschbase die (PL die Klatschbasen); 2 (scandal) Klatsch der. verb klatschen.

◇ IRREGULAR VERB: See the verb table in the centre of the dictionary

government noun Regierung die
(PL die Regierungen).

grab verb 1 packen; she grabbed my
arm sie packte mich am Arm; 2 to
grab something from somebody
jemandem etwas ←(ACC)
entreißen ◊; he grabbed the book
from me er hat mir das Buch
entrissen.

grade noun (mark) Note die (PL die
Noten); to get good grades gute
Noten bekommen.

gradual adjective allmählich.

gradually adverb allmählich; the
weather got gradually better das
Wetter wurde allmählich besser.

graffiti plural noun Graffiti (plural).

gram noun Gramm das; 100 grams
of salami hundert Gramm Salami.

grammar noun Grammatik die.

grammar school noun
Gymnasium das (PL die
Gymnasien).

gran noun Oma die (PL die Omas).

grandchildren plural noun
Enkelkinder (plural).

granddad noun Opa der (PL die
Opas).

granddaughter noun Enkelin die
(PL die Enkelinnen).

grandfather noun Großvater der
(PL die Großväter).

grandma noun Oma die (PL die
Omas).

grandmother noun
Großmutter die (PL die
Großmütter).

grandpa noun Opa der (PL die
Opas).

grandparents plural noun
Großeltern (plural).

grandson noun Enkel der (PL die
Enkel).

granny noun Omi die (PL die Omis).

grape noun Weintraube die (PL die
Weintrauben); a grape eine
Weintraube; to buy some grapes
Weintrauben kaufen; do you like
grapes? magst du Weintrauben?;
a bunch of grapes eine ganze
Weintraube.

grapefruit noun Grapefruit die (PL
die Grapefruits).

grasp verb festhalten ◊ SEP.

grass noun 1 Gras das; to lie on the
grass im Gras liegen; 2 (lawn)
Rasen der (PL die Rasen); to cut the
grass den Rasen mähen.

grasshopper noun
Heuschrecke die (PL die
Heuschrecken).

grate verb reiben ◊; grated cheese
geriebener Käse.

grateful adjective dankbar; to be
grateful to somebody jemandem
dankbar sein.

grater noun Reibe die (PL die
Reiben).

grave noun Grab das (PL die
Gräber).

△ NEW SPELLING: See page xii

graveyard noun Friedhof der (PL die Friedhöfe).

gravy noun Soße die (PL die Soßen).

grease noun Fett das.

greasy adjective 1 fettig; **to have greasy skin** fettige Haut haben; 2 (food) fett.

great adjective 1 groß; **a great poet** ein großer Dichter; 2 (terrific) großartig; **it was a great party** das war eine großartige Party; **great!** großartig!, prima! (informal); 3 **a great deal of** sehr viel; **a great many** sehr viele.

Great Britain noun Großbritannien das.

Greece noun Griechenland das.

greedy adjective gierig; (with food) gefräßig.

Greek noun 1 (person) Grieche der (PL die Griechen), Griechin die (PL die Griechinnen); 2 (language) Griechisch das.
adjective griechisch; **she's Greek** sie ist Griechin.

green noun 1 (colour) Grün das; **a pale green** ein Hellgrün; 2 **the Greens** (ecologists) die Grünen.
adjective 1 grün; **a green door** eine grüne Tür; 2 **the Green Party** die Grünen (plural).

greengrocer noun Obst- und Gemüsehändler der (PL die Obst- und Gemüsehändler).

greenhouse noun Gewächshaus das (PL die Gewächshäuser).

greenhouse effect noun Treibhauseffekt der.

greetings plural noun Grüße (plural); **Season's Greetings** fröhliche Weihnachten und ein glückliches neues Jahr.

greetings card noun Glückwunschkarte die (PL die Glückwunschkarten).

grey adjective grau.

grief noun Trauer die.

grill noun Grill der (PL die Grills).
verb grillen; **I'm going to grill the sausages** ich grille die Würstchen.

grin verb grinsen.

grind verb mahlen.

grip verb (hold on to) festhalten ◇ SEP.

groan noun Stöhnen das.
verb stöhnen.

grocer noun Lebensmittelhändler der (PL die Lebensmittelhändler).

groceries plural noun Lebensmittel (plural).

grocer's noun Lebensmittelgeschäft das (PL die Lebensmittelgeschäfte).

groom noun Bräutigam der (PL die Bräutigame); **the bride and groom** das Brautpaar.

gross adjective 1 **a gross injustice** ein schreiendes Unrecht; 2 grob; **a gross error** ein grober Fehler; 3 (disgusting) ekelhaft; **the food was gross!** das Essen war ekelhaft!

◇ IRREGULAR VERB: See the verb table in the centre of the dictionary

ground noun 1 Boden der; **to sit on the ground** auf dem Boden sitzen; 2 (for sport) Sportplatz der (PL die Sportplätze); **football ground** der Fußballplatz.
adjective gemahlen; **ground coffee** gemahlener Kaffee.

ground floor noun Erdgeschoss △ das; **they live on the ground floor** sie wohnen im Erdgeschoss.

group noun Gruppe die (PL die Gruppen).

grow verb (get bigger) 1 wachsen ✧ (PERF sein); **your hair grows very quickly** deine Haare wachsen sehr schnell; **my little sister's grown quite a bit this year** meine kleine Schwester ist dieses Jahr ein ganzes Stück gewachsen; **the number of students is still growing** die Zahl der Studenten wächst noch; 2 anbauen SEP (fruit, vegetables); 3 **to grow a beard** sich ←(DAT) einen Bart wachsen lassen; 4 (become) werden ✧ (PERF sein); **to grow old** alt werden.

● **to grow up** 1 erwachsen werden; **the children are growing up** die Kinder werden erwachsen; 2 aufwachsen ✧ SEP (PERF sein); **she grew up in Scotland** sie ist in Schottland aufgewachsen.

growl verb knurren.

grown-up noun Erwachsene der/die (PL die Erwachsenen).

growth noun Wachstum das.

grudge noun **to bear a grudge against somebody** etwas gegen jemanden haben; **she bears me a grudge** sie hat etwas gegen mich.

grumble verb 1 murren; **he's always grumbling** er murrt immer; 2 **to grumble about something** sich über etwas ←(ACC) beklagen; **what's she grumbling about?** worüber beklagt sie sich?

guarantee noun Garantie die (PL die Garantien); **a year's guarantee** ein Jahr Garantie.
verb garantieren.

guard noun 1 prison **guard** der Gefängniswärter, die Gefängniswärterin; 2 (on a train) Zugführer der (PL die Zugführer), Zugführerin die (PL die Zugführerinnen); 3 **security guard** der Wächter, die Wächterin.
verb bewachen.

guard dog noun Wachhund der (PL die Wachhunde).

guess noun **have a guess!** rate mal!; **it's a good guess** gut geraten.
verb 1 raten ✧; **guess who I saw last night** rate mal, wen ich gestern Abend gesehen habe; 2 (guess something correctly) es erraten ✧; **you'll never guess!** du errätst es nie!

guest noun Gast der (PL die Gäste); **we've got guests coming tonight** wir haben heute Abend Gäste; **a paying guest** ein zahlender Gast.

guide noun 1 (person) Führer der (PL die Führer), Führerin die (PL die Führerinnen); 2 (book) Reiseführer der (PL die Reiseführer).

3 (*girl guide*) Pfadfinderin die (PL die Pfadfinderinnen).

guidebook noun **1** Reiseführer der (PL die Reiseführer); **2** (*to a museum or monument*) Handbuch das (PL die Handbücher).

guide dog noun Blindenhund der (PL die Blindenhunde).

guilty adjective **1** schuldig; **2 to feel guilty** ein schlechtes Gewissen haben; **I felt guilty about the noise** ich hatte ein schlechtes Gewissen wegen des Lärms.

guinea pig noun
1 (*pet*) Meerschweinchen das (PL die Meerschweinchen);
2 (*in an experiment*) Versuchskaninchen das (PL die Versuchskaninchen).

guitar noun Gitarre die (PL die Gitarren); **to play the guitar** Gitarre spielen.

gum noun **1** (*in your mouth*) Zahnfleisch das; **2** (*chewing gum*) Kaugummi der (PL die Kaugummi).

gun noun **1** Pistole die (PL die Pistolen); **2** (*rifle*) Gewehr das (PL die Gewehre).

guy noun **1** Typ der (PL die Typen); (*informal*) **he's a nice guy** er ist ein netter Typ; **that guy from Newcastle** der Typ aus Newcastle.

gym noun **1** (*school lesson*) Turnen das; **2** (*building*) Turnhalle die (PL die Turnhallen); **3** (*health club*) Fitnesscenter △ das (PL die Fitnesscenter); **to go to the gym** ins Fitnesscenter gehen.

gymnasium noun Turnhalle die (PL die Turnhallen).

gymnast noun Turner der (PL die Turner), Turnerin die (PL die Turnerinnen).

gymnastics noun Turnen das.

gym shoe noun Turnschuh der (PL die Turnschuhe).

H h

habit noun Gewohnheit die (PL die Gewohnheiten); **it's a bad habit** es ist eine schlechte Gewohnheit.

haddock noun Schellfisch der; **smoked haddock** der Haddock.

hail noun Hagel der.

hailstone noun Hagelkorn das (PL die Hagelkörner).

hailstorm noun Hagelschauer der (PL die Hagelschauer).

hair noun **1** Haare (*plural*); **to comb your hair** sich ←(DAT) die Haare kämmen; **to wash your hair** sich ←(DAT) die Haare waschen; **to have your hair cut** sich ←(DAT) die Haare schneiden lassen; **she's had her hair cut** sie hat sich die Haare schneiden lassen; **2 a hair** ein Haar.

hairbrush noun Haarbürste die (PL die Haarbürsten).

haircut noun **1** Haarschnitt der (PL die Haarschnitte); **2 to have a haircut** sich ←(DAT) die Haare schneiden lassen.

◇ **IRREGULAR VERB: See the verb table in the centre of the dictionary**

hairdresser noun Friseur der (PL die Friseure), Friseuse die (PL die Friseusen); **at the hairdresser's** beim Friseur.

hair drier noun Föhn △ der (PL die Föhne).

hair gel noun Haargel das (PL die Haargele).

hairgrip noun Haarklemme die (PL die Haarklemmen).

hairslide noun Haarspange die (PL die Haarspangen).

hairspray noun Haarspray das (PL die Haarsprays).

hairstyle noun Frisur die (PL die Frisuren).

half noun **1** Hälfte die (PL die Hälften); **half of** die Hälfte von (+DAT); **I gave him half of the money** ich habe ihm die Hälfte des Geld gegeben; **half of it** die Hälfte davon; **2 half an apple** ein halber Apfel; **3 to cut something in half** etwas halbieren; **4** (as a fraction) halb; **three and a half** dreieinhálb; **5** (in time) halb; **half an hour** eine halbe Stunde; **an hour and a half** anderthalb Stunden; **it's half past three** es ist halb vier (literally: half on the way to four); **6** (in weights and measures) halb; **half a litre** ein halber Liter.

half hour noun halbe Stunde die; **every half hour** jede halbe Stunde.

half price adjective, adverb zum halben Preis; **half-price CDs** CDs zum halben Preis.

half-time noun Halbzeit die; **at half-time the score is 0–0** zur Halbzeit steht es null zu null.

halfway adverb **1** auf halbem Weg; **halfway to Frankfurt** auf halbem Weg nach Frankfurt; **2 to be halfway through doing something** halb fertig mit etwas sein; **I'm halfway through my homework** ich bin halb fertig mit meinen Hausaufgaben.

hall noun **1** (in a house) Diele die (PL die Dielen); **2** (public) Saal der (PL die Säle); **village hall** der Gemeindesaal; **concert hall** der Konzertsaal.

Hallowe'en noun der Tag vor Allerheiligen (in Germany there are no particular customs for this date).

ham noun Schinken der; **a ham sandwich** ein Schinkenbrot.

hamburger noun Hamburger der (PL die Hamburger).

hammer noun Hammer der (PL die Hammer).

hamster noun Hamster der (PL die Hamster).

hand noun **1** Hand die (PL die Hände); **to have something in your hand** etwas in der Hand haben; **to hold somebody's hand** jemandes Hand halten; **2 to give somebody a hand** jemandem helfen ◇; **can you give me a hand to move the table into the corner?** kannst du mir helfen, den Tisch in die Ecke zu rücken?; **do you need a hand?** kann ich dir helfen?; **3 on the other hand** ... andererseits ...; **4** (of a watch or clock) Zeiger der (PL die Zeiger); **the**

hour hand der Stundenzeiger.

verb **to hand something to somebody** jemandem etwas geben ◇; **I handed him the keys** ich gab ihm die Schlüssel.

● **to hand something in** etwas abgeben ◇ SEP; **hand in your homework** gebt eure Hausaufgaben ab.

● **to hand something out** etwas austeilen SEP.

handbag *noun* Handtasche *die* (PL die Handtaschen).

handcuffs *plural noun* Handschellen (*plural*).

handful *noun* **a handful of** eine Hand voll △.

handicapped *adjective* behindert.

handkerchief *noun* Taschentuch *das* (PL die Taschentücher).

handle *noun* **1** (*of a door, drawer, bag, or knife*) Griff *der* (PL die Griffe); **2** (*on a cup, jug, or basket*) Henkel *der* (PL die Henkel); **3** (*of a frying pan or broom*) Stiel *der* (PL die Stiele).

verb **1** erledigen; **Gina handles the correspondence** Gina erledigt die Korrespondenz; **2** umgehen ◇ SEP (PERF *sein*) mit; **she's good at handling people** sie kann gut mit Menschen umgehen; **3** fertig werden △ ◇ (PERF *sein*) mit; **he can't handle problems** er kann mit Problemen nicht fertig werden.

handlebars *plural noun* Lenkstange *die* (PL die Lenkstangen).

hand luggage *noun* Handgepäck *das*.

handmade *adjective* handgemacht.

handsome *adjective* gut aussehend △; **he's a handsome guy** er ist ein gut aussehender Typ.

handwriting *noun* Handschrift *die* (PL die Handschriften).

handy *adjective* **1** praktisch; **this little knife's very handy** dieses kleine Messer ist sehr praktisch; **2** griffbereit; **I always keep a notebook handy** ich habe immer ein kleines Notizbuch griffbereit.

hang *verb* **1** hängen ◇; **there was a mirror hanging on the wall** an der Wand hing ein Spiegel; **2** aufhängen SEP; **to hang a mirror on the wall** einen Spiegel an der Wand aufhängen.

● **to hang around** rumhängen ◇ SEP (PERF *sein*) (*informal*); **we were hanging around outside the cinema** wir haben vor dem Kino rumgehangen.

● **to hang on** warten; **hang on a second!** warten Sie einen Moment!

● **to hang up** (*on the phone*) auflegen SEP; **she hung up on me** sie hat einfach aufgelegt.

● **to hang something up** etwas aufhängen SEP.

hangover *noun* Kater *der* (PL die Kater).

happen *verb* **1** passieren (PERF *sein*); **what happened?** was ist passiert?; **it happened in June** es ist im Juni passiert; **2** what's happening? was ist los?; **what's happened to Jill?** was ist mit Jill los?; **3** what's happened to the can-opener?** wo ist der Dosenöffner?; **4** if you happen to see him** wenn du ihn

◇ IRREGULAR VERB: *See the verb table in the centre of the dictionary*

zufällig triffst; **Leila happened to be there** Leila war zufällig da.

happily *adverb* **1** glücklich; **2** (*willingly*) gerne; **I'll happily do it for you** ich tu es gerne für dich.

happiness *noun* Glück *das*.

happy *adjective* glücklich; **a happy child** ein glückliches Kind; **Happy Birthday** herzlichen Glückwunsch zum Geburtstag.

harbour *noun* Hafen *der* (PL *die* Häfen).

hard *adjective* **1** hart; **2** (*difficult*) schwer; **a hard question** eine schwere Frage; **it's hard to know ...** es ist schwer zu wissen ...
adverb **1** to work hard hart arbeiten; **2** to try hard sich sehr bemühen.

hard disk *noun* Festplatte *die* (PL *die* Festplatten).

hardly *adverb* **1** kaum; **I can hardly hear him** ich kann ihn kaum hören; **there was hardly anybody there** es war kaum jemand da; **we've got hardly any milk** wir haben kaum Milch; **hardly anything** kaum etwas; **he ate hardly anything** er hat kaum etwas gegessen; **2** hardly ever fast nie; **I hardly ever see him** ich sehe ihn fast nie.

hard up *adjective* **to be hard up** knapp bei Kasse sein.

harm *noun* **it won't do any harm** es kann nichts schaden.
verb **1** to harm somebody jemandem etwas tun; **they didn't harm him** sie haben ihm nichts

getan; **2** schaden (+DAT) (*health, environment, reputation*); **a cup of coffee won't harm you** eine Tasse Kaffee schadet nicht.

harmful *adjective* schädlich.

harmless *adjective* unschädlich.

hat *noun* Hut *der* (PL *die* Hüte).

hate *verb* hassen; **I hate geography** ich hasse Erdkunde.

hatred *noun* Hass△ *der*.

have *verb* **1** haben ◇; **Anna has three brothers** Anna hat drei Brüder; **how many sisters do you have?** wie viele Schwestern hast du?; **2 what have you got in your hand?** was hast du in der Hand?; **he has (got) flu** er hat die Grippe; **3** (*to form past tenses, some verbs in German take 'haben' and others 'sein'*) **I've finished** ich bin fertig; **have you seen the film?** hast du den Film gesehen?; **Rosie hasn't arrived yet** Rosie ist noch nicht angekommen; **4 to have to do something** etwas tun müssen ◇; **I have to phone my mum** ich muss meine Mutter anrufen; **5** (*'have' is often translated by a more specific German verb*) **we had a coffee** wir haben einen Kaffee getrunken; **what will you have?** was nehmen Sie?; **I'll have an omelette** ich nehme ein Omelett; **I'm going to have a shower** ich dusche jetzt; **to have lunch** zu Mittag essen; **to have dinner** (*in the evening*) zu Abend essen; **6** (*get*) bekommen ◇; **Emma had a letter from Sam yesterday**

gestern bekam Emma einen Brief von Sam; **she had a baby** sie hat ein Baby bekommen; **7 to have something done** etwas machen lassen ◇; **I'm going to have my hair cut** ich lasse mir die Haare schneiden; **8 to have on** (*be wearing*) anhaben ◇ SEP; **to have nothing on** nichts anhaben.

hay fever *noun* Heuschnupfen *der*.

hazelnut *noun* Haselnuss Δ *die* (PL *die* Haselnüsse).

he *pronoun* er; **he lives in Manchester** er wohnt in Manchester.

head *noun* **1** Kopf *der* (PL *die* Köpfe); **he shook his head** er schüttelte den Kopf; **2** (*of a school*) Direktor *der* (PL *die* Direktoren), Direktorin *die* (PL *die* Direktorinnen); **3** (*of a firm*) Chef *der* (PL *die* Chefs), Chefin *die* (PL *die* Chefinnen); **4** (*when tossing a coin*) **'heads or tails?'** 'Kopf oder Zahl?'.

● **to head for something** auf etwas ←(ACC) zusteuern SEP (PERF *sein*); **Liz headed for the door** Liz steuerte auf die Tür zu.

headache *noun* Kopfschmerzen (*plural*); **I've got a headache** ich habe Kopfschmerzen.

headlight *noun* Scheinwerfer *der* (PL *die* Scheinwerfer).

headline *noun* Schlagzeile *die* (PL *die* Schlagzeilen).

headmaster *noun* Direktor *der* (PL *die* Direktoren).

headmistress *noun* Direktorin *die* (PL *die* Direktorinnen).

headphones *noun* Kopfhörer *der* (PL *die* Kopfhörer).

headteacher *noun* Direktor *der* (PL *die* Direktoren), Direktorin *die* (PL *die* Direktorinnen).

health *noun* Gesundheit *die*.

health centre *noun* Ärztezentrum *das* (PL *die* Ärztezentren).

healthy *adjective* gesund.

heap *noun* Haufen *der* (PL *die* Haufen); **I've got heaps of work** ich habe einen Haufen Arbeit (*informal*).

hear *verb* hören; **I can't hear anything** ich kann überhaupt nichts hören; **I hear you've bought a dog** ich habe gehört, dass ihr einen Hund gekauft habt.

● **to hear about something** von etwas ←(DAT) hören; **have you heard about the concert?** hast du von dem Konzert gehört?

● **to hear from somebody** von jemandem hören.

heart *noun* **1** Herz *das* (PL *die* Herzen); **2 to learn something by heart** etwas auswendig lernen; **3** (*in cards*) Herz *das*; **the jack of hearts** der Herzbube.

heat *noun* Hitze *die*.
verb **1 to heat something** etwas heiß machen; **I'll go and heat the soup** ich mache die Suppe heiß; **2 the soup's heating** die Suppe wird warm; **3** heizen (*a room*);

◇ IRREGULAR VERB: *See the verb table in the centre of the dictionary*

● **to heat something up** etwas aufwärmen SEP; **I'm heating the sauce up** ich wärme die Soße auf.

heater noun Heizgerät das (PL die Heizgeräte).

heather noun Heidekraut das.

heating noun Heizung die.

heatwave noun Hitzewelle die (PL die Hitzewellen).

heaven noun Himmel der.

heavy adjective 1 schwer; **my rucksack's really heavy** mein Rucksack ist sehr schwer; 2 (busy) **I've got a heavy day tomorrow** ich habe morgen viel zu tun; 3 (in quantity) stark; **heavy rain** starker Regen.

hectic adjective hektisch; **a hectic day** ein hektischer Tag.

hedge noun Hecke die (PL die Hecken).

hedgehog noun Igel der (PL die Igel).

heel noun 1 (of foot or sock) Ferse die (PL die Fersen); 2 (of a shoe) Absatz der (PL die Absätze).

height noun 1 (of a person) Größe die; **what height are you?** wie groß bist du?; 2 (of a building, mountain) Höhe die; **what height is it?** wie hoch ist es?

helicopter noun Hubschrauber der (PL die Hubschrauber).

hell noun Hölle die; **hell!** verdammt! (informal).

hello exclamation 1 (polite) guten Tag!; 2 (informal, and on the phone) hallo!

helmet noun Helm der (PL die Helme).

help noun Hilfe die; **do you need any help?** kann ich dir helfen?; (in a shop) kann ich Ihnen behilflich sein?
verb 1 helfen ♢ (+DAT); **to help somebody (to) do something** jemandem helfen, etwas zu tun; **can you help me lay the table?** kannst du mir helfen, den Tisch zu decken?; 2 **to help yourself to something** sich ←(DAT) etwas nehmen ♢; **help yourself to vegetables** nimm dir Gemüse; **help yourself!** greif zu!; 3 **help!** Hilfe!; 4 **he can't help it** er kann nichts dafür.

helpful adjective (person) hilfsbereit.

hen noun Henne die (PL die Hennen).

her pronoun (in German this pronoun changes according to the function it has in the sentence or the preposition it follows) 1 (as a direct object in the accusative) sie; **I know her** ich kenne sie; **I saw her last week** ich habe sie letzte Woche gesehen; 2 (after prepositions +ACC) sie; **without her** ohne sie; **we've heard a lot about her** wir haben viel über sie gehört; 3 (as an indirect object or after verbs that take the dative) ihr; **I gave her my address** ich habe ihr meine Adresse gegeben; **we helped her** wir haben ihr

△ NEW SPELLING: See page xii

geholfen; **4** (*after prepositions* +DAT)
ihr; **with her** mit ihr; **5** (*in comparisons*) sie; **he's older than her** er ist älter als sie; **6** (*in the nominative*) sie; **it was her** sie war es.
adjective **1** (*before a masculine noun*) ihr; **her brother** ihr Bruder;
2 (*before a feminine noun*) ihre; **her sister** ihre Schwester; **3** (*before a neuter noun*) ihr; **her house** ihr Haus; **4** (*before a plural noun*) ihre; **her children** ihre Kinder; **5** (*with parts of the body*) der/die/das, die (*plural*); **she had a glass in her hand** sie hatte ein Glas in der Hand; **she's washing her hands** sie wäscht sich die Hände.

herb *noun* Kraut *das* (PL *die* Kräuter).

here *adverb* **1** (*in or at this place*) hier; **not far from here** nicht weit von hier; **here's my address** hier ist meine Adresse; **I want to stay here** ich möchte hier bleiben; **2** (*to this place*) hierher; **when Peter came here** als Peter hierher kam; **3 here they are!** da sind sie!; **Tom isn't here at the moment** Tom ist im Moment nicht da.

hero *noun* Held *der* (PL *die* Helden).

heroin *noun* Heroin *das*.

heroine *noun* Heldin *die* (PL *die* Heldinnen).

herring *noun* Hering *der* (PL *die* Heringe).

hers *pronoun* **1** (*for a masculine noun*) ihrer; **my coat is blue and hers is red** mein Mantel ist blau und

ihrer ist rot; **I took my hat and she took hers** ich nahm meinen Hut und sie nahm ihren; **2** (*for a feminine noun*) ihre; **I gave Ann my address and she gave me hers** ich habe Ann meine Adresse gegeben und sie hat mir ihre gegeben; **3** (*for a neuter noun*) ihr(e)s; **my bike is new but hers is old** mein Rad ist neu, aber ihrs ist alt; **4** (*for masculine/feminine/neuter plural nouns*) ihre; **I showed Emma my photos and she showed me hers** ich habe Emma meine Fotos gezeigt und sie hat mir ihre gezeigt; **5 the CDs are hers** die CDs gehören ihr; **it's hers** das gehört ihr.

herself *pronoun* **1** (*reflexive*) sich; **she's hurt herself** sie hat sich wehgetan; **2** (*stressing something*) selbst; **she said it herself** sie hat es selbst gesagt; **3 she did it by herself** sie hat es ganz allein gemacht.

hesitate *verb* zögern.

heterosexual *adjective* heterosexuell.
noun Heterosexuelle *der*/*die* (PL *die* Heterosexuellen).

hi *exclamation* hallo!

hiccups *plural noun* **to have the hiccups** einen Schluckauf haben.

hidden *adjective* verborgen.

hide *verb* **1** sich verstecken; **she hid behind the door** sie hat sich hinter der Tür versteckt; **2 to hide something** etwas verstecken.

hi-fi *noun* Hi-Fi-Anlage *die* (PL *die* Hi-Fi-Anlagen).

✧ IRREGULAR VERB: *See the verb table in the centre of the dictionary*

high *adjective* 1 hoch; **how high is the wall?** wie hoch ist die Mauer?; **the wall is two metres high** die Mauer ist zwei Meter hoch; **the shelf is too high** das Regal ist zu hoch; *(the adjective 'hoch' loses its* c *when it has an ending, becoming hoher/hohe/hohes)* **a high tower** ein hoher Turm; **a high wall** eine hohe Mauer; **at high speed** mit hoher Geschwindigkeit; **a high voice** eine hohe Stimme; 2 **high winds** starker Wind.
adverb hoch.

high-heeled *adjective* hochhackig.

high jump *noun* Hochsprung *der*.

hijack *verb* to hijack a plane ein Flugzeug entführen.

hijacker *noun* Entführer *der* (PL *die* Entführer).

hike *noun* Wanderung *die* (PL *die* Wanderungen).

hilarious *adjective* lustig.

hill *noun* 1 *(large hill)* Berg *der* (PL *die* Berge); **you can see the hills** man kann die Berge sehen; 2 *(smaller)* Hügel *der* (PL *die* Hügel); **to walk up the hill** den Hügel hinaufgehen; 3 *(hillside)* Hang *der* (PL *die* Hänge); **the house on the hill** das Haus am Hang.

him *pronoun* (*in German this pronoun changes according to the function it has in the sentence or the preposition it follows*) 1 *(as a direct object in the accusative)* ihn; **I know him** ich kenne ihn; **I saw him last week** ich habe ihn letzte Woche gesehen; 2 *(after prepositions +*ACC*)* ihn; **he fought against him** er hat gegen ihn gekämpft; **without him** ohne ihn; 3 *(as an indirect object or after verbs that take the dative)* ihm; **I gave him my address** ich habe ihm meine Adresse gegeben; **you must help him** du musst ihm helfen; 4 *(after prepositions +*DAT*)* ihm; **with him** mit ihm; 5 *(in comparisons)* er; **she's older than him** sie ist älter als er; 6 *(in the nominative)* er; **it was him** er war es.

himself *pronoun* 1 *(reflexive)* sich; **he's hurt himself** er hat sich wehgetan; 2 *(stressing something)* selbst; **he said it himself** er hat es selbst gesagt; 3 **he did it by himself** er hat es ganz allein gemacht.

Hindu *adjective* hinduistisch.

hip *noun* Hüfte *die* (PL *die* Hüften).

hippie *noun* Hippie *der* (PL *die* Hippies).

hire *noun* 1 Vermietung *die*; **car hire** die Autovermietung; 2 **for hire** zu vermieten.
verb mieten.

his *adjective* 1 *(before a masculine noun)* sein; **his brother** sein Bruder; 2 *(before a feminine noun)* seine; **his sister** seine Schwester; 3 *(before a neuter noun)* sein; **his house** sein Haus; 4 *(before a plural noun)* seine; **his children** seine Kinder; 5 *(with parts of the body noun)* der/die/das, die *(plural)*; **he had a glass in his hand** er hatte ein Glas in der Hand; **he's washing his hands** er wäscht sich ←(DAT) die Hände.

△ NEW SPELLING: *See page xii*

pronoun **1** (*for a masculine noun*) seiner; **my hat is red and his is blue** mein Hut ist rot und seiner ist blau; **2** (*for a feminine noun*) seine; **I gave him my address and he gave me his** ich habe ihm meine Adresse gegeben und er hat mir seine gegeben; **3** (*for a neuter noun*) sein(e)s; **my book is new but his is old** mein Buch ist neu, aber seins ist alt; **4** (*for masculine/feminine/ neuter plural nouns*) seine; **I've invited my parents and Steve's invited his** ich habe meine Eltern eingeladen und Steve hat seine eingeladen; **5 the green car's his** das grüne Auto gehört ihm; **it's his** das gehört ihm.

history *noun* Geschichte *die*.

hit *noun* **1** (*song*) Hit *der* (PL die Hits); **their latest hit** ihr neuester Hit; **2** (*success*) Erfolg *der* (PL die Erfolge); **the film is a huge hit** der Film ist ein großer Erfolg.
verb **1** treffen ◇; **to hit the ball** den Ball treffen; **2 to hit your head on something** sich ←(DAT) den Kopf an etwas ←(DAT) stoßen; **I hit my head on the door** ich habe mir den Kopf an der Tür gestoßen; **3** prallen gegen (+ACC) (PERF *sein*); **the car hit a wall** das Auto ist gegen eine Wand geprallt; **4 to be hit by a car** von einem Auto angefahren werden.

hitch *noun* Problem *das* (PL die Probleme); **there's been a slight hitch** ein kleines Problem ist aufgetaucht.
verb **to hitch a lift** per Anhalter fahren ◇ (PERF *sein*).

hitchhike *verb* per Anhalter fahren ◇ (PERF *sein*); **we hitchhiked to Heidelberg** wir sind per Anhalter nach Heidelberg gefahren.

hitchhiker *noun* Anhalter *der* (PL die Anhalter), Anhalterin *die* (PL die Anhalterinnen).

HIV-negative *adjective* HIV-negativ.

HIV-positive *adjective* HIV-positiv.

hobby *noun* Hobby *das* (PL die Hobbys).

hockey *noun* Hockey *das*.

hockey stick *noun* Hockeyschläger *der* (PL die Hockeyschläger).

hold *verb* **1** halten ◇; **to hold something in your hand** etwas in der Hand halten; **can you hold the torch?** kannst du die Taschenlampe halten?; **2** (*be able to contain*) fassen; **the jug holds a litre** der Krug fasst einen Liter; **3 to hold a meeting** eine Versammlung abhalten ◇ SEP; **4 can you hold the line, please?** bleiben Sie bitte am Apparat; **5 hold on!** (*wait*) warten Sie!; (*on the phone*) bleiben Sie am Apparat.
● **to hold on to something** (*to stop yourself from falling*) sich an etwas ←(DAT) festhalten ◇ SEP.
● **to hold somebody up** (*delay*) jemanden aufhalten ◇ SEP; **I was held up at the dentist's** ich bin beim Zahnarzt aufgehalten worden.
● **to hold something up** (*raise*) etwas hochhalten ◇ SEP.

hold-up *noun* **1** Verzögerung *die* (PL

◇ IRREGULAR VERB: *See the verb table in the centre of the dictionary*

die Verzögerungen); 2 (*traffic jam*) Stau *der* (PL *die* Staus); 3 (*robbery*) Überfall *der* (PL *die* Überfälle).

hole *noun* Loch *das* (PL *die* Löcher).

holiday *noun* 1 Ferien (*plural*), Urlaub *der* (PL *die* Urlaube) (*students, schoolchildren, and families usually have 'Ferien'; people in paid employment usually have 'Urlaub'*); **where are you going for your holiday?** wo fahrt ihr in den Ferien hin?; **have a good holiday!** schöne Ferien!, schönen Urlaub!; **to be away on holiday** auf Urlaub sein, in Ferien sein; **to go on holiday** in Urlaub fahren, in die Ferien fahren; **the school holidays** die Schulferien; 2 (*day off work*) freie Tag *der* (PL *die* freien Tage); **I'm taking two days' holiday next week** ich nehme mir nächste Woche zwei Tage frei; 3 **public holiday** *der* Feiertag; **Monday's a holiday** Montag ist ein Feiertag.

Holland *noun* Holland *das*.

holy *adjective* heilig.

home *noun* 1 **I was at home** ich war zu Hause; **to stay at home** zu Hause bleiben; 2 **make yourself at home** mach es dir bequem.
adverb 1 (*to home*) nach Hause; **Susie's gone home** Susie ist nach Hause gegangen; **on my way home** auf dem Weg nach Hause; **to get home** nach Hause kommen; **we got home at midnight** wir sind um Mitternacht nach Hause gekommen; 2 (*at home*) zu Hause; **I'll be home in the afternoon** ich bin am Nachmittag zu Hause.

homeless *adjective* obdachlos; **the homeless** die Obdachlosen.

homemade *adjective* selbst gemacht△; **homemade biscuits** selbst gebackene Kekse.

homeopathic *adjective* homöopathisch.

homesick *adjective* **to be homesick** Heimweh haben.

homework *noun* Hausaufgaben (*plural*); **I did my homework** ich habe meine Hausaufgaben gemacht; **my German homework** meine Deutschhausaufgaben.

homosexual *adjective* homosexuell.
noun Homosexuelle *der/die* (PL *die* Homosexuellen).

honest *adjective* ehrlich.

honestly *adverb* ehrlich.

honesty *noun* Ehrlichkeit *die*.

honey *noun* Honig *der* (PL *die* Honige).

hood *noun* 1 Kapuze *die* (PL *die* Kapuzen); 2 (*on a car*) Verdeck *das* (PL *die* Verdecke).

hook *noun* 1 Haken *der* (PL *die* Haken); 2 **to take the phone off the hook** das Telefon aushängen SEP.

hooligan *noun* Hooligan *der* (PL *die* Hooligans).

hooray *exclamation* hurra!

hoover *verb* saugen; **I hoovered my bedroom** ich habe mein Schlafzimmer gesaugt.

△ NEW SPELLING: See page xii

Hoover™ noun Staubsauger der (PL die Staubsauger).

hope noun Hoffnung die (PL die Hoffnungen); **to give up hope** die Hoffnung aufgeben.
verb 1 hoffen; **we hope you'll be able to come** wir hoffen, ihr könnt kommen; **I'm hoping to see you on Friday** ich hoffe, dich am Freitag zu sehen; 2 **I hope so** hoffentlich; **I hope not** hoffentlich nicht.

hopefully adverb hoffentlich; **hopefully, the film won't have started** hoffentlich hat der Film noch nicht angefangen.

hopeless adjective miserabel (informal); **I'm hopeless at geography** ich bin miserabel in Erdkunde.

horn noun 1 (of an animal, instrument) Horn das (PL die Hörner); 2 (of a car) Hupe die (PL die Hupen).

horoscope noun Horoskop das (PL die Horoskope).

horrible adjective 1 furchtbar; **the weather was horrible** das Wetter war furchtbar; 2 (person) gemein; **she's really horrible** sie ist richtig gemein; **he was really horrible to me** er war richtig gemein zu mir.

horror noun Entsetzen das.

horror film noun Horrorfilm der (PL die Horrorfilme).

horse noun Pferd das (PL die Pferde).

hospital noun Krankenhaus das (PL die Krankenhäuser); **in hospital** im

Krankenhaus; **to be taken into hospital** ins Krankenhaus kommen.

hospitality noun Gastfreundschaft die.

host noun 1 Gastgeber der (PL die Gastgeber); 2 (on a TV programme) Moderator der (PL die Moderatoren).

hostage noun Geisel die (PL die Geiseln).

hostel noun youth hostel Jugendherberge.

hostess noun 1 Gastgeberin die (PL die Gastgeberinnen); 2 (on a TV programme) Moderatorin die (PL die Moderatorinnen); 3 **air hostess** die Stewardess.

hot adjective 1 heiß; **be careful, the plates are hot** sei vorsichtig, die Teller sind heiß; **it's hot today** heute ist es heiß; 2 (person) **I'm very hot** mir ist sehr heiß; 3 (spicy) scharf; **the curry's too hot for me** das Curry ist mir zu scharf; 4 **a hot meal** ein warmes Essen.

hotel noun Hotel das (PL die Hotels).

hour noun Stunde die (PL die Stunden); **two hours later** zwei Stunden später; **we waited for two hours** wir haben zwei Stunden lang gewartet; **I've been waiting for hours** ich warte schon seit Stunden; **two hours ago** vor zwei Stunden; **to be paid by the hour** pro Stunde bezahlt werden; **every hour** jede Stunde; **half an hour** eine halbe Stunde; **a quarter of an hour** eine Viertelstunde; **an hour and a half** anderthalb Stunden.

house noun 1 Haus das (PL die

◇ IRREGULAR VERB: See the verb table in the centre of the dictionary

Häuser); **2 at somebody's house**
bei jemandem; **I'm at Judy's house**
ich bin bei Judy; **I'm going to Sid's
house tonight** ich gehe heute Abend
zu Sid; **I phoned from Jill's house**
ich habe von Jill angerufen.

housewife noun Hausfrau die (PL
die Hausfrauen).

housework noun Hausarbeit die;
he does the housework er macht
den Haushalt (informal).

hovercraft noun
Luftkissenfahrzeug das (PL die
Luftkissenfahrzeuge).

how adverb **1** wie; **how did you do
it?** wie hast du das gemacht?; **how
are you?** wie geht es dir?; **how
many?** wie viele?; **how many
brothers do you have?** wie viele
Brüder hast du?; **how old are you?**
wie alt bist du?; **how far is it?** wie
weit ist es?; **how far is it to York?**
wie weit ist es bis York?; **how long
will it take?** wie lange dauert es?;
how long have you known her? wie
lange kennst du sie?; **2 how much?**
wie viel?; **how much money do you
have?** wie viel Geld hast du?; **how
much is it?** wie viel kostet das?

however adverb **1** jedoch; **2** (in
questions) **however did she do it?**
wie hat sie das nur gemacht?; **3
however famous he is** wie
berühmt er auch sein mag.

hug noun **to give somebody a hug**
jemanden umarmen; **she gave me
a hug** sie hat mich umarmt.

huge adjective riesig.

hum verb summen.

human adjective menschlich.

human being noun Mensch der
(PL die Menschen).

humour noun Humor der; **to have
a sense of humour** Humor haben.

hundred number hundert; **two
hundred** zweihundert; **two
hundred and ten** zweihundertzehn;
a hundred people hundert
Menschen; **about a hundred** um die
hundert; **hundreds of people**
hunderte von Menschen.

Hungary noun Ungarn das.

hunger noun Hunger der.

hungry adjective **to be hungry**
Hunger haben; **I'm hungry** ich habe
Hunger.

hunting noun Jagd die; **fox-
hunting** die Fuchsjagd.

hurry noun **to be in a hurry** es eilig
haben; **I'm in a hurry** ich habe es
eilig; **there's no hurry** es eilt nicht.
verb **1** sich beeilen; **I must hurry** ich
muss mich beeilen; **hurry up!** beeil
dich!; **2 he hurried home** er ging
schnell nach Hause.

hurt verb **1 to hurt somebody**
jemandem wehtun ◇ SEP; **you're
hurting me!** du tust mir weh!; **that
hurts!** das tut weh!; **2 my arm
hurts** der Arm tut mir weh; **3 to hurt
yourself** sich ∼ (DAT) wehtun ◇ SEP;
did you hurt yourself? hast du dir
wehgetan?
adjective **1** (in an accident) verletzt;
three people were hurt drei
Menschen wurden verletzt; **2** (in

△ NEW SPELLING: See page xii

feelings) gekränkt; **she felt hurt** sie fühlte sich gekränkt.

husband *noun* Ehemann *der* (PL *die* Ehemänner).

hymn *noun* Kirchenlied *das* (PL *die* Kirchenlieder).

hypermarket *noun* Großmarkt *der* (PL *die* Großmärkte).

hyphen *noun* Bindestrich *der* (PL *die* Bindestriche).

I i

I *pronoun* ich; **I have two sisters** ich habe zwei Schwestern.

ice *noun* Eis *das*.

ice cream *noun* Eis *das*; **two chocolate ice creams** zwei Schokoladeneis.

ice hockey *noun* Eishockey *das*.

ice rink *noun* Eisbahn *die* (PL *die* Eisbahnen).

ice-skating *noun* **to go ice-skating** Schlittschuh laufen ◊ (PERF *sein*).

icy *adjective* 1 vereist (*road*); 2 (*very cold*) eiskalt.

idea *noun* 1 Idee *die* (PL *die* Ideen); **what a good idea!** was für eine gute Idee!; 2 **I've no idea** ich habe keine Ahnung.

ideal *adjective* ideal.

identical *adjective* identisch.

identification *noun* 1 Identifizierung *die*; 2 (*proof of identity*) Ausweispapiere (*plural*).

identity card *noun* Personalausweis *der* (PL *die* Personalausweise).

idiot *noun* Idiot *der* (PL *die* Idioten).

idiotic *adjective* idiotisch.

i.e. *abbreviation* d.h. (*das heißt*).

if *conjunction* 1 wenn; **if it rains** wenn es regnet; **if I won the lottery** wenn ich in der Lotterie gewinnen sollte; **if not** wenn nicht; **if only** wenn nur; **if only you'd told me** wenn du mir das nur gesagt hättest; 2 **even if** selbst wenn; **even if it snows** selbst wenn es schneit; 3 **if I were you** an deiner Stelle; 4 (*whether*) ob; **I wonder if he'll come** ich bin gespannt, ob er kommt; **as if** als ob.

ignore *verb* 1 ignorieren; 2 überhören (*what somebody says*).

ill *adjective* krank; **to fall ill, to be taken ill** krank werden; **I feel ill** ich fühle mich krank.

illegal *adjective* illegal.

illustration *noun* Illustration *die* (PL *die* Illustrationen).

image *noun* Bild *das* (PL *die* Bilder); ★ **he's the spitting image of his father** er ist das Ebenbild seines Vaters.

imagination *noun* Phantasie *die*.

imaginative *adjective* phantasievoll.

◊ IRREGULAR VERB: *See the verb table in the centre of the dictionary*

imagine verb sich ←(DAT) vorstellen; **imagine that you're very rich** stell dir vor, du bist sehr reich; **you can't imagine how hard it was** du kannst dir nicht vorstellen, wie schwer es war.

imitate verb nachahmen SEP.

immediate adjective 1 (without delay) unmittelbar; **2 the immediate family** die engste Familie.

immediately adverb 1 sofort; **I rang them immediately** ich habe sie sofort angerufen; **2 immediately before** unmittelbar davor; **immediately after** unmittelbar danach.

immigrant noun Einwanderer der (PL die Einwanderer), Einwanderin die (PL die Einwanderinnen).

immigration noun Einwanderung die.

impatience noun Ungeduld die.

impatient adjective 1 ungeduldig; **2 to be impatient with somebody** ungeduldig mit jemandem sein.

impatiently adverb ungeduldig.

importance noun Wichtigkeit die.

important adjective wichtig.

impossible adjective unmöglich; **it's impossible to find a telephone** es ist unmöglich, ein Telefon zu finden.

impressed adjective beeindruckt; **to be impressed by something** von etwas ←(DAT) beeindruckt sein.

impressive adjective eindrucksvoll.

improve verb 1 **to improve something** etwas verbessern; **2** (get better) besser werden; **the weather is improving** das Wetter wird besser.

improvement noun Verbesserung die (PL die Verbesserungen).

in preposition 1 in (+DAT or, with movement into, +ACC); **it is in my pocket** es ist in meiner Tasche; (with movement) **he put it in his pocket** er hat es in die Tasche gesteckt; **she sat in the sun** sie saß in der Sonne; **I read it in the newspaper** ich habe es in der Zeitung gelesen; **in Oxford** in Oxford; **in Germany** in Deutschland; **2 the biggest city in the world** die größte Stadt auf der Welt; **a house in the country** ein Haus auf dem Land; **in the street** auf der Straße; **3** (wearing and with colours) in (+DAT); **the girl in the pink shirt** das Mädchen im rosa Hemd; **4 in German** auf Deutsch; **5** (time expressions) in (+DAT); **in May** im Mai; **in 1994** (im Jahre) 1994; **in winter** im Winter; **in summer** im Sommer; **in the night** in der Nacht; **I'll phone you in ten minutes** ich rufe dich in zehn Minuten an; **she was ready in five minutes** sie war in fünf Minuten fertig; **6 in the morning** am Morgen; **at eight in the morning** um acht Uhr morgens; **7** (among people or in literature) bei (+DAT); **it's rare in children** das ist selten bei Kindern; **in Shakespeare** bei

△ NEW SPELLING: See page xii

Shakespeare; **in the army** beim Militär; **8 in time** rechtzeitig.
adverb **1** *(inside)* hinein-, herein-, rein- (*informal*); (*Herein-, hinein-, and rein- form prefixes to separable verbs. 'Herein-' is used with verbs like kommen, which have the sense of moving towards the speaker. 'Hinein-' is used with verbs like gehen, which have the sense of going away from the speaker. The informal 'rein-' can be used with either movement.*) **to come in** hereinkommen ◆ SEP (PERF *sein*); **to go in** hineingehen ◆ SEP (PERF *sein*); **he was not allowed to go into the room** er durfte nicht ins Zimmer reingehen; **to run in** reinlaufen ◆ SEP (PERF *sein*) (*informal*); **2 to be in** da sein; **Mick's not in at the moment** Mick ist im Moment nicht da; **3** (*at home*) zu Hause; **4** (*indoors*) drinnen; **in here** hier drinnen; **in there** da drinnen.

include *verb* einschließen ◆ SEP; **service is included in the price** die Bedienung ist im Preis inbegriffen.

including *preposition*
1 einschließlich (+GEN); **everyone, including the children** alle, einschließlich der Kinder; **£50 including postage** fünfzig Pfund einschließlich Porto; **including Sundays** einschließlich sonntags; **2 not including Sundays** außer sonntags.

income *noun* Einkommen *das* (PL *die* Einkommen).

income tax *noun*
Einkommensteuer *die* (PL *die* Einkommensteuern).

increase *noun* Erhöhung *die* (PL *die* Erhöhungen) (*in price, for example*).
verb **1** steigen ◆ (PERF *sein*); **the price has increased by £10** der Preis ist um zehn Pfund gestiegen; **2** erhöhen (*salary*).

incredible *adjective* unglaublich.

incredibly *adverb* (*very*) unwahrscheinlich; **the film's incredibly boring** der Film ist unwahrscheinlich langweilig.

indeed *adverb* **1** (*to emphasize*) wirklich; **she's very pleased indeed** sie hat sich wirklich sehr gefreut; **2** (*certainly*) natürlich; **'can you hear the radio?' – 'indeed I can!'** 'kannst du das Radio hören?' – 'ja, natürlich!'; **3 thank you very much indeed** vielen herzlichen Dank.

indefinite article *noun* unbestimmte Artikel *der.*

independence *noun* Unabhängigkeit *die.*

independent *adjective* unabhängig; **independent school** *die* Privatschule.

India *noun* Indien *das.*

Indian *noun* **1** Inder *der* (PL *die* Inder), Inderin *die* (PL *die* Inderinnen); **2** (*a Native American*) Indianer *der* (PL *die* Indianer), Indianerin *die* (PL *die* Indianerinnen).

◆ IRREGULAR VERB: *See the verb table in the centre of the dictionary*

indicate verb **1** zeigen auf (+ACC) (*a person or a thing*); **2** (*of a car or driver*) blinken.

indigestion noun Magenverstimmung die (PL die Magenverstimmungen).

individual noun Einzelne △ der/die (PL die Einzelnen).
adjective **1** einzeln (*serving, contribution*); **2** individual tuition der Einzelunterricht.

indoor adjective an indoor swimming pool ein Hallenbad; indoor games Spiele im Haus; (*in sports*) Hallenspiele.

indoors adverb drinnen; it's cooler indoors drinnen ist es kühler; to go indoors ins Haus gehen.

industrial adjective industriell.

industrial estate noun Industriegebiet das (PL die Industriegebiete).

industry noun Industrie die (PL die Industrien); the car industry die Autoindustrie.

inevitable adjective unvermeidlich.

inevitably adverb zwangsläufig.

inexperienced adjective unerfahren.

infant school noun Vorschule die (PL die Vorschulen).

adjective **1** indisch; he's Indian er ist Inder; **2** (*Native American*) indianisch; she's Indian sie ist Indianerin.

infection noun Infektion die (PL die Infektionen); eye infection die Augeninfektion; throat infection die Halsentzündung.

infectious adjective ansteckend.

infinitive noun Infinitiv der (PL die Infinitive).

inflammable adjective feuergefährlich.

inflatable adjective inflatable mattress die Luftmatratze; inflatable boat das Schlauchboot.

influence noun Einfluss △ der (PL die Einflüsse); to be a good influence on somebody einen guten Einfluss △ auf jemanden haben.
verb beeinflussen.

inform verb informieren; to inform somebody of something jemanden über etwas ←(ACC) informieren.

informal adjective **1** zwanglos (*meal or event*); **2** ungezwungen (*language, tone*).

information noun Auskunft die; where can I get information about flights to Berlin? wo kann ich Auskunft über Flüge nach Berlin bekommen?

information desk, information office noun Auskunftsbüro das (PL die Auskunftsbüros).

information technology noun Informatik die.

ingredient noun Zutat die (PL die Zutaten).

inhabitant noun Einwohner der (PL die Einwohner), Einwohnerin die (PL die Einwohnerinnen).

initials plural noun Initialen (plural).

injection noun Spritze die (PL die Spritzen).

injure verb verletzen.

injury noun Verletzung die (PL die Verletzungen).

ink noun Tinte die (PL die Tinten).

in-laws noun Schwiegereltern (plural).

innocent adjective unschuldig.

insane adjective 1 geisteskrank; 2 (foolish) wahnsinnig.

insect noun Insekt das (PL die Insekten); **insect bite** der Insektenstich.

insect repellent noun Insektenvertilgungsmittel das.

inside noun on the inside innen; **the inside of the oven is black** innen ist der Herd schwarz. preposition in (+DAT, or, with movement towards a place, +ACC); **inside the cinema** im Kino; **to go inside (the house)** ins Haus gehen. adverb drinnen; **she's inside, I think** ich glaube, sie ist drinnen.

inside out adjective, adverb (clothing) links.

insist verb darauf bestehen ◊; **if you insist** wenn du darauf bestehst; **to insist on doing something** darauf bestehen, etwas zu tun; **he insists**

on paying er besteht darauf zu zahlen; **to insist that …** darauf bestehen, dass …; **Ruth insisted I was wrong** Ruth hat darauf bestanden, dass ich Unrecht hatte.

inspector noun 1 (on a bus or train) Kontrolleur der (PL die Kontrolleure), Kontrolleurin die (PL die Kontrolleurinnen); 2 (in the police) Kommissar der (PL die Kommissare), Kommissarin die (PL die Kommissarinnen).

install verb installieren.

instalment noun (of a story or serial) Folge die (PL die Folgen).

instance noun **for instance** zum Beispiel.

instant noun Augenblick der (PL die Augenblicke); **come here this instant!** komm sofort hier! adjective 1 Instant- (coffee, tea); 2 (immediate) sofortig.

instantly adverb sofort.

instead adverb 1 **Ted couldn't come, so I came instead (of him)** Ted konnte nicht kommen, also bin ich an seiner Stelle gekommen; 2 **instead of** statt (+GEN or +DAT); **he bought a bike instead of a car** er hat ein Fahrrad statt eines Autos gekauft; **instead of cake I had cheese** statt Kuchen habe ich Käse genommen; **instead of playing tennis we went swimming** statt Tennis zu spielen, sind wir schwimmen gegangen.

instinct noun Instinkt der (PL die Instinkte).

institute noun Institut das (PL die Institute).

instructions plural noun Anweisung die (PL die Anweisungen); **follow the instructions on the packet** befolgen Sie die Anweisung auf der Packung; **'instructions for use'** 'Gebrauchsanweisung'.

instructor noun Lehrer der (PL die Lehrer), Lehrerin die (PL die Lehrerinnen); **my skiing instructor** mein Skilehrer.

instrument noun Instrument das (PL die Instrumente); **to play an instrument** ein Instrument spielen.

insulin noun Insulin das.

insult noun Beleidigung die (PL die Beleidigungen).
verb beleidigen.

insurance noun Versicherung die (PL die Versicherungen); **travel insurance** die Reiseversicherung.

intelligence noun Intelligenz die.

intelligent adjective intelligent.

intend verb beabsichtigen; **as I intended** wie beabsichtigt; **to intend to do something** beabsichtigen, etwas zu tun; **we intend to spend the night in Rome** wir beabsichtigen, in Rom zu übernachten.

intention noun Absicht die (PL die Absichten); **I have no intention of paying** ich habe nicht die Absicht zu zahlen.

interest noun 1 Interesse das (PL die Interessen); **to have lots of interests** viele Interessen haben; **he has an interest in jazz** er hat Interesse an Jazz; **2** (financial) Zinsen (plural).
verb interessieren; **that doesn't interest me** das interessiert mich nicht.

interested adjective **to be interested in something** sich für etwas ←(ACC) interessieren; **Sean's interested in cooking** Sean interessiert sich für Kochen.

interesting adjective interessant.

interfere verb 1 **to interfere with something** (to fiddle with it) sich ←(DAT) an etwas ←(DAT) zu schaffen machen; **don't interfere with my computer!** mach dir nicht an meinem Computer zu schaffen!; **2 to interfere in something** sich in etwas ←(ACC) einmischen SEP (somebody else's affairs).

interior designer noun Innenarchitekt der (PL die Innenarchitekten), Innenarchitektin die (PL die Innenarchitektinnen).

international adjective international.

Internet noun Internet das; **on the Internet** im Internet.

interpret verb (act as an interpreter) dolmetschen.

interpreter noun Dometscher der (PL die Dolmetscher), Dolmetscherin die (PL die Dometscherinnen).

interrupt verb unterbrechen ◊.

interruption noun
Unterbrechung die (PL die
Unterbrechungen).

interval noun (in a play or concert)
Pause die (PL die Pausen).

interview noun 1 (for a job)
Vorstellungsgespräch das (PL die
Vorstellungsgespräche); to go for an
interview sich vorstellen SEP; 2 (in
a newspaper, on TV, or radio)
Interview das (PL die Interviews).
verb interviewen (on TV, radio).

interviewer noun Interviewer der (PL
die Interviewer), Interviewerin
die (PL die Interviewerinnen).

into preposition 1 (in (+ACC); he's
gone into the garden er ist in den
Garten gegangen; I put the ball into
the bag ich habe den Ball in die
Tasche getan; we all got into the car
wir sind alle ins Auto eingestiegen; to
go into town in die Stadt gehen; to
get into bed ins Bett gehen; to
translate into German ins Deutsche
übersetzen; to change pounds into
marks Pfund in Mark wechseln;
2 (against) gegen (+ACC); he drove
into the wall er ist gegen die Wand
gefahren; 3 to be into jazz auf Jazz
abfahren ◇ SEP (PERF sein)
(informal).

introduce verb vorstellen SEP; she
introduced me to her brother sie
hat mich ihrem Bruder vorgestellt;
she introduced my brother to me
sie hat mir ihren Bruder vorgestellt;
can I introduce you to my mother?
darf ich Sie meiner Mutter
vorstellen?

introduction noun (in a book)
Einleitung die (PL die Einleitungen).

invade verb einfallen ◇ SEP in (PERF
sein) (+ACC).

invalid noun Kranke der/die (PL die
Kranken).

invent verb erfinden ◇.

invention noun Erfindung die (PL
die Erfindungen).

inverted commas plural noun
Anführungszeichen (plural);
in inverted commas in
Anführungszeichen.

investigation noun
Untersuchung die (PL die
Untersuchungen); an investigation
into the incident eine
Untersuchung des Vorfalls.

invisible adjective unsichtbar.

invitation noun Einladung die (PL
die Einladungen); an invitation to
dinner eine Einladung zum
Abendessen.

invite verb einladen ◇ SEP; Kirsty
invited me to lunch Kirsty hat mich
zum Mittagessen eingeladen; he's
invited me out on Tuesday er hat
mich eingeladen, Dienstag mit ihm
auszugehen; they invited us round
sie haben uns zu sich eingeladen.

inviting adjective verlockend.

involve verb 1 erfordern; it involves
a lot of time es erfordert viel Zeit;
2 (include) beteiligen; the game will
involve everybody alle können sich
an dem Spiel beteiligen; to be
involved in something an etwas
←(DAT) beteiligt sein; I am involved in
the new project ich bin an dem

◇ IRREGULAR VERB: See the verb table in the centre of the dictionary

neuen Projekt beteiligt;
3 (*implicate*) verwickeln; **to get
involved in something** in etwas
←(ACC) verwickelt werden; **two cars
were involved in the accident** zwei
Autos waren in den Unfall
verwickelt; 4 **to get involved with
somebody** sich mit jemandem
einlassen ◇ SEP.

Iran noun Iran der.

Iraq noun Irak der.

Ireland noun Irland das; **the
Republic of Ireland** die Republik
Irland.

Irish noun 1 (*the language*)
Irisch das; 2 (*the people*) **the Irish**
die Iren.
adjective irisch; **he's Irish** er ist Ire;
she's Irish sie ist Irin.

Irishman noun Ire der (PL die Iren).

Irish Sea noun Irische See die.

Irishwoman noun Irin die (PL die
Irinnen).

iron noun 1 (*for clothes*)
Bügeleisen das (PL die Bügeleisen);
2 (*the metal*) Eisen das.
verb bügeln.

ironing noun Bügeln das; **to do the
ironing** bügeln.

ironing board noun
Bügelbrett das (PL die Bügelbretter).

ironmonger's noun
Haushaltswarengeschäft das (PL die
Haushaltswarengeschäfte).

irregular adjective unregelmäßig.

irritable adjective reizbar.

irritate verb ärgern.

irritating adjective ärgerlich.

Islam noun Islam der.

Islamic adjective islamisch.

island noun Insel die (PL die Inseln).

isolated adjective 1 (*remote*)
abgelegen; 2 (*single*) einzeln;
isolated cases Einzelfälle.

Israel noun Israel das.

Israeli noun Israeli der/die (PL die
Israelis).
adjective israelisch.

issue noun 1 (*something you
discuss*) Frage die (PL die Fragen);
a political issue eine politische
Frage; 2 (*of a magazine*)
Ausgabe die (PL die Ausgaben).
verb (*hand out*) ausgeben ◇ SEP.

it pronoun 1 (*as the subject*)
er (*standing for a masculine noun*),
sie (*standing for a feminine noun*),
es (*standing for a neuter noun*);
**'where's my key?' – 'it's in the
kitchen'** 'wo ist mein Schlüssel?' –
'er ist in der Küche'; **'where's my
bag?'- 'it's in the living-room'**
'wo ist meine Tasche?' - 'sie ist im
Wohnzimmer'; **'how old is your
car?' - 'it's five years old'** 'wie alt
ist dein Auto?' - 'es ist fünf Jahre alt';
2 (*as the direct object, in the
accusative*) ihn (*standing for a
masculine noun*), sie (*standing for a
feminine noun*), es (*standing for a
neuter noun*); **'where's your
umbrella?' - 'I've lost it'** 'wo ist
dein Regenschirm?'- 'ich habe ihn
verloren'; **'have you seen my bag?' -**

'I saw it in the kitchen' 'hast du meine Tasche gesehen?' – ' ich habe sie in der Küche gesehen'; **'have you read his new book?'** – **'I've just bought it'** 'hast du sein neues Buch gelesen?' – 'ich habe es gerade gekauft'; **3 to it** ihm (*masculine*), ihr (*feminine*), ihm (*neuter*); **4 yes, it's true** ja, das stimmt; **it doesn't matter** das macht nichts; **5 who is it?** wer ist da?; **it's me** ich bins; **what is it?** was ist los?; **6 it's raining** es regnet; **it's Monday** es ist Montag; **it's two o'clock** es ist zwei Uhr; **7 of it** davon; **8 out of it** daraus.

Italian noun **1** (*the language*) Italienisch das; **2** (*person*) Italiener der (PL die Italiener), Italienerin die (PL die Italienerinnen). adjective **1** italienisch; **Italian food** die italienische Küche; **2 my Italian class** mein Italienischunterricht.

italics noun Kursivschrift die; **in italics** kursiv.

Italy noun Italien das.

itch verb **1 my back's itching** mein Rücken juckt; **2 this jumper itches** dieser Pullover kratzt.

item noun **1** Gegenstand der (PL die Gegenstände); **2** (*for sale in a shop*) Artikel der (PL die Artikel).

its adjective **1** sein (*for a masculine noun*), ihr (*for a feminine noun*), sein (*for a neuter noun*); **the dog has lost its collar** der Hund hat sein Halsband verloren; **the cat's in its basket** die Katze ist in ihrem Korb; **the horse is brown and its mane is black** das Pferd is braun und seine

Mähne ist schwarz; **2** (*for a plural noun*) seine (*standing for a masculine noun*), ihre (*standing for a feminine noun*), seine (*standing for a neuter noun*); **its toys** seine Spielsachen, ihre Spielsachen.

itself pronoun **1** (*reflexive*) sich; **the cat's washing itself** die Katze wäscht sich; **2 he left the dog by itself** er hat den Hund allein gelassen.

ivy noun Efeu der.

J j

jack noun **1** (*in cards*) Bube der (PL die Buben); **the jack of clubs** der Kreuzbube; **2** (*for a car*) Wagenheber der (PL die Wagenheber).

jacket noun Jacke die (PL die Jacken).

jackpot noun Jackpot der (PL die Jackpots); **to win the jackpot** das große Los ziehen.

jam noun **1** Marmelade die (PL die Marmeladen); **raspberry jam** die Himbeermarmelade; **2 traffic jam** der Stau.

January noun Januar der; **in January** im Januar.

Japan noun Japan das.

Japanese noun **1** (*the language*) Japanisch das; **2** (*person*) Japaner der (PL die Japaner),

Japanerin die (PL die Japanerinnen); **the Japanese** die Japaner. *adjective* japanisch.

jar noun 1 (*small*) Glas das (PL die Gläser); **a jar of jam** ein Glas Marmelade; 2 (*large*) Topf der (PL die Töpfe).

javelin noun Speer der (PL die Speere).

jaw noun Kiefer der (PL die Kiefer).

jazz noun Jazz der.

jealous *adjective* eifersüchtig; **to be jealous of somebody** eifersüchtig auf jemanden sein.

jeans plural noun Jeans (plural); **my jeans** meine Jeans; **a pair of jeans** ein Paar Jeans.

jelly noun 1 Gelee das (PL die Gelees); 2 (*dessert*) Götterspeise die (PL die Götterspeisen).

jellyfish noun Qualle die (PL die Quallen).

jersey noun 1 (*jumper*) Pullover der (PL die Pullover); 2 (*for football*) Trikot das (PL die Trikots).

Jesus noun Jesus der; **Jesus Christ** Jesus Christus.

jet noun (*a plane*) Jet der (PL die Jets).

Jew noun Jude der (PL die Juden), Jüdin die (PL die Jüdinnen).

jewel noun Edelstein der (PL die Edelsteine).

jeweller noun Juwelier der (PL die Juweliere).

jeweller's noun Juweliergeschäft das.

jewellery noun Schmuck der.

Jewish *adjective* jüdisch.

jigsaw noun Puzzlespiel das (PL die Puzzlespiele).

job noun 1 (*paid work*) Stelle die (PL die Stellen), Job der (PL die Jobs); (*informal*); **a job as a secretary** eine Stelle als Sekretärin; 2 (*a task*) Arbeit die (PL die Arbeiten); **it's not an easy job** das ist keine leichte Arbeit; 3 **she made a good job of it** sie hat es gut gemacht.

jobless *adjective* arbeitslos.

jog verb joggen ◇ (PERF sein).

join verb 1 (*become a member of*) beitreten ◇ SEP (+DAT) (PERF sein); **I've joined the tennis club** ich bin dem Tennisklub beigetreten; 2 (*to meet up with*) treffen ◇; **I'll join you later** ich treffe euch später.
● **to join in** 1 mitmachen SEP; **Kylie never joins in** Kylie macht nie mit; 2 **to join in something** bei etwas ←(DAT) mitmachen SEP; **won't you join in the game?** willst du bei dem Spiel nicht mitmachen?

joint noun 1 (*of meat*) Braten der (PL die Braten); **a joint of beef** ein Rinderbraten; 2 (*in your body*) Gelenk das (PL die Gelenke).

joke noun Witz der (PL die Witze); **to tell a joke** einen Witz erzählen. *verb* Witze machen; **you must be joking!** du machst wohl Witze!

joker noun (*in cards*) Joker der (PL die Joker).

△ NEW SPELLING: See page xii

journalism noun
Journalismus der.

journalist noun Journalist der (PL die Journalisten), Journalistin die (PL die Journalistinnen); **Sean's a journalist** Sean ist Journalist.

journey noun 1 (a long one) Reise die (PL die Reisen); **on our journey to Italy** auf unserer Reise nach Italien; 2 (shorter; to work or school) Fahrt die (PL die Fahrten); **bus journey** die Busfahrt.

joy noun Freude die (PL die Freuden).

judge noun 1 (in court) Richter der (PL die Richter); 2 (in sporting events) Schiedsrichter der (PL die Schiedsrichter); 3 (in a competition) Preisrichter der (PL die Preisrichter).
verb schätzen (time or distance).

judo noun Judo das; **he does judo** er macht Judo.

jug noun Krug der (PL die Krüge).

juice noun Saft der; **two orange juices please** zwei Orangensaft bitte.

juicy adjective saftig.

jukebox noun Jukebox die (PL die Jukeboxes).

July noun Juli der; **in July** im Juli.

jumble sale noun Basar der (PL die Basare).

jump noun Sprung der (PL die Sprünge); **parachute jump** der Fallschirmsprung.
verb springen ✧ (PERF sein).

jumper noun Pullover der (PL die Pullover).

June noun Juni der; **in June** im Juni.

jungle noun Dschungel der.

junior adjective jünger; **junior school** die Grundschule; **the juniors** (at primary school) die Grundschüler, die Grundschülerinnen.

junk noun Trödel der.

junk food noun ungesunde Essen das.

just adverb 1 (very recently) gerade; **to have just done something** gerade etwas getan haben; **Tom has just arrived** Tom ist gerade angekommen; 2 **to be just doing something** gerade dabei sein, etwas zu tun; **I'm just doing the food** ich bin gerade dabei, Essen zu machen; 3 **just before midday** kurz vor Mittag; **just after 4 o'clock** kurz nach vier Uhr; 4 (only) nur; **just for fun** nur zum Vergnügen; **he's just a child** er ist doch nur ein Kind; **just me and Justine are coming** nur ich und Justine kommen; 5 **just a minute!** einen Moment!; 6 **just coming!** ich komme schon!; 7 (exactly) **just as** genauso wie; **he's got just as many friends** er hat genauso viele Freunde.

justice noun Gerechtigkeit die.

✧ IRREGULAR VERB: See the verb table in the centre of the dictionary

K k

kangaroo noun Känguru △ das (PL die Kängurus).

karate noun Karate das.

kebab noun Kebab der (PL die Kebabs).

keen adjective 1 (enthusiastic or committed) begeistert; **he's a keen photographer** er ist ein begeisterter Fotograf; **you don't seem too keen** du scheinst nicht gerade begeistert zu sein; 2 **to be keen on** mögen ◇; **I'm not keen on fish** ich mag Fisch nicht; 3 **to be keen on doing** (or **to do**) **something** etwas gerne tun.

keep verb 1 behalten ◇; **you can keep the book** du kannst das Buch behalten; **to keep a secret** ein Geheimnis für sich behalten; 2 **will you keep my seat?** können Sie meinen Platz freihalten?; 3 **to keep somebody waiting** jemanden warten lassen; 4 (store) aufbewahren SEP; **can I keep my watch in your desk?** kann ich meine Uhr in deinem Schreibtisch aufbewahren?; **where do you keep saucepans?** wo hast du die Töpfe?; 5 (not throw away) aufheben ◇ SEP; **I kept all his letters** ich habe alle seine Briefe aufgehoben; 6 **to keep on doing something** etwas weiter tun; **she kept on talking** sie hat weitergeredet; **keep straight on** weiter geradeaus gehen; 7 **to keep**

on doing something (time after time) dauernd etwas tun; **he keeps on ringing me up** er ruft mich dauernd an; 8 (maintain) halten ◇; **to keep the food warm** das Essen warm halten; **to keep a promise** ein Versprechen halten; 9 (stay) bleiben ◇ (PERF sein); **to keep calm** ruhig bleiben; **to keep out of the sun** im Schatten bleiben.

kerb noun Randstein der.

kettle noun Kessel der (PL die Kessel); **to put the kettle on** Wasser aufsetzen.

key noun 1 (for a lock) Schlüssel der (PL die Schlüssel); **bunch of keys** das Schlüsselbund; 2 (on a piano or keyboard) Taste die.

keyboard noun (for a computer) Tastatur die (PL die Tastaturen).

keyring noun Schlüsselring der (PL die Schlüsselringe).

kick noun 1 (from a person or a horse) Tritt der (PL die Tritte); **to give somebody a kick** jemandem einen Tritt geben; 2 (in football) Schuss △ der (PL die Schüsse); ★ **to get a kick out of doing something** etwas nur zum Spaß tun.
verb 1 **to kick somebody** jemandem einen Tritt geben; 2 **to kick the ball** den Ball schießen.
● **to kick off** anstoßen ◇ SEP.

kick-off noun Anstoß der.

kid noun (child) Kind das (PL die Kinder); **Dad's looking after the kids** Vati passt auf die Kinder auf.

kidnap verb entführen.

kidney noun Niere die (PL die Nieren).

kill verb 1 töten (an animal); 2 (murder) umbringen ◇ SEP; **he killed the girl** er brachte das Mädchen um; 3 **she was killed in a car accident** sie kam bei einem Autounfall ums Leben.

killer noun Mörder der (PL die Mörder), Mörderin die (PL die Mörderinnen).

kilo noun Kilo das (PL die Kilo); **a kilo of sugar** ein Kilo Zucker; **ten marks a kilo** zehn Mark das Kilo.

kilogram noun Kilogramm das.

kilometre noun Kilometer der (PL die Kilometer).

kilt noun Kilt der (PL die Kilts).

kind noun 1 Art die (PL die Arten); **this kind of book** diese Art Buch; **all kinds of people** alle möglichen Leute; 2 (brand) Sorte die (PL die Sorten).
adjective nett; **she was very kind to me** sie war sehr nett zu mir.

kindness noun Freundlichkeit die.

king noun König der (PL die Könige); **the king of hearts** der Herzkönig.

kingdom noun Königreich das (PL die Königreiche); **the United Kingdom** das Vereinigte Königreich.

kipper noun Räucherhering der (PL die Räucherheringe).

kiss noun Kuss △ die (PL die Küsse); **to give somebody a kiss** jemandem einen Kuss geben.
verb küssen; **kiss me!** küss mich!;

we kissed each other wir haben uns geküsst.

kit noun 1 (of tools) Werkzeug das; 2 (in a box) **a tool kit** ein Werkzeugkasten; 3 (clothes) Sachen (plural); **where's my football kit?** wo sind meine Fußballsachen?; 4 (for making a model, a piece of furniture, etc.) Bausatz der (PL die Bausätze).

kitchen noun Küche die (PL die Küchen); **the kitchen table** der Küchentisch.

kitchen foil noun Alufolie die.

kitchen roll noun Küchenrolle die (PL die Küchenrollen).

kite noun Drachen der; **to fly a kite** einen Drachen steigen lassen.

kitten noun Kätzchen das (PL die Kätzchen).

kiwi fruit noun Kiwi die (PL die Kiwis).

knee noun Knie das (PL die Knie); **on (your) hands and knees** auf allen vieren.

kneel verb knien; **to kneel (down)** sich hinknien SEP.

knickers plural noun Schlüpfer der (PL die Schlüpfer); **two pairs of knickers** zwei Schlüpfer.

knife noun Messer das (PL die Messer).
verb einstechen ◇ SEP auf (+ACC); (kill) erstechen ◇.

knight noun (in chess) Springer der (PL die Springer).

knit verb stricken.

◇ IRREGULAR VERB: See the verb table in the centre of the dictionary

knitting noun Strickerei die.

knob noun 1 (on a door or walking stick) Knauf der (PL die Knäufe); 2 (control on a radio or machine) Knopf der (PL die Knöpfe); 3 knob of butter das Butterklümpchen.

knock noun Schlag der (PL die Schläge); a knock on the head ein Schlag auf den Kopf; a knock at the door ein Klopfen an der Tür. verb 1 (to bang) stoßen ◇; I knocked my arm on the table ich habe mir den Arm am Tisch gestoßen; 2 to knock on something an etwas ←(ACC) klopfen.

● to knock down 1 (in a traffic accident) anfahren ◇ SEP (a person); 2 (to demolish) abreißen ◇ SEP (an old building).

● to knock out 1 (to make unconscious) bewusstlos △ schlagen ◇; 2 (in sport, to eliminate) k.o. schlagen ◇.

knot noun Knoten der (PL die Knoten); to tie a knot einen Knoten machen.

know verb 1 (know a fact) wissen ◇; do you know where Tim is? weißt du, wo Tim ist?; I know they've moved house ich weiß, dass sie umgezogen sind; yes, I know ja, weiß ich; you never know! man kann nie wissen!; I know how to get to town ich weiß, wie man in die Stadt kommt; 2 (be personally acquainted with) kennen ◇; do you know the Jacksons? kennst du die Jacksons?; all the people I know alle Leute, die ich kenne; I don't know his mother ich kenne seine Mutter

nicht; 3 to know how to do something etwas tun können; Steve knows how to make potato salad Steve kann Kartoffelsalat machen; Liz knows how to mend it Liz kann es reparieren; 4 to know about Bescheid wissen über (+ACC) (items in the news); 5 to know about sich auskennen ◇ SEP mit (machines, cars, etc.); Lindy knows about computers Lindy kennt sich mit Computern aus; 6 to get to know somebody jemanden kennen lernen △.

knowledge noun Wissen das.

Koran noun Koran der.

kosher adjective koscher.

L l

lab noun Labor das (PL die Labors).

label noun Etikett das (PL die Etikette).

laboratory noun Labor das (PL die Labors).

lace noun 1 (for a shoe) Schnürsenkel der (PL die Schnürsenkel); to tie your laces sich ←(DAT) die Schnürsenkel binden; 2 (fabric or trimming) Spitze die.

ladder noun 1 (for climbing) Leiter die (PL die Leitern); 2 (in your tights) Laufmasche die (PL die Laufmaschen).

ladies noun (*lavatory*)
Damentoilette die (PL die
Damentoiletten); (*on a sign*)
'Ladies' 'Damen'.

lady noun Dame die (PL die Damen);
ladies and gentlemen meine
Damen und Herren.

lager noun helle Bier das (PL die
hellen Biere), Helle das (PL die
Hellen) (*informal*); **a lager,
please** ein Helles bitte.

laid-back adjective gelassen.

lake noun See der (PL die Seen); **Lake
Geneva** der Genfer See.

lamb noun Lamm das (PL die
Lämmer); **leg of lamb** die
Lammkeule.

lamp noun Lampe die (PL die
Lampen).

lamp-post noun
Laternenpfahl der (PL die
Laternenpfähle).

lampshade noun
Lampenschirm der (PL die
Lampenschirme).

land noun 1 (*when at sea*) Land das;
2 (*property*) Grundstück das; **piece
of land** das Grundstück.
verb 1 (*plane, passenger*) landen
(PERF sein); 2 (*leave a ship*) an Land
gehen.

landing noun 1 (*between flights of
stairs*) Treppenabsatz der (PL die
Treppenabsätze); (*passage*)
Treppenflur der; 2 (*of a plane or
ship*) Landung die (PL die
Landungen).

landlady noun 1 (*of a house or
room*) Vermieterin die (PL die

Vermieterinnen); 2 (*of a pub*)
Gastwirtin die (PL die
Gastwirtinnen).

landlord noun 1 (*of a house or room*)
Vermieter der (PL die Vermieter);
2 (*of a pub*) Gastwirt der (PL die
Gastwirte).

lane noun 1 (*small road*) Weg der
(PL die Wege); 2 (*of a motorway*)
Spur die (PL die Spuren).

language noun 1 (*German, Italian,
etc.*) Sprache die (PL die Sprachen);
foreign language die
Fremdsprache; 2 (*way of speaking*)
Ausdrucksweise die; **bad language**
Kraftausdrücke (*plural*).

lap noun 1 Schoß der (PL die
Schöße); 2 (*in races*) Runde die (PL
die Runden).

laptop noun Laptop der (PL die
Laptops).

larder noun Speisekammer die (PL
die Speisekammern).

large adjective groß.

last adjective letzter/letzte/letztes;
last week letzte Woche; **for the last
time** zum letzten Mal; **last night**
gestern Nacht.
adverb 1 (*in final position*) als
Letzter/als Letzte/als Letztes; **Rob
arrived last** Rob kam als Letzter an;
2 **at last!** endlich!; 3 (*most
recently*) zuletzt; **I last saw him in
May** ich habe ihn zuletzt im Mai
gesehen.
verb dauern; **the film lasted two
hours** der Film dauerte zwei
Stunden.

◇ IRREGULAR VERB: See the verb table in the centre of the dictionary

late *adjective, adverb* **1** spät; **I'm late** ich bin spät dran; **we were five minutes late** wir haben uns fünf Minuten verspätet; **they arrived late** sie sind zu spät angekommen; **to be late for something** zu spät zu etwas ←(DAT) kommen; **we were late for the party** wir kamen zu spät zur Party; **2 to be late** (*of a bus or train*) Verspätung haben; **the train was an hour late** der Zug hatte eine Stunde Verspätung; **3** (*late in the day*) spät; **we got up late** wir sind spät aufgestanden; **the chemist is open late** die Apotheke hat bis spät auf; **late last night** gestern spät in der Nacht; **too late!** zu spät!

lately *adverb* in letzter Zeit.

later *adverb* später; **I'll explain later** ich erkläre es später; **see you later!** bis später!

latest *adjective* **1** neuester/neueste/neuestes; **the latest news** die neuesten Nachrichten; **2 at the latest** spätestens.

Latin *noun* Latein *das*.

laugh *noun* Lachen *das*; **to do something for a laugh** etwas aus Spaß machen.
verb **1** lachen; **everybody laughed** alle haben gelacht; **to laugh about something** über etwas ←(ACC) lachen; **2 to laugh at somebody** jemanden auslachen SEP; **they'll only laugh at me** sie lachen mich bestimmt aus.

launderette *noun* Waschsalon *der* (PL *die* Waschsalons).

lavatory *noun* Toilette *die* (PL *die* Toiletten); **to go to the lavatory** auf die Toilette gehen.

lavender *noun* Lavendel *der*.

law *noun* **1** Gesetz *das* (PL *die* Gesetze); **to break the law** gegen das Gesetz verstoßen; **2 it's against the law** das ist verboten; **3** (*subject of study*) Jura (*plural*).

lawn *noun* Rasen *der* (PL *die* Rasen).

lawnmower *noun* Rasenmäher *der* (PL *die* Rasenmäher).

lawyer *noun* Rechtsanwalt *der* (PL *die* Rechtsanwälte), Rechtsanwältin *die* (PL *die* Rechtsanwältinnen).

lay *verb* **1** (*put*) legen; **she laid the cards on the table** sie legte die Karten auf den Tisch; **2 to lay the table** den Tisch decken.

lay-by *noun* Parkplatz *der* (PL *die* Parkplätze).

layer *noun* Schicht *die* (PL *die* Schichten).

lazy *adjective* faul.

lead[1] *noun* **1** (*when you are ahead*) Führung *die*; **to be in the lead** in Führung liegen; **Baxter's in the lead** Baxter liegt in Führung; **to take the lead** in Führung gehen; **2** (*electric*) Schnur *die* (PL *die* Schnüre); **3** (*for a dog*) Leine *die* (PL *die* Leinen); **on a lead** an der Leine; **4** (*role*) Hauptrolle *die* (PL *die* Hauptrollen); **5** (*an actor*) Hauptdarsteller *der* (PL *die* Hauptdarsteller), Hauptdarstellerin *die* (PL *die* Hauptdarstellerinnen).

verb **1** führen; **the path leads to the sea** der Weg führt zum Meer; **to lead by three points** mit drei Punkten führen; **2 to lead the way** vorangehen ◇ SEP (PERF *sein*); **3 to lead to something** zu etwas ←(DAT) führen (*an accident or problems, for example*).

lead² *noun* (*metal*) Blei *das*.

leader *noun* **1** (*of a political party*) Vorsitzende *der/die* (PL *die* Vorsitzenden); **2** (*of an expedition or group*) Leiter *der* (PL *die* Leiter), Leiterin *die* (PL *die* Leiterinnen); **3** (*in a competition*) Erste *der/die* (PL *die* Ersten); **4** (*of a gang*) Anführer *der* (PL *die* Anführer), Anführerin *die* (PL *die* Anführerinnen).

lead singer *noun* Leadsänger *der* (PL *die* Leadsänger), Leadsängerin *die* (PL *die* Leadsängerinnen).

leaf *noun* Blatt *das* (PL *die* Blätter).

leaflet *noun* **1** (*with instructions*) Merkblatt *das* (PL *die* Merkblätter); **2** (*for advertising*) Reklameblatt *das* (PL *die* Reklameblätter).

leak *noun* **1** (*in a roof, tent*) undichte Stelle *die* (PL *die* undichten Stellen); **2 gas leak** der Gasausfluss△; **3** (*in a boat*) Leck *das* (PL *die* Lecks).
verb (*of a bottle or a roof*) undicht sein.

lean *adjective* (*meat*) mager.
verb **1 to lean on something** sich an etwas ←(ACC) lehnen; **he leaned against the door** er hat sich gegen die Tür gelehnt; **2** sich lehnen; **she was leaning out of the window** sie

lehnte sich aus dem Fenster; **3 to lean forward** sich vorbeugen SEP.

leap year *noun* Schaltjahr *das* (PL *die* Schaltjahre).

learn *verb* lernen; **to learn German** Deutsch lernen; **to learn (how) to drive** Auto fahren lernen.

learner *noun* **1** Lerner *der* (PL *die* Lerner); **to be a fast learner** schnell lernen; **2** (*beginner*) Anfänger *der* (PL *die* Anfänger), Anfängerin *die* (PL *die* Anfängerinnen).

least *adjective, pronoun*
1 wenigster/wenigste/wenigstes; **to have least time** am wenigsten Zeit haben; **Tony has the least money** Tony hat das wenigste Geld; **2** (*the slightest*) geringster/geringste/geringstes; **I haven't the least idea** ich habe nicht die geringste Ahnung.
adverb **1** am wenigsten; **I like the blue shirt least** ich mag das blaue Hemd am wenigsten; **2 the least expensive hotel** das billigste Hotel; **3 at least** (*at a minimum*) mindestens; **at least twenty people** mindestens zwanzig Leute; **4 at least** (*at any rate*) wenigstens; **she's a teacher, at least I think she is** sie ist Lehrerin, glaube ich wenigstens.

leather *noun* Leder *das*; **leather jacket** die Lederjacke.

leave *noun* Urlaub *der*; **three days' leave** drei Tage Urlaub.
verb **1** (*go away*) gehen ◇ (PERF *sein*); (*by car*) fahren ◇ SEP (PERF *sein*); (*a train or bus*) abfahren ◇ SEP

◇ IRREGULAR VERB: *See the verb table in the centre of the dictionary*

(PERF *sein*); **they're leaving tomorrow evening** sie fahren morgen Abend; **we left at six** wir sind um sechs Uhr gegangen; **the train leaves Munich at ten** der Zug fährt um zehn Uhr von München ab; **2** (*go away from or go out of*) verlassen ◇; **I left the office at five** ich habe das Büro um fünf verlassen; **he left his wife** er hat seine Frau verlassen; **3** (*deposit or allow to remain in the same state*) lassen ◇; **you can leave your coats in the hall** Sie können Ihre Mäntel in der Diele lassen; **to leave the door open** die Tür offen lassen; **leave it until tomorrow** lass es bis morgen; **4** to **leave somebody something** jemandem etwas hinterlassen ◇ (*a message or money*); **he didn't leave a message** er hat keine Nachricht hinterlassen; **5** (*not do*) stehen lassen ◇ △; **leave the washing up** lass den Abwasch stehen; **6** (*forget*) vergessen ◇; **he left his umbrella on the train** er hat seinen Regenschirm im Zug vergessen; **7** be left übrig sein (PERF *sein*); **there are two pancakes left** zwei Pfannkuchen sind noch übrig; **I don't have any money left** ich habe kein Geld mehr übrig; **we have ten minutes left** wir haben noch zehn Minuten Zeit.

lecture *noun* **1** (*at university*) Vorlesung *die* (PL *die* Vorlesungen); **2** (*public*) Vortrag *der* (PL *die* Vorträge).

leek *noun* Lauch *der*.

left *noun* **on the left** links; **to drive on the left** links fahren; **on my left** links von mir.
adverb links; **turn left at the church** an der Kirche links abbiegen.
adjective linker/linke/linkes; **his left foot** sein linker Fuß.

left-hand *adjective* **the left-hand side** die linke Seite.

left-handed *adjective* linkshändig.

leg *noun* **1** Bein *das* (PL *die* Beine); **my left leg** mein linkes Bein; **to break your leg** sich ←(DAT) das Bein brechen; **2** (*in cooking*) Keule *die* (PL *die* Keulen); **leg of lamb** die Lammkeule; ★ **to pull somebody's leg** jemanden auf den Arm nehmen.

leggings *plural noun* Leggings (*plural*).

leisure *noun* Freizeit *die*; **in my leisure time** in meiner Freizeit.

lemon *noun* Zitrone *die* (PL *die* Zitronen).

lemonade *noun* Limonade *die* (PL *die* Limonaden).

lemon juice *noun* Zitronensaft *der* (PL *die* Zitronensäfte).

lend *verb* leihen ◇; **to lend something to somebody** jemandem etwas leihen; **I lent Judy my bike** ich habe Judy mein Rad geliehen; **will you lend it to me?** kannst du es mir leihen?

length *noun* Länge *die* (PL *die* Längen).

lens *noun* **1** (*in a camera*) Objektiv *das* (PL *die* Objektive); **2** (*in spectacles*) Brillenglas *das* (PL *die* Brillengläser); **3** contact lenses Kontaktlinsen (*plural*).

△ NEW SPELLING: See page xii

Lent noun Fastenzeit die.

lentil noun Linse die (PL die Linsen).

less pronoun, adjective, adverb weniger ('*weniger*' *never changes*); **Ben eats less** Ben isst weniger; **less time** weniger Zeit; **less than** weniger als; **less than three hours** weniger als drei Stunden; **you spent less than me** du hast weniger als ich ausgegeben; **less and less** immer weniger.

lesson noun (*class*) Stunde die (PL die Stunden); **German lesson** die Deutschstunde; **driving lesson** die Fahrstunde.

let¹ verb 1 (*allow*) lassen ✧; **to let somebody do something** jemanden etwas tun lassen; **she lets me drive her car** sie lässt mich mit ihrem Auto fahren; **the police let us through** die Polizei hat uns durchgelassen; **let me in** lass mich herein; 2 (*as a suggestion or a command*) **let's go!** gehen wir!; **let's not talk about it** reden wir nicht mehr darüber; **let's eat out** essen wir im Restaurant.

● **to let off** 1 hochgehen lassen ✧ (*fireworks*); 2 (*to excuse from*) befreien von (+DAT) (*homework*).

let² verb (*to rent out*) vermieten; '**flat to let**' 'Wohnung zu vermieten'.

letter noun 1 Brief der (PL die Briefe); **a letter for you from Delia** ein Brief für dich von Delia; 2 (*of the alphabet*) Buchstabe der (PL die Buchstaben).

letter box noun Briefkasten der (PL die Briefkästen).

lettuce noun Salat der; **two lettuces** zwei Kopf Salat.

level noun Höhe die; **at eye level** in Augenhöhe.
adjective 1 eben (*ground or floor*); 2 (*horizontal*) waagerecht (*shelf*); 3 (*at the same height*) auf gleicher Höhe; **to be level with the ground** auf gleicher Höhe mit dem Boden sein.

level crossing noun Bahnübergang der (PL die Bahnübergänge).

lever noun Hebel der (PL die Hebel).

liar noun Lügner der (PL die Lügner), Lügnerin die (PL die Lügnerinnen).

liberal adjective 1 tolerant; 2 (*in politics*) liberal; **the Liberal Democrats** die Liberaldemokraten.

Libra noun Waage die; **Sean's Libra** Sean ist Waage.

librarian noun Bibliothekar der (PL die Bibliothekare), Bibliothekarin die (PL die Bibliothekarinnen).

library noun Bibliothek die (PL die Bibliotheken); **public library** die öffentliche Bücherei.

licence noun 1 (*for a TV*) Genehmigung die (PL die Genehmigungen); 2 (*driving licence*) Führerschein der (PL die Führerscheine).

lick verb lecken.

lid noun Deckel der (PL die Deckel).

lie noun Lüge die (PL die Lügen); **to tell a lie** (or **lies**) lügen ✧.
verb 1 (*to be stretched out*) liegen ✧;

he's lying on the sofa er liegt auf dem Sofa; my coat lay on the bed mein Mantel lag auf dem Bett; **2 to lie down** (*for a rest*) sich hinlegen SEP; **I'm going to lie down for a little** ich lege mich ein bisschen hin; **3** (*tell lies*) lügen ✧.

lie-in noun **to have a lie-in** ausschlafen ✧ SEP.

life noun Leben das (PL die Leben); **all her life** ihr ganzes Leben lang; **full of life** voller Leben; **that's life!** so ist das Leben!

life-style noun Lebensstil der (PL die Lebensstile).

lift noun **1** Aufzug der (PL die Aufzüge); **let's take the lift** fahren wir mit dem Aufzug; **2** (*a ride*) **to give somebody a lift to the station** jemanden zum Bahnhof mitnehmen ✧ SEP; **Khaled's giving me a lift** Khaled nimmt mich mit; **would you like a lift?** möchtest du mitfahren?
verb hochheben ✧ SEP; **he lifted the box** er hob die Kiste hoch.

light noun **1** Licht das; **will you turn the light on?** kannst du das Licht anmachen?; **to turn off the light** das Licht ausmachen; **are your lights on?** hast du Licht an?; **2** (*in the street*) Straßenlampe die (PL die Straßenlampen); **3** (*a lamp*) Lampe die (PL die Lampen); **4 traffic lights** die Ampel (*singular*); **the lights are green** die Ampel ist grün; **5** (*for a cigarette*) **have you got a light?** hast du Feuer?
adjective **1** (*not dark*) hell; **a light blue dress** ein hellblaues Kleid; **it**

gets light at six es wird um sechs hell; **2** (*not heavy*) leicht; **a light coat** ein leichter Mantel; **a light breeze** eine leichte Brise.
verb **1** anzünden SEP (*the fire, a match, the gas*); **we lit a fire** wir zündeten ein Feuer an; **2 to light a cigarette** sich ←(DAT) eine Zigarette anzünden.

light bulb noun Glühbirne die (PL die Glühbirnen).

lighter noun Feuerzeug das (PL die Feuerzeuge).

lightning noun Blitz der; **flash of lightning** der Blitz; **to be struck by lightning** vom Blitz getroffen werden.

like¹ preposition, conjunction **1** wie; **like me** wie ich; **like a duck** wie eine Ente; **like I said** wie gesagt; **what's it like?** wie ist es?; **what was the weather like?** wie war das Wetter?; **2 like this/that** so; **3** ähnlich (+DAT); **to look like somebody** jemandem ähnlich sehen; **Cindy looks like her father** Cindy sieht ihrem Vater ähnlich.

like² verb **1** mögen ✧; **I like vegetables** ich mag Gemüse; **I don't like meat** ich mag Fleisch nicht; **I like Dürer best** ich mag Dürer am liebsten; **2 to like doing something** etwas gerne tun; **Mum likes reading** Mutti liest gerne; **3 I would like ...** ich möchte gerne ...; **would you like a coffee?** möchten Sie einen Kaffee?; **what would you like to eat?** was möchten Sie essen?; **yes, if you like** ja, wenn du willst; **4 I like**

△ NEW SPELLING: See page xii

the dress das Kleid gefällt mir; **how do you like it?** wie gefällt es dir?

likely *adjective* wahrscheinlich; **she's likely to phone** wahrscheinlich ruft sie an.

lime *noun* Kalk *der*.

limit *noun* Grenze *die* (PL die Grenzen); **speed limit** die Geschwindigkeitsbeschränkung.

limp *noun* **to have a limp** hinken.

line *noun* 1 Linie *die* (PL die Linien); **a straight line** eine gerade Linie; **to draw a line** eine Linie ziehen; 2 (*in writing*) Zeile *die* (PL die Zeilen); **six lines of text** sechs Zeilen Text; 3 (*railway*) Bahnlinie *die* (PL die Bahnlinien) (*from one place to another*); **on the line** (*the track*) auf der Strecke; 4 (*a queue of people or cars*) Schlange *die* (PL die Schlangen); **to stand in line** Schlange stehen; 5 (*telephone*) Leitung *die* (PL die Leitungen); **the line's bad** die Verbindung ist schlecht; **hold the line, please** bitte bleiben Sie am Apparat.
verb füttern (*a coat*).

linen *noun* Leinen *das*; **a linen jacket** eine Leinenjacke.

lining *noun* Futter *das* (PL die Futter).

link *noun* Verbindung *die* (PL die Verbindungen); **what's the link between the two?** was für eine Verbindung besteht zwischen den beiden?
verb verbinden ✧ (*two places*); **the two towns are linked by a railway line** die beiden Städte sind durch

eine Bahnlinie miteinander verbunden.

lion *noun* Löwe *der* (PL die Löwen).

lip *noun* Lippe *die* (PL die Lippen).

lip-read *verb* von den Lippen lesen ✧.

lipstick *noun* Lippenstift *der* (PL die Lippenstifte).

liquid *noun* Flüssigkeit *die* (PL die Flüssigkeiten).
adjective flüssig.

list *noun* Liste *die* (PL die Listen).

listen *verb* 1 zuhören SEP; **I wasn't listening** ich habe nicht zugehört; **to listen to somebody** jemandem zuhören; **you're not listening to me** du hörst mir nicht zu; 2 **to listen to something** etwas ⇒(ACC) zuhören; **to listen to the radio** Radio hören.

listener *noun* (*to the radio*) Hörer *der* (PL die Hörer), Hörerin *die* (PL die Hörerinnen).

litre *noun* Liter *der* (PL die Liter); **a litre of milk** ein Liter Milch.

litter *noun* (*rubbish*) Abfall *der*.

litter bin *noun* Abfalleimer *der* (PL die Abfalleimer).

little *adjective, pronoun* 1 (*small*) klein; **a little boy** ein kleiner Junge; **a little break** eine kleine Pause; 2 (*not much*) wenig; **we have very little time** wir haben sehr wenig Zeit; 3 **a little** ein wenig; **we have a little left** wir haben ein wenig übrig; 4 **just a little, please** nur ein bisschen, bitte; **it's a little late** es ist ein bisschen spät;

✧ IRREGULAR VERB: See the verb table in the centre of the dictionary

a little more ein bisschen mehr; **a little less** ein bisschen weniger; ★ **little by little** nach und nach.

live[1] *verb* **1** (*in a house or town*) wohnen; **she lives in York** sie wohnt in York; **we live in a flat** wir wohnen in einer Wohnung; **2** (*be or stay alive, spend one's life*) leben; **we're living in the country now** wir leben jetzt auf dem Land; **they live on fruit** sie leben von Obst; **they live apart** sie leben getrennt.

live[2] *adjective, adverb* **1** live (*broadcast*); **a live programme** eine Livesendung; **live music** die Livemusik; **a broadcast live from Wembley** eine Übertragung live aus Wembley; **to broadcast a concert live** ein Konzert live senden; **2** (*alive*) lebend.

lively *adjective* lebhaft.

liver *noun* Leber *die* (PL *die* Lebern).

living *noun* Lebensunterhalt *der*; **to earn a living** sich ←(DAT) seinen Lebensunterhalt verdienen.

living room *noun* Wohnzimmer *das* (PL *die* Wohnzimmer).

load *noun* **1** (*on a lorry*) Ladung *die* (PL *die* Ladungen); **a (lorry-)load of bricks** eine Ladung Ziegelsteine; **2 a bus-load of tourists** ein Bus voll Touristen; **3 loads of** massenhaft (*informal*); **loads of tourists** massenhaft Touristen; **they've got loads of money** die haben einen Haufen Geld (*informal*).

verb **1** beladen ◊ (*a vehicle*);

2 to load a camera einen Film einlegen SEP.

loaf *noun* Brot *das* (PL *die* Brote); **a loaf of white bread** ein Weißbrot.

loathe *verb* hassen; **I loathe getting up early** ich hasse es, früh aufzustehen.

local *noun* **1** (*a pub*) Stammkneipe *die* (PL *die* Stammkneipen); **2 the locals** (*people*) die Einheimischen. *adjective* **1** hiesig; **the local library** die hiesige Bücherei; **2 local newspaper** die Lokalzeitung.

lock *noun* Schloss △ *das* (PL *die* Schlösser). *verb* abschließen ◊ SEP (*a door, room, or bicycle*); **have you locked the door?** hast du abgeschlossen?

lodger *noun* Untermieter *der* (PL *die* Untermieter), Untermieterin *die* (PL *die* Untermieterinnen).

loft *noun* Dachboden *der* (PL *die* Dachböden).

log *noun* **1** Baumstamm *der* (PL *die* Baumstämme); **2** (*as firewood*) Holzscheit *das* (PL *die* Holzscheite); **a log fire** ein offenes Feuer.

lollipop *noun* Lutscher *der* (PL *die* Lutscher).

London *noun* London *das*.

Londoner *noun* Londoner *der* (PL *die* Londoner), Londonerin *die* (PL *die* Londonerinnen).

lonely *adjective* einsam; **to feel lonely** sich einsam fühlen.

△ NEW SPELLING: *See page* xii

long adjective, adverb **1** lang; **a long film** ein langer Film; **a long day** ein langer Tag; **it's five metres long** es ist fünf Meter lang; **the film is an hour long** der Film dauert eine Stunde; **2 a long time** lange; **he stayed for a long time** er ist lange geblieben; **I've been here for a long time** ich bin schon lange hier; **a long time ago** vor langer Zeit; **this won't take long** das dauert nicht lange; **3 how long?** wie lange?; **how long have you been here?** wie lange sind Sie schon hier?; **long ago** vor langer Zeit; **4 a long way** weit; **it's a long way to the cinema** bis zum Kino ist es weit; **5 all night long** die ganze Nacht; **6 no longer** nicht mehr; **he doesn't work here any longer** er arbeitet nicht mehr hier.

verb **to long to do something** sich danach sehnen, etwas zu tun; **I'm longing to see you** ich sehne mich danach, dich zu sehen.

long jump noun Weitsprung der.

longlife milk noun H-Milch die.

loo noun Klo das (PL die Klos) (informal).

look noun **1** (a glance) Blick der (PL die Blicke); **to take a look at somebody** einen Blick auf jemanden werfen; **2** (a tour) **to have a look at the school** sich ←(DAT) die Schule ansehen; **to have a look round the town** sich ←(DAT) die Stadt ansehen; **3** **to have a look for** suchen.

verb **1** sehen ◇; **to look out of the window** aus dem Fenster sehen; **I**

wasn't looking ich habe nicht hingesehen; **2** **to look at** ansehen ◇ SEP; **he looked at the girl** er hat das Mädchen angesehen; **to look at something** sich ←(DAT) etwas ansehen; **I'm looking at the photos** ich sehe mir die Fotos an; **3** (to seem) aussehen ◇ SEP; **she looks sad** sie sieht traurig aus; **the salad looks delicious** der Salat sieht köstlich aus; **to look like** aussehen wie; **what does the house look like?** wie sieht das Haus aus?; **4** (resemble) **to look like somebody** jemandem ähnlich sehen; **she looks like her aunt** sie sieht ihrer Tante ähnlich; **they look like each other** sie sehen sich ähnlich.

● **to look after** **1** sich kümmern um (+ACC); **Dad's looking after the children** Vati kümmert sich um die Kinder; **2** aufpassen SEP auf (+ACC) (luggage).

● **to look for** suchen; **I'm looking for my keys** ich suche meine Schlüssel.

● **to look forward to** sich freuen auf (+ACC) (a party or a trip, for example).

● **to look out** (to be careful) aufpassen SEP; **look out, it's hot!** pass auf, das ist heiß!

● **to look up** nachschlagen ◇ SEP (in a dictionary or directory); **he's looking it up in the dictionary** er schlägt es im Wörterbuch nach.

loose adjective **1** (screw or knot) locker; **2** (garment) weit; **3 loose change** das Kleingeld; ★ **I'm at a loose end** ich habe nichts zu tun.

lorry noun Lastwagen der (PL die Lastwagen).

◇ IRREGULAR VERB: See the verb table in the centre of the dictionary.

lorry driver *noun*
Lastwagenfahrer *der* (PL *die* Lastwagenfahrer).

lose *verb* 1 verlieren ◇; **we lost** wir haben verloren; **we lost the match** wir haben das Spiel verloren; **Sam's lost his watch** Sam hat seine Uhr verloren; 2 **to get lost** sich verlaufen ◇; **we got lost in the woods** wir haben uns im Wald verlaufen; 3 **to lose weight** abnehmen ◇ SEP.

loss *noun* Verlust *der* (PL *die* Verluste).

lost property *noun* Fundsachen (*plural*).

lot *noun* 1 **a lot** viel; **Wilbur eats a lot** Wilbur isst viel; **I spent a lot** ich habe viel ausgegeben; **he's a lot better** es geht ihm viel besser; **a lot of** viel; **a lot of coffee** viel Kaffee; 2 (*many*) **a lot of** viele; **a lot of books** viele Bücher; 3 **lots of** eine Menge (*informal*); **lots of people** eine Menge Leute.

lottery *noun* Lotterie *die* (PL *die* Lotterien); **to win the lottery** in der Lotterie gewinnen.

loud *adjective* 1 laut; **in a loud voice** mit lauter Stimme; 2 **to say something out loud** etwas laut sagen.

loudly *adverb* laut.

loudspeaker *noun* Lautsprecher *der* (PL *die* Lautsprecher).

lounge *noun* 1 (*in a house*) Wohnzimmer *das* (PL *die* Wohnzimmer); 2 (*in a hotel or an* airport) Halle *die* (PL *die* Hallen); (*departure* airport) die Abflughalle.

love *noun* 1 Liebe *die*; **for love** aus Liebe; 2 **to be in love with somebody** in jemanden verliebt sein; **she's in love with Jake** sie ist in Jake verliebt; 3 **Gina sends her love** Gina lässt grüßen; **with love from Charlie** herzliche Grüße von Charlie; 4 (*in tennis*) null.
verb 1 lieben (*a person*); **I love you** ich liebe dich; 2 sehr gerne mögen ◇ (*a place or food*); **she loves London** sie mag London sehr gerne; **Wayne loves chocolate** Wayne mag Schokolade sehr gerne; 3 **to love doing something** etwas sehr gerne tun; **I love dancing** ich tanze sehr gerne; 4 **I'd love to come** ich würde sehr gerne kommen.

lovely *adjective* schön; **a lovely dress** ein schönes Kleid; **we had lovely weather** wir hatten schönes Wetter; **we had a lovely day** es war sehr schön.

low *adjective* 1 niedrig; **a low table** ein niedriger Tisch; **at a low price** zu einem niedrigen Preis; 2 (*not loud*) leise; **in a low voice** mit leiser Stimme.

lower *adjective* (*not as high*) tiefer.
verb senken.

luck *noun* 1 Glück *das*; **good luck!** viel Glück!; **with a bit of luck** wenn wir Glück haben; 2 **bad luck!** so ein Pech!

luckily *adverb* zum Glück; **luckily for them** zu ihrem Glück.

△ NEW SPELLING: See page xii

lucky adjective 1 to be lucky Glück haben; we were lucky wir haben Glück gehabt; 2 to be lucky (bringing luck) Glück bringen; it's supposed to be lucky es soll Glück bringen; my lucky number meine Glückszahl.

luggage noun Gepäck das; my luggage is in the boot mein Gepäck ist im Kofferraum.

lump noun 1 Klumpen der (PL die Klumpen); 2 (of sugar or butter) Stück das (PL die Stücke).

lunch noun Mittagessen das (PL die Mittagessen); to have lunch zu Mittag essen; we had lunch in Oxford wir haben in Oxford zu Mittag gegessen.

lunch break noun Mittagspause die (PL die Mittagspausen).

lunch hour, lunch time noun Mittagszeit die.

lung noun Lungenflügel der; lungs die Lunge (singular).

luxurious adjective luxuriös.

lyrics plural noun Text der.

M m

mac noun Regenmantel der (PL die Regenmäntel).

macaroni noun Makkaroni (plural).

machine noun 1 Maschine die (PL die Maschinen); 2 (a slot machine) Automat der (PL die Automaten).

mackerel noun Makrele die (PL die Makrelen).

mad adjective 1 verrückt; she's completely mad! sie ist total verrückt!; 2 (angry) wütend; to be mad at somebody wütend auf jemanden sein; 3 to be mad about something ganz verrückt auf etwas ←(ACC) sein; she's mad about horses sie ist ganz verrückt auf Pferde.

madman noun Verrückte der (PL die Verrückten).

madness noun Wahnsinn der.

magazine noun Zeitschrift die (PL die Zeitschriften); (with mostly photos) Magazin das (PL die Magazine).

magic noun Zauber der; (conjuring tricks) Zauberei die. adjective 1 Zauber-; magic wand der Zauberstab; 2 (great) super (informal).

magician noun 1 (wizard) Zauberer der (PL die Zauberer); 2 (conjurer) Zauberkünstler der (PL die Zauberkünstler).

magnifying glass noun Lupe die (PL die Lupen).

maiden name noun Mädchenname der (PL die Mädchennamen).

mail noun Post die.

mail order noun Bestellung per Post die; to buy something by mail

✧ IRREGULAR VERB: See the verb table in the centre of the dictionary

order etwas bei einem Versandhaus bestellen; **mail order catalogue** *der* Versandhauskatalog.

main *adjective* Haupt-; **main entrance** *der* Haupteingang.

mainly *adverb* hauptsächlich.

main road *noun* Hauptstraße *die* (PL *die* Hauptstraßen).

major *adjective* 1 (*important*) groß; 2 (*serious*) schwer; **a major accident** ein schwerer Unfall.

Majorca *noun* Mallorca *das*.

majority *noun* Mehrheit *die*.

make *noun* Marke *die* (PL *die* Marken); **the make of a car** *die* Automarke.

verb 1 machen; **to make a meal** Essen machen; **I made breakfast** ich habe Frühstück gemacht; **she made her bed** sie hat ihr Bett gemacht; **to make somebody happy** jemanden glücklich machen; **it makes you tired** das macht einen müde; 2 herstellen SEP; **they make computers** sie stellen Computer her; **'made in Germany'** 'in Deutschland hergestellt'; 3 **he made me wait** er ließ mich warten; **she makes me laugh** sie bringt mich zum Lachen; 4 verdienen; **he makes forty pounds a day** er verdient vierzig Pfund pro Tag; **to make a living** seinen Lebensunterhalt verdienen; 5 (*force*) zwingen ◇; **to make somebody do something** jemanden zwingen, etwas zu tun; **she made him give the money back** sie hat ihn gezwungen, das

Geld zurückzugeben; 6 (*the verb 'make' is often translated by a more specific verb*) **to make a cake** einen Kuchen backen; **to make a phone call** telefonieren; **to make a dress** ein Kleid nähen; 7 **to make friends with somebody** sich mit jemandem anfreunden SEP; 8 **I can't make it tonight** ich kann heute Abend nicht kommen; 9 **two and three make five** zwei und drei ist fünf.

• **to make something up** 1 etwas erfinden ◇; **she made up an excuse** sie hat eine Ausrede erfunden; 2 **to make it up** (*after a quarrel*) sich versöhnen; **they've made it up again** sie haben sich wieder versöhnt.

make-up *noun* 1 Make-up *das*; **I don't wear make-up** ich trage kein Make-up; 2 **to put on your make-up** sich schminken; **Jo's putting on her make-up** Jo schminkt sich.

male *adjective* 1 männlich; **male voice** *die* Männerstimme; 2 **male animal** *das* Männchen; **male rat** *das* Rattenmännchen; 3 **male student** *der* Student.

male chauvinist *noun* Chauvi *der* (PL *die* Chauvis) (*informal*).

man *noun* 1 Mann *der* (PL *die* Männer); **an old man** ein alter Mann; 2 (*the human race*) *der* Mensch.

manage *verb* 1 leiten (*a business, team*); **she manages a travel agency** sie leitet ein Reisebüro; 2 (*cope*) zurechtkommen ◇ SEP (PERF *sein*); **I can manage** ich

△ NEW SPELLING: See page xii

komme schon zurecht; **3 to manage
to do something** es schaffen, etwas
zu tun; **he managed to push the
door open** er hat es geschafft, die
Tür aufzustoßen; **I didn't manage to
get in touch with her** ich habe es
nicht geschafft, sie zu erreichen.

management noun
1 Management das (PL die
Managements); **management
course** der Managementkurs;
2 Leitung die.

manager noun **1** (of a company or
bank) Direktor der (PL die
Direktoren); **2** (of a shop or
restaurant) Geschäftsführer der (PL
die Geschäftsführer); **3** (in football)
Trainer der (PL die Trainer); **4** (in
entertainment) Manager der (PL die
Manager).

manageress noun (of a shop or
restaurant) Geschäftsführerin die
(PL die Geschäftsführerinnen).

mania noun Manie die (PL die
Manien).

maniac noun Wahnsinnige der/die
(PL die Wahnsinnigen); **she drives
like a maniac** sie fährt wie eine
Wahnsinnige.

man-made adjective **man-made
fibre** die Kunstfaser.

manner noun **1 in a manner of
speaking** mehr oder weniger;
2 manners (plural); **to
have good manners** gute Manieren
haben; **it's bad manners to talk like
that** es gehört sich nicht, so zu reden.

mantelpiece noun Kaminsims der
(PL die Kaminsimse).

manual noun Handbuch das (PL die
Handbücher).

manufacture verb herstellen SEP.

manufacturer noun
Hersteller der (PL die Hersteller).

many adjective, pronoun **1** viele;
does she have many friends? hat
sie viele Freunde?; **we didn't see
many people** wir haben nicht viele
Leute gesehen; **not many** nicht
viele; **many of them forgot** viele
haben es vergessen; **there were too
many people** es waren zu viele
(Leute) da; **how many?** wie viele?;
how many were there? wie viele
waren da?; **how many sisters have
you got?** wie viele Schwestern hast
du?; **how many are there left?** wie
viele sind übrig geblieben?; **I've
never had so many presents** ich
habe noch nie so viele Geschenke
bekommen; **2** (a lot) **so many** so
viel; **I have so many things to do**
ich habe so viel zu tun; **3** (as much
as) **as many as** so viel wie; **take as
many as you like** nimm so viel wie
du willst; **4** (too much) **that's far too
many** das ist viel zu viel.

map noun **1** Karte die (PL die
Karten); **2** (of a town) Stadtplan (PL
die Stadtpläne).

marathon noun Marathonlauf der
(PL die Marathonläufe).

marble noun **1** Marmor der;
2 (for playing) Murmel die (PL die
Murmeln); **to play marbles**
Murmeln spielen.

March noun März der; **in March** im
März.

◇ **IRREGULAR VERB: See the verb table in the centre of the dictionary**

match

march noun Marsch der (PL die Märsche).
verb marschieren (PERF sein).

mare noun Stute die (PL die Stuten).

margarine noun Margarine die.

margin noun Rand der (PL die Ränder).

marijuana noun Marihuana das.

mark noun 1 (at school) Note die (PL die Noten); 2 (stain) Fleck der (PL die Flecke); 3 (the unit of German currency used before the euro) Mark die (PL die Mark).
verb 1 korrigieren; **the teacher marks our homework** die Lehrerin korrigiert unsere Hausaufgaben; 2 (in sports) decken.

market noun Markt der (PL die Märkte).

marketing noun Marketing das.

marmalade noun Orangenmarmelade die.

maroon adjective kastanienbraun.

marriage noun 1 Ehe die (PL die Ehen); 2 (wedding) Hochzeit die (PL die Hochzeiten).

married adjective 1 verheiratet; **they've been married for twenty years** sie sind seit zwanzig Jahren verheiratet; 2 **married couple** das Ehepaar.

marry verb 1 **to marry somebody** jemanden heiraten; **she married a Frenchman** sie hat einen Franzosen geheiratet; 2 **to get married**

heiraten; **they got married in July** sie haben im Juli geheiratet.

marvellous adjective wunderbar.

marzipan noun Marzipan das.

mascara noun Wimperntusche die.

masculine noun (in German and other grammars) männlich.

mash verb stampfen.

mashed potatoes plural noun Kartoffelbrei der (singular).

mask noun Maske die (PL die Masken).

mass noun 1 **a mass of** eine Menge; 2 **masses of** massenhaft (informal); **they've got masses of money** sie haben massenhaft Geld; **there's masses left over** es ist massenhaft übrig geblieben; 3 (religious) Messe die (PL die Messen); **to go to mass** zur Messe gehen.

massage noun Massage die (PL die Massagen).

massive adjective riesig.

master verb 1 meistern; 2 **to master a language** eine Sprache beherrschen.

mat noun 1 (doormat) Matte die (PL die Matten); 2 (to put under a hot dish) Untersetzer der (PL die Untersetzer); 3 **table mat** das Platzdeckchen.

match noun 1 (for lighting) Streichholz das (PL die Streichhölzer); **box of matches** die Streichholzschachtel; 2 (in sports)

Spiel *das* (PL *die* Spiele); **football
match** *das* Fußballspiel; **to watch
the match** das Spiel sehen; **to win
the match** das Spiel gewinnen; **to
lose the match** das Spiel verlieren.
verb passen zu (+DAT); **the jacket
matches the skirt** die Jacke passt
zu dem Rock.

mate *noun* Freund *der* (PL *die*
Freunde); **I'm going to the pub with
my mates** ich gehe mit meinen
Freunden in die Kneipe.

material *noun* 1 (*fabric, also
information*) Stoff *der* (PL *die*
Stoffe); 2 (*substance*) Material *das*
(PL *die* Materialien).

mathematics *noun*
Mathematik *die*.

maths *noun* Mathe *die* (*informal*);
I like maths ich mag Mathe gerne;
Anna's good at maths Anna ist gut
in Mathe.

matter *noun* **what's the matter?**
was ist los?
verb 1 **that's what matters most**
das ist am wichtigsten; **it matters a
lot to me** es ist mir sehr wichtig;
does it really matter? ist das
wirklich so wichtig?; 2 **it doesn't
matter** es macht nichts; **it doesn't
matter if it rains** es macht nichts,
wenn es regnet; 3 **you can write it
in German or English, it doesn't
matter** du kannst es auf Deutsch
oder Englisch schreiben, das ist egal;
4 **to matter to somebody**
jemandem etwas ausmachen SEP;
**does it matter to you if I leave
earlier?** macht es dir etwas aus,
wenn ich früher gehe?

mattress *noun* Matratze *die* (PL *die*
Matratzen).

May *noun* Mai *der*; **in May** im Mai.

may *verb* 1 **she may be ill** vielleicht
ist sie krank; **we may go to Spain**
wir fahren vielleicht nach Spanien;
2 (*expressing permission*) dürfen ✧;
may I close the door? darf ich die
Tür zumachen?

maybe *adverb* vielleicht; **maybe
they've got lost** vielleicht haben sie
sich verlaufen.

May Day *noun* der Erste Mai.

mayonnaise *noun* Majonäse △ *die*.

mayor *noun* Bürgermeister *der* (PL
die Bürgermeister), Bürgermeisterin
die (PL *die* Bürgermeisterinnen).

me *pronoun* (*in German this pronoun
changes according to the function it
has in the sentence or the preposition
it follows*) 1 (*as a direct object in the
accusative*) mich; **she knows me**
sie kennt mich; 2 (*after a
preposition that takes the accusative*)
mich; **they left without me** sie sind
ohne mich abgefahren; **wait for me!**
warte auf mich!; 3 (*as an indirect
object or following a verb that takes
the dative*) mir; **can you give me
your address?** kannst du mir deine
Adresse geben?; **he helped me** er
hat mir geholfen; 4 (*after a
preposition that takes the dative*)
mir; **she never talks to me** sie redet
nie mit mir; 5 (*in comparisons*) **than
me** als ich; **she's older than me** sie
ist älter als ich; 6 (*in the
nominative*) ich; **it's me** ich bin's;
not me ich nicht.

✧ IRREGULAR VERB: *See the verb table in the centre of the dictionary*

meal noun 1 Essen das (PL die Essen); **to cook a meal** Essen kochen; 2 **to go for a meal** essen gehen.

mean verb 1 (signify) bedeuten; **what does that mean?** was bedeutet das?; 2 (intend to say) meinen; 3 **what do you mean?** was meinst du?; **that's not what I meant** das habe ich nicht gemeint; 4 **to mean to do something** etwas tun wollen; **I meant to phone my mother** ich wollte meine Mutter anrufen; 5 **to be meant to do something** etwas tun sollen; **she was meant to be here at six** sie sollte um sechs hier sein. adjective 1 (with money) geizig; 2 (unkind) gemein; **she's really mean to her brother** sie ist richtig gemein zu ihrem Bruder; **what a mean thing to do!** das ist gemein!

meaning noun Bedeutung die (PL die Bedeutungen).

means noun 1 Mittel das (PL die Mittel); **means of transport** das Verkehrsmittel; **a means of earning money** eine Möglichkeit, Geld zu verdienen; 3 **by means of** mit Hilfe (+GEN); 4 **by all means!** selbstverständlich!

meantime adverb **for the meantime** einstweilen; **in the meantime** in der Zwischenzeit.

measles noun Masern (plural).

measure verb messen ✧.

measurements plural noun Maße (plural); **the measurements of the room** die Maße des Zimmers; **my measurements** meine Maße.

mechanic noun Mechaniker der (PL die Mechaniker), Mechanikerin die (PL die Mechanikerinnen).

mechanical adjective mechanisch.

medal noun Medaille die (PL die Medaillen); **the gold medal** die Goldmedaille.

media noun **the media** die Medien (plural).

medical noun 1 ärztliche Untersuchung die (PL die ärztlichen Untersuchungen); 2 **to have a medical** sich untersuchen lassen. adjective 1 medizinisch; 2 ärztlich (examination, treatment).

medicine noun 1 (drug) Medikament das (PL die Medikamente); 2 (subject of study) Medizin die; **she's studying medicine** sie studiert Medizin; 3 **alternative medicine** die Alternativmedizin.

Mediterranean noun **the Mediterranean (Sea)** das Mittelmeer.

medium adjective mittlerer/mittlere/mittleres.

medium-sized adjective mittelgroß.

meet verb 1 (by chance) treffen ✧; **I met Rosie at the baker's** ich habe Rosie beim Bäcker getroffen; 2 (by appointment) sich treffen mit (+DAT); **I'll meet you outside the cinema** ich treffe mich mit dir vor dem Kino; 3 sich treffen; **we're**

△ NEW SPELLING: See page xii

meeting at six wir treffen uns um sechs; **4** (*get to know*) kennen lernen △; **I met a German girl last week** ich habe letzte Woche eine Deutsche kennen gelernt; **5 I've never met Oskar** ich kenne Oskar nicht; **6** (*off a train or bus, for example*) abholen SEP; **my dad's meeting me at the station** mein Vater holt mich vom Bahnhof ab.

meeting noun **1** (*by arrangement*) Treffen *das* (PL die Treffen); **2** (*in business*) Besprechung *die* (PL die Besprechungen); **she's in a meeting** sie ist in einer Besprechung; **3** (*by chance, in sports*) Begegnung *die* (PL die Begegnungen).

melon noun Melone *die* (PL die Melonen).

melt verb **1** schmelzen ◇ (PERF sein); **the snow has melted** der Schnee ist geschmolzen; **2** (*in cookery*) zerlassen ◇ (*butter, fat*); **melt the butter in a saucepan** Butter im Topf zerlassen.

member noun Mitglied *das* (PL die Mitglieder).

Member of Parliament noun Abgeordnete *der/die* (PL die Abgeordneten).

membership noun Mitgliedschaft *die*.

membership card noun Mitgliedskarte *die* (PL die Mitgliedskarten).

membership fee noun Mitgliedsbeitrag *der* (PL die Mitgliedsbeiträge).

memorize verb **to memorize something** etwas auswendig lernen.

memory noun **1** (*of a person*) Gedächtnis *das*; **you have a good memory** du hast ein gutes Gedächtnis; **2** (*of the past*) Erinnerung *die* (PL die Erinnerungen); **I have good memories of our stay in Italy** ich habe schöne Erinnerungen an unseren Urlaub in Italien; **3** (*of a computer*) Speicher *der*.

mend verb **1** reparieren; **2** (*by sewing*) ausbessern SEP.

mental adjective **1** geistig; **2 mental illness** die Geisteskrankheit; **mental hospital** die psychiatrische Klinik.

mention verb erwähnen.

menu noun **1** (*in a restaurant*) Speisekarte *die* (PL die Speisekarten); **2** (*in computing*) Menü *das* (PL die Menüs).

meringue noun Baiser *das* (PL die Baisers).

merit noun **1** Verdienst *das* (PL die Verdienste); **2** (*good feature or advantage*) Vorzug *der* (PL die Vorzüge).

merry adjective **1** fröhlich; **Merry Christmas** fröhliche Weihnachten; **2** (*from drinking*) angeheitert.

mess noun **1** Durcheinander *das*; **my papers are in a complete mess** meine Unterlagen sind ein einziges Durcheinander; **what a mess!** was für ein Durcheinander!; **2 to make**

◇ IRREGULAR VERB: *See the verb table in the centre of the dictionary*

a mess Unordnung machen; 3 to clear up the mess aufräumen SEP.

● to mess about herumalbern SEP; stop messing about! hör auf herumzualbern!

● to mess about with something mit etwas ←(DAT) herumspielen SEP; it's dangerous to mess about with matches es ist gefährlich, mit Streichhölzern herumzuspielen.

● to mess something up 1 etwas durcheinander bringen △ ✧; you've messed up all my papers Sie haben meine Unterlagen völlig durcheinander gebracht; 2 (make dirty) etwas schmutzig machen; 3 (botch) etwas verpfuschen.

message noun 1 Nachricht die (PL die Nachrichten); a telephone message eine telefonische Nachricht; 2 to give somebody a message jemandem etwas ausrichten SEP.

messy adjective 1 (dirty) it's a messy job das ist ein dreckiger Job; 2 he's a messy eater er bekleckert sich beim Essen; 3 her writing's really messy sie hat eine furchtbare Schrift; 4 (untidy) she's very messy sie ist sehr unordentlich.

metal noun Metall das (PL die Metalle).

meter noun 1 (electricity, gas, taxi) Zähler der (PL die Zähler); to read the meter den Zähler ablesen ✧ SEP; 2 parking meter die Parkuhr.

method noun Methode die (PL die Methoden).

Methodist noun Methodist der (PL die Methodisten), Methodistin die (PL die Methodistinnen).

metre noun Meter der (PL die Meter).

metric adjective metrisch.

microphone noun Mikrofon das (PL die Mikrofone).

microscope noun Mikroskop das (PL die Mikroskope).

microwave (oven) noun Mikrowellenherd der (PL die Mikrowellenherde).

midday noun Mittag der; at midday mittags.

middle noun 1 Mitte die; in the middle of the room in der Mitte des Zimmers; in the middle of June Mitte Juni; in the middle of the night mitten in der Nacht; 2 to be in the middle of doing something gerade dabei sein, etwas zu tun; when she phoned I was in the middle of washing my hair als sie anrief, war ich gerade dabei, mir die Haare zu waschen.

middle-aged adjective mittleren Alters; a middle-aged lady eine Dame mittleren Alters.

middle-class adjective der Mittelschicht; a middle-class family eine Familie der Mittelschicht.

Middle-East noun the Middle East der Nahe Osten.

midge noun Mücke die (PL die Mücken).

midnight noun Mitternacht die; at midnight um Mitternacht.

△ NEW SPELLING: See page xii

Midsummer's Day noun
Sommersonnenwende die.

might verb 1 'are you going to
phone him?' – 'I might' 'rufst du
ihn an?' – 'vielleicht'; 2 I might invite
Jo vielleicht lade ich Jo ein; he
might have forgotten vielleicht hat
er es vergessen; 2 she might be
right sie könnte Recht haben.

mike noun (microphone) Mikro das
(PL die Mikros) (informal).

mild adjective mild.

mile noun 1 Meile die (PL die Meilen)
(Germans use kilometres for
distances; to convert miles to
kilometres, multiply by 8 and divide
by 5); it's ten miles to Oxford es
sind sechzehn Kilometer bis Oxford;
2 it's miles better das ist viel besser.

milk noun Milch die; full-cream
milk die Vollmilch; skimmed milk
die Magermilch; semi-skimmed
milk die fettarme Milch.
verb melken.

milk chocolate noun
Milchschokolade die.

milkman noun Milchmann der (PL
die Milchmänner).

milk shake noun
Milchmixgetränk das (PL die
Milchmixgetränke).

millimetre noun Millimeter der (PL
die Millimeter).

million noun Million die (PL die
Millionen); a million people eine
Million Menschen; two million
people zwei Millionen Menschen.

millionaire noun Millionär der (PL
die Millionäre); Millionärin die (PL
die Millionärinnen).

mince noun Hackfleisch das.

mind noun 1 Sinn der; it never
crossed my mind to ask them for
help es kam mir überhaupt nicht in
den Sinn, sie um Hilfe zu bitten;
2 Meinung die; to change your
mind seine Meinung ändern; I've
changed my mind ich habe meine
Meinung geändert; 3 to make up
your mind to do something sich
entschließen ◇, etwas zu tun; I can't
make up my mind which dress to
wear ich kann mich nicht
entschließen, welches Kleid ich
anziehe; 4 I've made up my mind
ich habe mich entschieden.
verb 1 aufpassen SEP auf (+ACC); can
you mind my bag for me? können
Sie auf meine Handtasche
aufpassen?; could you mind the
baby for ten minutes? könntest du
zehn Minuten auf das Baby
aufpassen?; 2 do you mind closing
the door? würden Sie bitte die Tür
zumachen?; 3 do you mind if ...?
würde es Ihnen etwas ausmachen SEP,
wenn ...?; do you mind if I open the
window? würde es Ihnen etwas
ausmachen, wenn ich das Fenster
aufmache?; I don't mind es macht
mir nichts aus; I don't mind the heat
die Hitze macht mir nichts aus;
4 never mind macht nichts.

mine[1] noun Bergwerk das (PL die
Bergwerke); coal mine das
Kohlenbergwerk.

mine[2] pronoun 1 (for a masculine

noun) mein; **she took her coat and I took mine** sie hat ihren Mantel genommen und ich habe meinen genommen; **2** (*for a feminine noun*) meine; **she gave me her address and I gave her mine** sie hat mir ihre Adresse gegeben und ich habe ihr meine gegeben; **3** (*for a neuter noun*) meins; **her dress is red and mine is blue** ihr Kleid ist rot und meins ist blau; **4** (*for masculine/ feminine/neuter plural nouns*) meine; **she showed me her photos and I showed her mine** sie hat mir ihre Fotos gezeigt und ich habe ihr meine gezeigt; **5 a friend of mine** ein Freund von mir; **it's mine** das gehört mir.

miner *noun* Bergarbeiter *der* (PL *die* Bergarbeiter).

mineral water *noun* Mineralwasser *das*.

minibus *noun* Kleinbus *der* (PL *die* Kleinbusse).

minimum *noun* Minimum *das* (PL *die* Minima); **a minimum of** ein Minimum von.
adjective Mindest-; **the minimum age** das Mindestalter; **minimum wage** *der* Mindestlohn.

miniskirt *noun* Minirock *der* (PL *die* Miniröcke).

minister *noun* **1** (*in government*) Minister *der* (PL *die* Minister), Ministerin *die* (PL *die* Ministerinnen); **2** (*of a church*) Geistliche *der/die* (PL *die* Geistlichen).

ministry *noun* Ministerium *das* (PL *die* Ministerien).

mint *noun* **1** (*herb*) Minze *die* (PL *die* Minzen); **2** (*sweet*) Pfefferminzbonbon *der* (PL *die* Pfefferminzbonbons).

minus *preposition* minus (+GEN); **seven minus three is four** sieben minus drei ist vier; **it was minus ten this morning** es war minus zehn heute Morgen.

minute[1] *noun* **1** Minute *die* (PL *die* Minuten); **I'll be ready in two minutes** ich bin in zwei Minuten fertig; **it's five minutes' walk from here** es ist fünf Minuten zu Fuß von hier; **2** Moment *der*; **just a minute!** einen Moment bitte!; **3 in a minute** gleich.

minute[2] *adjective* winzig; **the bedrooms are minute** die Schlafzimmer sind winzig.

miracle *noun* Wunder *das* (PL *die* Wunder).

mirror *noun* Spiegel *der* (PL *die* Spiegel); **he looked at himself in the mirror** er hat sich im Spiegel betrachtet.

misbehave *verb* sich schlecht benehmen ◇.

miserable *adjective* **1** unglücklich; **he was miserable without her** er war unglücklich ohne sie; **2 I feel really miserable today** ich fühle mich heute richtig elend; **3** mies; **it's miserable weather** das Wetter ist mies; **she gets paid a miserable salary** sie bekommt ein mieses Gehalt.

△ NEW SPELLING: See page xii

miss verb 1 verpassen; **she missed her train** sie hat ihren Zug verpasst; **I missed the film** ich habe den Film verpasst; **to miss an opportunity** eine Gelegenheit verpassen; 2 nicht treffen ◇; **the stone missed me** der Stein hat mich nicht getroffen; **the ball missed the goal** der Schuss ging am Tor vorbei; **missed!** nicht getroffen!; 3 versäumen; **he's missed his classes** er hat den Unterricht versäumt; 4 vermissen (a person or thing); **I miss you** ich vermisse dich; **she's missing her sister** sie vermisst ihre Schwester; **I miss England** ich vermisse England.

Miss noun Fräulein das; **Miss Jones** Fräulein Jones, Frau Jones (adult women are usually addressed as 'Frau', whether or not they are married).

missing adjective 1 fehlend; **she's found the missing pieces** sie hat die fehlenden Teile gefunden; **the missing link** das fehlende Glied; 2 **to be missing** fehlen; **there's a plate missing** ein Teller fehlt; **there are three forks missing** drei Gabeln fehlen; 3 **to go missing** verschwinden ◇ (PERF sein); **several things have gone missing lately** mehrere Sachen sind kürzlich verschwunden; 4 **three children are missing** drei Kinder werden vermisst.

missionary noun Missionar der (PL die Missionare), Missionarin die (PL die Missionarinnen).

mist noun Nebel der.

mistake noun 1 Fehler der (PL die Fehler); **spelling mistake** der Rechtschreibfehler; **you've made lots of mistakes** du hast viele Fehler gemacht; 2 **to make a mistake** (be mistaken) sich irren; **sorry, I made a mistake** Entschuldigung, ich habe mich geirrt; 3 **by mistake** aus Versehen.
verb **I mistook you for your brother** ich habe dich mit deinem Bruder verwechselt.

mistaken adjective **to be mistaken** sich täuschen; **you're mistaken** du täuschst dich.

mistletoe noun Mistel die (PL die Misteln).

misty adjective dunstig; **a misty morning** ein dunstiger Morgen.

misunderstand verb missverstehen △ ◇; **I misunderstood** ich habe es missverstanden.

misunderstanding noun Missverständnis △ das (PL die Missverständnisse); **there's been a misunderstanding** da liegt ein Missverständnis vor.

mix noun Mischung die (PL die Mischungen); **a good mix** eine gute Mischung; **cake mix** die Backmischung.
verb 1 vermischen; **mix the ingredients together** die Zutaten vermischen; **mix the cream into the sauce** die Sahne in die Soße rühren; 2 **to mix with** verkehren mit (+DAT); **she mixes with lots of interesting people** sie verkehrt mit vielen interessanten Leuten.

◇ IRREGULAR VERB: See the verb table in the centre of the dictionary.

● **to mix up** 1 durcheinander bringen △ ◇; **you've mixed up all the papers** du hast alle Unterlagen durcheinander gebracht; **you've got it all mixed up** du hast alles durcheinander gebracht; 2 (*confuse*) verwechseln; **I get him mixed up with his brother** ich verwechsele ihn mit seinem Bruder.

mixed *adjective* 1 bunt; **a mixed programme** ein buntes Programm; 2 gemischt; **a mixed salad** ein gemischter Salat.

mixture *noun* Mischung *die* (PL die Mischungen); **it's a mixture of jazz and rock** es ist eine Mischung aus Jazz und Rock.

moan *verb* (*complain*) jammern; **stop moaning!** hör auf zu jammern!

mobile home *noun* Wohnwagen *der* (PL die Wohnwagen).

mobile phone *noun* Mobiltelefon *das* (PL die Mobiltelefone), Handy *das* (PL die Handys).

mock *noun* (*mock exam*) Übungsprüfung *die* (PL die Übungsprüfungen).
verb sich lustig machen über (+ACC); **stop mocking me** hör auf, dich über mich lustig zu machen.

model *noun* 1 Modell *das* (PL die Modelle); **his car is the latest model** sein Auto ist das neueste Modell; **a model of Westminster Abbey** ein Modell von der Westminsterabtei; 2 (*fashion*

model) Mannequin *das* (PL die Mannequins); **she's a model** sie ist Mannequin.

model aeroplane *noun* Modellflugzeug *das* (PL die Modellflugzeuge).

model railway *noun* Minieisenbahn *die* (PL die Minieisenbahnen).

modem *noun* Modem *der* (PL die Modems).

modern *adjective* modern.

modernize *verb* modernisieren.

modern languages *noun* neuere Sprachen (*plural*).

modest *adjective* bescheiden.

modify *verb* abändern SEP.

moisture *noun* Feuchtigkeit *die*.

moisturizer *noun* Feuchtigkeitscreme *die*.

mole *noun* 1 (*animal*) Maulwurf *der* (PL die Maulwürfe); 2 (*on the skin*) Leberfleck *der* (PL die Leberflecke).

moment *noun* 1 Moment *der* (PL die Momente); **at any moment** jeden Moment; **at the moment** im Moment, im Augenblick; **at the right moment** im richtigen Moment; 2 Augenblick *der* (PL die Augenblicke); **wait a moment!** einen Augenblick!; 3 **he'll be ready in a moment** er ist gleich fertig.

monarchy *noun* Monarchie *die*.

Monday *noun* 1 Montag *der*; **on Monday** am Montag; **I'm going to**

A NEW SPELLING: See page xii

see him on Monday ich sehe ihn am
Montag; **see you on Monday!** bis
Montag!; **every Monday** jeden
Montag; **last Monday** letzten
Montag; **next Monday** nächsten
Montag; **2 on Mondays** montags;
the museum is closed on Mondays
das Museum ist montags
geschlossen.

money noun Geld das; **I don't have
enough money** ich habe nicht
genug Geld; **to make money** Geld
verdienen.

monitor noun (of a computer)
Monitor der (PL die Monitoren).

monkey noun Affe der (PL die
Affen).

monotonous adjective eintönig.

monster noun Ungeheuer das (PL
die Ungeheuer).

month noun Monat der; **in the
month of May** im Mai; **this month**
diesen Monat; **next month** nächsten
Monat; **last month** letzten Monat;
for three months drei Monate lang;
every month jeden Monat; **every
three months** alle drei Monate; **in
two months' time** in zwei Monaten;
at the end of the month am
Monatsende.

monthly adjective monatlich;
monthly payment die monatliche
Zahlung; **monthly ticket** die
Monatskarte.

monument noun Denkmal das (PL
die Denkmäler).

mood noun **1** Laune die (PL die
Launen); **to be in a good mood**

gute Laune haben; **to be in a bad
mood** schlechte Laune haben;
2 I'm not in the mood ich habe
keine Lust dazu; **I'm not in the mood
for working** ich habe keine Lust zum
Arbeiten.

moon noun Mond der (PL die
Monde); **by the light of the moon**
im Mondschein; ★ **to be over the
moon** im siebten Himmel sein
(literally: to be in seventh heaven).

moonlight noun Mondschein der;
by moonlight im Mondschein.

moped noun Moped das (PL die
Mopeds).

moral noun Moral die; **the moral of
the story** die Moral der Geschichte.
adjective moralisch.

morals noun Moral die.

more adverb **1** (followed by an
adjective) (in German the ending
'-er' is added to the adjective to show
the comparative) **more interesting**
interessanter; **the book's more
interesting than the film** das Buch
ist interessanter als der Film; **more
difficult** schwieriger; **more slowly**
langsamer; **more easily** einfacher;
**books are getting more and more
expensive** Bücher werden immer
teurer; **2 not any more** (no longer)
nicht mehr; **she doesn't live here
any more** sie wohnt nicht mehr hier.
adjective **1** mehr ('mehr' never
changes); **more friends** mehr
Freunde; **more ... than** mehr ... als;
they have more money than we do
sie haben mehr Geld als wir; **2 no
more** kein; **there's no more milk**

◇ IRREGULAR VERB: See the verb table in the centre of the dictionary

es ist keine Milch mehr da; **3** (of something you have already) noch; **would you like some more cake?** möchtest du noch etwas Kuchen?; **a few more glasses** noch ein paar Gläser.

pronoun 1 mehr; **he eats more than me** er isst mehr als ich; **no more, thank you** nichts mehr, danke; **2** (of something you have already) noch; **we need three more** wir brauchen noch drei; **any more?** noch etwas?; **3 more and more** immer mehr; **it takes more and more time** es beansprucht immer mehr Zeit; **4 more or less** mehr oder weniger; **it's more or less finished** es ist mehr oder weniger fertig.

morning noun **1** Morgen der (PL die Morgen); **in the morning** am Morgen; **this morning** heute Morgen; **tomorrow morning** morgen früh; **yesterday morning** gestern Morgen; **on Friday morning** am Freitagmorgen; **2 in the morning** (regularly) morgens; **she doesn't work in the morning** sie arbeitet morgens nicht; **on Friday mornings** freitagmorgens; **at six o'clock in the morning** um sechs Uhr morgens; **3** (as opposed to afternoon) Vormittag der (PL die Vormittage); **I spent the whole morning waiting for him** ich habe den ganzen Vormittag auf ihn gewartet.

Moscow noun Moskau das.

Moslem noun Moslem der (PL die Moslems), Moslime die (PL die Moslimen).

mosque noun Moschee die (PL die Moscheen).

mosquito noun Mücke die (PL die Mücken); **mosquito bite** der Mückenstich.

most adjective, pronoun **1** (followed by a plural noun) die meisten; **most children like chocolate** die meisten Kinder mögen Schokolade; **most of my friends** die meisten von meinen Freunden; **2** (followed by a singular noun) der meiste/die meiste/das meiste; **they've eaten most of the ice-cream** sie haben das meiste Eis gegessen; **3 the most** (followed by a noun or a verb) am meisten; **I've got the most time** ich habe am meisten Zeit; **4 most of the time** die meiste Zeit; **most of them** die meisten.

adverb **1** (followed by an adjective) (in German the ending '-(e)st' is added to the adjective to show the superlative) **the most interesting film** der interessanteste Film; **the most exciting story** die spannendste Geschichte; **the most boring book** das langweiligste Buch; **2** am meisten; **the noise bothers me most** der Lärm stört mich am meisten; **3** (very) höchst; **it's most unlikely** es ist höchst unwahrscheinlich.

moth noun **1** Nachtfalter der (PL die Nachtfalter); **2** (clothes moth) Motte die (PL die Motten).

mother noun Mutter die (PL die Mütter); **Kate's mother** Kates Mutter.

△ NEW SPELLING: See page xii

mother-in-law noun
Schwiegermutter die (PL die
Schwiegermütter).

Mother's Day noun Muttertag der
(PL die Muttertage).

motor noun Motor der (PL die
Motoren).

motorbike noun Motorrad das (PL
die Motorräder).

motorcyclist noun
Motorradfahrer der (PL die
Motorradfahrer), Motorradfahrerin
die (PL die Motorradfahrerinnen).

motorist noun Autofahrer der (PL
die Autofahrer), Autofahrerin die (PL
die Autofahrerinnen).

motor racing noun
Autorennen das.

motorway noun Autobahn die (PL
die Autobahnen).

mouldy adjective schimmelig.

mountain noun Berg der (PL die
Berge); **in the mountains** in den
Bergen.

mountain bike noun
Mountainbike das (PL die
Mountainbikes).

mountaineer noun
Bergsteiger der (PL die Bergsteiger),
Bergsteigerin die (PL die
Bergsteigerinnen).

mountaineering noun
Bergsteigen das; **to go
mountaineering** Bergsteigen gehen.

mountainous adjective gebirgig.

mouse noun Maus die (PL die
Mäuse) (also for a computer).

moustache noun Schnurrbart der
(PL die Schnurrbärte).

mouth noun 1 (of a person)
Mund der (PL die Münder); 2 (of an
animal) Maul das (PL die Mäuler);
3 (of a river) Mündung die (PL die
Mündungen).

mouthful noun (food) Happen der
(PL die Happen) (informal).

mouth organ noun
Mundharmonika die (PL die
Mundharmonikas); **to play the
mouth organ** Mundharmonika
spielen.

move noun 1 (to a different house)
Umzug der (PL die Umzüge); 2 (in a
game) Zug der (PL die Züge); **your
move!** du bist am Zug!
verb 1 sich bewegen; **she didn't
move** sie hat sich nicht bewegt; **2 to
move up** vorrücken SEP; **move
up a bit** rücken Sie etwas vor;
3 wegnehmen ◇ SEP; **can you move
your bag, please?** können Sie Ihre
Handtasche bitte wegnehmen?; **4 to
move something somewhere else**
etwas woandershin stellen; **I've
moved the chest into the cellar** ich
habe die Truhe in den Keller gestellt;
5 (car) fahren ◇ SEP;
6 (traffic) vorwärtskommen ◇ SEP
(PERF sein); 7 (driver) wegfahren ◇
SEP; **could you move your car,
please?** würden Sie bitte Ihr Auto
wegfahren?; **8 to move forward**
(person) vorrücken SEP (PERF sein);
(vehicle) vorwärts fahren ◇ (PERF
sein); 9 (move house) umziehen ◇
SEP (PERF sein); **we're moving on
Tuesday** wir ziehen am Dienstag

◇ IRREGULAR VERB: *See the verb table in the centre of the dictionary*

um; **they've moved to London** sie sind nach London umgezogen; **10 to move away** (*live somewhere else*) wegziehen ◇ SEP (PERF *sein*); **11 to move in** einziehen ◇ SEP (PERF *sein*); **she's moving in with friends** sie zieht bei Freunden ein.

movement *noun* Bewegung *die* (PL die Bewegungen).

movie *noun* Film *der* (PL die Filme); **to go to the movies** ins Kino gehen.

moving *adjective* **1** fahrend; **a moving car** ein fahrendes Auto; **2** (*emotionally*) ergreifend.

mow *verb* mähen.

mower *noun* Rasenmäher *der* (PL die Rasenmäher).

MP *noun* Abgeordnete *der/die* (PL die Abgeordneten).

Mr *noun* Herr *der*; (*in an address*) **Mr Angus Brown** Herrn Angus Brown; (*in a letter*) **Dear Mr Brown** Sehr geehrter Herr Brown.

Mrs *noun* Frau *die*; **Mrs Mary Hendry** Frau Mary Hendry; (*in a letter*) **Dear Mrs Hendry** Sehr geehrte Frau Hendry.

Ms *noun* Frau *die* (*there is no direct equivalent to 'Ms' in German, but 'Frau' may be used whether the woman is married or not*).

much *adjective, adverb, pronoun* **1** viel; **she doesn't eat much for breakfast** sie isst nicht viel zum Frühstück; **much more** viel mehr; **much quicker** viel schneller; **we**

don't have much time wir haben nicht viel Zeit; **2 not much** nicht viel; **'do you have a lot of work?'** – **'no, not much'** 'hast du viel Arbeit?' – ' 'nein, nicht viel'; **3 so much** so viel; **I have so much to do** ich habe so viel zu tun; **you shouldn't have given me so much** du hättest mir nicht so viel geben sollen; **4 as much as** so viel; **take as much as you like** nimm so viel du willst; **5 too much** zu viel Δ; **she gets too much money from her parents** sie bekommt zu viel Geld von ihren Eltern; **that's far too much** das ist viel zu viel; **6 how much?** wie viel? Δ; **how much is it?** wie viel kostet es?; **how much do you want?** wie viel möchten Sie?; **how much money do you need?** wie viel Geld brauchst du?; **7** (*greatly*) sehr; **he loved her very much** er hat sie sehr geliebt; **too much** zu sehr; **so much** (so) sehr; **we liked it so much** es hat uns sehr gefallen; **8** (*often*) oft; **I don't watch television much** ich sehe nicht oft fern; **we don't go out much** wir gehen nicht oft aus; **9 thank you very much** vielen Dank.

mud *noun* Schlamm *der*.

muddle *noun*
1 Durcheinander *das*; **2 to be in a muddle** durcheinander sein.

mug *noun* Becher *der* (PL die Becher); **a mug of milk** ein Becher Milch.
verb **to mug somebody** jemanden überfallen ◇; **to be mugged** überfallen werden.

Δ NEW SPELLING: See page xii

multiplication noun
Multiplikation die.

multiply verb multiplizieren; **six multiplied by four** sechs multipliziert mit vier.

mum, mummy noun Mutti die (PL die Muttis); **Tom's mum** Toms Mutti; **I'll ask my mum** ich frage die Mutti.

mumps noun Mumps der.

Munich noun München das.

murder noun Mord der (PL die Morde).
verb ermorden.

murderer noun Mörder der (PL die Mörder), Mörderin die (PL die Mörderinnen).

muscle noun Muskel der (PL die Muskeln).

muscular adjective muskulös.

museum noun Museum das (PL die Museen); **to go to the museum** ins Museum gehen.

mushroom noun Pilz der (PL die Pilze), Champignon der (PL die Champignons); **mushroom salad** der Champignonsalat.

music noun Musik die; **pop music** die Popmusik; **classical music** die klassische Musik.

musical noun Musical das (PL die Musicals).
adjective 1 **musical instrument** das Musikinstrument; 2 **they're a very musical family** sie sind eine sehr musikalische Familie.

musician noun Musiker der (PL die Musiker), Musikerin die (PL die Musikerinnen).

Muslim noun Moslem der (PL die Moslems), Moslime die (PL die Moslimen).

mussel noun Muschel die (PL die Muscheln).

must verb 1 müssen ◇; **we must leave now** wir müssen jetzt gehen; **you must learn the vocabulary** du musst die Vokabeln lernen; 2 (with a negative) dürfen ◇; **you mustn't do that** das darfst du nicht tun; 3 (expressing probability) müssen ◇; **you must be tired** du musst müde sein; **it must be five o'clock** es muss fünf Uhr sein; **he must have forgotten** er muss es vergessen haben.

mustard noun Senf der (PL die Senfe).

mutter verb murmeln.

my adjective 1 (before a masculine noun) mein; **my brother** mein Bruder; **they don't like my dog** sie mögen meinen Hund nicht; 2 (before a feminine noun) meine; **my sister** meine Schwester; 3 (before a neuter noun) mein; **that's my new car** das ist mein neues Auto; **we can go in my car** wir können mit meinem Auto fahren; 4 (before masculine/feminine/neuter plural nouns) meine; **my children** meine Kinder; 5 (with parts of the body) der/die/das (plural: die); **I had a glass in my hand** ich hatte ein Glas in der Hand; **I'm washing my hands** ich wasche mir die Hände.

◇ **IRREGULAR VERB: See the verb table in the centre of the dictionary**

myself pronoun 1 (reflexive and after a preposition taking the accusative) mich; **I've cut myself** ich habe mich geschnitten; **I've addressed the letter to myself** ich habe den Brief an mich adressiert; 2 (reflexive and after a preposition taking the dative) mir; **I've hurt myself** ich habe mir wehgetan; **I said to myself** ich habe mir gesagt; 3 (stressing something) selbst; **I said it myself** ich habe es selbst gesagt; 4 **by myself** allein.

mysterious adjective rätselhaft.

mystery noun 1 Rätsel das (PL die Rätsel); 2 (book) Krimi der (PL die Krimis) (informal).

mythology noun Mythologie die (PL die Mythologien).

N n

nail noun (on your finger or toe, also metal) Nagel der (PL die Nägel). verb nageln.

nailbrush noun Nagelbürste die (PL die Nagelbürsten).

nailfile noun Nagelfeile die (PL die Nagelfeilen).

nail polish noun Nagellack der.

nail polish remover noun Nagellackentferner der.

name noun 1 Name der (PL die Namen); **I've forgotten her name** ich habe ihren Namen vergessen;

what's your name? wie heißt du?; **my name's Joy** ich heiße Joy; 2 (of a book or film) Titel der (PL die Titel).

napkin noun Serviette die (PL die Servietten).

nappy noun Windel die (PL die Windeln).

narrow adjective schmal; **a narrow street** eine schmale Straße.

nasty adjective 1 (mean) gemein; **that was a nasty thing to do** das war gemein; 2 (unpleasant, bad) scheußlich; **that's a nasty job** das ist eine scheußliche Arbeit; **a nasty smell** ein scheußlicher Geruch.

nation noun Nation die (PL die Nationen).

national adjective national.

national anthem noun Nationalhymne die (PL die Nationalhymnen).

nationality noun Nationalität die (PL die Nationalitäten).

national park noun Nationalpark der (PL die Nationalparks).

natural adjective natürlich.

naturally adverb natürlich.

nature noun Natur die.

nature reserve noun Naturschutzgebiet das (PL die Naturschutzgebiete).

naughty adjective unartig.

△ NEW SPELLING: See page xii

navy noun Marine die; **my uncle's in the navy** mein Onkel ist bei der Marine.

navy-blue adjective marineblau.

near adjective 1 nah(e); 2 (the superlative of nah(e) is der/die/das nächste) **the nearest park** der nächste Park; **the nearest bank** die nächste Bank; **the nearest shop** das nächste Geschäft.
preposition nahe an (+DAT); **near (to) the station** nahe am Bahnhof.
adverb 1 nah (in spoken German 'nah' is more common); **they live quite near** sie wohnen ganz nah; 2 **to come nearer** näher kommen.

nearly adverb fast; **nearly empty** fast leer.

neat adjective 1 (well organized, tidy) ordentlich; **a neat room** ein ordentliches Zimmer; 2 adrett (clothes or the way you look).

necessarily adverb **not necessarily** nicht unbedingt.

necessary adjective nötig; **if necessary** falls nötig.

neck noun 1 (of a person) Hals der (PL die Hälse); 2 (of a garment) Kragen der (PL die Kragen).

necklace noun Halskette die (PL die Halsketten).

need noun **there's no need, I've already done it** das ist nicht nötig, ich habe es schon gemacht; **there's no need to wait** du brauchst nicht zu warten.
verb 1 brauchen; **we need bread** wir brauchen Brot; **everything you need** alles, was man braucht; 2 (to have to) müssen ◇; **I need to go to the bank** ich muss zur Bank gehen; 3 (with a negative) **you needn't wait** du brauchst nicht zu warten.

needle noun Nadel die (PL die Nadeln).

negative das (of a photo) Negativ die (PL die Negative).

neighbour noun Nachbar der (PL die Nachbarn), Nachbarin die (PL die Nachbarinnen); **we're going round to the neighbours'** wir besuchen die Nachbarn.

neighbourhood noun Nachbarschaft die; **in our neighbourhood** in unserer Nachbarschaft.

neither conjunction 1 **neither ... nor** weder ... noch; **I have neither the time nor the money** ich habe weder die Zeit noch das Geld; 2 **neither do I** ich auch nicht; **'I don't like fish' – 'neither do I'** 'ich mag keinen Fisch' – 'ich auch nicht'; **'I didn't like the film' – 'neither did Kirsty'** 'mir hat der Film nicht gefallen' – 'Kirsty hat er auch nicht gefallen'.
pronoun keiner von beiden/keine von beiden/keins von beiden; **'which do you like?' – 'neither'** 'welches gefällt dir?' – 'keins von beiden'.

nephew noun Neffe der (PL die Neffen).

nerve noun Nerv der (PL die Nerven); 1 **to lose your nerve** die Nerven verlieren; **you've got a nerve!** du hast Nerven! (informal);

2 what a nerve! so eine Frechheit!; ★ he gets on my nerves er geht mir auf die Nerven (*informal*).

nervous *adjective* **1** (*afraid*) ängstlich; to feel nervous about something Angst vor etwas ←(DAT) haben; **2** (*highly strung*) nervös (*person*).

net *noun* Netz *das* (PL die Netze).

Netherlands *noun* Niederlande (*plural*); in the Netherlands in den Niederlanden.

nettle *noun* Nessel *die* (PL die Nesseln).

neutral *noun* (*neutral gear*) Leerlauf *der*; to be in neutral im Leerlauf sein.
adjective neutral.

never *adverb* **1** nie; Ben never smokes Ben raucht nie; I've never told him ich habe es ihm nie gesagt; never again nie wieder; **2** noch nie; 'have you ever been to Spain?' – 'no, never' 'warst du schon mal in Spanien?' – 'nein, noch nie'; **3** never mind macht nichts.

new *adjective* neu; have you seen their new house? hast du ihr neues Haus gesehen?

news *noun* **1** (*new information*) Nachricht *die* (PL die Nachrichten); I've got good news ich habe gute Nachrichten; **2** a piece of news eine Neuigkeit; any news? was gibt es Neues?; **3** (*on TV or the radio*) Nachrichten (*plural*); we saw it on the news wir haben es in den Nachrichten gesehen.

newsagent *noun* Zeitungshändler *der* (PL die Zeitungshändler).

newspaper *noun* Zeitung *die* (PL die Zeitungen).

newsreader *noun* Nachrichtensprecher *der* (PL die Nachrichtensprecher), Nachrichtensprecherin *die* (PL die Nachrichtensprecherinnen).

New Year *noun* Neujahr *das*; Happy New Year! ein gutes neues Jahr!

New Year's Day *noun* Neujahr *das*.

New Year's Eve *noun* Silvester *der*.

New Zealand *noun* Neuseeland *das*.

next *adjective* **1** nächster/nächste/ nächstes; the next train leaves at ten der nächste Zug fährt um zehn ab; next week nächste Woche; next Thursday nächsten Donnerstag; next year nächstes Jahr; next time I see you nächstes Mal, wenn ich dich sehe; **2** (*following*) next please! der Nächste bitte/die Nächste bitte; the next thing das Nächste; the next day am nächsten Tag; the letter arrived the next day der Brief kam am nächsten Tag an; **3** the week after next übernächste Woche; **4** (*next-door*) nebenan; I'm in the next room ich bin nebenan.
adverb (*afterwards*) danach; what did he say next? was hat er danach gesagt?; **2** (*now*) als Nächstes; what

△ NEW SPELLING: See page xii

shall we do next? was machen wir als Nächstes?; **3 next to** neben (+DAT, or +ACC *with movement towards a place*); **the house next to the baker's** das Haus neben dem Bäcker; **I sat down next to her** ich habe mich neben sie gesetzt.

next door *adverb* nebenan; **they live next door** sie wohnen nebenan; **the girl next door** das Mädchen von nebenan.

nice *adjective* 1 (*pleasant*) schön; **we had a nice evening** wir haben einen schönen Abend verbracht; **Brighton's a nice town** Brighton ist eine schöne Stadt; **we had nice weather** wir hatten schönes Wetter; **2 to have a nice time** sich amüsieren; **have a nice day!** viel Spaß!; **3** (*attractive to look at*) hübsch; **that's a nice dress** das ist ein hübsches Kleid; **4** (*kind, friendly*) nett (*person*); **she's really nice** sie ist wirklich nett; **5 to be nice to somebody** nett zu jemandem sein; **she's been very nice to me** sie war sehr nett zu mir; **6** (*tasting good*) gut; **it tastes nice** es schmeckt gut.

niece *noun* Nichte *die* (PL *die* Nichten).

night *noun* 1 (*after bedtime*) Nacht *die* (PL *die* Nächte); **during the night** während der Nacht; **Sunday night** Sonntag Nacht; **it's cold at night** nachts ist es kalt; **to stay the night** über Nacht bleiben; **I stayed the night at Emma's** ich habe bei Emma übernachtet; **2** (*before you go to bed*) Abend *der*

(PL *die* Abende); **what are you doing tonight?** was machst ihr heute Abend?; **one night** eines Abends; **tomorrow night** morgen Abend; **I met Greg last night** ich habe Greg gestern Abend getroffen; **on Friday night** am Freitagabend; **see you tonight!** bis heute Abend!

night club *noun* Nachtklub *der* (PL *die* Nachtklubs).

nightie *noun* Nachthemd *das* (PL *die* Nachthemden).

nightmare *noun* Alptraum *der* (PL *die* Alpträume).

nil *noun* (*in sport*) null; **they won four-nil** sie haben vier zu null gewonnen.

nine *number* neun.

nineteen *number* neunzehn.

ninety *number* neunzig.

ninth *number* neunter/neunte/neuntes; **on the ninth floor** im neunten Stock; **on the ninth of June** am neunten Juni.

no *adverb* nein; **I said no** ich habe nein gesagt; **no thank you** nein danke.
adjective 1 kein; **we've got no bread** wir haben kein Brot; **no problem!** kein Problem!; **2** (*on a notice*) **'no smoking'** 'Rauchen verboten'; **'no parking'** 'Parken verboten'.

nobody *pronoun* niemand; **'who's there?' – 'nobody'** 'wer ist da?' – 'niemand'; **there's nobody in the kitchen** es ist niemand in der

Küche; **nobody was at home**
niemand war zu Hause.

nod verb nicken; **he nodded in
agreement** er hat zustimmend
genickt.

noise noun Lärm der; **to make a
noise** Lärm machen.

noisy adjective laut.

none pronoun 1 (not one)
keiner/keine/keins; **none of us**
keiner von uns/ keine von uns; **'how
many students failed the exam?'** –
'none' 'wie viele Schüler sind durch
die Prüfung gefallen?' – 'keine';
none of the boys knows him keiner
der Jungen kennt ihn; 2 **there's
none left** es ist nichts mehr übrig.

nonsense noun Unsinn der; **to talk
nonsense** Unsinn reden;
nonsense! Unsinn!

non-stop adjective durchgehend
(train); Nonstop- (flight);
adverb ununterbrochen;
she talks non-stop sie redet
ununterbrochen.

noon noun Mittag der; **at (twelve)
noon** um zwölf (Uhr mittags).

no-one pronoun niemand; **'who's
there?'** – **'no-one'** 'wer ist da?' –
'niemand'; **there's no-one in the
kitchen** es ist niemand in der
Küche; **no-one was at home**
niemand war zu Hause.

nor conjunction 1 neither ... nor
weder ... noch; **I have neither the
time nor the money** ich habe weder
die Zeit noch das Geld; 2 **nor do I**
ich auch nicht; **'I don't like fish'** –

'nor do I' 'ich mag keinen Fisch' –
'ich auch nicht'; **nor do we** wir
auch nicht.

normal adjective normal.

normally adverb 1 (usually)
normalerweise; 2 (in a normal way)
normal.

north noun Norden der; **in the
north** im Norden.
adjective nördlich, Nord-; **the north
side** die Nordseite; **north wind** der
Nordwind.
adverb 1 (towards the north) nach
Norden; **to travel north** nach
Norden fahren; 2 **north of London**
nördlich von London.

North America noun
Nordamerika das.

northeast noun Nordosten der.
adjective **in northeast England** in
Nordostengland.

Northern Ireland noun
Nordirland das.

North Pole noun Nordpol der.

North Sea noun **the North Sea** die
Nordsee.

northwest noun Nordwesten der.
adjective **in northwest England** in
Nordwestengland.

Norway noun Norwegen das.

Norwegian noun 1 (person)
Norweger der (PL die Norweger),
Norwegerin die (PL die
Norwegerinnen); 2 (language)
Norwegisch das.
adjective norwegisch.

△ NEW SPELLING: See page xii

nose noun Nase die (PL die Nasen); **to blow your nose** sich ←(DAT) die Nase putzen.

not adverb 1 nicht; **not on Sundays** sonntags nicht; **not all alone** nicht ganz allein!; **not bad** nicht schlecht; **not at all** überhaupt nicht; **not yet** noch nicht; **Sam didn't phone** Sam hat nicht angerufen; **I hope not** hoffentlich nicht; 2 **not a** kein/keine; **he's not a specialist** er ist kein Fachmann; **not a bit** kein bisschen.

note noun 1 (a short letter) Zettel der (PL die Zettel) (informal), Brief der (PL die Briefe); 2 (in a class) Notiz die (PL die Notizen); **to take notes** sich ←(DAT) Notizen machen; 3 (a banknote) Schein der (PL die Scheine); **a ten-pound note** ein Zehnpfundschein; 4 (in music) Note die (PL die Noten).

notebook noun Notizbuch das (PL die Notizbücher).

notepad noun Notizblock der (PL die Notizblöcke).

nothing pronoun nichts; **'what did you say?' – 'nothing'** 'was hast du gesagt?' – 'nichts'; **nothing special** nichts Besonderes; **nothing new** nichts Neues; **I saw nothing** ich habe nichts gesehen; **there's nothing left** es ist nichts mehr übrig.

notice noun 1 (a sign) Anschlag der (PL die Anschläge); 2 (an advertisement) Anzeige die (PL die Anzeigen); 3 (advance warning) Ankündigung die; 4 **don't take any notice of her** nimm keine Notiz von ihr; 5 **at short notice** kurzfristig. verb bemerken; **I didn't notice anything** ich habe nichts bemerkt.

notice board noun Anschlagbrett das (PL die Anschlagbretter).

nought noun Null die (PL die Nullen).

noun noun Substantiv das (PL die Substantive).

novel noun Roman der (PL die Romane).

novelist noun Romanautor der (PL die Romanautoren), Romanautorin die (PL die Romanautorinnen).

November noun November der; **in November** im November.

now adverb 1 jetzt; **where is he now?** wo ist er jetzt?; **from now on** von jetzt an; 2 **he left just now** er ist gerade eben gegangen; **I saw her just now in the corridor** ich habe sie gerade eben im Gang gesehen; 3 **do it right now!** mach es sofort!; 4 **now and then** hin und wieder.

nowhere adjective nirgends; **there's nowhere to park** man kann nirgends parken.

nuclear adjective Kern-; **nuclear power** die Kernenergie; **nuclear power station** das Kernkraftwerk.

nude noun **in the nude** nackt. adjective nackt.

nuisance noun **it's a nuisance** das ist ärgerlich; **what a nuisance!** wie ärgerlich!

✦ IRREGULAR VERB: See the verb table in the centre of the dictionary.

numb adjective 1 (with cold)
gefühllos; 2 (emotionally)
benommen.

number noun 1 (of a house,
telephone, or account) Nummer die
(PL die Nummern); **I live at number
five** ich wohne Nummer fünf; **my
new phone number** meine neue
Telefonnummer; 2 (a written figure)
Zahl die (PL die Zahlen); 3 (amount)
Anzahl die; **the number of visitors**
die Anzahl der Besucher.

number plate noun
Nummernschild das (PL die
Nummernschilder).

nun noun Nonne die (PL die
Nonnen).

nurse noun Krankenschwester die
(PL die Krankenschwestern); **Janet's
a nurse** Janet ist Krankenschwester.

nursery noun 1 (for children)
Kindertagesstätte die (PL die
Kindertagesstätten); 2 (for plants)
Gärtnerei die (PL die Gärtnereien).

nursery school noun
Kindergarten der (PL die
Kindergärten).

nut noun 1 Nuss△ die (PL die Nüsse);
2 (for a bolt) Mutter die (PL die
Muttern).

nylon noun Nylon das.

O o

oak noun Eiche die (PL die Eichen).

oar noun Ruder das (PL die Ruder).

oats noun Hafer der; **porridge oats**
Haferflocken (plural).

obedient adjective gehorsam.

obey verb 1 gehorchen (+DAT); **to
obey somebody** jemandem
gehorchen; 2 **to obey the rules** sich
an die Vorschriften halten ◇.

object noun 1 (thing)
Gegenstand der (PL die
Gegenstände); 2 (aim) Zweck der;
3 (in grammar) Objekt das (PL die
Objekte).
verb etwas dagegen haben ◇; **if you
don't object** wenn Sie nichts
dagegen haben.

objection noun Einwand der (PL die
Einwände).

observe verb beobachten.

obsessed adjective besessen; **she's
really obsessed with her diet** sie
ist von ihrer Schlankheitskur ganz
besessen.

obstinate adjective starrsinnig.

obtain verb erhalten ◇.

obvious adjective eindeutig.

obviously adverb 1 (of course)
natürlich; 2 (looking at something)
offensichtlich; **the house is**

obviously empty das Haus steht offensichtlich leer.

occasion noun Gelegenheit die (PL die Gelegenheiten); **on special occasions** zu besonderen Gelegenheiten.

occasionally adverb gelegentlich.

occupation noun Beruf der (PL die Berufe).

occupied adjective 1 (taken) besetzt; **the seat is occupied** der Platz ist besetzt; 2 (lived in) bewohnt.

occur verb 1 **to occur to somebody** jemandem einfallen ◊ SEP (PERF sein); **it occurs to me that ...** mir fällt ein, dass ...; 2 **it never occurred to me** darauf wäre ich nie gekommen; 3 (happen) sich ereignen.

ocean noun Ozean der (PL die Ozeane).

o'clock adverb **at ten o'clock** um zehn Uhr; **it's three o'clock** es ist drei Uhr.

October noun Oktober der; **in October** im Oktober.

odd adjective 1 (strange) komisch; **that's odd, I'm sure I heard the bell** das ist komisch, ich habe es bestimmt klingeln gehört; 2 (number) ungerade; **three is an odd number** drei ist eine ungerade Zahl; 3 **the odd one out** die Ausnahme.

odds and ends plural noun Kleinkram der.

of preposition 1 von (+DAT); (instead of translating 'of' with 'von', the genitive case can be used) **the parents of the children** die Eltern von den Kindern, die Eltern der Kinder; **the name of the flower** der Name der Blume; **it's very kind of you** das ist sehr nett von Ihnen; 2 (with quantities 'of' is not translated) **a kilo of tomatoes** ein Kilo Tomaten; **a bottle of milk** eine Flasche Milch; **the three of us** wir drei; 3 **of it/them** davon (things); **of them** von ihnen (people); **how many of them didn't pay?** wie viele von ihnen haben nicht gezahlt?; **Ray has four cars but he's selling three of them** Ray hat vier Autos, aber er verkauft drei davon; **half of it** die Hälfte davon; **we ate a lot of it** wir haben viel davon gegessen; 4 **the sixth of June** der sechste Juni; 5 **made of** aus; **a bracelet made of silver** ein Armband aus Silber.

off adverb, adjective, preposition 1 (switched off) aus; **is the telly off?** ist der Fernseher aus?; **to turn off the lights** das Licht ausmachen SEP; 2 (electricity, water, gas) abgestellt; **the gas and electricity were off** Gas und Strom waren abgestellt; **to turn off the tap** den Wasserhahn zudrehen SEP; 3 **to be off** (to leave) gehen ◊ (PERF sein); (in a vehicle) fahren ◊ (PERF sein); **I must be off** ich muss gehen; 4 **on my day off** an meinem freien Tag; **to take three days off work** sich ◊ (DAT) drei Tage frei nehmen; **we were given two days off school** wir hatten zwei Tage schulfrei; **to be off sick** wegen Krankheit fehlen; **Maya's off school today** Maya fehlt heute in der

---

◊ IRREGULAR VERB: See the verb table in the centre of the dictionary

Schule; **5** (*cancelled*) abgesagt; **the match is off** das Spiel ist abgesagt worden; **6 '20% off shoes'** 'Schuhe 20% reduziert'.

offence *noun* **1** (*crime*) Straftat *die* (PL *die* Straftaten); **2 to take offence** beleidigt sein; **he takes offence easily** er ist schnell beleidigt.

offer *noun* **1** Angebot *das* (PL *die* Angebote); **job offer** *das* Stellenangebot; **2 on special offer** im Sonderangebot.
verb anbieten ◊ SEP (*a present, a reward, or a job*); **he offered her a chair** er bot ihr einen Stuhl an; **to offer to do something** anbieten, etwas zu tun; **he offered to drive me to the station** er hat angeboten, mich zum Bahnhof zu fahren.

office *noun* Büro *das* (PL *die* Büros); **he's still at the office** er ist noch im Büro.

office block *noun* Bürohaus *das* (PL *die* Bürohäuser).

official *adjective* offiziell.

off-licence *noun* Wein- und Spirituosenhandlung *die* (PL *die* Wein- und Spirituosenhandlungen).

often *adverb* **1** oft; **he's often late** er kommt oft zu spät; **how often? wie oft?; 2 more often** öfter; **couldn't you come more often?** könntest du nicht öfter kommen?

oil *noun* **1** (*crude oil*) Öl *das*; **2 olive oil** *das* Olivenöl; **suntan oil** *das* Sonnenöl.

ointment *noun* Salbe *die* (PL *die* Salben).

okay *adjective* **1** okay (*informal*); **tomorrow at ten, okay?** morgen um zehn, okay?; **is it okay if I don't come till Friday?** ist es okay, wenn ich erst Freitag komme?; **2** (*person*) in Ordnung; **Daisy's okay** Daisy ist in Ordnung; **3** (*nothing special, not ill*) ganz gut; **the film was okay** der Film war ganz gut; **I've been ill but I'm okay now** ich war krank, aber jetzt geht es mir ganz gut; **'how are you?' – 'okay'** 'wie geht's?' – 'ganz gut'; **4 it's okay by me** mir ist es recht.

old *adjective* **1** (*not young, not new, previous*) alt; **an old man** ein alter Mann; **an old lady** eine alte Dame; **an old tree** ein alter Baum; **old people** alte Leute; **bring some old clothes** bring ein paar alte Sachen mit; **I've only got their old address** ich habe nur ihre alte Adresse; **2** (*talking about age*) **how old are you?** wie alt bist du?; **James is ten years old** James ist zehn Jahre alt; **3 a two-year-old child** ein zweijähriges Kind; **4 my older sister** meine ältere Schwester; **she's older than me** sie ist älter als ich; **he's a year older than me** er ist ein Jahr älter als ich.

old age *noun* Alter *das*.

old age pensioner *noun* Rentner *der* (PL *die* Rentner), Rentnerin *die* (PL *die* Rentnerinnen).

old-fashioned *noun* altmodisch.

olive *noun* Olive *die* (PL *die* Oliven).

△ NEW SPELLING: *See page xii*

olive oil noun Olivenöl das (PL die Olivenöle).

Olympic Games, Olympics plural noun Olympische Spiele (plural).

omelette noun Omelett das (PL die Omelette); **a cheese omelette** ein Käseomelett.

on preposition 1 auf (+DAT, or +ACC with movement towards a place); **it's on the desk** es ist auf dem Schreibtisch; 2 (attached to) an (+DAT, or +ACC with movement towards a place); **on the wall** an der Wand; 3 **on the beach** am Strand; **on the right/left** rechts/links; 4 (in expressions of time) **on March 21st** am 21. März; **he's arriving on Tuesday** er kommt am Dienstag an; **it's shut on Sundays** es ist sonntags geschlossen; **on rainy days** an Regentagen; 5 (for buses, trains, etc.) **to go on the bus** mit dem Bus fahren; **I met Jackie on the train** ich habe Jackie im Zug getroffen; **let's go on our bikes** fahren wir mit dem Rad; 6 **on TV** im Fernsehen; **on the radio** im Radio; **on video** auf Video; 7 **on holiday** in den Ferien. adjective 1 (switched on) **to be or on** an sein; **the lights are on** das Licht ist an; **is the radio on?** ist das Radio an?; 2 (happening) **what's on TV?** was gibt's im Fernsehen?; **what's on this week at the cinema?** was läuft diese Woche im Kino?

once adverb 1 einmal; **I've tried once already** ich habe es schon einmal versucht; **try once more** versuch es noch einmal; **once a day**

einmal täglich; 2 **more than once** mehrmals; 3 **at once** (immediately) sofort; **the doctor came at once** der Arzt kam sofort; 4 **at once** (at the same time) gleichzeitig; **I can't do two things at once** ich kann nicht zwei Sachen gleichzeitig machen.

one number (when counting) eins; (with a noun) ein; **one son** ein Sohn; **one apple** ein Apfel; **if you want a biro I've got one** falls du einen Kugelschreiber brauchst, habe ich einen; **at one o'clock** um ein Uhr. pronoun 1 einer/eine/eins; **I saw the photos, can I have one of them?** ich habe die Fotos gesehen, kann ich eins davon haben?; 2 **this one** dieser/diese/dieses; **I'd prefer that bike, but this one's cheaper** ich würde lieber das Rad haben, aber dieses ist billiger; 3 **that one** der da/die da/das da; **'which video?' – 'that one'** welches Video?' – 'das da'; 4 **which one?** welcher/welche/welches?; **'my foot's hurting' – 'which one?'** 'mir tut der Fuß weh' – 'welcher?'; **she borrowed a skirt from me' – 'which one?'** 'sie hat sich einen Rock von mir geliehen' – 'welchen?'; 5 (you) man; **one never knows** man kann nie wissen.

one's adjective sein/seine/sein; **one pays for one's car** man zahlt für sein Auto.

oneself pronoun 1 (reflexive) sich; **to wash oneself** sich waschen; 2 (stressing something) selbst; **one**

---

has to do everything oneself man muss alles selbst machen.

one-way street noun Einbahnstraße die (PL die Einbahnstraßen).

onion noun Zwiebel die (PL die Zwiebeln).

only adjective 1 einziger/einzige/einziges; **the only free seat** der einzige freie Platz; **the only thing you could do** das Einzige, was du machen könntest; 2 **an only child** ein Einzelkind.
adverb, conjunction 1 nur; **they've only got two bedrooms** sie haben nur zwei Schlafzimmer; **Anne's only free on Fridays** Anne ist nur freitags frei; **there are only three left** es sind nur noch drei übrig; **I'd walk, only it's raining** ich würde zu Fuß gehen, nur regnet es; 2 (very recently) gerade erst; **he's only just got the message** er hat die Nachricht gerade erst bekommen; 3 (barely) gerade noch; **we've only just made it on time** wir sind gerade noch rechtzeitig angekommen.

onto preposition auf (+ACC).

open noun **in the open** im Freien.
adjective 1 offen; **the door's open** die Tür ist offen; **the baker's is not open** die Bäckerei ist nicht geöffnet; 2 **in the open air** im Freien.
verb 1 aufmachen SEP; **can you open the door for me?** kannst du mir die Tür aufmachen?; **the bank opens at nine** die Bank macht um neun auf; 2 (open up) sich öffnen; **the door opened slowly** die Tür öffnete sich langsam.

opera noun Oper die (PL die Opern).

operation noun 1 Operation die (PL die Operationen); 2 **to have an operation** operiert werden.

opinion noun Meinung die (PL die Meinungen); **in my opinion** meiner Meinung nach.

opinion poll noun Meinungsumfrage die (PL die Meinungsumfragen).

opportunity noun Gelegenheit die (PL die Gelegenheiten); **to have the opportunity of doing something** die Gelegenheit haben, etwas zu tun.

opposite noun Gegenteil das (PL die Gegenteile); **no, quite the opposite** nein, ganz im Gegenteil.
adjective 1 entgegengesetzt (direction); **she went off in the opposite direction** sie ging in die entgegengesetzte Richtung; 2 (facing) gegenüberliegend; **in the house opposite** im gegenüberliegenden Haus.
adverb gegenüber; **they live opposite** sie wohnen gegenüber.
preposition gegenüber (+DAT); **opposite the station** gegenüber dem Bahnhof.

optician noun Optiker der (PL die Optiker), Optikerin die (PL die Optikerinnen).

option noun Wahl die; **we have no option** wir haben keine andere Wahl.

optional adjective auf Wunsch erhältlich; **optional subject** das Wahlfach.

△ NEW SPELLING: See page xii

or *conjunction* 1 oder; **English or German?** Englisch oder Deutsch?; **today or Tuesday?** heute oder Dienstag?; 2 (*in negatives*) noch; **I don't have a cat or a dog** ich habe weder eine Katze noch einen Hund; **not in June or July** weder im Juni noch im Juli; 3 (*or else*) sonst; **phone Mum, or she'll worry** ruf Mutti an, sonst macht sie sich Sorgen.

oral *noun* (*an exam*) Mündliche *das* (*informal*); **my German oral** mein Deutschmündliches.

orange *noun* (*the fruit*) Orange *die* (PL die Orangen); **orange juice** *der* Orangensaft.
adjective orange ('*orange*' *never changes*); **my orange socks** meine orange Socken.

orchestra *noun* Orchester *das* (PL die Orchester).

order *noun* 1 (*sequence*) Reihenfolge *die* (PL die Reihenfolgen); **in the right order** in der richtigen Reihenfolge; **in the wrong order** nicht in der richtigen Reihenfolge; **in alphabetical order** in alphabetischer Reihenfolge; 2 (*in a restaurant, café, or shop*) Bestellung *die* (PL die Bestellungen); 3 '**out of order**' 'außer Betrieb'; 4 **in order to do something** um etwas zu tun.
verb 1 (*in a restaurant or a shop*) bestellen; **we ordered soup** wir haben Suppe bestellt; **have you ordered?** haben Sie schon bestellt?; 2 bestellen (*a taxi*).

ordinary *adjective* normal.

organ *noun* 1 (*the instrument*) Orgel *die* (PL die Orgeln); 2 (*of the body*) Organ *das* (PL die Organe).

organic *adjective* Bio- (*food*); **organic food** die Biokost.

organization *noun* Organisation *die* (PL die Organisationen).

organize *verb* 1 organisieren; 2 veranstalten (*a conference or festival*).

original *adjective* 1 ursprünglich; **the original plan was better** der ursprüngliche Plan war besser; 2 originell; **it's a really original novel** das ist ein wirklich origineller Roman.

originally *adverb* ursprünglich; **originally we wanted to go by car** ursprünglich wollten wir mit dem Auto fahren.

other *adjective* 1 anderer/andere/ anderes; **we took the other road** wir haben die andere Straße genommen; **where are the others?** wo sind die anderen?; **the other two cars** die anderen beiden Autos; 2 **give me the other one** gib mir den anderen/die andere/das andere (*the translation of 'the other one' depends on the gender of the noun it refers to*); 3 **the other day** neulich; 4 **every other week** jede zweite Woche; 5 **somebody or other** irgendjemand; **something or other** irgendetwas; **somewhere or other** irgendwo; 6 **any other questions?** sonst noch Fragen?

◇ **IRREGULAR VERB: See the verb table in the centre of the dictionary**

otherwise adverb, conjunction
sonst.

ought verb ('ought' is usually
translated by the subjunctive of
'sollen') **I ought to go** ich sollte
eigentlich gehen; **they ought to
have known the address** sie
hätten die Adresse kennen sollen;
**you oughtn't to have any
problems** du solltest keine
Probleme haben.

our adjective 1 (before a masculine
noun) unser; **our father** unser
Vater; 2 (before a feminine noun)
unsere; **our mother** unsere Mutter;
3 (before a neuter noun) unser; **our
house** unser Haus; 4 (before
masculine/feminine/neuter plural
nouns) unsere; **our parents** unsere
Eltern; 5 (with parts of the body)
der/die/das (plural: die); **we'll go
and wash our hands** wir waschen
uns die Hände.

ours pronoun 1 (for a masculine
noun) unserer; **their garden's
bigger than ours** ihr Garten ist
größer als unserer; 2 (for a feminine
noun) unsere; **their kitchen is
smaller than ours** ihre Küche ist
kleiner als unsere; 3 (for a neuter
noun) unsers; **their child is younger
than ours** ihr Kind ist jünger als
unsers; 4 (for plural nouns) unsere;
**they've invited their friends and
we've invited ours** sie haben ihre
Freunde eingeladen und wir haben
unsere eingeladen; 5 **the green car
is ours** das grüne Auto gehört uns;
it's ours es gehört uns; **a friend of
ours** ein Freund von uns.

ourselves pronoun 1 (reflexive)
uns; **we introduced ourselves** wir
haben uns vorgestellt; 2 (for
emphasis) selbst; **in the end we did
it ourselves** schließlich haben wir
es selbst gemacht.

out adverb 1 (outside) draußen; **it's
cold out there** es ist kalt da
draußen; **they're out in the garden**
sie sind draußen im Garten; 2 **to go
out** hinausgehen ◇ SEP (PERF sein),
rausgehen ◇ SEP (PERF sein)
(informal); **to go out shopping**
einkaufen gehen; 3 **get out!** raus!
(informal); 4 **the ball is out** der Ball
ist aus; 5 (absent) **to be out** nicht
da sein; **Mr Barnes is out** Herr
Barnes ist nicht da; 6 **to go out** (for
an evening or to the theatre or
cinema) ausgehen ◇ SEP (PERF sein),
weggehen ◇ SEP (PERF sein)
(informal); **are you going out this
evening?** gehst du heute Abend
weg?; **to be going out with
somebody** mit jemandem gehen;
Alison's going out with Danny now
Alison geht jetzt mit Danny; 7 **to ask
somebody out** jemanden
einladen ◇ SEP; **he's asked me out**
er hat mich eingeladen; 8 (light,
fire) aus; **are all the lights out?** ist
das Licht aus?
preposition **out of** aus (+DAT); **to go
out of the room** aus dem Zimmer
gehen; **he threw it out of the
window** er hat es aus dem Fenster
geworfen; **to drink out of a glass**
aus einem Glas trinken; **she took the
photo out of her bag** sie hat das
Foto aus der Tasche genommen.

△ NEW SPELLING: See page xii

outdoor adjective (activity or sport) im Freien; **outdoor games** Spiele im Freien.

outdoors adverb draußen; **to go outdoors** nach draußen gehen.

outing noun Ausflug der (PL die Ausflüge); **to go on an outing** einen Ausflug machen.

outline noun (of an object) Umriss der (PL die Umrisse).

out-of-date adjective 1 (no longer valid) ungültig; **my passport's out of date** mein Pass ist ungültig; 2 (old-fashioned) altmodisch (clothes, music).

outside noun Außenseite die; **it's blue on the outside** auf der Außenseite ist es blau.
adjective Außen-.
adverb draußen; **it's cold outside** es ist kalt draußen.
preposition vor (+DAT); **I'll meet you outside the cinema** ich treffe mich vor dem Kino mit dir.

oven noun Ofen der (PL die Öfen); **to put something in the oven** etwas in den Ofen tun.

over preposition 1 (above) über ←(DAT); **there's a mirror over the sink** über dem Waschbecken hängt ein Spiegel; 2 (involving movement) über (+ACC); **he threw the ball over the wall** er hat den Ball über die Mauer geworfen; 3 **over here** hier drüben; **the food is over here** das Essen ist hier drüben; 4 **over there** da drüben; **she's over there** sie ist da drüben; 5 (more than) über; **it will cost over**

a hundred pounds es wird über hundert Pfund kosten; **he's over sixty** er ist über sechzig; 6 (during) über (+ACC); **over Christmas** über Weihnachten; **over the weekend** übers Wochenende; 7 (finished) zu Ende; **when the meeting's over** wenn die Besprechung zu Ende ist; **it's all over** es ist vorbei; 8 **over the phone** am Telefon; **to ask someone over** jemanden einladen ✧ SEP; **to come over** herüberkommen ✧ SEP; **come over on Saturday** komm am Samstag zu uns herüber; **all over the place** überall; **I've been looking for it all over** ich habe überall danach gesucht.

overtake verb überholen.

overtime noun **to work overtime** Überstunden machen.

overweight adjective **to be overweight** Übergewicht haben.

owe verb schulden; **I owe him ten pounds** ich schulde ihm zehn Pfund.

owing adjective 1 (outstanding) ausstehend; **there's five pounds owing** fünf Pfund stehen aus; 2 **owing to** wegen (+GEN); **owing to the snow** wegen des Schnees.

owl noun Eule die (PL die Eulen).

own adjective 1 eigen; **my own computer** mein eigener Computer; **I've got my own room** ich habe mein eigenes Zimmer; 2 **on your own** allein; **Annie did it on her own** Annie hat es allein gemacht.
verb besitzen ✧.

✧ IRREGULAR VERB: See the verb table in the centre of the dictionary.

owner noun Besitzer der (PL die Besitzer), Besitzerin die (PL die Besitzerinnen).

oxygen noun Sauerstoff der.

ozone layer noun Ozonschicht die.

P p

pace noun 1 (a step) Schritt der (PL die Schritte); 2 (the speed you walk at) Tempo das (PL die Tempos).

Pacific noun the Pacific (Ocean) der Pazifik.

pack noun 1 Packung die (PL die Packungen); 2 pack of cards das Kartenspiel.
verb 1 packen (your case); I haven't packed yet ich habe noch nicht gepackt; I'll pack my case tonight ich packe meinen Koffer heute Abend; 2 einpacken SEP (clothes, shoes, etc.); have you packed my red shirt? hast du mein rotes Hemd eingepackt?

package noun Paket das (PL die Pakete).

packed lunch noun Lunchpaket das (PL die Lunchpakete).

packet noun 1 Päckchen das (PL die Päckchen); a packet of tea ein Päckchen Tee; (box) Schachtel die (PL die Schachteln); 3 (bag) Tüte die (PL die Tüten); a packet of crisps eine Tüte Chips.

pad noun (of paper) Block der (PL die Blöcke).

page noun Seite die (PL die Seiten); on page seven auf Seite sieben.

pain noun Schmerz der (PL die Schmerzen); to be in pain Schmerzen haben; I've got a pain in my leg ich habe Schmerzen im Bein; ★ Eric's a real pain (in the neck) Eric geht einem richtig auf den Wecker (informal).

painful adjective schmerzhaft.

paint noun Farbe die (PL die Farben); 'wet paint' 'frisch gestrichen'. verb malen (a picture); streichen ◇ (a room); to paint a room pink ein Zimmer rosa streichen.

paintbrush noun Pinsel der (PL die Pinsel).

painter noun Maler der (PL die Maler), Malerin die (PL die Malerinnen).

painting noun (picture) Gemälde das (PL die Gemälde); a painting by Picasso ein Gemälde von Picasso.

pair noun 1 Paar das (PL die Paare); a pair of socks ein Paar Socken; 2 a pair of scissors eine Schere; 3 a pair of trousers eine Hose; a pair of knickers eine Unterhose; 4 to work in pairs paarweise arbeiten.

Pakistan noun Pakistan das.

palace noun Palast der (PL die Paläste).

pale adjective blass △; to turn pale blass werden; pale green zartgrün.

△ NEW SPELLING: See page xii

palm noun **1** (*of your hand*)
Handfläche die (PL die
Handflächen); **2** (*a palm tree*)
Palme die (PL die Palmen).

pan noun **1** (*saucepan*) Topf der (PL
die Töpfe); **a pan of water** ein Topf
Wasser; **2** (*frying-pan*) Pfanne die
(PL die Pfannen).

pancake noun Pfannkuchen der
(PL die Pfannkuchen).

panel noun **1** (*for a discussion*)
Diskussionsrunde die; (*for a quiz*)
Rateteam das; **2** (*a piece of wood*)
Tafel die (PL die Tafeln).

panic noun Panik die.
verb in Panik geraten ◇; **don't
panic!** keine Panik!

pantomime noun
Märchenvorstellung die (PL die
Märchenvorstellungen).

pants plural noun Unterhose die (PL
die Unterhosen).

paper noun **1** Papier das; **a sheet of
paper** ein Blatt Papier; **2 paper
hanky** das Papiertaschentuch;
3 paper cup der Pappbecher;
4 (*newspaper*) Zeitung die (PL die
Zeitungen); **it was in the paper** es
stand in der Zeitung; **5 papers**
(*documents*) Unterlagen (plural).

paperback noun Taschenbuch das
(PL die Taschenbücher).

paperclip noun Büroklammer die
(PL die Büroklammern).

paper towel noun
Papierhandtuch das (PL die
Papierhandtücher).

parachute noun Fallschirm der (PL
die Fallschirme).

parade noun Umzug der (PL die
Umzüge).

paragraph noun Absatz der (PL die
Absätze); **'new paragraph'** 'Absatz'.

paralysed adjective gelähmt.

parcel noun Paket das (PL die
Pakete).

pardon noun **I beg your pardon** (*as
an apology*) Entschuldigung!;
pardon? wie bitte?

parent noun Elternteil der;
parents Eltern (plural); **my parents
live in Germany** meine Eltern
wohnen in Deutschland; **parents'
evening** der Elternabend.

park noun **1** Park der (PL die Parks);
theme park der (thematische)
Freizeitpark; **2 car park** der
Parkplatz.
verb **1** parken; **you can park outside
the house** du kannst vor dem Haus
parken; **2 to find somewhere to
park** einen Parkplatz finden.

parking noun Parken das; **'no
parking'** 'Parken verboten'.

parking meter noun Parkuhr die
(PL die Parkuhren).

parking space noun
Parklücke die (PL die Parklücken).

parking ticket noun
Strafzettel der (PL die Strafzettel).

parliament noun Parlament das
(PL die Parlamente).

parrot noun Papagei der (PL die
Papageien).

◇ IRREGULAR VERB: *See the verb table in the centre of the dictionary*

parsley noun Petersilie die.

part noun 1 Teil der (PL die Teile);
part of the garden Teil des Gartens;
the last part of the book der letzte
Teil des Buches; 2 that's part of
your job das gehört dazu; 3 to take
part in something an etwas ←(DAT)
teilnehmen ◇ SEP; 4 (spare part)
Teil das (PL die Teile) (for a machine
or an engine); 5 (a role in a play)
Rolle die (PL die Rollen).

particular adjective
besonderer/besondere/besonderes;
nothing in particular nichts
Besonderes.

particularly adverb besonders; not
particularly interesting nicht
besonders interessant.

partly adverb teilweise.

partner noun Partner der (PL die
Partner), Partnerin die (PL die
Partnerinnen).

part-time adjective Teilzeit-;
part-time work die Teilzeitarbeit.
adverb to work part-time Teilzeit
arbeiten.

party noun 1 (small, private) Party
die (PL die Partys), Feier die
(PL die Feiern); a Christmas party
eine Weihnachtsfeier; to have a
birthday party eine
Geburtstagsparty machen;
2 (more formal, in the evening)
Gesellschaft die (PL die
Gesellschaften); we've been invited
to a party at the Smiths' house wir
sind zu einer Gesellschaft bei Smiths
eingeladen worden; 3 (group)
Gruppe die (PL die Gruppen); a party
of schoolchildren eine Gruppe

Schulkinder; 4 (in politics)
Partei die (PL die Parteien).

party game noun
Gesellschaftsspiel das (PL die
Gesellschaftsspiele).

pass noun 1 (to let you in)
Ausweis der (PL die Ausweise); 2 bus
pass die Buskarte; 3 (over the
mountains) Pass ∆ der (PL die
Pässe); 4 (in an exam) to get a pass
in maths die Mathematikprüfung
bestehen.
verb 1 (walk past) vorbeigehen ◇
SEP (PERF sein) an (+DAT) (a place or
building); we passed your house
wir sind an deinem Haus
vorbeigegangen; 2 (drive past)
vorbeifahren ◇ SEP (PERF sein) an
(+DAT) (a place or building);
3 (overtake) überholen (a car);
4 (give) reichen; could you pass me
the sugar please? könnten Sie mir
bitte den Zucker reichen?; 5 (time)
vergehen ◇ (PERF sein); the time
passed slowly die Zeit verging
langsam; 6 bestehen ◇ (an exam);
to pass an exam eine Prüfung
bestehen; did you pass in German?
hast du die Deutschprüfung
bestanden?

passenger noun 1 (in a plane or
ship) Passagier der (PL die
Passagiere); 2 (in a train or bus)
Fahrgast der (PL die Fahrgäste);
3 (in a car) Mitfahrer der (PL die
Mitfahrer).

Passover noun Passah das.

passport noun Reisepass ∆ der (PL
die Reisepässe), Pass ∆ der (PL die
Pässe).

password noun Kennwort das (PL die Kennwörter).

past noun Vergangenheit die; **in the past** in der Vergangenheit.
adjective 1 (recent) letzter/letzte/letztes; **in the past few weeks** in den letzten paar Wochen; 2 (over) vorbei; **winter is past** der Winter ist vorbei.
preposition, adverb 1 **to walk past something** an etwas ←(DAT) vorbeigehen ◇ SEP (PERF sein); **we went past the school** wir sind an der Schule vorbeigegangen; **to go past** vorbeifahren ◇ (PERF sein); 2 (after) nach (+DAT); **it's just past the post office** es ist kurz nach der Post; 3 (talking about time) **ten past six** zehn nach sechs; **half past four** halb fünf; **a quarter past two** Viertel nach zwei.

pasta noun Nudeln (plural); **I don't like pasta** ich mag keine Nudeln.

pastry noun 1 (for baking) Teig der; 2 (cake) Gebäck das.

path noun Weg der (PL die Wege); (very narrow) Pfad der (PL die Pfade).

pathetic adjective (useless, hopeless) jämmerlich.

patience noun 1 Geduld die; 2 (card game) Patience die.

patient noun Patient der (PL die Patienten), Patientin die (PL die Patientinnen).
adjective geduldig.

patiently adverb geduldig.

patio noun Terrasse die (PL die Terrassen).

pattern noun 1 (on wallpaper or fabric) Muster das (PL die Muster); 2 (dressmaking, knitting) Schnitt der (PL die Schnitte).

pause noun Pause die (PL die Pausen).

pavement noun Bürgersteig der (PL die Bürgersteige); **on the pavement** auf dem Bürgersteig.

paw noun Pfote die (PL die Pfoten).

pawn noun (in chess) Bauer der (PL die Bauern).

pay noun (wage) Lohn der (PL die Löhne); (salary) Gehalt das (PL die Gehälter).
verb 1 zahlen; **I'm paying** ich zahle; **to pay cash** bar zahlen; **to pay by credit card** mit Kreditkarte zahlen; **they pay £8 an hour** sie zahlen acht Pfund pro Stunde; **to pay by cheque** mit Scheck zahlen; 2 bezahlen ('bezahlen' is used when you pay a person, a bill or for something); **to pay for something** etwas bezahlen; **Tony paid for the drinks** Tony hat die Getränke bezahlt; **it's all paid for** es ist alles bezahlt; 3 **to pay somebody back** (money) jemandem Geld zurückzahlen SEP; 4 **to pay attention** aufpassen SEP; 5 **to pay a visit to somebody** jemanden besuchen.

payment noun 1 Bezahlung die (of sum, bill, debt, or fine); 2 Zahlung die (PL die Zahlungen) (of interest, tax, or fee).

pay phone noun Münzfernsprecher der (PL die Münzfernsprecher).

◇ IRREGULAR VERB: See the verb table in the centre of the dictionary

PC noun (computer) PC der (PL die PC).

pea noun Erbse die (PL die Erbsen).

peace noun Frieden der.

peaceful adjective friedlich.

peach noun Pfirsich der (PL die Pfirsiche).

peak period (for holidays) Hauptferienzeit die (PL die Hauptferienzeiten).

peak rate noun (for phoning) Höchsttarif der (PL die Höchsttarife).

peak time noun (for traffic) Stoßzeit die (PL die Stoßzeiten).

peanut noun Erdnuss △ die (PL die Erdnüsse).

peanut butter noun Erdnussbutter △ die.

pear noun Birne die (PL die Birnen).

pearl noun Perle die (PL die Perlen).

pebble noun Kieselstein der (PL die Kieselsteine).

peculiar adjective komisch.

pedal noun Pedal das (PL die Pedale).
verb (on a bike) **to pedal off** (mit dem Rad) wegfahren ◇ (PERF sein).

pedestrian noun Fußgänger der (PL die Fußgänger), Fußgängerin die (PL die Fußgängerinnen).

pedestrian crossing noun Fußgängerüberweg der (PL die Fußgängerüberwege).

pedestrian precinct noun Fußgängerzone die (PL die Fußgängerzonen).

pee noun **to have a pee** pinkeln (informal).

peel noun Schale die (PL die Schalen).
verb schälen (fruit, vegetables).

peg noun 1 (hook) Haken der (PL die Haken); 2 **clothes peg** der Kleiderhaken; 3 (for a tent) Pflock der (PL die Pflöcke).

pen noun (ball-point) Kugelschreiber der (PL die Kugelschreiber); **felt pen** der Filzstift.

penalty noun 1 (a fine) Geldstrafe die (PL die Geldstrafen); 2 (in football) Elfmeter der (PL die Elfmeter).

pence plural noun Pence (plural).

pencil noun Bleistift der (PL die Bleistifte); **to write in pencil** mit Bleistift schreiben.

pencil case noun Federmäppchen das (PL die Federmäppchen).

pencil sharpener noun Bleistiftanspitzer der (PL die Bleistiftanspitzer).

penfriend noun Brieffreund der (PL die Brieffreunde), Brieffreundin die (PL die Brieffreundinnen); **my German pen-friend is called Heidi** meine deutsche Brieffreundin heißt Heidi.

penis noun Penis der (PL die Penisse)

penny

penny noun Penny der (PL die Pence).

pension noun Rente die (PL die Renten).

pensioner noun Rentner der (PL die Rentner), Rentnerin die (PL die Rentnerinnen).

people plural noun 1 Leute (plural), Menschen (plural); ('Menschen' is used in a more formal context); most people round here die meisten Leute hier; several people verschiedene Leute; nice people nette Leute; all the people in the world alle Menschen auf der Welt; a crowd of people eine Menschenmenge; 2 (when you're counting them) Personen (plural); for ten people für zehn Personen; how many people have you invited? wie viele Personen hast du eingeladen? 3 people say that … man sagt, dass …

pepper noun 1 (spice) Pfeffer der; 2 (vegetable) Paprikaschote die (PL die Paprikaschoten).

peppermill noun Pfeffermühle die (PL die Pfeffermühlen).

peppermint noun (plant) Pfefferminze die; peppermint tea der Pfefferminztee.

per preposition pro (+ACC); ten pounds per person zehn Pfund pro Person.

per cent adverb Prozent das; sixty per cent of students sechzig Prozent der Studenten.

percentage noun Prozentsatz der (PL die Prozentsätze).

percussion noun Schlagzeug das; to play percussion Schlagzeug spielen.

perfect adjective 1 perfekt; she speaks perfect English sie spricht perfekt Englisch; 2 (ideal) herrlich (day or weather).

perfectly adverb 1 (absolutely) vollkommen; 2 (faultlessly) perfekt.

perform verb 1 spielen (a piece of music or a part); 2 singen ◊ (a song); 3 to perform a play ein Theaterstück aufführen ◊

performance noun 1 (playing or acting) Darstellung die (PL die Darstellungen); his performance as Hamlet seine Darstellung des Hamlet; 2 (show or film) Vorstellung die (PL die Vorstellungen); the performance starts at eight die Vorstellung fängt um acht Uhr an; 3 (of a play or opera) Aufführung die (PL die Aufführungen).

performer noun Künstler der (PL die Künstler), Künstlerin die (PL die Künstlerinnen).

perfume noun Parfüm das (PL die Parfüme).

perhaps adverb vielleicht; perhaps he's missed the train vielleicht hat er den Zug verpasst.

period noun 1 (length of time) Zeit die (PL die Zeiten); trial period die Probezeit; 2 (a portion of time) Zeitraum der; a two-year period

---

◊ IRREGULAR VERB: See the verb table in the centre of the dictionary

ein Zeitraum von zwei Jahren;
3 (*in school*) Stunde *die* (PL *die*
Stunden); **4** (*menstruation*)
Periode *die* (PL *die* Perioden).

perm *noun* Dauerwelle *die* (PL *die*
Dauerwellen).

permanent *adjective* **1** ständig;
2 fest (*job or address, for example*).

permanently *adverb* **1** dauernd;
2 to be permanently employed fest
angestellt sein.

permission *noun* Erlaubnis *die*; **to
get permission to do something**
Erlaubnis zu etwas ←(DAT) erhalten.

permit *noun* Genehmigung *die* (PL
die Genehmigungen).
verb **1** erlauben; **to permit
somebody to do something**
jemandem erlauben, etwas zu tun;
smoking is not permitted Rauchen
ist nicht gestattet; **2 weather
permitting** bei entsprechendem
Wetter.

person *noun* **1** Person *die* (PL *die*
Personen); **there's still room for
one more person** wir haben noch
Platz für eine Person; **2 in person**
persönlich.

personal *adjective* persönlich.

personality *noun*
Persönlichkeit *die* (PL *die*
Persönlichkeiten).

personally *adverb* persönlich;
personally, I'm against it ich
persönlich bin dagegen.

perspiration *noun* Schweiß *der*.

persuade *verb* überreden; **to
persuade somebody to come**
jemanden überreden zu kommen.

pessimistic *adjective*
pessimistisch.

pest *noun* **1** (*greenfly, for example*)
Schädling *der* (PL *die* Schädlinge);
2 (*annoying person*) Nervensäge *die*
(PL *die* Nervensägen) (*informal*).

pet *noun* **1** Haustier *das* (PL *die*
Haustiere); **do you have a pet?**
habt ihr Haustiere?; **a pet dog** ein
Hund; **2 Julie is teacher's pet** Julie
ist der Liebling des Lehrers.

petrol *noun* Benzin *das* (PL *die*
Benzine); **to fill up with petrol**
tanken; **to run out of petrol** kein
Benzin mehr haben.

petrol station *noun* Tankstelle *die*
(PL *die* Tankstellen).

pharmacy *noun* Apotheke *die* (PL
die Apotheken).

pheasant *noun* Fasan *der* (PL *die*
Fasane).

phone *noun* Telefon *das* (PL *die*
Telefone); **she's on the phone** sie
telefoniert; **I was on the phone to
Sophie** ich habe mit Sophie
telefoniert; **you can book by phone**
du kannst telefonisch buchen.
verb **1** telefonieren; **while I was
phoning** während ich telefonierte;
2 to phone somebody jemanden
anrufen ◇ SEP; **I'll phone you
tonight** ich rufe dich heute Abend
an.

phone book *noun* Telefonbuch
das (PL *die* Telefonbücher).

△ NEW SPELLING: See page xii

phone box noun Telefonzelle die (PL die Telefonzellen).

phone call noun 1 Anruf der (PL die Anrufe); to get a phone call einen Anruf erhalten; 2 to make a phone call ein Telefongespräch führen; phone calls are free Telefongespräche sind gebührenfrei.

phone card noun Telefonkarte die (PL die Telefonkarten).

phone number noun Telefonnummer die (PL die Telefonnummern).

photo noun Foto das (PL die Fotos); to take a photo ein Foto machen; to take a photo of somebody ein Foto von jemandem machen.

photocopier noun Fotokopiergerät das (PL die Fotokopiergeräte).

photocopy noun Fotokopie die (PL die Fotokopien). verb fotokopieren.

photograph noun Fotografie die (PL die Fotografien); to take a photograph ein Foto machen. verb fotografieren.

photographer noun Fotograf der (PL die Fotografen), Fotografin die (PL die Fotografinnen).

photography noun Fotografie die.

physics noun Physik die.

physiotherapist noun Physiotherapeut der (PL die Physiotherapeuten), Physiotherapeutin die (PL die Physiotherapeutinnen).

physiotherapy noun Physiotherapie die.

piano noun Klavier das (PL die Klaviere); to play the piano Klavier spielen; piano lesson die Klavierstunde.

pick noun to take your pick sich ←(DAT) etwas aussuchen SEP. verb 1 (to select) wählen; he picked his words carefully er wählte seine Worte mit Bedacht; 2 (choose for oneself) sich ←(DAT) aussuchen SEP; pick any book such dir irgendein Buch aus; 3 to pick a team eine Mannschaft aufstellen; 4 pflücken (fruit); to pick strawberries Erdbeeren pflücken.
● to pick up 1 (lift) (in die Hand) nehmen ◇; he picked up the papers er hat die Unterlagen genommen; 2 (collect) abholen SEP; I'll pick you up at six ich hole dich um sechs Uhr ab; I'll pick up the keys tomorrow ich hole die Schlüssel morgen ab.

pickpocket noun Taschendieb der (PL die Taschendiebe).

picnic noun Picknick das (PL die Picknicke); to have a picnic ein Picknick machen.

picture noun 1 Bild das (PL die Bilder); 2 to go to the pictures (the cinema) ins Kino gehen.

pie noun 1 (sweet) Kuchen der (PL die Kuchen); apple pie der Apfelkuchen; 2 (savoury) Pastete die (PL die Pasteten).

piece noun 1 (a bit) Stück das (PL die Stücke); a big piece of cheese

◇ IRREGULAR VERB: See the verb table in the centre of the dictionary

ein großes Stück Käse; 2 (*that you fit together*) Teil das (PL die Teile); **the pieces of a jigsaw** die Teile von einem Puzzle; **to take something to pieces** etwas in Einzelteile zerlegen; 3 **piece of furniture** das Möbelstück; **a piece of information** eine Information; **a piece of luck** ein Glücksfall; 4 (*coin*) Stück das (PL die Stücke); **a five-pence piece** ein Fünf-Pence-Stück.

pierce *verb* 1 durchstechen ◇ SEP; 2 **to have pierced ears** Löcher in den Ohrläppchen haben.

pig *noun* Schwein das (PL die Schweine).

pigeon *noun* Taube die (PL die Tauben).

pigtail *noun* Zopf der (PL die Zöpfe).

pile *noun* 1 (*a neat stack*) Stapel der (PL die Stapel); **a pile of plates** ein Stapel Teller; 2 (*a heap*) Haufen der (PL die Haufen).

• **to pile something up** (*neatly*) etwas aufstapeln SEP; (*in a heap*) etwas auftürmen SEP.

pill *noun* Pille die (PL die Pillen).

pillow *noun* Kopfkissen das (PL die Kopfkissen).

pilot *noun* Pilot der (PL die Piloten), Pilotin die (PL die Pilotinnen).

pimple *noun* Pickel der (PL die Pickel).

pin *noun* 1 (*for sewing*) Stecknadel die (PL die Stecknadeln); **2 a three-pin plug** ein dreipoliger Stecker.

• **to pin up** 1 hochstecken SEP (*a hem*); 2 anschlagen ◇ SEP (*a notice*).

PIN *noun* (*personal identification number*) Geheimnummer die.

pinball *noun* Flippern das; **to play pinball** flippern; **pinball machine** der Flipper.

pinch *noun* (*of salt, for example*) Prise die (PL die Prisen).

verb 1 kneifen ◇; **she pinched my arm** sie hat mich in den Arm gekniffen; 2 klauen; **somebody's pinched my bike** jemand hat mein Rad geklaut.

pine *noun* Kiefer die (PL die Kiefern); **pine furniture** Kiefernmöbel (*plural*).

pineapple *noun* Ananas die (PL die Ananas).

ping-pong *noun* Tischtennis das; **to play ping-pong** Tischtennis spielen.

pink *adjective* rosa ('*rosa*' never changes); **pink hats** rosa Hüte.

pip *noun* (*in a fruit*) Kern der (PL die Kerne).

pipe *noun* 1 (*for gas or water*) Rohr das (PL die Rohre); 2 (*for smoking*) Pfeife die (PL die Pfeifen); **he smokes a pipe** er raucht Pfeife.

Pisces *noun* Fische (*plural*); **Amanda is Pisces** Amanda ist Fisch.

pitch *noun* Platz der (PL die Plätze); **football pitch** der Fußballplatz. *verb* **to pitch a tent** ein Zelt aufstellen SEP.

△ NEW SPELLING: See page xii

pity noun 1 (*feeling sorry for somebody*) Mitleid das; 2 what a pity! wie schade!; it would be a pity to miss the beginning es wäre schade, den Anfang zu verpassen. verb to pity somebody jemanden bemitleiden.

place noun 1 (*spot*) Ort der (PL die Orte); Salzburg is a wonderful place Salzburg ist ein schöner Ort; in place an Ort und Stelle; 2 all over the place überall; 3 (*a space*) Platz der (PL die Plätze); a place for the car ein Platz für das Auto; is there a place for me? gibt es Platz für mich?; will you keep my place? kannst du mir den Platz freihalten?; to change places die Plätze tauschen; 4 (*spot*) Stelle die (PL die Stellen); this is a good place to stop das ist eine gute Stelle zum Halten; 5 (*in a race*) Platz der (PL die Plätze); to gain first place den ersten Platz belegen; 6 at your place bei dir; we'll go round to Zafir's place wir gehen zu Zafir; 7 to take place stattfinden ◇ SEP; the competition will take place at four der Wettbewerb findet um vier Uhr statt. verb (*upright*) stellen; (*lying flat*) legen.

plain noun Ebene die (PL die Ebenen). adjective 1 einfach; plain food einfaches Essen; 2 (*unflavoured*) Natur-; plain yoghurt der Naturjoghurt; 3 (*not patterned*) einfarbig; plain curtains einfarbige Vorhänge.

plait noun Zopf der (PL die Zöpfe).

plan noun Plan der (PL die Pläne); we've made plans for the summer wir haben Pläne für den Sommer gemacht; to go according to plan nach Plan gehen; everything went according to plan alles ist nach Plan gegangen. verb 1 to plan to do something etwas vorhaben ◇ SEP; we're planning to leave at eight wir haben vor, um acht abzufahren; 2 (*make plans for, organize, design*) planen; she's planning a trip to Italy sie plant eine Reise nach Italien.

plane noun Flugzeug das (PL die Flugzeuge); we went by plane wir sind geflogen.

planet noun Planet der (PL die Planeten).

plant noun Pflanze die (PL die Pflanzen); a house plant eine Topfpflanze. verb pflanzen.

plaster noun 1 (*sticking plaster*) Pflaster das (PL die Pflaster); 2 (*for walls*) Verputz der; 3 Gips der; to have your leg in plaster das Bein in Gips haben.

plastic noun Plastik das; plastic bag die Plastiktüte.

plate noun Teller der (PL die Teller).

platform noun 1 (*in a station*) Bahnsteig der (PL die Bahnsteige); 2 the train is arriving at platform six der Zug fährt auf Gleis sechs ein; 3 (*for lecturing or performing*) Podium das (PL die Podien).

play noun (*in the theatre*) Stück das (PL die Stücke); television play das

◇ IRREGULAR VERB: See the verb table in the centre of the dictionary

Fernsehspiel; **we are putting on a play by Brecht at school** wir führen ein Stück von Brecht in der Schule auf.

verb **1** spielen; **the children are playing with a ball** die Kinder spielen Ball; **they play the piano and the guitar** sie spielen Klavier und Gitarre; **who's playing Hamlet?** wer spielt Hamlet?; **to play tennis** Tennis spielen; **they were playing cards** sie haben Karten gespielt; **2** (*in sport*) **to play somebody** gegen jemanden spielen; **Italy are playing Germany** Italien spielt gegen Deutschland; **3** (*a tape, CD, or record*) **play your new CD** spiele mal deine neue CD.

player *noun* **1** Spieler *der* (PL *die* Spieler), Spielerin *die* (PL *die* Spielerinnen); **football player** *der* Fußballspieler; **2** (*in the theatre*) Schauspieler *der* (PL *die* Schauspieler), Schauspielerin *die* (PL *die* Schauspielerinnen).

playground *noun* Spielplatz *der* (PL *die* Spielplätze); **school playground** *der* Schulhof.

playgroup *noun* Kindergarten *der* (PL *die* Kindergärten).

playing field *noun* Sportplatz *der* (PL *die* Sportplätze).

pleasant *adjective* angenehm.

please *adverb* bitte; **two coffees, please** zwei Kaffee bitte; **could you turn the TV off, please?** könntest du bitte den Fernseher ausmachen?

pleased *adjective* **1** erfreut; **I'm really pleased!** das freut mich wirklich!; **2 she was pleased with**

her present sie hat sich über ihr Geschenk gefreut; **3** (*joy*) **pleased to meet you!** freut mich!

pleasure *noun* **1** (*amusement*) Vergnügen *das*; **2** (*joy*) Freude *die*; **to get a lot of pleasure out of something** viel Freude an etwas ←(DAT) haben.

plenty *pronoun* **1** (*lots*) viel; **he's got plenty of money** er hat viel Geld; **2** (*enough*) genug; **that's plenty!** das ist genug!; **we've got plenty of time left** wir haben noch genug Zeit.

plot *noun* (*of a film or novel*) Handlung *die*.

plug *noun* **1** (*electrical*) Stecker *der* (PL *die* Stecker); **2** (*in a bath or sink*) Stöpsel *der* (PL *die* Stöpsel); **to pull out the plug** den Stöpsel herausziehen.

plum *noun* Pflaume *die* (PL *die* Pflaumen); **plum tart** *der* Pflaumenkuchen.

plumber *noun* Installateur *der* (PL *die* Installateure).

plural *noun* Mehrzahl *die*, Plural *der*; **in the plural** in der Mehrzahl, im Plural.

plus *preposition* plus (+DAT); **three children plus a baby** drei Kinder und ein Baby.

p.m. *abbreviation* nachmittags (*for times up to 6 p.m.*); abends (*for times after 6 p.m.*); **at two p.m.** um zwei Uhr nachmittags, um vierzehn Uhr; **at nine p.m.** um neun Uhr abends, um einundzwanzig Uhr (*in German you usually express times after*

△ NEW SPELLING: See page xii

midday in terms of the 24-hour clock).

pocket noun Tasche die (PL die Taschen).

pocket money noun Taschengeld das.

poem noun Gedicht das (PL die Gedichte).

poet noun Dichter der (PL die Dichter), Dichterin die (PL die Dichterinnen).

poetry noun Dichtung die.

point noun 1 (tip) Spitze die (PL die Spitzen); **the point of a nail** die Spitze eines Nagels; 2 (a tiny mark or dot) Punkt der (PL die Punkte); 3 (in time) Zeitpunkt der (PL die Zeitpunkte); **at that point** zu diesem Zeitpunkt; **to be on the point of doing something** gerade etwas tun wollen; 4 **that's not the point** darum geht es nicht; **there's no point phoning, he's out** es hat keinen Sinn anzurufen, er ist nicht da; **what's the point?** wozu?; 5 **that's a good point!** das stimmt!; **the point is …** es geht darum …; 6 **point of view** der Standpunkt; **from my point of view** von meinem Standpunkt aus; 7 **her strong point** ihre Stärke; 8 (in scoring) Punkt der (PL die Punkte); **to win by fifteen points** mit fünfzehn Punkten Vorsprung gewinnen; 9 (in decimals) 6 **point** 4 sechs Komma vier (in German, a comma is used for the decimal point).
verb 1 hinweisen ◆ SEP auf (+ACC); **a notice pointing to the station** ein Schild, das auf den Bahnhof

hinweist; 2 (with your finger) zeigen auf (+ACC); **he pointed at Tom** er zeigte auf Tom.

pointless adjective sinnlos; **it's pointless to keep on ringing** es ist sinnlos, dauernd zu klingeln.

poison noun Gift das (PL die Gifte). verb vergiften.

poisonous adjective giftig.

Poland noun Polen das.

pole noun 1 (for a tent) Stange die (PL die Stangen); 2 (for skiing) Stock der (PL die Stöcke); 3 **the North Pole** der Nordpol.

Pole noun (a Polish person) Pole der (PL die Polen), Polin die (PL die Polinnen).

police noun **the police** die Polizei; **the police are coming** die Polizei kommt.

police car noun Streifenwagen der (PL die Streifenwagen).

policeman noun Polizist der (PL die Polizisten).

police station noun Polizeiwache die (PL die Polizeiwachen).

policewoman noun Polizistin die (PL die Polizistinnen).

polish noun 1 (for furniture) Politur die; 2 (for shoes) Schuhcreme die; 3 (for the floor) Bohnerwachs das.
verb 1 polieren (furniture, silver); 2 **to polish your shoes** seine Schuhe putzen.

◇ IRREGULAR VERB: See the verb table in the centre of the dictionary

Polish noun (language)
Polnisch das.
adjective polnisch.

polite adjective höflich; **to be polite
to somebody** höflich zu jemandem
sein.

political adjective politisch.

politician noun Politiker der (PL die
Politiker), Politikerin die (PL die
Politikerinnen).

politics noun Politik die.

polluted adjective verschmutzt.

pollution noun
Verschmutzung die.

polo-necked adjective Rollkragen-;
a polo-necked jumper ein
Rollkragenpullover.

pond noun Teich der (PL die Teiche).

pony noun Pony das (PL die Ponys).

ponytail noun Pferdeschwanz der
(PL die Pferdeschwänze).

poodle noun Pudel der (PL die
Pudel).

pool noun 1 (swimming pool)
Schwimmbecken das (PL die
Schwimmbecken); 2 (pond)
Tümpel der (PL die Tümpel);
3 (puddle) Lache die (PL die
Lachen); 4 (game) Poolbillard das;
5 **the football pools** das Toto; **to do
the pools** Toto spielen.

poor adjective 1 arm; **a poor country**
ein armes Land; **a poor family** eine
arme Familie; 2 **poor Tanya's failed
her exam** die arme Tanya ist durch
die Prüfung gefallen; 3 (bad)

schlecht; **that's a poor result** das
ist ein schlechtes Ergebnis; **the
weather was pretty poor** das Wetter
war ziemlich schlecht.

pop noun Popmusik die; **pop
concert** das Popkonzert; **pop star**
der Popstar; **pop song** der Schlager.
● **to pop into: I'll just pop into the
bank** ich gehe kurz auf die Bank.

popcorn noun Puffmais der.

pope noun Papst der (PL die Päpste).

poppy noun Mohn der.

popular adjective beliebt.

population noun Bevölkerung die
(PL die Bevölkerungen).

porch noun Vorbau der (PL die
Vorbauten).

pork noun Schweinefleisch das;
pork chop das Schweinekotelett.

porridge noun Haferbrei der.

port noun 1 Hafen der (PL die
Häfen); 2 (wine) Portwein der (PL
die Portweine).

porter noun 1 (at a station or an
airport) Gepäckträger der (PL die
Gepäckträger); 2 (in a hotel)
Portier der (PL die Portiers).

portion noun (of food) Portion die
(PL die Portionen).

portrait noun Porträt das (PL die
Porträts).

Portugal noun Portugal das.

Portuguese noun 1 (language)
Portugiesisch das; 2 (a person)
Portugiese der (PL die Portugiesen).

△ NEW SPELLING: See page xii

Portugiesin *die* (PL *die* Portugiesinnen).

adjective portugiesisch.

posh *adjective* vornehm; **a posh area** eine vornehme Gegend.

position *noun* 1 Platz *der* (PL Plätze); 2 (*situation*) Lage *die* (PL *die* Lagen); 3 (*status, job*) Stellung *die* (PL *die* Stellungen).

positive *adjective* 1 (*sure*) sicher; **I'm positive he's sent it** ich bin mir sicher, dass er gegangen ist; 2 (*enthusiastic*) positiv; **her reaction was very positive** ihre Reaktion war sehr positiv.

possessions *plural noun* Sachen (*plural*); **all my possessions are in the flat** alle meine Sachen sind in der Wohnung.

possibility *noun* Möglichkeit *die* (PL *die* Möglichkeiten).

possible *adjective* möglich; **it's possible** es ist gut möglich; **if possible** wenn möglich; **as quickly as possible** so schnell wie möglich.

possibly *adverb* 1 (*maybe*) möglicherweise; **'will you be at home at midday?' – 'possibly'** 'bist du mittags zu Hause?' – 'möglicherweise'; 2 **how can you possibly believe that?** wie kannst du das nur glauben?; **I can't possibly arrive before Thursday** ich kann unmöglich vor Donnerstag ankommen.

post *noun* 1 Post *die*; **to send something by post** etwas per Post schicken; (*letters*) **is there any post for me?** ist Post für mich

gekommen?; 2 (*a pole*) Pfosten *der* (PL *die* Pfosten); 3 (*a job*) Stelle *die* (PL *die* Stellen).

verb **to post a letter** einen Brief abschicken SEP.

postbox *noun* Briefkasten *der* (PL *die* Briefkästen).

postcard *noun* Postkarte *die* (PL *die* Postkarten).

postcode *noun* Postleitzahl *die* (PL *die* Postleitzahlen).

poster *noun* 1 (*for decoration*) Poster *das* (PL *die* Poster); **I've bought an Oasis poster** ich habe ein Poster von Oasis gekauft; 2 (*advertising*) Plakat *das* (PL *die* Plakate); **I saw a poster for the concert** ich habe ein Plakat für das Konzert gesehen.

postman *noun* Briefträger *der* (PL *die* Briefträger).

post office *noun* Post *die*; **the post office is on the right** die Post ist auf der rechten Seite.

postpone *verb* verschieben ◇; **we've postponed the meeting until next week** wir haben die Besprechung auf nächste Woche verschoben.

postwoman *noun* Briefträgerin *die* (PL *die* Briefträgerinnen).

pot *noun* 1 (*jar*) Topf *der* (PL *die* Töpfe); **a pot of honey** ein Topf Honig; 2 (*teapot*) Kanne *die* (PL *die* Kannen); 3 **the pots and pans** die Töpfe und Pfannen.

◇ IRREGULAR VERB: *See the verb table in the centre of the dictionary*

potato noun Kartoffel die (PL die Kartoffeln); **fried potatoes** Bratkartoffeln (plural); **mashed potatoes** der Kartoffelbrei.

potato crisps plural noun Kartoffelchips (plural).

pottery noun 1 (craft) Töpferei die; 2 (objects) Töpferwaren (plural).

pound noun 1 (money) Pfund das (PL die Pfunde); **fourteen pounds** vierzehn Pfund; **three marks to the pound** drei Mark für ein Pfund; **a five pound note** ein Fünfpfundschein; 2 (in weight) Pfund das; **two pounds of apples** zwei Pfund Äpfel.

pour verb 1 gießen ◊ (liquid); **he poured milk into the pan** er hat Milch in den Topf gegossen; 2 eingießen ◊ SEP (a drink); **to pour the tea** den Tee eingießen; **I poured him a drink** ich habe ihm zu trinken eingegossen; 3 (with rain) **it's pouring** es gießt.

poverty noun Armut die.

powder noun 1 Pulver das (PL die Pulver); 2 (for face or body) Puder der (PL die Puder).

power noun 1 (electricity) Strom der; **a power cut** eine Stromsperre; 2 (energy) Energie die; **nuclear power** die Kernenergie; 3 (strength) Kraft die; 4 (over other people) Macht die; **to be in power** an der Macht sein.

powerful adjective (strong) stark; (influential) mächtig.

power station noun Kraftwerk das (PL die Kraftwerke).

practical adjective praktisch.

practice noun 1 (for sport) Training das; **hockey practice** das Hockeytraining; 2 Übung die; **to do your piano practice** Klavier üben; **to be out of practice** außer Übung sein.

practise verb 1 üben (an instrument, exercise, or skill); **to practise the piano** Klavier üben; 2 anwenden SEP (a language); **a week in Berlin to practise my German** eine Woche in Berlin, um mein Deutsch anzuwenden; 3 (in sport) trainieren; **the team practises on Wednesday** die Mannschaft trainiert Mittwoch.

praise verb loben; **to praise somebody for something** jemanden für etwas ←(ACC) loben.

pram noun Kinderwagen der (PL die Kinderwagen).

prawn noun Garnele die (PL die Garnelen).

pray verb beten.

prayer noun Gebet das (PL die Gebete).

precinct noun **shopping precinct** das Einkaufszentrum; **pedestrian precinct** die Fußgängerzone.

precisely adverb genau; **at eleven o'clock precisely** um genau elf Uhr.

prefer verb 1 vorziehen ◊ SEP; **I prefer Anna to her sister** ich ziehe Anna ihrer Schwester vor; 2 **to prefer to do something** etwas lieber tun; **I prefer to stay at home** ich bleibe lieber zu Hause.

△ NEW SPELLING: See page xii

pregnant adjective schwanger.

prejudice noun Vorurteil das (PL die Vorurteile); **to fight against racial prejudice** gegen Rassenvorurteile ankämpfen.

prejudiced adjective **to be prejudiced** voreingenommen sein.

prep noun Hausaufgaben (plural); **my English prep** meine Englischhausaufgaben.

preparation noun Vorbereitung die (PL die Vorbereitungen); **in preparation for something** in Vorbereitung auf etwas ←(ACC); **our preparations for Christmas** unsere Weihnachtsvorbereitungen.

prepare verb 1 vorbereiten SEP; **to prepare somebody for something** jemanden auf etwas ←(ACC) vorbereiten; 2 **to be prepared for the worst** sich auf das Schlimmste gefasst machen.

prepared adjective bereit; **I'm prepared to pay half** ich bin bereit, die Hälfte zu zahlen.

preposition noun Präposition die (PL die Präpositionen).

prep school noun private Grundschule die.

prescription noun Rezept das (PL die Rezepte); **on prescription** auf Rezept.

present noun 1 (a gift) Geschenk das (PL die Geschenke); **to give somebody a present** jemandem ein Geschenk machen; 2 (the time now) Gegenwart die;

in the present (tense) in der Gegenwart; 3 **that's all for the present** das ist vorläufig alles. adjective 1 (attending) anwesend; **Mr Blair is not present** Herr Blair ist nicht anwesend; **to be present at something** bei etwas ←(DAT) anwesend sein; **fifty people were present at the funeral** fünfzig Personen waren bei der Beerdigung anwesend; 2 (existing now) gegenwärtig; **the present situation** die gegenwärtige Lage; 3 **at the present time** zur Zeit. verb 1 überreichen (a prize); 2 (introduce) vorstellen SEP; 3 (on TV, radio) moderieren (a programme).

presenter noun (on TV) Moderator der (PL die Moderatoren), Moderatorin die (PL die Moderatorinnen).

president noun Präsident der (PL die Präsidenten), Präsidentin die (PL die Präsidentinnen).

press noun (the press) die Presse. verb 1 (to push) drücken; **press here!** hier drücken!; 2 drücken auf (+ACC) (a button or switch); **she pressed the button** sie hat auf den Knopf gedrückt.

press conference noun Pressekonferenz die (PL die Pressekonferenzen).

pressure noun Druck der; **to put pressure on somebody** jemanden unter Druck setzen.

pressure group noun Interessengruppe die (PL die Interessengruppen).

◇ IRREGULAR VERB: See the verb table in the centre of the dictionary

pretend verb to pretend that ... so tun, als ob ...; **he's pretending not to hear** er tut so, als ob er nicht hört.

pretty adjective hübsch; **a pretty dress** ein hübsches Kleid.
adverb ziemlich; **it was pretty silly** das war ziemlich blöd.

prevent verb to prevent somebody from doing something jemanden daran hindern, etwas zu tun; **there's nothing to prevent you from leaving** niemand kann dich daran hindern wegzugehen.

previous adjective 1 (earlier) früher (years, opportunity, or job); 2 (immediately preceding); **on the previous Tuesday** am vorigen Dienstag.

price noun Preis der (PL die Preise); **the price per kilo** der Preis pro Kilo; **CDs have gone up in price** CDs sind im Preis gestiegen; **what is the price of this?** was kostet das?

price list noun Preisliste die (PL die Preislisten).

price ticket noun Preisschild das (PL die Preisschilder).

prick verb stechen ◇; **to prick your finger** sich in den Finger stechen.

pride noun Stolz der.

priest noun Priester der (PL die Priester).

primary school noun Grundschule die (PL die Grundschulen).

primary (school) teacher noun Grundschullehrer der (PL die Grundschullehrer),

Grundschullehrerin die (PL die Grundschullehrerinnen).

prime minister noun Premierminister der (PL die Premierminister), Premierministerin die (PL die Premierministerinnen).

prince noun Prinz der (PL die Prinzen).

princess noun Prinzessin die (PL die Prinzessinnen).

principal noun (of a college) Direktor der (PL die Direktoren), Direktorin die (PL die Direktorinnen).
adjective (main) Haupt-.

principle noun Prinzip das (PL die Prinzipien); **on principle** im Prinzip; **that's true in principle** im Prinzip stimmt das.

print noun 1 (letters) Druck der; **in small print** klein gedruckt; 2 (a photo) Abzug der (PL die Abzüge); **colour print** der Farbabzug.

printer noun (for a computer) Drucker der (PL die Drucker).

print-out noun Ausdruck der (PL die Ausdrucke).

prison noun Gefängnis das (PL die Gefängnisse); **in prison** im Gefängnis.

prisoner noun Gefangene der/die (PL die Gefangenen).

private adjective 1 Privat-, privat; **private school** die Privatschule; **private property** das Privateigentum; **to have private**

△ NEW SPELLING: See page xii

lessons Privatstunden nehmen;
2 **in private** privat.

prize noun Preis der (PL die Preise);
to win a prize einen Preis
gewinnen.

prize-giving noun
Preisverleihung die (PL die
Preisverleihungen).

prizewinner noun Gewinner der
(PL die Gewinner), Gewinnerin die
(PL die Gewinnerinnen).

probable adjective wahrscheinlich.

probably adverb wahrscheinlich.

problem noun Problem das (PL die
Probleme); **it's a serious problem**
das ist ein ernstes Problem; **no
problem!** kein Problem!

process noun 1 Prozess△ der (PL die
Prozesse); 2 **to be in the process of
doing something** dabei sein, etwas
zu tun.

produce noun (food) Erzeugnisse
(plural).
verb 1 herstellen SEP (goods, food);
2 vorzeigen SEP (a ticket, document);
I produced my passport ich habe
meinen Pass vorgezeigt; 3 erzeugen
(interest, tension); **it produces heat**
es erzeugt Wärme; 4 **to produce a
film** einen Film produzieren; 5 **to
produce a play** ein Theaterstück
inszenieren.

producer noun (of a film or
programme) Produzent der (PL die
Produzenten).

product noun Produkt das (PL die
Produkte).

production noun 1 (of a film or an
opera) Produktion die (PL die
Produktionen); 2 (of a play)
Inszenierung die (PL die
Inszenierungen); **a new production
of Hamlet** eine neue Inszenierung
von Hamlet; 3 (by a factory)
Produktion die.

profession noun Beruf der (PL die
Berufe).

professional noun 1 (a trained
person) Fachmann der (PL die
Fachleute); 2 (in sport) Profi der (PL
die Profis).
adjective 1 professionell (work,
sportsman); **a professional
footballer** ein professioneller
Fußballer; 2 beruflich (career,
success); **she's a professional
singer** sie ist Sängerin von Beruf.

professor noun Professor der (PL
die Professoren), Professorin die (PL
die Professorinnen).

profile noun Profil das (PL die
Profile).

profit noun Gewinn der (PL die
Gewinne).

profitable adjective rentabel.

program noun **computer program**
das Programm.

programme noun 1 (for a play or an
event) Programm das (PL die
Programme); 2 (on TV or radio)
Sendung die (PL die Sendungen).

progress noun 1 Fortschritt der (PL
die Fortschritte); **to make progress**
Fortschritte machen; 2 **to be in
progress** im Gange sein.

◇ IRREGULAR VERB: See the verb table in the centre of the dictionary

project noun 1 (at school)
Arbeit die (PL die Arbeiten); 2 (a
plan) Projekt das (PL die Projekte);
a project to build a bridge ein
Brückenbauprojekt.

promise noun Versprechen das (PL
die Versprechen); **to make
somebody a promise** jemandem
ein Versprechen geben; **to keep a
promise** ein Versprechen halten; **it's
a promise!** ganz bestimmt!
verb **to promise something** etwas
versprechen ◇; **I've promised to
ring my mother** ich habe
versprochen, meine Mutter
anzurufen.

promote verb **to be promoted** (in
football) aufsteigen ◇ SEP (PERF
sein); (at work) befördert werden.

promotion noun
1 Beförderung die; 2
(in football) Aufstieg der; 3 (in
advertising) Reklame die.

pronoun noun Pronomen das (PL
die Pronomen).

pronounce verb aussprechen ◇
SEP; **you don't pronounce the 'c'**
das 'c' spricht man nicht aus.

pronunciation noun
Aussprache die.

proof noun Beweis der (PL die
Beweise); **there's no proof that ...**
es gibt keine Beweise dafür, dass ...

propaganda noun
Propaganda die.

propeller noun Propeller der (PL die
Propeller).

proper adjective 1 (correct, real,
genuine) richtig; **the proper
answer** die richtige Antwort; **he's
not a proper doctor** er ist kein
richtiger Arzt; 2 (decent) anständig;
I need a proper meal ich brauche
ein anständiges Essen; 3 in its
proper place an Ort und Stelle.

properly adverb 1 richtig;
2 (decent) anständig.

property noun 1 (your belongings)
Eigentum das; 2 (land, premises)
Besitz der; **'private property'**
'Privatbesitz'; 3 (house) Haus das
(PL die Häuser).

propose verb 1 (suggest)
vorschlagen ◇ SEP; 2 (marriage) **he
proposed to her** er hat ihr einen
Heiratsantrag gemacht.

protect verb schützen; **to protect
somebody from something**
jemanden vor etwas ←(DAT) schützen.

protection noun Schutz der.

protein noun Protein das (PL die
Proteine).

protest noun 1 Beschwerde die (PL
die Beschwerden); **to make a
protest** eine Beschwerde einlegen
SEP; 2 (disapproval) Protest der (PL
die Proteste); **in protest against
something** aus Protest gegen etwas
←(ACC).
verb **to protest** protestieren; **to protest about
something** gegen etwas ←(ACC)
protestieren.

Protestant noun Protestant der (PL
die Protestanten), Protestantin die
(PL die Protestantinnen).
adjective protestantisch.

△ NEW SPELLING: See page xii

protest march noun
Protestmarsch der (PL die
Protestmärsche).

proud adjective stolz; to be proud
about something stolz auf etwas
←(ACC) sein.

prove verb beweisen ✧.

provide verb zur Verfügung stellen.

provided, providing conjunction
vorausgesetzt; provided it doesn't
rain vorausgesetzt, es regnet nicht.

prune noun Backpflaume die (PL die
Backpflaumen).

psychiatrist noun Psychiater der
(PL die Psychiater), Psychiaterin die
(PL die Psychiaterinnen).

psychological adjective
psychologisch.

psychologist noun
Psychologe der (PL die
Psychologen), Psychologin die (PL
die Psychologinnen).

psychology noun Psychologie die.

PTO abbreviation b.w. (bitte
wenden).

pub noun Kneipe die (PL die
Kneipen) (informal).

public noun the public die
Öffentlichkeit; in public in aller
Öffentlichkeit.
adjective öffentlich.

public holiday noun gesetzliche
Feiertag der (PL die gesetzlichen
Feiertage); January 1st is a public
holiday der erste Januar ist ein
gesetzlicher Feiertag.

publicity noun 1 Publicity die;
2 (advertising) Werbung die.

public school noun
Privatschule die (PL die
Privatschulen).

public transport noun öffentliche
Verkehrsmittel (plural).

publish verb veröffentlichen.

publisher noun 1 Verleger der (PL
die Verleger), Verlegerin die (PL die
Verlegerinnen); 2 (company)
Verlag der (PL die Verlage).

pudding noun (dessert)
Nachtisch der (PL die Nachtische);
for pudding we've got
strawberries zum Nachtisch gibt es
Erdbeeren.

puddle noun Pfütze die (PL die
Pfützen).

puff noun (of smoke) Wölkchen das
(PL die Wölkchen).

puff pastry noun Blätterteig der.

pull verb 1 ziehen ✧; to pull a cart
einen Wagen ziehen; 2 ziehen an
(+DAT); to pull a rope an einem Seil
ziehen; he pulled a letter out of his
pocket er hat einen Brief aus der
Tasche gezogen; ★ he's pulling
your leg! er nimmt dich auf den Arm
(literally: he's picking you up in his
arms).
● to pull down 1 herunterziehen ✧
SEP; 2 (demolish) abreißen ✧ SEP (a
building).
● to pull in (at the roadside) an den
Straßenrand fahren ✧ (PERF sein).

pullover noun Pullover der (PL die
Pullover).

pump noun Pumpe die (PL die
Pumpen); bicycle pump die

✧ IRREGULAR VERB: See the verb table in the centre of the dictionary

Fahrradpumpe.
verb pumpen.
● **to pump up** aufpumpen SEP.

punch *noun* 1 (*in boxing*)
Faustschlag der (PL die
Faustschläge); 2 (*drink*) Bowle die
(PL die Bowlen).
verb 1 **he punched me in the
stomach** er hat mich in den Magen
geboxt; 2 lochen (*a ticket*).

punctual *adjective* pünktlich.

punctuation *noun*
Interpunktion die.

punctuation mark *noun*
Satzzeichen das (PL die
Satzzeichen).

puncture *noun* (*flat tyre*)
Reifenpanne die (PL die
Reifenpannen).

punish *verb* bestrafen.

punishment *noun* Strafe die (PL die
Strafen).

pupil *noun* Schüler der (PL die
Schüler), Schülerin die (PL die
Schülerinnen).

puppet *noun* Puppe die (PL die
Puppen).

puppy *noun* junge Hund der (PL die
jungen Hunde); **a boxer puppy** ein
junger Boxer.

pure *adjective* rein.

purple *adjective* lila ('lila' never
changes).

purpose *noun* 1 Zweck der (PL die
Zwecke); **what's the purpose of it?**
was hat das für einen Zweck?; 2 **on
purpose** absichtlich; **she did it on**

purpose das hat sie absichtlich
getan; **he closed the door on
purpose** er hat die Tür absichtlich
zugemacht.

purr *verb* schnurren.

purse *noun* Portemonnaie das (PL
die Portemonnaies).

push *noun* **to give something a
push** etwas schieben ✧.
verb 1 schubsen; **he pushed me** er
hat mich geschubst; 2 (*to press*)
drücken auf (+ACC) (*a bell or button*);
3 **to push somebody to do
something** jemanden zu etwas
drängen; **his teacher is pushing him
to sit the exam** sein Lehrer drängt
ihn, die Prüfung zu machen; 4 **to
push your way through the crowd**
sich durch die Menge drängen.
● **to push something away** etwas
wegschieben ✧ SEP; **she pushed her
plate away** sie schob ihren Teller
weg.

pushchair *noun* Sportwagen der
(PL die Sportwagen).

put *verb* 1 (*place generally*) tun ✧;
put some milk in your tea tu etwas
Milch in den Tee; **you can put the
butter in the fridge** du kannst die
Butter in den Kühlschrank tun; 2 (*lay
flat*) legen; **she put the pencil on the
desk** sie hat den Bleistift auf den
Schreibtisch gelegt; 3 (*place
upright*) stellen; **where did you put
my bag?** wo hast du meine
Handtasche hingestellt?; 4 (*write*)
schreiben ✧; **put your address
here** schreiben Sie Ihre Adresse
hierhin.
● **to put away** wegräumen SEP; **put**

away your things räume deine Sachen weg.

- **to put back** 1 zurücklegen SEP, zurückstellen SEP, zurücktun SEP (*the translation of 'put back' depends on the way it is done: if it's placed lying down, use 'zurücklegen'; if placed upright use 'zurückstellen' and if it could be either, use 'zurücktun'*); **I put it back in the drawer** ich habe es in die Schublade zurückgetan; 2 (*postpone*) verschieben ◇; **the meeting has been put back until Thursday** die Besprechung ist auf Donnerstag verschoben worden.

- **to put down** (*lying down*) hinlegen SEP; (*upright*) hinstellen SEP; **where can I put the vase down?** wo kann ich die Vase hinstellen?

- **to put off** 1 (*postpone*) verschieben ◇; **he's put off my lesson till Thursday** er hat meine Stunde auf Donnerstag verschoben; 2 (*turn off*) ausmachen SEP; **don't forget to put off the lights** vergiss nicht, das Licht auszumachen; 3 **to put somebody off something** jemandem die Lust an etwas ◆(DAT) verderben ◇; **it really put me off my food** das hat mir wirklich die Lust am Essen verdorben; 4 **to put somebody off doing something** jemanden davon abbringen ◇ SEP, etwas zu tun; **don't be put off** lass dich nicht davon abbringen.

- **to put on** 1 anziehen ◇ SEP (*clothes*); **I'll just put my shoes on** ich ziehe nur schnell meine Schuhe an; 2 auflegen SEP (*a CD or record*); **I'm putting on Oasis** ich lege Oasis auf; 3 (*switch on*) anmachen SEP (*a light*

or the heating); **could you put the lamp on?** kannst du die Lampe anmachen?

- **to put out** 1 (*put outside*) hinaustun ◇ SEP, raustun ◇ SEP (*informal*); **have you put the rubbish out?** hast du den Müll rausgetan?; 2 ausmachen SEP (*a light or cigarette*); **I've put the lights out** ich habe das Licht ausgemacht; 3 **to put out your hand** die Hand ausstrecken SEP.

- **to put up** 1 heben ◇ (*your hand*); 2 aufhängen SEP (*a picture or poster*); **I've put up some posters in my room** ich habe ein paar Poster in meinem Zimmer aufgehängt; 3 anschlagen SEP (*a notice*); 4 erhöhen (*the price*); **they've put up the fare** sie haben den Fahrpreis erhöht; 5 (*for the night*) **friends put me up** ich habe bei Freunden übernachtet; **can you put me up on Friday?** kann ich Freitag bei euch übernachten?

- **to put up with something** etwas aushalten ◇ SEP; **I don't know how she puts up with it** ich weiß nicht, wie sie das aushält.

puzzle noun (*jigsaw*) Puzzle das (PL die Puzzles).

puzzled adjective verdutzt.

pyjamas plural noun Schlafanzug der (PL die Schlafanzüge); **a pair of pyjamas** ein Schlafanzug; **where are my pyjamas?** wo ist mein Schlafanzug?

◇ IRREGULAR VERB: *See the verb table in the centre of the dictionary*

Q q

qualification noun 1 (*ability, experience*) Qualifikation *die* (PL *die* Qualifikationen); 2 (*on paper*) Zeugnis *das* (PL *die* Zeugnisse).

qualified *adjective* 1 ausgebildet; **she's a qualified ski instructor** sie ist eine ausgebildete Skilehrerin; 2 (*having a degree or a diploma*) Diplom-; **a qualified engineer** ein Diplomingenieur.

quality noun Qualität *die*; **good quality products** Waren von guter Qualität.

quantity noun Menge *die* (PL *die* Mengen).

quarrel noun Streit *der* (PL *die* Streite); **to have a quarrel** Streit haben.
verb sich streiten ◇; **they're always quarrelling** sie streiten sich dauernd.

quarter noun 1 Viertel *das* (PL *die* Viertel); **a quarter of the price** ein Viertel des Preises; **three quarters of the class** drei Viertel der Klasse; **it's a quarter past ten** es ist Viertel nach zehn; **it's a quarter to ten** es ist Viertel vor zehn; 2 **we meet at quarter to eight** wir treffen uns um Viertel vor acht; 3 **a quarter of an hour** eine Viertelstunde; 4 **three quarters of an hour** eine Dreiviertelstunde; 5 **an hour and a quarter** eineinviertel Stunden.

queen noun 1 Königin *die* (PL *die* Königinnen); 2 (*in chess, cards*) Dame *die* (PL *die* Damen).

question noun Frage *die* (PL *die* Fragen); **to ask somebody a question** jemandem eine Frage stellen; **I asked her a question** ich habe ihr eine Frage gestellt; **it's out of the question** das kommt nicht in Frage.
verb befragen (*a person*).

question mark noun Fragezeichen *das* (PL *die* Fragezeichen).

questionnaire noun Fragebogen *der* (PL *die* Fragebögen).

queue noun (*of people, cars*) Schlange *die* (PL *die* Schlangen); **to stand in a queue** Schlange stehen; **a queue of cars** eine Autoschlange.

quick *adjective* schnell; **to have a quick lunch** schnell etwas zu Mittag essen; **it's quicker on the motorway** auf der Autobahn geht es schneller; **to have a quick look at something** sich ←(DAT) schnell etwas ansehen; **be quick!** mach schnell!

quickly *adverb* schnell; **I'll just quickly phone my mother** ich rufe schnell meine Mutter an.

quiet *adjective* 1 (*silent*) still; **to keep quiet** still sein; **please keep quiet** sei bitte still; 2 (*not loud*) leise; **the children are very quiet** die Kinder sind ganz leise; **in a quiet voice** mit leiser Stimme; 3 (*peaceful*) ruhig; **a quiet street** eine ruhige Straße.

△ NEW SPELLING: See page xii

quietly adverb 1 (speak, move) leise;
he got up quietly er ist leise
aufgestanden; 2 (read or play) ruhig;
to sit quietly ruhig sitzen.

quilt noun Steppdecke die (PL die
Steppdecken).

quite adverb 1 (fairly) ziemlich; it's
quite cold outside es ist ziemlich
kalt draußen; quite often ziemlich
oft; quite a few ziemlich viele; quite
a few of our friends came ziemlich
viele unserer Freunde sind
gekommen; quite a few people
ziemlich viele Leute; that's quite a
good idea das ist eine ganz gute
Idee; 2 (completely) völlig; it was
quite amazing es war einfach
fantastisch; not quite nicht ganz;
she's not quite ready sie ist noch
nicht ganz fertig; 3 genau; I don't
quite know what he wants ich weiß
nicht genau, was er will; quite!
genau!

quiz noun Quiz das (PL die Quiz).

quotation noun (from a book)
Zitat das (PL die Zitate).

quotation marks plural noun
Anführungszeichen (plural); in
quotation marks in
Anführungszeichen.

quote noun 1 (from a book)
Zitat das (PL die Zitate);
2 (estimate) Kostenvoranschlag der
(PL die Kostenvoranschläge).
verb zitieren.

R r

rabbi noun Rabbi der (PL die
Rabbis).

rabbit noun Kaninchen das (PL die
Kaninchen).

race noun 1 (a sports event)
Rennen das (PL die Rennen); cycle
race das Radrennen; 2 to have a
race (running) um die Wette
laufen ◇ (PERF sein); (swimming)
um die Wette schwimmen ◇ (PERF
sein); 3 (an ethnic group) Rasse die
(PL die Rassen).

racetrack noun Rennbahn die (PL
die Rennbahnen).

racial adjective rassisch, Rassen-;
racial discrimination die
Rassendiskriminierung.

racing car noun Rennwagen der
(PL die Rennwagen).

racing driver noun
Rennfahrer der (PL die Rennfahrer).

racism noun Rassismus der.

racist noun Rassist der (PL die
Rassisten), Rassistin die (PL die
Rassistinnen).
adjective rassistisch.

racket noun 1 (for tennis)
Schläger der (PL die Schläger); my
tennis racket mein Tennisschläger;
2 (noise) Krach der.

radiator noun Heizkörper der (PL
die Heizkörper).

◇ IRREGULAR VERB: See the verb table in the centre of the dictionary

radio noun Radio das (PL die Radios); **to listen to the radio** Radio hören; **to hear something on the radio** etwas im Radio hören.

radioactive adjective radioaktiv.

radio station noun Rundfunkstation die (PL die Rundfunkstationen).

radish noun Radieschen das (PL die Radieschen).

rag noun Lumpen der (PL die Lumpen).

rage noun Wut die; **to fly into a rage** in Wut geraten ◇ (PERF sein); **she's in a rage** sie ist wütend; ★ **it's all the rage** das ist der letzte Schrei (literally: it's the last scream).

rail noun 1 (for a train) Schiene die (PL die Schienen); 2 (the railway) **to go by rail** mit der Bahn fahren; 3 (on a balcony, bridge, or stairs) Geländer das (PL die Geländer).

rail card noun Bahnpass∆ der (PL die Bahnpässe).

railing(s) noun Geländer das (PL die Geländer).

railway noun 1 (the system) Bahn die; **the railways** die Bahn; 2 **railway line** (from one place to another) Bahnstrecke die; 3 **on the railway line** (the track) auf dem Gleis.

railway carriage noun Eisenbahnwagen der (PL die Eisenbahnwagen).

railway station noun Bahnhof der (PL die Bahnhöfe).

rain noun Regen der; **in the rain** im Regen.
verb regnen; **it's raining** es regnet; **it's going to rain** es wird regnen.

rainbow noun Regenbogen der (PL die Regenbogen).

raincoat noun Regenmantel der (PL die Regenmäntel).

rainy adjective regnerisch.

raise verb 1 (lift up) hochheben ◇ SEP; 2 (increase) erhöhen (prices); 3 **to raise money for something** Geld für etwas aufbringen ◇ SEP.

raisin noun Rosine die (PL die Rosinen).

rally noun 1 (a meeting) Versammlung die (PL die Versammlungen); 2 (for cars) Rallye die (PL die Rallyes); 3 (in tennis) Ballwechsel der (PL die Ballwechsel).

rambler noun Wanderer der (PL die Wanderer), Wanderin die (PL die Wanderinnen).

rambling noun Wandern das.

range noun 1 (a choice) Auswahl die; **a wide range of travel brochures** eine große Auswahl an Reiseprospekten; 2 **a range of subjects** verschiedene Fächer; **in a range of colours** in verschiedenen Farben; 3 **a computer in this price range** ein Computer in dieser Preislage; **that's out of my price range** das kann ich mir nicht leisten.

rap noun Rap der (music).

∆ NEW SPELLING: See page xii

rape noun Vergewaltigung die (PL die Vergewaltigungen).
verb vergewaltigen.

rare adjective 1 selten; **a rare bird** ein seltener Vogel; 2 englisch gebraten (steak).

rarely adverb selten.

rash noun Ausschlag der (PL die Ausschläge).
adjective voreilig.

raspberry noun Himbeere die (PL die Himbeeren); **raspberry jam** die Himbeermarmelade.

rat noun Ratte die (PL die Ratten).

rate noun 1 (a charge) Gebühren (plural); **postage rates** Postgebühren; 2 **are there special rates for children?** gibt es Sonderpreise für Kinder?; **at reduced rates** zu ermäßigten Preisen; 3 **rate of exchange** der Wechselkurs; 4 **rate of pay** der Lohnsatz; 5 (a level) Rate die (PL die Raten); **a high cancellation rate** eine hohe Absagerate; 6 **at any rate** auf jeden Fall.

rather adverb 1 lieber; **I'd rather wait** ich warte lieber; **I'd rather you didn't go** es wäre mir lieber, wenn du nicht gingst; 2 ziemlich; **I'm rather busy** ich habe ziemlich viel zu tun; **I've got rather a lot of shopping to do** ich muss noch ziemlich viel einkaufen; 3 **rather than** eher als; **in summer rather than winter** eher im Sommer als im Winter.

rave noun (party) Fete die (PL die Feten) (informal).

raw adjective roh.

razor noun Rasierapparat der (PL die Rasierapparate).

razor blade noun Rasierklinge die (PL die Rasierklingen).

RE noun Religionsunterricht der.

reach noun Reichweite die; **out of reach** außer Reichweite; **within reach** leicht erreichbar; **to be within easy reach of Munich** von München aus leicht erreichbar sein.
verb 1 ankommen ◇ SEP (PERF sein) an (+DAT) (a place or point), ankommen ◇ SEP (PERF sein) in (+DAT) (a town or country); **when you reach the station** wenn du am Bahnhof ankommst; 2 kommen ◇ (PERF sein) zu (+DAT) (an agreement, a conclusion); **to reach a decision** zu einer Entscheidung kommen; 3 **to reach for something** nach etwas ←(DAT) greifen ◇.

react verb reagieren.

reaction noun Reaktion die (PL die Reaktionen).

read verb 1 lesen ◇; **what are you reading at the moment?** was liest du zur Zeit?; **I'm reading a detective novel** ich lese einen Krimi; 2 **to read out** vorlesen ◇ SEP; **he read out the list to the students** er hat die Liste den Studenten vorgelesen.

reading noun 1 (action) Lesen das; 2 (reading matter) Lektüre die; **some easy reading for the holidays** eine leichte Lektüre für die Ferien.

ready adjective 1 fertig; **supper's not ready yet** das Essen ist noch nicht

◇ **IRREGULAR VERB: See the verb table in the centre of the dictionary**

fertig; **we are not quite ready** wir sind noch nicht ganz fertig; **are you ready to leave?** seid ihr fertig?; (*on a journey*) seid ihr reisefertig?; **to get ready** sich fertig machen; **I'm getting ready to play tennis** ich mache mich zum Tennisspielen fertig; **I was getting ready for bed** ich war gerade dabei, ins Bett zu gehen; **2 to get something ready** (*complete*) etwas fertig machen, etwas vorbereiten SEP (*a room or food*); **I'll get your room ready** ich bereite dein Zimmer vor.

real *adjective* **1** (*genuine*) echt; **it's a real diamond** das ist ein echter Brillant; **he's a real coward** er ist ein echter Feigling; **2** (*true*) richtig; **is that her real name?** ist das ihr richtiger Name?; **3** (*not imagined*) wirklich; **it's a real pity you can't come** es ist wirklich schade, dass du nicht kommen kannst.

realistic *adjective* realistisch.

realize *verb* wissen ✧; **I hadn't realized** das wusste ich nicht; **I didn't realize he was French** ich habe nicht gewusst, dass er Franzose ist; **do you realize what time it is?** weißt du, wie viel Uhr es ist?

really *adverb* **1** wirklich; **the film was really good** der Film war wirklich gut; **really?** wirklich?; **2 not really** eigentlich nicht.

reason *noun* Grund *der* (PL die Gründe); **for that reason** aus diesem Grund; **the reason why I phoned** der Grund meines Anrufs.

reasonable *adjective* vernünftig.

receipt *noun* Quittung *die* (PL die Quittungen).

receive *verb* erhalten ✧.

receiver *noun* Hörer *der* (PL die Hörer); **to pick up the receiver** den Hörer abnehmen ✧ SEP.

recent *adjective* **1** kürzlich erfolgter/kürzlich erfolgte/ kürzlich erfolgtes; **the recent closure** die kürzlich erfolgte Schließung; **2 in recent years** in den letzten Jahren.

recently *adverb* **1** (*at a time not long ago*) kürzlich; **2** (*over the recent period*) in letzter Zeit.

reception *noun* **1** Rezeption *die* (PL die Rezeptionen); **he's waiting at reception** er wartet in der Rezeption; **2** Empfang *der* (PL die Empfänge); **a big wedding reception** ein großer Hochzeitsempfang; **3 to get a good reception** gut aufgenommen werden.

receptionist *noun* **1** Empfangsdame *die* (PL die Empfangsdamen); **2** (*in a doctor's surgery*) Sprechstundenhilfe *die* (PL die Sprechstundenhilfen).

recipe *noun* Rezept *das* (PL die Rezepte).

reckon *verb* glauben; **I reckon it's a good idea** ich glaube, das ist eine gute Idee.

recognize *verb* erkennen ✧.

recommend *verb* empfehlen ✧; **can you recommend a dentist?** kannst du mir einen Zahnarzt

△ NEW SPELLING: See page xii

empfehlen?; **I recommend the fish soup** ich empfehle die Fischsuppe.

record noun 1 Rekord der (PL die Rekorde); **it's a world record** das ist ein Weltrekord; **record sales** Verkaufsrekorde; 2 (of events) Aufzeichnung die (PL die Aufzeichnungen); **on record** aufgezeichnet; **to keep a record of something** sich ←(DAT) etwas notieren; 3 (music) Platte die (PL die Platten); **a Miles Davis record** eine Platte von Miles Davis; 4 records (office files) Unterlagen (plural); **I'll just check your records** ich prüfe nur Ihre Unterlagen.
verb (on tape) aufnehmen ✧ SEP; **I'm recording it on cassette** ich nehme es auf Kassette auf.

recorder noun 1 Blockflöte die (PL die Blockflöten); **to play the recorder** Blockflöte spielen; 2 **cassette recorder** der Kassettenrekorder; **video recorder** der Videorekorder.

recording noun (on tape or CD) Aufnahme die (PL die Aufnahmen); (on video) Aufzeichnung die (PL die Aufzeichnungen).

record player noun Plattenspieler der (PL die Plattenspieler).

recover verb sich erholen; **she's recovered now** sie hat sich wieder erholt.

recovery noun (from an illness) Erholung die; **to make a good recovery** sich gut erholen.

recycle verb recyceln.

red adjective rot; **a red car** ein rotes Auto; **to go red** rot werden; **to have red hair** rote Haare haben.

Red Cross noun **the Red Cross** das Rote Kreuz.

redcurrant noun Johannisbeere die (PL die Johannisbeeren); **redcurrant jelly** das Johannisbeergelee.

redecorate verb (with paint) neu streichen ✧; (with wallpaper) neu tapezieren; **they've redecorated the kitchen** sie haben die Küche neu gestrichen.

redo verb noch einmal machen.

reduce verb 1 **to reduce prices** Preise herabsetzen SEP; 2 **to reduce speed** die Geschwindigkeit verringern.

reduction noun 1 (in price) Ermäßigung die (PL die Ermäßigungen); 2 (in speed or number) Verringerung die.

redundant adjective **to be made redundant** entlassen werden.

referee noun (in sport) Schiedsrichter der (PL die Schiedsrichter), Schiedsrichterin die (PL die Schiedsrichterinnen).

reference noun 1 Referenz die (PL die Referenzen); 2 (for a job) **she gave me a good reference** sie hat mir gute Referenzen ausgestellt.

reference book noun Nachschlagewerk das (PL die Nachschlagewerke).

refill verb nachfüllen SEP.

✧ IRREGULAR VERB: See the verb table in the centre of the dictionary

reflect verb spiegeln; to be reflected sich spiegeln.

reflection noun 1 (in a mirror or on water) Spiegelung die (PL die Spiegelungen); to see your reflection in the mirror sich im Spiegel sehen; 2 (thought) Überlegung die; on reflection nach nochmaliger Überlegung.

reflexive adjective a reflexive verb ein reflexives Verb.

refreshing adjective erfrischend.

refrigerator noun Kühlschrank der (PL die Kühlschränke).

refugee noun Flüchtling der (PL die Flüchtlinge).

refund noun Rückzahlung die (PL die Rückzahlungen). verb zurückerstatten SEP.

refusal noun 1 Weigerung die (PL die Weigerungen); 2 (for a job) Absage die (PL die Absagen); to get a refusal eine Absage bekommen.

refuse noun (rubbish) Abfall der. verb sich weigern; I refused ich habe mich geweigert; he refuses to help er weigert sich zu helfen.

regards plural noun Grüße (plural); regards to your parents viele Grüße an deine Eltern; Nat sends his regards Nat lässt grüßen.

reggae noun Reggae der.

region noun Gebiet das (PL die Gebiete).

regional adjective regional.

register noun (in school) Anwesenheitsliste die (PL die Anwesenheitslisten), Klassenbuch das (PL die Klassenbücher) (kept by the teacher, it also contains notes about students' achievements). verb 1 eintragen ◇ SEP (a name); 2 (report) anmelden SEP.

registered letter noun Einschreiben das (PL die Einschreiben).

registration number noun Autonummer die (PL die Autonummern).

regret verb bedauern.

regular adjective regelmäßig; regular visits regelmäßige Besuche.

regularly adverb regelmäßig.

regulation noun Vorschrift die (PL die Vorschriften).

rehearsal noun Probe die (PL die Proben).

rehearse verb proben.

reheat verb aufwärmen SEP.

reject verb ablehnen SEP.

related adjective verwandt; we're not related wir sind nicht verwandt.

relation noun Verwandte der/die (PL die Verwandten).

relationship noun Beziehung die (PL die Beziehungen); I have a good relationship with my parents ich habe eine gute Beziehung zu meinen Eltern.

relative noun Verwandte der/die (PL die Verwandten).

relatively adverb relativ.

relax verb entspannen; **I'm going to relax and watch telly tonight** heute Abend entspanne ich und sehe fern.

relaxed adjective entspannt.

relaxing adjective entspannend.

relay race noun Staffel die (PL die Staffeln).

release noun (a film, CD, or book) 1 Neuerscheinung die (PL die Neuerscheinungen); **this week's new releases** die neuen Filme der Woche; 2 (of a prisoner or hostage) Freilassung die (PL die Freilassungen); verb 1 herausbringen ◇ SEP (a record, film, or video); 2 freilassen ◇ SEP (a person).

reliable adjective zuverlässig.

relief noun Erleichterung die; **what a relief!** da bin ich aber erleichtert!

relieve verb stillen (pain).

relieved adjective erleichtert; **I was relieved to hear you'd arrived** es hat mich erleichtert zu hören, dass du angekommen bist.

religion noun Religion die (PL die Religionen).

religious adjective religiös.

rely verb 1 (trust) to rely on somebody sich auf jemanden verlassen ◇; **I'm relying on your help for Saturday** ich verlasse mich darauf, dass du mir am Samstag

hilfst; 2 (be dependent on) to rely on angewiesen sein auf (+ACC).

remain verb (be left over) übrig bleiben ◇ △ (PERF sein); (stay) bleiben ◇ (PERF sein).

remark noun Bemerkung die (PL die Bemerkungen); **to make remarks about something** Bemerkungen über etwas ←(ACC) machen.

remarkable adjective bemerkenswert.

remarkably adverb bemerkenswert.

remember verb 1 sich erinnern (+ACC) (a person or an occasion); **I don't remember** daran kann ich mich nicht erinnern; **do you remember the holiday in Italy?** erinnerst du dich noch an die Ferien in Italien?; 2 **I can't remember his number** seine Nummer fällt mir nicht ein; 3 **to remember to do something** daran denken ◇, etwas zu tun; **remember to lock the door** denk daran abzuschließen; **I remembered to bring the CDs** ich habe daran gedacht, die CDs mitzubringen.

remind verb 1 erinnern; **to remind somebody to do something** jemanden daran erinnern, etwas zu tun; **remind your mother to pick me up** erinnere deine Mutter daran, mich abzuholen; **he reminds me of my brother** er erinnert mich an meinen Bruder; 2 **oh, that reminds me** ... dabei fällt mir ein, ...

remote adjective abgelegen.

◇ IRREGULAR VERB: *See the verb table in the centre of the dictionary*

remote control noun 1 (for a car or plane) Fernsteuerung die (PL die Fernsteuerungen); 2 (for TV or video) Fernbedienung die (PL die Fernbedienungen).

remove verb 1 entfernen (a stain, mark, or obstacle); 2 ausziehen ◇ SEP (clothes).

renew verb verlängern (a passport or licence).

rent noun Miete die (PL die Mieten). verb mieten; **Simon's rented a flat** Simon hat eine Wohnung gemietet.

reorganize verb umorganisieren.

repair noun Reparatur die (PL die Reparaturen). verb reparieren; **to get something repaired** etwas reparieren lassen; **we've had the television repaired** wir haben unseren Fernseher reparieren lassen.

repay verb zurückzahlen SEP.

repeat noun Wiederholung die (PL die Wiederholungen). verb wiederholen.

repeatedly adverb wiederholt.

repetitive adjective eintönig.

replace verb ersetzen.

reply noun Antwort die (PL die Antworten); **I didn't get a reply to my letter** ich habe keine Antwort auf meinen Brief bekommen; **there's no reply** niemand antwortet. verb antworten; **I still haven't replied to the letter** ich habe immer noch nicht auf den Brief geantwortet.

report noun 1 (of an event) Bericht der (PL die Berichte); 2 (school report) Zeugnis das (PL die Zeugnisse). verb 1 melden (a problem or an accident); **we've reported the theft** wir haben den Diebstahl gemeldet; 2 sich melden; **I had to report to reception** ich musste mich an der Rezeption melden; 3 (in the news) berichten; **to report on the strike** über den Streik berichten.

reporter noun Reporter der (PL die Reporter), Reporterin die (PL die Reporterinnen).

represent verb 1 darstellen SEP (a word, a thing, an idea); 2 vertreten ◇ (a group or company).

representative noun Vertreter der (PL die Vertreter), Vertreterin die (PL die Vertreterinnen).

republic noun Republik die (PL die Republiken).

reputation noun 1 Ruf der; **to have a good reputation** einen guten Ruf haben; 2 **she has a reputation for honesty** sie gilt als ehrlich.

request noun Bitte die (PL die Bitten); **at my mother's request** auf Bitte meiner Mutter. verb bitten ◇; **to request something** um etwas ←(ACC) bitten.

rescue noun Rettung die; **rescue operation** die Rettungsaktion; **to come to somebody's rescue** jemandem zu Hilfe kommen. verb retten; **they rescued the dog** sie haben den Hund gerettet.

△ NEW SPELLING: See page xii

rescue party noun
Rettungsmannschaft die (PL die
Rettungsmannschaften).

research noun 1 Forschung die;
for research into Aids für die
Aidsforschung; 2 **to do research**
forschen.
verb **to research into something**
etwas erforschen.

resemblance noun
Ähnlichkeit die (PL die
Ähnlichkeiten).

reservation noun (a booking)
Reservierung die (PL die
Reservierungen); **to make a
reservation (for a room)** (ein
Zimmer) reservieren lassen.

reserve noun 1 Reserve die (PL die
Reserven); **we have a few in
reserve** wir haben ein paar in
Reserve; 2 **nature reserve** das
Naturschutzgebiet; 3 (for a match)
Reservespieler der (PL die
Reservespieler), Reservespielerin
die (PL die Reservespielerinnen).
verb reservieren; **this table is
reserved** dieser Tisch ist reserviert.

resident noun Bewohner der (PL die
Bewohner), Bewohnerin die (PL die
Bewohnerinnen).

residential adjective Wohn-; **a
residential area** eine Wohngegend.

resign verb 1 (from your job)
kündigen; 2 (from an official post)
zurücktreten ◇ SEP.

resignation noun 1 Kündigung die
(PL die Kündigungen); 2 (from an
official post) Rücktritt der.

resist verb widerstehen ◇ (+DAT)
(an offer or temptation).

resit verb wiederholen (an exam).

resort noun 1 (for holidays) **holiday
resort** der Urlaubsort; **ski resort**
der Skiurlaubsort; **seaside resort**
das Seebad; 2 **as a last resort** als
letzter Ausweg.

respect noun Respekt der.
verb respektieren.

respectable adjective anständig.

responsibility noun
Verantwortung die (PL die
Verantwortungen).

responsible adjective
1 verantwortlich; **he was
responsible for the accident** er war
für den Unfall verantwortlich; **I'm
responsible for booking the rooms**
ich bin für die Zimmerreservierung
verantwortlich; 2 (reliable)
verantwortungsbewusst △; **he's not
very responsible** er ist nicht sehr
verantwortungsbewusst.

rest noun 1 the rest der Rest; **the
rest of the day** der Rest des Tages;
the rest of the bread der Brotrest,
der Rest vom dem Brot; 2 (the others)
the rest die Übrigen; **the rest have
gone home** die Übrigen sind nach
Hause gegangen; 3 Erholung die;
**he's going to the mountains for a
rest** er fährt zur Erholung ins
Gebirge; **ten days' rest** zehn Tage
Erholung; **to have a rest** sich
ausruhen SEP; 4 (a short break)
Pause die (PL die Pausen); **to stop for
a rest** eine Pause machen.
verb (have a rest) sich ausruhen SEP.

◇ IRREGULAR VERB: See the verb table in the centre of the dictionary

restaurant noun Restaurant das (PL die Restaurants).

restful adjective erholsam.

restless adjective unruhig.

restrain verb zurückhalten ◇ SEP.

result noun 1 Ergebnis das (PL die Ergebnisse); **the exam results** die Prüfungsergebnisse; 2 **as a result** infolgedessen; **as a result we missed the train** infolgedessen haben wir den Zug verpasst.

retire verb 1 (from work) aufhören zu arbeiten; (civil servant, teacher, soldier) sich pensionieren lassen; **she retires in June** sie lässt sich im Juni pensionieren; 2 **to be retired** nicht mehr arbeiten.

retirement noun Ruhestand der; **since his retirement** seitdem er in den Ruhestand gegangen ist.

return noun 1 (coming back) Rückkehr die; **the return journey** die Rückreise; 2 **by return of post** postwendend; 3 **in return for** für; **in return for his help** für seine Hilfe; 4 **in return** dafür; ★ **many happy returns!** herzlichen Glückwunsch zum Geburtstag.
verb 1 (come back) zurückkommen ◇ SEP (PERF sein); **he returned ten minutes later** er kam zehn Minuten später zurück; **to return from holiday** aus den Ferien zurückkommen; 2 (go back) zurückgehen ◇ SEP (PERF sein); (drive) zurückfahren ◇ SEP (PERF sein); **we are planning to return in the evening** wir wollen am Abend zurückfahren; 3 (to give back)

zurückgeben ◇ SEP; **Gemma's never returned the video** Gemma hat das Video nie zurückgegeben.

return fare noun Preis für eine Rückfahrkarte der; (for a flight) Preis für einen Rückflugschein der.

return ticket noun Rückfahrkarte die (PL die Rückfahrkarten); (for a flight) Rückflugschein der (PL die Rückflugscheine)

reveal verb enthüllen.

reverse verb 1 (in a car) rückwärts fahren ◇ (PERF sein); 2 **to reverse the charges** ein R-Gespräch führen.

review noun (of a book, play, or film) Kritik die (PL die Kritiken).
verb rezensieren (a book, play, or film).

revise verb 1 lernen (for an exam); **Tessa's busy revising for her exams** Tessa lernt jetzt für ihre Prüfung; 2 wiederholen; **to revise maths** Mathe wiederholen.

revision noun Wiederholung die.

revolting adjective eklig.

revolution noun Revolution die (PL die Revolutionen).

reward noun Belohnung die (PL die Belohnungen).
verb belohnen.

rewind verb zurückspulen SEP (a cassette or video).

rhubarb noun Rhabarber der.

rhyme noun Reim der (PL die Reime).

△ NEW SPELLING: See page xii

rhythm *noun* Rhythmus *der* (PL *die* Rhythmen).

ribbon *noun* Band *das* (PL *die* Bänder).

rice *noun* Reis *der*; **rice pudding** *der* Milchreis.

rich *adjective* **1** reich; **they are very rich** sie sind sehr reich; **2 the rich** die Reichen.

rid *adjective* **to get rid of something** etwas loswerden ✧ SEP (PERF *sein*) (*informal*); **we got rid of the car** wir sind das Auto losgeworden.

riddle *noun* Rätsel *das* (PL *die* Rätsel).

ride *noun* Fahrt *die* (PL *die* Fahrten); **to go for a ride (on a bike)** eine Fahrt machen; **to go for a ride (on a horse)** reiten gehen ✧ (PERF *sein*). *verb* **1 to ride a bike** Rad fahren ✧ △ (PERF *sein*); **can you ride a bike?** kannst du Rad fahren?; **I've never ridden a bike** ich bin noch nie Rad gefahren; **2 to ride (a horse)** reiten ✧ (PERF *sein*); **I've never ridden a horse** ich bin noch nie auf einem Pferd geritten.

ridiculous *adjective* lächerlich.

riding *noun* Reiten *das*; **to go riding** reiten gehen.

riding school *noun* Reitschule *die* (PL *die* Reitschulen).

right *noun* **1** (*not left*) rechte Seite *die*; **on the right** auf der rechten Seite; **on my right** rechts von mir; **2** (*to do something*) Recht *das* (PL *die* Rechte); **to have the right to something** ein Recht auf etwas ←(ACC) haben; **the right to work** das Recht auf Arbeit; **you have no right to say that** du hast kein Recht, das zu sagen.
adjective **1** (*not left*) rechter/rechte/rechtes; **my right hand** meine rechte Hand; **2** (*correct*) richtig; **the right answer** die richtige Antwort; **is this the right address?** ist das die richtige Adresse?; **3 to be right** (*of a person*) Recht haben; **you see, I was right** siehst du, ich hatte Recht; **4 you were right not to say anything** du hattest Recht, nichts zu sagen; **5 the clock is right** die Uhr geht richtig; **6 yes, that's right** ja, das stimmt; **is that right?** stimmt das?
adverb **1** (*direction*) rechts; **turn right at the lights** biege an der Ampel rechts ab; **2** (*correctly*) richtig; **you're not doing it right** du machst das nicht richtig; **3** (*completely*) ganz; **right at the bottom** ganz unten; **right at the beginning** ganz am Anfang; **4** (*exactly*) genau; **right in the middle** genau in der Mitte; **5 right now** sofort; **6** (*okay*) gut; **right, let's go** gut, gehen wir.

right-hand *adjective* **on the right-hand side** rechts.

right-handed *adjective* rechtshändig.

ring *noun* **1** (*on the phone*) **to give somebody a ring** jemanden anrufen ✧ SEP; **2** (*for your finger*) Ring *der* (PL *die* Ringe); **3** (*circle*) Kreis *der* (PL *die* Kreise); **4 there was a ring at the door** es hat geklingelt.

✧ IRREGULAR VERB: *See the verb table in the centre of the dictionary*

verb 1 (*a bell or phone*) klingeln; **the phone rang** das Telefon hat geklingelt; **2** (*phone*) anrufen ✧ SEP; **I'll ring you tomorrow** ich rufe dich morgen an; **3 to ring for a taxi** ein Taxi rufen.

- **to ring back** zurückrufen ✧ SEP; **I'll ring you back later** ich rufe dich später zurück.
- **to ring off** auflegen SEP.

ring road noun Ringstraße die (PL die Ringstraßen).

rinse verb spülen.

riot noun Aufstand der (PL die Aufstände).

rioting noun Unruhen (*plural*).

rip verb zerreißen ✧.

ripe adjective reif; **are the tomatoes ripe?** sind die Tomaten reif?

rip-off noun **it's a rip-off** das ist Nepp (*informal*).

rise noun **1** Anstieg der; **a rise in temperature** ein Temperaturanstieg; **2 pay rise** die Gehaltserhöhung.
verb **1** (*the sun*) aufgehen ✧ SEP (PERF sein); **2** (*prices*) steigen ✧ (PERF sein).

risk noun Risiko das (PL die Risiken); **to take a risk** ein Risiko eingehen.
verb riskieren; **he risks losing his job** er riskiert es, seine Stelle zu verlieren.

river noun Fluss △ der (PL die Flüsse).

road noun **1** Straße die (PL die Straßen); **the road to London** die Straße nach London; **2 the baker's is on the other side of the road** die Bäckerei ist auf der anderen Straßenseite; **3 across the road** gegenüber; **they live across the road from us** sie wohnen bei uns gegenüber.

road accident noun Verkehrsunfall der (PL die Verkehrsunfälle).

road map noun Straßenkarte die (PL die Straßenkarten).

roadside noun **by the roadside** am Straßenrand.

road sign noun Straßenschild das (PL die Straßenschilder).

roadworks plural noun Straßenarbeiten (*plural*).

roast noun Braten der (PL die Braten).
adjective gebraten; **roast potatoes** Bratkartoffeln; **roast beef** der Rinderbraten.

rob verb **1** berauben (*a person*); **2** ausrauben SEP (*a bank*).

robber noun Räuber der (PL die Räuber).

robbery noun Raub der (PL die Raube); **bank robbery** der Bankraub.

rock noun **1** (*a big stone*) Felsen der (PL die Felsen); **2** (*the material*) Fels der; **3** (*music*) Rock der; **rock band** die Rockband; **to dance rock and roll** Rock'n'Roll tanzen.

rock climbing noun Klettern das; **to go rock climbing** zum Klettern gehen.

△ NEW SPELLING: See page xii

rock star noun Rockstar der (PL die Rockstars).

rocky adjective felsig.

rod noun a fishing rod eine Angel.

role noun Rolle die (PL die Rollen); to play the role of Hamlet die Rolle des Hamlet spielen.

roll noun 1 Rolle die (PL die Rollen); a roll of film eine Rolle Film; a toilet roll eine Rolle Toilettenpapier; 2 bread roll das Brötchen, die Semmel (South German). verb rollen (PERF sein).

roller noun 1 (for hair) Lockenwickler der (PL die Lockenwickler); 2 (for paint) Rolle die (PL die Rollen).

rollerblades plural noun Inlineskates (plural), Inliners (plural).

roller skates plural noun Rollschuhe (plural).

Roman Catholic adjective römisch-katholisch.

romantic adjective romantisch.

roof noun Dach das (PL die Dächer).

roof rack noun Gepäckträger der (PL die Gepäckträger).

room noun 1 Zimmer das (PL die Zimmer); she's in the other room sie ist im anderen Zimmer; a three-room flat eine Dreizimmerwohnung; 2 (space) Platz der; enough room for two genug Platz für zwei; very little room wenig Platz; to make room Platz machen.

root noun Wurzel die (PL die Wurzeln).

rope noun Seil das (PL die Seile).

rose noun Rose die (PL die Rosen).

rot verb verfaulen (PERF sein).

rotten adjective verfault.

rough adjective 1 (scratchy) rauh; 2 (vague) grob (plan or estimate); 3 a rough idea eine vage Vorstellung; 4 (stormy) stürmisch; a rough sea eine stürmische See; 5 (difficult) to have a rough time es schwer haben; 6 to sleep rough im Freien schlafen.

roughly adverb (approximately) ungefähr; roughly ten per cent ungefähr zehn Prozent; it takes roughly three hours es dauert ungefähr drei Stunden.

round noun Runde die (PL die Runden); a round of talks eine Gesprächsrunde; a round of drinks eine Runde. adjective rund; a round table ein runder Tisch. preposition 1 um (+ACC); round the city um die Stadt; round my arm um meinen Arm; they were sitting round the table sie haben um den Tisch gesessen; it's just round the corner es ist gleich um die Ecke; 2 to go round a museum ein Museum besuchen. adverb 1 to go round to somebody's house jemanden besuchen←(DAT); 2 to invite somebody round jemanden zu sich←(DAT) einladen ◊ SEP; we invited Sally round for lunch wir

◊ **IRREGULAR VERB:** See the verb table in the centre of the dictionary

haben Sally zum Mittagessen eingeladen; **3 to look round the shops** sich in den Geschäften umsehen ◇ SEP; **4 all the year round** das ganze Jahr hindurch.

roundabout noun **1** (*for traffic*) Kreisverkehr der; **2** (*in a fairground*) Karussell das (PL die Karussells).

route noun **1** (*that you plan*) Route die (PL die Routen); **the best route is via Calais** die beste Route ist über Calais; **2 bus route** die Linie.

row¹ noun **1** Reihe die (PL die Reihen); **in the front row** in der ersten Reihe; **in the back row** in der letzten Reihe; **2 in a row** hintereinander; **four times in a row** viermal hintereinander.
verb (*in a boat*) rudern (PERF sein/haben); **we rowed across the lake** wir sind über den See gerudert; **he rowed us across the lake** er hat uns über den See gerudert.

row² noun **1** (*a quarrel*) Krach der (*informal*) (PL die Kräche); **to have a row** Krach haben; **they've had a row** sie haben Krach gehabt; **I had a row with my parents** ich habe Krach mit meinen Eltern gehabt; **2** (*noise*) Krach der; **they were making a terrible row** sie haben einen furchtbaren Krach gemacht.

rowing noun Rudern das; **to go rowing** rudern gehen.

rowing boat noun Ruderboot das (PL die Ruderboote).

royal adjective königlich; **the royal family** die königliche Familie.

rub verb reiben ◇; **to rub your eyes** sich ←(DAT) die Augen reiben.
● **to rub something out** etwas ausradieren SEP.

rubber noun **1** (*an eraser*) Radiergummi der (PL die Radiergummis); **2** (*material*) Gummi der; **rubber soles** Gummisohlen.

rubbish noun **1** (*for the bin*) Müll der; **2** (*nonsense*) Quatsch der (*informal*); **you're talking rubbish!** du redest Quatsch.
adjective blöd; **the film was rubbish** der Film war blöd; **they're a rubbish band** sie sind eine blöde Band.

rubbish bin noun Mülleimer der (PL die Mülleimer).

rucksack noun Rucksack der (PL die Rucksäcke).

rude adjective **1** unhöflich; **that's rude** das ist unhöflich; **2** unanständig; **a rude joke** ein unanständiger Witz.

rug noun **1** Teppich der (PL die Teppiche); **2** (*a blanket*) Decke die (PL die Decken).

rugby noun Rugby das.

ruin noun (*remains*) Ruine die (PL die Ruinen); **in ruins** in Trümmern.
verb **1** ruinieren; **you'll ruin your jacket** du ruinierst dir die Jacke; **2** verderben ◇ (*day, holiday*); **it ruined my evening** das hat mir den Abend verdorben.

rule noun **1** Regel die (PL die Regeln); **the rules of the game** die

△ NEW SPELLING: See page xii

Spielregeln; **as a rule** in der Regel; 2 (*administrative*) Vorschrift die (PL die Vorschriften); **according to the school rules** nach den Schulvorschriften.

ruler noun Lineal das (PL die Lineale); **I've lost my ruler** ich habe mein Lineal verloren.

rumour noun Gerücht das (PL die Gerüchte).

run noun 1 (*in games, sport, and for fitness*) Lauf der (PL die Läufe); **to go for a run** einen Lauf machen, joggen (PERF *sein*); 2 (*of a play*) Laufzeit die; 3 (*in skiing*) Abfahrt die (PL die Abfahrten); 4 **in the long run** auf lange Sicht. verb 1 laufen ✧ (PERF *sein*); **I ran ten kilometres** ich bin zehn Kilometer gelaufen; **he ran across the pitch** er ist über das Spielfeld gelaufen; 2 (*run fast*) rennen ✧ (PERF *sein*); **Kitty ran for the bus** Kitty rannte, um den Bus zu kriegen; 3 (*drive*) fahren ✧; **I'll run you home later** ich fahre dich später nach Hause; 4 (*organize*) veranstalten (*a course or competition*); **who's running this competition?** wer veranstaltet diesen Wettbewerb?; 5 (*manage*) leiten (*a business*); **she's been running the firm for years** sie leitet die Firma schon seit Jahren; **to run a shop** ein Geschäft führen; 6 (*a train or a bus*) fahren ✧ (PERF *sein*); **the buses don't run on Sundays** sonntags fahren keine Busse; 7 **to run a bath** ein Bad einlaufen lassen.
● **to run away** weglaufen ✧ SEP (PERF *sein*).

● **to run into something** gegen etwas ←(ACC) fahren ✧ (PERF *sein*); **the car ran into a tree** das Auto ist gegen einen Baum gefahren.

● **to run out of something: we've run out of bread** wir haben kein Brot mehr; **I'm running out of money** ich habe kaum noch Geld.

● **to run somebody over** jemanden überfahren ✧; **he nearly got run over** er ist beinahe überfahren worden.

runner noun Läufer der (PL die Läufer), Läuferin die (PL die Läuferinnen).

runner-up noun Zweite der/die (PL die Zweiten).

running noun (*for exercise*) Laufen das, Jogging das. adjective 1 **running water** fließendes Wasser; **2 three days running** drei Tage hintereinander; **to win three times running** dreimal hintereinander gewinnen.

runway noun 1 (*for take-off*) Startbahn die (PL die Startbahnen); 2 (*for landing*) Landebahn die (PL die Landebahnen).

rush noun (*a hurry*) **to be in a rush** in Eile sein; **sorry, I'm in a rush** Entschuldigung, ich bin in Eile. verb 1 (*hurry*) sich beeilen; **I must rush!** ich muss mich beeilen; 2 (*run*) rasen (PERF *sein*); **she rushed out** sie raste raus (*informal*); 3 **Louise was rushed to hospital** Louise ist schnellstens ins Krankenhaus gebracht worden.

✧ IRREGULAR VERB: *See the verb table in the centre of the dictionary*

rush hour noun Stoßzeit die (PL die Stoßzeiten); **in the rush hour** während der Stoßzeit.

Russia noun Russland △ das.

Russian noun 1 (a person) Russe der (PL die Russen), Russin die (PL die Russinnen); 2 (the language) Russisch das. adjective russisch; **he's Russian** er ist Russe.

rust noun Rost der.

rusty adjective rostig.

rye noun Roggen der.

S s

Sabbath noun 1 (Jewish) Sabbat der (PL die Sabbate); 2 (Christian) Sonntag der (PL die Sonntage).

sack noun 1 Sack der (PL die Säcke); 2 **to get the sack** rausgeschmissen werden (informal). verb **to sack somebody** jemanden rausschmeißen ◇ SEP (informal).

sad adjective traurig.

saddle noun Sattel der (PL die Sättel).

sadly adverb 1 traurig; **she looked at me sadly** sie hat mich traurig angesehen; 2 (unfortunately) leider.

safe adjective 1 (out of danger) sicher; **to feel safe from something** sich vor etwas ←(DAT) sicher fühlen;

2 **she's safe** sie ist in Sicherheit; 3 (not dangerous) ungefährlich; **the path is safe** der Weg ist ungefährlich; **it's not safe** das ist gefährlich.

safety noun Sicherheit die.

safety belt noun Sicherheitsgurt der (PL die Sicherheitsgurte).

safety pin noun Sicherheitsnadel die (PL die Sicherheitsnadeln).

Sagittarius noun Schütze der; **Kylie's Sagittarius** Kylie ist Schütze.

sail noun Segel das (PL die Segel).

sailing noun Segeln das; **to go sailing** segeln.

sailing boat noun Segelboot das (PL die Segelboote).

sailor noun Seemann der (PL die Seeleute).

saint noun Heilige der/die.

sake noun 1 **for your mother's sake** deiner Mutter zuliebe; 2 **for heaven's sake** um Gottes willen.

salad noun Salat der (PL die Salate); **tomato salad** der Tomatensalat.

salad dressing noun Salatsoße die (PL die Salatsoßen).

salary noun Gehalt das (PL die Gehälter).

sale noun 1 (selling) Verkauf der (PL die Verkäufe); **the sale of the house** der Verkauf des Hauses; **'for sale'** 'zu verkaufen'; 2 **the sales**

△ NEW SPELLING: See page xii

der Ausverkauf; **I bought it in the sales** ich habe es im Ausverkauf gekauft.

sales assistant noun
Verkäufer der (PL die Verkäufer), Verkäuferin die (PL die Verkäuferinnen).

salesman noun Verkäufer der (PL die Verkäufer).

saleswoman noun
Verkäuferin die (PL die Verkäuferinnen).

salmon noun Lachs der (PL die Lachse).

salt noun Salz das.

salty adjective salzig.

same adjective **the same** der gleiche/die gleiche/das gleiche; **she said the same thing** sie hat das gleiche gesagt; **her birthday's the same day as mine** sie hat am gleichen Tag Geburtstag wie ich; **at the same time** zur gleichen Zeit; **their car's the same as ours** sie haben das gleiche Auto wie wir.
adverb **1 the same** gleich; **the two bikes look the same** die beiden Fahrräder sehen gleich aus; **2 all the same** trotzdem.

sample noun Muster das (PL die Muster); **a free sample** ein unverkäufliches Muster, eine Warenprobe.

sand noun Sand der.

sandal noun Sandale die (PL die Sandalen); **a pair of sandals** ein Paar Sandalen.

sandwich noun Sandwich das (PL die Sandwichs), belegte Brot das (PL die belegten Brote); **ham sandwich** das Schinkenbrot.

sanitary towel noun
Damenbinde die (PL die Damenbinden).

Santa Claus noun der Weihnachtsmann.

sarcastic adjective sarkastisch.

sardine noun Sardine die (PL die Sardinen).

satchel noun Ranzen der (PL die Ranzen).

satellite noun Satellit der (PL die Satelliten).

satellite dish noun
Satellitenschüssel die (PL die Satellitenschüsseln).

satellite television noun
Satellitenfernsehen das.

satisfactory adjective
befriedigend.

satisfied adjective zufrieden.

satisfy verb befriedigen.

satisfying adjective **1** befriedigend; **2 a satisfying meal** ein sättigendes Essen.

Saturday noun **1** Samstag der (PL die Samstage), Sonnabend der (North German) (PL die Sonnabende); **on Saturday** am Sonnabend/am Samstag; **I'm going out on Saturday** ich gehe Sonnabend aus; **see you on Saturday!** bis Samstag!; **every Saturday** jeden Samstag; **last**

◇ IRREGULAR VERB: See the verb table in the centre of the dictionary

Saturday vorigen Sonnabend; **next Saturday** nächsten Sonnabend; **2 on Saturdays** samstags, sonnabends (*North German*); **the museum is closed on Saturdays** das Museum ist sonnabends/ samstags geschlossen; **to have a Saturday job** sonnabends/ samstags arbeiten.

sauce *noun* Soße die (PL die Soßen).

saucepan *noun* Kochtopf der (PL die Kochtöpfe).

saucer *noun* Untertasse die (PL die Untertassen).

sausage *noun* Wurst die (PL die Würste).

save *verb* **1** retten (*life*); **to save somebody's life** jemandem das Leben retten; **the doctors saved his life** die Ärzte haben ihm das Leben gerettet; **2** sparen (*money*); **I've saved £60** ich habe sechzig Pfund gespart; **I cycle to school to save money** ich fahre mit dem Rad zur Schule, um Geld zu sparen; **we'll take a taxi to save time** um Zeit zu sparen, nehmen wir ein Taxi; **3** (*on a computer*) speichern; **4** (*stop*) abwehren SEP (*a shot*); **to save a penalty** einen Elfmeter abwehren.

● **to save up** sparen; **I'm saving up for a car** ich spare auf ein Auto.

savings *plural noun* Ersparnisse (*plural*).

savoury *adjective* (*not sweet*) pikant.

sax *noun* Saxophon das (PL die Saxophone).

saxophone *noun* Saxophon das (PL die Saxophone); **to play the saxophone** Saxophon spielen.

say *verb* **1** sagen; **what did you say?** was hast du gesagt?; **she says she's tired** sie sagt, dass sie müde ist; **he said to wait here** er hat gesagt, wir sollen hier warten; **they say** man sagt; **2** to say something again etwas wiederholen; **3** that's to say das heißt.

saying *noun* Redensart die (PL die Redensarten); **it's just a saying** das ist so eine Redensart; **as the saying goes** wie man so sagt.

scale *noun* **1** (*of a map or model*) Maßstab der (PL die Maßstäbe); **2** (*extent*) Ausmaß das (PL die Ausmaße); **the scale of the disaster** das Ausmaß der Katastrophe; **3** (*in music*) Tonleiter die (PL die Tonleitern).

scales *plural noun* Waage die (PL die Waagen); **bathroom scales** die Personenwaage.

scandal *noun* **1** Skandal der (PL die Skandale); **2** (*gossip*) Klatsch der (*informal*).

Scandinavia *noun* Skandinavien das.

Scandinavian *adjective* skandinavisch.

scar *noun* Narbe die (PL die Narben).

scarce *adjective* knapp.

scare *noun* **1** Schrecken der (PL die Schrecken); **to give somebody a scare** jemandem einen Schrecken einjagen SEP; **2** (*general alarm*)

△ NEW SPELLING: See page xii

Panik *die* (PL *die* Paniken); **to cause a scare** eine Panik auslösen; **3 bomb scare** die Bombendrohung. *verb* **to scare somebody** jemanden erschrecken; **you scared me! du hast mich erschreckt!**

scared *adjective* **1 to be scared** Angst haben; **I'm scared** ich habe Angst; **to be scared of something** vor etwas ←(DAT) Angst haben; **he's scared of dogs** er hat vor Hunden Angst; **2 to be scared of doing something** sich nicht trauen, etwas zu tun; **I'm scared of telling him the truth** ich traue mich nicht, ihm die Wahrheit zu sagen.

scarf *noun* **1** (*silky*) Tuch *das* (PL *die* Tücher); **2** (*long, warm*) Schal *der* (PL *die* Schals).

scary *adjective* unheimlich.

scene *noun* **1** (*of an incident or event*) Schauplatz *der* (PL *die* Schauplätze); **to be on the scene** am Schauplatz sein; **the scene of the crime** der Tatort; **2** (*world*) **the music scene** die Musikszene; **on the fashion scene** in der Modewelt; **3** (*argument*) Szene *die* (PL *die* Szenen); **to make a scene** eine Szene machen.

scenery *noun* **1** (*landscape*) Landschaft *die*; **2** (*in the theatre*) Bühnenbild *das*.

schedule *noun* Programm *das* (PL *die* Programme).

scheme *noun* Projekt *das* (PL *die* Projekte).

scholarship *noun* Stipendium *das* (PL *die* Stipendien).

school *noun* Schule *die* (PL *die* Schulen); **at school** in der Schule; **to go to school** zur Schule gehen.

schoolbook *noun* Schulbuch *das* (PL *die* Schulbücher).

schoolboy *noun* Schüler *der* (PL *die* Schüler).

schoolchildren *plural noun* Schulkinder (*plural*).

schoolfriend *noun* Schulfreund *der* (PL *die* Schulfreunde), Schulfreundin *die* (PL *die* Schulfreundinnen).

schoolgirl *noun* Schülerin *die* (PL *die* Schülerinnen).

science *noun* Wissenschaft *die* (PL *die* Wissenschaften).

science fiction *noun* Sciencefiction △ *die*.

scientific *adjective* wissenschaftlich.

scientist *noun* Wissenschaftler *der* (PL *die* Wissenschaftler), Wissenschaftlerin *die* (PL *die* Wissenschaftlerinnen).

scissors *plural noun* Schere *die* (PL *die* Scheren); **a pair of scissors** eine Schere.

scooter *noun* **1** (*motor scooter*) Motorroller *der* (PL *die* Motorroller); **2** (*for a child*) Roller *der* (PL *die* Roller).

score *noun* Spielstand *der* (PL *die* Spielstände); **the score was three two** es stand drei zu zwei. *verb* **1 to score a goal** ein Tor schießen ◇; **2 to score three**

◇ IRREGULAR VERB: *See the verb table in the centre of the dictionary*

points drei Punkte erzielen; **3** (*keep score*) zählen.

Scorpio noun Skorpion *der*; **Neil is Scorpio** Neil ist Skorpion.

Scot noun Schotte *der* (PL die Schotten), Schottin *die* (PL die Schottinnen); **the Scots** die Schotten.

Scotland noun Schottland *das*; **from Scotland** aus Schottland; **Pauline's from Scotland** Pauline kommt aus Schottland; **to Scotland** nach Schottland.

Scots adjective schottisch.

Scotsman noun Schotte *der* (PL die Schotten).

Scotswoman noun Schottin *die* (PL die Schottinnen).

Scottish adjective schottisch; **he's Scottish** er ist Schotte.

scout noun Pfadfinder *der* (PL die Pfadfinder).

scrambled eggs noun Rührei *das*.

scrap noun Stück *das* (PL die Stücke); **a scrap of paper** ein Stück Papier.

scrapbook noun Album *das* (PL die Alben).

scrape verb **1** schaben (*potatoes or carrots*); **2** (*remove dirt or paint*) abkratzen SEP; **3** (*damage*) verschrammen.

scratch noun (*on your skin or a surface*) Kratzer *der* (PL die Kratzer); ★ **to start from scratch** von vorn anfangen ◇ SEP.

verb (*scratch yourself*) sich kratzen; **to scratch your head** sich am Kopf kratzen.

scream noun Schrei *der* (PL die Schreie).
verb schreien ◇.

screen noun **1** Bildschirm *der* (PL die Bildschirme) (*of a TV or computer*); **on the screen** auf dem Bildschirm; **2** (*in the cinema*) Leinwand *die* (PL die Leinwände).

screw noun Schraube *die* (PL die Schrauben).
verb schrauben.

screwdriver noun Schraubenzieher *der* (PL die Schraubenzieher).

scribble verb kritzeln.

scrub verb scheuern (*a saucepan or the floor*); **to scrub your nails** sich ←(DAT) die Nägel bürsten.

sculptor noun Bildhauer *der* (PL die Bildhauer), Bildhauerin *die* (PL die Bildhauerinnen); **Rebecca's a sculptor** Rebecca ist Bildhauerin.

sculpture noun Skulptur *die* (PL die Skulpturen).

sea noun Meer *das* (PL die Meere), See *die*; **by the sea** am Meer, an der See.

seafood noun Meeresfrüchte (*plural*); **I love seafood** ich esse Meeresfrüchte sehr gern.

search verb **1** absuchen SEP; **I've searched my desk but I can't find the letter** ich habe meinen Schreibtisch abgesucht, aber ich

△ NEW SPELLING: See page xii

kann den Brief nicht finden;
**2 durchsuchen; they searched the
building for him** sie haben das
Gebäude nach ihm durchsucht;
3 suchen; to search for something
nach etwas ←(DAT) suchen; **I've been
searching everywhere for my
scissors** ich habe überall nach
meiner Schere gesucht.

seasick adjective **to be seasick**
seekrank sein.

seaside noun **at the seaside** am
Meer.

season noun **1** Jahreszeit die (PL die
Jahreszeiten); **the four seasons** die
vier Jahreszeiten; **2** (period of social
or sporting activity) Saison die (PL
die Saisons); **the tennis season** die
Tennissaison; **off-season prices**
Preise außerhalb der Saison;
3 strawberries are not in season at
the moment jetzt ist nicht die
richtige Zeit für Erdbeeren.

season ticket noun
Dauerkarte die (PL die
Dauerkarten).

seat noun **1** Sitz der (PL die Sitze);
the front seat (in a car) der
Vordersitz; **the back seat** der
Rücksitz; **take a seat** nehmen Sie
Platz (formal); setz dich (informal);
2 (on a bus, in the home, etc.)
Platz der (PL die Plätze); **to book a
seat** einen Platz reservieren; **can
you keep my seat?** kannst du mir
meinen Platz freihalten?

seatbelt noun Sicherheitsgurt der
(PL die Sicherheitsgurte).

second noun Sekunde die (PL die
Sekunden); **can you wait a
second?** kannst du eine Sekunde
warten?
adjective **1** zweiter/zweite/zweites;
for the second time zum zweiten
Mal; **2 the second of July** der
zweite Juli.

secondary school noun **1** höhere
Schule die (PL die höheren Schulen)
(Germans define the type of secondary
school); **2** Gymnasium das (PL die
Gymnasien) (grammar school, from
age 10 to 19 when Abitur is taken);
3 Realschule die (PL die
Realschulen) (from age 10 to 16, less
academic than a Gymnasium).

secondhand adjective, adverb
gebraucht; **a secondhand bike** ein
gebrauchtes Fahrrad; **secondhand
car** der Gebrauchtwagen; **I bought
it secondhand** ich habe es
gebraucht gekauft.

secondly adverb zweitens.

secret noun Geheimnis das (PL die
Geheimnisse); **to tell somebody a
secret** jemandem ein Geheimnis
verraten; **in secret** heimlich.
adjective geheim; **a secret plan** ein
geheimer Plan; **to keep something
secret** etwas geheim halten.

secretary noun Sekretär der (PL die
Sekretäre), Sekretärin die (PL die
Sekretärinnen); **the secretary's
office** das Sekretariat.

secretly adverb heimlich.

sect noun Sekte die (PL die Sekten).

section noun Teil der (PL die Teile).

security noun Sicherheit die.

◇ **IRREGULAR VERB: See the verb table in the centre of the dictionary**

ecurity guard noun Wächter der (PL die Wächter), Wächterin die (PL die Wächterinnen).

ee verb 1 sehen ◇; I saw Lindy yesterday ich habe Lindy gestern gesehen; have you seen the film? hast du den Film gesehen?; I can't see anything ich kann überhaupt nichts sehen; 2 to go and see nachsehen ◇ SEP; I'll go and see ich sehe nach; 3 (visit) besuchen; why don't you come and see us in the summer? warum besucht ihr uns nicht im Sommer?; 4 to see somebody home jemanden nach Hause begleiten; 5 see you! tschüs! (informal); see you on Saturday! bis Samstag!; see you soon! bis bald!

to see to something sich um etwas ←(ACC) kümmern; Jo's seeing to the drinks Jo kümmert sich um die Getränke.

eed noun Samen der (PL die Samen).

eem verb 1 scheinen ◇; his story seems odd to me seine Geschichte kommt mir komisch vor; he seems shy er scheint schüchtern zu sein; the museum seems to be closed das Museum scheint geschlossen zu sein; 2 it seems (that) ... anscheinend ...; it seems he's left anscheinend ist er weggegangen; it seems that there are problems anscheinend gibt es Probleme.

elect verb auswählen SEP.

elf-confidence noun Selbstbewusstsein △ das; she doesn't have much self-

confidence sie hat sehr wenig Selbstbewusstsein.

self-employed adjective to be self-employed selbstständig △ sein; my parents are self-employed meine Eltern sind selbstständig.

selfish adjective egoistisch.

self-service adjective a self-service restaurant ein Selbstbedienungsrestaurant.

sell verb 1 verkaufen; to sell something to somebody jemandem etwas verkaufen; I sold him my bike ich habe ihm mein Rad verkauft; the house sold for a million das Haus wurde für eine Million verkauft; 2 the concert's sold out das Konzert ist ausverkauft; the tickets sold out very quickly die Karten waren schnell ausverkauft.

sell-by date noun Verfallsdatum das (PL die Verfallsdaten).

Sellotape™ noun Tesafilm™ der. verb to sellotape something etwas mit Tesafilm kleben.

semi noun Doppelhaushälfte die (PL die Doppelhaushälften).

semi-detached house noun Doppelhaushälfte die (PL die Doppelhaushälften).

semi-final noun Halbfinale das (PL die Halbfinale).

send verb schicken; to send something to somebody jemandem etwas schicken; I sent her a present for her birthday ich habe

△ NEW SPELLING: See page xii

ihr zum Geburtstag ein Geschenk geschickt.
- to send somebody back jemanden zurückschicken SEP.
- to send something back etwas zurückschicken SEP.

sender noun Absender der (PL die Absender).

senior citizen noun Senior der (PL die Senioren), Seniorin die (PL die Seniorinnen).

sensational adjective sensationell.

sense noun 1 (common sense) Verstand der; 2 (faculty) Sinn der (PL die Sinne); sense of smell der Geruchssinn; sense of touch der Tastsinn; to have a sense of humour Humor haben; she has no sense of humour sie hat keinen Sinn für Humor; 3 (meaning) Sinn der; this sentence makes no sense dieser Satz ergibt keinen Sinn; it doesn't make sense to do that es ist Unsinn, das zu machen; it makes sense to collect her first es ist sinnvoll, sie erst abzuholen.

sensible adjective vernünftig; be sensible sei vernünftig; that's a sensible suggestion das ist ein vernünftiger Vorschlag.

sensitive adjective empfindlich; for sensitive skin für empfindliche Haut.

sentence noun 1 (words) Satz der (PL die Sätze); 2 (prison) Strafe die (PL die Strafen); the death sentence die Todesstrafe.
verb verurteilen; to be sentenced to death zum Tode verurteilt

werden; to sentence somebody to a year in prison jemanden zu einem Jahr Gefängnis verurteilen.

separate adjective 1 extra ('extra' never has an ending); a separate pile ein extra Stapel; she wrote it on a separate sheet of paper sie hat es auf ein anderes Blatt Papier geschrieben; the drinks are separate die Getränke gehen extra; 2 (different) verschieden; two separate problems zwei verschiedene Probleme; 3 they have separate rooms sie haben getrennte Zimmer.
verb 1 trennen; 2 (a couple) sich trennen.

separately adverb 1 extra; 2 getrennt; they live separately sie leben getrennt.

separation noun Trennung die (PL die Trennungen).

September noun September der; in September im September.

sequel noun Folge die (PL die Folgen).

sergeant noun 1 (in the police) Polizeimeister der (PL die Polizeimeister), Polizeimeisterin die (PL die Polizeimeisterinnen); 2 (in the army) Feldwebel der (PL die Feldwebel).

serial noun
1 Fortsetzungsgeschichte die (PL die Fortsetzungsgeschichten); 2 (on TV or radio) Serie die (PL die Serien).

series noun Serie die (PL die Serien); television series die Fernsehserie.

◊ IRREGULAR VERB: See the verb table in the centre of the dictionary

serious *adjective* 1 ernst; a serious discussion eine ernste Unterhaltung; to be serious about something etwas ernst nehmen; are you serious? ist das dein Ernst?; 2 schwer (*accident or mistake*).

seriously *adverb* 1 im Ernst; seriously, I have to go now im Ernst, ich muss jetzt gehen; seriously? im Ernst?; 2 to take somebody seriously jemanden ernst nehmen; 3 (*gravely*) schwer; she is seriously ill sie ist schwer krank.

serve *noun* (*in tennis*) Aufschlag *der* (PL die Aufschläge); it's my serve ich habe Aufschlag.
verb 1 (*in tennis*) aufschlagen ◇ SEP; Becker is serving Becker schlägt auf; 2 servieren; can you serve the vegetables, please? können Sie bitte das Gemüse servieren?; ★ it serves him right das geschieht ihm recht.

service *noun* 1 (*in a restaurant, shop, etc.*) Bedienung *die*; service is included inklusive Bedienung; 2 (*from a company or firm to a customer*) Service *der*; 3 the emergency services *der* Notdienst; 4 (*church service*) Gottesdienst *der* (PL die Gottesdienste); 5 (*of a car or machine*) Wartung *die* (PL die Wartungen).

service charge *noun* Bedienung *die*; there is no service charge die Bedienung wird nicht extra berechnet.

service station *noun* Tankstelle *die* (PL die Tankstellen).

serviette *noun* Serviette *die* (PL die Servietten).

session *noun* Sitzung *die* (PL die Sitzungen).

set *noun* 1 (*for playing a game*) Spiel *das* (PL die Spiele); chess set *das* Schachspiel; 2 train set *die* Spielzeugeisenbahn; 3 (*in tennis*) Satz *der* (PL die Sätze).
adjective 1 fest (*hours, habits*); a set date ein festes Datum; at a time zu einer festgesetzten Zeit; 2 set menu *das* Menü.
verb 1 festlegen SEP (*a date, time*); 2 aufstellen SEP (*a record*); 3 to set the table den Tisch decken; to set an alarm clock einen Wecker stellen; I've set my alarm for seven ich habe meinen Wecker auf sieben gestellt; 4 to set your watch seine Uhr richtig stellen; 5 (*sun*) untergehen ◇ SEP;

● to set off aufbrechen ◇ SEP (PERF *sein*); we're setting off at ten wir brechen um zehn auf; they set off for Vienna yesterday sie sind gestern nach Wien aufgebrochen.

● to set off something 1 etwas auslösen SEP (*an alarm, reaction*); 2 etwas abbrennen ◇ SEP (*a firework*); 3 etwas explodieren lassen (*a bomb*).

● to set out aufbrechen ◇ SEP (PERF *sein*); they set out for Hamburg at ten sie sind um zehn nach Hamburg aufgebrochen.

settee *noun* Sofa *das* (PL die Sofas).

settle verb 1 bezahlen (a bill);
2 lösen (a problem); 3 beilegen SEP
(an argument).

seven number sieben; Rosie's
seven Rosie ist sieben.

seventeen number siebzehn; I'm
seventeen ich bin siebzehn.

seventh adjective
siebter/siebte/siebtes; on the
seventh floor im siebten Stock; the
seventh of July der siebte Juli.

seventies plural noun the
seventies die Siebzigerjahre △; in
the seventies in den
Siebzigerjahren.

seventieth adjective
siebzigster/siebzigste/siebzigstes;
it's her seventieth birthday es ist
ihr siebzigster Geburtstag.

seventy number siebzig; my
granny's seventy meine Oma ist
siebzig.

several adjective, pronoun
1 mehrere; I've read several of her
novels ich habe mehrere ihrer
Romane gelesen; 2 I've seen her
several times ich habe sie
mehrmals gesehen.

sew verb nähen.

sewing noun Nähen das; I like
sewing ich nähe gern.

sewing machine noun
Nähmaschine die (PL die
Nähmaschinen).

sex noun 1 (gender) Geschlecht das
(PL die Geschlechter); 2 (sexuality)
Sex der.

sex education noun
Aufklärungsunterricht der.

sexism noun Sexismus der.

sexist adjective sexistisch; sexist
remarks sexistische Bemerkungen

sexual adjective sexuell.

sexual harassment noun
sexuelle Belästigung die.

sexuality noun Sexualität die.

sexy adjective sexy.

shabby adjective schäbig.

shade noun 1 Ton der (PL die Töne);
a shade of green ein Grünton;
2 Schatten der; in the shade im
Schatten.

shadow noun Schatten der (PL die
Schatten).

shake verb 1 (tremble) zittern; I was
shaking with fear ich zitterte vor
Angst; 2 to shake something etwa
schütteln; to shake your head
(meaning no) den Kopf schütteln;
3 to shake hands with somebody
jemandem die Hand geben ◇; she
shook hands with me sie hat mir
die Hand gegeben; we shook hands
wir gaben uns die Hand.

shaken adjective erschüttert; I was
shaken by the news die Nachricht
hat mich erschüttert.

shall verb shall I come with you?
soll ich mitkommen?; shall we stop
now? sollen wir jetzt aufhören?

shallow adjective flach; stay in the
shallow end of the pool bleib am
flachen Ende des Beckens.

◇ IRREGULAR VERB: See the verb table in the centre of the dictionary

shambles noun Chaos das; it was a total shambles! es war ein völliges Chaos!

shame noun 1 Schande die; the shame of it! was für eine Schande!; 2 what a shame! wie schade!; it's a shame she can't come schade, dass sie nicht kommen kann.

shampoo noun Shampoo das (PL die Shampoos); Schampon das (PL die Schampons); I bought some shampoo ich habe Shampoo gekauft.

shamrock noun Klee der.

shandy noun Radler der (PL die Radler) (South German), Alsterwasser das (PL die Alsterwasser) (North German).

shape noun Form die (PL die Formen).

share noun 1 Anteil der (PL die Anteile); your share of the money dein Anteil am Geld; he paid his share er hat seinen Anteil gezahlt; 2 (in a company) Aktie die (PL die Aktien).
verb teilen; I'm sharing a room with Lucy ich teile ein Zimmer mit Lucy.

sharp adjective 1 (knife) scharf; this knife isn't very sharp dieses Messer ist nicht sehr scharf; 2 (pointed) spitz; a sharp pencil ein spitzer Bleistift; 3 a sharp bend eine scharfe Kurve; 4 (clever) clever.

shave verb 1 (have a shave) sich rasieren; 2 to shave your legs sich ←(DAT) die Beine rasieren; 3 to shave off your beard den Bart abrasieren SEP.

shaver noun Rasierapparat der (PL die Rasierapparate); electric shaver der Elektrorasierer.

shaving cream noun Rasiercreme die (PL die Rasiercremes).

shaving foam noun Rasierschaum der.

she pronoun sie; she's a student sie ist Studentin; she's a very good teacher sie ist eine sehr gute Lehrerin.

shed noun Schuppen der (PL die Schuppen).

sheep noun Schaf das (PL die Schafe).

sheepdog noun Schäferhund der (PL die Schäferhunde).

sheet noun 1 (for a bed) Laken das (PL die Laken); 2 a sheet of paper ein Blatt Papier; a blank sheet ein leeres Blatt; 3 (of glass or metal) Platte die (PL die Platten); ★ to be as white as a sheet leichenblass △ sein.

shelf noun 1 (in the home or a shop) Regal das (PL die Regale); a set of shelves ein Regal; 2 (in an oven) Schiene die (PL die Schienen).

shell noun 1 (of an egg or a nut) Schale die (PL die Schalen); 2 (seashell) Muschel die (PL die Muscheln).

shellfish noun 1 Schalentier das (PL die Schalentiere); 2 (in cookery) Meeresfrüchte (plural).

shelter noun Schutz der; in the shelter of im Schutz (+GEN); to take

shelter from the rain sich
unterstellen SEP.

sherry noun Sherry der (PL die
Sherrys).

Shetland Islands noun
Shetlandinseln (plural).

shift noun Schicht die (PL die
Schichten); the night shift die
Nachtschicht; to be on night shift
Nachtschicht haben.
verb to shift something etwas
verrücken.

shifty adjective verschlagen; he
looks shifty er sieht verschlagen
aus; a shifty-looking guy ein
verschlagener Typ.

shine verb scheinen ◇; the sun is
shining die Sonne scheint.

shiny adjective glänzend.

ship noun Schiff das (PL die Schiffe).

shipyard noun Werft die (PL die
Werften).

shirt noun 1 (man's) Hemd das (PL
die Hemden); 2 (woman's)
Bluse die (PL die Blusen).

shiver verb zittern.

shock noun 1 Schock der (PL die
Schocks); to get a shock einen
Schock bekommen; it gave me a
shock das hat mir einen Schock
versetzt; 2 electric shock der
Schlag.
verb (upset) erschüttern; (cause
scandal) schockieren.

shocked adjective schockiert.

shocking adjective schockierend.

shoe noun Schuh der (PL die
Schuhe); a pair of shoes ein Paar
Schuhe.

shoelace noun Schnürsenkel der
(PL die Schnürsenkel).

shoe polish noun Schuhcreme die
(PL die Schuhcremes).

shoe shop noun
Schuhgeschäft das (PL die
Schuhgeschäfte).

shoot verb 1 (fire) schießen ◇; to
shoot at somebody auf jemanden
schießen; she shot him in the leg
sie hat ihm ins Bein geschossen; he
was shot in the arm er wurde am
Arm getroffen; 2 (kill, execute)
erschießen ◇; he was shot by
terrorists er wurde von Terroristen
erschossen; 3 (in football, hockey)
schießen ◇; 4 to shoot a film einen
Film drehen.

shop noun Geschäft das (PL die
Geschäfte), Laden der (PL die
Läden); shoe shop das
Schuhgeschäft; to go round the
shops einen Ladenbummel
machen.

shop assistant noun
Verkäufer der (PL die Verkäufer),
Verkäuferin die (PL die
Verkäuferinnen).

shopkeeper noun
Ladenbesitzer der (PL die
Ladenbesitzer), Ladenbesitzerin die
(PL die Ladenbesitzerinnen).

shoplifter noun Ladendieb der (PL
die Ladendiebe), Ladendiebin die
(PL die Ladendiebinnen).

◇ IRREGULAR VERB: See the verb table in the centre of the dictionary

shoplifting noun
Ladendiebstahl der.

shopping noun 1 Einkäufe (plural);
can you put the shopping away?
kannst du die Einkäufe wegräumen?;
2 (activity) Einkaufen das;
shopping is fun Einkaufen macht
Spaß; to go shopping einkaufen
gehen.

shopping trolley noun
Einkaufswagen der (PL die
Einkaufswagen).

shop window noun
Schaufenster das (PL die
Schaufenster).

short adjective 1 kurz; a short dress
ein kurzes Kleid; she has short hair
sie hat kurze Haare; 2 a short break
eine kurze Pause; to go for a short
walk einen kurzen Spaziergang
machen; it's a short walk from the
bus stop es ist nicht weit zu Fuß von
der Bushaltestelle; 3 to be short of
something knapp mit etwas ←(DAT)
sein; we're a bit short of money at
the moment wir sind im Moment
etwas knapp mit Geld; we're getting
short of time wir sind knapp mit der
Zeit.

shortage noun Mangel der.

shortbread noun
Buttergebäck das.

shortcrust pastry noun
Mürbeteig der.

short cut noun Abkürzung die (PL
die Abkürzungen).

shortly adverb gleich; shortly
before I left kurz bevor ich ging;
shortly after kurz danach.

shorts plural noun Shorts (plural);
a pair of shorts ein Paar Shorts; my
red shorts meine roten Shorts.

short-sighted adjective
kurzsichtig; I'm short-sighted ich
bin kurzsichtig.

shot noun 1 (from a gun)
Schuss △ der (PL die Schüsse);
2 (a photo) Aufnahme die (PL die
Aufnahmen).

should verb 1 sollen ◊ ('should' is
usually translated by the imperfect
subjunctive of 'sollen'); you should
ask Simon du solltest Simon fragen;
the potatoes should be ready now
die Kartoffeln sollten jetzt fertig
sein; 2 ('should have' is translated by
'hätte sollen') you should have told
me du hättest es mir sagen sollen;
I shouldn't have stayed ich hätte
nicht bleiben sollen; you shouldn't
have said that das hättest du nicht
sagen sollen; 3 ('should' meaning
'would' is translated by 'würde')
I forget it if I were you an
deiner Stelle würde ich es vergessen;
4 I should think ich würde sagen;
I should think he's forgotten ich
würde sagen, er hat's vergessen;
5 this should be enough das
müsste eigentlich reichen.

shoulder noun Schulter die (PL die
Schultern).

shoulder bag noun
Umhängetasche die (PL die
Umhängetaschen).

shout noun Schrei der (PL die
Schreie).
verb 1 schreien ◊; stop shouting!

△ NEW SPELLING: See page xii

hör auf zu schreien!; 2 (call) rufen ✧; he shouted at us to come back er rief uns zu, wir sollten zurückkommen.

show noun 1 (on stage) Show die (PL die Shows); we went to see a show wir haben eine Show gesehen; 2 (on TV, radio) Sendung die (PL die Sendungen); 3 (exhibition) Ausstellung die (PL die Ausstellungen); **fashion show** die Modenschau.
verb 1 zeigen; to show something to somebody jemandem etwas zeigen; I'll show you my photos ich zeige dir meine Fotos; to show somebody how something works jemandem zeigen, wie etwas funktioniert; he showed me how to make pancakes er hat mir gezeigt, wie man Pfannkuchen macht; 2 it shows! das sieht man!
• to show off angeben ✧ SEP.

shower noun 1 (in a bathroom) Dusche die (PL die Duschen); to have a shower duschen; 2 (of rain) Schauer der (PL die Schauer).

show-jumping noun Springreiten das.

show-off noun Angeber der (PL die Angeber), Angeberin die (PL die Angeberinnen).

shriek verb kreischen.

shrimp noun Krabbe die (PL die Krabben).

shrink verb 1 schrumpfen (PERF sein); 2 (clothes) einlaufen ✧ SEP (PERF sein); my sweater has shrunk mein Pullover ist eingelaufen.

Shrove Tuesday noun Fastnachtsdienstag der.

shrug verb to shrug your shoulders die Achseln zucken.

shuffle verb to shuffle the cards die Karten mischen.

shut adjective zu; the shops are shut die Geschäfte haben zu.
verb zumachen SEP; can you shut the door please? kannst du die Tür bitte zumachen?; the shops shut at six die Geschäfte machen um sechs zu.
• to shut up den Mund halten ✧ (informal); shut up! halt den Mund!

shuttlecock noun Federball der (PL die Federbälle).

shy adjective schüchtern.

shyness noun Schüchternheit die.

Sicily noun Sizilien das.

sick adjective 1 (ill) krank; 2 to be sick (vomit) sich übergeben ✧; I was sick several times ich habe mich mehrmals übergeben; 3 I feel sick mir ist schlecht; 4 übel; a sick joke ein übler Witz; 5 to be sick of something etwas satt haben; I'm sick of staying at home every day ich habe es satt, jeden Tag zu Hause zu sitzen.

sickness noun Krankheit die (PL die Krankheiten).

side noun 1 Seite die (PL die Seiten); on the other side of the street auf der anderen Straßenseite; on the wrong side auf der falschen Seite;

✧ **IRREGULAR VERB: See the verb table in the centre of the dictionary**

I'm on your side (*I agree with you*) ich bin auf deiner Seite; **2** (*edge*) Rand der (PL die Ränder) (*of a pool, river*); **at the side of the road** am Straßenrand; **3** (*team*) Mannschaft die (PL die Mannschaften); **the winning side** die siegreiche Mannschaft; **she plays on our side** sie spielt bei uns mit; **4 to take sides** Partei ergreifen ◇; **he always takes sides against her** er ergreift immer gegen sie Partei; **5 side by side** nebeneinander.

ideboard noun Anrichte die (PL die Anrichten).

ideburns noun Koteletten (*plural*).

ide-effect noun Nebenwirkung die (PL die Nebenwirkungen).

ide street noun Seitenstraße die (PL die Seitenstraßen).

ieve noun Sieb das (PL die Siebe).

igh noun Seufzer der (PL die Seufzer).
verb seufzen.

ight noun **1** Anblick der; **it was a marvellous sight** es war ein herrlicher Anblick; **at first sight** auf den ersten Blick; **3** (*eyesight*) **to have poor sight** schlechte Augen haben; **to know somebody by sight** jemanden vom Sehen kennen; **out of sight** außer Sicht; **to lose sight of somebody** jemanden aus den Augen verlieren; **4 the sights** die Sehenswürdigkeiten; **to see the**

sights die Sehenswürdigkeiten besichtigen.

sightseeing noun Sightseeing das; **to do some sightseeing** einige Sehenswürdigkeiten besichtigen.

sign noun **1** (*notice*) Schild das (PL die Schilder); **there's a sign on the door** da hängt ein Schild an der Tür; **2** (*trace, indication*) Zeichen das (PL die Zeichen); **3** (*of the zodiac*) Sternzeichen das (PL die Sternzeichen); **what sign are you?** was für ein Sternzeichen bist du?
verb **1** unterschreiben ◇; **to sign a cheque** einen Scheck unterschreiben; **2** (*using sign language*) sich durch Zeichen verständigen.
● **to sign on** sich arbeitslos melden.

signal noun Signal das (PL die Signale).

signature noun Unterschrift die (PL die Unterschriften).

significant adjective bedeutend.

sign language noun Zeichensprache die (PL die Zeichensprachen).

signpost noun Wegweiser der (PL die Wegweiser).

silence noun Stille die.

silent adjective still.

silk noun Seide die (PL die Seiden).
adjective Seiden-; **a silk blouse** eine Seidenbluse.

silky adjective seidig.

△ NEW SPELLING: *See page xii*

silly *adjective* dumm; **it was a really silly thing to do** das war wirklich dumm.

silver *noun* Silber *das*.
adjective Silber-; **a silver medal** eine Silbermedaille.

similar *adjective* ähnlich; **it looks similar to my old bike** es sieht so ähnlich wie mein altes Rad aus.

similarity *noun* Ähnlichkeit *die* (PL die Ähnlichkeiten).

simple *adjective* einfach.

simply *adverb* einfach.

sin *noun* Sünde *die* (PL die Sünden).

since *preposition* 1 seit (+DAT); *(notice that German uses the present tense for an action starting in the past and still going on in the present)* **I have been in Berlin since Saturday** ich bin seit Samstag in Berlin; **since when?** seit wann?; 2 *(with a negative the perfect tense is used)* **I haven't seen her since Monday** ich habe sie seit Montag nicht gesehen. *conjunction* 1 seit; **since I have known him** seit ich ihn kenne; **since I've been learning German** seitdem ich Deutsch lerne; 2 *(because)* da; **since it was raining, the match was cancelled** da es regnete, wurde das Spiel abgesagt. *adverb* seitdem; **I haven't seen him since** ich habe ihn seitdem nicht mehr gesehen.

sincere *adjective* aufrichtig.

sincerely *adverb* **Yours sincerely** Mit freundlichen Grüßen.

sing *verb* singen ◇.

singer *noun* Sänger *der* (PL die Sänger), Sängerin *die* (PL die Sängerinnen).

singing *noun* 1 Singen *das*; **a singing lesson** eine Singstunde; 2 **I like singing** ich singe gern.

single *noun* 1 *(ticket)* einfache Fahrkarte *die* (PL die einfachen Fahrkarten); **a single to Munich, please** eine einfache Fahrkarte nach München bitte; 2 *(record, CD Single die* (PL die Singles). *adjective* 1 *(not married)* allein stehend ▲; **a single woman** eine allein stehende Frau; *(on forms)* ledig; 2 *(just one)* einzig; **I haven't had a single reply** ich habe keine einzige Antwort bekommen; 3 **not single one** kein Einziger/keine Einzige/kein Einziges ▲; 4 **single room** das Einzelzimmer; **single be** das Einzelbett.

single parent *noun* allein Erziehende ▲ *der/die* (PL die allein Erziehenden); **she's a single paren** sie ist allein erziehende Mutter; **a single-parent family** eine Einelternfamilie.

singles *plural noun* *(in tennis)* Einzel *das* (PL die Einzel); **the women's singles** das Dameneinze **the men's singles** das Herreneinzel.

singular *noun* Einzahl *die*; **in the singular** in der Einzahl.

sink *noun* Spülbecken *das* (PL die Spülbecken).
verb sinken ◇ (PERF sein).

◇ IRREGULAR VERB: *See the verb table in the centre of the dictionary*

sir noun Herr der (PL die Herren); (in German,' Sir' is usually not translated) **would you like another one, sir?** möchten Sie noch eins?; **yes, sir** ja, mein Herr.

sister noun Schwester die (PL die Schwestern); **my sister's ten** meine Schwester ist zehn.

sister-in-law noun Schwägerin die (PL die Schwägerinnen).

sit verb 1 (to sit down) sich setzen; **you can sit on the sofa** ihr könnt euch aufs Sofa setzen; **sit on the floor** setz dich auf den Boden; 2 (to be sitting) sitzen ◇; **Leila was sitting on the sofa** Leila saß auf dem Sofa; **to sit on the floor** auf dem Boden sitzen; 3 **to sit an exam** eine Prüfung machen.
to sit down sich setzen; **he sat down on the chair** er setzte sich auf den Stuhl; **do sit down** setzen Sie sich.

sitcom noun Situationskomödie die (PL die Situationskomödien).

site noun 1 **building site** die Baustelle; 2 **camping site** der Campingplatz; 3 **archaeological site** die archäologische Stätte.

sitting room noun Wohnzimmer das (PL die Wohnzimmer).

situated adjective **to be situated** liegen ◇; **the house is situated in a small village** das Haus liegt in einem kleinen Dorf.

situation noun 1 (location) Lage die (PL die Lagen);

2 (circumstances) Situation die (PL die Situationen).

six number sechs; **Harry's six** Harry ist sechs.

sixteen number sechzehn; **Alice is sixteen** Alice ist sechzehn.

sixth adjective sechster/sechste/sechstes; **on the sixth floor** im sechsten Stock; **on the sixth of July** am sechsten Juli.

sixty number sechzig; **she's sixty** sie ist sechzig.

size noun 1 Größe die (PL die Größen); **it depends on the size of the house** es kommt auf die Größe des Hauses an; 2 **what size is the window?** wie groß ist das Fenster?; 3 (in clothes) Größe die (PL die Größen); **what size do you take?** welche Größe haben Sie?; 4 (of shoes) Schuhgröße die (PL die Schuhgrößen); **I take a size thirty-eight** ich habe Schuhgröße achtunddreißig.

skate noun 1 (an ice skate) Schlittschuh der (PL die Schlittschuhe); 2 (a roller skate) Rollschuh der (PL die Rollschuhe).
verb 1 (ice-skate) Schlittschuh laufen ◇ (PERF sein); 2 (roller-skate) Rollschuh laufen ◇ (PERF sein).

skateboard noun Skateboard das (PL die Skateboards).

skateboarding noun Skateboardfahren das; **to go skateboarding** Skateboard fahren ◇ (PERF sein).

skating noun 1 (on ice) Schlittschuhlaufen das; **to go**

△ NEW SPELLING: See page xii

skating Schlittschuh laufen ◇ (PERF *sein*); 2 (*roller-skating*) Rollschuhlaufen *das*; **to go roller-skating** Rollschuh laufen ◇ (PERF *sein*).

skating rink noun 1 (*ice rink*) Eisbahn *die* (PL die Eisbahnen); 2 (*for roller-skating*) Rollschuhbahn *die* (PL die Rollschuhbahnen).

sketch noun 1 Skizze *die* (PL die Skizzen); 2 (*comedy routine*) Sketch *der* (PL die Sketche).

ski noun Ski *der* (PL die Skier). verb Ski fahren ◇ (PERF *sein*); **he can ski** er kann Ski fahren.

ski boot noun Skistiefel *der* (PL die Skistiefel).

skid verb schleudern (PERF *sein*); **the car skidded** das Auto ist geschleudert.

skiing noun Skifahren *das*; **to go skiing** Ski fahren ◇ (PERF *sein*).

ski lift noun Skilift *der* (PL die Skilifte).

skin noun Haut *die* (PL die Häute).

skinhead noun Skinhead *der* (PL die Skinheads).

skinny adjective dünn.

skip noun (*for rubbish*) Container *der* (PL die Container). verb 1 auslassen ◇ SEP (*a meal, part of a book*); **I skipped a few chapters** ich ließ ein paar Kapitel aus; 2 **to skip a lesson** ein Stunde schwänzen (*informal*).

skirt noun Rock *der* (PL die Röcke); **a long skirt** ein langer Rock; **a tigh[t] skirt** ein enger Rock; **a mini-skirt** ein Minirock.

sky noun Himmel *der* (PL die Himmel).

skyscraper noun Wolkenkratzer *der* (PL die Wolkenkratzer).

slam verb zuknallen SEP; **she slammed the door** sie hat die Tür zugeknallt; **the door slammed** die Tür ist zugeknallt.

slang noun Slang *der* (PL die Slangs).

slap noun Klaps *der* (PL die Klapse) (*in the face*) Ohrfeige *die* (PL die Ohrfeigen). verb **to slap somebody** (*across th[e] face*) jemanden ohrfeigen; (*on the bottom*) jemandem einen Klaps geben.

sledge noun Schlitten *der* (PL die Schlitten).

sledging noun **to go sledging** Schlitten fahren ◇ (PERF *sein*).

sleep noun Schlaf *der*; **you need more sleep** du brauchst mehr Schlaf; **I had a good sleep** ich hab[e] gut geschlafen; **to go to sleep** einschlafen ◇ SEP (PERF *sein*); **he's gone back to sleep** er ist wieder eingeschlafen. verb schlafen ◇; **she's sleeping** si[e] schläft.

sleeping bag noun Schlafsack *de[r]* (PL die Schlafsäcke).

sleeping pill noun Schlaftablette *die* (PL die Schlaftabletten).

◇ IRREGULAR VERB: See the verb table in the centre of the dictionary

sleepy *adjective* to be sleepy schläfrig sein; he was getting sleepy er wurde schläfrig.

sleet *noun* Schneeregen *der*.

sleeve *noun* Ärmel *der* (PL die Ärmel); a long-sleeved jumper ein Pullover mit langen Ärmeln; a short-sleeved shirt ein Hemd mit kurzen Ärmeln; to roll up your sleeves die Ärmel hochkrempeln.

slice *noun* Scheibe *die* (PL die Scheiben); a slice of bread eine Scheibe Brot.
verb to slice something etwas in Scheiben schneiden ◇.

slide *noun* 1 (*photo*) Dia *das* (PL die Dias); 2 (*hairslide*) Haarspange *die* (PL die Haarspangen); 3 (*for sliding down*) Rutschbahn *die* (PL die Rutschbahnen).

slight *adjective* klein; there is a slight problem es gibt ein kleines Problem.

slightly *adverb* etwas.

slim *adjective* schlank.
verb abnehmen ◇ SEP; I'm slimming ich mache eine Schlankheitskur.

sling *noun* Schlinge *die* (PL die Schlingen); to have your arm in a sling den Arm in der Schlinge haben.

slip *noun* 1 (*mistake*) Fehler *der* (PL die Fehler); 2 (*petticoat*) Unterrock *der* (PL die Unterröcke).
verb 1 (*slide*) ausrutschen SEP (PERF sein); 2 it slipped my mind es ist mir entfallen.
● to slip up einen Fehler machen.

slipper *noun* Hausschuh *der* (PL die Hausschuhe).

slippery *adjective* glatt.

slope *noun* Hang *der* (PL die Hänge).

slot *noun* Schlitz *der* (PL die Schlitze).

slot machine *noun* 1 (*vending machine*) Automat *der* (PL die Automaten); 2 (*games machine*) Spielautomat *der* (PL die Spielautomaten).

slow *adjective* 1 langsam; the service is a bit slow die Bedienung ist etwas langsam; 2 (*of a clock or watch*) to be slow nachgehen ◇ SEP (PERF sein); my watch is slow meine Uhr geht nach.
● to slow down langsamer werden.

slowly *adverb* langsam; he got up slowly er ist langsam aufgestanden; can you speak more slowly, please? können Sie bitte etwas langsamer sprechen?

sly *adjective* gerissen (*a person*);
★ on the sly heimlich.

smack *noun* Klaps *der* (PL die Klapse).
verb to smack somebody jemandem einen Klaps geben ◇.

small *adjective* klein; a small dog ein kleiner Hund.

smart *adjective* 1 (*well-dressed, posh*) elegant; a smart restaurant ein elegantes Restaurant; 2 (*clever*) clever.

smash *noun* (*collision*) Zusammenstoß *der* (PL die Zusammenstöße).

△ NEW SPELLING: See page xii

smashing verb 1 (break) zerschlagen ◇; they smashed a window pane sie haben eine Fensterscheibe zerschlagen; 2 (get broken) zerbrechen ◇ (PERF sein); the plate smashed der Teller ist zerbrochen.

smashing adjective klasse (informal).

smell noun Geruch der (PL die Gerüche); a nasty smell ein scheußlicher Geruch; a smell of gas ein Gasgeruch.
verb 1 riechen ◇; I can't smell anything ich kann nichts riechen; to smell of perfume nach Parfüm riechen; 2 (smell bad) stinken ◇; the drains smell der Abfluss stinkt.

smelly adjective 1 stinkend; her smelly dog ihr stinkender Hund; 2 to be smelly stinken ◇.

smile noun Lächeln das.
verb lächeln; to smile at somebody jemanden anlächeln SEP.

smoke noun Rauch der.
verb rauchen; she doesn't smoke sie raucht nicht.

smoking noun 'no smoking' 'Rauchen verboten'; to give up smoking mit dem Rauchen aufhören.

smooth adjective 1 glatt; a smooth surface eine glatte Oberfläche; 2 (person) aalglatt.

smug adjective selbstgefällig.

smuggle verb to smuggle something etwas schmuggeln.

smuggler noun 1 Schmuggler der (PL die Schmuggler), Schmugglerin die (PL die Schmugglerinnen); 2 drugs smuggler der Drogenschmuggler.

snack noun Snack der (PL die Snacks).

snail noun Schnecke die (PL die Schnecken).

snake noun Schlange die (PL die Schlangen).

snap noun (card game) Schnippschnapp das (PL die Schnippschnapp).
verb 1 (break) brechen ◇ (PERF sein); 2 to snap something etwas zerbrechen ◇; 3 to snap your fingers mit den Fingern schnalzen.

snapshot noun Schnappschuss△ der (PL die Schnappschüsse).

snarl verb knurren.

snatch verb 1 entreißen ◇; to snatch something from somebody jemandem etwas entreißen; she had her bag snatched man hat ihr die Handtasche entrissen; 2 he snatched it out of my hand er hat es mir aus der Hand gerissen.

sneak verb 1 to sneak in sich hineinschleichen ◇ SEP; to sneak out sich hinausschleichen ◇ SEP; 2 to sneak on somebody jemanden verpetzen (informal).

sneeze verb niesen.

sniff verb schnüffeln.

snob noun Snob der (PL die Snobs).

◇ IRREGULAR VERB: See the verb table in the centre of the dictionary

snobbery noun Snobismus der.

snooker noun Snooker das.

snore verb schnarchen.

snow noun Schnee der.
verb schneien; **it's snowing** es
schneit.

snowball noun Schneeball der (PL
die Schneebälle).

snowman noun Schneemann der
(PL die Schneemänner).

so conjunction, adverb 1 so; **he's so
lazy** er ist so faul; **not so** nicht so;
**our house is a bit like yours, but not
so big** unser Haus ist so ähnlich wie
eures, aber nicht so groß; **2 so much**
so sehr; **I hate it so much** ich hasse
es so sehr; **3 so much** so viel; **I have
so much work** ich habe so viel
Arbeit; **4 so many** so viele; **we've
got so many problems** wir haben
so viele Probleme; **5** (therefore) also;
**he got up late, so he missed his
train** er ist spät aufgestanden, also
hat er den Zug verpasst; **so what
shall we do?** also, was machen wir?;
6 so what? na und?; **7** (also) **so do
I, so did I** ich auch; **'I live in Leeds' –
'so do I'** 'ich wohne in Leeds' – 'ich
auch'; **I liked the film and so did he**
ich fand den Film gut und er auch; **so
am I** ich auch; **so do we** wir auch;
8 I think so ich glaube schon;
9 I hope so hoffentlich.

soak verb einweichen SEP.

soaked adjective patschnass Δ;
★ **to be soaked to the skin**
patschnass sein.

soap noun 1 Seife die (PL die Seifen);
2 (soap opera) Seifenoper die (PL die
Seifenopern).

soap powder noun
Seifenpulver das.

sober adjective nüchtern.
● **to sober up** nüchtern werden ◊
(PERF sein).

soccer noun Fußball der.

social adjective 1 sozial; **social
problems** soziale Probleme;
2 gesellschaftlich (engagement,
ambition); **social engagements**
gesellschaftliche Verpflichtungen;
social class die gesellschaftliche
Schicht; 3 (sociable) gesellig
(evening, person).

socialism noun Sozialismus der.

socialist noun, adjective
Sozialist der (PL die Sozialisten),
Sozialistin die (PL die
Sozialistinnen).

social security noun
1 Sozialhilfe die; **to be on social
security** Sozialhilfe bekommen;
2 (the system) Sozialversicherung
die.

social worker noun
Sozialarbeiter der (PL die
Sozialarbeiter), Sozialarbeiterin die
(PL die Sozialarbeiterinnen).

society noun Gesellschaft die (PL
die Gesellschaften).

sociology noun Soziologie die.

sock noun Socke die (PL die Socken);
a pair of socks ein Paar Socken.

socket noun (power point)
Steckdose die (PL die Steckdosen).

Δ NEW SPELLING: See page xii

sofa noun Sofa das (PL die Sofas).

sofa bed noun Schlafcouch die (PL die Schlafcouchs).

soft adjective 1 weich; 2 a soft option eine bequeme Lösung; ★ to have a soft spot for somebody eine Vorliebe für jemanden haben.

soft drink noun alkoholfreie Getränk das (PL die alkoholfreien Getränke).

soft toy noun Stofftier das (PL die Stofftiere).

software noun Software die.

soil noun Erde die.

solar energy noun Sonnenenergie die.

soldier noun Soldat der (PL die Soldaten).

solicitor noun 1 (dealing with lawsuits) Rechtsanwalt der (PL die Rechtsanwälte), Rechtsanwältin die (PL die Rechtsanwältinnen); 2 (dealing with property or documents) Notar der (PL die Notare), Notarin die (PL die Notarinnen).

solid adjective 1 (not flimsy) stabil; a solid structure ein stabiler Bau; 2 massiv; a table made of solid oak ein Tisch aus massiver Eiche; solid silver massives Silber.

solo noun Solo das (PL die Solos); guitar solo das Gitarrensolo. adjective Solo-; a solo act eine Solonummer. adverb solo.

soloist noun Solist der (PL die Solisten), Solistin die (PL die Solistinnen).

solution noun Lösung die (PL die Lösungen).

solve verb lösen.

some adjective, adverb 1 (followed by a singular noun) etwas; would you like some salad? möchtest du etwas Salat?; can you lend me some money? kannst du mir etwas Geld leihen?; have you got some bread? (some is often not translated) hast du Brot?; 2 (followed by a plural noun) (a few) ein paar; I've bought some apples ich habe ein paar Äpfel gekauft; 3 (followed by a plural noun) (a certain number but not all) einige; some of his films are too violent einige von seinen Filmen sind zu brutal; 4 (referring to something that has been mentioned) 'would you like tea?' – 'thanks, I've got some' 'möchten Sie Tee?' – 'nein danke, ich habe schon welchen'; he's eaten some of it er hat etwas davon gegessen; I'd like some ich möchte etwas; (with a plural noun) ich möchte welche; 5 (certain people or things) manche; some people think he's right manche Leute glauben, dass er Recht hat; 6 some day eines Tages.

somebody, someone pronoun jemand; there's somebody in the garden da ist jemand im Garten.

somehow adverb irgendwie; I've got to finish this essay somehow ich muss diesen Aufsatz irgendwie fertig schreiben.

✥ IRREGULAR VERB: See the verb table in the centre of the dictionary

omething pronoun 1 etwas; there's something I've got to tell you ich muss dir etwas erzählen; something new etwas Neues; something interesting etwas Interessantes; there's something wrong irgendetwas stimmt nicht; 2 their house is really something! ihr Haus ist einfach Klasse!

sometime adverb irgendwann; give me a ring sometime next week ruf mich irgendwann nächste Woche an.

sometimes adverb manchmal; I sometimes take the train manchmal fahre ich mit der Bahn.

somewhere adverb 1 (in a place) irgendwo; I've left my bag somewhere here ich habe meine Handtasche hier irgendwo liegen lassen; 2 (to a place) irgendwohin; I'd like to go somewhere warm ich möchte irgendwohin fahren, wo es warm ist.

son noun Sohn der (PL die Söhne).

song noun Lied das (PL die Lieder).

son-in-law noun Schwiegersohn der (PL die Schwiegersöhne).

soon adverb 1 bald; we'll soon be on holiday wir haben bald Ferien; see you soon! bis bald!; 2 as soon as she arrives sobald sie ankommt; as soon as possible so bald wie möglich; 3 it's too soon es ist zu früh.

sooner adverb 1 früher; we should have started sooner wir hätten früher anfangen sollen; sooner or later früher oder später; 2 I'd sooner wait ich würde lieber warten.

soprano noun Sopran der (PL die Soprane).

sore noun wunde Stelle die (PL die wunden Stellen).
adjective 1 (inflamed) wund; to have a sore throat Halsschmerzen haben; 2 he has a sore leg ihm tut das Bein weh; my arm's sore mir tut der Arm weh; ★ it's a sore point das ist ein wunder Punkt.

sorry adjective 1 I'm really sorry es tut mir wirklich Leid △; sorry to disturb you es tut mir Leid, dass ich dich störe; I'm sorry I forgot your birthday es tut mir Leid, dass ich deinen Geburtstag vergessen habe; I'm sorry, we're closing es tut mir Leid, aber wir machen jetzt zu; 2 sorry! Entschuldigung!; 3 sorry? wie bitte?; 4 I feel sorry for him er tut mir Leid △.

sort noun Art die (PL die Arten); a sort of dance music eine Art Tanzmusik; what sort of car have you got? was für ein Auto hast du?; all sorts of people alle möglichen Leute; for all sorts of reasons aus allen möglichen Gründen.
● to sort something out 1 Ordnung schaffen ◇ in (+DAT) (papers, desk, room, possessions); I must sort out my room tonight ich muss heute Abend in meinem Zimmer Ordnung schaffen; 2 klären (a problem, arrangement); Liz is sorting it out Liz klärt es.

so-so *adjective* so lala (*informal*); 'how was the film?' – 'so-so' 'wie war der Film?' – 'so lala'.

soul *noun* 1 Seele *die* (PL *die* Seelen); 2 (*music*) Soul *der*.

sound *noun* 1 (*noise*) Geräusch *das* (PL *die* Geräusche); 2 (*of voices, laughter, bell*) Klang *der*; **the sound of her voice** der Klang ihrer Stimme; **I can hear the sound of voices** ich kann Stimmen hören; 3 **without a sound** lautlos; 4 (*volume*) Lautstärke *die*; **to turn the sound down** leiser stellen.
verb 1 **it sounds easy** es hört sich einfach an; 2 **it sounds as if she's happy** sie scheint glücklich zu sein.

sound asleep *adverb* **to be sound asleep** fest schlafen ◇.

sound effect *noun* Geräuscheffekt *der* (PL *die* Geräuscheffekte).

soundtrack *noun* Soundtrack *der* (PL *die* Soundtracks).

soup *noun* Suppe *die* (PL *die* Suppen); **mushroom soup** *die* Pilzsuppe.

soup plate *noun* Suppenteller *der* (PL *die* Suppenteller).

soup spoon *noun* Suppenlöffel *der* (PL *die* Suppenlöffel).

sour *adjective* sauer.

south *noun* Süden *der*; **in the south** im Süden.
adjective Süd-, südlich; **the south side** die Südseite; **south wind** *der* Südwind.

adverb **south of Berlin** südlich von Berlin; **they went south** sie sind nach Süden gefahren.

South Africa *noun* Südafrika *das*.

South America *noun* Südamerika *das*.

southeast *noun* Südosten *der*. *adjective* **in southeast England** in Südostengland.

South Pole *noun* Südpol *der*.

southwest *noun* Südwesten *der*. *adjective* **in southwest England** in Südwestengland.

souvenir *noun* Souvenir *das* (PL *die* Souvenirs).

soya *noun* Soja *die*.

space *noun* 1 (*room*) Platz *der*; **there's enough space** es ist genug Platz da; **we've got enough space for two** wir haben genug Platz für zwei; 2 (*gap*) Zwischenraum *der* (PL *die* Zwischenräume); **to leave a large space between lines** einen großen Zwischenraum zwischen den Zeilen lassen; 3 (*parking*) space *die* Lücke; 4 (*outer space*) Weltraum *der*; **in space** im Weltraum.

spacecraft *noun* Raumschiff *das* (PL *die* Raumschiffe).

spade *noun* 1 Spaten *der* (PL *die* Spaten); 2 (*in cards*) Pik *das*; **the queen of spades** die Pikdame.

Spain *noun* Spanien *das*; **from Spain** aus Spanien; **to Spain** nach Spanien.

◇ IRREGULAR VERB: See the verb table in the centre of the dictionary

Spaniard noun Spanier der (PL die Spanier), Spanierin die (PL die Spanierinnen).

spaniel noun Spaniel der (PL die Spaniels).

Spanish noun 1 (language) Spanisch das; I'm learning Spanish ich lerne Spanisch; 2 the Spanish (people) die Spanier. adjective spanisch; Pedro is Spanish Pedro ist Spanier.

spare adjective Extra-; we have a spare ticket wir haben eine Extrakarte. verb to have time to spare Zeit haben; can you spare a moment? hast du einen Moment Zeit?

spare room noun Gästezimmer das (PL die Gästezimmer).

spare time noun Freizeit die; in my spare time in meiner Freizeit.

spare wheel noun Reserverad das (PL die Reserveräder).

sparkling adjective sparkling mineral water Mineralwasser mit Kohlensäure; sparkling wine der Schaumwein.

sparrow noun Spatz der (PL die Spätze).

speak verb 1 sprechen ◇; do you speak German? sprechen Sie Deutsch?; spoken German gesprochenes Deutsch; to speak to somebody about something mit jemandem über etwas ←(ACC) sprechen; she's speaking to Mike about it sie spricht mit Mike

darüber; 2 who's speaking? (on the phone) wer ist am Apparat?

speaker noun 1 (on a music system) Lautsprecher der (PL die Lautsprecher); 2 (at a public lecture) Redner der (PL die Redner), Rednerin die (PL die Rednerinnen).

special adjective 1 besonderer/ besondere/besonderes; on special occasions bei besonderen Anlässen; 2 special offer das Sonderangebot.

specialist noun Fachmann der (PL die Fachleute), Fachfrau die (PL die Fachfrauen).

specially adverb 1 besonders; not specially nicht besonders; it's specially good for babys es ist besonders gut für Babys; 2 (specifically) speziell; I made this cake specially for you ich habe diesen Kuchen speziell für dich gebacken.

spectacles noun Brille die (PL die Brillen).

spectacular adjective spektakulär.

spectator noun Zuschauer der (PL die Zuschauer), Zuschauerin die (PL die Zuschauerinnen).

speech noun Rede die (PL die Reden); to make a speech eine Rede halten.

speed noun 1 Geschwindigkeit die (PL die Geschwindigkeiten); at top speed mit Höchstgeschwindigkeit; what speed was he doing? wie schnell ist er gefahren?; 2 (gear) Gang der (PL die Gänge); a twelve-speed bike ein Rad mit zwölf Gängen.

△ NEW SPELLING: See page xii

● **to speed up 1** beschleunigen (*a car*); **2** (*of a person, car*) schneller werden.

speeding *noun* zu schnelle Fahren *das*; **he was fined for speeding** er hat wegen zu schnellen Fahrens einen Strafzettel bekommen.

speed limit *noun* Geschwindigkeitsbeschränkung *die*.

spell *noun* **1** (*of time*) Weile *die*; **for a spell** eine Weile; **2 cold spell** die Kälteperiode; **sunny spells** sonnige Wetterabschnitte.
verb **1** (*in writing*) schreiben ◇; **how do you spell it?** wie schreibt man das?; **how do you spell your surname?** wie schreibt man Ihren Nachnamen?; **2** (*out loud*) buchstabieren.

spelling *noun* Rechtschreibung *die*; **spelling mistake** *der* Rechtschreibfehler.

spend *verb* **1** ausgeben ◇ SEP (*money*); **I've spent all my money** ich habe mein ganzes Geld ausgegeben; **2** verbringen ◇ (*time*); **we spent three days in Munich** wir haben drei Tage in München verbracht; **she spends her time reading** sie verbringt ihre Zeit mit Lesen.

spice *noun* Gewürz *das* (PL *die* Gewürze).

spicy *adjective* scharf; **he doesn't like spicy food** er mag kein scharfes Essen.

spider *noun* Spinne *die* (PL *die* Spinnen).

spill *verb* verschütten; **I've spilled my wine on the carpet** ich habe meinen Wein auf dem Teppich verschüttet.

spinach *noun* Spinat *der*.

spire *noun* Kirchturm *der* (PL *die* Kirchtürme).

spirit *noun* **1** (*energy*) Energie *die*; **2 in the right spirit** mit der richtigen Einstellung.

spirits *noun* **1** (*alcohol*) Spirituosen (*plural*); **2 to be in good spirits** guter Laune sein.

spit *verb* **1** spucken; **2 to spit something out** etwas ausspucken SEP; **spit it out!** spuck es aus!

spite *noun* **1 in spite of** trotz (+GEN); **we decided to go in spite of the rain** wir beschlossen trotz des Regens zu gehen; **2** (*nastiness*) Boshaftigkeit *die*; **to do something out of spite** etwas aus Boshaftigkeit tun.

spiteful *adjective* gehässig.

splash *noun* **1** (*noise*) Platsch *der*; **2 splash of colour** *der* Farbfleck.
verb bespritzen.

splendid *adjective* herrlich.

split *verb* **1** (*with an axe or a knife*) spalten; **to split wood** Holz spalten. **2** (*come apart*) zerreißen ◇ (PERF *sein*); **the lining has split** das Futter ist zerrissen; **3** (*divide up*) teilen; **they split the money between**

◇ IRREGULAR VERB: See the verb table in the centre of the dictionary

them sie haben das Geld untereinander geteilt.

• **to split up 1** (*a group or crowd*) sich auflösen SEP; **2** (*a couple*) sich trennen; **she's split up with her husband** sie hat sich von ihrem Mann getrennt; **she's split up with Sam** sie hat mit Sam Schluss gemacht (*informal*).

spoil *verb* verderben◇; **it completely spoiled our evening** das hat uns den Abend völlig verdorben; **to spoil somebody's fun** jemandem den Spaß verderben.

spoiled *adjective* verwöhnt; **a spoiled child** ein verwöhntes Kind.

spokesman *noun* Sprecher *der* (PL die Sprecher).

spokeswoman *noun* Sprecherin *die* (PL die Sprecherinnen).

sponge *noun* Schwamm *der* (PL die Schwämme).

sponge cake *noun* Rührkuchen *der* (PL die Rührkuchen).

sponsor *noun* Sponsor *der* (PL die Sponsoren). *verb* sponsern.

spooky *adjective* gruselig; **a spooky story** eine gruselige Geschichte.

spoon *noun* Löffel *der* (PL die Löffel); **a spoon of sugar** ein Löffel Zucker; **soup spoon** der Suppenlöffel; **teaspoon** der Teelöffel.

spoonful *noun* Löffel *der* (PL die Löffel).

sport *noun* **1** Sport *der*; **to be good at sport** gut im Sport sein; **my favourite sport** mein Lieblingssport; **2** (*in games*) **to be a good sport** ein guter Verlierer sein.

sports bag *noun* Sporttasche *die* (PL die Sporttaschen).

sports car *noun* Sportwagen *der* (PL die Sportwagen).

sports centre *noun* Sportzentrum *das* (PL die Sportzentren).

sports club *noun* Sportverein *der* (PL die Sportvereine).

sportsman *noun* Sportler *der* (PL die Sportler).

sportswear *noun* Sportbekleidung *die*.

sportswoman *noun* Sportlerin *die* (PL die Sportlerinnen).

spot *noun* **1** (*pattern in fabric*) Punkt *der* (PL die Punkte); **a red shirt with black spots** ein rotes Hemd mit schwarzen Punkten; **2** (*on your skin*) Pickel *der* (PL die Pickel); **I've got spots** ich habe Pickel; **to be covered in spots** völlig verpickelt sein; **3** (*stain*) Fleck *der* (PL die Flecke); **you've got a spot on your shirt** du hast einen Fleck auf dem Hemd; **4** (*spotlight*) Scheinwerfer *der* (PL die Scheinwerfer); (*in the home*) Spot *der* (PL die Spots); **5 on the spot** (*immediately*) auf der Stelle; **we'll do it for you on the spot** wir machen es Ihnen auf der Stelle; **6** (*at hand*) **on the spot** zur Stelle; **7** (*at the same place*) **on the spot** an Ort

△ NEW SPELLING: See page xii

und Stelle.
verb entdecken; **he spotted his friend in the crowd** er entdeckte seinen Freund in der Menge.

spotlight *noun* 1 Scheinwerfer der (PL die Scheinwerfer); 2 (*in the home*) Spots der (PL die Spots).

spotty *adjective* (*pimply*) pickelig.

sprain *noun* Verstauchung die (PL die Verstauchungen).
verb **to sprain your ankle** sich ←(DAT) den Fuß verstauchen.

spray *noun* (*spray can*) Spray das (PL die Sprays).
verb sprühen.

spread *noun* Brotaufstrich der; **cheese spread** der Streichkäse.
verb 1 (*of news or a disease*) sich verbreiten; 2 streichen ◇ (*butter, jam, glue*).

spreadsheet *noun* (*on a computer*) Tabellenkalkulation die.

spring *noun* 1 (*the season*) Frühling der (PL die Frühlinge); **in the spring** im Frühling; **spring flowers** Frühlingsblumen; 2 (*made of metal*) Feder die (PL die Federn); 3 (*providing water*) Quelle die (PL die Quellen).

springtime *noun* Frühjahr das; **in springtime** im Frühjahr.

spring water *noun* Quellwasser das.

sprint *noun* Sprint der (PL die Sprints).
verb rennen ◇ (PERF sein).

sprinter *noun* Sprinter der (PL die Sprinter), Sprinterin die (PL die Sprinterinnen).

sprout *noun* (*Brussels sprout*) Rosenkohl der; **he likes sprouts** er mag Rosenkohl.

spy *noun* Spion der (PL die Spione), Spionin die (PL die Spioninnen).
verb **to spy on somebody** jemandem nachspionieren SEP; **he's spying on me** er spioniert mir nach.

squabble *verb* sich zanken.

square *noun* 1 (*shape*) Quadrat das (PL die Quadrate); 2 (*in a town or village*) Platz der (PL die Plätze); **the village square** der Dorfplatz.
adjective quadratisch; **a square box** eine viereckige Schachtel; **three square metres** drei Quadratmeter; **the room is four metres square** das Zimmer ist vier mal vier Meter; ★ **to go back to square one** noch einmal von vorn anfangen.

squash *noun* 1 (*drink*) Saft der; **orange squash** der Orangensaft; 2 (*sport*) Squash das.
verb zerquetschen.

squeak *verb* 1 (*door, hinge*) quietschen; 2 (*person, animal*) quieken.

squeeze *verb* 1 **to squeeze somebody's hand** jemandem die Hand drücken; 2 drücken (*toothpaste*).

stab *verb* stechen ◇; **to stab somebody** (*kill*) jemanden erstechen ◇.

◇ IRREGULAR VERB: See the verb table in the centre of the dictionary

stable noun Stall der (PL die Ställe). adjective stabil.

stack noun 1 Stapel der (PL die Stapel); 2 stacks of ein Haufen; she's got stacks of CDs sie hat einen Haufen CDs.

stadium noun Stadion das (PL die Stadien).

staff noun 1 (of a company) Personal das; 2 (in a school) Lehrkräfte (plural).

stage noun 1 (for a performance) Bühne die (PL die Bühnen); on stage auf der Bühne; 2 (phase) Phase die (PL die Phasen); at this stage of the project in dieser Phase des Projekts; at this stage it's hard to say im Augenblick ist es schwer zu sagen.

staggered adjective (amazed) verblüfft.

stain noun Fleck der (PL die Flecke). verb beflecken.

stainless steel noun Edelstahl der; a stainless steel sink ein Spülbecken aus Edelstahl.

stair noun 1 (step) Stufe die (PL die Stufen); 2 the stairs die Treppe (singular); I met her on the stairs ich habe sie auf der Treppe getroffen.

staircase noun Treppe die (PL die Treppen).

stale adjective alt.

stalemate noun (in chess) Patt das (PL die Patts).

stall noun 1 (at a market or fair) Stand der (PL die Stände); 2 (in a theatre) the stalls das Parkett.

stammer noun to have a stammer stottern.

stamp noun Briefmarke die (PL die Briefmarken). verb 1 frankieren (a letter); 2 to stamp your foot mit dem Fuß aufstampfen.

stamp album noun Briefmarkenalbum das (PL die Briefmarkenalben).

stamp collection noun Briefmarkensammlung die (PL die Briefmarkensammlungen).

stand verb 1 stehen ◊; several people were standing viele Leute standen; we stood outside the cinema wir haben vor dem Kino gestanden; 2 (bear) ausstehen ◊ SEP; I can't stand her ich kann sie nicht ausstehen; I can't stand waiting ich kann es nicht ausstehen, wenn man warten muss; 3 (keep going) aushalten ◊ SEP; I can't stand it any longer ich halte es nicht mehr aus. noun (in a stadium) Tribüne die (PL die Tribünen).

● to stand for something (be short for) bedeuten; UN stands for United Nations UN bedeutet United Nations.

● stand up aufstehen ◊ SEP (PERF sein); everybody stood up alle standen auf.

standard noun 1 (level) Niveau das; of high standard von hohem Niveau; 2 standard of living

der Lebensstandard; **3 she sets herself high standards** sie stellt hohe Ansprüche an sich selbst.
adjective **the standard size** die Normalgröße.

staple *noun* Heftklammer *die* (PL die Heftklammern).
verb heften; **to staple the pages together** die Seiten zusammenheften.

stapler *noun* Hefter *der* (PL die Hefter).

star *noun* **1** (*in the sky*) Stern *der* (PL die Sterne); **2** (*person*) Star *der* (PL die Stars); **he's a film star** er ist ein Filmstar.
verb **to star in a film** in einem Film die Hauptrolle spielen; **starring ...** in der Hauptrolle ...

stare *verb* **1** starren; **what are you staring at?** was starrst du so?; **2 to stare at somebody** jemanden anstarren SEP; **he's staring at the wall** er starrt die Wand an.

start *noun* **1** Anfang *der*; **at the start** am Anfang; **at the start of the film** am Anfang des Films; **from the start** von Anfang an; **we knew from the start that it was dangerous** wir wussten von Anfang an, dass es gefährlich war; **2 to make a start on something** mit etwas ←(DAT) anfangen ◇ SEP; **I've made a start on my homework** ich habe mit meinen Hausaufgaben angefangen; **3** (*of a race*) Start *der* (PL die Starts).
verb **1** anfangen ◇ SEP; **the film starts at eight** der Film fängt um acht an; **I've started the book** ich habe das Buch angefangen; **to start**

doing something anfangen, etwas zu tun; **I've started learning Spanish** ich habe angefangen, Spanisch zu lernen; **to start crying** anfangen zu weinen; **2 to start a business** ein Geschäft gründen; **3 to start a car** ein Auto starten; **she started the car** sie hat das Auto gestartet; **4 the car won't start** das Auto springt nicht an.

starter *noun* (*first course*) Vorspeise *die* (PL die Vorspeisen).

starve *verb* verhungern; **I'm starving!** ich bin schon am Verhungern!

state *noun* **1** Zustand *der* (PL die Zustände); **the house is in a very bad state** das Haus ist in einem sehr schlechten Zustand; **2** (*country*) Staat *der* (PL die Staaten); **the state** der Staat; **3 the States** (*USA*) die Staaten; **they live in the States** sie leben in den Staaten.
verb **1** erklären (*intention, reason*); **2** angeben ◇ SEP (*an address, income, a reason*).

stately home *noun* Schloss △ *das* (PL die Schlösser).

statement *noun* Erklärung *die* (PL die Erklärungen).

station *noun* **1** Bahnhof *der* (PL die Bahnhöfe); **at the railway station** am Bahnhof; **bus station** der Busbahnhof; **2 police station** die Polizeiwache; **3 radio station** der Rundfunksender.

stationer's *noun* Schreibwarengeschäft *das* (PL die Schreibwarengeschäfte).

◇ IRREGULAR VERB: *See the verb table in the centre of the dictionary*

statistics noun (subject)
Statistik die; **the statistics** (figures)
die Statistik.

statue noun Statue die (PL die
Statuen).

stay noun Aufenthalt der (PL die
Aufenthalte); **our stay in Cologne**
unser Aufenthalt in Köln; **enjoy your
stay!** einen schönen Aufenthalt!
verb **1** bleiben ◊ (PERF sein); **I'll stay
here** ich bleibe hier; **how long are
you staying?** wie lange bleibst du?;
2 (spend the night) **you can stay
with us** du kannst bei uns
übernachten; **to stay the night with
friends** bei Freunden übernachten; **3** (be temporarily lodged) wohnen;
where are you staying? wo wohnst
du?; **I'm staying in a hotel** ich
wohne im Hotel; **4** (be on a visit)
sein ◊ (PERF sein); **I'm going to stay
with my sister this weekend** ich bin
am Wochenende bei meiner
Schwester; **I stayed in Munich for a
couple of days** ich war ein paar
Tage in München.
● **to stay in** zu Hause bleiben ◊ (PERF
sein); **I'm staying in tonight** heute
Abend bleibe ich zu Hause.

steady adjective **1** fest; **a steady job**
eine feste Stelle; **2** gleichmäßig; **at a
steady pace** mit gleichmäßiger
Geschwindigkeit; **3** (hand, voice)
ruhig; **to hold something steady**
etwas ruhig halten; **4** (dependable)
zuverlässig.

steak noun Steak das (PL die Steaks);
steak and chips Steak mit Pommes
frites.

steal verb stehlen ◊.

steam noun Dampf der.

steel noun Stahl der.

steep adjective steil; **a steep slope**
ein steiler Hang.

steeple noun (spire) Kirchturm der
(PL die Kirchtürme).

steering wheel noun
Lenkrad das (PL die Lenkräder).

step noun **1** Schritt der (PL die
Schritte); **to take a step forwards**
einen Schritt nach vorn machen; **to
take a step backwards** einen
Schritt zurück machen; **2** (stair)
Stufe die (PL die Stufen).
● **to step back** zurücktreten ◊ SEP
(PERF sein).
● **to step forward** vortreten ◊ SEP (PERF
sein).

stepbrother noun Stiefbruder der
(PL die Stiefbrüder).

stepdaughter noun
Stieftochter die (PL die Stieftöchter).

stepfather noun Stiefvater der (PL
die Stiefväter).

stepladder noun Trittleiter die (PL
die Trittleitern).

stepmother noun Stiefmutter die
(PL die Stiefmütter).

stepsister noun Stiefschwester die
(PL die Stiefschwestern).

stepson noun Stiefsohn der (PL die
Stiefsöhne).

stereo noun Stereoanlage die (PL die
Stereoanlagen).

sterling noun Sterling der; **in
sterling** in Pfund (Sterling).

△ NEW SPELLING: *See page xii*

stew noun Eintopf der (PL die Eintöpfe).

steward noun Steward der (PL die Stewards).

stewardess noun Stewardess △ die (PL die Stewardessen).

stick noun 1 Stock der (PL die Stöcke); 2 hockey stick der Hockeyschläger.
verb 1 (with glue) kleben; 2 (put) tun ◇; stick them on my desk tu sie auf meinen Schreibtisch.

sticker noun Aufkleber der (PL die Aufkleber).

sticky adjective 1 klebrig; I've got sticky hands ich habe klebrige Hände; 2 a sticky label ein Aufkleber.

sticky tape noun Klebestreifen der.

stiff adjective 1 steif; to feel stiff steif sein; (after exercise) Muskelkater haben; to have a stiff neck einen steifen Hals haben; 2 to be bored stiff sich zu Tode langweilen; 3 to be scared stiff furchtbare Angst haben.

still adjective 1 sit still! sitz still!; keep still! halt still!; 2 still mineral water Mineralwasser ohne Kohlensäure.
adverb 1 noch; do you still live in London? wohnst du noch in London?; I've still not finished ich bin immer noch nicht fertig; he's still working er arbeitet noch; 2 (nevertheless) trotzdem; I told her not to, but she still did it ich habe

es ihr verboten, aber sie hat es trotzdem gemacht; 3 better still noch besser.

sting noun Stich der (PL die Stiche).
verb stechen ◇.

stink noun Gestank der.
verb stinken ◇; it stinks of fish in here es stinkt hier nach Fisch.

stir verb rühren.

stitch noun 1 (in sewing, surgical) Stich der (PL die Stiche); 2 (in knitting) Masche die (PL die Maschen); 3 (pain) Seitenstechen das.

stock noun 1 (in a shop) Warenbestand der; to have something in stock etwas auf Lager haben; to be out of stock ausverkauft sein; 2 (supply) Vorrat der (PL die Vorräte); I always have a stock of pencils ich habe immer einen Bleistiftvorrat; 3 (for cooking) Brühe die; chicken stock die Hühnerbrühe.
verb (in a shop) führen; they don't stock books sie führen keine Bücher.

stock cube noun Brühwürfel der (PL die Brühwürfel).

stocking noun Strumpf der (PL die Strümpfe).

stomach noun Magen der (PL die Mägen).

stomach-ache noun Magenschmerzen (plural); to have stomach-ache Magenschmerzen haben.

◇ IRREGULAR VERB: See the verb table in the centre of the dictionary

stone noun Stein der (PL die Steine);
stone wall die Steinmauer.

stool noun Hocker der (PL die
Hocker).

stop noun Haltestelle die (PL die
Haltestellen); **bus stop** die
Bushaltestelle.
verb 1 halten ◇; **does the train stop
in Stuttgart?** hält der Zug in
Stuttgart?; **2 to stop somebody/
something** jemanden/etwas
anhalten ◇ SEP; **the police stopped
the car** die Polizei hielt den Wagen
an; **3** (cease) aufhören SEP; **the noise
has stopped** der Lärm hat
aufgehört; **to stop doing
something** aufhören, etwas zu tun;
he's stopped smoking er hat
aufgehört zu rauchen; **she never
stops asking questions** sie hört nie
auf, Fragen zu stellen; **stop it!** hör
auf!; **4 to stop somebody doing
something** jemanden daran
hindern, etwas zu tun; **I can't stop
her ringing him** ich kann sie nicht
daran hindern, ihn anzurufen;
5 (prevent) verhindern (an accident,
a crime).

stopwatch noun Stoppuhr die (PL
die Stoppuhren).

store noun (shop) Geschäft das (PL
die Geschäfte); **department store**
das Kaufhaus.
verb 1 aufbewahren SEP; (in a
warehouse) lagern; **2** (on a
computer) speichern.

storey noun Stockwerk das (PL die
Stockwerke); **a four-storey house**
ein vierstöckiges Haus.

storm noun 1 Sturm der (PL die
Stürme); **2** (thunderstorm)
Gewitter das (PL die Gewitter).

stormy adjective stürmisch.

story noun Geschichte die (PL die
Geschichten); **to tell a story** eine
Geschichte erzählen.

stove noun (cooker) Herd der (PL
die Herde).

straight adjective 1 gerade; **a
straight line** eine gerade Linie;
2 to have straight hair glatte Haare
haben.
adverb 1 (in direction) straight
ahead geradeaus; **to go straight
ahead** geradeaus gehen;
2 (immediately, directly) sofort;
straight away sofort; **he went
straight to the doctor's** er ging
sofort zum Arzt.

straightforward adjective
einfach.

strain noun Stress △ der; **the strain
of the last few weeks** der Stress in
den letzten Wochen; **to be a strain**
anstrengend sein.
verb 1 zerren (a muscle);
2 verrenken (your arm, back); **he's
strained his back** er hat sich ←(DAT)
den Rücken verrenkt.

strange adjective seltsam; **his
strange behaviour** sein seltsames
Verhalten.

stranger noun Fremde der/die (PL
die Fremden).

strap noun 1 (on a case, bag, camera)
Riemen der (PL die Riemen); **2** (on a
garment) Träger der (PL die Träger);

△ NEW SPELLING: See page xii

3 (*of a watch*) Armband *das* (PL *die* Armbänder).

strapless *adjective* trägerlos.

straw *noun* **1** (*for drinking*) Strohhalm *der* (PL *die* Strohhalme); **2** (*the material*) Stroh *das*; **straw hat** *der* Strohhut.

strawberry *noun* Erdbeere *die* (PL *die* Erdbeeren); **strawberry jam** *die* Erdbeermarmelade.

stray *adjective* **a stray dog** ein streunender Hund.

stream *noun* Bach *der* (PL *die* Bäche).

street *noun* Straße *die* (PL *die* Straßen); **I met Simon in the street** ich habe Simon auf der Straße getroffen.

streetlamp *noun* Straßenlampe *die* (PL *die* Straßenlampen).

street map *noun* Stadtplan *der* (PL *die* Stadtpläne).

streetwise *adjective* gewieft.

strength *noun* Kraft *die* (PL *die* Kräfte).

stress *noun* Stress △ *der*. *verb* betonen; **to stress the importance of something** die Wichtigkeit von etwas betonen.

stretch *verb* **1** (*garment, shoes*) sich dehnen; **this jumper has stretched** der Pullover hat sich gedehnt; **2** **to stretch your legs** sich ←(DAT) die Beine vertreten ◇.

stretcher *noun* Trage *die* (PL *die* Tragen).

stretchy *adjective* elastisch.

strict *adjective* streng.

strike *noun* Streik *der* (PL *die* Streiks); **to go on strike** in den Streik treten ◇ (PERF sein); **to be/go on strike** streiken. *verb* **1** (*hit*) schlagen ◇; **the clock struck six** die Uhr schlug sechs; **2** (*be/go on strike*) streiken.

striker *noun* **1** (*in football*) Stürmer *der* (PL *die* Stürmer), Stürmerin *die* (PL *die* Stürmerinnen); **2** (*person on strike*) Streikende *der/die* (PL *die* Streikenden).

string *noun* **1** (*for tying*) Schnur *die* (PL *die* Schnüre); **2** (*on a musical instrument*) Saite *die* (PL *die* Saiten).

strip *noun* Streifen *der* (PL *die* Streifen). *verb* **1** (*undress*) sich ausziehen ◇ SEP; **2** (*remove paint from*) abbeizen SEP.

strip cartoon *noun* Comicstrip △ *der* (PL *die* Comicstrips).

stripe *noun* Streifen *der* (PL *die* Streifen).

striped *adjective* gestreift.

stroke *noun* **1** (*style of swimming*) Stil *der* (PL *die* Stile); **2** (*medical*) Schlaganfall *der* (PL *die* Schlaganfälle); **to have a stroke** einen Schlaganfall bekommen; ★ **a stroke of luck** ein glücklicher Zufall; **to have a stroke of luck** Glück haben. *verb* streicheln.

◇ **IRREGULAR VERB:** *See the verb table in the centre of the dictionary*

strong adjective 1 (person, drink, feeling) stark; 2 (sturdy) stabil (furniture); **strong shoes** feste Schuhe.

strongly adverb 1 (believe, oppose) fest; 2 (support) nachdrücklich; 3 (advise, recommend) dringend; 4 **she smelt strongly of garlic** sie hat stark nach Knoblauch gerochen.

struggle noun Kampf der (PL die Kämpfe); **the struggle for freedom** der Kampf für die Freiheit; **it's been a struggle** es war ein Kampf.
verb 1 (to obtain something) kämpfen; **to struggle to do something** kämpfen, um etwas zu tun; **she struggled for a place** sie kämpfte um einen Platz; 2 (physically, in order to escape or reach something) sich wehren; 3 (have difficulty in doing something) sich abmühen SEP; **they are struggling to pay the rent** sie mühen sich ab, ihre Miete zu zahlen; **he's struggling with his homework** er müht sich mit seinen Hausaufgaben ab.

stub noun cigarette stub die Kippe.
● **to stub out** ausdrücken SEP.

stubborn adjective stur.

stuck adjective 1 (jammed) **it's stuck** es klemmt; **the drawer's stuck** die Schublade klemmt; 2 **to get stuck** (person) stecken bleiben △ ◇ (in a lift, traffic jam, or place).

stud noun 1 (on clothes) Niete die (PL die Nieten); 2 (on a boot) Stollen der (PL die Stollen);

3 (earring) Ohrstecker der (PL die Ohrstecker).

student noun 1 (at college or university) Student der (PL die Studenten), Studentin die (PL die Studentinnen); 2 (at school) Schüler der (PL die Schüler), Schülerin die (PL die Schülerinnen).

studio noun 1 (film, TV) Studio das (PL die Studios); 2 (artist's) Atelier das (PL die Ateliers).

study verb 1 lernen; **he's busy studying for his exams** er lernt fleißig für seine Prüfung; 2 studieren; **she's studying medicine** sie studiert Medizin.

stuff noun (things, personal belongings) Zeug das (informal); **we can put all that stuff in the attic** wir können das ganze Zeug auf den Boden bringen; **you can leave your stuff at my house** du kannst dein Zeug bei mir lassen.
verb 1 (shove) stopfen; **she stuffed some things into a suitcase** sie hat ein paar Sachen in einen Koffer gestopft; 2 füllen (vegetables, turkey); **stuffed peppers** gefüllte Paprikaschoten.

stuffing noun (in cooking) Füllung die (PL die Füllungen).

stuffy adjective (airless) stickig.

stunned adjective sprachlos.

stunning adjective toll (informal).

stunt noun (in a film) Stunt der (PL die Stunts).

stuntman noun Stuntman der (PL die Stuntmen).

△ NEW SPELLING: See page xii

stupid adjective blöd; **that was really stupid** das war so blöd; **I did something stupid** ich habe etwas Blödes gemacht.

stutter noun **to have a stutter** stottern.
verb stottern.

style noun 1 Stil der (PL die Stile); **style of living** der Lebensstil; **he has his own style** er hat seinen eigenen Stil; 2 (fashion) Mode die; **it's the latest style** das ist die neueste Mode.

subject noun 1 Thema das (PL die Themen); **the subject of my talk** das Thema meiner Rede; 2 (at school) Fach das (PL die Fächer); **my favourite subject is biology** mein Lieblingsfach ist Biologie.

subscription noun Abonnement das (PL die Abonnements); **to take out a subscription to a magazine** eine Zeitschrift abonnieren.

subsidize verb subventionieren.

subsidy noun Subvention die (PL die Subventionen).

substance noun Substanz die (PL die Substanzen).

substitute noun (in sport) Ersatzspieler der (PL die Ersatzspieler), Ersatzspielerin die (PL die Ersatzspielerinnen).
verb ersetzen.

subtitled adjective mit Untertiteln.

subtitles plural noun Untertitel (plural).

subtract verb abziehen ◇ SEP.

suburb noun Vorort der (PL die Vororte); **a suburb of Edinburgh** ein Vorort von Edinburgh; **in the suburbs of London** in den Londoner Vororten.

suburban adjective Vorort-; **a suburban train** ein Vorortzug.

subway noun (underpass) Unterführung die (PL die Unterführungen).

succeed verb gelingen ◇ (PERF sein); **we've succeeded in contacting her** es ist uns gelungen, sie zu erreichen.

success noun Erfolg der (PL die Erfolge); **a great success** ein großer Erfolg.

successful adjective 1 erfolgreich; **he's a successful writer** er ist ein erfolgreicher Schriftsteller; 2 **to be successful in doing something** etwas mit Erfolg tun.

successfully adverb mit Erfolg.

such adjective, adverb 1 so; **they're such nice people** das sind so nette Leute; **I've had such a busy day** ich habe so einen hektischen Tag gehabt; **it's such a long way** es ist so weit; **it's such a pity** es ist so schade; 2 **such a lot of** (followed by a singular noun) so viel; **they've got such a lot of money** sie haben so viel Geld; 3 **such a lot of** (followed by a plural noun) so viele; **she's got such a lot of problems** sie hat so viele Probleme; 4 **such as** wie; **in big cities such as Glasgow** in großen Städten wie Glasgow;

◇ IRREGULAR VERB: See the verb table in the centre of the dictionary

5 there's no such thing so etwas gibt es nicht.

suck verb lutschen; **to suck your thumb** am Daumen lutschen.

sudden adjective plötzlich; ★ **all of a sudden** plötzlich.

suddenly adverb plötzlich; **he suddenly started to laugh** plötzlich hat er zu lachen angefangen zu lachen; **suddenly the light went out** plötzlich ging das Licht aus.

suede noun Wildleder das; **suede jacket** die Wildlederjacke.

suffer verb leiden ◇; **to suffer from asthma** an Asthma leiden.

sufficiently adverb genug.

sugar noun Zucker der; **do you take sugar?** nimmst du Zucker?

suggest verb vorschlagen ◇ SEP; **he suggested to speak to you about it** er hat vorgeschlagen, dass ich mit dir darüber sprechen soll.

suggestion noun Vorschlag der (PL die Vorschläge); **to make a suggestion** einen Vorschlag machen.

suicide noun Selbstmord der (PL die Selbstmorde); **to commit suicide** Selbstmord begehen.

suit noun 1 (man's) Anzug der (PL die Anzüge); 2 (woman's) Kostüm das (PL die Kostüme).
verb 1 (be convenient) passen (+DAT); **does Monday suit you?** passt Ihnen Montag?; 2 (look good on) stehen ◇ (+DAT); **hats suit her** ihr stehen Hüte gut.

suitable adjective 1 geeignet; **to be suitable for something** für etwas geeignet sein; **it's suitable for children** es ist für Kinder geeignet; 2 (convenient) passend; **at a suitable time** zur passenden Zeit; **Saturday is the most suitable day for me** Samstag passt mir am besten; 3 (for a social occasion) angemessen (clothes).

suitcase noun Koffer der (PL die Koffer).

sulk verb schmollen.

sum noun 1 Summe die (PL die Summen); **a sum of money** eine Geldsumme; 2 (calculation) Rechenaufgabe die (PL die Rechenaufgaben).
● **to sum up** zusammenfassen SEP.

summarize verb zusammenfassen SEP.

summary noun Zusammenfassung die (PL die Zusammenfassungen).

summer noun Sommer der (PL die Sommer); **in summer** im Sommer; **summer clothes** die Sommerkleidung; **the summer holidays** die Sommerferien.

summertime noun Sommer der; **in summertime** im Sommer.

summit noun Gipfel der (PL die Gipfel).

sun noun Sonne die (PL die Sonnen); **in the sun** in der Sonne.

sunbathe verb sich sonnen.

△ NEW SPELLING: **See page xii**

sunblock noun Sun-Block-Creme die (PL die Sun-Block-Cremes).

sunburned adjective **to get sunburned** einen Sonnenbrand bekommen.

Sunday noun 1 Sonntag der (PL die Sonntage); **on Sunday** am Sonntag; **I'm going to the cinema on Sunday** ich gehe (am) Sonntag ins Kino; **see you on Sunday!** bis Sonntag!; **every Sunday** jeden Sonntag; **last Sunday** vorigen Sonntag; **next Sunday** nächsten Sonntag; **2 on Sundays** sonntags; **the museum is closed on Sundays** das Museum ist sonntags geschlossen.

sunflower noun Sonnenblume die (PL die Sonnenblumen); **sunflower oil** das Sonnenblumenöl.

sunglasses plural noun Sonnenbrille die (PL die Sonnenbrillen).

sunlight noun Sonnenlicht das.

sunny adjective sonnig; **a sunny day** ein sonniger Tag; **sunny intervals** Aufheiterungen.

sunrise noun Sonnenaufgang der (PL die Sonnenaufgänge).

sunscreen noun Sonnenschutzcreme die (PL die Sonnenschutzcremes).

sunset noun Sonnenuntergang der (PL die Sonnenuntergänge).

sunshine noun Sonnenschein der.

sunstroke noun Sonnenstich der (PL die Sonnenstiche); **to get sunstroke** einen Sonnenstich bekommen.

suntan noun Bräune die; **to have a suntan** braun sein; **to get a suntan** braun werden.

suntan lotion noun Sonnenmilch die.

suntan oil noun Sonnenöl das.

super adjective klasse (informal) ('klasse' never changes); **we had a super time** es war wirklich klasse.

supermarket noun Supermarkt der (PL die Supermärkte).

supernatural adjective übernatürlich.

superstitious adjective abergläubisch.

supervise verb beaufsichtigen.

supper noun Abendessen das (PL die Abendessen); **I had supper at Sandy's** ich war bei Sandy zum Abendessen.

supplement noun 1 (to newspaper) Beilage die (PL die Beilagen); 2 (to fare) Zuschlag der (PL die Zuschläge).

supply noun 1 (stock) Vorrat der (PL die Vorräte); **2 to be in short supply** knapp sein.
verb 1 stellen; **the school supplies the books** die Schule stellt die Bücher; 2 (deliver) liefern; **to supply somebody with something** jemandem etwas liefern.

supply teacher noun Aushilfslehrer der (PL die Aushilfslehrer), Aushilfslehrerin die (PL die Aushilfslehrerinnen).

◇ IRREGULAR VERB: See the verb table in the centre of the dictionary.

support noun Unterstützung die;
in support zur Unterstützung.
verb 1 (back up) unterstützen; **her
teachers have really supported
her** die Lehrer haben sie sehr
unterstützt; **to support somebody
financially** jemanden finanziell
unterstützen; 2 **Will supports
Chelsea** Will ist ein Chelsea-Fan;
what team do you support? für
welche Mannschaft bist du?; 3 (keep,
provide for) ernähren; **to support a
family** eine Familie ernähren.

supporter noun 1 Fan der (PL die
Fans); **she's a Manchester United
supporter** sie ist ein Manchester-
United-Fan; 2 (of a party or cause)
Anhänger der (PL die Anhänger),
Anhängerin die (PL die
Anhängerinnen).

suppose verb annehmen ◊ SEP;
I suppose she's forgotten ich
nehme an, sie hat es vergessen.

supposed adjective **to be
supposed to do something** etwas
tun sollen; **you were supposed to
be here at six** du solltest um sechs
hier sein.

sure adjective 1 sicher; **are you
sure?** bist du sicher?; **are you
sure you saw her?** bist du sicher, dass du
sie gesehen hast?; 2 **sure!** klar!

surely adverb doch sicherlich;
surely she hasn't forgotten sie hat
es doch sicherlich nicht vergessen.

surface noun Oberfläche die (PL die
Oberflächen).

surfboard noun Surfbrett das (PL
die Surfbretter).

surfing noun Surfen das.

surgeon noun Chirurg der (PL die
Chirurgen), Chirurgin die (PL die
Chirurginnen).

surgery noun 1 **to have surgery**
operiert werden; 2 (doctor's)
Praxis die (PL die Praxen); **the
dentist's surgery** die
Zahnarztpraxis; 3 (surgery hours)
Sprechstunde die.

surname noun Nachname der (PL
die Nachnamen).

surprise noun Überraschung die
(PL die Überraschungen); **what a
surprise!** was für eine
Überraschung!

surprised adjective überrascht; **I
was surprised to see her** ich war
überrascht, sie zu sehen.

surprising adjective überraschend.

surround verb umgeben;
surrounded by umgeben von (+DAT);
she was surrounded by friends sie
war von Freunden umgeben.

survey noun Umfrage die (PL die
Umfragen).

survive verb überleben.

survivor noun
Überlebende der/die (PL die
Überlebenden).

suspect noun Verdächtige der/die
(PL die Verdächtigen).
adjective verdächtig.
verb verdächtigen.

suspend verb 1 **to be suspended**
(from school) vom Unterricht
ausgeschlossen werden; 2 (from a

△ NEW SPELLING: See page xii

team) sperren; **to suspend a player for four weeks** einen Spieler für vier Wochen sperren.

suspense *noun* Spannung *die*.

suspicious *adjective*
1 misstrauisch Δ; **to be suspicious of somebody** jemandem misstrauen; 2 (*suspicious looking*) verdächtig.

swallow *noun* (*bird*) Schwalbe *die* (PL *die* Schwalben).
verb schlucken.

swan *noun* Schwan *der* (PL *die* Schwäne).

swap *verb* tauschen; **do you want to swap?** willst du tauschen?; **he swapped his bike for a computer** er hat sein Rad gegen einen Computer getauscht; **we swapped seats** wir tauschten die Plätze.

swear *verb* (*use bad language*) fluchen.

swearword *noun* Kraftausdruck *der* (PL *die* Kraftausdrücke).

sweat *noun* Schweiß *der*.
verb schwitzen.

sweater *noun* Pullover *der* (PL *die* Pullover).

Swede *noun* Schwede *der* (PL *die* Schweden), Schwedin *die* (PL *die* Schwedinnen).

Sweden *noun* Schweden *das*; **from Sweden** aus Schweden; **to Sweden** nach Schweden.

Swedish *noun* (*the language*) Schwedisch *das*.

adjective schwedisch; **he's Swedish** er ist Schwede; **she's Swedish** sie ist Schwedin.

sweep *verb* fegen.

sweet *noun* 1 Bonbon *der* (PL *die* Bonbons); 2 (*dessert*) Nachtisch *der* (PL *die* Nachtische).
adjective 1 süß; **I try not to eat sweet things** ich versuche nichts Süßes zu essen; **she looks really sweet in that hat** sie sieht richtig süß mit dem Hut aus; 2 (*kind*) lieb; **she's a really sweet person** sie ist wirklich ein sehr lieber Mensch; **how sweet of him** wie lieb von ihm.

sweetcorn *noun* Mais *der*.

swell *verb* (*part of the body*) anschwellen ◇ SEP (PERF *sein*).

swim *noun* **to go for a swim** schwimmen gehen ◇ (PERF *sein*).
verb schwimmen ◇ (PERF *sein*); **can he swim?** kann er schwimmen?; **to swim across a lake** über einen See schwimmen.

swimmer *noun* Schwimmer *der* (PL *die* Schwimmer), Schwimmerin *die* (PL *die* Schwimmerinnen); **she's a strong swimmer** sie ist eine gute Schwimmerin.

swimming *noun* Schwimmen *das*; **to go swimming** schwimmen gehen.

swimming cap *noun* Badekappe *die* (PL *die* Badekappen).

swimming costume *noun* Badeanzug *der* (PL *die* Badeanzüge).

◇ IRREGULAR VERB: See the verb table in the centre of the dictionary

swimming pool noun
Schwimmbecken das (PL die
Schwimmbecken).

swimming trunks noun
Badehose die (PL die Badehosen).

swimsuit noun Badeanzug der (PL
die Badeanzüge).

swing noun Schaukel die (PL die
Schaukeln).

Swiss noun (person) Schweizer der
(PL die Schweizer), Schweizerin die
(PL die Schweizerinnen); **the Swiss**
die Schweizer.
adjective schweizerisch; **she is
Swiss** sie ist Schweizerin.

switch noun (for a light, radio, etc.)
Schalter der (PL die Schalter).
verb (change) wechseln; **to switch
places** die Plätze wechseln.

● **to switch something off** etwas
ausschalten SEP.

● **to switch something on** etwas
anschalten SEP.

Switzerland noun die Schweiz;
from Switzerland aus der Schweiz;
in Switzerland in der Schweiz; **to
Switzerland** in die Schweiz.

swollen adjective geschwollen.

swop verb SEE **swap**.

syllabus noun Lehrplan der (PL die
Lehrpläne); **to be on the syllabus**
auf dem Lehrplan stehen.

symbol noun Symbol das (PL die
Symbole).

sympathetic adjective
verständnisvoll.

sympathize verb **to sympathize
with somebody** mit jemandem
mitfühlen SEP; **I sympathize with
you** ich kann mit Ihnen mitfühlen.

sympathy noun Mitleid das.

symptom noun Symptom das (PL
die Symptome).

synthesizer noun Synthesizer der
(PL die Synthesizers).

synthetic adjective synthetisch.

syringe noun Spritze die (PL die
Spritzen).

system noun System das (PL die
Systeme).

T t

table noun Tisch der (PL die Tische);
to lay the table den Tisch decken;
to clear the table den Tisch
abräumen SEP.

tablecloth noun Tischdecke die (PL
die Tischdecken).

tablespoon noun Esslöffel △ der
(PL die Esslöffel); **a tablespoon of
flour** ein Esslöffel Mehl.

tablet noun Tablette die (PL die
Tabletten).

table tennis noun
Tischtennis das.

tackle verb 1 (in football or hockey)
angreifen ◇ SEP; 2 angehen ◇ SEP
(PERF sein) (a job or a problem).

tact noun Takt der.

tactful *adjective* taktvoll; **that wasn't very tactful** das war nicht sehr taktvoll.

tail *noun* **1** Schwanz der (PL die Schwänze); **2 'heads or tails?' – 'tails'** 'Kopf oder Zahl?' – 'Zahl'.

take *verb* **1** nehmen ◇; **he took a sweet** er nahm einen Bonbon; **take my hand** nimm meine Hand; **I took the bus** ich habe den Bus genommen; **do you take sugar?** nimmst du Zucker?; **2** (*with time*) dauern; **it takes two hours** es dauert zwei Stunden; **3** (*react to*) aufnehmen ◇ SEP; **he took the news calmly** er hat die Nachricht gelassen aufgenommen; **4** (*take to a place*) bringen ◇; **I'm taking Jake to my parents** ich bringe Jake zu meinen Eltern; **I must take the car to the garage** ich muss das Auto in die Werkstatt bringen; **to take somebody home** jemanden nach Hause bringen; **5 to take something up(stairs)** etwas heraufbringen ◇ SEP; **could you take the towels up?** könntest du die Handtücher heraufbringen?; **6 to take something down(stairs)** etwas herunterbringen ◇ SEP; **Cheryl's taken the cups down** Cheryl hat die Tassen heruntergebracht; **7** (*carry with you*) mitnehmen ◇ SEP; **she's taken some of the files home** sie hat einige der Akten mit nach Hause genommen; **I'm taking my Walkman** ich nehme meinen Walkman mit; **I'll take him next time** nächstes Mal nehme ich ihn mit; **8** annehmen ◇ SEP (*a credit card or a cheque*); **do you take cheques?** nehmen Sie Schecks an?; **9** machen (*an exam, a holiday, or a photo*); **she's taking her driving test tomorrow** sie macht morgen ihre Fahrprüfung; **to take a holiday** Ferien machen; **10** (*need*) brauchen; **it takes a lot of courage** dazu braucht man viel Mut; **it takes me at least two hours to read it** ich brauche mindestens zwei Stunden, um es zu lesen; **11** haben ◇ (*clothes size*); **what size do you take?** welche Größe haben Sie?

- **to take something apart** etwas auseinander nehmen △ ◇.
- **to take something back** etwas zurückbringen ◇ SEP.
- **to take off 1** (*plane*) abfliegen ◇ SEP (PERF *sein*); **2** ausziehen ◇ SEP (*clothes, shoes*); **take your jacket off** zieh die Jacke aus; **to take your clothes off** sich ausziehen; **3** abziehen ◇ SEP (*money*); **he took five pounds off the price** er hat fünf Pfund vom Preis abgezogen.
- **to take out something** (*from a bag or pocket*) etwas herausnehmen ◇ SEP; **Eric took out his wallet** Eric nahm seine Brieftasche heraus.
- **to take somebody out** jemanden einladen ◇ SEP; **to take somebody out for a meal** jemanden zum Essen einladen ◇ SEP.

takeaway *noun* **1** (*meal*) Essen zum Mitnehmen das (PL die Essen zum Mitnehmen); **an Indian takeaway** ein indisches Essen zum Mitnehmen; **2** (*where you buy it*) Restaurant mit Straßenverkauf das (PL die Restaurants mit Straßenverkauf).

◇ IRREGULAR VERB: *See the verb table in the centre of the dictionary*

take-off noun (of a plane) Abflug der (PL die Abflüge).

talent noun Talent das (PL die Talente); **to have a talent for painting** ein Talent zum Malen haben.

talented adjective talentiert; **he's really talented** er ist wirklich talentiert.

talk noun 1 (a chat) Gespräch das (PL die Gespräche); **we had a serious talk about it** wir hatten ein ernstes Gespräch darüber; 2 Vortrag der (PL die Vorträge); **she's giving a talk on Hungary** sie hält einen Vortrag über Ungarn.
verb 1 reden; **to talk to somebody** mit jemandem reden; **we talked about football** wir haben über Fußball geredet; **what's he talking about?** wovon redet er?; **we'll talk about it later** darüber reden wir später; **they're always talking** sie reden immer; 2 **to talk to somebody on the phone** mit jemandem telefonieren.

tall adjective 1 groß; **she's very tall** sie ist sehr groß; **I'm 1.7 metres tall** ich bin ein Meter siebzig groß; 2 hoch (building or tree).

tampon noun Tampon der (PL die Tampons).

tan noun Bräune die; **to have a tan** braun sein; **to get a tan** braun werden.

tank noun 1 (for petrol or water) Tank der (PL die Tanks); 2 **fish tank** das Aquarium; 3 (army) Panzer der (PL die Panzer).

tanned adjective braun.

tap noun Wasserhahn der (PL die Wasserhähne); **to turn on the tap** den Wasserhahn aufdrehen SEP; **to turn off the tap** den Wasserhahn zudrehen SEP; **the hot tap** der Warmwasserhahn.
verb klopfen; **to tap on the door** an die Tür klopfen.

tap-dancing noun Stepptanzen das.

tape noun 1 Kassette die (PL die Kassetten); **my tape of the Stones** meine Kassette von den Stones; **I've got it on tape** ich habe es auf Band; 2 **sticky tape** der Klebestreifen.
verb aufnehmen ◇ SEP; **I want to tape the film** ich will den Film aufnehmen.

tape measure noun Metermaß das (PL die Metermaße).

tape recorder noun Tonbandgerät das (PL die Tonbandgeräte).

target noun Ziel das (PL die Ziele).

tart noun Kuchen der (PL die Kuchen); **apple tart** der Apfelkuchen.

tartan adjective Schotten-; **a tartan skirt** ein Schottenrock.

task noun Aufgabe die (PL die Aufgaben).

taste noun 1 Geschmack der (PL die Geschmäcke); **a taste of onions** Zwiebelgeschmack; **she's got no taste** sie hat keinen Geschmack; 2 **in bad taste** geschmacklos.
verb 1 schmecken; **the soup tastes**

horrible die Suppe schmeckt
furchtbar; **2 to taste of something**
nach etwas ←(DAT) schmecken; **it
tastes of garlic** es schmeckt nach
Knoblauch; **3** (try a little)
probieren; **do you want to taste?**
möchtest du mal probieren?

tasty adjective schmackhaft.

tattoo noun Tätowierung die (PL die
Tätowierungen); **he's got a tattoo
on his arm** er hat eine Tätowierung
am Arm.

Taurus noun Stier der; **Josephine's
Taurus** Josephine ist (ein) Stier.

tax noun Steuer die (PL die Steuern)
(on goods, income).

taxi noun Taxi das (PL die Taxis);
to go by taxi mit dem Taxi fahren;
to take a taxi ein Taxi nehmen.

taxi driver noun Taxifahrer der (PL
die Taxifahrer), Taxifahrerin die (PL
die Taxifahrerinnen).

taxi rank noun Taxistand der (PL die
Taxistände).

tea noun **1** Tee der (PL die Tees); **a
cup of tea** eine Tasse Tee; **to have
tea** Tee trinken; **2** (evening meal)
Abendessen das (PL die
Abendessen).

teabag noun Teebeutel der (PL die
Teebeutel).

teach verb **1** beibringen ◇ SEP; **she's
teaching me to drive** sie bringt mir
das Autofahren bei; **to teach
yourself something** sich ←(DAT)
etwas beibringen ◇ SEP; **I taught
myself Italian** ich habe mir
Italienisch beigebracht; **3** that'll

teach you! das wird dir eine Lehre
sein!; **4** unterrichten; **her mum
teaches maths** ihre Mutter
unterrichtet Mathematik.

teacher noun Lehrer der (PL die
Lehrer), Lehrerin die (PL die
Lehrerinnen).

teaching noun Unterrichten das.

team noun Mannschaft die (PL die
Mannschaften); **football team** die
Fußballmannschaft.

teapot noun Teekanne die (PL die
Teekannen).

tear¹ noun (a rip) Riss△ der (PL die
Risse).
verb **1** zerreißen ◇; **she tore up my
letter** sie hat meinen Brief
zerrissen; **2** reißen ◇ (PERF sein); **the
net has torn** das Netz ist gerissen;
be careful, it tears easily sei
vorsichtig, es reißt leicht.

tear² noun (when you cry) Träne die
(PL die Tränen); **to be in tears** in
Tränen aufgelöst sein; **to burst into
tears** in Tränen ausbrechen.

tease verb **1** necken (a person);
2 quälen (an animal).

teaspoon noun Teelöffel der (PL die
Teelöffel); **a teaspoon of vinegar**
ein Teelöffel Essig.

teatime noun (evening meal)
Abendessenzeit die (PL die
Abendessenzeiten); **it's teatime!**
es gibt Abendessen!

tea towel noun Geschirrtuch das
(PL die Geschirrtücher).

technical adjective technisch.

technical college noun
Fachhochschule die (PL die
Fachhochschulen).

technician noun Techniker der (PL
die Techniker), Technikerin die (PL
die Technikerinnen).

technique noun Technik die (PL die
Techniken).

techno noun (music) Techno der.

technology noun
1 Technologie die; 2 information
technology die Informatik.

teddy bear noun Teddybär der (PL
die Teddybären).

teenage adjective 1 Teenage-;
2 they have a teenage son sie
haben einen Sohn im Teenageralter;
3 (films, magazines, etc.) für
Teenager; a teenage magazine eine
Zeitschrift für Teenager.

teenager noun Teenager der (PL die
Teenager); a group of teenagers
eine Gruppe von Teenagern.

teens plural noun the teens die
Teenagerjahre; he's in his teens er
ist ein Teenager.

tee-shirt noun T-Shirt das
(PL die T-Shirts).

telephone noun Telefon das (PL die
Telefone); on the telephone am
Telefon.
verb anrufen ◇ SEP; I'll telephone
the bank ich rufe die Bank an.

telephone box noun
Telefonzelle die (PL die
Telefonzellen).

telephone call noun
Telefongespräch das (PL die
Telefongespräche).

telephone directory noun
Telefonbuch das (PL die
Telefonbücher).

telephone number noun
Telefonnummer die (PL die
Telefonnummern).

televise verb im Fernsehen
übertragen ◇; they're televising
the match sie übertragen das Spiel
im Fernsehen.

television noun 1 Fernsehen das;
I saw it on television ich habe es
im Fernsehen gesehen; 2 to watch
television fernsehen ◇ SEP; I'm
watching television ich sehe fern.

television programme noun
Fernsehsendung die (PL die
Fernsehsendungen).

tell verb 1 sagen; to tell somebody
something jemandem etwas sagen;
if she asks, tell her sag's ihr, wenn
sie fragt; 2 to tell somebody to do
something jemandem sagen, er/sie
soll etwas tun; he told me to do it
myself er hat mir gesagt, ich soll es
selbst machen; she told me not to
wait sie hat mir gesagt, ich soll nicht
warten; 3 (explain) can you tell me
how to do it? kannst du mir sagen,
wie man das macht? 4 erzählen (a
story); tell me about your holiday
erzähl mir von deinen Ferien; 5 (to
see) sehen ◇; you can tell it's old
man sieht, dass es alt ist; I can't tell
them apart ich kann sie nicht
unterscheiden.

△ NEW SPELLING: See page xii

telly noun 1 (set) Fernseher der (PL die Fernseher); 2 to watch telly fernsehen ◇ SEP; I saw her on telly ich habe sie im Fernsehen gesehen.

temp noun Aushilfskraft die (PL die Aushilfskräfte).

temper noun to lose your temper wütend werden.

temperature noun 1 Temperatur die (PL die Temperaturen); what is the temperature? wie viel Grad sind es?; 2 to have a temperature Fieber haben.

temporary adjective vorübergehend.

temptation noun Versuchung die (PL die Versuchungen).

tempted adjective versucht; I'm really tempted to come ich bin wirklich versucht zu kommen.

tempting adjective verlockend.

ten number zehn; Harry's ten Harry ist zehn.

tend verb to tend to do something dazu neigen, etwas zu tun.

tender adjective 1 (loving) zärtlich; 2 (painful) empfindlich.

tennis noun Tennis das; to play tennis Tennis spielen.

tennis ball noun Tennisball der (PL die Tennisbälle).

tennis court noun Tennisplatz der (PL die Tennisplätze).

tennis player noun Tennisspieler der (PL die Tennisspieler), Tennisspielerin die (PL die Tennisspielerinnen).

tennis racket noun Tennisschläger der (PL die Tennisschläger).

tenor noun Tenor der (PL die Tenöre).

tenpin bowling noun Bowling das.

tense noun Zeit die; the present tense das Präsens; in the future tense im Futur.
adjective gespannt.

tent noun Zelt das (PL die Zelte).

tenth number zehnter/zehnte/zehntes; on the tenth floor im zehnten Stock; the tenth of April der zehnte April.

term noun (in school) Halbjahr das (PL die Halbjahre); (at university) Semester das (PL die Semester).

terminal noun 1 (at an airport) Terminal der (PL die Terminals); 2 bus terminal die Endstation; 3 (computer terminal) Terminal das (PL die Terminals).

terrace noun 1 (outside a house) Terrasse die (PL die Terrassen); 2 (row of houses) Häuserreihe die (PL die Häuserreihen); 3 the terraces (at a stadium) die Ränge (plural).

terrible adjective furchtbar.

terribly adverb 1 (very) sehr; not terribly clean nicht sehr sauber; 2 (badly) furchtbar; I played terribly ich habe furchtbar gespielt.

terrific adjective 1 irre (informal); a terrific amount eine irre Menge; 2 terrific! super! (informal).

◇ IRREGULAR VERB: See the verb table in the centre of the dictionary

terrified adjective verängstigt; **to be terrified** furchtbar Angst haben.

terrorism noun Terrorismus der.

terrorist noun Terrorist der (PL die Terroristen), Terroristin die (PL die Terroristinnen).

test noun 1 (in school) Klassenarbeit die (PL die Klassenarbeiten); **we've got a maths test tomorrow** wir schreiben morgen eine Mathearbeit; 2 (medical check, trial) Test der (PL die Tests); **eye test** der Sehtest; **blood test** die Blutprobe; 3 **driving test** die Fahrprüfung; **she's taking her driving test on Friday** sie macht am Freitag ihre Fahrprüfung; **he passed his driving test** er hat seine Fahrprüfung bestanden.
verb (in school) prüfen; **can you test me?** kannst du mich abfragen?

test tube noun Reagenzglas das (PL die Reagenzgläser).

text noun Text der (PL die Texte).

textbook noun Lehrbuch das (PL die Lehrbücher).

Thames noun die Thames die Themse.

than conjunction als; **they have more money than we do** sie haben mehr Geld als wir; **more than forty** mehr als vierzig; **more than thirty years** mehr als dreißig Jahre.

thank verb 1 **to thank somebody for something** sich bei jemandem für etwas ←(ACC) bedanken; 2 **thank you** danke; **thank you for looking after the children** danke, dass du auf die Kinder aufgepasst hast.

thanks plural noun 1 Dank der; **thanks a lot!** vielen Dank!; **many thanks** vielen Dank; 2 **no thanks** nein danke; **thanks for your letter** danke für deinen Brief; 3 **thanks to** dank (+DAT); **it was thanks to him that we made it** dank ihm haben wir es geschafft.

thank you adverb danke; **thank you very much for the cheque** herzlichen Dank für den Scheck; **no thank you** nein danke; **a thank-you letter** ein Dankbrief.

that adjective 1 dieser/diese/dieses; **that boy** dieser Junge; **that woman** diese Frau; **that house** dieses Haus; 2 **that one** der da/die da/das da; **'which cake would you like?' – 'that one, please'** 'welchen Kuchen möchten Sie?' – 'den da, bitte'; **I like all the dresses but I'm going to buy that one** mir gefallen alle Kleider, aber ich kaufe das da.
adverb so; **it's not that easy** es ist nicht so einfach.
pronoun 1 das; **what's that?** was ist das?; **who's that?** wer ist das?; **where's that?** wo ist das?; **is that Mandy?** ist das Mandy?; 2 das; **did you see that?** hast du das gesehen?; **that's my bedroom** das ist mein Schlafzimmer; 3 (in relative clauses) der/die/das (depending on the gender of the noun 'that' refers to); **the train that's leaving now** der Zug, der jetzt abfährt; **the flower that I picked** die Blume, die ich gepflückt habe; **the car that's red** das Auto, das rot ist.
conjunction dass △; **I knew that he was lying** ich wußte, dass er log.

△ NEW SPELLING: See page xii

the *definite article* **1** der/die/das (*the article changes according to the gender of the noun*); (*before a masculine noun*) **the dog** der Hund; (*before a feminine noun*) **the cat** die Katze; (*before a neuter noun*) **the car** das Auto; **2** (*before all plural nouns*) die; **the windows** die Fenster.

theatre *noun* Theater *das* (PL die Theater); **to go to the theatre** ins Theater gehen.

their *adjective* ihr; (*plural*) ihre; **their son** ihr Sohn; **their daughter** ihre Tochter; **their car** ihr Auto; **their presents** ihre Geschenke.

theirs *pronoun* **1** ihrer (*when standing for a masculine noun*); **our garden's smaller than theirs** unser Garten ist kleiner als ihrer; **2** ihre (*when standing for a feminine noun*); **your flat is bigger than theirs** deine Wohnung ist größer als ihre; **3** ihrs (*when standing for a neuter noun*); **our car was cheaper than theirs** unser Auto war billiger als ihrs; **4** ihre (*when standing for a plural noun*); **our children are older than theirs** unsere Kinder sind älter als ihre; **5** the yellow car's theirs das gelbe Auto gehört ihnen; **it's theirs** das gehört ihnen.

them *pronoun* **1** (*as a direct object in the accusative*) sie; **I know them** ich kenne sie; **I don't know them** ich kenne sie nicht; **2** (*after prepositions* +ACC) sie; **it's for them** das ist für sie; **3** (*as an indirect object or following a verb that takes the dative*) ihnen; **I told them a story** ich habe

ihnen eine Geschichte erzählt; **4** (*to them*) ihnen; **I gave them my address** ich habe ihnen meine Adresse gegeben; **5** (*after prepositions* +DAT) ihnen; **I'll go with them** ich gehe mit ihnen mit; **6** (*in comparisons*) **he's older than them** er ist älter als sie.

themselves *pronoun* **1** sich; **they enjoyed themselves** sie haben sich amüsiert; **2** (*for emphasis*) selbst; **the boys can do it themselves** die Jungen können es selbst machen.

then *adverb* **1** (*next*) dann; **I get up and then I make the bed** ich stehe auf und dann mache ich das Bett; **I went to the post office and then the bank** ich bin zur Post und dann auf die Bank gegangen; **2** (*at that time*) damals; **we were living in York then** wir haben damals in York gewohnt; **3** (*in that case*) dann; **then why worry?** warum machst du dir dann Sorgen?; **4** **since then** seitdem; **5** **from then on** von da an.

theory *noun* **1** Theorie *die* (PL die Theorien); **2** **in theory** theoretisch.

there *adverb* **1** (*in a fixed location*) da; **up there** da oben; **down there** da unten; **in there** da drin; **stay there** bleib da; **over there** da drüben; **she's over there with Mark** sie ist da drüben mit Mark; **2** (*with movement to a place*) dahin; **put it there** leg es dahin; **we're going there on Tuesday** wir fahren am Dienstag dahin; **4** (*further away*) dort; **I've seen photos of Oxford but I've never been there** ich habe Fotos von Oxford gesehen, aber ich

⬥ IRREGULAR VERB: See the verb table in the centre of the dictionary war noch nie dort; **5 there is** (*there exists*) da ist, es ist; **there's a cat in the garden** da ist eine Katze im Garten; **there's enough bread** es ist genug Brot da; **no, there's not enough** nein, es ist nicht genug da; **6 there is** es gibt; **there's only one hospital in this town** in dieser Stadt gibt es nur ein Krankenhaus; **7 there are** da sind, es sind; **there were lots of people in town** es waren viele Leute in der Stadt; **8 there are** (*there exist*) es gibt; **there are lots of museums here** es gibt hier viele Museen; **9** (*when drawing attention*) da; **there they are!** da sind sie!; **there's the bus coming!** da kommt der Bus!

therefore *adverb* deshalb.

thermometer *noun* Thermometer *das* (PL *die* Thermometer).

these *adjective* diese; **these glasses** diese Gläser. *pronoun* die; **these are cheaper** die sind billiger.

they *pronoun* **1** sie; 'where are the knives?' – 'they're in the drawer' 'wo sind die Messer?' – 'sie sind in der Schublade'; **2** man; **they say** man sagt.

thick *adjective* dick; **a thick layer of butter** eine dicke Schicht Butter.

thief *noun* Dieb *der* (PL *die* Diebe), Diebin *die* (PL *die* Diebinnen).

thin *adjective* dünn.

thing *noun* **1** (*an object*) Ding *das* (PL *die* Dinge); **they have lots of nice things** sie haben viele schöne Dinge;

she told me some strange things sie hat mir ein paar seltsame Dinge erzählt; **that thing next to the hammer** das Ding da neben dem Hammer; **2 things** (*belongings*) Sachen (*plural*); **you can leave your things in my room** du kannst deine Sachen in meinem Zimmer lassen; **3 the best thing to do is …** am besten wäre es …; **4** (*subject, affair*) Sache *die* (PL *die* Sachen); **the thing is, I've lost her address** die Sache ist die, ich habe ihre Adresse verloren; **5 how are things?** wie geht's?

think *verb* **1** (*believe*) glauben; **do you think they'll come?** glaubst du, sie kommen?; **no, I don't think so** nein, ich glaube nicht; **I think so** ich glaube schon; **I think he's already paid** ich glaube, er hat schon gezahlt; **2** denken ◇; **I'm thinking about you** ich denke an dich; **what are you thinking about?** woran denkst du?; **3 what do you think of that?** was halten Sie davon?; **I don't think much of her proposal** ich halte nicht viel von ihrem Vorschlag; **4 what do you think of my new jacket?** wie findest du meine neue Jacke?; **5** (*remember*) **to think to do something** daran denken, etwas zu tun; **he didn't think of locking the door** er hat nicht daran gedacht, die Tür abzuschließen; **6** (*to think carefully*) nachdenken ◇ SEP; **he thought for a moment** er hat einen Moment lang nachgedacht; **think about it!** denk darüber nach!; **7 I've thought it over carefully** ich habe es mir genau überlegt;

△ **NEW SPELLING: See page xii**

8 (*imagine*) sich ←(DAT) vorstellen SEP; **just think, we'll soon be in Spain!** stell dir nur vor, bald sind wir in Spanien!; **I never thought it would be like this** ich habe mir nie vorgestellt, dass es so sein würde.

third noun Drittel das (PL die Drittel); **a third of the population** ein Drittel der Bevölkerung. adjective dritter/dritte/drittes; **on the third floor** im dritten Stock; **on the third of March** am dritten März.

thirdly adverb drittens.

Third World noun Dritte Welt △ die.

thirst noun Durst der.

thirsty adjective durstig; **to be thirsty** Durst haben; **I'm thirsty** ich habe Durst; **we were all thirsty** wir hatten alle Durst.

thirteen number dreizehn; **Ahmed's thirteen** Ahmed ist dreizehn.

thirty number dreißig.

this adjective **1** dieser/diese/dieses; **this boy** dieser Junge; **this flower** diese Blume; **this car** dieses Auto; **at the end of this week** Ende dieser Woche; **2 this morning** heute Morgen; **this evening** heute Abend; **this afternoon** heute Nachmittag; **3 this one** der/die/das; (*with more emphasis*) dieser/diese/dieses; **if you need a pen you can have this one** wenn du einen Kugelschreiber brauchst, kannst du den haben; **I'll take this one** ich nehme diesen. pronoun **1** das; **can you hold this?** kannst du das festhalten?; **what's**

this? was ist das?; **2 this is my sister Carla** (*in introductions*) das ist meine Schwester Carla; **3 this is Tracy speaking** (*on the phone*) hier spricht Tracy.

thistle noun Distel die (PL die Disteln).

those adjective diese; **those books** diese Bücher. pronoun die da; **if you need more knives you can take those** wenn du mehr Messer brauchst, kannst du die da nehmen.

though conjunction obwohl; **though it's cold** obwohl es kalt ist. adverb aber; **it was a good idea, though** es war aber eine gute Idee.

thought noun Gedanke der (PL die Gedanken).

thousand number **1** tausend; **a thousand** eintausend; **three thousand** dreitausend; **2 thousands of** Tausende von; **there were thousands of tourists in Venice** Tausende von Touristen waren in Venedig.

thread noun Faden der (PL die Fäden). verb einfädeln (*a needle*).

threat noun Drohung die (PL die Drohungen); **is that a threat?** soll das eine Drohung sein?

threaten verb drohen (+DAT); **he threatened her** er hat ihr gedroht; **to threaten to do something** damit drohen, etwas zu tun.

three number drei; **Oskar's three** Oskar ist drei.

✧ IRREGULAR VERB: *See the verb table in the centre of the dictionary*

three-quarters noun
Dreiviertel das.
adverb **three-quarters full** drei
viertel △ voll.

thrilled adjective **to be thrilled** sich
wahnsinnig freuen.

thriller noun Thriller der (PL die
Thriller).

thrilling adjective spannend.

throat noun Hals der (PL die Hälse);
to have a sore throat
Halsschmerzen haben.

through preposition 1 (across, via)
durch (+ACC); **through the forest**
durch den Wald; **the train goes
through Leeds** der Zug fährt durch
Leeds; **through the window** durch
das Fenster; 2 **to let somebody
through** jemanden durchlassen ◇
SEP; **the police let us through** die
Polizei ließ uns durch; 3 **I know
them through my cousin** ich kenne
sie über meinen Vetter.

throw verb 1 werfen ◇; **I threw the
letter in the bin** ich habe den Brief
in den Mülleimer geworfen; 2 **to
throw something to somebody**
jemandem etwas zuwerfen ◇ SEP;
throw me the ball wirf mir den Ball
zu; **to throw something at
somebody** etwas nach jemandem
werfen.
● **to throw something away** etwas
wegwerfen ◇ SEP; **I'm throwing
away the old newspapers** ich werfe
die alten Zeitungen weg.
● **to throw somebody out** jemanden
rauswerfen ◇ SEP.

● **to throw something out** etwas
wegwerfen ◇ SEP (rubbish).

thumb noun Daumen der (PL die
Daumen).

thunder noun Donner der; **peal of
thunder** der Donnerschlag.

thunderstorm noun Gewitter das
(PL die Gewitter).

Thursday noun 1 Donnerstag der
(PL die Donnerstage); **on Thursday**
(am) Donnerstag; **I'm leaving on
Thursday** ich fahre am Donnerstag
ab; **see you on Thursday** bis
Donnerstag; **every Thursday** jeden
Donnerstag; **last Thursday** vorigen
Donnerstag; **next Thursday**
nächsten Donnerstag; 2 **on
Thursdays** donnerstags; **the
museum is closed on Thursdays**
das Museum ist donnerstags
geschlossen.

thyme noun Thymian der.

tick verb 1 (clock, watch) ticken;
2 (on paper) abhaken SEP.

ticket noun 1 (for an exhibition,
theatre, or cinema) Karte die (PL die
Karten); **two tickets for the concert**
zwei Karten für das Konzert; 2 (for
the underground, a bus, or a train)
Fahrkarte die (PL die Fahrkarten); **a
plane ticket** ein Flugschein, ein
Ticket; 3 (for left luggage, parking)
Schein der (PL die Scheine); 4 (for a
lottery or raffle) Los das (PL die
Lose); 5 **parking ticket** der
Strafzettel.

ticket office noun (at a station)
Fahrkartenschalter der (PL die
Fahrkartenschalter).

tickle verb kitzeln.

tidy adjective ordentlich.
verb aufräumen SEP; **I'll tidy (up)** the
kitchen ich räume die Küche auf.

tie noun 1 (necktie) Krawatte die (PL
die Krawatten); 2 (in a match)
Unentschieden das.
verb 1 binden ◊; **to tie your
shoelaces** sich ←(DAT) die
Schnürsenkel binden; 2 **to tie a knot
in something** einen Knoten in
etwas ←(ACC) machen; 3 (in a match)
we tied two all wir haben zwei zu
zwei gespielt.

tiger noun Tiger der (PL die Tiger).

tight adjective (close-fitting) eng;
the skirt's a bit tight der Rock ist
etwas eng; **these shoes are too tight**
diese Schuhe sind zu eng; **she was
wearing tight jeans** sie hatte enge
Jeans an.

tightly adverb fest.

tights plural noun Strumpfhose die
(PL die Strumpfhosen); **a pair of
purple tights** eine lila Strumpfhose.

tile noun 1 (on a floor) Fliese die (PL
die Fliesen); 2 (on a wall)
Kachel die (PL die Kacheln); 3 (on a
roof) Ziegel der (PL die Ziegel).

till[1] preposition, conjunction 1 bis;
they're staying till Sunday sie
bleiben bis Sonntag; **till he jetzt**;
dann; **till now** bis jetzt; 2 (when 'till'
is followed by a noun it is usually
translated as 'bis zu' +DAT) **till the
evening** bis zum Abend; 3 **not till**
erst; **she won't be back till ten** sie
kommt erst um zehn zurück; **we**

won't know till Monday wir werden
erst am Montag Bescheid wissen.

till[2] noun Kasse die (PL die Kassen);
please pay at the till bitte zahlen
Sie an der Kasse.

time noun 1 (on the clock) Zeit die;
it's time for breakfast es ist Zeit
zum Frühstücken; 2 **what time is it?**
wie viel Δ Uhr ist es?; **at what time
does it start?** um wie viel Uhr fängt
es an?; **ten o'clock German time**
zehn Uhr, deutsche Zeit; 3 **on time**
pünktlich; 4 (an amount of time)
Zeit die; **we've got lots of time** wir
haben viel Zeit; **I haven't got time
now** ich habe jetzt keine Zeit;
there's no time left to do it dafür
bleibt keine Zeit mehr; **from time to
time** von Zeit zu Zeit; **for a long
time** lange; 5 (moment)
Moment der (PL die Momente); **this
isn't a good time to discuss it** das
ist kein guter Moment, um sich
darüber zu unterhalten; **at the right
time** im richtigen Moment; **for the
time being** im Moment; **any time
now** jeden Moment; 6 **at times**
manchmal; 7 (in a series) Mal das
(PL die Male); **eight times** achtmal;
for the first time zum ersten Mal;
the first time I saw you das erste
Mal, als ich dich sah; **three times a
year** dreimal jährlich; 8 **three
times two is six** drei mal zwei ist
sechs; 9 **to have a good time** sich
amüsieren; **we had a really good
time** wir haben uns richtig gut
amüsiert; **have a good time!** viel
Vergnügen!

timetable noun 1 (in school)
Stundenplan der (PL die

◊ IRREGULAR VERB: See the verb table in the centre of the dictionary

Stundenpläne; **2** (for trains or buses) Fahrplan der (PL die Fahrpläne); **bus timetable** der Busfahrplan.

tin noun Dose die (PL die Dosen); **a tin of tomatoes** eine Dose Tomaten.

tinned adjective in Dosen; **tinned peas** Erbsen in Dosen.

tin opener noun Dosenöffner der (PL die Dosenöffner).

tiny adjective winzig.

tip noun **1** (end) Spitze die (PL die Spitzen); **2** (money) Trinkgeld das; **3** (useful hint) Tipp △ der (PL die Tipps) (informal).
verb (give money) ein Trinkgeld geben ◇ (+DAT); **we tipped the waiter** wir haben dem Kellner ein Trinkgeld gegeben.

tired adjective **1** müde; **I'm tired** ich bin müde; **you look tired** du siehst müde aus; **2** to be tired of something** etwas satt haben; **I'm tired of London** ich habe London satt; **I'm tired of watching TV every evening** ich habe es satt, jeden Abend fernzusehen.

tiring adjective ermüdend.

tissue noun (a paper hanky) Papiertaschentuch das (PL die Papiertaschentücher).

tissue paper noun Seidenpapier das.

title noun Titel der (PL die Titel).

to preposition **1** (to a country or town) nach; **to go to London** nach London fahren; **the motorway to**

Italy die Autobahn nach Italien; **they're going to Switzerland** sie fahren in die Schweiz; **2** (to the cinema, theatre, school, office) in (+ACC); **I'm going to school** ich gehe in die Schule; **she's gone to the office** sie ist ins Büro gegangen; **we want to go to town** wir wollen in die Stadt gehen; **3** (to a wedding, party, university, the toilet) auf (+ACC); **she's gone to the toilet** sie ist auf die Toilette gegangen; **4** (addressed or attached to) an (+ACC); **a letter to my parents** ein Brief an meine Eltern; **5** give the book to me** gib ihr das Buch; **he said to me that …** er hat mir gesagt, dass …; **6** (to somebody's house, a particular place, or person) zu (+DAT); **I went round to Paul's house** ich bin zu Paul nach Hause gegangen; **we're going to the Browns' for supper** wir gehen zu Browns zum Abendessen; **I'm going to the dentist tomorrow** morgen gehe ich zum Zahnarzt; **7** (talking about the time) **it's ten to nine** es ist zehn vor neun; **from eight to ten** von acht bis zehn; **from Monday to Friday** von Montag bis Freitag; **8** (in order to) um … zu (+ infinitive); **he gave me some money to buy a sandwich** er hat mir Geld gegeben, um ein Sandwich zu kaufen; **9** (in verbal phrases with the infinitive) zu; **I have nothing to do** ich habe nichts zu tun; **have you got something to eat?** hast du etwas zu essen?

toast noun **1** Toast der (PL die Toasts); **two slices of toast** zwei Scheiben Toast; **2** (to your health)

Toast *der* (PL die Toasts); **to drink a toast to somebody** auf jemanden trinken.

toaster *noun* Toaster *der* (PL die Toaster).

tobacco *noun* Tabak *der*.

tobacconist's *noun* Tabakladen *der* (PL die Tabakläden).

today *adverb* heute; **today's her birthday** sie hat heute Geburtstag.

toe *noun* Zeh *der* (PL die Zehen).

toffee *noun* Karamell △ *der*.

together *adverb* 1 zusammen; **we did it together** wir haben es zusammen gemacht; 2 (*at the same time*) gleichzeitig; **they all left together** sie sind alle gleichzeitig weggegangen.

toilet *noun* Toilette *die* (PL die Toiletten); **she's gone to the toilet** sie ist auf die Toilette gegangen.

toilet paper *noun* Toilettenpapier *das*.

toilet roll *noun* Rolle Toilettenpapier *die* (PL die Rollen Toilettenpapier).

token *noun* 1 (*for a machine or game*) Marke *die* (PL die Marken); 2 (*voucher*) Gutschein *der* (PL die Gutscheine); **gift token** *der* Geschenkgutschein.

toll *noun* Gebühr *die* (PL die Gebühren).

tomato *noun* Tomate *die* (PL die Tomaten); **tomato salad** *der* Tomatensalat; **tomato sauce** *die* Tomatensoße.

tomorrow *adverb* 1 morgen; **I'll do it tomorrow** ich mache es morgen; **tomorrow afternoon** morgen Nachmittag; **tomorrow morning** morgen früh; **tomorrow night** morgen Abend; 2 **the day after tomorrow** übermorgen.

tone *noun* (*on an answerphone, of a voice, or letter*) Ton *der* (PL die Töne).

tongue *noun* Zunge *die* (PL die Zungen); **to stick your tongue out at somebody** jemandem die Zunge herausstrecken; ★ **it's on the tip of my tongue** es liegt mir auf der Zunge.

tonic *noun* Tonic *das* (PL die Tonics); **a gin and tonic** ein Gin Tonic.

tonight *adverb* 1 (*this evening*) heute Abend △; **I'm going out with my friends tonight** ich gehe heute Abend mit meinen Freunden weg; 2 (*after bedtime*) heute Nacht △.

tonsillitis *noun* Mandelentzündung *die*; **Ahlem's got tonsillitis** Ahlem hat eine Mandelentzündung.

too *adverb* 1 zu; **it's too expensive** es ist zu teuer; **too often** zu oft; 2 **too much** zu viel; **I've spent too much** ich habe zu viel ausgegeben; **too many** zu viele; 3 (*as well*) auch; **Karen's coming too** Karen kommt auch; **me too!** ich auch!

tool *noun* Werkzeug *das* (PL die Werkzeuge).

tool kit *noun* Werkzeug *das*.

tooth *noun* Zahn *der* (PL die Zähne);

◇ **IRREGULAR VERB:** *See the verb table in the centre of the dictionary*

to brush your teeth sich ←(DAT) die Zähne putzen.

toothache noun Zahnschmerzen (plural).

toothbrush noun Zahnbürste die (PL die Zahnbürsten).

toothpaste noun Zahnpasta die (PL die Zahnpasten).

top noun 1 (highest part) Spitze die (PL die Spitzen); 2 (of a tree); **at the top of** oben auf (+DAT); **at the top of the ladder** oben auf der Leiter; **it's on top of the chest of drawers** es liegt oben auf der Kommode; 3 **at the top** oben; **there are four rooms at the top** oben sind vier Zimmer; **from top to bottom** von oben bis unten; 4 (of a container, jar, or box) Deckel der (PL die Deckel); 5 (of a mountain) Gipfel der (PL die Gipfel); 6 (a lid) Kappe die (PL die Kappen); (of a pen) Verschluss △ der (PL die Verschlüsse); (of a bottle); 7 (of a garment) Oberteil das (PL die Oberteile); 8 (in sport) **the top of the table** die Tabellenspitze; ★ **and on top of all that** obendrein; ★ **it was a bit over the top** es war leicht übertrieben.
adjective oberster/oberste/oberstes (step or floor); **on the top floor** im obersten Stockwerk.

topic noun Thema das (PL die Themen).

torch noun Taschenlampe die (PL die Taschenlampen).

torn adjective zerrissen.

tortoise noun Schildkröte die (PL die Schildkröten).

torture noun 1 (contact) Folter die (PL die Foltern); 2 **the exam was torture** die Prüfung war die Hölle (informal).
verb quälen.

Tory noun Konservative der/die (PL die Konservativen).

total noun 1 (number) Gesamtzahl die (PL die Gesamtzahlen); 2 (result of addition) Summe die (PL die Summen).
adjective gesamt.

totally adverb völlig.

touch noun 1 (contact) **to get in touch with somebody** sich mit jemandem in Verbindung setzen; **to stay in touch with somebody** mit jemandem in Verbindung bleiben; 2 **we've lost touch** wir haben keinen Kontakt mehr miteinander; **I've lost touch with Peter** ich habe keinen Kontakt mehr mit Peter; 3 (a little bit) **a touch of salt** eine Spur Salz; **it was a touch embarrassing** es war ein bisschen peinlich.
verb 1 berühren; 2 (get hold of) anfassen SEP; **don't touch that** fass das nicht an.

touched adjective gerührt.

touching adjective rührend.

tough adjective 1 hart; **she's had a tough time** sie hat eine harte Zeit hinter sich; **a tough guy** ein harter Kerl; 2 zäh; **the meat's tough** das Fleisch ist zäh; 3 fest (material, shoes, etc.); 4 **tough luck!** Pech!; **tough, you're too late** so'n Pech, du bist zu spät dran.

△ NEW SPELLING: See page xii

tour noun 1 Besichtigung die (PL die Besichtigungen); a tour of the city eine Stadtbesichtigung; we did a tour of the castle wir haben das Schloss besichtigt; 2 guided tour die Führung; 3 package tour die Pauschalreise; 4 (by a band or theatre group) Tournee die (PL die Tournees); to go on tour auf Tournee gehen.
verb (performer) auf Tournee sein ◇ (PERF sein); they're touring America sie sind auf Tournee in Amerika.

tour guide noun Reiseleiter der (PL die Reiseleiter), Reiseleiterin die (PL die Reiseleiterinnen).

tourism noun Tourismus der.

tourist noun Tourist der (PL die Touristen), Touristin die (PL die Touristinnen).

tourist information office noun Fremdenverkehrsbüro das (PL die Fremdenverkehrsbüros).

tournament noun Turnier das (PL die Turniere); tennis tournament das Tennisturnier.

tow verb to be towed away abgeschleppt werden ◇ (PERF sein).

towards preposition zu (+DAT); she went off towards the lake sie ist zum See gegangen; to come towards somebody auf jemanden zukommen ◇ SEP (PERF sein).

towel noun Handtuch das (PL die Handtücher).

tower noun Turm der (PL die Türme).

tower block noun Hochhaus das (PL die Hochhäuser).

town noun Stadt die (PL die Städte); to go into town in die Stadt gehen.

town centre noun Stadtmitte die (PL die Stadtmitten).

town hall noun Rathaus das (PL die Rathäuser).

toy noun Spielzeug das.

toyshop noun Spielzeuggeschäft das (PL die Spielzeuggeschäfte).

trace noun Spur die (PL die Spuren); there was no trace of the thieves es fehlte jede Spur von den Dieben.
verb 1 (find) finden ◇; 2 (follow) verfolgen; 3 (copy) durchpausen SEP.

tracing paper noun Pauspapier das.

track noun 1 (for sport) Bahn die (PL die Bahnen); cycling track die Radrennbahn; racing track (for cars) die Rennstrecke; 2 (a path) Weg der (PL die Wege); 3 (song) Stück das (PL die Stücke); this is my favourite track das ist mein Lieblingsstück.

track suit noun Trainingsanzug der (PL die Trainingsanzüge).

tractor noun Traktor der (PL die Traktoren).

trade noun 1 (a profession) Gewerbe das; 2 (skill, craft) Handwerk das; to learn a trade ein Handwerk erlernen.

◇ IRREGULAR VERB: See the verb table in the centre of the dictionary.

trade union noun
Gewerkschaft die (PL die Gewerkschaften).

tradition noun Tradition die (PL die Traditionen).

traditional adjective traditionell.

traffic noun Verkehr der.

traffic jam noun Stau der (PL die Staus).

traffic lights plural noun Ampel die (PL die Ampeln).

traffic warden noun Hilfspolizist der (PL die Hilfspolizisten), Politesse die (PL die Politessen).

tragedy noun Tragödie die (PL die Tragödien).

tragic adjective tragisch.

trailer noun Anhänger der (PL die Anhänger).

train noun Zug der (PL die Züge); he's coming by train er kommt mit dem Zug; I met her on the train ich habe sie im Zug getroffen; the train for York der Zug nach York.
verb 1 (for a career) ausbilden SEP; 2 she's training to be a nurse sie lässt sich als Krankenschwester ausbilden; 3 (in sport) trainieren; the team trains on Wednesdays die Mannschaft trainiert mittwochs.

trainer noun 1 (of an athlete or horse) Trainer der (PL die Trainer), Trainerin die (PL die Trainerinnen); 2 trainers Trainingsschuhe (plural).

training noun 1 (for a career) Ausbildung die; 2 (for sport) Training das.

train ticket noun Fahrkarte die (PL die Fahrkarten).

train timetable noun Bahnfahrplan der (PL die Bahnfahrpläne).

tram noun Straßenbahn die (PL die Straßenbahnen).

tramp noun Landstreicher der (PL die Landstreicher), Landstreicherin die (PL die Landstreicherinnen).

transfer noun Abziehbild das (PL die Abziehbilder).

transform verb verwandeln.

transistor noun Transistor der (PL die Transistoren).

translate verb übersetzen; to translate something into German etwas ins Deutsche übersetzen.

translation noun Übersetzung die (PL die Übersetzungen).

translator noun Übersetzer der (PL die Übersetzer), Übersetzerin die (PL die Übersetzerinnen).

transparent adjective durchsichtig.

transport noun Transport der (PL die Transporte); the transport of goods der Warentransport; public transport öffentliche Verkehrsmittel (plural).

trap noun Falle die (PL die Fallen).

travel noun Reisen das; foreign travel Auslandsreisen (plural).
verb reisen (PERF sein).

△ NEW SPELLING: See page xii

travel agency noun
Reisebüro das (PL die Reisebüros).

travel agent's noun
Reisebüro das (PL die Reisebüros).

traveller noun 1 Reisende der/die
(PL die Reisenden); 2 (gypsy)
Zigeuner der (PL die Zigeuner),
Zigeunerin die (PL die
Zigeunerinnen).

traveller's cheque noun
Reisescheck der (PL die
Reiseschecks).

tray noun Tablett das (PL die
Tabletts).

tread verb to tread on something
auf etwas ←(ACC) treten ◇ (PERF sein);
she trod on my foot sie ist mir auf
den Fuß getreten.

treasure noun Schatz der (PL die
Schätze).

treat noun 1 I took them to the
circus as a treat ich habe ihnen
eine besondere Freude gemacht und
sie in den Zirkus eingeladen; 2
(food) Leckerbissen der (PL die
Leckerbissen).
verb 1 behandeln; he treats his dog
well er behandelt seinen Hund gut;
the doctor who treated you der
Arzt, der dich behandelt hat; 2 to
treat somebody to something
jemandem etwas spendieren; I'll
treat you to an ice cream ich
spendiere euch ein Eis.

treatment noun Behandlung die
(PL die Behandlungen).

tree noun Baum der (PL die Bäume).

tremble verb zittern.

trend noun 1 (a fashion) Trend der
(PL die Trends); 2 (a tendency)
Tendenz die (PL die Tendenzen).

trendy adjective modern.

trial noun (in court) Prozess △ der
(PL die Prozesse).

triangle noun Dreieck das (PL die
Dreiecke).

trick noun 1 (a joke) Streich der (PL
die Streiche); to play a trick on
somebody jemandem einen Streich
spielen; 2 (a knack or by a conjuror)
Trick der (PL die Tricks); there must
be a trick to it da muss ein Trick
dabei sein.
verb hereinlegen SEP; he tricked
me! er hat mich hereingelegt!

tricky adjective verzwickt; it's a
tricky situation das ist eine
verzwickte Situation.

trim verb schneiden ◇ (hair).

trip noun 1 Reise die (PL die Reisen);
a trip to Florida eine Reise nach
Florida; he's going on a business
trip er macht eine Geschäftsreise;
2 (a day out) Ausflug der (PL die
Ausflüge); a day trip to France ein
Tagesausflug nach Frankreich.
verb (to stumble) stolpern (PERF
sein); Nicky tripped over a stone
Nicky ist über einen Stein gestolpert.

trolley noun 1 (for shopping)
Einkaufswagen der (PL die
Einkaufswagen); 2 (for luggage)
Kofferkuli der (PL die Kofferkulis).

trombone noun Posaune die (PL die
Posaunen).

◇ IRREGULAR VERB: See the verb table in the centre of the dictionary

roops *plural noun* Truppen (*plural*).

rophy *noun* Trophäe *die* (PL *die* Trophäen); (*in competitions*) Pokal *der* (PL *die* Pokale).

rot *verb* traben (PERF *sein*).

rouble *noun* 1 (*general difficulties*) Ärger *der*; **to make trouble** Ärger machen; **to get into trouble** Ärger bekommen; **we had trouble with the travel agency** wir hatten Ärger mit dem Reisebüro; 2 (*problem*) Problem *das* (PL *die* Probleme); **the trouble is, I've lost his phone number** das Problem ist, dass ich seine Telefonnummer verloren habe; **Steph's in trouble** Steph hat Probleme; **what's the trouble?** was ist los?; **it's no trouble!** das ist kein Problem; 3 (*difficulty, effort*) Mühe *die*; **to have trouble doing something** Mühe haben, etwas zu tun; **I had trouble finding a seat** ich hatte Mühe, einen Platz zu finden; **it's not worth the trouble** das ist nicht die Mühe wert.

rousers *plural noun* Hose *die* (PL *die* Hosen); **my old trousers** meine alte Hose; **a new pair of trousers** eine neue Hose.

rout *noun* Forelle *die* (PL *die* Forellen).

ruck *noun* Lastwagen *der* (PL *die* Lastwagen).

rue *adjective* 1 wahr; **a true story** eine wahre Geschichte; 2 **is that true?** stimmt das?; **it's true she's absent-minded** das stimmt, sie ist sehr vergesslich.

trump *noun* Trumpf *der* (PL *die* Trümpfe); **hearts are trumps** Herz ist Trumpf.

trumpet *noun* Trompete *die* (PL *die* Trompeten).

trunk *noun* 1 (*of a tree*) Stamm *der* (PL *die* Stämme); 2 (*of an elephant*) Rüssel *der* (PL *die* Rüssel).

trust *noun* Vertrauen *das*.
verb 1 (*believe*) **to trust somebody** jemandem vertrauen; 2 (*rely on*) **you can trust him** man kann sich auf ihn verlassen.

truth *noun* Wahrheit *die*.

try *noun* Versuch *der* (PL *die* Versuche); **it's my first try** es ist mein erster Versuch; **to have a try** es versuchen; **give it a try!** versuch's doch mal!
verb 1 versuchen; **to try to do something** versuchen, etwas zu tun; **I'm trying to open the door** ich versuche, die Tür aufzumachen; 2 (*taste*) probieren.

● **to try something on** etwas anprobieren SEP (*a garment*).

T-shirt *noun* T-Shirt *das* (PL *die* T-Shirts).

tube *noun* 1 Tube *die* (PL *die* Tuben); 2 (*the Underground*) **the Tube** die U-Bahn.

Tuesday *noun* 1 Dienstag *der* (PL *die* Dienstage); **on Tuesday** (am) Dienstag; **I'm going to the cinema on Tuesday** ich gehe Dienstag ins Kino; **see you on Tuesday!** bis Dienstag!; **every Tuesday** jeden Dienstag; **last Tuesday** vorigen Dienstag; **next Tuesday** nächsten

△ NEW SPELLING: *See page xii*

Dienstag; **2 on Tuesdays** dienstags; **the museum is closed on Tuesdays** das Museum ist dienstags geschlossen.

tuition noun **1** Unterricht der; **piano tuition** der Klavierunterricht; **2 extra tuition** Nachhilfestunden (plural).

tulip noun Tulpe die (PL die Tulpen).

tumble-drier noun Wäschetrockner der (PL die Wäschetrockner).

tuna noun Thunfisch der.

tune noun Melodie die (PL die Melodien).

tunnel noun Tunnel der (PL die Tunnel); **the Channel Tunnel** der Eurotunnel.

turkey noun Pute die (PL die Puten).

Turkey noun die Türkei; **from Turkey** aus der Türkei; **in Turkey** in der Türkei; **to Turkey** in die Türkei.

Turkish noun (language) Türkisch das.
adjective türkisch; **he is Turkish** er ist Türke; **she is Turkish** sie ist Türkin.

turn noun **1** (in a game) **it's your turn** du bist an der Reihe; **whose turn is it?** wer ist an der Reihe?; **it's Jane's turn** Jane ist an der Reihe; **2 to take turns** sich abwechseln; **to take it in turns to do something** abwechselnd etwas tun; **3** (in a road) Kurve die (PL die Kurven); **to take a right/left turn** nach rechts/links abbiegen.
verb **1** drehen; **turn the key to the**

right dreh den Schlüssel nach rechts; **turn your chair round** dreh deinen Stuhl herum; **2** (person, car) abbiegen ◇ SEP (PERF sein); **turn left at the next set of traffic lights** biegen Sie an der nächsten Ampel links ab; **3** (become) werden ◇ (PERF sein); **she turned red** sie ist rot geworden.
● **to turn back** umkehren SEP (PERF sein).
● **to turn off 1** (from a road) abbiegen ◇ SEP (PERF sein); **2** (switch off) ausmachen SEP (a light, an oven, a TV, or radio); zudrehen SEP (a tap) abstellen SEP (gas, electricity, or water); ausschalten SEP (an engine).
● **to turn on** anmachen SEP (a TV, radio or light); aufdrehen SEP (a tap); anschalten SEP (an oven); anlassen ◇ SEP (an engine).
● **to turn out 1 to turn out well** gut ausgehen ◇ SEP (PERF sein); **the discussions turned out badly** die Gespräche sind schlecht ausgegangen; **it all turned out all right in the end** am Ende ging alles gut aus; **2 it turned out that I was right** es stellte sich heraus, dass ich Recht hatte.
● **to turn up 1** (to arrive) aufkreuzen SEP (PERF sein); **they turned up an hour later** sie sind eine Stunde später aufgekreuzt; **2** (to make louder) lauter machen.

turquoise adjective türkis.

turtle noun Schildkröte die (PL die Schildkröten).

TV noun Fernsehen das; **I saw her on TV** ich habe sie im Fernsehen gesehen.

◇ **IRREGULAR VERB: See the verb table in the centre of the dictionary**

tweezers noun Pinzette die (PL die Pinzetten).

twelfth number zwölfter/zwölfte/zwölftes; **on the twelfth floor** im zwölften Stock; **the twelfth of May** der zwölfte Mai.

twelve number 1 zwölf; **Tara's twelve** Tara ist zwölf; **2 at twelve o'clock** um zwölf Uhr.

twenty number zwanzig; **Marie's twenty** Marie ist zwanzig; **twenty-one** einundzwanzig.

twice adverb 1 zweimal; **I've asked him twice** ich habe ihn zweimal gefragt; **twice a day** zweimal täglich; **2 twice as much** doppelt so viel.

twin noun Zwilling der (PL die Zwillinge); **Helen and Tim are twins** Helen und Tim sind Zwillinge; **her twin sister** ihre Zwillingsschwester. verb **Richmond is twinned with Konstanz** Richmond und Konstanz sind Partnerstädte.

twist verb 1 (bend out of shape) verbiegen ◇; **2 verdrehen** (words, meaning); **3 to twist your ankle** sich ←(DAT) den Knöchel verrenken.

two number zwei; **Ben's two** Ben ist zwei; **two by two** zu zweit.

type noun Art die; **what type of computer is it?** welche Art Computer ist es? verb (on a typewriter) Schreibmaschine schreiben ◇, tippen (informal); **I'm learning to type** ich lerne Schreibmaschine schreiben; **I'm just typing some**
letters ich tippe gerade ein paar Briefe.

typewriter noun Schreibmaschine die (PL die Schreibmaschinen).

typical adjective typisch.

tyre noun Reifen der (PL die Reifen).

U u

ugly adjective hässlich △.

UK noun (United Kingdom) Vereinigte Königreich das.

Ulster noun Ulster; **from Ulster** aus Ulster.

umbrella noun Regenschirm der (PL die Regenschirme).

umpire noun Schiedsrichter der (PL die Schiedsrichter), Schiedsrichterin die (PL die Schiedsrichterinnen).

UN noun (United Nations) UN (plural).

unable adjective **to be unable to do something** etwas nicht tun können; **he's unable to come** er kann nicht kommen.

unavoidable adjective unvermeidlich.

unbearable adjective unerträglich.

unbelievable adjective unglaublich.

uncertain adjective 1 (not sure) to
be uncertain whether ... sich
←(DAT) nicht sicher sein, ob ...;
2 (unpredictable) ungewiss △
(future or result).

uncle noun Onkel der (PL die
Onkel).

uncomfortable adjective
1 unbequem (shoes, chair, or
journey); 2 unangenehm (situation,
heat).

unconscious adjective (out cold)
bewusstlos △.

under preposition 1 (underneath)
unter (+DAT, or +ACC when there is
movement towards a place); the dog's
under the bed der Hund ist unter
dem Bett; the ball rolled under the
bed der Ball ist unter das Bett
gerollt; 2 under there da drunter;
perhaps it's under there vielleicht
ist es da drunter; 3 (less than) unter
(+DAT); under £20 unter zwanzig
Pfund; children under five Kinder
unter fünf.

under-age adjective to be under-
age minderjährig sein.

undercooked adjective nicht gar.

underestimate verb
unterschätzen.

underground noun (railway) U-
Bahn die (PL die U-Bahnen); I saw
her on the underground ich habe
sie in der U-Bahn gesehen; shall we
go by underground? fahren wir mit
der U-Bahn?
adjective unterirdisch (cave);

underground car park die
Tiefgarage.

underline verb unterstreichen ◈.

underneath preposition unter
(+DAT, or +ACC when there is movement
towards a place); it's underneath the
newspaper es ist unter der Zeitung
I put it underneath the newspaper
ich habe es unter die Zeitung gelegt.
adverb darunter; check
underneath sieh darunter nach.

underpants plural noun
Unterhose die (PL die Unterhosen);
my underpants meine Unterhose.

underpass noun Unterführung die
(PL die Unterführungen).

understand verb verstehen ◈; do
you understand? verstehst du?; I
couldn't understand what he was
saying ich konnte ihn nicht
verstehen; I can't understand why
she doesn't want to see him ich
kann nicht verstehen, warum sie ihn
nicht sehen will.

understandable adjective that's
understandable das ist
verständlich.

understanding noun
Verständnis das.
adjective verständnisvoll.

underwear noun
Unterwäsche die.

undo verb aufmachen SEP.

undone adjective to come undone
aufgehen ◈ SEP (PERF sein).

undress verb to get undressed
sich ausziehen ◈ SEP.

◈ IRREGULAR VERB: See the verb table in the centre of the dictionary

unemployed noun the **unemployed** die Arbeitslosen (plural).
adjective arbeitslos.

unemployment noun Arbeitslosigkeit die.

unexpected adjective unerwartet.

unexpectedly adverb (to happen, arrive) überraschend.

unfair adjective unfair; it's unfair on young people es ist jungen Leuten gegenüber unfair.

unfashionable adjective unmodern.

unfasten verb aufmachen SEP.

unfit adjective nicht fit; I'm terribly unfit ich bin nicht sehr fit.

unfortunate adjective unglücklich.

unfortunately adverb leider.

unfriendly adjective unfreundlich.

ungrateful adjective undankbar.

unhappy adjective 1 unglücklich; 2 (not satisfied) unzufrieden; to be unhappy about something mit etwas unzufrieden sein.

unhealthy adjective ungesund.

uniform noun Uniform die (PL die Uniformen).

union noun (trade union) Gewerkschaft die (PL die Gewerkschaften).

Union Jack noun the Union Jack die britische Nationalflagge.

unique adjective einzigartig.

unit noun 1 (for measuring, for example) Einheit die (PL die Einheiten); 2 (in a kitchen) Einbauschrank der (PL die Einbauschränke); 3 (a department) Abteilung die (PL die Abteilungen); the research unit die Forschungsabteilung.

United Kingdom noun Vereinigte Königreich das.

United Nations noun Vereinte Nationen (plural).

United States (of America) plural noun Vereinigte Staaten (von Amerika) (plural).

universe noun Universum das, Weltall das.

university noun Universität die (PL die Universitäten); to go to university auf die Universität gehen.

unkind adjective unfreundlich.

unknown adjective unbekannt.

unleaded petrol noun bleifreie Benzin das.

unless conjunction es sei denn; unless he does it es sei denn, er macht es; unless you write es sei denn, du schreibst.

unlike adjective 1 im Gegensatz zu (+DAT); unlike me, she hates dogs im Gegensatz zu mir hasst sie Hunde; 2 it's unlike her to be late es sieht ihr gar nicht ähnlich, zu spät zu kommen.

unlikely adjective unwahrscheinlich.

unload verb 1 ausladen ◇ SEP (luggage, car); 2 entladen ◇ (lorry).

unlock verb aufschließen ◇ SEP.

unlucky adjective 1 to be unlucky (person) Pech haben; I was unlucky, the shop was shut ich hatte Pech, das Geschäft war zu; 2 (bringing bad luck) Unglücks-; thirteen is an unlucky number dreizehn ist eine Unglückszahl; it's unlucky es bringt Unglück.

unnecessary adjective unnötig.

unpack verb auspacken SEP; I'm just unpacking my rucksack ich packe gerade meinen Rucksack aus; I'll just unpack and then come down ich packe nur noch aus und dann komme ich runter.

unpaid adjective unbezahlt.

unpleasant adjective unangenehm.

unplug verb to unplug the lamp den Stecker von der Lampe herausziehen ◇ SEP.

unpopular adjective unbeliebt.

unreasonable adjective uneinsichtig; he's being really unreasonable er ist so uneinsichtig.

unreliable adjective unzuverlässig; he's unreliable er ist unzuverlässig.

unsafe adjective gefährlich (wiring, for example).

unsatisfactory adjective unbefriedigend.

unscrew verb aufschrauben SEP.

unshaven adjective unrasiert.

unsuccessful adjective 1 erfolglos an unsuccessful attempt ein erfolgloser Versuch; 2 to be unsuccessful keinen Erfolg haben; I tried, but I was unsuccessful ich habe es versucht, aber ich hatte keinen Erfolg.

unsuitable adjective unpassend.

untidy adjective unordentlich; the house is always untidy das Haus ist immer unordentlich.

until preposition, conjunction 1 bis; until Monday bis Montag; until now bis jetzt; until then bis dahin; 2 (when 'until' is followed by a noun it is usually translated as 'bis zu' +DAT) until the tenth bis zum Zehnten; until the morning bis zum Morgen; 3 not until erst; not until September erst im September; it won't be finished until Friday es wird erst Freitag fertig sein.

unusual adjective ungewöhnlich; an unusual face ein ungewöhnliches Gesicht.

unwilling adjective to be unwilling to do something etwas nicht tun wollen.

unwrap verb auspacken SEP.

up preposition, adverb 1 (out of bed) to be up auf sein ◇ △ (PERF sein); Liz isn't up yet Liz ist noch nicht auf; I was up late last night ich war gestern bis spät auf; 2 to get up aufstehen ◇ SEP (PERF sein); we got up at six wir sind um sechs aufgestanden; 3 (higher up) auf (+DAT, or +ACC when there is movement towards a place); on the roof auf

◇ IRREGULAR VERB: See the verb table in the centre of the dictionary

dem Dach; **4 up here** hier oben; **up there** da oben; **to go up** (*upstairs*) nach oben gehen; **I went up** ich bin nach oben gegangen; **5 to go up the road** die Straße entlanggehen ◆ SEP (PERF *sein*); **it's further up the road** es ist weiter die Straße entlang; **6 to go up the hill** (*on foot*) hinaufgehen ◆ SEP (PERF *sein*); (*in a vehicle*) hinauffahren ◆ SEP (PERF *sein*); (*in spoken German the prefix 'rauf-' is most common*) **does the bus go up the hill?** fährt der Bus den Berg rauf?; **7 to come up** heraufkommen ◆ SEP (PERF *sein*), raufkommen ◆ SEP (PERF *sein*) (*informal*); **8** (*wrong*) **what's up?** was ist los? (*informal*); **what's up with him?** was ist mit ihm los?; **9 up to** bis; **up to here** bis hier; **up to last week** bis zur letzten Woche; **10 she came up to me** sie kam auf mich zu; **11 what's she up to?** was hat sie vor?; **12 it's up to you** (*it's for you to decide*) das hängt von dir ab; (*it concerns only you*) das ist deine Sache; ★ **time's up!** die Zeit ist um.

upheaval *noun* Unruhe *die* (PL *die* Unruhen).

upper-class *adjective* der Oberschicht; **an upper-class family** eine Familie der Oberschicht.

upright *adjective* aufrecht; **put it upright** stell es aufrecht; **to stand upright** aufrecht stehen.

upset *noun* stomach upset die Magenverstimmung.
adjective **1** (*annoyed*) ärgerlich; **he's upset** er ist ärgerlich; **2** (*distressed*) bestürzt; (*sad*)

betrübt.
verb **to upset somebody** (*hurt*) jemanden kränken; (*annoy*) jemanden ärgern.

upside down *adjective* verkehrt herum.

upstairs *adverb* **1** oben; **Mum's upstairs** Mutti ist oben; **2** (*with movement*) nach oben; **to go upstairs** nach oben gehen.

up-to-date *adjective* **1** (*in fashion*) modern; **2** (*information*) aktuell.

upwards *adjective* nach oben.

urgent *adjective* dringend.

US *noun* USA (*plural*).

us *pronoun* uns; **she knows us** sie kennt uns; **they saw us** sie haben uns gesehen; **with us** mit uns.

USA *noun* USA (*plural*).

use *noun* **1** Gebrauch *der*; **instructions for use** die Gebrauchsanweisung (*singular*); **2 it's no use** es hat keinen Zweck; **it's no use phoning** es hat keinen Zweck anzurufen.
verb benutzen; **we used the dictionary** wir haben das Wörterbuch benutzt; **to use something to do something** etwas zu etwas ◆(DAT) benutzen; **I used a towel to dry myself** ich habe ein Handtuch zum Abtrocknen benutzt.
● **to use up 1** aufbrauchen SEP (*food*); **2** verbrauchen (*money*).

used *adjective* **1 to be used to something** an etwas ◆(ACC) gewöhnt sein; **I'm used to cats** ich bin an Katzen gewöhnt; **I'm not used to it!**

△ NEW SPELLING: *See page xii*

ich bin nicht daran gewöhnt!; **I'm not used to eating in restaurants** ich bin nicht daran gewöhnt, in Restaurants zu essen; **2 to get used to something** sich an etwas ←(ACC) gewöhnen; **you'll soon get used to the new car** du wirst dich schnell an das neue Auto gewöhnen; **I've got used to living here** ich habe mich daran gewöhnt, hier zu wohnen; **you'll get used to it** du wirst dich schon daran gewöhnen.
verb **they used to live in the country** sie haben früher auf dem Land gewohnt; **she used to smoke** sie hat früher geraucht.

useful *adjective* nützlich.

useless *adjective* **1** unbrauchbar; **this knife's useless** dieses Messer ist unbrauchbar; **you're completely useless!** du bist wirklich zu nichts zu gebrauchen!; **2** nutzlos (*advice, information,* or *facts, for example*); **useless knowledge** nutzloses Wissen; **3** (*pointless*) zwecklos.

user-friendly *adjective* benutzerfreundlich.

usual *adjective* **1** üblich; **it's the usual problem** es ist das übliche Problem; **as usual** wie üblich; **2 it's colder than usual** es ist kälter als gewöhnlich.

usually *adjective* normalerweise; **I usually leave at eight** normalerweise gehe ich um acht weg.

V v

vacancy *noun* **1** (*in a hotel*) 'vacancies' 'Zimmer frei'; 'no vacancies' 'belegt'; **2** job vacancy die freie Stelle.

vacant *adjective* frei.

vaccination *noun* Impfung *die* (PL die Impfungen).

vacuum *verb* saugen; **I'm going to vacuum my room** ich sauge mein Zimmer.

vacuum cleaner *noun* Staubsauger *der* (PL die Staubsauger).

vagina *noun* Vagina *die* (PL die Vaginen).

vague *adjective* vage.

vain *adjective* eitel; **in vain** vergeblich.

Valentine's Day *noun* Valentinstag *der* (PL die Valentinstage).

valid *adjective* gültig.

valley *noun* Tal *das* (PL die Täler).

valuable *adjective* wertvoll.

value *noun* Wert *der* (PL die Werte). *verb* schätzen.

van *noun* Lieferwagen *der* (PL die Lieferwagen).

vandal *noun* Rowdy *der* (PL die Rowdies).

◇ IRREGULAR VERB: *See the verb table in the centre of the dictionary*

andalism *noun* Wandalismus △ *der*.

andalize *verb* mutwillig zerstören.

anilla *noun* Vanille *die*; **vanilla ice cream** *das* Vanilleeis.

anish *verb* verschwinden ◇ (PERF *sein*).

ariety *noun* 1 Abwechslung *die* (*in a routine, diet, or style*); **for the sake of variety** zur Abwechslung; 2 (*kind*) Sorte *die* (PL *die* Sorten); **a new variety of apple** eine neue Apfelsorte; 3 (*assortment*) Auswahl *die*.

arious *adjective* verschieden; **there are various ways of doing it** man kann es auf verschiedene Art und Weise machen.

ary *verb* 1 (*become different*) sich ändern; 2 **it varies a lot** es ist sehr unterschiedlich; 3 (*make different*) ändern (*a programme or method*).

ase *noun* Vase *die* (PL *die* Vasen).

AT *noun* Mehrwertsteuer *die* (PL *die* Mehrwertsteuern).

CR *noun* Videorecorder *der* (PL *die* Videorecorder).

DU *noun* Bildschirm *der* (PL *die* Bildschirme).

eal *noun* Kalbfleisch *das*.

egan *noun* Veganer *der* (PL *die* Veganer), Veganerin *die* (PL *die* Veganerinnen).

egetable *noun* Gemüse *das*; **fresh vegetables** frisches Gemüse.

vegetarian *noun* Vegetarier *der* (PL *die* Vegetarier), Vegetarierin *die* (PL *die* Vegetarierinnen). *adjective* vegetarisch.

vehicle *noun* Fahrzeug *das* (PL *die* Fahrzeuge).

vein *noun* Vene *die* (PL *die* Venen).

velvet *noun* Samt *der*.

vending machine *noun* Automat *der* (PL *die* Automaten).

verb *noun* Verb *das* (PL *die* Verben).

verdict *noun* Urteil *das* (PL *die* Urteile).

verge *noun* 1 (*roadside*) Bankette *die* (PL *die* Banketten); 2 **to be on the verge of doing something** im Begriff sein, etwas zu tun; **I was on the verge of leaving** ich war im Begriff zu gehen.

version *noun* Version *die* (PL *die* Versionen).

versus *preposition* gegen (+ACC); **Arsenal versus Chelsea** Arsenal gegen Chelsea.

very *adverb* sehr; **it's very difficult** es ist sehr schwer; **very much** sehr viel. *adjective* 1 **the very person I need!** genau der Mann, die ich brauche; genau die Frau, die ich brauche; **the very thing he's looking for** genau das, was er sucht; **in the very middle** genau in der Mitte; 2 **at the very end** ganz am Ende; **at the very front** ganz vorne.

vest *noun* Unterhemd *das* (PL *die* Unterhemden).

△ NEW SPELLING: *See page xii*

vet noun Tierarzt der (PL die Tierärzte), Tierärztin die (PL die Tierärztinnen); **she's a vet** sie ist Tierärztin.

via preposition über (+ACC); **we're going to Frankfurt via Brussels** wir fahren über Brüssel nach Frankfurt.

vicar noun Pfarrer der (PL die Pfarrer).

vicious adjective 1 bösartig (dog); 2 brutal (attack).

victim noun Opfer das (PL die Opfer).

victory noun Sieg der (PL die Siege).

video noun 1 (film, cassette) Video das (PL die Videos); **to watch a video** ein Video ansehen; **I've got it on video** ich habe es auf Video; **it's out on video** das gibt's als Video; 2 (video recorder) Videorecorder der (PL die Videorecorder). verb aufzeichnen SEP; **I'll video it for you** ich zeichne es für dich auf.

video camera noun Videokamera die (PL die Videokameras).

video cassette noun Videokassette die (PL die Videokassetten).

video game noun Videospiel das (PL die Videospiele).

video recorder noun Videorecorder der (PL die Videorecorder).

video shop noun Videothek die (PL die Videotheken).

Vienna noun Wien das; **to Vienna** nach Wien.

view noun 1 Aussicht die; **a room with a view of the lake** ein Zimmer mit Aussicht auf den See; 2 (opinion) Meinung die (PL die Meinungen); **in my view** meiner Meinung nach; **point of view** der Standpunkt.

viewer noun Zuschauer der (PL die Zuschauer), Zuschauerin die (PL die Zuschauerinnen).

vile adjective ekelhaft.

villa noun Villa die (PL die Villen).

village noun Dorf das (PL die Dörfer).

vine noun Weinrebe die (PL die Weinreben).

vinegar noun Essig der.

vineyard noun Weinberg der (PL die Weinberge).

violence noun Gewalt die.

violent adjective 1 gewalttätig (person, film, behaviour); 2 heftig (jolt, punch).

violin noun Geige die (PL die Geigen); **to play the violin** Geige spielen.

violinist noun Geiger der (PL die Geiger), Geigerin die (PL die Geigerinnen).

virgin noun Jungfrau die (PL die Jungfrauen).

Virgo noun Jungfrau die; **Robert's Virgo** Robert ist Jungfrau.

virtual reality noun virtuelle Realität die.

virus noun Virus das (PL die Viren).

◇ IRREGULAR VERB: **See the verb table in the centre of the dictionary**

isa *noun* Visum *das* (PL *die* Visa).

isit *noun* Besuch *der* (PL *die* Besuche); **I was in Berlin on a visit to friends** ich war in Berlin bei Freunden zu Besuch; **my last visit to Germany** mein letzter Deutschlandsbesuch.
verb **1** besuchen (*a person*); **2** besichtigen (*a building, town*).

isitor *noun* **1** Besucher *der* (PL *die* Besucher), Besucherin *die* (PL *die* Besucherinnen); **2 we've got visitors tonight** wir haben heute Abend Besuch; **3** (*in a hotel*) Gast *der* (PL *die* Gäste).

isual *adjective* visuell.

ital *adjective* unbedingt erforderlich; **it's vital to book** man muss unbedingt buchen.

itamin *noun* Vitamin *das* (PL *die* Vitamine).

ivid *adjective* lebhaft (*colours, memory*); **to have a vivid imagination** eine lebhafte Phantasie haben.

ocabulary *noun* Wortschatz *der*.

ocational *adjective* beruflich.

odka *noun* Wodka *der* (PL *die* Wodkas).

oice *noun* Stimme *die* (PL *die* Stimmen).

olcano *noun* Vulkan *der* (PL *die* Vulkane).

olleyball *noun* Volleyball *der*; **to play volleyball** Volleyball spielen.

olume *noun* **1** Lautstärke *die*; **could you turn down the volume?**

könntest du etwas leiser stellen?; **2** (*book*) Band *der* (PL *die* Bände).

voluntary *adjective* **1** freiwillig; **a voluntary worker** ein freiwilliger Helfer, eine freiwillige Helferin; **2 to do voluntary work** für einen wohltätigen Zweck arbeiten.

volunteer *noun* Freiwillige *der/die* (PL *die* Freiwilligen).
verb **to volunteer to do something** sich anbieten, etwas zu tun.

vote *verb* wählen; **to vote for somebody** jemanden wählen.

voucher *noun* Gutschein *der* (PL *die* Gutscheine).

vowel *noun* Vokal *der* (PL *die* Vokale).

vulgar *adjective* vulgär.

W w

wage(s) *noun* Lohn *der* (PL *die* Löhne).

waist *noun* Taille *die* (PL *die* Taillen).

waistcoat *noun* Weste *die* (PL *die* Westen).

waist measurement *noun* Taillenweite *die*.

wait *noun* Wartezeit *die*; **an hour's wait** eine Stunde Wartezeit.
verb **1** warten; **they're waiting in the car** sie warten im Auto; **she kept me waiting** sie hat mich warten lassen; **2 to wait for somebody** auf jemanden warten; **wait for me**

△ NEW SPELLING: See page xii

warte auf mich; **to wait for something** auf etwas ←(ACC) warten; **we waited for a taxi** wir haben auf ein Taxi gewartet; **3 to wait for somebody to do something** darauf warten, dass jemand etwas tut; **I'm waiting for him to ring** ich warte darauf, dass er anruft; **4 I can't wait to open it** ich kann's kaum erwarten, es aufzumachen.

waiter noun Kellner der (PL die Kellner); **waiter!** Herr Ober!

waiting room noun Wartezimmer das (PL die Wartezimmer); (*at a station*) Warteraum der (PL die Warteräume).

waitress noun Kellnerin die (PL die Kellnerinnen); **waitress!** Fräulein!

wake verb **1** wecken (*somebody*); **Jess woke me at six** Jess hat mich um sechs geweckt; **2** aufwachen SEP (PERF sein); **I woke (up) at six** ich bin um sechs aufgewacht; **wake up!** wach auf!

Wales noun Wales das; **from Wales** aus Wales; **to Wales** nach Wales.

walk noun **1** Spaziergang der (PL die Spaziergänge); **to go for walk** einen Spaziergang machen; **we'll go for a little walk through the village** wir machen einen kleinen Spaziergang durchs Dorf; **to take the dog for a walk** mit dem Hund spazieren gehen ◇ (PERF sein); **3 it's about five minutes' walk from here** es ist ungefähr fünf Minuten zu Fuß von hier.

verb **1** (*go, not run*) gehen ◇ (PERF sein); **he walks very slowly** er geht

sehr langsam; **I'll walk to the bus stop with you** ich gehe mit dir zur Bushaltestelle; **2** (*on foot rather tha[n] by car or bus*) zu Fuß gehen ◇ (PERF sein); **it's not far, we can walk** es i[st] nicht weit, wir können zu Fuß gehen; **3** (*walk around*) spazieren gehen ◇ △ (PERF sein); **we walked around the old town** wir sind in de[r] Altstadt spazieren gegangen; **4** (*move on foot*) laufen ◇ (PERF sein); **to learn to walk** laufen lernen; **the child can't walk yet** da[s] Kind kann noch nicht laufen.

walking noun (*hiking*) Wandern das; **to go walking** wandern (PERF sein).

walking distance noun **to be within walking distance** zu Fuß zu erreichen sein; **it's within walking distance of the sea** man kann das Meer zu Fuß erreichen.

walkman™ noun Walkman™ der (PL die Walkmen);

wall noun **1** (*inside a building*) Wand die (PL die Wände); **there's a picture on every wall** an jeder Wan[d] hängt ein Bild; **2** (*outside*) Mauer die (PL die Mauern).

wallet noun Brieftasche die (PL die Brieftaschen);

wallpaper noun Tapete die (PL die Tapeten);

walnut noun Walnuss △ (PL die Walnüsse).

wander verb **to wander around town** durch die Stadt bummeln

◇ IRREGULAR VERB: *See the verb table in the centre of the dictionary*

(PERF *sein*); **to wander off** weggehen ◇ SEP (PERF *sein*).

ant *verb* **1** wollen ◇; **do you want to come?** willst du mitkommen?; **what do you want to do?** was willst du machen?; **I don't want to bother him** ich will ihn nicht stören; **2** (*more polite*) mögen ◇ ('*ich möchte* is much politer than '*ich will*'); **do you want some more coffee?** möchtest du noch Kaffee?; **I want two pounds of apples please** ich möchte gern zwei Pfund Äpfel ('*möchte gern*' is particularly used when shopping).

ar *noun* Krieg *der* (PL die Kriege).

ardrobe *noun* Kleiderschrank *der* (PL die Kleiderschränke).

arm *adjective* **1** warm; **a warm coat** ein warmer Mantel; **it's warm today** heute ist es warm; **I keep your dinner warm** ich halte dir das Essen warm; **it's warm inside** drinnen ist es warm; **I am warm** mir ist warm; **2** (*friendly*) herzlich; **a warm welcome** ein herzlicher Empfang.

verb wärmen; **to warm the plates** die Teller wärmen.

• **to warm up 1** (*weather*) warm werden; **2** (*an athlete*) sich aufwärmen SEP; **3** (*to heat up*) aufwärmen SEP; **I'll warm the soup up for you** ich wärme dir die Suppe auf.

armth *noun* Wärme *die*.

arn *verb* **1** warnen; **I warn you, it's expensive** ich warne dich, es ist teuer; **to warn somebody not to do something** jemanden davor

warnen, etwas zu tun; **she warned me not to let him drive** sie hat mich davor gewarnt, ihn fahren zu lassen; **2 he warned me to lock the car** er hat mich ermahnt, das Auto abzuschließen.

warning *noun* Warnung *die* (PL die Warnungen).

wash *noun* **to give something a wash** etwas waschen ◇; **to have a wash** sich waschen.
verb **1** waschen ◇; **I've washed your jeans** ich habe deine Jeans gewaschen; **2** (*have a wash*) sich waschen ◇; **to get washed** sich waschen; **3 to wash your hands** sich ←(DAT) die Hände waschen; **I washed my hands** ich habe mir die Hände gewaschen; **to wash your hair** sich ←(DAT) die Haare waschen; **4 to wash the dishes** abwaschen ◇ SEP.

• **to wash up** abwaschen ◇ SEP.

washbasin *noun* Waschbecken *das* (PL die Waschbecken).

washing *noun* Wäsche *die*; **to do the washing** Wäsche waschen.

washing machine *noun* Waschmaschine *die* (PL die Waschmaschinen).

washing powder *noun* Waschpulver *das*.

washing-up *noun* Abwasch *der*; **to do the washing-up** den Abwasch machen.

washing-up liquid *noun* Spülmittel *das* (PL die Spülmittel).

△ NEW SPELLING: See page xii

wasp noun Wespe die (PL die Wespen).

waste noun Verschwendung die; **it's a waste of time** das ist eine Zeitverschwendung.
verb verschwenden.

waste-bin noun Mülltonne die (PL die Mülltonnen).

waste-paper basket noun Papierkorb der (PL die Papierkörbe).

watch noun Uhr die (PL die Uhren); **my watch is fast** meine Uhr geht vor; **my watch is slow** meine Uhr geht nach.
verb 1 (to look at) sich ←(DAT) ansehen ◇ SEP; **I was watching a film** ich habe mir einen Film angesehen; 2 **to watch TV** fernsehen ◇ SEP; 3 (keep a check on, look after) achten auf (+ACC); **watch the children** achte auf die Kinder; 4 (to be careful) aufpassen SEP; **watch you don't spill it** pass auf, dass du es nicht verschüttest; **watch out!** pass auf!; 5 (observe) beobachten; **they were being watched** sie wurden beobachtet.

water noun Wasser das.
verb gießen ◇ (plants).

waterfall noun Wasserfall der (PL die Wasserfälle).

watering can noun Gießkanne die (PL die Gießkannen).

waterproof adjective wasserdicht.

water-skiing noun Wasserskifahren das; **to go water-skiing** Wasserski fahren.

wave noun 1 (in the sea) Welle die (PL die Wellen); 2 (with your hand to give somebody a wave) jemandem zuwinken SEP; **she gave him a wave from the bus** sie winkte ihm vom Bus zu.
verb 1 (with your hand) winken; 2 (flap) schwenken (a flag, for example).

wax noun Wachs das.

way noun 1 (a route or road) Weg der (PL die Wege); **the way to town** der Weg in die Stadt; **we asked the way to the station** wir haben gefragt, wie man zum Bahnhof kommt; **on the way back** auf dem Rückweg; **on the way** unterwegs; **be in the way** im Weg sein; **to be somebody's way** jemandem in Weg sein; **to get out of the way** aus dem Weg gehen; 2 **to lose your way** sich verlaufen ◇; (in a car) sich verfahren ◇; 3 **'way in'** 'Eingang' **'way out'** 'Ausgang'; 4 (direction) Richtung die (PL die Richtungen); **which way did he go?** in welche Richtung ist er gegangen?; **this way** in diese Richtung; 5 (side) **the right way up** richtig herum; **the wrong way round** falsch herum; **the other way round** andersherum; 6 (distance) **it's a long way** es ist weit weg; **we still had a little way to go** wir mussten noch ein kleines Stück gehen; 7 (manner) Art und Weise die; **my way of learning German** meine Art und Weise, Deutsch zu lernen; **he does it his way** er macht es auf seine Art und Weise; **I've done it the wrong way** ich habe es falsch gemacht; **in a way**

◇ IRREGULAR VERB: *See the verb table in the centre of the dictionary*

in gewisser Weise; **8 no way!** auf keinen Fall!; **9 by the way** übrigens.

'e *pronoun* wir; **we're going to the cinema tonight** wir gehen heute Abend ins Kino.

'eak *adjective* **1** (*feeble*) schwach; **in a weak voice** mit schwacher Stimme; **2** dünn (*coffee or tea*).

'ealthy *adjective* reich.

'eapon *noun* Waffe *die* (PL *die* Waffen).

'ear *noun* **children's wear** *die* Kinderkleidung; **sports wear** *die* Sportkleidung.
verb tragen ◇, anhaben ◇ SEP (*informal*); **she often wears red** sie trägt oft Rot; **Tamsin's wearing her jeans** Tamsin hat ihre Jeans an.

'eather *noun* **1** Wetter *das*; **what's the weather like?** wie ist das Wetter?; **in fine weather** bei schönem Wetter; **the weather is terrible** das Wetter ist furchtbar; **2 in wet weather** wenn es regnet; **the weather was cold** es war kalt.

'eather forecast *noun* Wettervorhersage *die*; **the weather forecast says it will rain** der Wettervorhersage zufolge soll es regnen.

'edding *noun* Hochzeit *die* (PL *die* Hochzeiten).

'ednesday *noun* **1** Mittwoch *der* (PL *die* Mittwoche); **on Wednesday** (am) Mittwoch; **I'm going to the cinema on Wednesday** ich gehe Mittwoch ins Kino; **see you on Wednesday!** bis Mittwoch!; **every**

Wednesday jeden Mittwoch; **last Wednesday** vorigen Mittwoch; **next Wednesday** nächsten Mittwoch; **2 on Wednesdays** mittwochs; **the museum is closed on Wednesdays** das Museum ist mittwochs geschlossen.

weed *noun* Unkraut *das*.

week *noun* Woche *die* (PL *die* Wochen); **last week** vorige Woche; **next week** nächste Woche; **this week** diese Woche; **for weeks** wochenlang; **a week today** heute in einer Woche; **in three weeks' time** in drei Wochen.

weekday *noun* **on weekdays** wochentags.

weekend *noun* Wochenende *das* (PL *die* Wochenenden); **last weekend** voriges Wochenende; **next weekend** nächstes Wochenende; **they're coming for the weekend** sie kommen übers Wochenende; **I'll do it at the weekend** ich mache es am Wochenende; **have a nice weekend!** ein schönes Wochenende!

weigh *verb* **1** wiegen ◇; **to weigh something** etwas wiegen; **to weigh yourself** sich wiegen; **2 how much do you weigh?** wie viel wiegst du?; **I weigh 50 kilos** ich wiege fünfzig Kilo.

weight *noun* **1** Gewicht *das* (PL *die* Gewichte); **2 to put on weight** zunehmen ◇ SEP; **3 to lose weight** abnehmen ◇ SEP.

weird *adjective* seltsam.

△ NEW SPELLING: *See page xii*

welcome noun 1 they gave us a warm welcome sie haben uns herzlich empfangen; 2 welcome to Oxford! herzlich willkommen in Oxford!
adjective willkommen; you're welcome any time du bist immer willkommen; 'thank you!' – 'you're welcome!' 'danke!' – 'bitte!'.
verb begrüßen; to welcome somebody jemanden begrüßen.

well adverb 1 to be well gesund sein; I'm very well, thank you danke, es geht mir gut; get well soon! gute Besserung!; 2 gut; Terry played well Terry hat gut gespielt; it's well paid es wird gut bezahlt; well done! gut gemacht!; 3 as well auch; Kevin's coming as well Kevin kommt auch; 4 na ja; well, never mind na ja, macht nichts; 5 gut; it may well be that ... es ist gut möglich, dass ...; very well then, you can go also gut, du kannst gehen.

well-behaved adjective artig.

well-done adjective durchgebraten (steak).

wellington (boot) noun Gummistiefel der (PL die Gummistiefel).

well-known adjective bekannt.

well-off adjective wohlhabend.

Welsh noun 1 the Welsh (people) die Waliser (plural); 2 (language) Walisisch das.
adjective walisisch; he's Welsh er ist Waliser; she's Welsh sie ist Waliserin.

Welshman noun Waliser der (PL die Waliser).

Welshwoman noun Waliserin die (PL die Waliserinnen).

west noun Westen der; in the west im Westen.
adjective West-; the west side die Westseite; west wind der Westwind; west of westlich von; it's west of Munich es liegt westlich von München.
adverb nach Westen.

western noun (film) Western der (PL die Western).

West Indian noun Westinder der (PL die Westinder), Westinderin die (PL die Westinderinnen).
adjective westindisch.

West Indies plural noun die Westindischen Inseln (plural); in the West Indies auf den Westindischen Inseln.

wet adjective 1 nass Δ; we got wet wir sind nass geworden; 2 a wet day ein regnerischer Tag.

whale noun Wal der (PL die Wale).

what pronoun, adjective 1 (in questions) was; what did you say? was hast du gesagt?; what's she doing? was macht sie?; what did you buy? was hast du gekauft?; what is it? was ist das?; what's the matter was ist los?; what's happened? was ist passiert?; what? was?; 2 what's your address? wie ist Ihre Adresse; what's her name? wie heißt sie?; what was it like? wie war's?; 3 (asking for an amount) wie viel Δ

◇ IRREGULAR VERB: See the verb table in the centre of the dictionary

at what time? um wie viel Uhr?; **4** (*that which*) was (*relative pronoun*); **she told me what had happened** sie hat mir gesagt, was passiert ist; **do what I tell you** tu, was ich dir sage; **5** (*which*) welcher/welche/welches; **what country is it in?** in welchem Land ist es?; **what colour is it?** welche Farbe hat es?; **what make is it?** welche Marke ist es?; **6 what for?** wozu?

wheat *noun* Weizen *der*.

wheel *noun* Rad *das* (PL die Räder); **the spare wheel** das Reserverad; **the steering wheel** das Lenkrad.

wheelbarrow *noun* Schubkarre *die* (PL die Schubkarren).

wheelchair *noun* Rollstuhl *der* (PL die Rollstühle).

when *adverb* wann; **when is she arriving?** wann kommt sie an?; **when's your birthday?** wann hast du Geburtstag?
conjunction **1** (*with the past*) als; **I was out shopping when you rang** ich war beim Einkaufen, als du anriefst; **2** (*with the present or future*) wenn; **when she comes I'll ring** wenn sie kommt, rufe ich an.

where *adverb, conjunction* wo; **where do you live?** wo wohnst du?; **where are you going?** wo gehst du hin?; **I don't know where they live** ich weiß nicht, wo sie wohnen.

whether *conjunction* ob; **I don't know whether he's back** ich weiß nicht, ob er schon zurück ist.

which *adjective, pronoun*
1 welcher/welche/welches; **which CD did you buy?** welche CD hast du gekauft?; **2 which (one)** welcher/welche/welches (*depending on the gender of the noun the question refers to*); **'I met your brother' – 'which one?'** 'ich habe deinen Bruder getroffen' – 'welchen?'; **'I met your sister' – 'which one?'** 'ich habe deine Schwester getroffen' – 'welche?'; **'have you seen my book?' – 'which one?'** 'hast du mein Buch gesehen?' – 'welches?'; **3** (*relative pronoun*) der/die/das (*depending on the gender of the noun 'which' refers to*); (*plural*) die; **the film which is showing now** der Film, der gerade läuft; **the lamp which is on the table** die Lampe, die auf dem Tisch steht; **the book which I lent you** das Buch, das ich dir geliehen habe; **the books which I've read** die Bücher, die ich gelesen habe.

while *noun* **for a while** eine Weile; **she worked here for a while** sie hat eine Weile hier gearbeitet; **after a while** nach einer Weile.
conjunction während; **you can make some coffee while I'm finishing my homework** du kannst Kaffee kochen, während ich meine Hausaufgaben fertig mache.

whip *noun* Peitsche *die* (PL die Peitschen).
verb schlagen ◇ (*cream*); **whipped cream** die Schlagsahne.

whisky *noun* Whisky *der* (PL die Whiskys).

△ NEW SPELLING: See page xii

whisper noun Flüstern das; in a whisper im Flüsterton.
verb flüstern.

whistle noun Pfeife die (PL die Pfeifen).
verb pfeifen ◈.

white noun Weiß das; egg white das Eiweiß.
adjective weiß; a white shirt ein weißes Hemd.

white coffee noun Kaffee mit Milch der (PL die Kaffees mit Milch).

Whitsun noun Pfingsten das (PL die Pfingsten).

who pronoun 1 (in questions) wer; who wants some chocolate? wer möchte Schokolade? 2 (in the accusative) wen; who did you ring? wen hast du angerufen? 3 (in the dative) wem; who did you give it to? wem hast du es gegeben? 4 (relative pronoun) der/die/das (depending on the gender of the noun 'who' refers to); (plural) die; my boy friend who lives in Liverpool mein Freund, der in Liverpool wohnt; my girl friend who lives in Berlin meine Freundin, die in Berlin wohnt; the child who's staying with us das Kind, das bei uns wohnt; the friends who are coming to see us tonight die Freunde, die heute Abend kommen.

whole noun the whole of the class die ganze Klasse; the whole of Germany ganz Deutschland; on the whole im Großen und Ganzen.
adjective ganz; the whole family die ganze Familie; the whole

morning den ganzen Morgen; the whole time die ganze Zeit; the whole world die ganze Welt.

wholemeal adjective Vollkorn-; wholemeal bread das Vollkornbrot.

whom pronoun 1 den/die/das; (plural) die; the man whom I saw der Mann, den ich sah; the woman whom I saw die Frau, die ich sah; the child whom I saw das Kind, das ich sah; 2 (in the dative) dem/der/dem; (plural) denen; the girl to whom I wrote das Mädchen, dem ich geschrieben habe; 3 (in questions) wen; whom did you see? wen haben Sie gesehen?; 4 to whom did you give it? wem haben Sie es gegeben?

whose pronoun, adjective 1 (in questions) wessen; whose is this jacket? wessen Jacke ist das?; whose shoes are these? wessen Schuhe sind das?; 2 whose is it? wem gehört das?; I know whose it is ich weiß, wem es gehört; 3 (as a relative pronoun) dessen/deren/dessen (depending on the gender of the noun 'whose' refers to); (plural) deren; the man whose car I'm buying der Mann, dessen Auto ich kaufe; the woman whose bag I found die Frau, deren Tasche ich gefunden habe; the girl whose sister I know das Mädchen, dessen Schwester ich kenne; the people whose children he teaches die Leute, deren Kinder er unterrichtet.

why adverb 1 warum; why did she phone? warum hat sie angerufen?; why not? warum nicht?; 2 that's

◈ **IRREGULAR VERB:** See the verb table in the centre of the dictionary why I don't want to come darum will ich nicht kommen.

wide *adjective* **1** breit; **it's a very wide road** es ist eine sehr breite Straße; **the shelf is 30 cm wide** das Regal ist dreißig Zentimeter breit; **wide screen** *das* Breitbild; **2** groß; **a wide range** eine große Auswahl. *adverb* **the door was wide open** die Tür stand weit offen.

wide awake *adjective* hellwach.

widow *noun* Witwe *die* (PL *die* Witwen).

widower *noun* Witwer *der* (PL *die* Witwer).

width *noun* Breite *die*.

wife *noun* Ehefrau *die* (PL *die* Ehefrauen).

wig *noun* Perücke *die* (PL *die* Perücken).

wild *adjective* **1** wild; **wild animals** wilde Tiere; **2** (*crazy*) verrückt (*idea, party, person*); **3** **to be wild about something** scharf auf etwas ←(ACC) sein.

wildlife *noun* Tierwelt *die*; **a programme on wildlife in Africa** eine Sendung über die afrikanische Tierwelt.

wildlife park *noun* Wildpark *der* (PL *die* Wildparks).

will *verb* **1** (*in German the present tense is often used to express future actions and intentions*) **I'll wait for you at the bus stop** ich warte an der Bushaltestelle auf dich; **he'll be pleased to help you** er hilft dir gern; **that won't be a problem** das ist kein Problem; **I'll phone them at once** ich rufe sie sofort an; **2** (*the German future tense is used when firm intention is stressed, when referring to the more distant future and when some doubt about the future is expressed*) werden ◇; **he will definitely come** er wird ganz bestimmt kommen; **she'll probably ring before leaving** sie wird wahrscheinlich anrufen, bevor sie geht; **3** (*in questions and requests*) **will you have some more tea?** möchten Sie noch Tee? **will you help me?** hilfst du mir?; **'will you write to me?'** – **'of course I will!'** 'schreibst du mir?' – 'ja, natürlich'; **'he won't like it'** – **'yes he will'** 'es wird ihm nicht gefallen' – 'doch'; **4** wollen ◇; **he won't help us** er will uns nicht helfen; **the car won't start** das Auto will nicht anspringen.

willing *adjective* **to be willing to do something** bereit sein, etwas zu tun; **I'm willing to pay half** ich bin bereit, die Hälfte zu zahlen.

willingly *adverb* gern.

win *noun* Sieg *der* (PL *die* Siege); **our win over Everton** unser Sieg über Everton.
verb **1** gewinnen ◇; **we won!** wir haben gewonnen!; **2** **to win a prize** einen Preis bekommen.

wind[1] *noun* Wind *der* (PL *die* Winde).

wind[2] *verb* **1** wickeln (*a wire or rope, for example*); **2** aufziehen ◇ SEP (*a clock*).

△ NEW SPELLING: *See page xii*

wind instrument noun
Blasinstrument das (PL die
Blasinstrumente).

window noun 1 Fenster das (PL die
Fenster); **to look out of the window**
aus dem Fenster sehen; 2 (in a shop)
Schaufenster das (PL die
Schaufenster).

windscreen noun
Windschutzscheibe die (PL die
Windschutzscheiben).

windscreen wiper noun
Scheibenwischer der (PL die
Scheibenwischer).

windy adjective windig; **it's windy
today** heute ist es windig.

wine noun Wein der (PL die Weine);
a glass of white wine ein Glas
Weißwein.

wing noun Flügel der (PL die Flügel).

wink verb **to wink at somebody**
jemandem zuzwinkern SEP.

winner noun Sieger der (PL die
Sieger), Siegerin die (PL die
Siegerinnen).

winning adjective siegreich.

winnings plural noun Gewinn der.

winter noun Winter der (PL die
Winter); **in winter** im Winter.

wipe verb 1 abwischen SEP; **I'll just
wipe the table** ich wische schnell
den Tisch ab; **to wipe your nose** sich
←(DAT) die Nase abwischen; 2 **to wipe
the floor** den Boden wischen; 3 **to
wipe your feet** sich ←(DAT) die
Schuhe abtreten SEP.

• **to wipe up** abtrocknen SEP (dishes).

wire noun Draht der (PL die Drähte);
electric wire die Leitung.

wise adjective weise.

wish noun 1 Wunsch der (PL die
Wünsche); **to make a wish** sich
←(DAT) etwas wünschen; **make a
wish!** wünsch dir was!; 2 **best
wishes on your birthday** alles Gut[e]
zum Geburtstag; 3 (in a letter) with
best wishes mit freundlichen
Grüßen.
verb 1 **I wish she were here** ich
wünschte, sie wäre hier; 2 **to wish
for something** sich ←(DAT) etwas
wünschen; 3 **to wish somebody a
happy Christmas** jemandem froh[e]
Weihnachten wünschen; **I wished
him happy birthday** ich habe ihm
alles Gute zum Geburtstag
gewünscht.

with preposition 1 mit (+DAT); **with
me** mit mir; **with pleasure** mit
Vergnügen; **he went on holiday wi[th]
his friends** er ist mit seinen
Freunden in die Ferien gefahren; **a
girl with red hair** ein Mädchen mit
roten Haaren; 2 (at the house of) b[ei]
(+DAT); **we're staying the night with
friends** wir übernachten bei
Freunden; 3 vor (+DAT); **to shiver
with cold** vor Kälte zittern; **to
tremble with fear** vor Angst zitter[n];
4 **I haven't got any money with m[e]**
ich habe kein Geld dabei.

without preposition ohne (+ACC);
without you ohne dich; **without a
sweater** ohne einen Pullover;
without knowing ohne zu wissen.

◆ IRREGULAR VERB: *See the verb table in the centre of the dictionary*

witness noun Zeuge der (PL die Zeugen), Zeugin die (PL die Zeuginnen).

witty adjective geistreich.

woman noun Frau die (PL die Frauen); **a woman friend** eine Freundin; **a woman doctor** eine Ärztin.

wonder noun Wunder das (PL die Wunder); **it's no wonder you're tired** es ist kein Wunder, dass du müde bist.

verb 1 sich fragen; **I wonder why she did that** ich frage mich, warum sie das getan hat; **2 I wonder who?** wer wohl?; **I wonder where Jake is** wo Jake wohl ist?; **3** (in polite requests) **I wonder if you could tell me ...?** könnten Sie mir vielleicht sagen ...?

wonderful adjective wunderbar.

wood noun Holz das; **the lamp is made of wood** die Lampe ist aus Holz.

wooden adjective Holz-, hölzern; **wooden toys** das Holzspielzeug.

woodwork noun (craft) Tischlerei die.

wool noun Wolle die.

word noun **1** Wort das (PL die Wörter) (the plural 'Wörter' is used when the words are unrelated); **a long word** ein langes Wort; **what's the German word for 'window'?** wie heißt 'window' auf Deutsch?; **I've learned ten German words today** ich habe heute zehn deutsche Wörter gelernt; **words in the dictionary** Wörter im Wörterbuch; **2** Wort das (PL die Worte) (the plural

'Worte' is used when the words are connected in a text or conversation); **he wanted to say a few words** er wollte nur ein paar Worte sagen; **in other words** mit anderen Worten; **to have a word with somebody** mit jemandem sprechen; **3** (promise) Wort das; **to keep your word** sein Wort halten; **he broke his word** er hat sein Wort gebrochen; **4 the words of a song** der Text von einem Lied.

word processing noun Textverarbeitung die.

word processor noun Textverarbeitungssystem das.

work noun Arbeit die; **I enjoy my work** meine Arbeit macht mir Spaß; **she's looking for work** sie sucht Arbeit; **I've got some work to do** ich habe noch etwas Arbeit; **he's out of work** er hat keine Arbeit; **to be off work** nicht arbeiten; **Ben's off work** (sick) Ben ist krank; **to go to work on the tube** mit der U-Bahn zur Arbeit fahren.

verb **1** arbeiten; **she works in an office** sie arbeitet in einem Büro; **Mum works as a dentist** Mutti ist Zahnärztin; **he works part-time** er arbeitet halbtags; **2** (to operate) sich auskennen ◇ SEP mit; **can you work the video?** kennst du dich mit dem Videorecorder aus?; **3** (function) funktionieren; **the washing machine's not working** die Waschmaschine funktioniert nicht; **4** (a plan or idea) klappen; **that worked really well** das hat prima geklappt.

△ NEW SPELLING: *See page xii*

- **to work out 1** (*understand*) verstehen ◇; **I can't work out why** ich kann nicht verstehen, warum; **2** (*exercise*) trainieren; **3** (*to go well*) klappen; **4** (*calculate*) ausrechnen SEP (*a sum*); **I'll work out how much it would cost** ich rechne aus, wie viel es kosten würde; **5** (*solve*) lösen (*a problem*).

worker noun Arbeiter der (PL die Arbeiter), Arbeiterin die (PL die Arbeiterinnen).

work experience noun Praktikum das (PL die Praktika); **to do work experience** ein Praktikum machen.

working-class adjective der Arbeiterschicht; **a working-class family** eine Familie der Arbeiterschicht.

workshop noun Werkstatt die (PL die Werkstätten).

world noun Welt die; **the biggest tree in the world** der größte Baum der Welt; **all over the world** auf der ganzen Welt; **the Western world** die westliche Welt.

World Cup noun the World Cup die Weltmeisterschaft.

world war noun Weltkrieg der (PL die Weltkriege); **the Second World War** der Zweite Weltkrieg.

worm noun Wurm der (PL die Würmer).

worn out adjective **1** (*person*) erschöpft; **2** (*clothes or shoes*) abgetragen.

worried adjective **1** besorgt; **his**

worried parents seine besorgten Eltern; **2 to be worried about somebody** sich ←(DAT) um jemanden Sorgen machen; **we're worried about Susan** wir machen uns um Susan Sorgen.

worry noun Sorge die (PL die Sorgen).
verb sich ←(DAT) Sorgen machen; **don't worry!** keine Sorge!; **don't worry about it** mach dir darum keine Sorgen.

worrying adjective beunruhigend.

worse adjective **1** (*more unpleasant*) schlimmer (*problem, pain, illness*); **things couldn't be worse** es kann nicht schlimmer kommen; **2** (*less good*) schlechter; **it was even worse than the last time** es war noch schlechter als letztes Mal; **to get worse** schlechter werden; **the weather's getting worse** das Wetter wird schlechter; **she's getting worse** (*in health*) es geht ihr schlechter.

worst adjective **1** (*most unpleasant*) schlimmster/schlimmste/ schlimmstes; **the worst** der/die/das Schlimmste; **it was the worst day of my life** es war der schlimmste Tag meines Lebens; **if the worst comes to the worst** wenn es zum Schlimmsten kommt; **2** (*least good*) schlechtester/schlechteste/ schlechtestes; **it's his worst film** das ist sein schlechtester Film; **French my worst subject** in Französisch bin ich am schlechtesten.

worth adjective **to be worth** wert sein; **how much is it worth?** wie viel ist es wert?; **it's worth buying**

◇ IRREGULAR VERB: See the verb table in the centre of the dictionary

das lohnt sich zu kaufen; **it's worth it** das lohnt sich; **it's not worth it** es lohnt sich nicht.

would verb 1 **would you like something to eat?** möchtest du etwas essen?; **what would you like?** was möchten Sie?; 2 **I wouldn't do it** ich würde das nicht machen; **I would buy it, but I haven't got any money at the moment** ich würde es kaufen, aber ich habe zur Zeit kein Geld; **I'd like to go to the cinema** ich würde gern ins Kino gehen; **she said she'd help us** sie hat gesagt, sie würde uns helfen; 3 **that would be a good idea** das wäre ein gute Idee; **if we had asked her she would have helped us** wenn wir sie gefragt hätten, hätte sie uns geholfen; 4 **he wouldn't answer** er wollte nicht antworten; **the car wouldn't start** das Auto wollte nicht anspringen.

wound noun Wunde die (PL die Wunden).
verb verwunden.

wrap verb einwickeln SEP; **I'm going to wrap (up) my presents** ich wickele meine Geschenke ein; **could you wrap it for me please?** können Sie es bitte in Geschenkpapier einwickeln?

wrapping paper noun Geschenkpapier das.

wreck noun 1 Wrack das (PL die Wracks); 2 **I feel a wreck** ich bin völlig kaputt.
verb 1 zerstören (a building or machinery); 2 kaputtfahren ◇ SEP (a car); 3 verderben ◇ (a party, holidays); **it completely wrecked**

my evening das hat mir den Abend völlig verdorben; 4 zunichte machen (plans).

wrestler noun Ringer der (PL die Ringer), Ringerin die (PL die Ringerinnen).

wrestling noun Ringen das.

wrist noun Handgelenk das (PL die Handgelenke).

write verb schreiben ◇; **to write to somebody** jemandem schreiben; **I'll write a letter** ich schreibe ihr einen Brief; **to write to a firm** an eine Firma schreiben.
● **to write down** aufschreiben ◇ SEP; **I wrote down her name** ich schrieb ihren Namen auf; **she wrote it down for me** sie hat es mir aufgeschrieben.

writer noun Schriftsteller der (PL die Schriftsteller), Schriftstellerin die (PL die Schriftstellerinnen).

writing noun Schrift die.

wrong adjective 1 (not correct) falsch; **the wrong answer** die falsche Antwort; **it's the wrong address** das ist die falsche Adresse; 2 **you've got the wrong number** Sie haben sich verwählt; 3 **to be wrong** (be mistaken) sich irren; **I must have been wrong** ich muss mich geirrt haben; 4 (out of order) **to be wrong** nicht stimmen; **there's something wrong** etwas stimmt nicht; 5 (dishonest) unrecht; **it's wrong to make him pay for it** es ist unrecht, dass er dafür zahlen muss; **he's wrong** er hat Unrecht; **you're quite wrong there, cars pollute the**

△ NEW SPELLING: See page xii

environment da haben Sie aber Unrecht, Autos verschmutzen die Umwelt; **6 what's wrong?** was ist los?

adverb **1** (*false*) falsch; **he's got it wrong** er hat es falsch gemacht; **2 to go wrong** (*break*) kaputtgehen ✧ SEP (PERF *sein*) (*informal*); **3 to go wrong** schief gehen △ ✧ (*plan*).

X x

xerox™ *noun* Fotokopie *die* (PL *die* Fotokopien).
verb fotokopieren.

X-ray *noun* Röntgenaufnahme *die* (PL *die* Röntgenaufnahmen); **to have an X-ray** geröntgt werden ✧ (PERF *sein*).
verb röntgen; **they X-rayed her ankle** sie haben ihren Knöchel geröntgt.

Y y

yacht *noun* **1** (*sailing boat*) Segelboot *das* (PL *die* Segelboote); **2** (*large luxury boat*) Jacht *die* (PL *die* Jachten).

yawn *verb* gähnen.

year *noun* **1** Jahr *das* (PL *die* Jahre); **six years ago** vor sechs Jahren; **the whole year** das ganze Jahr; **2 they lived in Moscow for years** sie haben jahrelang in Moskau gewohnt; **3 to be seventeen years old** siebzehn Jahre alt sein; **a two-year-old child** ein zweijähriges Kind; **4** (*in school*) Klasse *die* (PL *die* Klassen) *in German secondary schools the years go from the 'fünfte Klasse' to the 'dreizehnte Klasse'*); **I'm in Year 10** (*in Britain*) ich gehe in die zehnte Klasse; **he'll be in Year 11** (*in Britain*) er kommt in die elfte Klasse.

yellow *adjective* gelb.

yes *adverb* **1** ja; **yes please** ja bitte; **'is Tom in his room?'** – **'yes, he is'** 'ist Tom im Zimmer?' – 'ja'; **2** (*answering a negative*) doch; **'you don't want to come with us, do you?'** – **'yes, I do!'** 'du willst nicht mitkommen?' – 'doch!'; **'you haven't finished, have you?'** – **'yes I have'** 'Sie sind noch nicht fertig, oder?' – 'doch!'.

yesterday *adverb* **1** gestern; **I saw her yesterday** ich habe sie gestern gesehen; **yesterday afternoon** gestern Nachmittag; **yesterday morning** gestern früh; **2 the day before yesterday** vorgestern.

yet *adverb* **1 not yet** noch nicht; **it's not ready yet** es ist noch nicht fertig; **2** (*in questions*) schon; **has she mentioned it yet?** hat sie es schon erwähnt?

yoghurt *noun* Joghurt *der* (PL *die* Joghurt).

✧ **IRREGULAR VERB:** *See the verb table in the centre of the dictionary*

yolk noun Eigelb das (PL die Eigelbe).

you pronoun **1** (as the subject of the sentence and in comparisons) du (familiar form, singular); Sie (polite form, singular and plural); ('du' is the familiar way of talking to family members, close friends, and people of your own age; 'Sie' is more polite) **do you want to go to the cinema tonight?** möchtest du heute Abend ins Kino gehen?; **can you tell me where the station is, please?** können Sie mir bitte sagen, wo der Bahnhof ist?; **he's older than you** er ist älter als du, er ist älter als Sie; **2** (the object form of 'du' and 'Sie', in the dative) dir (familiar form, singular); Ihnen (polite form, singular and plural); **I'll lend you my bike** ich leihe dir mein Rad; **I'll write to you** ich schreibe Ihnen; **I'll come with you** ich komme mit Ihnen mit; **3** (the object form of 'du' and 'Sie', in the accusative) dich (familiar form, singular); Sie (polite form, singular and plural); **I saw you** ich habe dich gesehen, ich habe Sie gesehen; **4** (as the subject of the sentence) ihr (familiar form, plural); **do you all want to come?** wollt ihr alle kommen?; **5** (the object form, in the accusative and the dative) euch; **I'll invite you all!** ich lade euch alle ein!; **I'll give it to you later** ich gebe es euch später.

young adjective jung; **young people** junge Leute; **he's younger than me** er ist jünger als ich; **Tessa's two years younger than me** Tessa ist zwei Jahre jünger als ich.

your adjective **1** (familiar form, singular) dein; (this is the familiar way of talking to family members, close friends, and people of your own age; 'Ihr' is more polite) **I met your brother** ich habe deinen Bruder getroffen; **I met your sister** ich habe deine Schwester getroffen; **I drove your car** ich bin mit deinem Auto gefahren; **I know your brothers** ich kenne deine Brüder; **2** (familiar form, plural) euer; **your brother** euer Bruder; **your sister** eure Schwester; **your car** euer Auto; **your friends are waiting downstairs** eure Freunde warten unten; **3** (polite form, singular and plural) Ihr; **your brother** Ihr Bruder; **your sister** Ihre Schwester; **your car is in the garage** Ihr Auto ist in der Garage; **you can all bring your friends** Sie können alle Ihre Freunde mitbringen.

yours pronoun **1** (familiar form, singular) deiner/deine/deins; (this is the familiar way of talking to family members, close friends, and people of your own age; 'Ihrer/Ihre/Ihrs' is more polite) **my brother's younger than yours** mein Bruder ist jünger als deiner; **my sister is older than yours** meine Schwester ist älter als deine; **I enjoyed that book – is it yours?** das Buch hat mir gefallen – ist es deins?; **my shoes are more expensive than yours** meine Schuhe sind teurer als deine; **2** (familiar form, plural) euer/eure/eures; **my children are younger than yours** meine Kinder sind jünger als eure; **3** (polite form, singular and

△ NEW SPELLING: See page xii

plural) Ihrer/Ihre/Ihrs; **his father must be older than yours** sein Vater muss älter als Ihrer sein; **she's a friend of yours** sie ist eine Freundin von Ihnen; **these books are yours** diese Bücher gehören Ihnen; **5** (*in letters*) Yours sincerely Mit freundlichen Grüßen.

yourself *pronoun* **1** (*when translated by a reflexive verb in German*) dich; (*formal*) sich; **ask yourself** frage dich, fragen Sie sich; **2** (*as a reflexive dative pronoun*) dir; (*formal*) sich; **did you hurt yourself?** hast du dir wehgetan?, haben Sie sich wehgetan?; **3** (*for emphasis*) selbst; **did you do it yourself?** hast du es selbst gemacht?; **4 all by yourself** ganz allein.

yourselves *pronoun* **1** euch; (*formal*) sich; **make yourselves comfortable** macht es euch gemütlich, machen Sie es sich gemütlich; **did you do it yourselves?** habt ihr es selbst gemacht?; **3 by yourselves** allein.

youth hostel *noun* Jugendherberge *die* (PL *die* Jugendherbergen).

Yugoslavia *noun* Jugoslawien *das*; **in the former Yugoslavia** im ehemaligen Jugoslawien.

Z z

zany *adjective* verrückt.

zebra *noun* Zebra *das* (PL *die* Zebras).

zebra crossing *noun* Zebrastreifen *der* (PL *die* Zebrastreifen).

zero *noun* Null *die* (PL *die* Nullen).

zigzag *verb* **1** im Zickzack laufen ✧(PERF *sein*); **2** (*in a car*) im Zickzack fahren ✧(PERF *sein*).

zip *noun* Reißverschluss △ *der* (PL *die* Reißverschlüsse).

zodiac *noun* Tierkreis *der*; **the signs of the zodiac** die Sternzeichen (*plural*).

zone *noun* Zone *die* (PL *die* Zonen).

zoo *noun* Zoo *der* (PL *die* Zoos).

zoom lens *noun* Zoomobjektiv *das* (PL *die* Zoomobjektive).

✧ IRREGULAR VERB: *See the verb table in the centre of the dictionary*

OXFORD
Dictionaries and Thesauruses
for home and school

Oxford Very First Dictionary
Oxford First Dictionary
Oxford First Thesaurus

Oxford Illustrated Junior Dictionary
Oxford Illustrated Junior Thesaurus
Oxford Junior Dictionary
Oxford Junior Thesaurus

Oxford Primary Dictionary
Oxford Primary Thesaurus
Oxford Children's Dictionary
Oxford Children's Thesaurus

Oxford Practical School Dictionary
Oxford Concise School Dictionary
Oxford Concise School Thesaurus
Oxford School Dictionary
Oxford School Thesaurus
Oxford Pocket School Dictionary
Oxford Pocket School Thesaurus
Oxford Mini School Dictionary
Oxford Mini School Thesaurus

Oxford Student's Dictionary

Large print
Oxford Young Readers' Dictionary
Oxford Young Readers' Thesaurus

Notes

Notes

Notes

Notes

Notes